SOCIAL COGNITION:
The Ontario Symposium
Volume 1

SOCIAL COGNITION
The Ontario Symposium
Volume 1

Edited by
E. Tory Higgins
University of Western Ontario
C. Peter Herman
University of Toronto
Mark P. Zanna
University of Waterloo

 LAWRENCE ERLBAUM ASSOCIATES, PUBLISHERS
1981   Hillsdale, New Jersey

Lawrence Erlbaum Associates, Inc., Publishers
365 Broadway
Hillsdale, New Jersey 07642

Library of Congress Cataloging in Publication Data
Ontario Symposium on Personality and Social Psychology,
    1st, University of Western Ontario, 1978
    Social cognition.

    Bibliography: p.
    Includes index.
    1. Cognition—Congresses. 2. Social perception—
Congresses. I. Higgins, Edward Tory, 1946– .
II. Herman, C. Peter, 1946–   . III. Zanna, Mark P.
IV. University of Western Ontario. V. Title.
BF311.057 1978   153.7'5   80-27757
ISBN 0-89859-049-3

Printed in the United States of America

Contents

Preface   ix

PART I: ORGANIZATION AND REPRESENTATION
OF SOCIAL INFORMATION   1

1.   **The Organization of Social Information**   3
     Thomas M. Ostrom, John B. Pryor, David D. Simpson
     The Organization of Social Information   3
     Analysis of the Cognitive Organization
       of Social Information   6
     Contributions of Previous Clustering Research
       to Person Perception   10
     Research on the Organization of Social Information
       According to Persons   15
     Discussion   30

2.   **Schematic Principles in Human Memory**   39
     Reid Hastie
     Introduction   39
     Verbal Learning and Memory Research   47
     Visual Schemata   54
     Social Group Schemata   58
     Individual Person Schemata   64
     Point-of-View Schemata   71
     Discussion   75
     Conclusion   79

3. **Schematic Bases of Social Information Processing**   *89*
   Shelley E. Taylor and Jennifer Crocker
   What is a Schema?   *89*
   The Functions of Schemas   *93*
   Liabilities of Schematic Processing   *114*
   Summary, Conclusions, and Future Considerations   *123*

4. **Cognitive Representations of Persons**   *135*
   David L. Hamilton
   Some Thoughts on a Social Cognition Approach
      to Person Perception   *136*
   Organization Processes in the Development of
      Cognitive Representations of Persons   *140*
   Toward a Conceptual Framework for Understanding
      Cognitive Representations of Persons   *149*

5. **Category Accessibility: Some Theoretical and
   Empirical Issues Concerning the Processing of
   Social Stimulus Information**   *161*
   Robert S. Wyer, Jr. and Thomas K. Srull
   A Theoretical Description of Social Inference
      Processes   *163*
   The Role of Schemata in Memory for Episodic
      Information   *173*
   Effects of Prior Judgments on Subsequent Ones   *176*
   The Effects of Category Accessibility on the
      Interpretation of New Information   *177*
   Conclusions   *193*

PART II: PROCESSING FACTORS AND BIASES
           IN SOCIAL COGNITION   199

6. **What Grabs You? The Role of Attention in
   Impression Formation and Causal Attribution**   *201*
   Leslie Zebrowitz McArthur
   Introduction   *201*
   Object Perception   *203*
   Impressions   *205*
   Causal Attributions   *227*
   Mediation   *234*
   Conclusions   *240*

7. Cognitive Processes in Inferences About
A Person's Personality 247
Ebbe B. Ebbesen
Research on Personality 247
Processes By Which Raters Construct Responses 254
Research on the Construction of Personality 259
Implications 267

8. Seek, And Ye Shall Find:
Testing Hypotheses About Other People 277
Mark Snyder
Formulating Strategies for Testing Hypotheses About
Other People: A Paradigmatic Investigation 280
In Search of the Limits of Confirmatory
Hypothesis Testing 283
The Consequences of Confirmatory Strategies for
Testing Hypotheses About Other People 290
Hypothesis Testing: A Theoretical Analysis 295
Hypothesis Testing and the Social Nature of
Social Knowledge 298

9. Self-centered Biases in Attributions of
Responsibility: Antecedents and Consequences 305
Michael Ross
Pervasiveness of Self-centered Biases
in Judgments of Responsibility 306
Determinants of the Self-centered Bias
in Judgments of Responsibility 307
Availability and Judgments of Responsibility 308
The Interaction Hypothesis 309
Determinants of the Availability Bias 312
Group Centered Biases in Availability
and Responsibility 314
Exceptions 316
Intentionality 317
Participant Involvement 317
Valence of Outcome 318
Consequences of Self-centered Biases
in Responsibility 319

10. Impression Formation, Impression Management,
and Nonverbal Behaviors 323
Robert M. Krauss

11.   The "Communication Game": Implications for
      Social Cognition and Persuasion   *343*
      E. Tory Higgins
      General Rules of the "Communication Game"   *348*
      The "Communication Game" as Purposeful Social
         Interaction   *375*
      General Summary and Conclusions   *383*

PART III: COMMENTARY   393

12.   Social Cognition: A Need to Get Personal   *395*
      E. Tory Higgins, Nicholas A. Kuiper, James M. Olson
      The Role of Personal Experience in Social Cognition   *398*
      The Role of Affect in Social Cognition   *407*
      The Role of Personal Relevance in Social Cognition   *413*
      Concluding Remarks   *415*

Author Index   *421*

Subject Index   *433*

Preface

This volume presents papers from the first Ontario Symposium on Personality and Social Psychology, which was held at the University of Western Ontario over a 3-day period, from August 25 to 27, 1978. The general theme of the symposium was social cognition. More specifically, the participants were selected to present various perspectives on the cognitive structures and processes underlying social judgment and social behavior. We were fortunate enough to bring together an exciting group of psychologists who were actively engaged in expanding and formulating various aspects of social cognition and whose enthusiasm about their own and others' pursuits was still ascendant. In addition to the contributors to this volume, Robert Zajonc and Lee Ross also presented papers at the symposium that further contributed to the intellectual stimulation and success of the conference. Unfortunately, it is not possible to capture in print the excitement and sense of common purpose that was felt throughout the conference. The papers have benefited significantly from the interchange and discussion at the conference, as well as from the comments that the participants provided one another on earlier drafts of their papers. As editors, we would like to thank the authors for their editorial contribution to this volume.

The 12 chapters contained in the volume have been grouped into two major parts. Chapters 1 to 5 focus on the implications of cognitive structures for social cognition, with particular emphasis on the nature of social schemata and the organization of social information. Chapters 6 to 11 focus on the consequences for social cognition of various cognitive processes and mechanisms, including verbal and nonverbal communicative processes, category accessibility, salience and selective attention, hypothesis-testing, and self-centered biases. Chapter 12 comments on the general perspectives taken in the previous chapters and suggests some additional directions for future consideration.

The purpose of the symposium and this volume was two-fold: first, to report on current research programs and critically review major areas in social cognition; and, second, to propose new perspectives on traditional issues in social cognition as well as to suggest new approaches and questions for future research. We hope that this volume will generate new ideas and inspire new research in the rapidly expanding field of social cognition.

The symposium on social cognition represented in this volume was the first Ontario Symposium on Personality and Social Psychology. The second Ontario Symposium concerns the variability and consistency of social behavior, with special emphasis on attitude-behavior consistency and person-situation interactions. There are a number of purposes behind our idea of an Ontario Symposium on Personality and Social Psychology. We expect that this symposium will become an annual, or at least biannual, conference similar to those already established in the areas of development and cognition. Fellow psychologists have frequently expressed the need for an international symposium in personality and social psychology and the desire that one be organized. We felt that a symposium would provide a major service by creating a forum in which scholars concerned with the same issue might meet to discuss common concerns and attempt to integrate their findings into a unified picture. The book that derives from each conference is intended to provide the most up-to-date sourcebook in the particular area being considered. Each individual conference could be of great service for the particular area that is being considered. By providing an opportunity for psychologists and nonpsychologists actively involved in an important, evolving area to meet, exchange ideas, and hopefully arrive at some common conclusions, the conference could further our understanding of the issue concerned and guide further research.

We would like to express our sincere gratitude to W. J. McClelland, Chairman of the Department of Psychology, and B. B. Kymlicka, Dean of Social Science, University of Western Ontario, for their encouragement and financial assistance regarding this first Ontario Symposium. We are grateful to Pat Steele for her help in the initial preparation of the conference. We are also indebted to P. T. Johnson, General Manager, and the staff at Spencer Hall for contributing to the success of the symposium by their courteous, friendly, and professional assistance throughout the conference. We owe a particular debt to Larry Erlbaum for his enthusiastic response to our idea of an Ontario Symposium as well as his editorial guidance. Finally, we wish to thank Janet Polivy, Lorraine Rocissano, and Betsy Zanna for their helpful suggestions and continuous support throughout the project.

E. Tory Higgins
University of Western Ontario

C. Peter Herman
University of Toronto

Mark P. Zanna
University of Waterloo

ORGANIZATION AND REPRESENTATION OF SOCIAL INFORMATION

1 The Organization of Social Information

Thomas M. Ostrom
Ohio State University

John B. Pryor
University of Notre Dame

David D. Simpson
Carroll College

THE ORGANIZATION OF SOCIAL INFORMATION

In the course of their day-to-day activities, people receive an enormous amount of information about a large number of other people, obtained either directly through interaction and observation or indirectly through secondary sources. As has been recognized for a long time (e.g., Lippman, 1922), people cannot hope to hold in memory each discrete item of information they encounter. To make living more manageable, people need to classify and organize this information as it is received. The manner in which people organize social information has an important bearing on the extent to which they will, for example, trust, seek out, or cooperate with others, as well as how much they will discriminate against, aggress against, or reject others.

This chapter is concerned with the manner in which people cognitively organize social information. We use the term "social information" in its broadest sense. It refers to the temporal flow of information about other people, with special emphasis on situations in which people receive two or more units of information about each of two or more persons. Most past work in the area of impression formation has studied settings in which subjects are given information about only one stimulus person. We argue that new considerations arise when the stimulus field contains information items about a variety of persons.

3

Historical Prelude

Soloman Asch (1946) was one of the first social psychologists to study the organization of person impressions. He started from the premise that items of information about a single person would form a perceptual unit. The resulting "gestalt" would influence the interpretation of each of the elements so as to make them consistent with the overall theme of the impression. First impressions, then, were viewed as being thematically organized into a coherent whole.

Asch explored two possible determinants of the organizing theme, trait centrality and order of presentation. Some traits (or, more generally, person features) were thought to be especially salient, vivid, or otherside dominant so as to emerge as the focus of organization. In his research, traits such as warm and cold appeared to occupy this central position. In a similar vein, sociological literature has argued that person features that are "deviant" within a particular culture may also provide such a central organizing function in person perception. The second variable studied by Asch was order of presentation. He found evidence in support of the view that the first items in the sequence of person information provide a thematic organization into which the later items are integrated.

Subsequent work on the variables of centrality and order moved away from the question of impression organization and looked instead at the effects of these (and other) variables on trait inference and impression favorability judgments (see N. H. Anderson, 1974; Rosenberg & Sedlak, 1972). Not until very recently (e.g., Anderson & Hastie, 1974; Hastie, Ostrom, Ebbesen, Wyer, Jr., Hamilton, & Carlston, 1980; Lingle & Ostrom, 1980; Wyer & Carlston, 1979) have social psychologists returned to Asch's original concern regarding the thematic organization of person impressions and attitudes.

There has now emerged a healthy interest in the cognitive organization of social information. This interest has extended beyond understanding the organization of information about a single person (Asch's objective) to the organization in memory of information about several other persons (e.g., Picek, Sherman, & Shiffrin, 1975), as well as about the self (e.g, Markus, 1977; Rogers, Kuiper, & Kirker, 1977).

This renewed attention to the manner in which people organize social information is not only welcome, but it represents an important advance over previous work in the field of impression formation and person perception. It allows us to theorize about which items of social information get categorized together, how one thought follows from another thought, and the manner in which people retrieve previously learned items.

Objectives of This Chapter

Previous research in this area of person perception has uncritically accepted the assumption made by Asch regarding the "unity" of person impressions. It was assumed by Asch, as well as by those who followed, that people automatically form a "person gestalt" when exposed to information about other persons. This tendency can be seen in the nature of both theory and research practices in person perception.

In constructing theories of person impressions, social psychologists have dealt only with the case of a single person, with no recognition given to the fact that information about one person is acquired and processed in the midst of information about a variety of other people. This is true of theories from a Gestalt perspective (Asch, 1946; deCharms, 1968; Heider, 1958; Krech & Crutchfield, 1948) a reinforcement perspective (Byrne, 1971), an information integration perspective (Anderson, 1974), an attribution theory perspective (Kelley, 1967), and a cognitive structure perspective (Rosenberg & Sedlak, 1972; Scott, 1969). They all appear to be based on the premise that people naturally isolate all the items of information about each person and somehow treat it as a collective when making impression responses. None of these theories provide an understanding of when or how people do, in fact, organize the flow of information according to persons. It is as if all these theorists take it for granted that the person is the only meaningful focus of organization.

This assumption has also affected research practices. The empirical paradigms used by most investigators have the effect of perceptually isolating the information about one person from the information about another. For example, in both the trait judgment task (Anderson, 1974; Asch, 1946) and the similarity-attraction paradigm (Byrne, 1971) information is blocked by stimulus persons. That is, the information about one person is exhaustively presented in a block before information about anyone else is given. This, of course, is quite discrepant from what occurs in day-to-day life. Except for certain occupations (a psychiatrist who sees patients in sequentially blocked time periods) most of us have repeated intermittent encounters with a variety of persons over the course of a typical day. Despite the relative frequency of such intermittently acquired information in day-to-day life, nearly all contemporary social psychological research on person perception presents information to subjects in a "blocked" fashion. There is clearly a need to develop empirical procedures for studying how people organize social information when the flow of information about one person is arbitrarily interspersed among information items about other persons.

This chapter explores the possibility that there are a variety of factors that determine the strength of the "person gestalt." When the stimulus field contains a variety of information items about several people, there may be circumstances under which the information items are not organized around persons at all. We view the problem of discovering the determinants of the strength of the "person gestalt" as being fundamental to all work in person perception. If there is no cognitive unit representing the person, there can be no within-person organization of information. Under such conditions, it would not make sense to talk about an organized impression of the person.

The remainder of this chapter is divided into four major sections. The first provides an analysis of the concept of organization by person and outlines a methodology (clustering in free recall) by which person organization can be studied. The second section reviews relevent previous research that employed this methodology. The implications of these findings for understanding person perception is also described. The third section presents data that refutes the assumption that social information is always organized around persons. It then introduces the notion that prior familiarity with the person serves as a primary determinant of the strength of the "person gestalt." The last section describes the implications of the present approach for other problems in social and personality psychology. We also provide suggestions for future research in that section.

ANALYSIS OF THE COGNITIVE ORGANIZATION OF SOCIAL INFORMATION

An item of social information refers to any feature or characteristic of a person that is descriminable (i.e., represents an identifiable unit) by the observer. It may be an observed behavior sequence, a belief about the person's past, a physical feature, a trait, or any other of a multitude of such possible characteristics. Naturally enough, features are associated with a specific person at the time they are perceived. In the language of associative network theories (e.g., Anderson & Bower, 1973; Collins & Loftus, 1975; Kintsch, 1974), a person node is created in memory when the first item of information is received and a pathway is established between the person node and a node representing the feature. As additional characteristics of a person are observed, new feature nodes and their pathways to the person node are created. Such models of person perception have been proposed by Anderson and Hastie (1974), Ostrom, Lingle, Pryor, and Geva (1980) and Wyer and Carlston (1979).

Consider a hypothetical person named Bill. He is remembered as being a shy, male coal miner who smiles a lot and whom the perceiver met at a party last New Year's Eve.

Feature Nodes

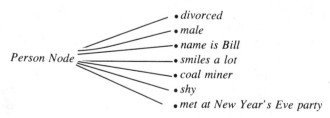

This drawing provides an illustration of social information being organized by a "person gestalt"; all items are related to each other by virtue of having pathways to a common node, the person node. Asch (1946) no doubt created such an associative network in his research on impression formation because his subjects were given a list of traits, all of which characterized a single stimulus person. This traditional impression formation methodology offers no competing items of information (about other people), or about nonperson objects and events) that could interfere with person organization.

Consider, on the other hand, that our observer met two other persons (besides Bill) at the New Year's Eve party. Susan was an attractive airline stewardess who was unmarried, and Abe, who likes to drink beer, was a surgeon with four kids. The observer may have encountered the several items of social information in the following temporal sequence:

Bill is divorced.
Susan is attractive.
Susan is a stewardess.
Abe likes to drink beer.
Bill is a coal miner.
Susan is unmarried.
Bill is shy.
Abe is a surgeon.
Abe has four kids.

When trying to remember these items of social information the morning after (on New Year's Day), it is by no means certain that they will be organized by person. The observer may remember meeting a divorced person, an unmarried person, and a person with four children, but not remember which person was the surgeon, the airline stewardess, or the coal miner. At a later point in this chapter, we discuss several alternatives to person organization. Our concern at this point, however, is to establish the plausibility that alternative modes of organization exist and may well be adopted under some circumstances. We turn next to describing a methodology that will allow us to study the conditions under which people do and do not organize social information by persons.

Clustering in Free Recall

The manner in which an observer organizes information about persons in memory will affect the way in which the information items are later recalled. One technique for studying organization is to have subjects learn a list of words and then to recall them in the order in which they come to mind (e.g., Bousfield, 1953). For example, subjects may be given a list of words that contain the names of animals randomly interspersed among the names of flowers. It is found that the order in which items are listed in free recall reflects their associative organization in memory. Subjects tend to cluster the animals in one part of the recall sequence and the flowers in another part. This is interpreted to mean that despite the random order of presentation in the learning phase, subjects mentally compartmentalize the two categories of stimulus items. Items within a category are more strongly associated with one another than they are with the items in the other category. When asked to recall the entire set of items, the sequence of recall is determined by the strongest associative pathways. Analogously, if social information is organized around the person, it would be expected that person clustering should emerge in free recall. In the earlier example, there should be a tendency for the Susan items to group together, the Abe items to appear together, and the Bill items to be together if the items had been organized by person.

Measures of Clustering in Free Recall

This section describes two alternative indices that can be used for measuring clustering in free recall. Because the presentation is somewhat technical and detailed, it may distract the reader from the more substantive concerns in this chapter. However, we believe that because most social psychologists are unfamiliar with these procedures, a brief digression at this point should not only help the reader to better understand our findings, but should also be of use to other researchers who wish to adopt this methodology.

During the last 10 years, numerous measures have been proposed to assess memorial organization of lists of words. All of these measures to date have been guided more by intuitive criteria than by theory (Colle, 1972; Sternberg & Tulving, 1977), and there is as yet little consensus as to which measure is most appropriate, or even under what circumstances a given measure is appropriate (Shuell, 1969). Discussed in turn are two of the measures of categorical clustering we have used in our research.

SCR.   In 1966, A. K. Bousfield and W. A. Bousfield proposed a formula for a deviation measure of categorical clustering that was to stimulate a great deal of research as well as a plethora of other clustering indices mathematically related to it. In distinction to the "Ratio of Repetition" measure that the latter author had originally proposed (Bousfield, 1953), the new formula assumed that all items presented were not equally available at recall.

The basic unit of analysis for measuring categorical clustering is the repetition. A repetition is defined as occurring any time two items from the same conceptual category are reported contiguously. As observed Stimulus Category Repetition (SCR), then, indicates the amount of clustering represented by the number of repetitions. The expected number of repetitions in a list is represented by the following formula:

$$E(SCR) = \frac{\Sigma m^2}{N} - 1$$

where m is the number of words recalled in a category k, and N is the total number of words recalled. The deviation measure of categorical clustering is therefore O(SCR) $-$ E(SCR) and reflects the degree to which the observed number of repetitions differs from the number expected by chance.

One potential limitation of this deviation clustering index is that there is no fixed upper limit. As has been pointed out by other researchers (e.g., Roenker, Thompson, & Brown, 1971), this characteristic may introduce ambiguity of interpretation in those situations where there are large differences in the number of items recalled. For example, although perfect clustering might be achieved in a shorter list, the SCR value could be smaller than that obtained in a longer list where perfect clustering was not achieved.

ARC. Roenker, Thompson, and Brown (1971) and Gerjouy and Spitz (1966) separately proposed a measure of categorical clustering that has proven especially useful.

Like *SCR,* the Adjusted Ratio of Clustering (ARC) has chance clustering set at zero. Unlike SCR, however, perfect clustering is set at unity (1) for ARC. The ARC score in effect represents the ratio of obtained category repetitions above chance to the total possible category repetitions above chance. Its usefulness is enhanced by the fact that it is minimally affected by the number of categories recalled, the total number of items recalled, and the distribution of items across categories. Therefore, direct comparisons can meaningfully be made between and within subjects and experiments. It is computed by the following formula:

$$\text{ARC} = \frac{R - E(R)}{\text{Max } R - E(R)}$$

where R equals the total number of observed repetitions, $E(R)$ equals the chance number of category repetitions and is computed with the Bousfield and Bousfield (1966) formula for E(SCR) and *Max R* equals the maximum number of category repetitions (i.e., Max R $= N - k$ where k is the number of recalled categories). Over several different studies, Simpson (1979) found that ARC correlated .90 or better with several other indices of clustering (including SRC). We have found this to be the most useful of the several indexes and report it exclusively in the empirical portion of this chapter.

One potential limitation of ARC as an index of categorical clustering is that a negative score does not have the same meaning as a positive score under many circumstances (Frankel & Cole, 1971). This is because, whereas the upper limit of ARC is 1.00 and chance is zero, the lower limit is not -1.00. This problem can be particularly acute in situations where recall is poor. Consider the following hypothetical example where a subject recalls two words from one conceptual category and only one word from another with the single instance intervening between the other two (e.g., the recall sequence: Bill is divorced, Susan is attractive, Bill is a coal miner). For this particular case, $R = 0$, $E(R) = 0.67$, Max $R = 1.00$, ARC $= -2.03$. Fortunately, we have rarely encountered such large negative values in this research.

CONTRIBUTION OF PREVIOUS CLUSTERING RESEARCH TO PERSON PERCEPTION

By and large, most previous clustering research has employed rather austere stimulus material, frequently composed of sets of nouns that can be classified consensually into a priori categories (e.g., foods, trees, cities, etc.). On the other hand, information about persons is far more varied in content. It may include appearance, traits, attitudes, behavior episodes, memberships, friendships, and demographic characteristics. There are also differences in the manner in which information is acquired by the observer. Most clustering research presents the stimuli sequentially one word at a time, with no direct connection made between the word and the a priori categories. In learning about persons, information generally must be extracted from a much more complicated stimulus field. Furthermore, one directly apprehends a linkage between the person and the information item. That is, in clustering research, the subject is not explicitly told that the term "oak" is an instance of a "building materials" category. However, in person perception such a linkage is almost always explicit. The memory item "surgeon" is directly associated with the person Abe.

Despite these clear differences between most clustering research and the nature of person organization processes, it will still prove useful to selectively review past clustering research and relate it to issues in person perception. In the following section, we discuss several variables that have been found to affect the degree to which information is clustered by category or associative strength in recall.

Temporal Blocking of Information.   Blocking (i.e., presenting all items from a single category contiguously during list presentation) enhances clustering compared to random presentation for both high and low frequency words (Cofer, 1967; Cofer, Bruce, & Reicher, 1966; Cofer & Reicher, 1963; Dallet, 1964; Puff, 1973). This superiority in clustering for blocked over random presentation of words also holds when the stimuli consist of factual material presented in complex sentences (Balser, 1972). This body of research suggests that there would be a greater likelihood of subjects organizing their recall of facts about persons according to persons if they acquired all the information about one person before learning information about a new person. Temporal blocking of information occurs in such structured and unstructured social encounters as job interviews and meeting strangers on a plane trip.

Task Orientation.   A second variable that affects organization of recall is the task orientation (set) of subjects. For example, Marshall and Cofer (1961) presented subjects with mixed lists of categorized or uncategorized word pairs at two levels of associative strength under either a set or a no-set condition. In the set condition, subjects were instructed that they might notice relations among some of the words that would facilitate recall. The results showed that such a set enhanced clustering for both categorized and uncategorized pairs of words that shared a high number of associated but no differential effect for instructions occurred when associative strength was low.

Another kind of task orientation manipulation that has been shown to reliably affect clustering of recall is that used by Jenkins and his colleagues (Hyde, 1973; Hyde & Jenkins, 1969; and recently by Mueller, 1978). In investigations using this procedure, subjects are presented with a list of words (say, four filler words and 12 pairs of medium strength associates) in a random order. Some subjects are required to perform a semantic orienting task (e.g., rating each word for pleasantness), whereas other subjects are engaged in a nonsemantic task (e.g., searching for words that have the letter "e" in them). The typical result is that the semantic orienting task results in reliably greater clustering than the nonsemantic task.

In a number of research contexts, social psychologists have shown an interest in the effects of task orientation on impressions. Zajonc's (1960) theory of cognitive tuning predicts that a person who expects to transmit a message to another person should have a rigid, polarized cognitive orientation toward stimulus information, whereas a person not expecting to transmit information should have a more flexible cognitive structure. Hence, one's cognitive set may mediate impressions formed of another person. In accord with this formulation, research by Brock and Fromkin (1968), Cohen (1961), and Harvey, Harkins, and Kagehiro (1976) has demonstrated that such a task variable affects receptivity to supportive information, polarization of impressions, and attributions of causality. One might also expect that such a cognitive tuning manipulation would affect the organization of recall of person information with transmitters demonstrating more clustering than receivers.

Another task variable of recent interest to social psychologists is that of an impression versus a recall task orientation. Hamilton, Katz, and Leirer (1980) have found that recall of person information is greater for subjects having an impression set than for subjects having a recall set. Using a similar manipulation, but presenting subjects with videotapes of person behaviors, Cohen and Ebbesen (1979) have found that impression subjects use fewer but larger temporal units than memory subjects and that the boundaries of the units used by impression subjects do not correspond to those of memory subjects. (Subjects indicated the boundaries of the units they were employing by pressing a button as they observed the behavioral stream.) It would seem worthwhile to explore how such a task orientation would affect the organization of the information recalled.

Number of Learning Trials. A third variable that affects organization of recall is the number of learning trials. Bousfield and Cohen (1953), for example, presented a four-category, 40-item list to subjects for either one, two, three, four, or five trials prior to a single free recall period and found that clustering was directly related to the number of presentations. Other research (Bousfield, Berkowitz, & Whitmarsh, 1959; Marshall, 1967; Robinson, 1966) using an alternating study-recall procedure has also shown that clustering increases progressively as a function of trials. This has also been demonstrated to hold true for idiosyncratic subjective organization (Bousfield, Puff, & Cowan, 1964; Tulving, 1962). Cofer and his associates (Cofer, 1967, Cofer, Bruce, & Reicher, 1966; Gonzalez & Cofer, (1959) have investigated changes in clustering from an immediate-recall test to a second test 5 minutes later. In general, they have found an increase in clustering and a decrease in recall as a function of delay.

The results of this group of studies suggest the potential usefulness of examining how organization of person impressions change over time and with repeated presentations of stimulus information. This research also seems germane to some recent research in social psychology concerning the effects of thinking about an attitude object. Tesser and his colleagues (Clary, Tesser, & Downing, 1978; Sadler & Tesser, 1973; Tesser, 1978; Tesser & Cowan, 1977; Tesser & Leone, 1977) have recently argued that: (1) persons have well-developed schemas for processing information about other persons; and (2) under certain theory-specified circumstances, thinking about an attitude object (e.g., a person) can polarize the attitude. Sadler and Tesser (1973), for example, presented subjects with either negative or positive information about a potential partner, had subjects indicate their liking for the individual, and then either distracted subjects from thinking about the individual or encouraged thinking about the individual before subjects rated the partner for a second time. Thought-condition subjects tended to polarize their second judgments compared to distraction-condition subjects. In order to understand this phenomenon, it is paramount to find indices other than the usual polarization index that are sensitive to manipulations of the amount of time spent thinking. The two explanations advanced (i.e., thought generates consistent congitions and thought results in reinterpretation of inconsistent cognitions) to explain this polarization phenomenon lead one to predict that thought should result in enhanced clustering of related facts about a person that are initially presented in a random order. Clustering of these cognitions about a person should provide a more consistent representation of the individual.[*]

Organizational Strategies

The studies just reviewed describe conditions that increase the likelihood of categorical clustering, but do not specify the alternative categorical bases people might use. When a subject is presented a list of stimuli in a free recall task, several alternative memory strategies could be adopted.

Serial Order.   One strategy is simply to attempt to recall the information on the basis of serial order. Mandler and Dean (1969) have demonstrated that subjects show a marked tendency to recall information in the same order in which it was presented. It seems unlikely that such a strategy would prove useful in an impression formation situation unless one were presented a minimum of information, were expecting no intervening events between input and need to recall, or wished to retain the information for only a short time.

Category Salience.   A second strategy subjects tend to use when presented a list in a free recall task is to group the stimulus information in terms of the most salient organizational categories. There is considerable evidence indicating that as conceptual categories become more salient and easy to discover there is a greater likelihood of subjects organizing their recall in terms of those categories (Bousfield, Cohen, & Whitmarsh, 1958; Cofer, 1965; Mandler, 1967; Shuell, 1969). One might expect, then, that if a subject was presented with information about several persons whose most salient difference was, for example, occupation, race, or sex, these differences might function as the most salient categories. Facts about all the males may be put together in one category and facts about the females in another. Organization of the person information in memory might reflect that salience (see Taylor, Fiske, Etcoff, & Ruderman, 1978). When, on the other hand, no obvious categorical scheme is available, subjects will find more subtle relationships among stimuli. Even then there often will still be substantial commonality among subjects in the manner in which they group their recall (Earhard, 1967; Tulving, 1962, 1965).

Competing Categories.   An especially interesting situation arises when (or if) people organize information in more than one way. The concern here is with determining the factors that increase or decrease the relative utilization of one organizational heuristic over another. For example, Dolinsky (1972) presented subjects with a list of words that could be grouped only according to associations, only according to rhymes, or in terms of both. When subjects could choose to organize their recall either according to associates or according to rhymes they overwhelmingly chose the former strategy, and this associative clustering increased across trials. When subjects could only organize recall according to rhymes there was weak but reliable rhyme clustering, which also increased across trials. When subjects could organize their recall only according to associations, subjects did so to a reliably greater degree than when they could only organize by rhymes.

Other studies in a similar vein have compared the relative utilization of taxonomic (categorical) versus alphabetical organization in lists (Lauer & Battig, 1972). When a stimulus list composed of words that can be organized either alphabetically or categorically is blocked alphabetically at input, subjects demonstrate greater categorical than alphabetical clustering. Similar subject preference for categorical over alphabetical clustering has been found by Mueller (1978). Assuming that the two potential organizational heuristics were equally salient to subjects in these studies (an assumption that was not tested), it is conceivable that subjects may have chosen to organize their recall in the manner they were most accustomed to using. That is, it is reasonable to assume that subjects do not ordinarily organize information according to rhyme or initial letter of the alphabet.

Studies such as the foregoing and those described immediately following, then, suggest a procedure by which one could compare the relative strength of a tendency to organize information according to persons versus according to other organizational schemes.

Divesta, Schultz, and Dangel (1973) and Perlmutter and Royer (1973) have examined the effect of competing organizational schemes on organization of recall of prose passages. In the Perlmutter and Royer (1973) study, subjects were presented prose paragraphs concerning the climate, language, chief agricultural products, chief industrial products, and geography of five fictitious countries. The test stimuli were five paragraphs of five sentences each, organized either by the country's name, attributes, or randomly presented. Subjects were required to recall the information either organized by name, by attribute, or in the order that things came to mind. For all subjects, a distractor task of counting backward was interpolated between stimulus presentation and recall. The results indicated that independent of input organization subjects tended to cluster their recall according to how they were requested to organize it. That is, subjects were equally able to organize their recall according to names or according to attributes.

Free recall subjects in the Perlmutter and Royer (1973) study showed a strong tendency to organize their recall according to names and almost no tendency to organize their recall according to attributes. Similar preference for name over attribute clustering has been found by Frase (1969); Schultz and Divesta (1972); and Myers, Pezdek, and Coulson (1973). On the basis of this evidence, it has been suggested that name organization is the more spontaneous and natural strategy (Shimmerlik, 1978). If this is the case, then one might expect that subjects presented information about persons that could be organized either according to attributes or names should show a preference for organization according to names. Herstein, Carroll, and Hayes (in press) provide some support for this prediction.

On the basis of this review of research dealing with the role of organization in memory, there appear to be a number of variables that are likely to affect the organization of person information. A free recall paradigm appears useful to study the organization of person information and the variables affecting such organization.

RESEARCH ON THE ORGANIZATION OF SOCIAL INFORMATION ACCORDING TO PERSONS

The research just reviewed supports the hypothesis that social information should, in general, be organized by persons. The long-time assumption of social psychologists that there exists a "person gestalt" would seem warranted. Often the information about others is blocked, is acquired under an impression set, and (especially for appearance and mannerism) is encountered on repeated occasions. All three of these factors were shown to increase the extent of clustering in free recall. This section describes the results of our investigations on the questions of when and how social information is organized around persons.

Pilot Research

In an initial pilot investigation, the possibility of persons serving as organizing foci in memory was explored using the free recall paradigm. It was hypothesized that subjects ordinarily would tend to cluster their recall of social information on a person-by-person basis. Subjects ($N = 20$) were verbally presented three items of familiar information about each of three well-known persons (a total of nine items) and asked to recall all the items in the order in which they came to mind. The three persons were designated by the letter A, S, and Q, rather than their real names (the facts referred to Elvis Presley, George Washington, and Abraham Lincoln). The nine items were read to the subjects three times, each time in a different random order. (The order was randomized with the constraint that if subjects recalled all nine items in the order they were read, clustering would occur at exactly chance level). Following each of the readings, subjects wrote down as many of the items as they could remember.

As mentioned previously, the ARC measure was used as our index of clustering in all our studies. Chance clustering of this index has a value of zero and perfect clustering has a value of 1.0. Averaging over all three trials in the pilot investigation, overall person clustering was substantially greater than chance ($\bar{X} = .68$, $p < .001$). Also, a significant increase in clustering was observed over the three trials ($\bar{X}$'s = .54, .71, & .80; $p < .001$). These data provide clear support for the conclusion that social information can be organized around persons in memory, and that this organization influences the patterning of free recall.

The foregoing findings are perfectly consistent with Asch's assumption that social perception is organized around persons. It should be noted, however, that this study used familiar facts about well-known persons. This is in contrast to most person perception research, which employs Asch's approach of studying "first impressions" of hypothetical or unfamiliar stimulus persons. It is possible that information sequences concerning such unfamiliar persons are not so readily organized on a person-by-person basis. We next describe a series of studies that analyzes the contribution of familiarity to a person-focused organization of social information.

Familiarity as a Determinant of the Organization of Person Information

In analyzing the contribution of person familiarity to a person-by-person organization of social information, our first goal was to develop a methodology by which we could assess the relative degree of person-focused organization of the same information under varying conditions of familiarity. To this end, a group of 38 undergraduate subjects participated in a pretest study in which they were asked to write down the names of the first three well-known persons that came to mind. Subsequently, subjects were asked to list the first three familiar facts that came to mind about each of the three persons they had listed. These names and facts were tabulated across subjects and the 20 most frequently mentioned names were selected. These names were divided into four sets of five on the basis of maximizing the heterogeneity within each set. Five of the most frequently mentioned facts about each person were selected and converted to generalities that would not uniquely distinguish the person. For example, "George Washington was the first president of the United States" was converted to "George Washington was a leader." These generalities are henceforth referred to as *descriptors*. It should be noted that descriptors were either nouns or adjectives.

For purposes of manipulating person familiarity, five names and the accompanying five descriptors for each name were arranged into 5 × 5 matrices, such as the one shown in Fig. 1.1. The rows in this matrix provide the description of the five familiar persons, and the columns represent the five unfamiliar persons. The particular positioning of descriptors within the rows of these matrices was first randomly determined and subsequently rearranged when the unfamiliar persons (represented by the columns) were inconsistent or improbable. The names of the unfamiliar persons were equated in letter length to the familiar names for each set. Using this counterbalancing scheme, it is possible to construe the same set of 25 descriptors in terms of both familiar and unfamiliar persons. In the

UNFAMILIAR PERSONS

	Stephan Falcoln	Don Carr	Alexander Cox	Clark Patterson	Chuck Cooke
Abraham Lincoln	TALL	HONEST	SELF-TAUGHT	LEADER	BEARDED
Bob Hope	GOLFER	OLD	CONSERVATIVE	COMEDIAN	HARD-WORKING
Muhamed Ali	RELIGIOUS	ATHLETE	CHAMPION	BLACK	OPINIONATED
Clint Eastwood	TOUGH	ACTOR	HANDSOME	RUGGED	VIRILE
Jerry Brown	OUTSPOKEN	BACHELOR	POLITICIAN	CALIFORNIAN	INDEPENDENT

(FAMILIAR PERSONS — row label at left margin)

FIG. 1.1.   Example of a stimulus set used in the first familiarity study.

following studies, information items were formed by combining familiar or unfamiliar names with descriptors in sentences with the verbs "is" or "was."

In an initial study (Pryor & Ostrom, 1979), 48 undergraduate subjects were verbally presented with all four stimulus sets, two in the familiar version and two in the unfamiliar version. Following each presentation, subjects were instructed to recall the information items and write them down in the order in which they came to mind. The exposure/recall sequence was presented twice for each stimulus set. A booklet of paper slips was provided, and subjects were instructed to write one recalled item on each consecutive slip without looking back.

In addition to the procedures mentioned thus far, this experiment also examined the generality of organizational factors across different set sizes. The 5 × 5 information matrices as shown in Fig. 1.1 were used to generate three additional set types. From each of these matrices, a 3 person × 3 descriptor matrix, a 3 person × 5 descriptor matrix, and a 5 person × 3 descriptor matrix were generated for both familiar and unfamiliar versions. These four stimulus set types constituted two two-level between-subjects variables.

ARC scores were computed for the recall protocols with persons considered as categories. As in the pilot study, errors were ignored in this computation. A recall response was considered correct in this analysis only if both name and descriptor were correct (analyses based on a less restrictive definition of error yielded comparable results). Figure 1.2 shows how clustering was affected by trials and by levels of person familiarity. An analysis of variance indicated significant main effects for familiarity F (1, 32) = 22.70, $p < .001$ and for trials F (1, 32) = 15.58, $p < .001$. No interactions or main effects involving number of persons or number of descriptors were obtained (all p's > .20). In Fig. 2.2, the mean ARC scores were significantly different from zero (p's

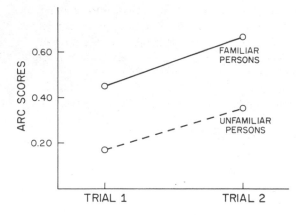

FIG. 1.2. Mean clustering index (ARC) as a function of person familiarity and trial.

< .001) in all cells except in the first trial of the unfamiliar condition [$p > .10$].

Thus, subjects tended to organize their recall around persons more if the information concerned familiar (or famous) persons than if it pertained to unfamiliar persons. Person-by-person organization also increased as subjects had more experience with the information sets. It is interesting to note that no significant degree of person-by-person organization existed in the first trial with the unfamiliar persons. This finding implies that studies of first impressions of unfamiliar stimulus persons should not necessarily assume that the person constitutes an integral unit of social perception.

Additional analyses were performed upon the number of items recalled correctly (where correct items represent a correct name and descriptor pairing) and the number of errors across experimental conditions. Noteworthy in these analyses is that the number recalled was higher in the familiar than in the unfamiliar condition and higher on trial 2 than on trial 1. Also, more errors were made in the unfamiliar than in the familiar conditions. The possibility exists, then, that the obtained clustering differences resulted from differences in amount recalled.

Roenckner, Thompson, and Brown (1971) point out that a distinct advantage in using ARC as a measure of clustering is that it should not be affected by the number of recalled items. An analysis of the average within-cell correlation between ARC and (1) the number of items recalled ($r = .13$, $p > .10$) and (2) number of errors ($r = -.15$, $p > .10$) bore this out in the present data. This shows that individual differences in the size of the recall set do not automatically produce a higher clustering score (as would be the case with the SCR index). When size of the memory set was experimentally manipulated by exposing 9 (the 3 × 3 matrix), 15 (the 3 × 5 matrices), or 25 (5 × 5 matrix) stimulus items, again no effects were found on the amount of clustering.

Three Explanations of the Familiarity Effect.   The high and low familiarity stimulus sets used in the preceding studies differed from one another in two ways. The names used to designate the stimulus person were selected to be either familiar or unfamiliar. Second, the information items describing each person were either familiar or unfamiliar. That is, because the items were selected so that they all pertained to one well-known person, the items may have a high degree of associative overlap. The interitem associations may be stronger in the familiar than in the unfamiliar sets. Note in Fig. 1.1 that Bob Hope is old and conservative; Clint Eastwood is tough, rugged, and virile; and Jerry Brown is outspoken and independent. Although occasional instances of semantic related-ness occur for the unfamiliar persons (e.g., tough and outspoken for Stephan Falcon in Fig. 1.1), they seem to occur much less frequently.

This potential confound was purposely retained in our stimulus sets to insure inclusion of the two kinds of familiarity that exist in day-to-day life. In this research, name familiarity results from having frequently encountered informa-tion about that person in the past. On the other hand, information about a new person may ''seem'' familiar because of high interitem associations. The infor-mation may fit together in a way that suggests a ''type'' of person, such as the high-achiever student or the cantankerous old curmudgeon. Including both types of familiarity in the manipulation insured that if either affects clustering in free recall, those effects would be detected. Now that such effects have been ob-tained, the next step is to isolate the separate contribution of each.

Distinguishing between name familiarity and interitem association strength is the first step in providing a theoretical analysis of the processes that underly the effects of familiarity on clustering. The overall effect may have been produced by one (or more) of the following three processes:

1. *Name discriminability* could have operated by providing a greater incen-tive to recall the information by name for familiar than for unfamiliar names. Familiar names would be easier to recall and therefore provide a more convenient starting point for memory search during the retrieval stage. According to this explanation, the nature of the information describing the person is irrelevent. If correct, it suggests that our findings were not necessarily due to the organization of information in memory, but due primarily to the nature of the information search at the retrieval stage. If this is the case, then familiarity of name should affect clustering independently of the information in the stimulus set.

2. The *strength of interitem associations* could have produced the effect independent of whether a person name was linked to the information items. If the familiar information sets do, in fact, possess high interitem associations in com-parison to the unfamiliar sets, then the clustering effects could have resulted from this differential associative structure. That is, accessing one item from a high association set will readily bring to mind other items from that set (and therefore the subject will record them contiguously in the recall task). This is less likely to occur in the low association sets. This explanation of the clustering effects assumes they are due to the nature of information organization in memory rather

than a result of retrieval processes. If the obtained clustering effects were due to this explanation, then the association value of the information sets should have the same effects on clustering, regardless of name familiarity.

3. A third explanation stems from the possibility that subjects use specific *person schemata* in their organization of new information about familiar persons, but not with unfamiliar persons. For famous persons, the schema involves strong associative bonds between the person's name and a number of other facts about the person. When information items are encountered, the person may fit them into this already existing structure. Because no such schemata are available for unfamiliar persons, little person clustering should occur with unfamiliar names, regardless of whether they are linked to high or low association stimulus sets.

Two versions of the third explanation can be identified. It may be that schemata only affect clustering when the stimulus item is either already a part of the schema or is strongly linked to an existing schema element. Such strong associative pathways may be a prerequisite for the recall of one information item to elicit another item in the same schema. If true, it would mean that the only time that strong person clustering would occur is when the information items to be recalled are relevent to the schema. If low association stimulus sets were linked to familiar names, the amount of person clustering would be low and similar to that obtained when the low association sets were linked to unfamiliar names.

A second version of the person schema explanation is based on the possibility that a person schema can affect clustering even for information items that were not originally a part of the schema. Although most of the items in the low association stimulus sets were not selected to be part of the schema of the famous persons, it is possible that subjects could find meaningful linkages between them and the person schema. For example, there is a sense in which Muhammed Ali is self-taught, handsome, and a politician. To the extent that this version of the person schema explanation holds, it would be expected that the amount of person clustering observed when low association items are paired with a familiar name should be greater than when they are paired with an unfamiliar name. However, because these linkages to the schema would be weaker than for information directly related to the familiar person schema, the amount of clustering should be less than is found in the completely familiar case.

Tests of the Three Explanations.   An experiment conducted by Pryor and Ostrom was designed to assess the base-rate clustering that might be attributable to interitem associations in the stimulus sets used in the foregoing experiment. If the effect of familiarity was exclusively due to high versus low interitem associations, similar clustering differences would be expected, even if no names were attached to the descriptors at the time of stimulus presentation.

Twenty-four subjects were presented with the 25 descriptors from each of the four stimulus sets. The descriptors were presented without any person names attached. Subjects read through each stimulus set three times (the desciptors were printed on index cards), each time in a different shuffled order. They then were instructed to recall the descriptors, writing them down in the order they came to mind. Subsequently, subjects were given one additional exposure and a second recall trial. The order of the four stimulus sets was counterbalanced across subjects.

Each recall protocol was given two clustering scores. The familiar person categorization of descriptors (e.g. the rows in Fig. 1.1) were used for computing one score, and the unfamiliar person categories (the columns in Fig. 1.1) were used for the other. The resulting two clustering indices were analyzed as repeated measures. The means of these two ARC scores were .07 for the familiar (or high association) sets and $-.02$ for the unfamiliar (or low association) sets. Although this difference is small, and both values are near zero, the difference was statistically reliable [$F(1, 20) = 11.76$, $p < .01$]. No effects were found due to trials or stimulus replications. These results indicate that a difference in interitem association may have accounted for some part of the clustering results of the first experiment. When the very small magnitude of clustering observed in this study is compared to the relatively robust clustering tendencies observed in the first experiment, the additional influence of other processes is suggested.

The next study, also conducted by Pryor and Ostrom was designed to simultaneously assess all three alternative explanations of the familiarity effect (name discriminability, interitem association, and person schema). The basic variables involved in this study are perhaps best understood by referring back to Fig. 1.1. In this study the pairing of names and descriptor sets was manipulated orthogonally. Familiar names were presented in conjuction with either the high association or low association descriptor sets (the rows or columns, respectively, from Fig. 1.1). Likewise, unfamiliar names were presented with either high or low association descriptor sets. The basic experimental design, then, was a 2 (familiar vs. unfamiliar names) by 2 (high vs. low association descriptor sets) factorial. Subjects saw all four of these conditions, each with a different stimulus replication (replications were latin square counterbalanced across conditions over subjects). Another factor in this experiment was stimulus set size. Half the subjects received nine item sets (3 persons × 3 descriptors) and half received 25 item sets (5 persons × 5 descriptors).

Thirty-two subjects participated in this experiment. Subjects were told that the experiment concerned their memory for information about persons. The information items for each stimulus set were printed on index cards in the form of sentences.

The descriptor word in each sentence was underlined. Subjects were instructed to remember the underlined words as they read through each stimulus deck, saying the sentences aloud. The rationale for having subjects remember only the descriptors involved reducing the number of recall errors by simplifying the response task. It should also help solve an interpretive problem with the previous procedure. It should reduce subjects' tendency to use the name written down on the preceding response as a retrieval cue for the next response.

The subjects went through two exposure and two recall trials for each of the four stimulus decks. The order of cards within each deck was arbitrarily determined by shuffling for each exposure. Subjects' recall protocols were scored for clustering around the stimulus persons.

Each of the three alternative explanations for the familiarity effect makes a different prediction for this study. The name discriminability explanation predicts that the only significant effect should be the name familiarity main effect. Name discriminability should be just as influential when paired with low or high association item sets. Conversely, the interitem association explanation predicts only a main effect due to the item set factor. This effect should occur under both levels of name familiarity.

If person schemata are activated in this research task, an interaction between the two factors just discussed would be expected. As noted previously, there are two versions of the person schema explanation, both involving the prediction of an interaction. They have in common the expectation that when an unfamiliar name is used, no person schema should be evoked. Consequently, they both predict that there will be no difference between the high and low association stimulus sets when an unfamiliar name is presented.

The first version of the person schema explanation required that the information sets contain items that were already a part of the schema before the schema would facilitate clustering. This means that the familiar name/high assocaition association value condition should produce higher clustering than the other three and that those three should not differ from one another. The second version of the person schema explanation relaxed the requirement that the information item be an explicit part of the preexisting schema. It allowed for the possibility that people could discover or create lines of association between each stimulus item and one or more elements of the schema. In this case, it would be expected that the familiar name/low association value condition be lower than the familiar name/high association value condition, but higher than the other two.

The data of this study (see Table 1.1) clearly favored the name discriminability and interitem association explanations over either version of the person schema explanation. The main effect for name familiarity was significant [F (1, 24) = 13.58, $p < .001$], which supports the name discriminability explanation. Also, the main effect for item set was significant [F (1, 24) = 13.61, $p < .001$], which supports the interitem association explanation. Consistent with both was the finding that the interaction was not significant [F (1, 24) = 1.19, p = n.s.]. All the foregoing findings held for both the small (3 × 3) and large (5 × 5) stimulus sets.

The absence of a significant interaction is contrary to the predictions of the person schema explanation. The second (or more relaxed) version came closest in that it correctly predicted that the familiar name/low association cell should be

TABLE 1.1
Mean Clustering Scores (ARC)
as a Function of Name
Familiarity
and Descriptor Set
Association Value[a]

		Association Value of Descriptor Set	
		Low	High
Names	Familiar	.37[b]	.66[b]
	Unfamiliar	.17	.37[b]

[a]Perfect clustering is indicated by an ARC of 1.0 and chance by zero.
[b]Mean ARC greater than chance, $p < .05$

between the familiar name/high association and unfamiliar name/low association conditions. However, neither version anticipated that the unfamiliar name/high association condition would be above the baseline established by the unfamiliar name/low association condition.

It is clear that the first (or strong) version of the person schema explanation cannot account for the outcome of this study. However, with some adjustment, it is possible that the more relaxed version could have been operating. It may have been that in the unfamiliar name/high association condition that some of the subjects were able to recognize the famous person from the descriptor set and employed the schema for that person during recall. Even though the tall, bearded, honest, self-taught leader was given the name of Stephen Falcoln in this condition, some subjects may have thought to themselves that this stimulus person sounded like Abraham Lincoln. Unfortunately, subjects were not asked at the end of this study whether any of the unfamiliar persons remined them of other well-known persons.

This study, then, ruled out only one explanation of the familiarity effect on clustering in free recall—that being the strong version of the person schema explanation. This still leaves three possibilities. Although the more relaxed version of the person schema explanation has the advantage of accounting for all the findings in terms of just one theoretical process, we cannot rule out the simultaneous operation of the name discriminability and interitem association explanations.

One clear conclusion from this study is that the original familiarity effect cannot be fully explained on the basis of processes operating at the time of retrieval. Name discriminability, a retrieval process, could account for the name familiarity main effect, but not for the effect of high versus low association value item sets. At least one component of person familiarity, then, reflects the nature of how information is organized in memory. Whether the effect of name familiarity on clustering was a retrieval process (via name discriminability) or an organizational process (via person schema) remains to be determined.

One useful approach to this problem is through the use of "multiple operations." Pryor and Ostrom (1979) have shown that person familiarity affects other kinds of responses besides clustering in free recall. At least one of these, speed of descriptor recognition, supports the view that organizational processes underlie the familiarity effects. This is consistent with other research using a recognition time methodology to study the organization of person information. Smith, Adams, and Schorr (1978) have shown that descriptors thematically related to the person schema are recognized more quickly than unrelated ones. Anderson (1977) has shown that with repetition, items of person information become more strongly linked to the organizing node of the person. Both these factors would appear to differentiate our familiar from our unfamiliar persons at the organizational level.

In both the first and third studies of this series, unfamiliar information about strangers was not organized in recall according to persons. The clustering indices in those conditions were not significantly greater than chance. Among other concerns that arise from this finding is the question that if the information is not organized according to persons, then how is it organized? The next series of studies was aimed at exploring alternative ways people might be organizing social information in memory.

Alternatives to Person Organization

The previous studies indicated that social information is most likely to be cognitively organized according to persons when the information constitutes familiar descriptors concerning familiar persons. The organization of unfamiliar information about strangers according to persons emerged only under repeated exposures. It is important to note that the information sets used in these experiments could not readily be organized in any other manner except according to persons. Efforts were made to keep the stimulus persons within a set relatively distinct from one another and the information items were randomly ordered. Therefore, it seems reasonable to infer that other types of cognitive organization might typify the mental representations of information concerning strangers.

In our laboratory, two types of competing cognitive organizations have been studied in conjunction with person information: (1) descriptor organization; and (2) temporal organization. Descriptor organization refers to an organization based upon semantically related descriptor items. For example, information items might be cognitively classified as being instances of hometowns, part-time jobs, or hobbies. Temporal organization in our research refers to an organization based on the temporal order in which blocks of information are received. For example, information items may be presented in consecutive blocks on different pages of a questionnaire, where a block contains one item about each of the persons.

Two experiments that examine the role of competing organizations in the recall of person information are presented in the following section. Unlike the preceding studies, these structure the information sets in a manner that makes available explicit alternatives to person organization. In addition, these experiments also explored the role of different task demands in mentally organizing person information.

Descriptor Organization.   Simpson (1979) conducted several studies employing competing descriptor category designs. Three of these studies involved unfamiliar descriptors about strangers. Because the results of these studies are quite similar, only one will be described in any detail. Following is an example stimulus set used in Simpson's research:

Dave is a part-time usher.
Dave is from Witchita, Kansas.
Tom is from Richmond, Virginia.
Tom enjoys collecting beer cans.
John enjoys collecting coins.
Tom is a part-time dishwasher.
John is from Denver, Colorado.
Dave enjoys tinkering with cars.
John is a part-time farmworker.

There are two alternative ways this information can be organized. The information items may be grouped according to the persons Dave, Tom, and John. Or they may be seen as instances of the categories: part-time jobs, hobbies, and hometowns. Thus, person and descriptor organizations are orthogonal within this set.

Subjects in this experiment (N = 32) were presented with nine information items like those in the foregoing set. They were in a written format with each item on a consecutive page. The order of the items was arranged so that if subjects recalled all of the items in the order they were presented, clustering would occur at exactly a chance level for both the person and descriptor organizations.

In the previous studies, subjects were in a learning set when they received the information. The present study had subjects focus on forming impressions from the information. Two kinds of impression sets were used.

Half of the subjects were given the task of forming impressions of how compatible the three persons in a stimulus set would be as college roommates for an academic year. The other half were asked to form an impression of which person in each group would least fit in as a roommate for an academic year. The second judgment task was intended to promote the cognitive individuation of the stimulus set according to persons; the first was inteded to merely encourage the subject to attend to the information.

As a matter of procedure, the subjects were: (1) informed of the judgment task and given the names of the persons to be judged; (2) presented the stimulus set; (3) required to make the judgment; (4) given a distractor task; and (5) tested for recall. This exposure/recall sequence was repeated one additional time. The purpose of including a distractor (which in this case involved picking the names of famous psychologists from a letter matrix) was to insure that recall was not just a function of regurgitating the contents of short-term memory.

An analysis of the ARC indices derived from the recall protocols revealed several interesting results. First, there was no evidence that subjects organized their recall according to persons. The mean ARC for person clustering was .05, which was not significantly different from chance ($F < 1$).[1] Nor was this index affected by exposure/recall trials ($F < 1$). However, there was evidence that subjects organized their recall according to descriptor categories [$\bar{X} = 0.24$, F (1, 16) $= 5.59$, $p < .03$]. This measure was also unaffected by exposure/recall repetition ($F < 1$). The between subjects variable, task orientation failed to produce any significant effects with regard to either person or descriptor clustering.

The main results of this study were duplicated in another experiment, also reported in Simpson (1979), in which photographs were substituted for the names in the stimulus sets. In this replication, only the group-compatibility-as-roommates judgment was required of subjects.

The results of these studies are congruent with the preceding findings that unfamiliar persons are not likely to serve as organizing foci for social information. Physical information such as age, race, height, and sex are all readily apparent when meeting a number of new people (e.g., attending a cocktail party or starting a new job). In such circumstances, one might remember that all the women were outspoken, but not remember which woman said what. One might expect such descriptor organizations to dominate the representation of information about unfamiliar persons.

Another factor that appears to affect the organization of information about unfamiliar others is the amount of information (or memory load) acquired about the persons. Rothbart, Fulero, Jensen, Howard, and Birrell (1978) found that under high memory load, information is organized by trait characteristics, and

---

[1]The scoring of the recall protocols for clustering in this experiment involved a slightly different strategy than was used in experiments hitherto described. Recall responses were included for analysis if they involved only a correct descriptor (without a name) or if they involved a correct name/ descriptor pairing. Again errors were ignored.

under low memory load, it is organized by person. Presumably, then, the tendency of Simpson's (1979) subjects to organize by descriptor would have been even greater had he used a larger number of stimulus items.

One question left unanswered in this study is: How is information about familiar (compared to unfamiliar) persons cognitively organized when such salient competing descriptor categories are present? Although the next and final study reported in this series does not use a competing category design that involves descriptor categories, it nevertheless addresses the general question. Indeed, the competing categories involved in the following study are perhaps even more immediately salient than those involved in the last one.

Temporal Organization.   One of the variables that potentially influences the cognitive organization of the social information we encounter is the spatial–temporal sequence of our experience. For example, we may remember several facts that we encountered concerning the people with whom we had lunch today, several items of information that were discussed in a faculty meeting this afternoon, and several news items heard on the radio coming home from work. Significant spatial–temporal contexts may thus serve to organize our experiences. In studies from the cognitive literature, this sort of organization is often operationalized by "blocking" stimulus information into discrete groups. Whereas social experience is perhaps not often blocked into units as distinct as those employed in cognitive experiments,[2] there are chronological conventions such as general times of the day (morning, afternoon, night) or even days of the week that may serve as organizing foci.

The present experiment (conducted by Pryor & Ostrom) attempted to operationalize blocking in a manner that would seem relevent to the manner in which we usually encounter social information. The principle aim of the experiment was to observe the organizational influence of temporal categories upon person information across varying conditions of person familiarity. A secondary concern was to further explore the possibility that differential judgmental sets may mediate organizational tendencies.

Forty-eight subjects participated in this experiment. Half of the subjects were given Memory Set instructions and the other half were given Impression Set instructions. In the Memory Set condition, subjects were merely told that they would be given information sets about persons and would subsequently be asked to recall the information. In the Impression Set condition, subjects were given the same memory instructions and, in addition, they were told that they would have to make favorability ratings of each of the several persons described in the information sets. These person ratings were to be made from memory. It was hypothesized that the Impression Set instructions would tend to encourage a

---

[2]It should be noted that some theorists (e.g., Newtson, Ridner, Miller, & La Cross, 1978) maintain that the stream of social experience is organized into discrete, consensually perceived units.

person-by-person representation of the information in comparison to the Memory Set instructions.

The information sets used in this study were the same 3 persons × 3 descriptors sets used in our original familiarity study (see Fig. 1.1). The information items included names and descriptors. The descriptors were underlined and subjects were told to try to remember the underlined words. Each subject received two familiar and two unfamiliar sets. Order of the stimulus sets and familiarity conditions was counterbalanced. Each stimulus information set was blocked into three groups of three items each. Within a block was contained one item concerning each stimulus person in the set. Blocks were presented on consecutive pages in a test booklet. At the top of the page containing the first block was: "Imagine that on *Monday* you found out the following information." The second block was labeled *Tuesday* and the third, *Wednesday*. The information items were randomly ordered within each block.

Following presentation of a stimulus set, subjects were given a 1-minute distractor task that involved counting backwards from a three-digit number (e.g., 697) by threes. Next, subjects were asked to recall all of the descriptors they could and write them on a single page in the order they came to mind. Finally, subjects in the Impression Set condition made a favorability rating of each stimulus person on a seven-point scale. Each subject went through this entire procedure for each stimulus set three times. The order of the information items within a block was counterbalanced over trials.

Each recall protocol was given two clustering scores, one based on persons and one on the temporal blocks (day of the week). These two ARC indices were treated as repeated measures. The variables of theoretical interest in this experiment constituted a 2 (set) × 2 (person familiarity) × 2 (ARC index) factorial design.

One of the main reasons for doing this study was to explain whether person familiarity affected the extent to which nonperson forms of information organization would be used. Of primary interest, then, is the interaction between person familiarity and clustering index. Figure 1.3 shows that, as in the previous

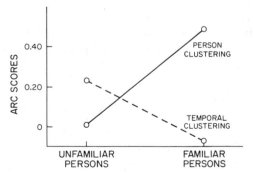

FIG. 1.3.   Mean person and temporal clustering indices (ARC's) as a function of person familiarity.

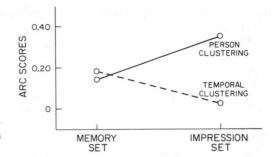

FIG. 1.4.   Mean person and temporal clustering indices (ARC's) as a function of instructional set.

studies, little person clustering is found with unfamiliar stimulus persons. There was a significant interaction [F (1, 32) = 87.54, $p < .001$] that was caused by temporal clustering being greater for unfamiliar than familiar persons. This finding, along with that in the preceding study, establishes that people tend to prefer nonperson bases of cognitive organization when the social information is about unfamiliar persons.

There was also a significant two-way interaction between the set manipulation and cluster index, [F (1, 32) = 7.17, $p < .02$]. This interaction is depicted in Fig. 1.4. When the subjects' task is to form an impression, they show a strong preference of person organization over temporal organization; however under Memory Set conditions, neither organization clearly dominated over the other. Thus, the Impression Set instructions functioned as hypothesized.

Another interaction was obtained between the Familiarity and the Set factors [F (1, 32) = 5.60 p $< .03$]. The basic nature of this interaction was that, summing over person and temporal clustering, more clustering was detected in the Familiar, Impression Set condition than in the other conditions. One interpretation of this finding is that more overall organization of social information occurred in this condition than in the others. Subjects were able to use person organization and temporal organization simultaneously. However, because the person and temporal ARC indices tended to be negatively correlated, any interpretation would seem somewhat speculative. Finally, it should be noted that the number of presentation trials had no clear effect on organizational tendencies.

These results replicate the findings of the familiarity series of experiments: Person-by-person organizations of social information tended to occur only under familiar conditions. Furthermore, other forms of cognitive organization seemed to emerge and dominate when information concerned unfamiliar persons. It is also interesting to note that person-by-person organizations of familiar person information seemed to be utilized in recall even when salient competing organizational categories were present.

The findings vis-a-vis the set manipulation suggest that situational demands concerning the expected uses of person information may affect the manner in which it is organized in memory. Thus, these findings suggest ways in which different cognitive organizations of person information may be encouraged. This is particularly important considering that, as we note in the following, the way social information is cognitively organized may have important implications for social behavior.

DISCUSSION

Previous research in person perception has not questioned the assumption that social information is organized according to persons. The research reported in this chapter suggests that such an organization only occurs under certain circumstances, one of which is when the information concerns familiar persons. A variety of other implications arise when one questions the "person organization" assumption made by previous researchers. In this section we discuss: (1) alternative forms of cognitive organization; (2) behavioral consequences of person organization; (3) possible individual differences; and (4) affective considerations.

Alternative Ways of Organizing Social Information

One of the first questions of interest has to do with identifying alternative modes of organization. When people are not organizing social information by person, how are they organizing it?

The last two studies reported in the foregoing section confirm the existence of two alternative modes of organization: descriptor and temporal organizations. We now suggest other organizational modes and describe how the several alternatives relate to the Anderson and Bower (1973) model of associative memory.

As an item of social information is received, the perceiver no doubt forms many associative linkages. In a computer stimulation of Human Associative Memory (HAM) developed by Anderson and Bower (1973), information is "parsed" or organized according to several idea nodes. The first two nodal divisions assigned to incoming information are a "fact node," and a "context node." The "fact node" is further divided into a subject node (which is comparable to the person node under investigation in the present studies) and a predicate node. The predicate node is further subdivided into verb and object nodes (These latter nodes refer to the person features conveyed by the information items.)

The second major nodal division (the "context node") is subdivided into location and time nodes. They refer to the place (or context) and time (or sequence) in which the factual information items occurred. This latter nodal organization is quite similar to the temporal organization operationalized by blocking in the study mentioned previously.

Nodes are interconnected in a hierarchical fashion through associative pathways for each information item. A person feature (i.e., the "predicate node") will frequently be linked to superordinate descriptor categories. In the Simpson

(1979) study, the person feature "enjoys tinkering with cars" had a preexisting linkage to the descriptor category "hobby." Similarly, a skin color feature (e.g., yellow) has a preexisting linkage to a racial category (e.g., oriental).

In terms of human associative memory, the organizational influence of any node in this network is determined by the associative strength of the pathways connecting it to other relevant nodes. Associative strength is thought to be determined by the number of intervening nodes and the frequency with which the pathway between nodes has been activated (Anderson & Bower, 1973; Collins & Loftus, 1975).

The theoretical framework provided by Anderson and Bower suggests three ways social information can be organized in addition to a person-oriented organization. The fact that social information is temporally ordered (or blocked) provides one alternative form of organization that was verified in one of our studies. This temporal information is represented by the time node. For example, in some coffee shops two or more waitresses frequently serve the same customer. As a customer, you may recall the sequence of acts on the part of the waitresses (e.g., brought menu, took order, poured coffee, and looked impatient while you were finishing). You may, however, not be able to identify which one of the several waitresses did each of the acts. Not only can people organize on the basis of temporal sequence, but they can organize around specific dates. Most older people can probably remember what they were doing on their 21st birthday; Yarmey and Bull (1978) found that 97% of a large sample of Americans and Canadians could remember (when asked in 1976) what they were doing on November 22, 1963.

A second alternative to person organization is organization around situational or contextual features of the social information setting. This is represented by Anderson and Bower's location node. For example, people find it easy to recall social encounters that occurred when on vacation, while attending costume parties, or while visiting public restrooms.

The third alternative emerges from the nature of the person features stored in the predicate node (which consists of the verb and object). Many features can readily be classified into broader descriptor categories. One of our studies showed that for unfamiliar persons, items of social information may be linked more strongly to nodes representing these descriptor categories than to person nodes. For example, you may come away from a party remembering you met a policeman and a fireman, and that one was in his 20s, and one was in his 40s. However, you may find it impossible to recall which was which. It would be clear in this instance that the information was organized by the descriptor categories of occupation and age rather than by the persons.

A fourth form of social information organization of particular interest to social psychologists (and one not directly suggested by the HAM model) is organization according to the self. We may organize person features on the basis of being similar or dissimilar to ourselves (e.g., Markus, 1977; Rogers, Kuiper, &

Kirker, 1977). This form of cognitive organization would go beyond the immediate factual nature of information and emphasize an integration with one's recollections of one's own past experiences.

One issue that has yet to be addressed is whether social information can be simultaneously organized according to two or more of these alternatives. The associative network model would allow for this possibility because information items are linked to a variety of these organizational nodes. The data from our study on person versus temporal clustering (where the total amount of person plus temporal clustering was greatest for familiar persons) suggests that the ability to access social information through several organizational alternatives occurs primarily for familiar persons.

Descriptor Organization and Stereotyping.   Of these four alternative organizational modes, perhaps the most relevent to past work in social psychology is the third—organization by descriptor. When a particular behavior or person feature dominates the organization of information concerning some person, other behaviors or characteristics of that person may become less accessible in memory. We believe it is this type of organization that forms the basis of stereotyping.

It is interesting to note that stereotyping is one area in social psychology that has not adopted the assumption that social information is organized around persons. Stereotypes represent exactly the opposite process; social information is organized around a descriptor category (e.g., ethnic label, gender designation, mental illness label), and the unique features of each group member are ignored or forgotten. Studies that would contrast a person-dominated organization to a descriptor-dominated organization offer the potential of integrating person perception processes and stereotyping processes under the same conceptual structure.

Two kinds of settings appear promising in studying descriptor organization: settings that contain *crossed* and settings that contain *nested* information ensembles. Crossed information ensembles refer to circumstances under which the observer receives the exact same categories of information about all persons. The study by Simpson (1979) is an example of this sort of design. We may infer that organizing by descriptor categories obfuscates the relationship of particular descriptors to particular persons.

Nested information ensembles refer to settings in which there is only one dominant feature used to classify persons (e.g., race or sex) and several distinct (noncrossed) items of information are received about each person in each category. For example, say you meet two whites and two blacks and learn several different facts about each. You may remember the facts about the whites and the facts about the blacks, but not be able to recall which fact went with each person within a racial category. This was the situation studied by Taylor et al. (1978).

Through systematic variation of the qualities that are potentially important to the formation of person nodes, it should be possible to gain an understanding of how person nodes can come to exert an influence in the context of highly influential descriptor nodes. Such a line of research has a rich potential for the understanding of stereotyping and how one might encourage the consideration of persons as individuals.

A final point to be mentioned regarding person versus descriptor organization is the potential effects of memory on decision making. Memory-based judgments are dependent on the accuracy and specificity of information available from memory. The mode of organization is certain to affect the amount of information one can retrieve from the original information ensemble, and the nature of the reconstructive errors introduced.

Behavioral Consequences of Person Organization

Another avenue for future investigation involves the overt behavioral manifestations of cognitive organization. Research by Wilder (1977) has already examined some conceptual issues that are relevant to this concern. Wilder found that the social influence of persons in a conformity situation was greater when subjects were encouraged to perceive the persons as individual "social entities" than when subjects were encouraged to perceive them as members of a group. Although Wilder did not directly assess the cognitive representation of the stimulus persons in his experiments, it is reasonable to suggest that a single node was used to represent all persons when they were perceived as members of the same group and that each person was represented by a separate node when he or she was perceived as a separate social entity. Future research may be designed to combine the methodologies proposed in this chapter with the methodologies described by Wilder. In this way, cognitive and behavioral indices of person node formation may be assessed within the same setting.

An additional question that may be posed in this same conceptual vein is: Are persons who are cognitively represented in terms of highly organized person nodes more likely to be *treated* as individuals in a behavioral sense? Research along these lines might ultimately lead to a better understanding of the cognitive bases of discriminatory behaviors. Are administrators more likely to withhold resources from a group cognitively organized by descriptor (e.g., an out group) than from a group organized (at least in part) by persons?

Individual Differences

Another direction for future research involves the role of individual differences. There may be individual preferences for cognitively organizing social information according to person or descriptor categories. It may be that people with a chronic inability to relate to others as individuals suffer from a deficit in their capacity to organize social information by person. If so, it would be worthwhile to develop training programs to facilitate person organization.

Certain descriptor categories may be dispositionally preferred to other categories. This is directly implied by the work of Kelly (1955) and Rosenberg (1977). Also, there may be general organizational preferences related to self-schemata (Markus, 1977; Rogers, Kuiper, & Kirker, 1977). Organizational preferences may also evolve from past experiences that impose a highly organized categorical structure upon person information, e.g., the reliance on particular diagnostic categories (Chapman & Chapman, 1969).

Affective Considerations

The final conceptual factor that we mention as a possible avenue of future investigations is the role of affect. How does affect (or emotion) influence the formation of person nodes? At least two possibilities should be explored. In relation to discriminability, sentiments may influence one's focus of attention. A person may become a salient organizing theme because the feelings that an observer has toward that person may consistently direct the observer's focus of attention toward the person.

On a different level of analysis, one might suggest that the associative dynamics of memory that have been described in this chapter are primarily characteristic of nonaffective thought processes. Although the trends in cognitive psychology direct us to explore rational information processing, it is possible that emotional factors circumvent rational processes. On the other hand, emotional states may serve only to intensify the influence of a dominant organizational mode. In either case, the influence of emotional factors deserves further attention in experimental investigations.

ACKNOWLEDGMENTS

This research was sponsored in part by the Organizational Effectiveness Research Program, Office of Naval Research (Contract No. N00014-79-C-0027, NR 170-882). We wish to acknowledge helpful comments on an earlier draft provided by M. Hyde, J. Lingle, M. Mitchell, W. Wallace, and R. Wyer.

REFERENCES

Anderson, J. R. Memory for information about individuals. *Memory and Cognition*, 1977, *5*, 430–442.

Anderson, J. R., & Bower, G. H. *Human associative memory*. Washington, D.C.: Winston & Sons, 1973.

Anderson, J. R., & Hastie, R. Individuation and reference in memory: Proper names and definite descriptions. *Cognitive Psychology*, 1974, *6*, 495–514.

Anderson, N. H. Information integration theory: A brief survey. In D. Krantz, R. Atkinson, R.

Luci, & P. Suppes (Eds.), *Contemporary developments in mathematical psychology* (Vol. 2). San Francisco: Freeman, 1974.

Asch, S. E. Forming impressions of personality. *Journal of Abnormal and Social Psychology,* 1946, *41,* 258–290.

Balser, E. The free recall and category clustering of factual material presented in complex sentences. *Psychonomic Science,* 1972, *27,* 327–328.

Bousfield, A. K., & Bousfield, W. A. Measurement of clustering and of sequential constancies in repeated free recall. *Psychological Reports,* 1966, *19,* 935–942.

Bousfield, W. A. The occurrence of clustering in the recall of randomly arranged associates. *Journal of General Psychology,* 1953, *49* 229–240.

Bousfield, W. A., Berkowitz, H., & Whitmarsh, G. A. Associative clustering in the recall of minimally meaningful geometric designs. *Canadian Journal of Psychology,* 1959, *13,* 281–287.

Bousfield, W. A., & Cohen, B. H. The effects of reinforcement on the occurrence of clustering in the recall of randomly arranged associates. *Journal of Psychology,* 1953, *36,* 67–81.

Bousfield, W. A., Cohen, B. H., & Whitmarsh, G. A. Associative clustering in the recall of words of different taxonomic frequencies of occurrence. *Psychological Reports,* 1958, *4,* 39–44.

Bousfield, W. A., Puff, C. R., & Cowan, T. M. The development of constancies in sequential organization during repeated free recall. *Journal of Verbal Learning and Verbal Beahvior,* 1964, *3,* 489–495.

Brock, T. C., & Fromkin, H. L. Cognitive tuning set and behavioral receptivity to discrepant information. *Journal of Personality,* 1968, *36,* 108–125.

Byrne, D. *The attraction paradigm.* New York: Academic Press, 1971.

Chapman, L. J., & Chapman, J. P. Illusory correlations as an obstacle to the use of valid psychodiagnostic signs. *Journal of Abnormal Psychology,* 1969, *74,* 271–280.

Clary, E. G., Tesser, A., & Downing, L. L. Influence of a salient schema on thought-induced cognitive change. *Personality and Social Psychology Bulletin,* 1978, *4* 39–44.

Cofer, C. N. On some factors in the organizational characteristics of free recall. *American Psychologist,* 1965, *20,* 261–272.

Cofer, C. N. Does conceptual organization influence the amount retained in immediate free recall. In B. Kleinmuntz (Ed.), *Concepts and the structure of memory,* New York: John Wiley & Sons, 1967.

Cofer, C. N., Bruce, D., & Reicher, G. M. Clustering in free recall as a function of certain methodological variations. *Journal of Experimental Psychology,* 1966, *71,* 858–866.

Cofer, C. N., & Reicher, G. M. *The effects of grouping during presentation and of immediate recall on clustering in free recall.* Paper read at the Western Psychological Convention, Santa Monica, Calif., April 1963.

Cohen, A. R. Cognitive tuning as a factor affecting impression formation. *Journal of Personality.* 1961, *29,* 235–245.

Cohen, C. E., & Ebbesen, E. B. Observational goals and schema activation: A theoretical framework for behavior perception. *Journal of Experimental Social Psychology,* 1979, *15,* 305–329.

Colle, H. A. The reification of clustering. *Journal of Verbal Learning and Verbal Behavior,* 1972, *11,* 624–633.

Collins, A. M., & Loftus, E. A spreading activation theory of semantic processing. *Psychological Review,* 1975, *82,* 407–428.

Dallett, K. M. Number of categories and category information in free recall. *Journal of Experimental Psychology,* 1964, *68,* 1–12.

deCharms, R. C. *Personal causation: The internal affective determinants of behavior.* New York: Academic Press, 1968.

Divesta, F. J., Schultz, C. B., & Dangel, T. R. Passage organization and imposed learning strategies in comprehension and recall of connected discourse. *Memory and Cognition,* 1973, *1,* 471–476.

Dolinsky, R. Clustering and free recall with alternative organizational cues. *Journal of Experimental Psychology*, 1972, *95*, 159–163.

Earhard, M. Subjective organization and list organization as determinants of free recall and serial-recall memorization. *Journal of Verbal Learning and Verbal Behavior*, 1967, *6*, 501–507.

Frankel, F., & Cole, M. Measures of category clustering in free recall. *Psychological Bulletin*, 1971, *76*, 39–44.

Frase, L. T. Paragraph organization of written materials: The influence of conceptual clustering upon the level and organization of recall. *Journal of Educational Psychology*, 1969, *60*, 394–401.

Gerjouy, T. R., & Spitz, H. H. Associative clustering in free recall: Intellectual and developmental variables. *American Journal of Mental Deficiency*, 1966, *70*, 918–927.

Gonzalez, R. C., & Cofer, C. N. Exploratory studies of verbal context by means of clustering in free recall. *Journal of Genetic Psychology*, 1959, *95*, 293–320.

Hamilton, D. L., Katz, L., & Leirer, V. Organizational processes in impression formation. In R. Hastie, T. Ostrom, E. Ebbesen, R. Wyer, Jr., D. Hamilton, & D. Carlson (Eds.), *Person memory: The cognitive basis of social perception.* Hillsdale, N.J.: Lawrence Erlbaum Associates, 1980.

Harvey, J. H., Harkins, S. G., & Kagehiro, D. K. Cognitive tuning and the attribution of causality. *Journal of Personality and Social Psychology*, 1976, *34*, 708–715.

Hastie, R., Ostrom, T., Ebbesen, E. Wyer, Jr., R., Hamilton, D., & Carlston, D. (Eds.). Person memory: The Cognitive basis of social perception. Hillsdale, N. J.: Lawrence Erlbaum Associates, 1980.

Heider, F. *The psychology of interpersonal relations.* New York: John Wiley & Sons, 1958.

Herstein, J. A., Carroll, J. S., & Hayes, J. R. The organization of knowledge about people and their attributes in long-term memory. *Representative Research in Social Psychology,* in press.

Hyde, T. S. Differential effects of effort and type of orienting task on recall and organization of highly associated words. *Journal of Experimental Psychology*, 1973, *79*, 111–113.

Hyde, T. S., & Jenkins, J. J. Differential effects of incidental tasks on the organization of recall of a list of highly associated words. *Journal of Experimental Psychology*, 1969, *82*, 472–481.

Kelley, H. H. Attribution theory in social psychology. In D. Levine (Ed.), *Nebraska Symposium on Motivation* (Vol. 15). Lincoln: University of Nebraska Press, 1967.

Kelly, G. A. *The psychology of personal constructs.* New York: Norton, 1955.

Krech, D., & Crutchfield, R. *Theory and problems of social psychology.* New York: McGraw–Hill, 1948.

Kintsch, W. *The representation of meaning in memory.* Hillsdale, N. J.: Lawrence Erlbaum Associates, 1974.

Lauer, P. A., & Battig, W. F. Free recall of taxonomically and alphabetically organized word lists as a function of storage and retrieval cues. *Journal of Verbal Learning and Verbal Behavior*, 1972, *11*, 333–342.

Lingle, J. H., & Ostrom, T. M. Principles of memory and cognition in attitude formation. In R. Petty, T. Ostrom, & T. Brock (Eds.), *Cognitive responses in persuasion.* Hillsdale, N.J.: Lawrence Erlbaum Associates, 1980.

Lippman, W. *Public opinion.* New York: Harcourt, Brace, 1922.

Mandler, G. Organization and memory. In K. Spence & J. Spence (Eds.), *The psychology of learning and motivation* (Vol. 1). New York: Academic Press, 1967.

Mandler, G., & Dean, P. J. Seriation: Development of serial order in free recall. *Journal of Experimental Psychology*, 1969, *81*, 207–215.

Markus, H. Self-schemata and processing information about the self. *Journal of Personality and Social Psychology*, 1977, *35*, 63–78.

Marshall, G. R. Stimulus characteristics contributing to organization in free recall. *Journal of Verbal Learning and Verbal Behavior*, 1967, *6*, 364–374.

Marshall, G. R., & Cofer, C. N. *Associative, category, and set factors in clustering among word pairs and triads* (Tech. Rep. No. 4). New York University. Contract Nohr 285(47), Office of Naval Research, 1961.

Mueller, J. H. The effects of individual differences in test anxiety and type of orienting task on levels of organization in free recall. *Journal of Research in Personality,* 1978, *12,* 100–116.

Myers, J. L., Pezdek, K., & Coulson, D. Effect of prose organization upon free recall. *Journal of Educational Psychology,* 1973, *65,* 313–320.

Newtson, D., Rindner, R., Miller, R., & La Cross, K. Effects of availability of feature changes on behavior sequentation. *Journal of Experimental Social Psychology,* 1978, *14,* 379–388.

Ostrom, T. M., Lingle, J. H., Pryor, J. B., & Geva, N. Cognitive organization of person impressions. In R. Hastie, T. Ostrom, E. Ebbesen, R. Wyer, Jr., D. Hamilton, & D. Carlton (Eds.), *Person memory: The cognitive basis of social perception.* Hillsdale, N. J.: Lawrence Erlbaum Associates, 1980.

Perlmutter, J., & Royer, J. M. Organization of prose materials: Stimulus, storage and retrieval. *Canadian Journal of Psychology,* 1973, *27,* 200–209.

Picek, J. S., Sherman, S. J., & Shiffrin, R. M. Cognitive organization and coding of social structures. *Journal of Personality and Social Psychology,* 1975, *31,* 758–768.

Pryor, J. B., & Ostrom, T. M. *The cognitive organization of person information: A multiple operationism approach-* Unpublished manuscript, Ohio State University, 1979.

Puff, C. R. Effects of types of input structure upon recall and different clustering scores. *Bulletin of the Psychonomic Society,* 1973, *2,* 271–272.

Robinson, J. A. Category clustering in free recall. *Journal of Psychology,* 1966, *62,* 279–285.

Roencker, D. L., Thompson, C. P., & Brown, S. C. Comparison of measures for the estimation of clustering in free recall. *Psychological Bulletin,* 1971, *76,* 45–48.

Rogers, T. B., Kuiper, N. A., & Kirker, W. S. Self-reference and the encoding of personal information. *Journal of Personality and Social Psychology,* 1977, *35,* 677–688.

Rosenberg, S. New approaches to the analysis of person constructs in person perception. In J. Cole & A. Landsfield (Eds.), *Nebraska Symposium on Motivation* (Vol. 24). Lincoln: University of Nebraska Press, 1977.

Rosenberg, S., & Sedlak, A. Structural representations of implicit personality theory. In L. Berkowitz (Ed.), *Advances in experimental social psychology* (Vol. 6). New York: Academic Press, 1972.

Rothbart, M., Fulero, S., Jensen, C., Howard, J., & Birrell, P. From individual in group impressions: Availability heuristics in stereotype formation. *Journal of Experimental Social Psychology,* 1978, *14,* 237–255.

Sadler, O., & Tesser, A. Some effects of salience and time upon interpersonal hostility and attraction during social isolation. *Sociometry,* 1973, *36,* 99–112.

Schultz, C. B., & Divesta, F. J. The effects of passage organization and note-taking on the selection of clustering strategies and on recall of textual materials. *Journal of Educational Psychology,* 1972, *63,* 244–252.

Scott, W. A. Structure of natural cognitions. *Journal of Personality and Social Psychology,* 1969, *12,* 261–278.

Shimmerlik, S. M. Organization theory and memory for prose: A review of the literature. *Review of Educational Research,* 1978, *48,* 103–120.

Shuell, T. J. Clustering and organization in free recall. *Psychological Bulletin,* 1969, *72,* 353–374.

Simpson, D. D. *Four empirical investigations of organization of person information in memory.* Unpublished doctoral dissertation, Ohio State University, 1979.

Smith, E. E., Adams, N., & Schorr, D. Fast retrieval and the paradox of interference. *Cognitive Psychology,* 1978, *10,* 438–464.

Sternberg, R. J., & Tulving, E. The measurement of subjective organization in free recall. *Psychological Bulletin,* 1977, *84,* 539–556.

Taylor, S. E., Fiske, S. T. Etcoff, N. L., & Ruderman, A. J. Categorical and contextual bases of person memory and stereotyping. *Journal of Personality and Social Psychology*, 1978, *36*, 778–793.

Tesser, A. Self-generated attitude change. In L. Berkowitz (Eds.), *Advances in experimental social psychology* (Vol. 11). Academic Press: New York, 1978.

Tesser, A., & Cowan, C. L. Some attitudinal and cognitive consequences of thought. *Journal of Research in Personality*, 1977, *11*, 216–226.

Tesser, A., & Leone C. Cognitive schemas and thought as determinants of attitude change. *Journal of Experimental Social Psychology*, 1977, *13*, 340–356.

Tulving, E. Subjective organization in free recall of "unrelated" words. *Psychological Review*, 1962, *69*, 344–354.

Tulving, E. The effect of order of presentation on learning of "unrelated" words. *Psychonomic Science*, 1965, *3*, 337–338.

Wilder, D. Perception of groups, size of opposition, and social influence. *Journal of Experimental Social Psychology*, 1977, *13*, 253–268.

Wyer, R. S., & Carlston, D. E. *Social cognition, inference and attribution*. Hillsdale, N. J.: Lawrence Erlbaum Associates, 1979.

Yarmey, A. D., & Bull, M. P., III. Where were you when President Kennedy was assassinated? *Bulletin of the Psychonomic Society*, 1978, *11*, 133–135.

Zajonc, R. B. The process of cognitive tuning in communication. *Journal of Abnormal and Social Psychology*, 1960, *61*, 159–167.

2 Schematic Principles in Human Memory

Reid Hastie
Harvard University

INTRODUCTION

This chapter is a review of empirical studies of learning, memory, and social judgment that are concerned with the effects of cognitive schemata or expectancies on memory for specific events. The primary goal of this paper is to provide a framework in which questions about schema relevance and memorability can be clearly stated. The second goal is to review some of the major experimental approaches to the issue. The third goal is to summarize the conceptual tools, available in current theories of memory, that will help to frame answers to these questions.

Let us begin the analysis by stating the focus of the review as a question. *When a person perceives specific, concrete events that are related to a general, abstract schema, how will each event's relation to the schema affect its availability for later recall or cognitive utilization?*

In the remainder of this introduction, we review the nature and origins of the schema construct, suggest methods to measure schema-event relationships and memorability, and introduce the cognitive approach to psychological theorizing.

Three Types of Schemata

For the purposes of this review, we include almost any of the abstract hypotheses, expectations, organizing principles, frames, implicational molecules, scripts, plans, or prototypes that have been proposed as abstract mental organizing systems or memory structures in our use of the word "schema." Within particular content domains, researchers have made specific claims about the nature of these mental structures and their functions as parts of larger perception, memory, and decision systems. In our view, three distinct conceptions of the term "schema" are represented in recent cognitive theory: central tendency schemata, template schemata, and procedural schemata.

First, and simplest, are what we label central tendency schemata. These are prominent theoretical constructs in the work of Posner (1969), Reed (1972, 1973), and Rosch (Rosch & Mervis, 1975), where they are called prototype schemata. There are at least two slight variations on the notion of a prototype schema in current use. Reed and Posner often use the term to refer to a member of a stimulus set that is located at the statistical center of the distribution of items in the set. A variant on this definition, deriving from philosophical notions of family resemblance (Wittgenstein, 1953) and statistical notions of cue validity (Beach, 1964), has been applied by Rosch in her analysis of categorical concepts. This analysis (Rosch & Mervis, 1975; Tversky, 1977) defines a prototype as the member of a category with the most attributes in common with other members of the category and the fewest attributes in common with members of other contrasting categories. The second type of cognitive schemata under review in this paper is labeled *template schemata*. This type of schema is a filing system for classifying, retaining, and coordinating incoming sensory data. The most useful definitions of template schemata have been proposed by cognitive scientists and artificial intelligence researchers, who are developing general theories of knowledge while attempting to construct language production and comprehension machines. For example, according to Norman and Bobrow, 1975: "A *schema* consists of a framework for tying together the information about any given concept or event, with specifications about the types of interrelations and restrictions upon the way things fit together. Schemata can activate procedures capable of operating upon local information and a common pool of data [p. 125]."

Tesser (1978) presents a closely related definition of schema in his discussion of social attitudes:

A schema is a naive theory of some stimulus domain and the individual using it a "naive scientist".... When we apply a particular schema for thinking about some stimulus object it does two things. First, it tells us what to attend to. Like a scientific theory, it makes some attributes relevant, that is salient, while allowing others to be ignored. Second, a schema contains the network of associations that is believed to hold among the attributes of the stimulus and thereby provides rules for thinking about the stimulus. Thus, if information conveying some relevant attribute is unavailable from the stimulus itself or is ambiguous or is unavailable from memory, the schema allows for the "filling in" of such information with "default options" [p. 290].

Note that the distinction between static structures and dynamic procedures is starting to blur. Template schemata have certain elementary processing capacities: to add "default" information to the schematic structure when anticipated information is not supplied perceptually; to modify acceptability constraints on one subset of information given the nature of another subset of input; and to perform tests on a subset of information to verify inferences about its proper classification.

We call the third and most complex type of schemata *procedural schemata*. This type is probably closest to Bartlett's (1932) description of a schema as, "... an active organization of past reactions, or of past experiences, which must be supposed to be operating in any well-adapted organic response [p. 20]," (Oldfield & Zangwill, 1942, 1943; Zangwill, 1972). It is also close to Piaget's concept of schema, (Flavell, 1963): "... as a cognitive structure which has reference to a class of similar action sequences, these sequences of necessity being strong, bonded totalities in which the constituent behavioral elements are tightly interrelated [p. 52]." (Freud should probably also be credited with a similar conception of dynamic memory traces [Paul, 1967; Thompson, 1967].) Neisser's (1976) discussion is probably the clearest recent expression of the procedural schema notion:

> A schema is that portion of the entire perceptual cycle which is internal to the perceiver, modifiable by experience, and somehow specific to what is being perceived. The schema accepts information as it becomes available at sensory surfaces and is changed by that information; it directs movements and exploratory activities that make more information available, by which it is further modified... The functions of schemata may be clarified by some analogies. In one sense, when it is viewed as an information-accepting system, a schema is like a *format* in a computer-programming language. Formats specify that information must be of a certain sort if it is to be interpreted coherently... A schema is not merely like a format; it also functions as a *plan* of the sort described by Miller, Galanter, and Pribram in their seminal book. Perceptual schemata are plans for finding out about objects and events, for obtaining more information to fill in the format... The analogy between schemata and formats and plans is not complete. Real formats and plans incorporate a sharp distinction between form and content, but this is not true of schemata. The information that fills in the format at one moment in the cyclic process becomes a part of the format in the next, determining how further information is accepted. The schema is not only the plan but also the executor of the plan. It is a pattern of action as well as a pattern *for* action. [p. 54].

For present pruposes, the critical features of the concept of a schema are that it is an abstract, general structure that establishes relations between specific events or entities; and, that any specific event or entity can be evaluated as congruent, or irrelevant with reference to the schema.

Origins of the Schema Construct

We would like to add several brief notes on the historical origins, theoretical status, and theoretical power of the schema construct. First, it is important to keep in mind that the use of the schema construct in psychological theory is chiefly motivated as a reaction to a simple associationist theoretical analysis. This is very clear in Bartlett's (1932) work, where he spends considerable energy contrasting his schematic account with the theoretical and methodological tradition represented by Ebbinghaus' (1885) associationist analysis. Thus, many "schematic" empirical findings are best understood, not as cases that unequivocally support a schema model, but as cases that are difficult for associationist models to explain. For example, the Jenkins (1974) and Bransford (e.g., Bransford & Franks, 1971) results, which are so frequently cited in discussions of schema models, are important primarily because of the problems they pose for traditional associationism rather than for their clear support of well-defined schema models.

A further historical point that characterizes the essense of the association-schema distinction is concerned with the nature of mental representation. Early association models emphasized the extent to which mental representation was a literal reflection of physical stimulus properties. Aristotle's wax tablet metaphor (Aristotle, 1931) and Mill's (1869) analysis of the concept of house into its constituent *sensory* building blocks express this *copy* theory very clearly. In fact, several critiques of the associationist enterprise have focused on the copy theory of mental representation (e.g., Bever, Fodor, & Garrett, 1968, on the terminal metapostulate).

Memory theorists began to express their discomfort with the copy theory shortly after Ebbinghaus introduced it to psychology and began to talk about *trace* theories of representation (e.g., Koffka, 1935). The trace concept departed from the copy model in that the direct almost isomorphic relation between stimulus and idea was relaxed and traces were embued with certain active self-organizing properties (e.g., Helson, 1925, 1926). The recent transition to *schema* theories postulates large differences between the structure and content of the stimulus and its mental representation. The representation may be both more general and more detailed than the stimulus because of the operation of abstraction (e.g., Bransford & Franks, 1971; Kahneman & Tversky, 1972) and inference (e.g., Johnson, Bransford, & Solomon, 1973; Kintsch, 1974) processes.

Second, both associationist (e.g., Anderson & Bower, 1973) and schema theories (e.g., Norman & Bobrow, 1975) have been advanced considerably by the development of complex computing languages and machines on which to interpret them (Newell & Simon, 1972; Winston, 1977). One critically important conclusion from modern automata theory (e.g., Estes, 1975; Hopcroft & Ullman, 1969) is that associationist and schematic theories are equivalent with reference to computational power. This means that no experimental results can strongly separate the two *classes* of models. Rather, *particular* process models must be framed within the constraints of the general theoretical orientation and then experimental results can be used to evaluate the relative plausibility of the specific process configurations.

This specific competitive model-testing approach has only recently come to dominate the empirical evaluation of cognitive models. Furthermore, the most discriminating results have not usually been obtained in the relatively simple memory tasks considered in the present review. Rather, complex reasoning (Anderson, 1976), problem-solving (Newell & Simon, 1972), and language processing (Schank & Abelson, 1977) have presented the largest obstacles for associationist models. However, when problematic results can be obtained in relatively simple perception (Garner, 1974) and memory (e.g., Jenkins, 1974) tasks, the implications for the schema-association controversy are especially clear and compelling.

Third, an important property of schema representations is that distinct schemata may be linked to one another, embedded within one another, and (in the case of procedural schemata) call one another to accomplish mental tasks (e.g., Rumelhart & Ortony, 1977). The notion of interdependent, interacting schemata is significant in the present discussion in that it implies that the three levels of schemata previously distinguished—central tendency, template, and procedural—may all be appropriate in the theoretical explanation of performance in memory tasks. For example, we might imagine a heirarchy of embedded schemata to characterize the processes and products of story comprehension. At the most elementary level in our schematic heirarchy would be central tendency schemata to characterize individual actors, locations, goals, and actions. At the next level of complexity these central tendency schemata would be linked together into template structures to organize information episodes, scenes, or events. Finally, template schemata would provide direction for more active procedural schemata that would make and store inferences, initiate information search in the environment or in memory, and even create new template schemata. Abelson (1973), Rumelhart (1975), and others have promoted similar heirarchical organization plans for belief and comprehension systems.

Schema-Event Relationships

Our focal question requires an adequate conceptual definition of the relationships between a schema and possible experienced events. Probably the clearest definition can be phrased in terms of probabilities. More precisely, we think of a general schema as having a status like a hypothesis or theory in science and a specific event as data or evidence that has been related or connected to the hypothesis. (The reader will doubtless recognize the analogy of the social perceiver as a naive scientist [Heider, 1958; Kelley, 1973; Piaget, 1954]). The three relationships are defined as ranges of values along the probability continuum relating the hypothesis to the data: probability (data/hypothesis). When this probability is high, we think of the data being "congruent" with or fitting the hypothesis; when it is low the data are "incongruent" with the hypothesis; and when it is in the middle range, close to .50, we think of the data as irrelevant or undiagnostic to the hypothesis. The analogy to our event-to-schema relationship is obvious.

Note that this definition does not include event-event relationships. The assumption is that two events cannot be related cognitively without specifying an abstract schema or dimension along which congruence can be defined. For example, it is possible to speak of conditional probabilities between the occurrences of two events (e.g., probability [$event_2$/$event_1$]); however, conceptually this case usually reduces to a consideration of the two events *in the context of a causal schema* (e.g., L.Cohen, 1977).

The probability analogy we have used to define schema-event relations is borrowed from the conditional probability axiom that is central in Bayesian inference (Ajzen & Fishbein, 1975; Edwards, Lindman, & Savage, 1963; Leamer, 1978). However, it would divert us from the purposes of this review to trace out the usefulness of Bayes' theorem, as a model of the mind. Our commitment is to the usefulness of the conditional probability concept in *summarizing* schema-event relations for the purposes of this review. A thorough cognitive analysis of a schema-event relationship would involve reducing the summary conditional probability to more fundamental memory (Tverksky & Kahneman, 1973), representation (Kahneman & Tversky, 1972), and inference (Tversky & Kahneman, 1980) processes.

The Cognitive Approach

Figure 2.1 depicts a simple flowchart that indicates the major events that occur when a person perceives and memorizes an event. The diagram emphasizes the activation and application of a schema to structure and transform event information. The asumption is that the use of schemata is necessary in any perceptual act. This fits current developmental (Piaget, 1954, 1963) and cognitive (Neisser, 1976; Rumelhart, 1977) theorizing. The central characterization of the performing organism in the cognitive view is as an active, goal-seeking, purposive creature (Bower, 1975; Tolman, 1932). A key ingredient in every current cognitive theory is a mental model of the current *"subjective world"* of the information processor and a set of *goals* and associated *plans* that are executed to act on the current environment to change this environment toward a more highly valued state (Bower, 1978; Newell & Simon, 1972; Powers, 1978). The construct of a *schema* is a convenient theoretical device to represent the subject's expectations about structure of future and past events in the world or to represent desirable, valued patterns of events.

Figure 2.2 helps us summarize the aspects of schematic processing that any complete model must address. The body of this paper is a review of a number of experiments studying schematic perception. The specifics of each theoretical analysis, available in the original reports of the research, provide detail for the skeletal flowchart.

Methodological Note

Although questions concerning the relative memory of schema-congruent, schema-incongruent, and schema-irrelevant information are often posed, there are very few experiments that examine memory along the full range of the

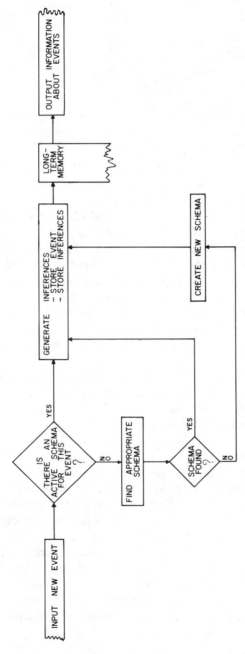

FIG. 2.1. Flowchart diagram to represent a schematic perception and memory information-processing system. Arrows indicate the flow of information among subparts of the system.

45

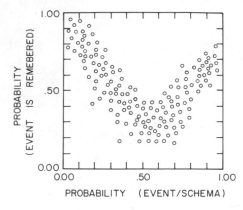

FIG. 2.2. Graphical representation of the hypothesized empirical relationship between schema-event relatedness and the memorability of event information.

schema-event relationship dimension. As we shall see, most research designed to study schema-relatedness and memory compares recall or recognition of schema-congruent and schema-irrelevant events. To express this point more clearly, we might imagine the structure of an ideal experiment to study such effects. First, we would like to be able to measure memory for events from the full range of points on our schema-event relationship dimension. Second, we want to insure that no stimulus properties or task conditions covary with manipulation of schema-event relatedness. Thus, we want to avoid the frequent confounding of item set size and degree of incongruence that is observed in many experiments.

In our ideal experiment, we would manipulate the schema-event relationship such that individual events would appear at various locations on that dimension. This unconfounding of stimulus item properties with schema-relatedness can be accomplished by varying the schema. For example, if the to-be-remembered information were in the form of behavioral descriptions and the relevant schemata were personality trait impressions (Cantor & Mischel, 1977; Hastie & Kumar, 1979), a single event (e.g., the description of an aggressive act) would be congruent, incongruent, or irrelevant in the context of various trait attributions (e.g., aggressive, meek, artistic). Thus, our ideal experiment would begin with a large sample of events and schemata in which each event appeared in congruent, incongruent, and irrelevant relationships across varying schemata. Then, experimental materials would be constructed such that congruent, incongruent, and irrelevant events would appear in equal set sizes, unconfounded with input serial position or other task factors. Between list or between subject counterbalancing plans would be used to insure that each individual event was represented in each schema-event relationship. Finally, several measures of mnemonic availability including recall and recognition tests would be employed.

No single experiment in the current memory literature matches this ideal plan. However, it is possible to piece together a tentative picture of the relationship between schema relatedness and availability. Furthermore, a thorough review of the literature relevant to our focal question is the foundation for research that can provide definite answers to the question. Because we believe that the question of schematic effects on event memory has considerable theoretical and practical significance, the review is worthwhile even if only tentative conclusions can be reached at this time.

VERBAL LEARNING AND MEMORY RESEARCH

Early Word List Learning Research

Research in the associationist verbal learning tradition was designed to avoid complex schematic effects by using unfamiliar "nonsense" materials and highly controlled paired associate and serial learning tasks (Ebbinghaus, 1885; McGeoch, 1942; Postman, 1971). Gestalt psychologists, early critics of the associationists, produced experiments designed to demonstrate clear schematic effects. Item isolation effects in paired associate, serial, and free recall learning tasks were some of the earliest results intepreted as evidence for schema-event relationship effects on memory (Calkins, 1896; von Restorff, 1933; Wallace, 1965). In these experiments, selected items were "isolated" by making their appearance dissimilar from other items in the list. For example, the isolated item might be printed in a novel color or typeface, underlined, or selected from a novel semantic (e.g., Tulving, 1969) or material category. The typical result of the isolation manipulation was elevated recall of the isolated event. The Gestalters' interpretation of the isolation effect (Koffka, 1935) was that the homogeneous items in the list created a general impression, background, or schematic context that became an undifferentiated *ground* against which the isolated item stood out as a perceptually vivid *figure*. In terms of the summary of schema-event relationships advanced in this review, the isolated items are incongruent events. Thus, isolation effects are evidence for relatively high recall of incongruent events. The qualification on this interpretation is that set size is confounded with the schema-congruence factor, such that perceptually striking incongruent events are in a small minority in the lists in which they occur.

The Gestalt tradition produced a large literature of demonstrations showing schematic organizational effects on memory. Asch and Ebenholtz (1962), Garner and Whitman (1965), Katona (1940), and Turving and Pearlstone (1966) provide a diverse set of experiments that illustrate the point that a meaningfully organized list is better remembered than a list with an unfamiliar or hidden structure. These experiments were all problematic for simple association theory; however, they are not directly pertinent to our interest in the relative recall of schema-congruent, schema-incongruent, and schema-irrelevant events.

Complex Linguistic Schemata

Recent research on human memory has departed from the verbal learning tradition by exploring the operation of more and more complex schemata. Probably a major motivation of this movement is still to show that simple associative linkage models are inadequate or, at least, very implausible (Jenkins, 1974). One obvious tactic in this endeavor is to demonstrate that subjects possess, generate, and apply extremely complex perceptual and mnemonic schemata.

Bransford and Franks (1971) conducted what is probably the most often cited experiment in the literature on schematic memory processes. Their subjects listened to a series of short sentences expressing parts of the meaning of a very long sentence. The long sentence was composed of four interrelated propositions. The sentences to which the subjects were exposed contained from one to three of the propositions related to a single long sentence. Subsequent recognition memory confidence ratings showed that subjects were unable to discriminate between presented and nonpresented sentences. Recognition confidence was directly related to the number of propositions in a test sentence. Sentences containing fewer propositions were rated as less familiar. Finally, sentences that were not presented and that were incongruent (semantically inconsistent) with the propositions expressed in the long sentence were accurately rated as very unfamiliar.

Probably the major contribution of the Bransford and Franks experiments was to popularize the false recognition method they used to draw inferences about schematic processing. The method focuses on the rates of recognition responses to distractor sentences appearing only on the recognition test. By manipulating the relationship between these sentences and the presented materials, it is possible to draw conclusions about the structure of memory traces. The logic of the method is sensible, and the technique is sensitive to variations in experimental materials and tasks. However, we must be careful not to overgeneralize from *false* recognition of "lure items" to draw conclusions about *accuracy* of recall, or *accuracy* of recognition for acquisition set items.

The results of the Bransford and Franks experiment are suggestive evidence for the operation of an interpropositional sentence schema. The critical result from the experiments is easily interpreted as a schema-event congruence effect. Longer test sentences composed of propositions from the long base sentence were rated as more familiar than shorter sentences regardless of whether or not they had appeared in the acquisition list. Thus, the greater the overlap of the test sentence and the four-proposition sentence schema, the higher the recognition familiarity rating. However, these results can only be treated as suggestive evidence for the operation of a linguistic schema. The same pattern of results has been obtained in experiments using nonlinguistic materials (Park & Whitten, 1977; Reitman & Bower, 1973), and a nonschematic associative model provides a convincing account for results in both linguistic and nonlinguistic domains (Anderson & Bower, 1973).

Sir Frederick Bartlett (1932) is probably the best known researcher to study memory for complex narrative materials. His research and theorizing were obvious reactions to the nonschematic, associationist tradition represented by the work of Ebbinghaus. It is of interest to note that Bartlett introduced the term *schema* as a description of a hypothetical mental structure controlling encoding and reconstruction of memory traces (Oldfield & Zangwill, 1942, 1943). His usage of the term was close to our modern usage, although not as precise or general as some of the example definitions cited (see the foregoing discussion). Bartlett's use of the term emphasized the dynamic, generative character of mental schemata to an extent that is matched by few contemporary narrative grammars. Bartlett's empirical analysis was primitive by current methodological standards. He focused on errors in the recall protocols of subjects who were asked to repeatedly reproduce unfamiliar folktales. (Note the similarity to Bransford and Frank's focus on false alarm *errors* of commission on recognition memory tests.) Bartlett developed a taxonomy of errors of commission and omission in recall and postulated four schematic mechanisms underlying these errors: assimilation to a schema, simplification, retention of unimportant details, construction based on a schema. Bartlett's work has been extremely influential, and much of the modern research on memory for narrative discourse can be viewed as the development of Bartlett's concept of schema with an emphasis on accounting for accurate reproduction as well as for errors.

Research on memory for narrative discourse has tended to emphasize the weaknesses in Bartlett's methods and theory. Gauld and Stephenson (1967) demonstrated that a considerable portion of the errors identified by Bartlett were *deliberate* constructions at recall, not inadvertant mistakes. Zangwill (1972) and Gomulicki (1956) argued that story recall followed *abstractive* rather than *reconstructive* principles. Their assertion was based on the preponderance of errors of omission over errors of commission in their subjects' protocols. Dawes (1966) introduced a very precise formulation of a schema using formal set theory notation and identified systematic errors of commission in research that included controls for "response bias" interpretations.

The tradition of research illustrated by the post-Bartlett story memory citations retained the schematic emphasis of Bartlett's formulation. However, none of this research addressed our focal question concerning the relative memorability of information varying in schema-relatedness. Recent research by Bransford and his colleagues (Bransford, McCarrell, Franks, & Nitsch, 1977) is more relevant to our review. These researchers emphasize dynamic schematic processing and also focus on relatively simple statements of schematic principles. A considerable amount of this research examines causal reasoning in sentence and paragraph comprehension (e.g., Bransford, Barclay, & Franks, 1972) using the false alarm technique as its primary method. The results consistently show that *implicit* causal inferences that are consistent with a model based on information in presented sentences are (falsely) recognized as having been presented. Bransford and Johnson (1972) departed from the heavy reliance on recognition data to study subjects' use of paragraph themes as schemata in a free recall task. Subjects were presented paragraphs describing a series of events such as "washing clothes at a laundromat." The paragraphs were written so that subjects were unable to infer the prerequisite context for comprehension without assistance from the experimenter in the form of a title or picture. The primary result of the research was the finding of dramatic increases in recall when the schematic theme or context was presented. Furthermore, some experimental paragraphs were constructed to fit two possible titles (e.g., "Watching a Parade" or "A Space Trip to an Inhabited Planet"). When one title was presented, information that was congruent with that title was well recalled in contrast to information that was irrelevant to it (e.g., sentences describing "the landing," in a paragraph titled "Watching a Parade"). However, when an alternate title was presented such that the previously irrelevant information was now congruent with the schematic context (e.g., "the landing" paired with "A Space Trip to an Inhabited Planet") recall increased dramatically. This result is clear evidence for the higher recall of schema-congruent events than schema-irrelevant events.

A next level of complexity of narrative schemata is exhibited by the network schemata for discourse proposed by Bower (1978), Frederikson (1975), Restle (1975), and Schank and Abelson (1977). Bower (1978) and his students have demonstrated that causal schemata governing social perception serve as organizing principles for the storage and retrieval or simple story narratives. Subjects use inferred goals and motives to structure mental representations as "causal chains." When story titles, prologues, task instructions, or hypnotic inductions were used to vary the perceived goal of a central character, memory for events in the story shifted.

Schank and Abelson's (1977) script and goal analysis is the most thoroughgoing effort to characterize causal reasoning underlying story comprehension and memory (cf., Frase, 1969; Fredericksen, 1975; Minsky, 1975). A script is a conceptual structure outlining the roles, objects, conditions, and results that occur in a stereotyped sequence of events such as "eating in a restaurant," "visiting a doctor," or "taking a plane flight." Bower, Black, and Turner (1979) collected a set of conventional script action "recipes," demonstrated that script-coherent event sequences were more readily comprehended than unconventional sequences, and then explored the recall, recognition, and temporal reordering of events with reference to script organization. The results were clear evidence for script-driven memory processing with congruent events and orderings dominating recall and recognition (including both measures of accurate reproduction and false alarm or intrusion errors).

One of Bower, Black, and Turner's (1979) experiments is especially relevant to our review in that it studied memory for events that were congruent, irrelevant, and incongruent to a script schema. Congruent events were routine actions in the context of the dominant script (e.g., ordering a hamburger in a restaurant setting). Incongruent events were script interruptions that Schank and Abelson

(1977) had called obstacles, errors, or distractions; events that block or divert the flow of events essential to the script (e.g., the protagonist is unable to read a foreign language menu, the waiter brings the wrong dish, or the waiter spills the order). Irrelevant events were descriptions of details of the scene unrelated to script actions. Recall was highest for incongruent events, and lowest for irrelevant events.

Smith, Adams, and Schorr (1978) have also studied the operation of script schemata in memory for simple narratives. They used reaction times to verify sentences as their primary dependent variable and demonstrated that script-congruent lure sentences (sentences that were falsely asserted to have been previously presented) produced relatively slow reaction times compared to script-irrelevant lures. This can be interpreted as evidence for higher availability of congruent than incongruent events in much the same fashion as the Bransford and Franks false alarm data. Probably the most fascinating result from the Smith, Adams, and Schorr (1978) research was the conclusion that script structures controlled verification performance *only* when the relevant sentences were integrated into a coherent, unitary story at presentation. The same materials, when studied under rote learning conditions that discouraged integration, did not reveal schematic effects at retrieval.

A second class of schematic models for narrative discourse represent the underlying organization of paragraphs and stories as hierarchical structures. Kintsch (1974) has proposed a system to characterize paragraph structures as heirarchies of propositions and has recently extended the approach to model story structure (Kintsch & van Dijk, 1978). Rumelhart (1975, 1977) has developed a complicated parser that separates the story into setting (location, characters, time), theme (events and goals), plot (episodes), and resolution (states) categories; these categories are broken down further into individuals, objects, and relations between them. Most of the critical structural relationships in the model are causal connections of the sort discussed by Schank and Abelson (1977). Research by Thorndyke (1977) and Mandler (Mandler & Johnson, 1977; Mandler, 1978) has shown that the degree to which a story's structure at presentation matches the ideal schematic structure predicts story recall; that subjects tended to recall higher level story elements more readily than lower level elements; and that events were reordered at recall to more closely match the ideal structure.

The results from research on the Kintsch and the Rumelhart story structure models show that information that is central in a schematic representation (higher in the organizational hierarchy) is better remembered than peripheral information. This can be interpreted as evidence that schema-congruent information is more available than schema-irrelevant information. However, this conclusion must be kept tentative because several factors co-varied with schematic relatedness in these experiments. For example, central events or propositions were typically represented in simpler linguistic formats, presented earlier in the stories, and differed in vividness of depiction from peripheral events.

Category Concept Acquisition

Laboratory research on concept induction has included experiments studying recall and recognition of events during acquisition trials (Dominowski, 1965). This research was motivated by the focus on assumptions about memory capacity in early mathematical models for concept attainment (Gregg & Simon, 1967; Restle, 1962; Trabasso & Bower, 1968). Generally, memory for instances presented during the acquisition of artificial concepts is extremely low (Bourne & O'Bannion, 1969; Coltheart, 1971; Trabasso & Bower, 1964) and barely exceeds chance levels of performance. In the few experiments where presentation rate was adjusted to produce moderately accurate memory performance, no difference was reported between memory for positive (rule-fitting) and negative (rule-exception) instances. However, one clear result was that memory for all types of instances was higher at the end of a sequence in which the rule was successfully learned as compared to a sequence in which the induction problem was not solved (Calfee, 1969). It seems reasonable to consider this result a demonstration of schematic memory processing. The concept or classification rule is a schema, and successful induction of the schema promotes accurate recall and recognition of schema relevant instances. However, there is no evidence for differential memorability of instances varying in congruence with the schema.

Rosch and her students have extended our understanding of natural categories by demonstrating that within-category structure is an important determinant of perception and memory (Rosch, 1973). One clear demonstration that the internal structure of categories affects memorability appears in a series of experiments by Rosch, Simpson, and Miller (1976). Using a variety of visual and verbal stimuli, these researchers showed that the typicality or centrality of an instance within a category determined ease of learning and classification speed after learning. If we think of Rosch's visual object, color, and linguistic categories as schemata, it is plausible to connect congruity and typicality. Central, typical category instances are most congruent with the category schema, whereas peripheral, atypical instances are less congruent. However, it is not clear that Rosch's results demonstrate low rates of learning and memory for schema-*in*congruent events. We are hesitant to identify incongruent, schema-contradicting events with Rosch's peripheral item materials. In terms of our schema-event relationship summary, the peripheral items probably correspond to intermediate levels along the schema-relatedness dimension.

Grammatical Structures

A few experiments have examined the effects of a grammatical schema on memory for grammatical and ungrammatical events in grammar induction tasks. Smith's (1973) research program on recall of exceptions in verbal reconstructive memory is an example of this approach. Smith's subjects performed a letter bigram learning task in which sixteen two-letter bigrams, generated according to a simple rule, were presented and followed by a free recall task. The intrusion rate, appearance of *non*presented items in the recall protocols, followed a schematic principle such that bigrams congruent with the generation rule (but not presented in the acquisition list) were more likely to be falsely recalled than ungrammatical, generation rule incongruent items. Furthermore, when an exception to the generation rule (i.e., an incongruent item) was *presented* in the list, relative recall for that item was quite high—higher than for congruent items. Note that item incongruence is defined in an unusually complex manner. Exceptional does not mean "printed in a distinctive color" or "not a member of the same semantic category" as other to-be-remembered items; rather Smith's subjects had to induce the unfamiliar letter position rule *before* the rule could serve as a schema against which items could be classified as congruent or incongruent.

Despite the complex manner in which Smith operationalized a grammatical schema, these experiments provide some of the clearest results to evaluate our question about the relative memorability of congruent and incongruent events. Interestingly, the conclusion from Smith's work is that exceptions to the schema, incongruent items, will be best recalled. Smith does place several limitations on this conclusion noting that the schema-item relations were clear, subjects had time to optionally allocate rehearsal and attention during the study phase of each trial, and, incongruent items were always in the minority in any to-be-learned list. This last condition is especially important as it means that the congruent-incongruent factor is confounded with a set size variable.

Summary

Research on the recall and recognition of verbal materials has been a battleground for associationist and schematic theorists since the earliest scientific empirical research on human memory. Despite recent valiant efforts to preserve the associationist position (e.g., Anderson & Bower, 1973), there seems to be an emerging consensus that schematic principles are necessary to provide economical accounts for inference and memory task performances (e.g., Anderson, 1976; Estes, 1979; Jenkins, 1974). Our brief review of verbal learning research has selected results that are problematic for the associationist position and that support schematic interpretations. Interestingly, only a small subset of this research addresses our focal question concerning the relative memorability of events varying along a dimension of schema-event relatedness. A tentative conclusion from this review is that schema-irrelevant events are relatively poorly remembered compared to schema-relevant (congruent or incongruent) events. This literature does not clearly indicate whether congruent or incongruent events are more memorable. There is a hint in the research on item isolation effects in list memory (Wallace, 1965), episode recall from stories (Bower, Black & Turner, 1979), and recall of letter strings in a grammar induction task (Smith,

1973) that schema-incongruent events will be slightly better remembered than schema-congruent events. However, in each case, variables such as set size and vividness were confounded with the schematic relationship.

VISUAL SCHEMATA

Schematic models have a long history in theorizing about memory for pictorial information. Early schema theorists (e.g., Bartlett, 1932; Koffka, 1935) relied heavily on examples of memory for pictures to illustrate their arguments. There is also a lengthy tradition of research on the influence of linguistic labels on memory for visual forms started by Carmichael, Hogan, and Walter (1932). Recently there has been considerable research on the perception and memory of complex visual scenes (e.g., Biederman, 1972; Loftus, 1972; Mandler & Parker, 1976). Theoretical accounts for the more complex cases are particularly likely to include elaborate schema structures (e.g., Friedman, 1979; Minsky, 1975).

Memory for Form

Riley (1962) has reviewed the history of research on memory for form with reference to opposing interpretations of changes in reproduction advanced by associationist (e.g., Postman, 1954) and gestalt theoreticians (e.g., Wulf, 1922). Associationist accounts emphasized fading or decay of the original memory trace and interference with the trace caused by experience with other similar forms. The gestalt account introduced the notion of autonomous change occurring as distortions toward "good figure" were produced by physiological processes underlying the memory trace.

Woodworth's (1938) classic discussion of the "schema with correction" conception of memory processes was motivated by his review of research on memory for form (cf., Rock, Halper, & Clayton, 1972). Woodworth noted that regular, schematic figures were best remembered, whereas memorability of irregular figures was dependent on the nature of their deviation from regularity. His interpretation of these results included a very "modern" conception of mental schemata that were activated at encoding and then guided the formation of memory traces.

An important tangent from research on memory for form was started by the research of Carmichael, Hogan, and Walter (1932). These researchers demonstrated that a verbal label attributed to a to-be-remembered form produced systematic errors on later drawn reproductions of the form. For example, a form shaped like an infinity sign would be elongated when accompanied by the label, "dumbells," and compressed when labeled "eyeglasses." Research on this phenomenon has had a lively history (Cohen, 1966; Cooper, 1974; Daniel, 1972;

Hanawalt, 1937; Hanawalt & Demarest, 1939; Steinfeld, 1967). Recent interpretations have emphasized the integration of linguistic and visual information to alter the memory trace (Loftus, 1975; Loftus & Palmer, 1974; Pezdek, 1977) or the influence of linguistic schema on initial visual encoding processes (Jörg & Hormann, 1978).

A third type of experiment relevant to schematic interpretations of visual perception and memory concerns the abstraction of iconic concepts. Posner and his colleagues (Posner, 1969) conducted an important series of experiments on the formation of prototype schemata for visual materials. In one series of studies, Posner and Keele (1968, 1970) investigated the abstraction of prototype schema from a set of distortions of dot patterns. The stimuli were nonsense patterns generated by randomly moving nine dots from an original prototype pattern. Subjects learned to associate *distortions* of each prototype with a category label, but they were never shown the prototypes. The subjects were then presented a set of dot patterns to classify on the basis of the learning trials. Classification of never-seen prototypes was typically as good as classification of previously seen patterns and, after a week's delay, performance was better for prototypes than for patterns from the study set. Subjects were also unable to distinguish between "new" prototype patterns and "old" study set patterns under strict recognition test instructions (Posner, 1969). Nonprototypic new patterns were classified or recognized as category members at a decreasing rate at they were less similar to the prototype pattern. Franks and Bransford (1971) conducted an experiment using geometric line drawings as stimuli and replicated the essential features of these results. In related research, conducting experiments using line-drawing faces as stimuli, Reed (1972, 1973) had concluded that prototype-item relatedness determined classification and recognition performance.

Our review of research on memory for form provides considerable evidence for schematic processing and evidence that schema-irrelevant events are poorly remembered in comparison with high congruent, prototypic events. However, we cannot draw any conclusions about memory for highly incongruent events.

Memory for Scenes

A considerable amount of theorizing has appeared recently on scene analysis by computing machines (e.g., Minsky, 1975; Waltz, 1975.) The motivation for this research is the design of robots that can negotiate natural environments and identify objects in natural settings. However, the theorizing has a strong cognitive flavor, and psychologists are beginning to cite these artificial intelligence models as general, precise schematic processing theories.

Research by Mandler illustrates the current work by psychologists on schematic factors in memory for scenes. Mandler and Stein (1974) showed subjects line drawings of complex scenes and tested memory with pictorial recognition and verbal recall. Half of the stimulus pictures were presented with constituent objects organized into a conventional scene (e.g., a living room), and half were presented with the objects arranged in an unnatural scrambled pattern. Recognition and recall performance was considerably higher for organized scenes than for jumbled ensembles. Mandler and Parker (1976) used similar stimulus materials to investigate within-picture object recognition and location reproduction. Scene organization did not affect memory for details of individual objects; however, memory for the relative locations of objects within a scene was considerably lower for disorganized than organized scenes. Finally, Mandler and Ritchey (1977) tested recognition performance for pictures over a 4-month retention interval and studied the effects of organization—the extent to which interobject relationships conformed to typical patterns in real-world scenes. The degree of organization was related to recognition accuracy for interobject spatial relationships and for inventory memory of exactly which objects were included in the scene but did not enhance memory for details of the overall picture composition or detailed descriptions of the component objects.

Mandler concluded that real world scene schemata include inventory and spatial location information but lack detailed object or composition information. It is not clear what status to accord the spatial location information: Were Mandler's jumbled scenes schema-incongruent or schema-irrelevant? Related research by Biederman (1972) on scene perception demonstrated that schema-incongruent jumbled scenes produced considerable decrements in encoding accuracy in an object indentification task. This suggests that when an object is presented in a schema-incongruent location (even when the subject knows where to look and what to look for), it will be difficult to perceive and probably difficult to remember. We should note that a major tradition in research on memory for pictures has emphasized aschematic associative accounts for scene memory results (e.g., Loftus, 1972; Loftus & Bell, 1975; Nelson, Metzler, & Reed, 1974; Shepard, 1967).

An interesting variation on the scene memory research tradition that strongly supports schematic interpretations is Chase and Simon's (1973, 1975) effort to explain novice–master differences in memory for chessboard displays. Chess masters exhibit extraordinarily accurate memory for unfamiliar but sensible game positions (typically locating 20 out of 25 pieces correctly after a short exposure), novices perform at a much lower level (placing five pieces correctly under similar exposure conditions). However, a master's performance plummets to the novice level if pieces are arranged on the board at random (nonsensically). Chase and Simon have developed a process model account for these results that postulates the development of elaborate schemata by master players over the course of their experience with the game. When a novel but plausible constellation of pieces is presented, a chess master "chunks" the pieces according to schematic properties of the configuration yielding an economical encoding of the board. The novice lacks cognitive schemata for constellations of pieces and produces an unwieldy mnemonic representation that identifies and locates only a few pieces.

Several recent papers dispute the Simon and Chase conclusion that short-term memory chunking is the crucial difference between master and novice memorizers. For example, Charness (1976) and Frey and Adesman (1976) argue that experts process board configurations rapidly to a deep level of meaning producing a more elaborate, more durable long-term memory trace. Furthermore, masters have a considerable advantage at reconstruction tests where their long-term memory advantage over novices allows them to "guess" more accurately when episode specific information is lacking (e.g., Allport, 1975).

Goldin (1978) has elaborated the Chase and Simon explanation by demonstrating that a *prototype plus deviations* representation (cf., Woodworth, 1938) provides a more accurate account of the subtleties of master performance. Goldin also included control groups in her empirical research to rule out guessing accounts for the masters' superior memory performance. Goldin's research is pertinent to our interest in the relative memorability of events varying in schema-relatedness. In her research, prototypical patterns (schema-congruent patterns in the present vocabulary) were the best recalled and recognized configurations. Less schematically expected patterns, corresponding to our schema-irrelevant events, were less well remembered.

These results are persuasive evidence for schematic processing. However, again it is difficult to derive the implications for relative memorability of schema-irrelevant and schema-incongruent events. We suspect that the master's dramatically poor memory for random board configurations is evidence that schema-incongruent information is poorly remembered in this task. This is an interesting case in that it is quite obvious that the subject is attempting to apply chess schemata, but most of the to-be-remembered information is contradictory to schematic principles. Chase and Simon's hypothesis is that the master is actively searching through a mental library of thousands of piece-constellation schemata. Of course, none of the learned schemata will fit random board configurations, and the master is reduced to the novice's level of performance.

Memory for Event Sequences

Experimental psychologists have conducted very little research on schematic effects in the perception and memory of coherent sequences of events. Social psychologists (e.g., Ebbesen, Chapter 7, this volume; Newtson, 1976) have been much more active in this area. One exception is the recent research by Jenkins (Jenkins, Wald, & Pittenger, 1978; Kraft & Jenkins, 1977) on memory for component scenes in an everyday sequence such as a telephone conversation, making tea, or a walk across a familiar campus. In a series of demonstration experiments, Jenkins and his students showed that if the sequence of scenes comprises a coherent event schema, subjects are unable to remember exactly which schema-congruent events were in the sequence. These findings appear as high failure to (correctly) reject lure scenes, directly analogous to the Bransford and Franks false-alarm method. This does not diminish the relevance of Jenkins' results to the conclusion that schematic processing is occurring. However, we hesitate to draw conclusions about the memorability of schema-incongruent scenes. In fact, our intuitions are that schema-incongruent events would be dramatically well remembered in a task such as Jenkins'.

Summary

Research on recognition memory for geometric patterns, scenes, and visually presented event sequences provides a solid foundation for schematic interpretations. However, none of the research reviewed here thoroughly studies the schema-relatedness dimension that we are especially concerned with. The range in variation along our hypothetical schema-event dimension covers only the schema-congruent to schema-irrelevant values. Within this range it seems clear that congruent events are likelier to be remembered accurately than irrelevant events. However, we can draw no firm conclusions about memory for incongruent events.

SOCIAL GROUP SCHEMATA

Linear Ordering Principles

There is a long tradition of research on schemata and memory in social psychology. Probably the earliest work in this tradition was performed to study memory for social structures of relations between people that fit or contradicted elementary mathematical principles of symmetry, transitivity, and completeness. For example, De Soto (1960) hypothesized that the relation "influences" would be readily learned (and well remembered) if its application in a series of propositions was consistent by principles of asymmetry, transitivity, and completeness. Using the number of trials required to learn a set of propositions to a criterion of two perfect trials as a measure of difficulty, De Soto found that certain predicted mathematical structures yielded optimal performance for the relationships; "influences," "likes," and "confides." Similar results have been obtained in more recent work using reaction times (Huttenlocher, 1968; Mayer, 1979; Potts, 1974), recognition confidence ratings (Tsujimoto, Wilde, & Robertson, 1978), and other measures of memory (Henly, Horsfall, & De Soto, 1969).

These experiments are not directly relevant to our question concerning the relative recall of schema congruent and incongruent events. The problem is that it is difficult to identify single incongruent propositions; rather, entire structures of schema propositions are congruent or distorted. The Tsujimoto, Wilde, and Robertson (1978) experiments are an exception to this rule, single "propositions" (actually pictures) were inconsistent with a linear ordering schema to various degrees. As in other similar experiments employing the Bransford and Franks (1971) false recognition paradigm, the focus was on *in*correct recognition of nonpresented lure items (e.g., Barclay & Reid, 1974). Nonetheless, there is a strong suggestion that schema congruent items will be quickly learned and slowly forgotten.

Social Balance Schemata

Heider (1946, 1958) first proposed the uniquely social, logical structure of the balance principle. For example, if we observe the sentiments among three people, triads containing three positive relations or one positive and two negative are defined as balanced. Triads including two positive sentiment relations and one negative relation or three negative relations are defined as unbalanced. Heider hypothesized that a cognitive "force" would tend to change unbalanced structures into balanced structures. Consequently, balanced structures should be easier to learn and more accurately recalled than unbalanced structures. One approach to evaluate the psychological reality of the balance principle has followed from Heider's (1958) hypothesis that balanced structures would be better remembered than unbalanced. Most early experiments in this vein (Rubin & Zajonc, 1969; Zajonc & Burnstein, 1965a, 1965b; Zajonc & Sherman, 1967) did not find that balanced structures were learned faster or retained longer than unbalanced. One exception to this result is an experiment by Press, Crockett, and Rosenkrantz (1969). They pointed out that the difficult paired-associate anticipation method used by Zajonc and his students may have been insensitive to balance schema effects. Press, Crockett, and Rosenkrantz found that subjects classified as low in cognitive complexity learned balanced structures more quickly than unbalanced, confirming Heider's prediction. However, high cognitive complexity subjects did not perform in accordance with the balance theory prediction.

Recently, Picek, Sherman, and Shiffrin (1975) have reopened this line of research using what seems to be a more sensitive method than the paired-associate learning task. Subjects in this experiment were given two stories each describing the relationships between four people. The stories were either complete (all six dyadic sentiment relations were stated) or incomplete (with only four relations stated explicitly). After reading two of the stories, subjects attempted to recall each *presented* relationship. First, balanced or (incomplete) balanceable structures were better recalled than unbalanced or unbalanceable, although the magnitude of the effect was quite small. The authors were able to show, with a careful analysis of input serial order effects, that the difference in recallability for balanced and unbalanced structures was localized at the first contradictory (*in*congruent) relationship. When the first dyadic relationship that could not exist in a balanced structure with earlier relationships appeared (it was always the third), recall for that specific relationship dropped. An analysis of intrusion data also supported the dominance of schema-congruent elements in recall. When subjects (incorrectly) remembered having read about a relationship in one of the incomplete structure stories, they tended to recall a relationship that would balance the structure if it was balanceable (see also Sentis & Burnstein, 1979).

The Picek, Sherman, and Shiffrin, and Sentis and Burnstein results are convincing evidence that balance schemata are used to structure memory for social relations. Furthermore, the results are clear support for the conclusion that schema-congruent events are better remembered than schema-incongruent events. The balance principle is an unusual schema in that the schematic principle *by itself* does not specify whether or not a single element (dyadic sentiment relationship) is congruent with the schema. Rather, the schema *plus* a minimum of two relationships must be established; then it is possible to determine if a third relationship is congruent, incongruent, or irrelevant.

Bear and Hodun (1975) conducted an experiment in which subjects were given an explicit, balance principle rule (e.g., if a man feels positive toward some cause, then if this cause displeases a friend of his, the man will reaffirm his own belief about the cause) and trained to apply it to example propositions. Subsequent to the rule learning task, subjects were shown a list of sentences and then asked to recall them. No mention was made in this acquisition task of the possibility of using the previously learned rule. Nonetheless, subjects' sentence recall was influenced by the nature of the rule. The results were consistently in agreement with the general conclusion that sentences congruent with the rule would be better recalled than incongruent or irrelevant sentences. In addition, when subjects distorted material at recall, the changes from the original tended to alter propositions to conform to the rule. Finally, when sentences that had not been presented were fabricated by subjects and appeared as intrusions in recall protocols, they tended to be congruent with the schematic rule.

This experiment provides some of the clearest results in favor of relatively high recall of schema-congruent information. As in the case of Heider's balance principle, the schema *plus* some propositions serve to define the congruence or incongruence of other propositions.

Group Stereotypes

Allport (1954) was one of the first psychologists to outline a cognitive point of view of the antecedents and consequences of group stereotyping. His suggestion was that stereotyping effects were irresistible products of human cognitive processing. Perceptual and mnemonic processes inevitably select, simplify, and categorize information in the social environment, and this produces the biases in judgment that are often associated with ethnic group evaluation. Campbell (1967) has presented a similar analysis based on principles of learning theory and Brunswik's functionalist analysis of perception. Several demonstration experiments by Allport and his colleagues were illustrations of the continuity of expectancy effects across social and nonsocial materials. A clever demonstration in a nonsocial perceptual task is the Bruner and Postman (1949) playing card identification experiment in which subjects were shown anomalous card markings (e.g., a red spade) in a series of ordinary symbols. For the most part, these sharp violations of schematic expectancies were ignored. An analogous demonstration with social stereotype-based expectancies involved presenting subjects with a drawing of a subway car scene (Allport & Postman, 1945). There were black and white characters in the scene and a white man was holding an open straight razor. On a memory test, white subjects frequently reported that the razor was in a black man's hands. Presumably white subjects' stereotyped image of violent black men produced the error.

These demonstrations are extremely suggestive evidence for schematic processing. Alternate associationist accounts have difficulty explaining the particular patterns of expectancies and responses to violations of expectancies observed in these experiments. However, the "psycho-logic" that predicts stereotype-based inferences is easily described in schematic vocabularies.

Although these demonstrations offer support for the general notion of schematic processing in perception, they are not directly relevant to our focal question concerning the memorability of events of varying degrees of schema-relatedness. There is a hint in the research that dramatically schema-incongruent events will not be perceived and hence would not be remembered. However, the crude but powerful demonstration method does not allow us to confidently locate the incongruent events along our schema-event relatedness dimension, and the dependent measures employed in this research are not clearly measures of accuracy of memory. Erdelyi (1974) provides an important analysis of one of the major flaws in the Allport–Bruner–Postman "new look" research on schematic effects in perception. These early cognitive theorists did not posit a thorough processing stage account for their experimental results. Consequently, it seemed paradoxical that schematic expectancy effects appeared to occur before stimuli had been "perceived." Erdelyi points out that a more modern conception of perception as a sequence of partially overlapping stages eliminates the apparent paradox (cf. Dixon, 1971).

Recently, Tajfel and his associates (e.g., Billig & Tajfel, 1973; Tajfel & Billig, 1974; Tajfel, Sheikh, & Gardner, 1964) have followed a program of research that has shown that even arbitrarily assigned group membership can produce many of the perception and judgment effects associated with stereotyping. Taylor, Fiske, Etcoff, and Ruderman (1978) have reported some of the most interesting research in this tradition. Subjects viewed a simulated group meeting in which the relative proportions of men and women or blacks and whites were varied. When subjects were asked to recall which specific group members had made remarks during the meeting, gender and ethnic category membership influenced the pattern of memory errors.

Taylor's results, especially some of her judgment data, are evidence for schematic processing. However, the foregoing particular memory result is not directly relevant to our present interest in schema-relatedness. The greater confusion of within-group than between-group behaviors (i.e., conversational sentences) is consistent with schematic explanations but it is also easily accounted for by traditional associationist approaches. Furthermore, Taylor was not attempting to address the question of the relative recall of schema-congruent and schema-incongruent events in her experimental design.

Hamilton and his colleagues have also studied the cognitive bases of stereotyping effects (Hamilton, 1979; Hamilton & Gifford, 1976). For example, Hamilton and Gifford investigated the tendency to over-attribute undesirable acts to members of minority groups. They reasoned that the statistical infrequency of minority group members and the nonnormative, unexpectedness of undesirable behaviors would combine to make the performance of an undesirable behavior by a minority group member dramatically striking or salient. They concluded that recall of undesirable minority group member behaviors would be relatively high and that the frequency of such acts would be overestimated. Hamilton and Gifford tested this hypothesis by presenting lists of behavior-actor pairings in which desirable and undesirable behaviors were attributed to members of a large (majority) or small (minority) group. Members of the minority group and undesirable behaviors were distinctive because they were both relatively infrequent. However, the *proportions* of undesirable acts were equal for the two groups. As predicted, recall for the distinctive event was relatively high and the frequency of undesirable acts performed by minority group members was overestimated. Jones, Stoll, Solernau, Noble, Fiala, and Miller (1976) systematically replicated these results presenting desirable events less frequently (hence more distinctive) and using different stimulus materials.

Two features of these results and the Hamilton and Gifford interpretation are important to the present review. First, the rather subtle "distinctiveness hypothesis" reverses the usual hypothesis about the schema-event memory relationship. Hamilton's prediction is based on the assumption that infrequent, distinctive events will be well recalled. In other words, instances that are exceptional, disconfirm expectations, or are schema-incongruent will be salient and memorable. Second, an issue that is raised in our review of individual impression research concerns the dependence of an impression on specific events or instances. Some researchers have taken the extreme view that *once formed,* an impression is independent of the specific event information on which it is based. At least with reference to group stereotype, Hamilton, Jones, and their colleagues appear to believe that impressions continue to depend on the availability of specific events, even after they are established.

A second series of experiments has come from Rothbart's laboratory (Rothbart, Evans, & Fulero, 1979; Rothbart, Fulero, Jensen, Howard, & Birrell, 1978). This research emphasizes even more strongly the dependence of general group stereotypes on specific events. In his earliest research on the topic, Rothbart (Rothbart, Fulero, Jensen, Howard, & Birrell, 1978) attempted to establish that group impressions were strongly dependent on the availability to memory of specific information about individual group members. In a sense this research concentrates on a question that is the mirror image of the question around which this review is organized: To what extent does the creation of a schema depend on the memorability of the specific information to which it applies? Rothbart used a complex design manipulating the structure and amount of information attributed to group members to generate a convincing argument that the availability of specific behaviors controlled group stereotype formation.

Subsequent research by Rothbart has turned to the question we are directly concerned with in this review: To what extent does the creation or selection of a (group) schema determine memory for specific information relevant to that schema? Rothbart, Evans, and Fulero (1978) led subjects to expect that members of a hypothetical group would be either intellectual or friendly. Members of the group were then described as performing 17 friendly, 17 intelligent, 3 unfriendly, 3 nonintelligent, and 10 trait-unrelated acts. On a subsequent memory test, subjects recalled relatively more behaviors congruent with their expectancy if the expectancy was induced *prior* to presentation of the acts. Other groups of subjects, given the ''expectation'' *after* the behaviors were presented, did not exhibit the bias to recall congruent information. The set size manipulation (confounded with behavior type) and restriction of the expectancy manipulation to positive acts (intelligent, friendly) limits the generality of conclusions from this research. Nonetheless, this is one of the few designs in which the issue of the relative recall of congruent and incongruent information is addressed directly. Furthermore, even with our reservations about generality, the results are evidence that schema confirmatory or congruent information is well recalled. The major interpretive problem is that when set size is controlled (intelligent, [17 acts] *vs.* friendly [17 acts] or nonintelligent [three acts] *vs.* unfriendly [3 acts]) relative recall of the expected acts is higher. However, note that the nonconfirmatory acts are irrelevant rather than incongruent in terms of our schema-event relationship summary.

Taken together, the Rothbart experiments provide several examples of higher recall of schema-congruent events than schema-incongruent events. Throughout this research, the schematic organizing principle, labeled a stereotype, was hypothesized to be an evaluative trait impression.

The present review of social ordering, balance, and stereotype schemata consistently supports the conclusion that irrelevant information will be poorly remembered as compared to schema-congruent information. It also seems clear that schema-incongruent information is less well remembered than schema-congruent information. This conclusion is somewhat at odds with the consistent finding (in the verbal learning and visual memory literature) that congruent information was not quite as well retained as incongruent. We will reserve our discussion of possible accounts for this discrepancy until after we have reviewed the effects of other social schemata on memory.

INDIVIDUAL PERSON SCHEMATA

Trait-Based Impressions

The first experiment, to our knowledge, studying the relationship between a general evaluative impression and memory for specific trait information on which it is based was conducted by Norman Anderson (Anderson & Hubert, 1963). Anderson and Hubert were studying the persistence of impression primacy effects under various task conditions. In their experiment, subjects studied a sequence of personality trait adjectives, rated the hypothetical character's likeability, and then *on some trials* recalled the original trait ensemble. Two of Anderson and Hubert's conclusions are relevant to our interest in schematic memory. First, when the character of the traits in an ensemble changed dramatically (from positive evaluation to negative or the reverse), there was no reflection of the change in memory serial position curves. We might interpret this result in schematic terms by supposing that the general evaluative impression being induced by the subject is a schema. Traits in the first half of our example list would be congruent with the emerging schema whereas traits in the second half, at least the first few, would be strikingly incongruent. Anderson and Hubert's result suggests that the evaluative impression is not related to specific event memorability. Anderson and Hubert's second major conclusion is that, once formed, the impression schema is independent of the traits on which it was based. This conclusion is derived from the result that primacy effects typically appear in impression ratings, but recency effects are strongest in trait recall (cf. Dreben, Fiske, & Hastie, 1979; Riskey, 1979 for concurring opinions, and Chalmers & Byde, 1973; Rywick & Schaye, 1974 for a contrary view).

Recently, Ostrom and his students conducted a series of experiments that also explore the impression-trait relationship (Lingle & Ostrom, 1979; Lingle, Geva, Ostrom, Leippe, & Baumgardner, 1979; Ostrom, Lingle, Pryor, & Geva, 1980). The experiments reported in Lingle and Ostrom (1979) exemplify the method common to all of this research. A subject was presented with an ensemble of traits immediately followed by a request for a decision about the occupational suitability of an individual described by the traits. A few seconds after this judgment was registered, the subject was asked for a second occupation suitability decision. The timing of the decisions, the relation between the two occupations (similar or disimilar), the number of traits presented, and several other variables were manipulated in a series of experiments to infer the extent to which the second judgment was based directly on the traits or on the first decision. By analogy with our discussion of the Asch impression formation task employed by Anderson and Hubert (1963), we view the decision as following from abstract schematic impressions. The original trait ensemble corresponds to the specific events or data that are associated with the schema.

The Lingle and Ostrom method is a more powerful methodology than Anderson and Hubert, including great variations in the trait ensemble and using sensitive reaction time measures, but their conclusions were essentially the same. The second decision was quite impervious to variations in the original stimulus ensemble, strongly implying that it was dominated by the first judgment. The general conclusion was that the impression and the traits on which it was based were independent of one another. (There was some subsidiary indication that subjects were searching the original trait ensemble stored in memory for negative trait information.) The authors did suggest that the relatively heavy dependence on the impression schema with the accompanying disregard of specific trait information was an optional decision strategy. The implication is that subjects would optionally select a trait-scanning strategy if incentives and instructions were varied. However, no direct evidence on this speculation was presented.

The results of these experiments bear on the question of the extent to which an impression depends on recall of relevant events, but our primary interest concerns the reverse relationship. In other experiments using this method (Lingle, Geva, Ostrom, Leippe, & Baumgardner, 1979), the effect of the decision on recall of trait items was explored. The conclusion that traits *relevant* to the decision were better recalled than *irrelevant* traits was clearly supported. However, no results directly on the question of relative recall of congruent and incongruent traits (both relevant to the decision) were reported.

A third research program that has covered the trait impression–trait memory relationship has been led by Cantor (Cantor & Mischel, 1977). This research used a variation on the Bransford and Franks false alarm recognition method to study the organization of impressions in memory. Subjects were shown a sequence of traits that were generally consistent with an impression of introversion or extraversion. Subsequently, in a recognition test format, subjects gave impression-congruent traits higher ratings of familiarity than unrelated or impression-incongruent items. Tsujimoto (1978) has replicated this result and extended it to "nonnormative" impressions. Both Cantor and Mischel and Tsujimoto have labeled their impression schemata "prototypes." However, in both cases they define prototype as the "central tendency" of the set of trait items presented in the acquisition list. It is clear that Cantor and Mischel conceptualize the subject's impression formation performance as "activating" an appropriate pattern stored in long-term memory. Tsujimoto on the other hand has replicated Cantor and Mischel's results with novel, nonnormative "prototypes." One implication of Tsujimoto's results is that it is not necessary to have a preexisting prototype available in memory to produce the pattern of false alarm results obtained by Cantor and Mischel.

Our conclusion from these findings is that Cantor and Mischel; Tsujimoto, Lingle and Ostrom; and Anderson and Hubert are all studying the effects of an impression formed by *integrating* the specific trait information in the list. We treat these impressions as schemata because: (1) they establish relationships between the specific (trait adjective) events on which they are based; and (2) because it is sensible to speak of traits as congruent, incongruent, or irrelevant to such an impression.

The Cantor and Mischel and Tsujimoto results are another indication that impression schemata affect memory for specific information. The suggestion is that schema-congruent items are better remembered (high recognition familiarity ratings) than schema-incongruent items. There are a few features of these results that lead us to qualify this conclusion. As in all of the false recognition results we have examined, the conclusion is based on subjects' responses to *non*presented distractor items—appearing only on the recognition test. Furthermore, in none of these experiments did subjects' recognition confidence for nonpresented items approach their ratings of presented items—in fact, the mean ratings of *non*-presented items never crossed the midpoints of the confidence scales.

A general conclusion from this review of trait impressions as schemata affecting memory for specific trait items is that there is scant evidence for the conclusion that schema-congruent events will be better remembered than schema-incongruent events. Most of the research concludes that there is little or no relationship between the schema, once it is formed or activated, and the availability of specific trait information. The work by Cantor and Mischel and Tsujimoto is suggestive that schema-congruent items will be better remembered than incongruent items. But the limits of the false alarm recognition method in these experiments make this conclusion suggestive rather than convincing on the congruent–incongruent memory issue.

Impression Schemata and Behavioral Events

A number of experiments have studied the extent to which trait, role, or intention schema attributed to an individual, affects memory for information about that individual's actions. This research addresses the question of the relative memorability of schema-congruent and schema-incongruent (behavioral) events more directly than the other research we have reviewed on memory for social materials.

A series of experiments by Zadny and Gerard (1974) are typical of this approach. One experiment manipulated subjects' beliefs about a character's academic major field of study and clearly demonstrated that memory for the character's course enrollment schedule and objects carried by the character was affected. Information that fit the academic major schema was best recalled. For example, if the subject was told that the character was a chemistry major, the subject remembered a preponderance of science courses from the course schedule and recalled the titles of science books, a slide rule, and so forth. If the major was psychology or music, the recall pattern changed to reflect the major. In a second study, subjects watched a videotape of two students wandering around in a livingroom talking about drug use, theft, and the police. Subjects were told that the tape depicted two burglars, two friends attempting to conceal illegal drugs, or two students waiting for a friend. Subjects given the burglar-theft intention-schema before viewing the tape recalled more theft-related objects and more theft-related conversation than subjects in the "drug concealment" or "waiting friends" conditions. This result was small in magnitude, but clearly represented better memory for intention-schema relevant material. The other intention manipulations did not affect the recall measures.

The third experiment in the series demonstrated that a shopper's intention (shopping for a male or female gender-typed gift) affected recall for gift items considered during a shopping trip. Again, intention-schema congruent items were better recalled than irrelevant items, although the effect was small in magnitude and must be qualified by a higher order interaction with gender of subject. The schema-congruent recall result held only when the subject was the same sex as the recipient of the gift.

In summary, if we view these experiments as manipulating the subject's schema for the main character's intention, the results show consistent but small effects of the schema on recall of objects and conversation. Again, it is important to note that the comparison is between recall of schema-congruent material and schema-*irrelevant* material. The stories did not appear to include schema-*incongruent* material as we have defined it. An important issue raised by Zadny and Gerard concerns the effects of a schema on memory for events when the schema is activated *before* the events or *after* the events. In their second experiment, these researchers manipulated timing of the theft *versus* drug *versus* waiting-intention schema. The effects of the schema were only detectable when the schema was activated before the videotape was presented.

Hastie and Kumar (1979) have conducted a series of experiments that directly addresses the issue of relative recall of congruent and incongruent behaviors. Subjects read sentences describing a series of behaviors attributed to a single fictional character with instructions to form an impression of the character. We attempted to insure that subjects activated or induced particular trait impression schemas by preceding each list of behaviors with an ensemble of trait adjectives, all consistent with a unitary trait impression (e.g., friendly, gregarious, outgoing, extraverted, sociable). In most of this research, the lists of behaviors included a mixture of schema-congruent and schema-incongruent behaviors (analogous to Cantor and Mischel's trait-inconsistent characters). The analysis of the experiment concentrated on comparing the relative recall of congruent and incongruent behaviors. First, recall was differential with consistently higher proportions of incongruent behaviors recalled. This result must be qualified by the observation that set size (the numbers of congruent and incongruent items in the list) was a primary determinant of recall performance. When incongruent items were relatively uncommon (e.g., $1/14$, $3/14$), incongruent item recall was extremely probable; however, when the set sizes were equal (seven congruents and seven incongruents), recall was almost equal (although incongruent items were still slightly more memorable than congruent).

These results were interpreted as evidence that trait schemata are determinants of behavior recall. The differential recall of congruent and incongruent behaviors was explained with reference to a levels-of-processing framework (Craik & Lockhart, 1972). Incongruent behaviors were salient or attention catching. Subjects attempting to obey the instruction to form a clear impression of the character to whom the behaviors were attributed spent more time and (perhaps) invoked more complex perception and comprehension strategies to account for incongruent material. Thus, incongruent acts were processed longer and perhaps more deeply than congruent acts. The deeper and more extensive processing produced richer, more durable, and more retrievable memory traces for incongruent items.

Cohen (1977) has used a similar experimental paradigm to study the effects of an occupational role schema on memory for actions of a person. In her experiments, subjects viewed a 5-minute videotape that they were told was of a librarian or of a waitress. On a subsequent recall test, subjects recalled slightly more information congruent with the salient occupation schema. Again, the results do not have direct implications for our concern with congruent versus incongruent item recall. It is quite plausible to think of waitress-congruent information as irrelevant to, but not incongruent with, the librarian schema. But, of course, we view the results as further evidence for schematic memory processes.

Sulin and Dooling (1974) provide another source of evidence for schematic processes in person memory. Their subjects were told that the character described in a paragraph was an actual person who was either unknown (e.g., Jerry Olson) or famous (Aldolf Hitler). Information congruent with the famous character's reputation (e.g., "hated the Jewish people") was slightly better remembered when attributed to the famous person than the unknown. Even more dramatic effects appeared when false alarm recognition rates for nonpresented items were summarized. The commonly found high recognition ratings of schema-congruent distractor items were obtained. Again, we think that these results are good evidence for the importance of schematic concepts in a theoretical analysis of person memory. However, the experiment does not directly study the relative recall of schema-congruent and schema-incongruent events.

Hamilton and his students (Hamilton & Katz, 1975; Hamilton, Katz, & Leirer, 1980) have conducted a series of experiments on subjects' optional use of organizational strategies in remembering a sequence of acts attributed to a single character. These studies concentrate on evidence that a general categorical person schema is being used when the subject attempts to integrate information to form an impression.

Briefly, Hamilton, Katz, and Leirer conducted a series of experiments studying the increases in recall and organization of behavior descriptions over a series of presentations in a multitrial free recall learning task. The major finding was that subjects who were instructed to form a clear impression of the character tended to structure the to-be-remembered material according to categories representing domains of activity (e.g., intellectual pursuits, athletic endeavors, religious beliefs). When instructed to concentrate on recalling the behavioral information, subjects did not utilize these organizational groupings as consistently as under impression instructions. An interesting result was a small but consistent recall advantage for subjects in the impression conditions. Thus, instructions to concentrate on memorization were less effective than instructions to form an impression in producing a high level of recall.

The interpretation of these results favored by the authors is that subjects given the impression instructions activate a person schema, probably based on a hierarchical ordering of trait categories, and that this schema facilitates encoding, comprehension, and retrieval of behavioral information. Memory instruction subjects are less likely to apply natural, effective social schemas in the task, and consequently their recall performance suffers.

To summarize, these results converge nicely with other empirical arguments for schematic memory processes. However, they do not help us answer our question concerning the relative memorability of congruent and incongruent events.

An experiment by Hastie and Mazur (1978) may help us understand the consistent finding that schema-congruent information is better remembered than schema-irrelevant material, whereas schema-incongruent material is best remembered of all. Hastie and Mazur showed films of characters behaving in a series of social episodes to subjects and followed the sequence with an unexpected instruction to recall as much information from the films as possible. As in the Hastie and Kumar (1979) experiments, subjects were instructed to form impressions of the central character in the films, and each film sequence was preceded by a trait ensemble to insure that a particular initial impression schema was selected. Set sizes of acts congruent and incongruent with the schema in each series were also varied. Finally, a new variable was introduced in the design to vary the nature of the acts in each sequence. Every sequence included two sets of acts; acts congruent with the initial trait ensemble (*base* acts) and acts from a second trait category (*contrast* acts). There were three types of contrast acts and only one type appeared in any single sequence: (1) incongruent contrast acts selected to be congruent with a trait opposite in meaning to the initial trait impression (e.g., hostile acts would be incongruent for a friendly character); (2) intermediate contrast acts, selected to be opposite to the base acts in evaluative valence, but to represent behaviors on an orthogonal trait dimension (e.g., stupid acts would be intermediate contrast acts for a friendly character); (3) low contrast acts, selected to match the base trait in evaluative valence, but to represent behaviors on an orthogonal trait dimension (e.g., intelligent acts would be low contrast acts for a friendly character [cf., Rosenberg & Sedlak, 1972]).

Recall test results for the incongruent contrast behaviors replicated the findings of the Hastie and Kumar experiments that had used written materials rather than films. Set size was the major determinant of incongruent item recall and the smaller the set of incongruent items, the higher the probability of recalling any particular item. When set sizes were equal (five congruent acts vs. five incongruent acts), recall was almost exactly equal. The pattern of recall for intermediate contrast acts was quite different. Overall there was no recall advantage for contrast acts. Finally, for the low contrast condition, recall of low contrast acts was significantly lower than recall of base (congruent) acts. Our interpretation of these results is that the initial trait impression controls encoding and comprehension processes. Highly unexpected, incongruent acts receive extra processing during encoding and, therefore, are well retained and recalled. However, intermediate and low contrast acts do not receive special treatment during encoding. Furthermore, low contrast acts are irrelevant to the final impression and are especially difficult to recall. Thus, within one experimental task, we observe the von Restorff-like heightened recall of unexpected events and the common, lowered recall of schema-irrelevant events.

There seems to be one experiment in the literature that clearly contradicts the emerging generalization that Schema *incongruent* events will be better remembered than congruent events, whereas schema *irrelevant* events will be more poorly remembered than congruent events.

In an experiment performed by Snyder and Uranowitz (1978), subjects read a three-page narrative about the life of a woman. *After* finishing the story, either immediately or 1 week later, subjects were given information about her lifestyle. One-third of the subjects were told that her sexual perferences were lesbian, one-third that she was heterosexual, and one-third were told nothing about her sexual preferences. A recognition memory test administered one week after the story had been read, found evidence that information congruent with the life style schema was likelier to be remembered than information that was incongruent with the schema. Subjects given the lesbian life style label exhibited a bias to falsely recognize more items that fit a stereotype of lesbianism than subjects given no information about sexuality. The heterosexual label did not produce a corresponding bias in the opposite direction. However, the heterosexual label did produce a bias toward heterosexuality for correctly recognized items. The corresponding pattern did not appear for lesbian label subjects.

The Snyder and Uranowitz results are problematic for our summary interpretation because they are a clear comparison of memory for schema-congruent and schema-incongruent events. For the moment, we will merely acknowledge the finding without attempting to interpret it. The schema-congruent memory advantage over schema-incongruent items was miniscule in magnitude, did not appear consistently in all analyses of the Snyder and Uranowitz data, and may be limited to the particular materials employed in that research. Furthermore, the sexual preference information was presented *after* the biographical narrative, making our ''extra processing at imput'' explanation for differential memory untenable.

Until the result is replicated with other schemata and story materials, we will reserve judgment of its importance and stay with the simple generalization outlined earlier.

POINT-OF-VIEW SCHEMATA

A number of theoreticians have suggested that a perceiver's attitudes, perspective, and self-concept operate as schemata to control perception and memory. Examples of point-of-view schemata from the attitude change, attribution, and personality literatures are considered in this section of our review.

Social Attitudes

Several experiments have been conducted to evaluate the role of a subject's social attitudes in the acquisition and retention of attitude-relevant statements. For example, Levine and Murphy (1943) had pro- and anti-Communist subjects repeatedly study and recall a pro- and an anti-Communist paragraph about the Soviet Union. Their actual results were extremely weak, but they concluded that "an individual notes and remembers material which supports his social attitudes better than material which conflicts with these attitudes [p. 515]." Several other experiments are also cited as demonstrating selective memory for information relevant to political attitudes (Edwards, 1941; Watson & Hartmann, 1939), racial attitudes (Seeleman, 1940; Taft, 1954), and gender concepts (Alper & Korchin, 1952; Clark, 1940; Zillig, 1928). Probably the most substantial early experiments were conducted by Jones and Aneshansel (1956) and Jones and Kohler (1958) studying selective learning of statements relevant to racial segregation attitudes. In the Jones and Kohler (1958) experiment, subjects read aloud and then recalled 12 statements on the segregation issue. The statements could be divided into four sets of three arguments: plausible prosegregation, implausible prosegregation, plausible antisegregation, implausible antisegregation. Subjects scoring high on an attitude scale measuring racial prejudice recalled more plausible prosegregation and more implausible antisegregation statements than low-prejudice subjects. Low-prejudice subjects recalled implausible prosegregation and plausible antisegregation statements at a higher rate than high-prejudice subjects.

Waly and Cook (1966) have disputed the conclusions from all of this early research arguing that differential familiarity with particular material is the explanatory factor and that general attitudinal schemata need not be invoked to account for the results. Even more telling was these authors' failure to replicate the Jones and Kohler results in a series of careful experiments closely modeled on the original task.

More recently, Greenwald and Sakumura (1967) have failed to obtain clear attitude schema effects on the learning of statements about the United States involvement in the Vietnam War. These researchers concentrated on unconfounding attitude orientation and prior familiarity with the material and studied memory under intentional and incidental learning conditions. Surprisingly, their results did not demonstrate either schema-relatedness or familiarity effects of the expected kind. They did note a tendency for statements unsympathetic to United States involvement in Vietnam, a category that was relatively unfamiliar to subjects, to be better recalled than statements supporting involvement. Greenwald and Sakumura tentatively concluded that information novelty might *facilitate* learning.

The results of research on attitude schemata and memory do not yield any simple summary conclusions for the purposes of this review. It seems that an attitudinal orientation (e.g., antisegregation, pro-United States invovement in Vietnam conflict) fits our initial prescription for a mental schema and that pro- and con- argument statements are suitable examples of schema-related events. Thus, it is easy to restate many of the hypotheses tested in this literature as expressions of functional relations between schema relatedness and event memory. However, no consistent conclusion about the form of this functional relation is apparent in the relevant literature. Furthermore, it is obvious that systematic presentation of arguments from a full range of locations on the schema-event relation dimension was not achieved in this research. Rather, only arguments from the two ends of the continuum, schema-congruent and schema-incongruent, were presented.

An interesting variation on the traditional attitude and argument memory research method is provided by an experiment conducted by Bem and McConnell (1970; replicated by Wixon & Laird, 1976). Subjects' opinions on an attitude issue were measured and then subsequently changed using a role-playing technique. When subjects were asked to recall their original opinions, they erroneously responded with their current (changed) opinions. The schematic interpretation of this finding is that current attitudes serve as a guide to construct a judgment of the original attitude. Thus, schema-congruent opinions are constructed and judged to have been held initially. (Ross, Lepper, & Hubbard, 1975, have demonstrated a related phenomenon operating on a belief about the self.)

Perspective Schemata

A number of recent experiments have manipulated the subject's set, identification, or narrative perspective before presenting a sequence of to-be-remembered events. Abelson and Pinto (reported in Abelson, 1975, 1976) appear to be the vanguards in this area. They showed that subjects instructed to comprehend a story from the vantage point of the main character recalled best details that were prominent in that character's "perceptual field." Vantage point was varied for a second group of subjects, who were instructed to view the study from the position of an observer on a balcony above the central scene. These subjects' recall reflected their perspective.

Bower (1978) and his colleagues have produced a series of clever variations on the Abelson and Pinto experiment that replicate and explore the effects of perspective in considerable detail. In one study, subjects were induced to identify with one of three central characters by reading different first paragraphs of a single story about filming a television commercial. Subjects recalled information that was relevant to their character's actions and feelings, and subjects' ratings on a recognition test revealed a pattern of false alarm errors that placed a sympathetic interpretation on their character's actions and intentions. Anderson and Prichert (1978) conducted a similar series of experiments in which subjects took the perspective of a burglar or a housebuyer while reading *or* recalling a story that included a detailed description of a house. The most interesting finding in this research was that a manipulation of perspective, at retrieval only, produced small but reliable effects on the pattern of recall.

Bower's most recent work has explored some of the conditions that produce identification with one character or another. For example, Bower and Monteiro (reported in Bower, 1978; see also Bower, Monteiro, & Gilligan, 1978) have used hypnotic suggestion to vary subjects' moods. They found that subjects identified with the character in a story whose mood matched their hypnotically induced emotion.

Several social psychologists have studied perspective effects in order to account for the effects of varying social attention on causal attribution. For example, Taylor and Fiske (1975) and McArthur and Post (1977) varied subjects' attention as observers of a two-person conversation and subsequently measured memory for events during the conversation. Perspective effects were extremely weak but generally in the direction of more accurate recall of the focal character's actions.

It is easy to interpret these results as evidence for schematic perception and memory processing. It would be difficult to explain both the memory and causal judgment results with an associationist account. However, once again, the results are not directly useful in assessing the effects of schema relatedness along a full range of schema-event congruence values. The difficulty is that it is uncertain what type of information would constitute highly incongruent events. Conversation and action in the two-person situation could be classified as varying in importance or relevance to the subject's perspective, but this would only seem to yield congruent and irrelevant schema-related events.

Self-Concept Schemata

The concept of a constellation of generalizations about the self that serves as a basis for experience has a long history in philosophy and psychology (McGuire, McGuire, Child, Fujioka, 1978; McGuire & Padawer-Singer, 1976; Wylie, 1974). Recently, experimental psychologists have started to explore the influence of self-schemata on memory for personally relevant information.

Mischel, Ebbesen, and Zeiss (1976) manipulated subjects' expectations of success or failure on a (bogus) test of intellectual ability as well as classifying subjects according to the repression-sensitization personality scale. Subsequently each subject was shown information that was claimed to describe positive and negative sides of their character. Expectations about performance on the intellectual abilities test affected memory such that subjects expecting to succeed more accurately recognized statements from the positive personality feedback file than from the negative feedback file. There were no differences in recognition accuracy between a no-expectancy control group and the failure-expectancy group. This result is consistent with a schematic account that predicts that schema-congruent (success expectancy-positive character attributes) information will be best remembered. However, this conclusion is weakened by the lack of symmetric effects for failure-expectancy subjects and the fact that the recognition results are weak even when summarized by a complex sensitivity score.

Markus (1977) has studied the effects of differences in self-schemata along an independent–dependent personality trait dimension in several information-processing tasks. Markus' research concentrated on attentional selectivity and on the amount of time required to verify statements about the self. Thus, she did not directly address questions concerning the accurate acquisition and retrieval of information in memory. However, her general conclusion—that information that is congruent with one's self-concept is processed more easily and confidently than incongruent or irrelevant information—has clear implications for the relative memorability of personal information. The suggestion is that schema-irrelevant information will be processed and retained with difficulty, whereas schema-congruent material will be processed quickly and retained relatively easily. Schema-incongruent information would be remembered at intermediate levels.

A final experiment that is often cited as evidence for schematic effects in person memory was conducted by Rogers, Kuiper, and Kirker (1977) as part of a larger research program. In this experiment, personality traits were presented and rated on various dimensions. When subjects were asked to judge the extent to which a trait applied to themselves, performance on a subsequent recognition test was very high. The researchers concluded that this result is strong evidence that relating the trait to a "self-schema" produces powerful retrieval cues for later recall or recognition. There are two problems with this interpretation for our present purposes. First, it is not clear that it is *self*-reference per se that is responsible for the high recall of trait materials. It may be that judgments involving any elaborate reference schema (e.g., a pet dog, a familiar geographic location, or a symphony) would yield relatively high recognition accuracy. Second, the authors do not report any effects of degree of applicability (congruence between the trait and self-schema); thus, their result is not directly pertinent to our question about the relative recall of congruent and incongruent information.

DISCUSSION

When a person perceives specific, concrete events that are related to a general, abstract schema, how will each event's relation to the schema affect its availability for later recall or cognitive utilization? Almost none of the empirical research we have reviewed meets the strict methodological conditions for a clear investigation of this question outlined in the introduction of this paper. Very little of this research explicitly addressed our theme question; however, almost all of the research did include some reference to the issue of schema-congruence and memory.

Our conclusion is that the typical relationship between schema-event relatedness and memory is best summarized as a nonmonotonic U-shaped function (see Fig. 2.2). Infromation that is highly congruent or highly incongruent with reference to a currently active schema is best remembered. Information that is undiagnostic, or irrelevant to the applicability of the schema is worst remembered, all other factors being equal.

Our summary conclusion is based on two aspects of the empirical findings. First, in almost all of the areas of research reviewed there are some results exhibiting a pattern of increasingly accurate memory with increasing schema-event congruence and other results showing increasingly accurate memory with increasing schema-event *in*congruence. A careful examination of both result patterns suggests that lowest recall and recognition performance occurred when schema-event relatedness was closest to the midpoint of our hypothetical scale (the abcissa in Fig. 2.2). Second, in five of the investigations covered in this review (Bower, Black, & Turner, 1979; Hastie & Kumar, 1979; Hastie & Mazur, 1978; Lingle & Ostrom, 1979; Smith, 1973), where it was plausible that schema-event relatedness values spanned a wide range on the relatedness dimension, U-shaped functions were observed.

Our conclusion should be qualified by summarizing some of the task conditions that prevailed throughout the literature we reviewed. First, the schema that defines the congruence of to-be-remembered events must be prominent in the subject's perception of the materials. Second, the pace at which to-be-remembered information occurs was leisurely in all of the research. This allowed the subject to optionally deploy attentional and working memory capacities during the study phase of the experimental tasks. The qualifications implied by these conditions are obvious. The subject must be using the schema that is hypothesized to control perception and memory, and the subject must have time and capacity to vary processing strategies under the schema's direction.

How should we conceptualize the relationships between an abstract schema and specific events? The theoretical focus of this review has concerned the specification of the mental relationships between an abstract schema and the specific events encountered while that schema is cognitively available. Our preliminary approach was to suppose that these relationships, at least the most important relationships in the analysis of memory tasks, could be summarized as a conditional probability: probability (event/schema). This conceptual summary was a useful device to organize our review of individual experiments to focus on the connection between memory (recall, recognition, etc.) and schema relatedness (probability; [event/schema]) relationship (see Fig. 2.2).

Now it is time to review the schema-relatedness index critically. There are two major problems with the conditional probability index. First, it collapses or equates some schema-relatedness relationships that should probably be treated separately. Second, from a practical point of view, we have presented no specific plan for the measurement of the conditional probability index.

The first difficulty is clearest in the case of events that are associated with intermediate conditional probabilities (near .50). We have called these events irrelevant with respect to the current schema; however, the types of events receiving this intermediate classification are extremely heterogeneous. For example, events that are pertinent to the schema but that are undiagnostic would be equated with events that are completely removed from the schema's domain of application. Thus, if we were evaluating personality trait schema-behavioral event relationships, events such as "combed her hair" and "it rained on Wednesday" might receive equivalent ratings. The example is problematic because we would expect schema-relevant information to be responded to differently than irrelevant information. One solution is to restrict our application of the conditional probability index to events that are relevant to, or belong in, the "domain of discourse" of the schema of interest. The weakness of this solution is that we must rely on the researcher's or reader's intuitive sense of pertinence to distinguish between relevant and irrelevant events (cf., Quine, 1969). However, the reliance on intuitions to specify the applicability of social science theories is widespread and quite reasonable when we are explicit about its occurrence.

We believe if we can distinguish between pertinent but undiagnostic events and events outside of the schema's range of application that the conditional probability index of schema-event relatedness is very useful. Of course, we look forward to the development of more complex theoretical analyses of schematic processing that provide empirically justified structural accounts for the cognitive relations underlying the conditional probability summary (e.g., Tversky & Kahneman, 1974).

The second problem with the conditional probability index, designing procedures to measure it, requires empirical rather than conceptual analysis. For the present, we would propose using direct ratings of stimulus materials to produce a relatively crude index of relatedness. Such an index is probably adequate to permit researchers to establish a preliminary summary of schema-event relatedness and memory relationships.

Note on Processing

It is interesting to note the extent to which research on schematic effects has concentrated on the gap-filling inferential processes that produce reorderings, intrusions, false recognitions, and other *errors* of commission at the time memory is tested. The present review concludes that there is a need for schematic accounts for the relative rates of *correct* recall and recognition of various types of material.

To date, theoretical accounts for the relative memorability of schema-congruent, schema-irrelevant, and schema-incongruent events are virtually nonexistent. Schank and Abelson (1977) suggest that when *obstacles, errors,* or *distractions* occur during comprehension of a story that detour paths will be added to a script representing the products of comprehension. This account suggests that script-incongruent events will be linked to the base script in a different manner than script-congruent events. However, the Schank and Abelson discussion does not yield specific predictions about relative memorability of direct- and detour-linked events. Bower, Black, and Turner (1979) have based their theoretical analysis on the Schank and Abelson model and predict "that interruptions (script-incongruent events) will be remembered better than script actions (script-congruent events) and that irrelevancies will be remembered less well than either [p. 210]." However, they admit that this conclusion is based on intuition rather than the script theory.

Bobrow and Norman (1975) have also addressed the issue of the relative memorability of *expected* and *unexpected* events. They argue that *un*expected events will be given priority in processing. This means that a search for a conceptual schema that will account for the unexpected "data" occurs. If the data are important or "cannot readily be accounted for," then they will tend to be processed deeply (cf., Cermak & Craik, 1979). Deep processing produces better memory; thus, Bobrow and Norman predict that unexpected events will be better remembered than expected events.

Thorndyke and Hayes-Roth (1979) are concerned about the nebulous character of current schema theories and cite as an example the present concern. "So, for example, it is not clear what a schema theory would predict about memory for an anomalous datum—(i.e., "a constituent detail in a set of information that did not fit the schema invoked to comprehend that information [p. 84]." However, their own theoretical analysis does not yield clear predictions about memory and schema relatedness.

As a summary, there seem to be three theoretical approaches to describe the mental representation of schema-event connections for events varying in schema relatedness. First, it may be that schema-congruent events are directly linked (by "pointers") to the schema structure's "slots," whereas incongruent or irrelevant events are connected ("tagged") to the base structure by special links that differ qualitatively from direct links. The properties of these various *types of links* with respect to memory processes have not yet been established. Second, the expectedness of an event may determine the amount of mental resource that will be allocated to comprehend an event. The more resources, the *more links* (of any type) will be formed from schema to event. Important unexpected events are hypothesized to receive the greatest amounts of comprehension resources and would be relatively well-remembered. Third, the *overall pattern of associations* between events and schemata may have to be considered to predict relative memorability of events. An event that is associated with many schemata will tend to be well-remembered, and the fewer events associated with a particular schema, the more accessible each event will be. Anomalous events might be predicted to be associated with fewer schemata than unsurprising events, but anomalous events would also tend to be associated with less crowded schemata. Thus, the prediction of memory for events varying in schema relatedness is complicated and requires the specification of the relative importance to recall or recognition of event-to-schema and schema-to-event association ratios.

As a final comment on schematic processing, we present the speculative scenario that we favor for the processes occurring for a typical subject in any of the memory tasks we have reviewed. During the acquisition stage of a memory task, the subject selects a schema from conceptual memory and proceeds to comprehend to-be-remembered events by referring to the schema and to task-specific information already stored in event memory. When a schema-incongruent event occurs, the subject identifies the event as unexpected as it is initially perceived. If the processing requirements during acquisition permit it (i.e., if the subject is not "cognitively overloaded"), the subject devotes extra processing time to the comprehension of the incongruent event. This additional time will be used to link the event to other events relevant to the schema and often the time will be used to causally analyze the event. For instance, in a task such as Hastie and Mazur's (1978), where subjects observe the behavior of a target character, subjects would react to incongruent events by reviewing other information in memory relevant to that character to find an explanation for the unexpected behavior. This review would result in the creation of a large number of links between the incongruent event and other events in memory. Thus, incongruent events would typically be given special treatment during acquisition producing a later advantage for these events on memory tests. Second, at the time of retrieval, the subject would use the memory schema to guide and control search processes. However, at retrieval, schematic effects would favor congruent information. The extent to which the schema was used to select a subset of memory to scan carefully and the extent to which the schema controlled response thresholds would both emphasize the selection and affirmation of schema-congruent events.

Relying on current characterizations of acquisition and retrieval stages, we have concluded that the advantage in memory for schema-congruent events derives primarily from retrieval processes. On the other hand, the advantage for schema-incongruent events derives from acquisition stage processes. The empirical significance of this speculation is that the left-hand portion (congruence) of the curve in Fig. 2.2 will be responsive to variations in retrieval conditions, whereas the right-hand (incongruence) portion will be more sensitive to acquisition task variations.

CONCLUSION

The concept of the mental schema pervades theorizing in cognitive psychology despite the fact that its basic meaning is indefinite, its usage by theorists is highly individualistic, and its operational connection to empirical events is tenuous. One motive of the present survey of research, in which memory measures were the primary criterial tasks, was to identify a common core of meaning for the term *schema* and its variants. Our conclusion was that a typology of overlapping meanings would be necessary to capture the rudiments of its current usage. Furthermore, we found that large portions of the catalogue of experimental studies relevant to the concept of a schema were chaotic and incomplete. We also emphasized the central ambiguity of the definition of schema-event relationships in the planning, execution, and discussion of research on schematic effects in memory.

As a final positive note, theory and research on schematic processing have reached levels of sophistication that greatly exceed the powers of common sense. The schema theoretic terminology, although often confused, is rich, subtle, and occasionally precise. The results of many experiments to study schematic principles are formidable obstacles for associationist interpretation and defy common-sense analysis. It seems obvious that schema theories have advanced our thinking about the human mind. The resolution of the ambiguities and problems identified in this review pose questions that can only be answered by future research.

ACKNOWLEDGMENTS

This paper was prepared for presentation at the first annual Ontario Symposium on Personality and Social Psychology. The writing of the paper was supported by NIMH Grant No. MH 28928. The author is grateful to James Bartlett, Tory Higgins, Marcia Penrod, Shelley Taylor, and the Eleventh Floor Personality and Cognition Lunch Seminar for useful comments on preliminary versions of this paper.

REFERENCES

Abelson, R. P. The structure of belief systems. In R. C. Schank & K. Colby (Eds.), *Computer models of thought and language*. San Francisco: Freeman, 1973.

Abelson, R. P. Does a story understander need a point of view? In R. Schank & B. L. Nash-Webber (Eds.), *Theoretical issues in natural language processing*. Proceedings of a conference at the Massachusetts Institute of Technology, Cambridge, June 1975.

Abelson, R. P. Script processing in attitude formation and decision making. In J. Carroll & J. Payne (Eds.), *Cognition and social behavior*. Hillsdale, N. J.: Lawrence Erlbaum Associates, 1976.

Ajzen, I., & Fishbein, M. A Bayesian analysis of attribution processes. *Psychological Bulletin*, 1975, *82*, 261–277.

Allport, D. A. The state of cognitive psychology. *Quarterly Journal of Experimental Psychology*, 1975, *27*, 141–152.

Allport, G. W. *The nature of prejudice*. Cambridge: Addison–Wesley, 1954.

Allport, G. W., & Postman, L. J. The basic psychology of rumor. *Transactions of the New York Academy of Sciences, Series II*, 1945, *8*, 61–81.

Alper, T. G., & Korchin, S. J. Memory for socially relevant material. *Journal of Abnormal and Social Psychology*, 1952, *47*, 25–37.

Anderson, J. R. *Language, memory, and thought*. Hillsdale, N.J.: Lawrence Erlbaum Associates, 1976.

Anderson, J. R., & Bower, G. H. *Human associative memory*. Washington, D.C.: V. H. Winston, 1973.

Anderson, N. H., & Hubert, S. Effects of concomitant verbal recall on order effects in personality impression formation. *Journal of Verbal Learning and Verbal Behavior*, 1963, *2*, 379–391.

Anderson, R. C., & Prichert, J. W. Recall of previously unrecallable information following a shift in perspective. *Journal of Verbal Learning and Verbal Behavior*, 1978, *17*, 1–12.

Aristole. [On memory and recollection.] In W. D. Ross (Ed.; J. I. Beare, trans), *The works of Aristotle* (Vol. 3). Oxford: Clarendon Press, 1931.

Asch, S. E., & Ebenholtz, S. M. The principle of associative symmetry. *Proceedings of the American Philosophical Society*, 1962, *106*, 135–163.

Barclay, J. R., & Reid, M. Characteristics of memory representations of sentence sets describing a linear array. *Journal of Verbal Learning and Verbal Behavior*, 1974, *13*, 133–137.

Bartlett, F. C. *Remembering: A study in experimental and social psychology*. Cambridge: Cambridge University Press, 1932.

Beach, L. R. Cue probabilism and inference behavior. *Psychological Monographs*, 1964, *78*, 1–20.

Bear, G., & Hodun, A. Implicational principles and the cognition of confirmatory, contradictory, incomplete, and irrelevant information. *Journal of Personality and Social Psychology*, 1975, *32*, 594–604.

Bever, T. G., Fodor, J. A., & Garrett, M. A. A formal limitation of associationism. In T. R. Dixon & D. L. Horton (Eds.), *Verbal behavior and general behavior theory*. Englewood Cliffs, N.J.: Prentice-Hall, 1968.

Bem, D. J., & McConnell, H. K. Testing the self-perception explanation of dissonance phenomena: On the salience of premanipulation attitudes. *Journal of Personality and Social Psychology*, 1970, *14*, 23–31.

Biederman, I. Perceiving real-world scenes. *Science*, 1972, *177*, 77–79.

Billig, M., & Tajfel, H. Social categorization and similarity in intergroup behavior. *European Journal of Social Psychology*, 1973, *3*, 27–52.

Bobrow, D. G., & Norman, D. A. Some principles of memory schemata. In D. G. Bobrow & A. Collins (Eds.), *Representation and understanding: Studies in cognitive science*. New York: Academic Press, 1975.

Bourne, L. E., Jr., & O'Banion, K. Memory for individual events in concept identification. *Psychonomic Science*, 1969, *16*, 101–103.

Bower, G. H. Cognitive psychology: An introduction. In W. K. Estes (Ed.), *Handbook of learning and cognitive processes* (Vol. 1). Hillsdale, N.J.: Lawrence Erlbaum Associates, 1975.

Bower, G. H. Experiments on story comprehension and recall. *Discourse Processes*, 1978, *1*, 211–232.

Bower, G. H., Black, J. B., & Turner, T. J. Scripts in memory for text. *Cognitive Psychology*, 1979, *11*, 177–220.

Bower, G. H., Monteiro, K. P., & Gilligan, S. G. Emotional mood as a context for learning and recall. *Journal of Verbal Learning and Verbal Behavior*, 1978, *17*, 573–585.

Bransford, J. D., Barclay, J. R., & Franks, J. J. Sentence memory: A constructive versus interpretive approach. *Cognitive Psychology*, 1972, *3*, 193–209.

Bransford, J. D., & Franks, J. J. The abstraction of linguistic ideas. *Cognitive Psychology*, 1971, *2*, 331–350.

Bransford, J. D., & Johnson, M. K. Contextual prerequisities for understanding: Some investigations of comprehension and recall. *Journal of Verbal Learning and Verbal Behavior*, 1972, *11*, 717–726.

Bransford, J. D., McCarrell, N. S., Franks, J. J., & Nitsch, K. E. Toward unexplaining memory. In R. Shaw & J. Bransford (Eds.), *Perceiving, acting, and knowing: Toward an ecological psychology*. Hillsdale, N.J.: Lawrence Erlbaum Associates, 1977.

Bruner, J. S., & Postman, L. J. On the perception of incongruity: A paradigm. *Journal of Personality*, 1949, *18*, 206–223.

Calfee, R. C. Recall and recognition memory in concept identification. *Journal of Experimental Psychology*, 1969, *81*, 436–440.

Calkins, M. W. Association: An essay analytic and experimental. *Psychological Review Monograph Supplement*, 1896, *3*, 32–49.

Campbell, D. T. Stereotypes and the perception of group differences. *American Psychologist*, 1967, *22*, 817–829.

Cantor, N., & Mischel, W. Traits as prototypes: Effects on recognition memory. *Journal of Personality and Social Psychology*, 1977, *35*, 38–48.

Carmichael, L., Hogan, H. P., & Walter, A. A. An experimental study of the effect of language on the reproduction of visually perceived form. *Journal of Experimental Psychology*, 1932, *15*, 73–86.

Cermak, L. S., & Craik, F. I. M. (Eds.). *Levels of processing in human memory*. Hillsdale, N.J.: Lawrence Erlbaum Associates, 1979.

Chalmers, D. K., & Byde, R. W. *The relation between impression judgment and verbal recall*. Paper read at Psychonomic Society, November 1973.

Charness, N. Memory for chess positions: Resistance to interference. *Journal of Experimental Psychology: Human Learning and Memory*, 1976, *2*, 641-653.

Chase, W. G., & Simon, H. A. Perception in chess. *Cognitive Psychology*, 1973, *4*, 55-81.

Chase, W. G., & Simon, H. A. The mind's eye in chess. In W. G. Chase (Ed.), *Visual information processing*. New York: Academic Press, 1975.

Clark, K. B. Some factors influencing the remembering of prose material. *Archives of Psychology*, 1940 (No. 253).

Cohen, L. J. *The probable and the provable*. Oxford, Eng.: Oxford University Press, 1977.

Cohen, C. E. *Cognitive basis of stereotyping*. Paper presented at the American Psychological Association Annual Meeting, San Francisco, September 1977.

Cohen, R. L. The effect of verbal levels on the recall of a visually perceived simple figure: Recognition or reproduction. *Perceptual and Motor Skills*, 1966, *23*, 859-862.

Coltheart, V. Memory for stimuli and memory for hypotheses in concept identification. *Journal of Experimental Psychology*, 1971, *89*, 102-108.

Cooper, R. M. The control of eye fixations by the meaning of spoken language. *Cognitive Psychology*, 1974, *6*, 84-107.

Craik, F. I. M., & Lockhart, R. S. Levels of processing: A framework for memory research. *Journal of Verbal Learning and Verbal Behavior*, 1972, *11*, 671-684.

Daniel, T. C. Nature of the effect of a verbal label on recognition memory for form. *Journal of Experimental Psychology*, 1972, *96*, 152-157.

Dawes, R. M. Memory and distortion of meaningful written material. *British Journal of Psychology*, 1966, *57*, 77-86.

De Soto, C. B. Learning a social structure. *Journal of Abnormal and Social Psychology*, 1960, *60*, 417-421.

Dixon, N. F. *Subliminal perception: The nature of a controversy*. London: McGraw-Hill, 1971.

Dominowski, R. L. Role of memory in concept learning. *Psychological Bulletin*, 1965, *63*, 271-280.

Dreben, E. K., Fiske, S. T., & Hastie, R. Independence of evaluation and item information: Impression and recall order effects in behavior based impression formation. *Journal of Personality and Social Psychology*, 1979, *37*, 1758-1768.

Ebbinghaus, H. [Über das Gedächtnis]. Leipzig, Germany: Duncker and Humblot, 1885. (Translation by H. A. Ruger and C. E. Bussenius, *Memory: A contribution to experimental psychology*. New York: Dover, 1964.)

Edwards, A. L. Political frames of reference as a factor influencing recognition. *Journal of Abnormal and Social Psychology*, 1941, *36*, 34-50.

Edwards, W., Lindman, H., & Savage, L. J. Bayesian statistical inference for psychological research. *Psychological Review*, 1963, *70*, 193-242.

Erdelyi, M. H. A new look at the New Look: Perceptual defense and vigilance. *Psychological Review*, 1974, *81*, 1-25.

Estes, W. K. Structural aspects of associative models for memory. In C. N. Cofer (Ed.), *The structure of human memory*. San Francisco: Freeman, 1975.

Estes, W. K. On the organization and core concepts of learning theory and cognitive psychology. In W. K. Estes (Ed.), *Handbook of learning and cognitive processes* (Vol. 6). Hillsdale, N.J.: Lawrence Erlbaum Associates, 1979.

Flavell, J. H. *The developmental psychology of Jean Piaget*. Princeton, N.J.: Van Nostrand, 1963.

Franks, J. J., & Bransford, J. D. Abstraction of visual patterns. *Journal of Experimental Psychology*, 1971, *90*, 65-74.

Frase, L. T. Structural analysis of knowledge that results from thinking about text. *Journal of Educational Psychology Monograph*, 1969, *60* (2), 1-16.

Frederiksen, C. Representing logical and semantic structure of knowledge acquired from discourse. *Cognitive Psychology*, 1975, *7*, 371-458.

Frey, P. W., & Adesman, P.   Recall memory for visually presented chess positions. *Memory and Cognition*, 1976, *4*, 541–547.

Friedman, A.   Framing pictures: The role of knowledge in automatized encoding and memory for gist. *Journal of Experimental Psychology: General*, 1979, *108*, 316–355.

Garner, W. R.   *The processing of information and structure*. Potomac, Md.: Lawrence Erlbaum Associates, 1974.

Garner, W. R., & Whitman, J. R.   Form and amount of internal structure as factors in free-recall learning of nonsense words. *Journal of Verbal Learning and Verbal Behavior*, 1965, *4*, 257–266.

Gauld, A., & Stephenson, G. M.   Some experiments relating to Bartlett's theory of remembering. *British Journal of Psychology*, 1967, *58*, 39–49.

Goldin, S. E.   Memory for the ordinary: Typicality effects in chess memory. *Journal of Experimental Psychology: Human Learning and Memory*, 1978, *4*, 605–616.

Gomulicki, B. R.   Recall as an abstractive process. *Acta Psychologica*, 1956, *12*, 77–94.

Greenwald, A. G., & Sakumura, J. S.   Attitude and selective learning: Where are the phenomena of yesteryear. *Journal of Personality and Social Psychology*, 1967, *7*, 387–397.

Gregg, L. W., & Simon, H. A.   Process models and stochastic theories of simple concept formation. *Journal of Mathematical Psychology*, 1967, *4*, 246–276.

Hamilton, D. L.   A cognitive attributional analysis of stereotyping. In L. Berkowitz (Ed.), *Advances in experimental social psychology* (Vol. 12). New York: Academic Press, 1979.

Hamilton, D. L., & Gifford, R. K.   Illusory correlation in interpersonal perception: A cognitive basis of stereotypic judgments. *Journal of Experimental Social Psychology*, 1976, *12*, 392–407.

Hamilton, D. L., & Katz, L. B.   *A process-oriented approach to the study of impressions*. Paper read at American Psychological Association Meeting, Chicago, 1975.

Hamilton, D. L., Katz, L., & Leirer, V.   Organizational processes in impression formation. In R. Hastie, T. M. Ostrom, E. Ebbesen, R. S. Wyer, Jr., D. L. Hamilton, & D. Carlston (Eds.), *Person memory: The cognitive basis of social perception*. Hillsdale, N.J.: Lawrence Erlbaum Associates, 1980.

Hanawalt, N. G.   Memory trace for figures in recall and recognition. *Archives of Psychology*, 1937, (No. 216).

Hanawalt, N. G., & Demarest, I. H.   The effect of verbal suggestion on the reproduction of visually perceived forms. *Journal of Experimental Psychology*, 1939, *25*, 159–174.

Hastie, R., & Kumar, P. A.   Person memory: Personality traits as organizing principles in memory for behaviors. *Journal of Personality and Social Psychology*, 1979, *37*, 25–38.

Hastie, R., & Mazur, J. E.   *Memory for information about people presented on film*. Unpublished manuscript, Harvard University, 1978.

Heider, F.   Attitudes and cognitive organization. *Journal of Psychology*, 1946, *21*, 107–112.

Heider, F.   *The psychology of interpersonal relations*. New York: Wiley, 1958.

Helson, H.   The psychology of Gestalt. *American Journal of Psychology*, 1925, *36*, 342–370.

Helson, H.   The psychology of Gestalt. *American Journal of Psychology*, 1926, *37*, 25–62, 189–216.

Henley, N. M., Horsfall, R., & De Soto, C. B.   Goodness of figure and social structure. *Psychological Review*, 1969, *76*, 194–204.

Hopcroft, J. E., & Ullman, J. D.   *Formal languages and their relation to automata*. Reading, Mass.: Addison-Wesley, 1969.

Huttenlocher, J.   Constructing spatial images: A strategy in reasoning. *Psychological Review*, 1968, *75*, 550–560.

Jenkins, J. J.   Remember that old theory of memory? Well, forget it! *American Psychologist*, 1974, *29*, 785–795.

Jenkins, J. J., Wald, J., & Pittenger, J. B.   Apprehending pictorial events: An instance of psychological cohesion. In C. W. Savage (Ed.), *Minnesota studies in the philosophy of science* (Vol. 9). University of Minnesota Press, 1978.

Johnson, M. K., Bransford, J. D., & Solomon, S. Memory for tacit implications of sentences. *Journal of Experimental Psychology,* 1973, *98,* 203-205.

Jones, E. E., & Aneshansel, J. The learning and utilization of contravalent material. *Journal of Abnormal and Social Psychology,* 1956, *53,* 27-33.

Jones, E. E., & Kohler, R. The effects of plausibility on the learning of controversial statements. *Journal of Abnormal and Social Psychology,* 1958, *57,* 315-320.

Jones, R. A., Stoll, J., Solernau, J., Noble, A., Fiala, J., & Miller, K. *Availability and stereotype formation.* Unpublished manuscript, University of Kentucky, 1976.

Jörg, S., & Hormann, H. The influence of general and specific verbal labels on the recognition of labeled and unlabeled parts of pictures. *Journal of Verbal Learning and Verbal Behavior,* 1978, *17,* 445-454.

Kahneman, D., & Tversky, A. Subjective probability: A judgement of representativeness. *Cognitive Psychology,* 1972, *3,* 430-454.

Katona, G. *Organizing and memorizing.* New York: Columbia University Press, 1940.

Kelley, H. H. The processes of attribution. *American Psychologist,* 1973, *28,* 107-128.

Kintsch, W. *The representation of meaning in memory.* Hillsdale, N.J.: Lawrence Erlbaum Associates, 1974.

Kintsch, W., & van Dijk, T. A. Toward a model of text comprehension and production. *Psychological Review,* 1978, *85,* 363-394.

Koffka, K. *Principles of Gestalt psychology.* New York: Harcourt, Brace, & World, 1935.

Kraft, R. N., & Jenkins, J. J. Memory for lateral orientation of slides in picture stories. *Memory and Cognition,* 1977, *5,* 397-403.

Leamer, E. E. *Specification searches.* New York: John Wiley & Sons, 1978.

Levine, J. M., & Murphy, G. The learning and forgetting of controversial material. *Journal of Abnormal and Social Psychology,* 1943, *38,* 507-517.

Lingle, J. H., Geva, N., Ostrom, T. M., Leippe, M. R., & Baumgardner, M. H. Thematic effects of person judgments on impression organization. *Journal of Personality and Social Psychology,* 1979, *37,* 674-687.

Lingle, J. H., & Ostrom, T. M. Retrieval selectivity in memory-based judgments. *Journal of Personality and Social Psychology,* 1979, *37,* 180-194.

Loftus, E. F. Leading questions and the eyewitness report. *Cognitive Psychology,* 1975, *7,* 560-572.

Loftus, E. F., & Palmer, J. P. Reconstruction of automobile destruction: An example of the interaction between language and memory. *Journal of Verbal Learning and Verbal Behavior,* 1974, *13,* 585-589.

Loftus, G. R. Eye fixations and recognition memory for pictures. *Cognitive Psychology,* 1972, *3,* 525-551.

Loftus, G. R., & Bell, S. M. Two types of information in picture memory. *Journal of Experimental Psychology: Human Learning and Memory,* 1975, *104,* 103-113.

Mandler, J. M. A code in the node: The use of a story schema in retrieval. *Discourse Processes,* 1978, *1,* 14-35.

Mandler, J. M., & Johnson, N. J. Remembrance of things parsed: Story structure and recall. *Cognitive Psychology,* 1977, *9,* 111-151.

Mandler, J. M., & Parker, R. E. Memory for descriptive and spatial information in complex pictures. *Journal of Experimental Psychology: Human Learning and Memory,* 1976, *2,* 38-48.

Mandler, J. M., & Ritchey, G. H. Long-term memory for pictures. *Journal of Experimental Psychology: Human Learning and Memory,* 1977, *3,* 386-396.

Mandler, J. M., & Stein, N. L. Recall and recognition of pictures by children as a function of organization and distractor similarity. *Journal of Experimental Psychology,* 1974, *102,* 657-669.

Markus, H. Self-schemata and processing information about the self. *Journal of Personality and Social Psychology*, 1977, *35*, 63–78.

Mayer, R. E. Qualitatively different encoding strategies for linear reasoning premises: Evidence for single association and distance theories. *Journal of Experimental Psychology: Human Learning and Memory*, 1979, *5*, 1–10.

McArthur, L. Z., & Post, D. D. Figural emphasis and person perception. *Journal of Experimental Social Psychology*, 1977, *13*, 520–535.

McGeoch, J. A. *The psychology of human learning*. New York: Longmans, Green, 1942.

McGuire, W. J., McGuire, W. J., Child, P., Fujioka, T. Salience of ethnicity in the spontaneous self-concept as a function of one's ethnic distinctiveness in the social environment. *Journal of Personality and Social Psychology*, 1978, *36*, 511–520.

McGuire, W. J., & Padawer-Singer, A. Trait salience in the spontaneous self-concept. *Journal of Personality and Social Psychology*, 1976, *33*, 743–754.

Mill, J. *Analysis of the phenomena of the human mind*. London: Longmans, Green, Reader, & Dyer, 1869.

Minsky, M. A framework for representing knowledge. In P. H. Winston (Ed.), *The psychology of computer vision*. New York: McGraw-Hill, 1975.

Mischel, W., Ebbesen, E., & Zeiss, A. M. Determinants of selective memory about the self. *Journal of Consulting and Clinical Psychology*, 1976, *44*, 92–103.

Neisser, V. *Cognitive and reality: Principles and implications of cognitive psychology*. San Francisco: Freeman, 1976.

Nelson, T. O., Metzler, J., & Reed, D. A. Role of details in the long-term recognition of pictures and verbal descriptions. *Journal of Experimental Psychology*, 1974, *102*, 184–186.

Newell, A., & Simon, H. A. *Human problem solving*. Englewood Cliffs, N.J.: Prentice-Hall, 1972.

Newtson, D. The foundations of attribution: The unit of perception of ongoing behavior. In J. H. Harvey, W. J. Ickes, & R. F. Kidd (Eds.), *New directions in attribution research* (Vol. 1). Hillsdale, N.J.: Lawrence Erlbaum Associates, 1976.

Norman, D. A., & Bobrow, D. G. On the role of active memory processes in perception and cognition. In C. Cofer (Ed.), *The structure of human memory*. San Francisco: Freeman, 1975.

Oldfield, R. C., & Zangwill, O. L. Head's concept of schema and its application in contemporary British psychology. *British Journal of Psychology*, 1942, *32*, 267–286; and 1943, *33*, 58–64, 113–129, 143–149.

Ostrom, T. M., Lingle, J. H., Pryor, J., & Geva, N. Cognitive organization of person impressions. In R. Hastie, T. M. Ostrom, E. Ebbesen, R. S. Wyer, Jr., D. L. Hamilton, & D. Carlston (Eds.), *Person memory: The cognitive basis of social perception*. Hillsdale, N.J.: Lawrence Erlbaum Associates, 1980.

Park, D. C., & Whitten, W. The abstraction of linguistic, imaginal, and pictorial ideas. *Journal of Experimental Psychology: Human Learning and Memory*, 1977, *3*, 525–538.

Paul, I. H. The concept of schema in memory theory. *Psychological Issues*, 1967, *5*, 219–258.

Pezdek, K. Cross-modality semantic integration of sentence and picture memory. *Journal of Experimental Psychology: Human Learning and Memory*, 1977, *3*, 515–524.

Piaget, J. *The construction of reality in the child*. New York: Basic Books, 1954.

Piaget, J. *The origins of intelligence*. New York: Norton, 1963.

Picek, J. S., Sherman, S. J., & Shiffrin, R. M. Cognitive organization and coding of social structures. *Journal of Personality and Social Psychology*, 1975, *31*, 758–768.

Posner, M. I. Abstraction and the process of recognition. In G. H. Bower & J. T. Spence (Eds.), *The psychology of learning and motivation* (Vol. 3). New York: Academic Press, 1969.

Posner, M. I., & Keele, S. W. On the genesis of abstract ideas. *Journal of Experimental Psychology*, 1968, *77*, 353–363.

Posner, M. I., & Keele, S. W. Retention of abstract ideas. *Journal of Experimental Psychology*, 1970, *83*, 304–308.

Postman, L. Learned principles in the organization of memory. *Psychological Monographs*, 1954, *67*, 315–320.

Postman, L. Transfer, interference, and forgetting. In J. W. Kling & L. A. Riggs (Eds.), *Woodworth and Schlossberg's experimental psychology*. New York: Holt, Rinehart & Winston, 1971.

Potts, G. R. Storing and retrieving information about ordered relationships. *Journal of Experimental Psychology*, 1974, *102*, 431–439.

Powers, W. T. Quantitative analysis of purposive systems: Some spadework at the foundations of scientific psychology. *Psychological Review*, 1978, *85*, 417–435.

Press, A. N., Crockett, W. H., & Rosenkrantz, P. S. Cognitive complexity and the learning of balanced and unbalanced social structures. *Journal of Personality*, 1969, *37*, 541–553.

Quine, W. V. O. Natural kinds. In W. V. O. Quine, (Ed.), *Ontological relativity and other essays*. New York: Columbia University Press, 1969.

Reed, S. K. Pattern recognition and categorization. *Cognitive Psychology*, 1972, *3*, 382–407.

Reed, S. K. *Psychological processes in pattern recognition*. New York: Academic Press, 1973.

Reitman, J. S., & Bower, G. H. Storage and later recognition of exemplars of concepts. *Cognitive Psychology*, 1973, *4*, 194–206.

Restle, F. The selection of strategies in cue learning. *Psychological Review*, 1962, *69*, 329–343.

Restle, F. Answering questions from cognitive structures. In F. Restle, R. M. Shiffrin, N. J. Castellan, H. R. Lindman, & D. B. Pisoni (Eds.), *Cognitive theory* (Vol. 1). Hillsdale, N.J.: Lawrence Erlbaum Associates, 1975.

Riley, D. A. Memory for form. In L. Postman (Ed.), *Psychology in the making*. New York: Alfred Knopf, 1962.

Riskey, D. R. Verbal memory processes in impression formation. *Journal of Experimental Psychology: Human Learning and Memory*, 1979, *5*, 271–281.

Rock, I., Halper, F., & Clayton, T. The perception and recognition of complex figures. *Cognitive Psychology*, 1972, *3*, 655–673.

Rogers, T. B., Kuiper, N. A., & Kirker, W. S. Self-reference and the encoding of personal information. *Journal of Personality and Social Psychology*, 1977, *35*, 677–688.

Rosch, E. On the internal structure of perceptual and semantic categories. In T. E. Moore, (Ed.), *Cognitive development and the acquisition of language*. New York: Academic Press, 1973.

Rosch, E., & Mervis, C. B. Family resemblances: Studies in the internal structure of categories. *Cognitive Psychology*, 1975, *7*, 573–605.

Rosch, E., Simpson, C., & Miller, R. S. Structural bases of typicality effects. *Journal of Experimental Psychology: Human Perception and Performance*, 1976, *2*, 491–502.

Rosenberg, S., & Sedlak, A. Structural representations of implicit personality theory. In L. Berkowitz (Ed.), *Advances in experimental social psychology* (Vol. 6). New York: Academic Press, 1972.

Ross, L., Lepper, M., & Hubbard, M. Perserverence in self perception and social perception: Biased attributional processes in the debriefing paradigm. *Journal of Personality and Social Psychology*, 1975, *32*, 880–892.

Rothbart, M., Evans, M., & Fulero, S. Recall for confirming events: Memory processes and maintenance of social stereotypes. *Journal of Experimental Social Psychology*, 1979, *15*, 342–353.

Rothbart, M., Fulero, S., Jensen, C., Howard, J., & Birrell, P. From individual to group impressions: Availability heuristics in stereotype formation. *Journal of Experimental Social Psychology*, 1978, *14*, 237–256.

Rubin, Z., & Zajonc, R. B. Structural bias and generalization in the learning of social structures. *Journal of Personality*, 1969, *27*, 310–324.

Rumelhart, D. E. Notes on a schema for stories. In D. G. Bobrow & A. Collins, (Eds.), *Representation and understanding: Studies in cognitive science*. New York: Academic Press, 1975.

Rumelhart, D. E. *Introduction to human information processing*. New York: Wiley, 1977.

Rumelhart, D. E., & Ortony, A. The representation of knowledge in memory. In R. C. Anderson,

R. J. Spiro, & W. E. Montague, (Eds.), *Schooling and the acquisition of knowledge.* Hillsdale, N.J.: Lawrence Erlbaum Associates, 1977.

Rywick, T., & Schaye, P. Use of long-term memory in impression formation. *Psychological Reports,* 1974, *34,* 939–945.

Schank, R., & Abelson, R. *Scripts, plans, goals and understanding: An inquiry into human knowledge structures.* Hillsdale, N.J.: Lawrence Erlbaum Associates, 1977.

Seeleman, V. The influence of attitude upon the remembering of pictorial material. *Archives of Psychology,* 1940 (No. 258).

Sentis, K. P., & Burnstein, E. Remembering schema-consistent information: Effects of a balance schema on recognition memory. *Journal of Personality and Social Psychology,* 1979, *37,* 2200–2211.

Shepard, R. N. Recognition memory for words, sentences, and pictures. *Journal of Verbal Learning and Verbal Behavior,* 1967, *6,* 156–163.

Smith, E. E., Adams, N., & Schorr, D. Fact retrieval and the paradox of interference. *Cognitive Psychology,* 1978. *10,* 438–464.

Smith, K. H. Effect of exceptions on verbal reconstructive memory. *Journal of Experimental Psychology,* 1973, *97,* 119–139.

Snyder, M., & Uranowitz, S. W. Reconstructing the past: Some cognitive consequences of person perception. *Journal of Personality and Social Psychology,* 1978, *38,* 941–950.

Steinfeld, G. J. Concept of set and availability and their relations to the reorganization of ambiguous pictorial stimuli. *Psychological Review,* 1967, *74,* 505–522.

Sulin, R. A., & Dooling, D. J. Intrusion of thematic ideas in retention of prose. *Journal of Experimental Psychology,* 1974, *103,* 255–262.

Taft, R. Selective recall and memory distortion of favorable and unfavorable material. *Journal of Abnormal and Social Psychology,* 1954, *49,* 23–28.

Tajfel, H., & Billig, M. Familiarity and categorization in intergroup behavior. *Journal of Experimental Social Psychology,* 1974, *10,* 159–170.

Tajfel, H., Sheikh, A. A., & Gardner, R. C. Content of stereotypes and the interference of similarity between the members of stereotyped groups. *Acta Psychologica,* 1964, *22,* 191–201.

Taylor, S. E., & Fiske, S. T. Point of view and perceptions of causality. *Journal of Personality and Social Psychology,* 1975, *32,* 439–445.

Taylor, S. E., Fiske, S. T., Etcoff, N. L., & Ruderman, A. J. Categorical and contextual bases of person memory and stereotyping. *Journal of Personality and Social Psychology,* 1978, *36,* 778–793.

Tesser, A. Self-generated attitude change. In L. Berkowitz (Ed.), *Advances in experimental social psychology* (Vol. 11). New York: Academic Press, 1978.

Thompson, J. W. Psycholinguistics, psychoanalysis, and Bartlett's concept of schema. *Human Relations,* 1967, *20,* 251–257.

Thorndyke, P. W. Cognitive structures in comprehension and memory of narrative discourse. *Cognitive Psychology,* 1977, *9,* 77–110.

Thorndyke, P. W., & Hayes-Roth, B. The use of schemata in the acquisition and transfer of knowledge. *Cognitive Psychology,* 1979, *11,* 82–106.

Tolman, E. C. *Purposive behavior in animals and men.* Berkeley; University of California Press, 1932.

Trabasso, T., & Bower, G. H. Memory in concept identification. *Psychonomic Science,* 1964, *1,* 133–134.

Trabasso, T., & Bower, G. H. *Attention in learning: Theory and research.* New York: Wiley, 1968.

Tsujimoto, R. N. Memory bias toward normative and novel trait prototypes. *Journal of Personality and Social Psychology,* 1978, *36,* 1391–1401.

Tsujimoto, R. N., Wilde, J., & Robertson, D. R. Distorted memory for examplars of social structure: Evidence for schematic memory processes. *Journal of Personality and Social Psychology,* 1978, *38,* 1402–1414.

Tulving, E. Retrograde amnesia in free recall. *Science,* 1969, *164,* 88–90.

Tulving, E., & Pearlstone, Z. Availability versus accessibility of information in memory for words. *Journal of Verbal Learning and Verbal Behavior,* 1966, *5,* 381–391.

Tversky, A. Features of similarity. *Psychological Review,* 1977, *84,* 327–352.

Tversky, A., & Kahneman, D. Availability: A heuristic for judging frequency and probability. *Cognitive Psychology,* 1973, *5,* 207–232.

Tversky, A., & Kahneman, D. Judgment under uncertainty: Heuristics and biases. *Science,* 1974, *185,* 1124–1131.

Tversky, A., & Kahneman, D. Causal schemata in judgments under uncertainty. In M. Fishbein (Ed.), *Progress in social psychology.* Hillsdale, N.J.: Lawrence Erlbaum Associates, 1980.

von Restorff, H. Über die Wirkung von Bereichsbildungen im Spurenfeld. *Psychologische Forschung,* 1933, *18,* 299–342.

Wallace, W. P. Review of the historical empirical, and theoretical status of the von Restorff phenomenon. *Psychological Bulletin,* 1965, *63,* 410–424.

Waltz, D. Understanding line drawings of scenes with shadows. In P. H. Winston (Ed.), *The psychology of computer vision.* New York: McGraw-Hill, 1975.

Waly, P., & Cook, S. W. Attitude as a determinant of learning and memory: A failure to confirm. *Journal of Personality and Social Psychology,* 1966, *4,* 280–288.

Watson, W. S.,& Hartmann, G. W. The rigidity of a basic attitudinal frame. *Journal of Abnormal and Social Psychology,* 1939, *34,* 314–335.

Winston, P. H. *Artificial intelligence.* Reading, Mass.: Addison-Wesley, 1977.

Wittgenstein, L. *Philosophical investigations.* New York: Macmillan, 1953.

Wixon, D. R., & Laird, J. D. Awareness and attitude change in the forced-compliance paradigm: The importance of when. *Journal of Personality and Social Psychology,* 1976, *34,* 376–384.

Woodworth, R. S. *Experimental psychology.* New York: Henry Holt, 1938.

Wulf, F. Uber die Veränderung von Verstellungen. *Psychologische Forschung,* 1922, *1,* 333–373.

Wylie, R. C. *The self concept.* Lincoln: University of Nebraska Press, 1974.

Zadny, J., & Gerard, H. B. Attributed intentions and informational selectivity. *Journal of Experimental Social Psychology,* 1974, *10,* 34–52.

Zajonc, R. B., & Burnstein, E. The learning of balanced and unbalanced social structures. *Journal of Personality,* 1965, *33,* 153–163. (a).

Zajonc, R. B., & Burnstein, E. Structural balance, reciprocity, and positivity as sources of cognitive bias. *Journal of Personality,* 1965, *33,* 570–583. (b).

Zajonc, R. B., & Sherman, S. J. Structural balance and the induction of relations. *Journal of Personality,* 1967, *35,* 635–650.

Zangwill, O. L. Remembering revisited. *Quarterly Journal of Experimental Psychology,* 1972, *24,* 123–138.

Zillig, M. Einstellung und aussage. *Zeitschrift für Psychologie,* 1928, *106,* 58–106.

3 Schematic Bases of Social Information Processing

Shelley E. Taylor
Jennifer Crocker
Harvard University

> *Speculations, he says, are useless until you have all the facts. But I've noticed often enough that it isn't like that with him, really. He begins speculating straight away, if you ask me, and his speculations suggest what factors to hunt for next. . . . I really believe that he is guessing all the time, and this is what makes him so good a Detective Inspector.*
>
> —M. Innes (1946/1977, p. 97)

Embedded in this remark about the detection methods of Inspector Cadover is a more serious issue about the nature of information processing. Do we use the data our senses bring to us to construct hypotheses about how the world works, or do we use our hypotheses about how the world works to determine what data to process? The answer is that we do both, but we here advance the position that, at least in the adult social perceiver, hypothesis-driven processing is very much the rule, being both common and maximally efficient. In this paper, we pursue the theme that hypothesis-driven processing is often determined by abstract schematic conceptions that people hold about how the world works. As will be clear, there is a voluminous literature on social schemas dating back at least 20 years. Accordingly, an important goal of our paper is to address a central question raised by this literature: Is there now a basis for a schema theory?

WHAT IS A SCHEMA?

The term, schema, appears to have been first used by Bartlett in 1932 in his work on recall of perceptual experience. Since that time, it has been adopted as a descriptive or explanatory concept by more than 150 researchers in social psychology, most of whose work is reviewed in this paper. To what extent has this work provided us with the basis of a schema theory?

First, one must ask what constitutes a theory in social science. As Deutsch and Krauss (1965) note, the social psychologist's criteria for a theory are considerably less rigorous than those adopted by researchers in the natural sciences. To constitute a theory, we require only "a set of interrelated hypotheses . . . which are in part a summary of known 'facts' and in part conjecture about the implications of facts and the probable relationships among them [Shaw & Costanzo, 1970, p. 8]." Though not all social psychologists adopt precisely this definition, a quick review of other definitions (See Deutsch & Krauss, 1965; Shaw & Costanzo, 1970) will reveal little if any incompatibility with these minimal assumptions. Accordingly, in reviewing the schema literature, we can ask if the literature furnishes a set of interrelated hypotheses about the nature of schemas.

A minimal theory is not, however, necessarily a good theory, and so one may want to inquire of the schema's literature not only if the minimum criterion of a theory has been met, but if it is a good theory. A good theory, must have several additional attributes. First, it must have maximum conceptual clarity. Because the term schema has been used in so many different contexts, we need to know not only what schemas are, but what they are *not* and how they differ from seemingly related structural conceptions. In other words, are schemas just reinventing the wheel? Second, as Shaw and Costanzo (1970) note, a good theory must be internally consistent and not generate contradictory propositions. Third, a good theory must fit the data, both old and new. And finally, a theory must be testable; a corollary of this last point is that a good theory must be falsifiable. These elements of a good theory can constitute a focus for reviewing the schema's literature as well as a set of criteria against which the literature will be evaluated following the review.

Why do we need the concept of a schema? The processing of information involves scanning the environment, selecting items to attend to, taking in information about those items, and either storing it in some form, so that it can be retrieved later for consideration, or using it as a basis for action. It goes without saying that there is necessarily a tremendous amount of selectivity in this process, because we cannot notice every detail in the environment. To select the information that is useful and to process it quickly and efficiently, the perceiver needs selection criteria and guidelines for processing. Hypotheses about how the world works provide such criteria and guidelines. Hypothesis-driven processing is processing that is guided by expectations or preconceptions. The hypotheses, whatever their nature, tell the social perceiver what data to look for and how to interpret the data that is found. Hypotheses lend focus, structure, and sequence to search behavior and subsequently provide a basis for how the information will be used (see also Nisbett & Ross, 1979).

Neisser (1976) has called this kind of processing *schematic processing*. He draws an analogy between a format statement, which enables a computer to take in information, and a schema, which enables the person to take in information. As in the computer analogy, nothing for which there is no format gets into the system. For example, if we do not have a conception of a chair, we do not recognize a chair when one is before us; we recognize it only if we have a schema or theory about what a chair is. Although Neisser is talking primarily about perception and the perception of individual objects in particular, the analogy is appropriate to the processing of large chunks of social information as well. Data do not have meaning unless they fit into a cognitive context, a schema about the meaning of the stimulus.

A schema is a cognitive structure that consists in part of the representation of some defined stimulus domain. The schema contains general knowledge about that domain, including a specification of the relationships among its attributes, as well as specific examples or instances of the stimulus domain. As such, one of the chief functions of a schema is to provide an answer to the question. ''what is it?'' The schema provides hypotheses about incoming stimuli, which include plans for interpreting and gathering schema-related information (See Markus, 1977; Miller, Galanter, & Pribram, 1960; Minsky, 1975; Schank & Abelson, 1977; Tesser, 1978). It may also provide a basis for activating actual behavior sequences or expectations of specific behavior sequences, i.e. scripts for how an individual behaves in a social situation (Schank & Abelson, 1977).

We are concerned in this paper with social schemas, i.e., constructions of how the social world works. Three general classes of social schemas, not necessarily exhaustive, are commonly used by the social perceiver, and they also reflect somewhat independent research areas. One is person schemas, which include prototypic conceptions like extravert and introvert (Cantor & Mischel, 1977), person impressions or representations of specific individuals (e.g., Hamilton, Katz, & Leirer, 1980), and self-schemata (Markus, 1977). A second is role schemas, which include schemas for particular occupations like fireman, professor, cowboy, or politician; schemas for social roles like lover or parent; and stereotypic conceptions of social groups like blacks or women. A third type of social schema, which we might call ''event'' schemas, include schemas for such happenings as cocktail party, or department meeting; routine, well-practiced behavioral scripts (Schank & Abelson, 1977); and stories (e.g., Bower, Black, & Turner, 1979). Social perceivers, then, have schemas about types of personalities, social events, and social roles. When they encounter a new stimulus person or event, they draw upon their representation of that kind of person or event (i.e. their schema) and use it to both fill out the attributes of the stimulus configuration before them and generate predictions about other attributes and subsequent events.

Before discussing whether or not a schema theory can be culled from the literature, two questions that have concerned researchers in this area merit comment: (1) whether schemas are content-free processing structures, content-specific knowledge structures, or both; and (2) what the level of abstraction of schemas is. These problems are amply illustrated by the catalog of schema-like concepts that are available in the literature. Just a few examples are balance

(Picek, Sherman, & Shiffrin, 1975), reciprocity (DeSoto, 1969), causal schemata (Kelley, 1972), scripts (Schank & Abelson, 1977), expectations (e.g. Aronson & Carlsmith, 1962), perceptual readiness (Bruner, 1957), frames (Minsky, 1975), plans (Miller, Galanter, & Pribram, 1960), and some applications of the attitudinal work on cognitive consistency (e.g. Jervis, 1976; Zajonc, 1968).

As a partial solution to these problems, we make two assumptions. On the first point, we make the assumption that social schemas are content-specific. Rules such as balance and reciprocity and causation may apply to certain content-specific schemas (e.g., attributes of a friendship group are balance and reciprocity), and they may help to structure incoming data, but structural characteristics such as balance or reciprocity are not social schemas themselves.

On the second point, regarding the level of abstraction of schemas, because we are operating with a "picture in the head" of what schemas look like, we spell it out here. A schema can be thought of as a pyramidal structure, hierarchically organized with more abstract or general information at the top and categories of more specific information nested within the general categories. The lowest level in the hierarchy consists of specific examples or instances of the schema (e.g., specific people or events). The schema is connected to other schemas through a rich web of associations, particularly at the lower levels of greater specificity. Thus, for example, one event may be represented in each of several schemas, with connections among the schemas, indicating these cross references. In addition, one can have schemas for the lower level specific instances of another schema. For example, one's friend, Susan, may be included as a specific example of an extraverted person, and at the same time one can have a schema for Susan including a representation of her attributes, and specific behaviors she has engaged in as examples of those attributes. Schemas can be accessed either from the top down, (i.e., from the more general to the specific), from the bottom up, or laterally through the web of associations.

There is nothing special or novel about the assumptions made here. This conception is very similar to suggestions made by Abelson (e.g., 1975), to hypotheses about the representation of semantic memory (e.g. Collins & Quillian, 1969) and to arguments regarding the structure of conceptual prototypes (Cantor & Mischel, 1977). There is, however, a difference among these various formulations as to the level of specificity they posit. For example, Abelson talks about the highest level of abstraction being overarching themes within which are nested more specific scripts and acts. Cantor and Mischel (1977) talk about a prototype that has a trait at its highest level and more specific behaviors lower down. Bower, Black, and Turner (1979) talk about hierarchical structures that move from stories to scripts to events to actions, as one moves farther down in the hierarchy. So far, this issue, namely the level of abstraction at which schemas exist, has not proven to be an important problem, at least for the goal of understanding schematic information processing. The reason is that schematic processing appears so far to occur roughly in the same ways at each level of abstraction in the schema hierarchy. As the relevant literature is reviewed, the reader will see this point illustrated repeatedly. What the trait prototype of extravert does for lists of behaviors (Cantor & Mischel, 1977), the story theme does for series of scripts (Bower, 1977). What the self-schema of independence does for independence behaviors (Markus, 1977), an occupational background does for processing complex information in a resumé (Taylor, Livingston, & Crocker, in progress). What the single expectation does for specific feedback (e.g., Aronson & Carlsmith, 1962), the overarching theory or stereotype does for more complex material (Wyatt & Campbell, 1951). This apparent consistency of processing functions across levels of abstraction makes the researcher's task both easier and more difficult. On the one hand, it lends a certain persimony to models of schematic processing. On the other hand, it obscures the issue of how one determines the level at which information is being processed. It may be that important processing differences dependent upon levels of abstraction will emerge with more research, but as yet these differences have not materialized.[1]

To return to the central question: Is there a schema theory? The answer (using the minimal criterion of a set of interrelated hypotheses) is a qualified *yes*. As the following review illustrates, the literature quite clearly suggests a set of interrelated processing functions that both summarize known facts in the literature consistently and lead to the generation of subsequent hypotheses and predictions. The next sections discuss the more specific functions and influences that schematic processing may have on how the perceiver acquires social knowledge and acts on it.

THE FUNCTIONS OF SCHEMAS

Given some stimulus configuration in the environment, it would be prohibitively time-consuming to match it against all prior experiences and given some problem to solve, the problem would never get solved quickly enough if one were to try out every possible solution. Even if the stimulus configuration were identified quickly and a strategy for solving a problem were selected immediately, it would still be prohibitively costly to process data piece by piece instead of in larger chunks. What schemas do is enable the perceiver to identify stimuli quickly, "chunk" an appropriate unit, fill in information missing from the stimulus configuration, and select a strategy for obtaining further information,

---

[1]One promising point at which processing differences in levels of abstraction are likely to become important is the issue of the "best level" of abstraction, i.e., the level at which most inference occurs (where the processing action is). Rosch, Mervis, Gray, Johnson, and Boyes-Braem (1976) have suggested that for taxonomies of objects there is a basic category level that is maximally informative. This may also be true of other hierarchical knowledge structures like schemas (see also Cantor & Mischel, 1979).

solving a problem, or reaching a goal. In the following sections, we have arbitrarily grouped the functions of schemas into two general categories. The first is encoding and representation functions, which include the ways in which schemas enable the individual to acquire information from the environment and represent it in short-term memory. The second is interpretive or inferential functions; once the social perceiver has imputed meaning to the data in the environment, how is the meaning used to solve problems, set goals, or select a behavior? The reader will note a certain fuzziness in these categories, which is unavoidable, given that encoding and interpretation are processes that draw on each other and occur in rapid succession.

The Encoding and Representation Functions of Schemas

Schemas Lend Structure to Experience.   When a stimulus configuration is encountered in the environment, it is matched against a schema, and the ordering and relations among the elements of the schema are imposed on the elements of the stimulus configuration. This process of ordering and structuring the elements of the stimulus configuration is important because it lays the groundwork for subsequent inferences. The elements of the schema are linked to each other through various kinds of relationships (such as balance, hierarchy, grouping, or affect). Thus, knowing the schema enables one to identify the elements of the stimulus configuration and their relationships to one another and to impute meaning to behavior. For example, when one goes to a circus there are a number of characters, acts, and events. Having a schema for a circus enables one to relate those elements to each other: The ringmaster is in charge, and the aerialists, clowns, and acrobats form three distinct groupings. There are subunits within a schema such as particular roles (e.g. the clown) or events (e.g. the acrobats' act).

The circus example is an easy one. How do schemas provide structure in ambiguous situations? Suppose we see a room full of people chatting pleasantly and drinking. There are roughly equal numbers of men and women, and one man in the corner is talking at length to a group of assembled listeners. If we are told that this is an office party, we will probably assume, however incorrectly, that the men are executives, the women are secretaries, and the pontificating individual in the corner is the boss. Informed that the same group is a room full of friends, we will assume that the people are of equal status, the men and women are husbands and wives, and the pontificating individual is merely pompous.

Earlier, we made the assumption that all schemas are hierarchically organized, with more abstract or general elements "higher up" than more concrete or specific elements. In addition to this abstract to concrete structure, the elements of the schema may have other organizational properties, such as grouping, categorization, balance, and temporal sequence. These organizational properties represent an individual's knowledge about the way the world is organized.

How is structure manifested? We would argue that evidence of grouping or categorization, balance, and the imputation of relations of similarity, proximity, reciprocity, and dominance in a perceiver's construction of a stimulus configuration is de facto evidence of the structuring functions of social schemas. A considerable amount of literature within social psychology, interpretable from a schematic point of view, points to this structuring function. Keuthe (1962; 1964) for example, presented subjects with groups of cut-out figures of objects and persons and had them select figures and arrange them on a board in front of them. Persons were almost always grouped together, apart from objects. Within the person figures, the adult man, adult woman, and child figures were seen as going together and as doing so in particular ways; the child was almost always placed closer to the woman than to the man and was usually placed between the two adults. Apparently subjects drew upon their family schema and knowledge of its subunits and tasks to generate this construction. Little (1964) used a similar procedure and found that friends versus acquaintances were placed closer together. (See also DeSoto & Albrecht, 1968a, 1968b; DeSoto, Henley & London, 1968; Rabbie & Horwitz, 1969). Stereotyping processes rely upon this grouping of function of schemas. Taylor, Fiske, Etcoff, and Ruderman (1978), for example, found that race and sex were used as categorical systems for organizing incoming information. Information was recalled as a function of race (or sex) of speaker and was also a function of the number of persons of that race or sex present in the group. Other evidence of grouping included the fact that subjects tended to mix up members of a given race or sex with each other, but less frequently made cross-racial or cross-sexual errors.

Studies comparing the effects of memory set versus impression set on recall also point to the structuring function of schemas. In these studies, subjects are typically given lists of behavioral descriptions of an individual and are told either to memorize the list (memory set) or to try to form an impression of the person (impression set). Presumably, under the impression-set manipulation, subjects are organizing the material into some conceptually good figure on the basis of their schematic conceptions of personality types. Hamilton, Katz, and Leirer (1980) have used this procedure and in a series of six studies found that impression-set subjects organize the behavior descriptions into sets of related behaviors, as measured by a Bousfield (1953) clustering of output paradigm. That is, for example, when reiterating the original set of stimulus behaviors, impression-set subjects organized the information into personality-relevant schematic categories to a greater extent than did subjects given memory instructions.

Other types of structures besides groupings that schemas may impose on social stimuli include balance and linear ordering. Balanced structure seems to be particularly characteristic of schemas for interpersonal sentiment relations. In the circus example, if there are three aerialists, Renaldo, Pietro, and Maria, and we know that Maria loves Renaldo, then we are likely to assume that Renaldo loves

Maria. If we also know that Pietro and Renaldo are enemies, we are likely to assume that Maria also dislikes Pietro. In fact, deviations from balanced interpersonal sentiment relations are assumed to be unstable and require some sort of resolution (e.g. if Maria loves Renaldo, Renaldo hates Pietro, and Pietro loves Maria, will the aerialists split up?). Such interpersonal relations are better remembered when they are balanced than when they are not balanced (Cottrell, Ingraham, & Monfort, 1971; Picek, Sherman, & Shiffrin, 1975) and single-paired associates from balanced interpersonal and sentiment structures are easier to learn than single-paired associate items from inbalanced structures (DeSoto et al., 1968; Press, Crockett, & Rosencrantz, 1969; Zajonc & Burnstein, 1965a,b). Whereas balance is an important organization for schemas for sentiment relations, schemas in which dominance and influence are important are characterized by a linear ordering organization (Henley, Horsfall, & DeSoto, 1969; Poitou, 1970; Van Kreveld & Zajonc, 1966). That is, if I can order you around, then you probably can't order me around, but you probably can order someone else around. Potts (1972) found that subjects impose linear ordering on social elements. He presented subjects with an incomplete social unit and found that, in a recognition memory test, they tended to order items linearly, filling in the relationships missing from the unit, and storing the completed unit. In general, then, it is easier to learn hypothetical social relationships when they are consistent with prevalent schemas for those relationships than when they are inconsistent (Delia & Crockett, 1973; DeSoto, 1961; Van Kreveld & Zajonc, 1966); balance and linear ordering seem to be particularly "good" preferred organizations.

Thus far, we have discussed the structure of schemas for persons and social groups. Research on schemas for stories and events suggests that event schemas also have structure. In an investigation of social scripts, Bower, Black, & Turner (1979) found substantial intersubject agreement as to how to segment scripts (e.g. visiting the supermarket) into lower-level action sequences of "scenes" (e.g. going through the checkout line). They interpreted these results to mean that scripts are hierarchically organized in memory with each script composed of scenes and actions within scenes, much as others (e.g. Cantor & Mischel, 1977) have assumed person schemas to be structured.

Schemas for social events may also be organized according to their causal relations. Evidence for the causative structure of social scripts comes from efforts to develop procedures to classify episodes and ideas in passages according to their causal dependencies (c.f. Schank, 1975a, 1975b). For example, in the statement "Sue liked John because he gave her flowers for the dance," "Sue liked John" would be the superordinate episode or central theme, and "because he gave her flowers" and "for the dance" would be subordinate causative episodes. Several different techniques have been developed for classifying texts, and all of them have found that subjects are most likely to remember the central theme of the passage and less likely to remember subordinate episodes. (c.f. Frederiksen, 1975; Mandler & Johnson, 1977; Rumelhart, 1975; Thorndyke, 1977).

Action schemas (e.g., scripts or events) appear to have not only a hierarchical organization, but a temporal one as well. Bower, Black, and Turner (1979), for example, found that subjects given script scenes in a scrambled order (e.g., she made coffee, got up, started the car, put on her coat, drank coffee) tended to output them in a free recall task in the temporal order in which they logically occurred (she got up, made coffee, drank coffee, put on her coat, and started the car). The temporal structure of event schemas appears to reflect the goal sequence of the action. For routine actions, the goal sequence is implicit in the temporal sequence. For nonroutine actions, the goal sequence must be inferred. Owens, Bower, and Black (1977) have investigated the structuring effects of schemas for events. They presented subjects with a series of bland, neutral vignettes—making a cup of coffee, visiting a doctor, attending a lecture, going shopping in a grocery store, and attending a cocktail party. Some subjects read the series of vignettes with only the name of the character—Nancy or Jack. Other subjects were presented with a three-sentence introduction to the story. The Nancy introduction read, "Nancy woke up feeling sick again and wondered if she really were pregnant. How would she tell the professor she had been seeing? And the money was another problem." The Jack introduction indicated that he was a wrestler who wanted to gain weight. Subjects were tested on recall 24 hours after reading the vignettes. Subjects in the "pregnant Nancy" or "wrestler Jack" character conditions recalled more of the vignettes and recalled them in the correct order more often than control subjects. Subjects in the character conditions also interpreted the vignettes as successive scenes in the character's day, adding connective bridges between the scenes. Bower (1977) interpreted these results to mean that, "if a reader conceives of a main character trying to resolve a specific problem, then he uses that as an organizational framework for interpreting actions and events even in an uneventful story—for deciding what is relevant and important, for inferring what must have happened between the lines and why. That framework helps to integrate separate episodes of the text, and it serves as a retrieval prompt for recall [p. 14]." These data are consistent with the idea that the temporal structure of action schemas or scripts derives from the causal chains or goal sequences in those schemas (Rumelhart, 1975; Schank & Abelson, 1977).

To summarize, then, when a stimulus configuration is matched against a schema, elements in the configuration come to be ordered in a manner that reflects the structure of the schema. The basic structure imputed to the configuration is a hierarchical one based on levels of abstraction. In addition, schemas enable the perceiver to group classes of observations together and to order them in particular ways (e.g. balance or linear ordering). In the case of event schemas, temporal sequence ordering based on imputed goals appears to be an important organizational principle.

The structuring function of schemas is important because it influences subsequent recall of information and provides the basis for inferences and predictions. Evidence that the structuring schemas impose on stimuli influences recall is discussed in the following section.

Schemas Determine What Information Will be Encoded or Retrieved from Memory.   When confronted with a social stimulus configuration such as an individual or a social situation, one could conceivably recall any of many attributes of that stimulus configuration. Information is easier to recall, however, if it is structured in some way, and there is evidence that people will structure stimuli so as to facilitate recall (e.g., Bousfield, 1953). Because a schema provides a means of structuring and ordering the information in a stimulus configuration, one should find, first, that a good match to a schema facilitates recall overall, and second, that schema-relevant material will be recalled better than schema-irrelevant information.

On the first point, the research suggests that either imposing a schema on a stimulus configuration or encountering a stimulus configuration that is a good match to a schema does increase recall. Cantor and Mischel (1977) presented subjects with profiles of individuals that were either internally consistent (extravert, introvert), mixed (varied but not inconsistent), or internally inconsistent (both introverted and extraverted). The consistent characters presumably evoked a prototype or schema for that kind of character, whereas the mixed and inconsistent characters presumably evoked weak or conflicting schemas. When asked to recall attributes of the characters, more material and more correct material was recalled about pure than mixed inconsistent characters. This effect replicated across type of schema (introvert or extravert) and was not influenced by whether the recall task was immediate or delayed. Marginal effects in the same direction were found in a second study. Similar effects occur for semantic material. Recall for sentences and prose is facilitated when the passage is preceded by a thematic title (Bransford & Johnson, 1973; Dooling & Mullet, 1973). Thus it appears that recall is improved when a stimulus configuration is a good match to a preexisting schema, or when the schema is made explicit through a thematic lead-in. (See also Owens, Bower, & Black, 1977).

It also appears that schematic structuring of an otherwise disjointed set of information improves recall. In a study cited earlier, Hamilton et al. (1980) had subjects read a list of 15 behaviors enacted by an individual; half the subjects were told to memorize the information, and half were told to form an impression of the individual. Presumably, the "impression-set" subjects matched the behavior descriptions to organized structured personality-type schemas. The subjective organization in their recall of the descriptions reflected categorization by personality types, or traits, whereas the recall of subjects in the memory-set conditions showed an equal amount of subjective organization, but it was not based on any obvious person schemas. Most important to the point here, impression-set subjects, who apparently were using person schemas to organize the information, had better recall of the information than memory-set subjects, who apparently did not use person schemas to organize the information.

A good match to a schema should not only facilitate recall overall, it should facilitate recall of schema-relevant material. This selective encoding function of schemas has also been demonstrated experimentally. For example, Taylor, Livingston, and Crocker (in progress) presented graduate students in different departments with an academic folder of a hypothetical student. Subjects were later tested on recall: English graduate students recalled more English-relevant material (courses, language, writing skill); and psychology graduate students, more psychology-relevant material (research experience, psychology courses, math background), even though the experimental task had not required selective use of this material. In a study of occupational stereotypes (Cohen, 1977), subjects observed a videotape of a woman performing some daily activities, having been told either that she was a waitress or that she was a librarian. In a free recall task, subjects recalled stereotype-consistent information more accurately than irrelevant or inconsistent information. (See also Hamilton & Rose, 1978; Picek, Sherman, & Shiffrin, 1975; Potts, 1972; Rothbart, Evans, & Fulero, 1979; Sulin & Dooling, 1974; Woll & Yopp, 1978).

Recall of events and episodes is similarly affected in that when such items are set into an overall story or even just a title or briefly stated theme, recall is selectively improved. For example, Zadny and Gerard (1974) had subjects observe a videotape of two people poking around an apartment. Some subjects were told the people were anticipating a drug bust and were looking for their dope so they could remove it. Others were told that the two intended to burgle the apartment, and a third group was told the two were waiting for a friend and had become stir crazy. Results showed that subjects remembered more sentences and features of the scene appropriate to the particular scenario they had been given than features or sentences related to the other scenarios. These effects were replicated in two other studies. Other studies have shown that the presence of a theme predicts what specific items, in a set of information items, will later be recalled (Bower, Black, & Turner, 1979; Frederiksen, 1975; Rumelhart, 1975; Schank, 1975a, 1975b; Thorndyke, 1977).

Selective recall is not a completely reliable effect of schematic processing, however. Under some circumstances, information that is moderately inconsistent with a schema may be recalled better than schema-consistent information (Hastie & Anderson, in progress; Hastie & Kumar, 1979). In these studies, subjects were given lists of traits (or behaviors) that described an individual. A set of adjectives varying in congruency (high, medium, low) with the majority of the adjectives was included in the list. In some cases, the medium level incongruent adjectives were better recalled than the high or low incongruent adjectives. These findings have been explained as follows: Information that is consistent can be assimilated into a schema relatively easily, where it may become confused with other nonpresented semantically related adjectives. Highly inconsistent information is rejected or discounted as not being a valid reflection of the individual's character. A good deal of cognitive work is performed on moderately inconsistent adjectives, however, to make them consistent with the overall impression, and so those adjectives are remembered well. If this explanation is true, then recalled moderately inconsistent adjectives might be rated as more consistent with the overall impression than unrecalled ones; there might be more idiosyncratic intrusions around moderately inconsistent than consistent material; and moderately inconsistent information might generate more idiosyncratic associations or behavioral predictions than might consistent information.[2]

However, this discussion also underscores the fact that recall often involves a tradeoff between attention and encoding or storage, and many factors affect attention and storage in opposite ways. Inconsistency is just such a factor. Incongruent or inconsistent stimuli may be more easily recalled because they draw attention, but less easily recalled because they are more difficult to encode or store with a schema and are not "cued" by schema-relevant material. The conditions under which inconsistent material is recalled better must be addressed by future research.

A remaining question in this area is whether schematically based biases in recall represent an encoding or a retrieval bias. In order to see if the selective recall bias is one of encoding or retrieval, Rothbart, Evans, and Fulero (1979) gave subjects stereotypic expectancies either before or after they saw behavioral descriptions that were consistent, inconsistent, or irrelevant to the stereotype. They found selective retrieval when subjects were given an expectancy before, but not after, seeing the behavioral descriptions. In another study, Zadny and Gerard (1974) gave half their subjects a label before they observed an experimental skit, and half were given the label after. Results suggested that the bias was primarily an encoding rather than a retrieval bias, because selective retrieval effects were stronger when subjects were given the scenario label before observing the interaction. However, a selective retrieval bias has also been observed using a similar format. Snyder and Uranowitz (1978) had subjects read an account of a case history of a woman and later told them either that she was currently involved in a lesbian or a heterosexual experience. When reconstructing the case history, subjects showed a bias toward recalling lesbian-consistent or heterosexual-consistent background information, depending on the label they had been given (see also Bower, 1977). Most of the other studies in this area have looked for either an encoding or a retrieval bias but not both. Those studies that have looked at both have found that encoding biases are stronger than retrieval biases, although both kinds of biases are implicated.

To summarize, either imposing a schema on a stimulus configuration or encountering a stimulus configuration that is a good match to a schema increases overall recall, especially recall of schema-relevant material. Under some circum-

---

[2]Similarly, in their exploration of scripts, Bower, Black, and Turner (1979) found that subjects remembered certain kinds of deviations from scripts better than more characteristic script actions; the recalled deviations were typically nonvisual but goal-relevant deviations, thus being consistent with the Hastie and Kumar (1979) analysis.

stances, moderately inconsistent information will be recalled better than schema-consistent information. The effects of schemas on recall seem to be due to both encoding and retrieval biases, although encoding biases seem to be stronger.

Schemas Affect Processing Time, Speed of Information Flow, and Speed of Problem Solving. The assumptions underlying any schematic model of information processing include some acknowledgment that such a system must be efficient and capable of moving information through capacity with reasonable speed. A large literature within cognitive psychology consistently shows faster processing times for schema-relevant versus schema-irrelevant material. These assumptions in turn have led to the prediction that, if a perceiver has a social schema for a particular stimulus domain, information relevant to that domain will be processed more quickly than irrelevant information or information for which there is not a schema.

Some evidence for this point comes from a study by Markus (1977) on self-schemata. Markus identified two groups of subjects who had schemas about themselves for the traits of dependence or independence and a third group of subjects who were aschematic on these traits. She then had them read sentences describing behaviors and press a button indicating whether or not the behaviors were self-descriptive. Subjects with self-schemata were able to respond faster to schema-relevant statements than were aschematics. Taylor, Crocker, and D'Agostino (1978) obtained similar effects on a problem-solving task. They gave subjects problems that included a schema-relevant cue, a schema-irrelevant cue, or no cue (control). Problems with schema-relevant cues were solved faster than control problems, and control problems were solved faster than problems with schema-irrelevant cues.

Other data, however, suggest that some schema-relevant material takes longer to process than schema-irrelevant material. Markus (1977) found that false feedback on an attribute was processed more slowly by people who held a schema for that attribute (schematics) than by those who did not (aschematics). More recently, Markus, Sentis, and Hammill (1978) found that subjects with "weight schemas" (e.g. obese subjects) took longer to process schema-relevant information than did aschematics. In a conceptually similar analysis, Rogers, Kuiper, and Kirker (1977) had subjects process material under conditions of self-reference or various non-self-relevant strategies (structural, phonemic, or semantic associations). They found that subjects who encoded trait information in terms of self-reference took longer to identify the traits in a recall task than did subjects who encoded the information through structural, phonemic, or semantic associations.

Why does schematic processing of schema-relevant material sometimes take longer and sometimes take less time than other kinds of processing or processing of other kinds of material? Markus (1974) explains these inconsistencies by suggesting that under some circumstances when schema-relevant material is processed, a data base of experience is evoked by the input, and accordingly, processing time is increased because both the input and the data base that has been evoked must be processed; however, to date, there are no suggestions as to what mediating circumstances might lead to shorter versus longer processing times.

Another possible explanation, not necessarily incompatible with Markus's explanation, is that under certain circumstances, the person processing schema-relevant material shifts from automatic to controlled processing (see Schneider & Shiffrin, 1977). Controlled "thoughtful" processing involves a slower search than does automatic processing. When schema-relevant material is processed in a controlled fashion, more information and/or a richer structure is brought to bear on the data than when schema-irrelevant material is processed in a controlled fashion, thus leading to longer processing times.

What kinds of conditions might prompt a shift into controlled processing or otherwise lengthen processing time? Information that is highly redundant and/or central to the schema might be processed faster than schema-irrelevant material, whereas information that has novel implications for the schema and/or is peripheral to the schema might be processed more slowly. One can envision, for example, a shy person responding quickly to the question "would you be shy at a party?", whereas a response to the question "would you be shy with a psychiatrist?" might take longer to process if the person had little experience with a psychiatrist and considered interactions with a psychiatrist to be a less central situation on which the schema of shyness might bear. It is also possible that more highly valenced material and/or material that evokes an evaluatively mixed data base would take longer to process than material that is less evaluative or that evokes an evaluatively consistent data base; in the former two cases, the implications of the input would be more far-reaching and/or more complex than in the latter two cases. Consider, for example, persons who consider themselves shy, who are asked if they would be shy on an important job interview; processing time might be long because the implications are profound, as compared with, for example, being shy in a bus terminal.

Before closing this section, two caveats are warranted regarding the current available literature and the design of experiments to test hypotheses regarding length of processing time. The first is that it is relatively easy to manipulate task constraints so as to increase or decrease processing time (see, for example, Baddeley, 1978; Craik & Tulving, 1975) and accordingly, one must be cautious that effects due to irrelevant task constraints are not misinterpreted as effects due to systematic manipulation of stimulus material. The inconsistent effects of schemas on processing time also suggest a second caveat in the form of a possible liability of borrowing too heavily from research findings in cognitive psychology. In the cognitive literature, where faster processing times for schema-

relevant material are the rule, the experimental materials tend to be highly redundant stimulu in impoverished environments. In contrast, in the social world
schema-relevant information is likely to be complex and embedded in a rich
environmental and/or affective context. Accordingly, whereas the functions of
perceptual and other simple congitive schemas may be to identify stimuli quickly
and move information through capacity efficiently, the functions of the more
elaborate social schemas may instead be to identify that information on which
one should lavish extended processing time. Probably social schemas do both:
i.e., enable the perceiver to process some information faster and other information in more depth.

Overall, then, one can summarize the literature on reaction-time differences in
processing schema-relevant versus schema-irrelevant input with a hypothesis:
whether or not schema-relevant material is processed faster than schema-
irrelevant material depends on the valence, centrality, evaluative consistency,
novelty, and implications of the material.

The Inferential and Interpretive Functions of Schemas: Beyond the Information Given

*Schemas Enable the Social Perceiver to Fill in Data Missing from an Input
Stimulus Configuration.*   This process can occur in several ways. First, the
schema can direct a search for data. That is, as a preexistent structure, the
schema contains characteristic attributes and dimensions associated with a particular stimulus domain. When a configuration is matched to a schema and the
configuration is missing certain attributes usually found in that domain, search
behavior may proceed for those attributes so as to obtain a fuller match. For
example, if I go to a circus, and do not immediately see any clowns, I may
wonder where they are and look around for them. Research has not, to our
knowledge, focused specifically on this search direction aspect of schemas.
However, a common procedure used in cognitive psychology could be employed
and/or adapted for such a purpose—namely, providing subjects with the opportunity to request additional information. An analysis of those requests would
elucidate the kinds of information subjects feel it is necessary to have before
they make schema-based inferences (Carroll & Payne, 1976). For example,
Garland, Hardy, and Stephenson (1975) used this procedure in an investigation of Kelley's ANOVA model of social cognition to see if subjects' spontaneous requests about a "person–acts–object" scenario would center around
consensus, consistency and distinctiveness information. What they found, instead, was that many of the subjects' requests for information focused on other
qualities of the person, suggesting that subjects were trying to identify what kind
of person was involved in the activity. The "request for information" format,

then, may be a useful tool for identifying not only the dimensions along which subjects are seeking out information to fill out a match to a known schema, but it may also be a useful way of discovering *what* schema or general class of schemas the subject is using, (e.g., person schema vs. event schema).

Schemas also fill in missing data in a second, more interesting way. When data along some dimension or attribute is missing, the schema may fill in the missing values with best guesses regarding what the value should be and insert this value in the configuration. Minsky (1975) terms these best guesses *default options*. These default options presumably develop from experience with instances of the schema and thus are typical qualities of the stimulus domain in question. For example, if I tell you that my brother is a fireman and ask you what color his boots are, you will probably say "black"; if I tell you that my boyfriend is a cowboy, and ask you what his hat lookes like, you are unlikely to infer that he wears a beret. The assumptions of black boots and cowboy hat constitute the default for the schemas of fireman and cowboy. In common parlance, "no news" is regarded as "good news," or as a communication that the news is or probably would be schema-consistent.

Default options may not only be inserted when a particular piece of data is missing; they may also be inserted in the stimulus configuration if there is too much information for the perceiver to process. That is, with highly complex configurations, there may be so much detail that the perceiver cannot notice each bit. When reconstructing the configuration from memory, the perceiver may insert default options for those missing values he or she failed to notice. Thus, if the stimulus configuration is out of focus, presented only briefly or otherwise incomplete, and possibilities for a direct search are limited, the social perceiver can fill in the missing data with best guesses from the schema. Default options can be inserted when the stimulus configuration is first encountered, when it is rehearsed in memory, or when some relevant response is required. Schemas, then, not only lead to systematic omissions in reconstructions of persons or events as noted in the work on volume and selectivity of recall, they also lead to systematic constructions or additions to those stimulus configurations. There is a considerable amount of research evidence on this point.

Spiro (1977) had subjects read a story about a couple's plans regarding whether or not to marry and later have children; instructions were to either form an impression of the couple or to memorize the information. Subjects were then given information stating either that the couple had split up or that they had married and lived happily ever after. On a recall task, "impression" subjects invented data that was consistent with the outcome they had been given, despite encouragement to reproduce the information exactly as it had been provided; the effect was more pronounced the longer the delay between the story and the recall task. Cantor and Mischel (1977) found that among subjects who formed inferences about internally consistent prototypical persons (e.g. extravert, introvert), recollections of those persons' behavior was biased toward including conceptually related but nonpresented behaviors. In her study of occupational stereotypes, Cohen (1977) found that subjects intruded stereotype-consistent but nonpresented details in their recall of the activities of the person they had viewed. (see also Loftus & Palmer, 1974; Snyder & Uranowitz, 1978).

Self-relevant material shows similar affects. Rogers, Rogers, and Kuiper (cited in Rogers, Kuiper, & Kirker, 1977) had subjects rate a series of adjectives for their self-descriptiveness; 2½ months later, subjects were shown both the old and new adjectives in a recognition memory task. Subjects were more likely to identify self-relevant but nonpresented adjectives as part of the original set, compared with non-self-relevant, nonpresented adjectives.

In their investigation of scripts, Bower, Black, and Turner (1979) found a strong tendency for subjects to falsely recall actions that were not part of the original text, but which were strongly implied by the script. For example, if the script stated that the person waited in the checkout line at the supermarket and then wheeled her groceries to the car, subjects were likely to remember that she had paid the checkout girl for her food (see also Picek, Sherman, & Shiffrin, 1975; Potts, 1972; Sulin & Dooling, 1974).

The finding that subjects' reconstructions of persons and events show schema-relevant intrusions is extremely robust. However, though the default options explanation seems to make some sense, it is not immediately consistent with the evidence and speculation on another issue, namely, whether subjects' mental representations of incoming data configurations constitute a full or a partial copy of the schema. The nature of this inconsistency will be made clear following an explanation of the full versus partial copy issue.

The issue is: When a data configuration is instantiated as a match to a particular schema, is the mental representation of that configuration fleshed out in short-term memory as a full or a partial copy of the schema? Bower, Black, and Turner (1979) raise this issue at length in the context of their research on scripts and conclude, for reasons too lengthy to reiterate here, that a partial copy model fits the data better. We take the same position, and a simple examination of the costs of a full copy model illustrates some of the reasons. That is, fleshing out a stimulus configuration is a fair amount of work, and there are probably many instances in which a full match to the schema is not required in order to use it for some purpose. I can tell you a story about my fireman brother without your knowing or caring what color his boots are. Or you can ask me about my cowboy boyfriend's cowpunching style without making explicit an inference about what his hat looks like. The social perceiver can flesh out those attributes if he or she chooses, but probably need not do so in order to utilize the schema. It would be cognitively costly to flesh out every stimulus configuration. Furthermore, the process of fleshing out, itself, would be endless, because each missing value that is filled in with data or a default option lays the groundwork for more assumptions and the prospect for more data and default options. Matches to schemas are probably only fleshed out under certain circumstances.[3]

However, if we accept both the partial copy model of data representation and the evidence on default options, it follows that we need some explanation of which default options are inserted and which are left empty. Bower et al. (1979) proposed that the strength of the activation trace associated with a particular slot in the schema will determine whether or not it is falsely recalled as having occurred in the stimulus configuration. Assuming this to be true, what might lead to a strong activation trace for nonpresented schema-relevant details? The following points are largely speculative, but suggest some directions in which to move. First, details that have almost always been part of the schema-relevant scenario before might be inserted more frequently than less usual details, because the former presumably have a stronger cumulative memory trace. For example, in the supermarket scenario, a perceiver would probably falsely recall that the groceries were put into brown paper bags before recalling that sardines was one of the purchases. Second, highly salient (e.g. vibrant, colorful, dramatic) details in a prior instance of a schema seem to have a stronger memory trace, because they are more commonly recalled and more easily brought to mind (see Taylor & Fiske, 1978); accordingly, they might also be good candidates as intrusions in subsequent matches to schemas. Consistent with this point, research by Thompson, Reyes, and Bower (1978) found that vivid courtroom details exerted a stronger effect on judgments about evidence after a delay than immediately after presentation of stimulus materials. Third, if the stimulus configuration contains data on a schema-relevant detail, but detail regarding some precondition of causal relationship is missing, those latter details might be good candidates for insertion of default options. For example, if you are told that a woman wore a red outfit, it might be necessary to instantiate the outfit as something, specific, like a suit, in order to have the detail "red" be meaningful. Details in a schema that are adjacent or subsequent to actually presented details in a hierarchical or temporal sequence may be intruded. For example, if you are told that a person carried groceries to the car and drove home, the likelihood of assuming the person started the car is high, because it is part of that temporal sequence. Finally, schema-relevant details that were recently activated by a highly related but nonidentical dataset, are more likely to be intruded than not recently-activated details (Bower et al., 1979; Rholes, 1977).

Though there are clear implications for research in these hypotheses, there are two unfortunate drawbacks in actually conducting the implied research. The first

---

[3]Input data configurations may be fleshed out by the schema if there is a demand from the environment (as for example, a question from some individual) or if one needs the information to generate subsequent assumptions, to plan one's own behavior, to advance toward a coal state, or if the situation is highly involving or affectively laden.

is that subject output does not necessarily reflect cognitive processes, especially on this issue of default options. Subjects do not always intrude obvious schema- or script-relevant details precisely because such details *are* obvious; subjects expect the audience to insert these default options. For example, in describing a visit to the doctor, the subject may say that the patient was examined by the doctor, but will not add the detail that the doctor said, "Say 'Ahh'," because they assume the audience will know this. The second problem in conducting this kind of research is in distinguishing what people *do* do from what they *can* do. Because subjects can flesh out a schema endlessly and relatively effortlessly, the risk is that they will do so when prompted merely to report on their representation. For example, if I am told that the prince rescued the princess and am asked if I have a picture of the princess' dress, I can describe it right down to the pastel embroidery on the hem, but such detail would not be a normal part of my rescue scene. Thus, research procedures may inadvertently extend a representation rather than merely tap it. If a methodology can be developed that overcomes these problems, then a study of the predictors of intrusions can proceed.

Schemas Provide Bases for Solving Problems. Within the last few years, there has been a debate in the problem-solving literature concerning how "rational" the social perceiver is in selecting and using his or her problem-solving and decision-making strategies (see, for example, Fischoff, 1976; Slovic & Lichtenstein, 1971). Evidence has mounted to the effect that, instead of considering all available information evenhandedly, thoroughly, and in an unbiased fashion, the social perceiver employs shortcuts or heuristics that simplify and shorten the process. Kahneman and Tversky (1973) have identified three such heuristics: availability, representativeness, and anchoring. Of these, the first two relate directly to schemas.

Representativeness is the degree to which a given stimulus or evidentiary base matches the essential features of some class of stimuli or of some outcome. For example, Hitler may be thought of as representative of the class of dictators, and Bozo, of the class of clowns. According to Kahneman and Tversky, people use the representativeness heuristic when judging such problems as how likely it is that a given person is a member of a category or how likely a given outcome is to be explained by a particular set of antecedent conditions. For example, given the description, "John is a meek and tidy soul who likes order in his life," people are more likely to infer that John is a librarian than a salesman, and ignore baserate information regarding the absolute numbers of librarians versus salesmen that exist in the population. The relationship between the representativeness heuristic and schematic processing is clear. The representativeness of a particular stimulus cannot be judged without invoking the schema against which it will be compared. In the previous example, the perceiver presumably matches what he knows about John against what he knows about librarians and salesmen and comes to the conclusion that John is a more typical instance of a librarian than of a salesman (see also Cantor & Mischel, 1979; Taylor, Crocker, & D'Agostino, 1978; Trope, 1978; Tversky & Kahneman, 1974).

In addition to providing a strategy for solving problems, the representativeness heuristic influences what evidence one brings to bear in solving social problems and making inferences. The research on this point is sketchy but intriguing. Ajzen (1977) found that subjects were more likely to use statistically relevant baserate information to make predictions if the baserate information fit their assumptions about the causes of the event they were predicting. For example, subjects were asked to predict the grade point average (GPA) of several students, given certain data about the specific students and baserate information relating the student data to GPA. The student data either fit subjects' intuitive theories about factors related to GPA (I.Q. and the number of hours spent studying each week) or was intuitively unrelated to GPA (dollars earned each week and number of miles between the student's residence and the college). Ajzen found that subjects used the baserate information that was consistent with their causal theories about I.Q. but not base rate information that did not fit their causal theories. In a similar study, Tversky and Kahneman (1977) found that subjects instructed to estimate probabilities used baserate information that fit their causal theories of events, but did not use the same baserate information when it did not fit their causal theories of events. This research leads to the conclusion that the social perceiver incorporates those aspects of evidence that represent the essential features of an outcome, paying relatively less attention to information that is not representative.

Availability is often used as a heuristic for judging frequency or probability. Tversky and Kahneman (1973) define the use of availability as a problem-solving heuristic as follows: "A person is said to employ the availability heuristic whenever he estimates frequency or probability by the ease with which instances or associations could be brought to mind. To assess availability, it is not necessary to perform the actual operations of retrieval or construction. It suffices to assess the ease with which these operations could be performed [p. 208]." Thus, the speed with which an association is made is used to judge its strength, which in turn provides a basis for estimating frequency. Many of these associations will involve reference to a schema. For example, clinicians were asked to examine a set of draw-a-person protocols by patients with particular symptoms. When asked to recall certain co-occurrences such as how frequently the symptom of suspiciousness was paired with the drawing characteristic of enlarged eyes, the clinicians over-estimated the frequency of co-occurrence, presumably because their schemas for paranoia prompted them to make a rapid association between suspiciousness and enlarged eyes (see Tversky & Kahneman's [1974] interpretation of Chapman & Chapman, [1969]).

In addition to prompting past associations, availability acts as a schema-based problem-solving strategy through the ease with which instances can be brought to mind. Speed of accessing instances leads one to infer high frequency or probability. For example, when asked to judge the percentage of the population that is divorced in a given community, one may do so by bringing to mind the number of people within one's friendship group who are divorced. The relationship between schematic processing and this use of availability, then, is through the database that a schema provides. A query to the social perceiver evokes a schema, and the examples of its occurrence are counted. Consistent with this point is Markus's (1977) data showing that subjects who had schemas for particular traits were able to provide more examples of that behavior type faster than were aschematics.

There are, of course, many uses of the availability heuristic that are not schema-related. Information that is colorful, novel, distinctive, or otherwise salient is highly available without being made so through reference to a schema (see Taylor, 1980). In contrast, the representativeness heuristic is intrinsically bound up in schematic processing of information, because there can be no judgement of representativeness without recourse to some abstract cognitive representation.

Schemas Provide a Basis for Evaluating Experience. A schema represents a normative structure, and as such, specific instances can be matched against it for goodness of fit. There are several implications of this point. One is that if schema-relevant expectations are generated prior to encountering any given stimulus configuration, the configuration is judged against these expectations. Expectations, in turn, exert a powerful influence on emotions and behavior. There is an enormous literature on the role of expectations as mediators of psychological feelings of disappointment or satisfaction in the areas of interpersonal attraction (e.g. Aronson & Linder, 1965; Mettee, Taylor, & Friedman, 1973), income satisfaction (e.g. Martin, 1977), job satisfaction (e.g. Lawler, 1973; Mitchell, 1974), and achievement (e.g. Aronson & Carlsmith, 1962). Failure to satisfy expectations has been posited to mediate behavior as varied as school performance (Radloff, 1966), romantic breakups (Aronson & Linder, 1965), and riot behavior (e.g. Sears & McConahay, 1973). (See Pettigrew, 1967, for a review.) Obviously, not all expectations come from schemas, but many can and so the role of expectations in determining satisfaction in these domains suggests some of the psychological consequences of matching a schema to a stimulus configuration for goodness of fit.

The normative aspect of schemas also functions as a standard for explicit evaluations of the stimulus configuration. The overall evaluation of the stimulus depends on whether the stimulus configuration is a good match or good instance of the schema, and whether the schema itself is evaluated positively or nega-tively. Data consistent with this point are provided by Higgins and Rholes (1976). They had subjects rate the desirability of occupation/trait combinations: Overall desirability ratings were a function of the desirability or social value of the role, and the degree to which the trait was central to and fulfilled the role.

A stimulus configuration should be a better instance of a schema the more it has the central attributes of the schema. For example, if one's schema for an Irishman indicates that he must have pink cheeks and a brogue, then an Irishman who has very pink cheeks and a strong brogue is a very good Irishman indeed. If a stimulus configuration includes attributes that are not central to the schema, it may be evaluated more negatively as an instance of the schema, even if the attribute is independently evaluated as positive. This may be especially true if the noncentral attribute is relatively unusual (see Higgins & Rholes, 1976). For example, a salesman who recites poetry is not as good a salesman as one who does not have that attribute, even to people who like poetry. Thus, we may like people who fit our schemas or stereotypes for them, even if we have a generally negative evaluation of that type of person or role. People who stay true to type, or in-role, are easier to predict, they confirm our expectations, they enable us to plan our behavior, and they simply make a good cognitive gestalt. However, we probably prefer these good cognitive gestalts only if they are being evaluated as instances of a *schema*. For example, a librarian who likes rock music may not be considered a very good librarian; however, he or she may be a more interesting person than a stereotypic librarian. (See Cantor & Mischel, 1979, for a discus-sion of some of these issues.)

A third implication of the normative function of schemas is that people who have highly developed schemas will make more extreme evaluations for schema-relevant material than will people whose schemas are less well de-veloped. Some evidence on this point is provided by Tesser and his colleagues (Tesser, 1978; Tesser & Leone, 1977). In a series of studies, they found that the more a person attends to a particular stimulus, the more extreme his or her evaluation of that stimulus becomes; this result has been interpreted in attentional terms (see Taylor & Fiske, 1978) and is not, in itself, relevant here. What is relevant is that people who have articulated schemas for those stimuli show those effects more strongly than do people without such schemas. For example, people who have an artistic background show more polarization in their evaluations of pictures than do people without an artistic background, and people who have a schema for football show more polarized evaluations of football plays than do people with less football experience. Tesser's (1978) explanation is that schemas provide criteria for evaluation, and so people with highly developed schemas make more confident and extreme evaluations more quickly than do people without schemas. Schematics, then, may show more disappointment or satisfac-tion when schema-relevant expectations are frustrated or confirmed respectively.

They may also show polarized evaluations of schema-relevant stimuli not usually evaluative in tone.

Overall, the evaluative component of schemas has received considerable attention within the context of some literatures (e.g. the expectancy literature) and very little in other areas (e.g. person or role schemas). Some possible extensions have been suggested here. Two additional points warrant mention. Although we have stated that expectations function as a basis for evaluating experience, nothing has been said about how this process occurs, save vague reference to a matching process. A more fine-grained analysis of this problem is needed (see Tversky, 1977, for a possible attack on this problem). Second, the area of expectations and evaluations would seem to be a good context in which to study schemas that have a strong affective component versus those that do not to see what the important differences are between them. For example, are there processing differences between schemas that are affectively toned and those which are not?

Schemas Provide a Basis for Anticipating the Future, Setting Goals, Making Plans, and Developing Behavioral Routines to Deal with Them. First, people seem to be able to predict the future faster and more confidently if they have a schema for the stimulus domain than if they do not. Some evidence for this point comes from the work on self-schemata. Markus (1977) asked her subjects who were either dependents, independents, or aschematics to predict how they would behave in hypothetical situations involving dependent or independent behaviors. She found that subjects were able to generate predictions for their own behavior faster and more confidently if they had a schema for that dimension than if they did not. Schematics also predicted a higher likelihood of engaging in subsequent schema-related behaviors; they were more resistant to counter-schematic feedback than were aschematics; and they showed more consistency over time in their self-descriptions than did aschematics (see also Bem & Allen, 1974; Sorrentino & Short, 1977). Similar effects have been found for other kinds of schemas. Fiske and Kinder (1978), for example, found that subjects who had been given schematic lead-ins to accounts of political turmoil in a foreign country were more confident in their predictions and more extreme in their judgments compared with subjects with no schematic lead-in.

A corollary of this phenomenon also seems to be true, at least under some circumstances—namely, that coming to think about a situation schematically leads to overestimating the likelihood of its occurrence. In a series of intriguing studies on what they call the perseverance effect, Ross and his colleagues found that when instructed to imagine an event, subjects subsequently came to regard its occurence as more likely, even when the event was subsequently discredited (Ross, Lepper, Strack, & Steinmetz, 1977). By way of explaining this phenomenon, Ross et al. (1977) argued that anticipating how an event might come about makes cause-effect linkages salient, which remain salient even after the outcome is discredited. To test this point, Carroll (1978) had some subjects just image the events in question and others explain how the events in question might come about. The absence of differences in the subjective probability that the events would transpire as a function of the manipulation suggests that mere imaging alone can produce the effect; however, there is no way of knowing whether or not subjects who merely imaged the events also thought about how the events might come about. One can argue that even more imaging evokes the temporal sequence of events in the schema, so that the causal chain is activated.[4]

Schemas enable the perceiver to set goals and enact the appropriate behavior sequences. Having structured representations of events, persons, roles, or relationships enables a social perceiver to envision a state toward which he or she would like to move. For example, a person who wishes to be successful can maintain an idealized conception of personal success in his or her head and test each new work experience against that ideal conception. Because event schemas are temporally ordered, the schema also provides a basis for moving from a current state toward the ideal state by specifying, at least roughly, what intermediate events are required to move from the initial state to the goal state. This, in turn, provides a basis for selecting the appropriate behavior sequence. As Abelson (1976) and others have noted (see, for example, Snyder, 1977), abstract knowledge representations of events, particularly scripts, include an action sequence. Abelson points out, "scripts handle stylized everyday situations . . . [a script] is a pre-determined, stereotyped sequence of actions that defines a well-known situation (Schank & Abelson, 1977)." For example, the cocktail party script involves arriving stylishly late, greeting one's host and making one's way to the bar, getting a drink, finding a congenial small group to chat with for about 20 minutes, moving on, and then leaving when one becomes bored or drunk, or the right number of other people have left or the party is clearly over (e.g., the hostess yawns conspiciously). The point here is that not only does the social perceiver know what one does at a cocktail party, he or she also knows how to do it and so can move from the abstract representation of what to do into the actual doing of the behavior through some as yet unspecified mechanism. Because considerably more sophisticated work than what we could attempt here has already been done on this problem, no further elaboration is needed. (The reader is referred to Abelson, 1976; Schank & Abelson, 1977.)

---

[4]Interestingly enough, when subjects are instructed to image scripts (e.g., having a cup of coffee, losing one's wallet), the imaging process does not lead to higher expectations of occurrence. Perhaps scripts are a "basic level" of event schemas that require no active construction on the part of the social perceiver; to get perseveration effects, the social perceiver may have to be engaging in higher order combinations of scripts.

Schematic conceptions of how the world works can also help create the reality they anticipate, even in the absence of objective bases for it in the environment. False feedback studies that lead actors to behave in ways consistent with the feedback (e.g. Aronson & Mettee, 1968) are testimony to this fact. One's own behavior is not the only behavior so affected. The expectations for others' behaviors that are generated by a powerful schema can lead to those others' adopting the anticipated behavior as well. An eerie little book, *Cards of Identity* by Nigel Dennis (1955), develops the thesis that a person who is put into a new environment in which all feedback is consistent with a new schema for that situation will come to adopt that new schema, even if it means completely disassembling his or her old identity and taking on a new one. In this book, a caretaker, investigating some new tenants, is drugged and wakes up to discover that everyone is responding to him as if he were the house butler who had gone on a bender. The puzzled caretaker comes, in the short space of 40 pages, to accept the definition and is a most proper butler for the entire remainder of the book.

Somewhat less Mephistophelian demonstrations of this effect have been achieved by Rosenthal and Jacobson (1968) and by Snyder and his colleagues. Rosenthal and Jacobson provided teachers with feedback suggesting that certain of their students were potential "late bloomers," students who could be expected to show their true ability if properly nurtured. Over the space of a year, these students showed increases in both academic performance and I.Q., though there had in fact been nothing to distinguish them from their peers at the outset of the study. Snyder and Swann (1976) found that subjects' expectations that a partner would be hostile led these subjects to exhibit behavior that evoked hostility in the partner. The result was an escalating spiral of aggression. Snyder, Tanke, and Berscheid (1977) led subjects to believe that a female partner they were interacting with but whom they could not see, was either highly attractive or unattractive. Not only was the partner treated differently by the subject depending on his expectations, but she came to take on more attractive or unattractive behavior as a result of the false expectations that had been generated about her (see also Word, Zanna, & Cooper, 1974; Zanna & Pack, 1975).

In a third set of studies (Snyder & Swann, 1978), subjects were led to believe that a partner might have a particular trait (e.g. extraversion) and were instructed to find out if it were true, using an interview format. Results indicated that subjects slanted their questions primarily toward the hypothesis they were trying to test with the result that they obtained primarily information that supported the hypothesis. When asked if the hypothesis was valid, subjects gave strong affirmative answers, apparently oblivious to the biases they had introduced into their own data sampling. The labeling of social deviants has been interpreted in similar terms. Expectations communicated by labelers to the target individual can lead to what is termed "secondary deviance," in which the target confirms the appropriateness of the label by playing out the behavior that is expected. This kind of analysis has been used to explain criminal behavior, the development of stigmatized identities (Goffman, 1963), and mental illness (Scheff, 1966), among other kinds of social deviance. (See, for example, Becker, 1963; Schur, 1971).

To summarize, then, schemas enable the perceiver to predict the future by specifying what events, abilities, or behaviors have a high likelihood of occurrence when activated; they also prompt the perceiver to see schema-relevant events, attributes, or behaviors as more likely to occur, even when the schema is subsequently discredited. Under some circumstances, the knowledge portion of the schema is tied to guidelines for action, thus enabling the individual to act in service of relevant goals (see for example, Snyder, 1977; Snyder & Swann, 1976). When this schema is strongly enough evoked and schema-relevant behaviors are set in motion, the implications of the schema may be strong enough to actually create the reality that is implied.

In these four sections, we have reviewed what evidence there is to date on the processing functions of schemas, i.e., how schematic processing serves the perceiver well. In the following section, we consider how schematic processing can be a liability.

LIABILITIES OF SCHEMATIC PROCESSING

In my view, the human condition would be greatly improved if . . . confrontations and willingness to reject hypotheses were a regular part of our social, political, economic, religious, and cultural lives [Sagan, 1977, p. 193].

Scientific investigation could not be carried out if men were too open-minded. Pure empiricism is impossible: facts do not speak for themselves . . . Although the rejection of discrepant information may lead to incorrect conclusions, this process is a necessary part of theory-building [Jervis, 1976, p. 158].

All of us are cognitive gamblers—some more than others, but most of us are more than we realize [Miller, Galanter, & Pribram, 1960, p. 92].

The foregoing quotations reflect a fundamental tension in the functions of social schemas, a tension that is generated by the perceiver's simultaneous needs to both invoke and avoid schematic interpretations of the world. On the one hand, schemas are essential to imputing structure and meaning to incoming data, and on the other hand, schemas lead to stale interpretations, closing off new definitions and solutions. We have thus far focused on the processing advantages of schemas. Here we focus on their liabilities.

Because schemas lead to selectivity in attention, encoding, representation, and retrieval, schemas also lead to information loss. Accordingly, virtually any of the properties of schematic functioning that are useful under some circumstances will be liabilities under others. Like all gamblers, cognitive gamblers sometimes lose. Much has been made of biases in the social cognition literature of late, a bias being a systematic and often pervasive departure from some normative model of processing (see for example, Kahneman & Tversky, 1973; Ross, 1977; Ross, 1978; Slovic & Lichtenstein, 1971). A schematic model of thought is descriptive, rather than normative, and so "bias" has a somewhat different meaning in this context. We use here the terms "bias," "error," or "liability" interchangeably to refer to the systematic ways in which the social perceiver is simply wrong in the judgment that is made or the generalizations that are drawn about stimuli. Thus, our focus is on the question: Given that a schematic conception will sometimes lead to wrong answers, what are the most probable ways and reasons for this happening?

In this section, we consider several kinds of liabilities in schematic processing: biases due to using the wrong schema; the illusory database; type one error biases; and biases in perceived co-occurrence, such as illusory correlations.

Errors Due to Using the Wrong Schema

The fact that any advantage of schema can also be a disadvantage under certain stimulus conditions has been repeatedly demonstrated by social psychologists. Indeed, many of the studies we have already cited to demonstrate the processing advantages of schemas have used a "biases" format for demonstrating their points. For example, Langer and Abelson (1974) had subjects listen to a tape of two men interacting, having told one group that the tape was a job interview and another group that it was a psychiatric intake interview. Subjects, who in this case were therapists, "found" more pathology in the behavior of the to-be-committed individual (psychiatric interview tape) and distorted the background data presented to be consistent with their schema, compared with subjects who believed the man was a job applicant. (See also Bower, 1977; Cohen, 1977; Snyder & Uranowitz, 1978; Taylor, Livingston, & Crocker, in progress; Zadny & Gerard, 1974). In these studies, errors arise at several points: selectivity in recall, the insertion of default options, and the reinterpretation of otherwise ambiguous data.

A wrong theory applied to a stimulus configuration also slows down information gathering and problem solving. Bruner and Potter (1964), for example, demonstrated that subjects induced to form a (usually incorrect) hypothesis about an out-of-focus stimulus configuration took longer to identify the configuration when it came into focus, presumably because the early incorrect hypotheses interfered with stimulus recognition. In the previously described problem-solving study by Taylor, Crocker, and D'Agostino (1978), subjects who used schema-irrelevant cues as a basis for solving a "common attribute" task had slower decision times than did subjects with schema-relevant cues or no cues.

Another consequence of employing the wrong schema is illustrated by a set of experiments cited earlier (Ross, Lepper, Strack & Steinmetz, 1977) on what is called the perseverance effect. In one experiment, subjects were given a description of a young woman and, after reading it, were told either that she had committed suicide or that she had made substantial financial contributions to the Peace Corps. They were then asked to write an explanation of how this event came about. After they had written their account, subjects were told that the event they had written about had not actually occurred. They were then asked to estimate the likelihood of several events occurring in the woman's life, including the event they had written about. Subjects consistently overestimated the probability that the event they had written about would occur, compared to other events, presumably because their writing exercise had made them aware of the ways in which the event could have come about and the factors in the woman's background that would lead to the event's occurrence (Ross, Lepper, Strack, & Steinmetz, 1977; see also, Ross, Lepper, & Hubbard, 1975; Wyatt & Campbell, 1951.) Perseverance, then, is another usually helpful process gone awry. That is, it is undoubtedly customarily helpful to encode new information in a manner that fleshes out its meaning rather than to simply record events as they transpire. The disadavantage of perseverance is that when the schema is discredited, the perceiver has difficulty disembedding the raw data from the inferential structure that surrounds it.

Psychologists are not the only people who are fascinated by biases due to using the wrong schema. Playwrights have used "the misunderstanding" as a comic device for centuries. Goldsmith's *She Stoops to Conquer* is an example. The leading character in this play is a young man who is shy and awkward with those of his own class (especially women), but arrogant, blustery, and lustful with those of lower class origins. He is on his way to meet an upperclass young lady, a prospective bride, when he tires and stops off at what he thinks is an inn. In fact, the inn is the very house where the prospective bride and her father reside. Believing himself to be in the company of an innkeeper, the young man orders his prospective father-in-law about, criticizes and sends back the food, complains of his accommodations, and generally behaves as any dissatisfied customer would, to the astonishment of the father-in-law and delight of the servants. Similarly, believing his prospective bride to be a serving wench, he pursues her with a single-mindedness she finds appealing, if a bit over-zealous. In the end, of course, all deception is unmasked, the young man loses his shyness, the father-in-law forgives, and the couple marries.

Classical comedy draws on the wrong schema theme for several reasons. Everyone has had enough experience with mistaken identities and erroneously defined situations to appreciate the acute embarrassment and opportunity for humor that results. Because many schemas are held in common by large numbers of people, the audience understands both the actual flow of events and the erroneous construction that the duped character has made of it. Accordingly, the audience can see how employing the wrong schema prompts the mislead character to selectively encode all the wrong data, define ambiguous or contradictory information as being consistent with the schema, evaluate behavior using the wrong criteria, generate incorrect expectations about future events, and employ behavioral scripts that are completely inappropriate to the situation.

Illusory Data Base

A second set of liabilities in schematic processing derive, not from employing a wrong schema, but from employing a correct one too enthusiastically. Such enthusiasm leads to an illusory data base. An illusory data base is a set of assumptions, inferences, or bits of information that are not actually present in the stimulus configuration encountered by the perceiver, but that rather constitute the contribution the schema makes to the stimulus configuration. In the mind of the perceiver the actual attributes of the configuration and information provided by the schema become indistinguishable. There are at least three ways in which a schema can provide an illusory data base. The first is through the use of default options. As noted earlier, schemas contain best guesses of the attributes of the stimulus configurations that match it. When the perceiver encounters a stimulus configuration and a schema is evoked, if the value of some particular attribute is missing in the stimulus configuration, under some circumstances, the schema fills it in with the best guess (i.e. the default option). These kinds of intrusions may then be misrecalled as having actually occurred in the original configuration, providing additional "confirmation" of the validity of the schema, or additional "data" from which subsequent inferences can be generated.

A second kind of illusory data base is provided by the inferences one draws about the stimulus configuration using the schema. When evidence is evaluated schematically, inferences are drawn which may then, themselves, be stored as data independent of the initial stimulus configuration. There is some evidence for this hypothesis. (See, for example, Baumgardner, Leippe, & Ostrom, 1976; Geva, Lingle, Ostrom, Leippe, & Baumgardner, 1978; Lingle & Ostrom, 1977.) In one study, subjects were given a list of traits describing an individual and then asked to judge the suitability of that individual for a particular occupation (e.g. pilot vs. comedian). After completing this task, subjects were told to list traits they thought might be characteristic of the person. Subjects were found to list traits that were judged to be more descriptive of the occupation they had judged than the occupation they had not judged, even though in theory all subjects had exactly the same information about the individual. Apparently, then, subjects had convinced themselves that the target person was suitable for the particular occupation and then used this inference to guide their subsequent guesses regarding his or her other attributes. Consistent with the idea that inferences are stored as data, Greenwald (1968) found that the inferences and abstractions subjects generated when exposed to a persuasive communication were better predictors of attitude change than recall of persuasive arguments presented in the communication (cited in Lingle & Ostrom, 1977; see also Ross, Lepper, & Hubbard, 1975, on this point [p. 889]).

A third kind of illusory data base that stems from schematic processing is the indiscriminate application of the schema to stimulus configurations when the match is less than perfect. We know of no experimental evidence on this point, but anecdotes abound. The recent convert to a social movement, who sees exploitation everywhere, is one example. It is a standard saw among physicians that when a patient presents a complaint, the internist sees something to be medicated, the suregon sees something removable, and the psychiatrist sees something shrinkable. In the political area, Kearns (1976) states:

> National leaders tend to fit incoming information about other nations into existing theories about their own nation. Experience with his own system typically determines what a leader perceives in another system. It is hard for any leader to see that issues important to him are not important to others, and even more difficult to realize that others may be governed by very different values and assumptions. Perception is always influenced by personal and historic memory. Historical analogies often precede rather than follow a careful analysis of the situation [pp. 268–269].

Thus, in a number of ways, schematic conceptions that people have about persons and events do not merely restructure, order, and select the information the perceiver makes use of in the stimulus configuration; they actually contribute to the data base, providing information that later becomes indistinguishable from the original data.

Type 1 Error Bias

Another pervasive schematic bias, one which follows logically from the illusory data base, is a chronic propensity for type 1 errors: accepting data as consistent with a schema when it is either neutral or even inconsistent. This bias stems, we would argue, from several different sources. First, the data base that is stored with a schema is a data base of confirming instances. Second, the criteria for a "match" to a schema are broadly defined and admit neutral or even mildly inconsistent information. Third, disconfirmations of a schema lead to greater differentiation of that schema rather than revision of the schema. Fourth, the social perceiver is single-minded, employing one fairly unqualified schema at a time and thereby does not cross-check what appear to be confirmations of a schema against other equally plausible or qualifying schemas. We now elaborate on each of these four points.

In the opening sections of the paper, we suggested that a schema includes a data base of examples that is stored with the knowledge structure portion of the schema. Examples are, by definition, confirming instances. How would this fact lead to a propensity to make the type 1 errors? The study by Ross, Lepper, and Hubbard (1975) cited previously suggests how. In this study, subjects were given false feedback, leading them to believe that they were either very good or very bad at a test of social sensitivity, i.e., discriminating real from bogus suicide notes. Later on, subjects were debriefed concerning the falsity of the feedback, but their impressions of themselves as socially sensitive or insensitive persisted despite the debriefing. Ross et al. (1975) reasoned that subjects may have searched their memories for evidence consistent with the feedback that they were either socially sensitive or insensitive. When the debriefing occurred, it removed only one piece of what was now a highly buttressed opinion. Thus, the data base was left intact. Ross et al. explained this effect by suggesting that the perceiver engaged in a biased search for hits (positive examples), although they did not explain exactly why a biased search should occur. Our own explanation is somewhat different, maintaining that there need not be anything biased about the search; rather, the bias may be structural, being a function of the data base that is stored with the schema. That is, rather than actively searching for hits, the perceiver may simply draw on the relevant portion of the schema (e.g. sensitive me) and find examples of the behavior (e.g., me being sensitive) stored with the schema.

A second condition that leads to type 1 errors is that the criteria for a match to a schema seem to be broadly defined, thereby leading to identifying neutral or even mildly disconfirming stimulus configurations as instances of a schema. Research previously cited as labeling effects is evidence for this point. For example, in the Langer and Abelson (1974) study in which subjects listened to a tape, believing it to be either a psychiatric intake interview or a job interview, the same piece of data was frequently used as support for either construction of reality. For example, the fact that the individual had argued with a previous boss was taken to mean variously that he could not establish social relations or that he had high ideals, which he was not willing to compromise in his job. (See also Bower, 1977, Zadny & Gerard, 1974.)

A third source of type 1 errors lies in the impact of disconfirming data. Schemas seem to resist disconfirmation. (See, for example, Kuhn, 1970, for a discussion of this issue in the context of the conduct of scientific research.) It may be that, from a developmental perspective, whether cognitive or scientific, it is better to have a faulty schema than no schema at all. If one has no schema, information cannot be meaningfully encoded, whereas with a faulty schema, information can at least be processed, if not entirely accurately. Whether or not this is the case, we would argue that disconfirming instances of a schema rarely lead to revision of the basic schema itself, but rather provide a basis for differentiation of the schema, e.g., the creation of subtypes. One can observe this phenomenon quite readily in stereotyping. For example, if a man believes that women are basically passive, quiet, and none too bright, it would seem that encountering an aggressive, outgoing, and smart woman should challenge this stereotype. Rarely, however, does this happen. Rather, he may simply develop a new stereotype such as "castrating female" or "career woman," keeping his original stereotype for most women and considering his new stereotype to be a kind of exception to the rule. Eventually, as his experience increases, the number of stereotypes he has available also increases—mother, princess, bitch, castrating female, showgirl—and any behavior a female performs can fit within at least one of these sterotypic conceptions without disconfirming the overarching stereotype. In a study of stereotyping, Taylor et al. (1978) found that stereotypes were exhibited at this level and that the same behavior could be interpreted as both masculine- or feminine-stereotyped depending on which sex did it. For example, behavior seen as fatherly when a man did it was perceived as motherly when a woman did it, and male behavior that was cynical was bitchy when a woman did it. More research on the development of schemas is needed to bear out these conjectures (see also Taylor, 1980).

A fourth condition that may lead to type 1 errors in schematic processing is that the social perceiver is single-minded, employing one fairly unqualified schema at a time without checking what appear to be confirmations against equally plausible or qualifying schemas. Perhaps the clearest case of this point is what Ross (1977) calls the fundamental attribution error, i.e., the propensity to see the behavior of an individual as reflecting some dispositional quality of that individual. That is, there seems to be a general bias toward making inferences about persons, a bias that may stem from any of several sources. People are good units. They have clear boundaries, unlike events, for example; they intend things, unlike objects or events; they are salient because they move around and make noise, unlike other features of the environment; and when action occurs, they are frequently responsible for it. Thus the social perceiver seems to define his or her chief task as finding out what kind of people inhabit the social world. The fundamental attribution error, though, consists not only of a person bias but a bias toward perceiving stability and consistency in the person's behavior. Instead of qualifying inferences about people on the basis of the situational context in which the behavior occurred, the social perceiver instead labels the person in terms of the behavior. For example, a person may be perceived as an extravert whether she or he is extraverted at a football game, where extraversion is the norm, or in a library, where the behavior is clearly non-normative (Taylor & Crocker, 1978). (See also Jones & Harris, 1967; Ross, 1977; Ross, Amabile, & Steinmetz, 1977, for evidence on this point.)

Why are person attributions made when more plausible situational explanations would suffice? Taylor and Crocker (1978) have pointed out that subjects in these tasks are asked to make person inferences in the dependent measures employed. If the form of the inference task defines the type of schema that will be evoked (i.e., a person schema) then presumably, the target person's behavior is matched against a relevant person schema and a judgment is made as to how well the behavior fits the schema. There is nothing in the inference task that prompts the subject to call up schemas for the situation, and so a person attribution is made, relatively unqualified by the context in which the behavior occurred. According to this line of reasoning, if subjects were called upon to make situation judgments, the appropriate event schema would be called up and the situation would be matched against it. Under such circumstances, relevant data about persons might go unnoticed. (See Taylor & Crocker, 1978, for a fuller account of this line of reasoning.)

A number of conditions, then, lay the ground work for a substantial type 1 error bias in schematic processing.

Errors in the Assessment of Covariation

One of the tasks frequently performed by social perceivers is the assessment of the degree of covariation between two categories of events. Implicit personality theories, for example, reflect judgements about what traits covary with one another (cf. Hastorf, Schneider, & Polefka, 1970). Social perceivers also make covariation judgments about what traits are characteristic of members of an occupation, race, sex, or other category; what behaviors are likely to co-occur in an individual or situation (such as giving up one's seat in the subway and holding a door open for someone); and the degree to which outcomes covary with behavior (e.g., "every time I tell him to do something he does the opposite").

Systematic errors in judgments of the degree of covariation between two categories of events are called illusory correlations. Illusory correlations can occur when individuals hold relevant schemas or hypotheses about the relationship between the events in question. Considerable research on the assessment of covariation points to this conclusion. The Chapmans, in a clever series of studies, have shown that psychiatric clinicians and college students tend to overestimate correlations that they expect to be present (between exaggerating the eyes on the Draw-a-Person psychiatric test, and having paranoia, for example), but underestimate or fail to report correlations that are present but unexpected (Chapman, 1967; Chapman & Chapman, 1967, 1969). In a further demonstration of the impact of schemas on covariation judgments, Jennings, Amabile, & Ross (1980) have shown that people overestimate the degree of covariation between things that they believe to be associated (such as the ability to delay gratification and the ability to resist temptation to cheat), but they are very conservative when estimating the degree of covariation in data when they have no clear-cut expectations.

How does schematic processing produce illusory correlations? There are two functions of schemas that might lead to errors in the assessment of covariation. One possibility is that schemas or theories influence the evidence one brings to bear in assessing covariations. A second possibility is that schemas make certain types of evidence more available (i.e. easier to recall) and, therefore, that evidence is over-represented in judgments. We consider each of these explanations in turn.

That schemas influence the type of evidence one searches for and uses in assessing covariation is consistent with evidence that schemas influence the evidence one brings to bear in such inference tasks as predicting future behavior (Ajzen, 1977; Taylor & Crocker, 1978) and estimating probabilities (Tversky & Kahneman, 1977). Specifically, this process would involve searching for and using information that is consistent with one's schema, rather than information that is inconsistent or irrelevant, to estimate the degree of covariation between two categories of events. Research that shows subjects over-rely on the number of "hits" or instances that confirm the relationship they are assessing and believe to exist (such as a cloud-seeding/rain covariation), is consistent with this process of over-utilization of schema-consistent instances as evidence of covariation (Jenkins & Ward, 1965; Smedslund, 1963; Snyder & Swann, 1978; Ward & Jenkins, 1965; also, see Crocker & Taylor, 1978, for further discussion of schematic processing, theory testing, and the use of evidence in assessing covariation.)

Schemas might also produce illusory correlations by making schema-consistent instances more available, or easier to bring to mind (Kahneman & Tversky, 1973). If one can recall more schema-consistent instances (such as extraverted salesmen), than schema-inconsistent (introverted salesmen), or schema-irrelevant (dependent salesmen) instances, then schema-consistent instances should be over-represented in judgments of covariation. Instances need not actually be retrieved for availability to influence judgments of frequency. If an association between two categories is strong, then one may judge that instances could easily be brought to mind, and therefore estimate that such instances occur frequently. Tversky and Kahneman (1974) provide the following discussion of the influence of availability on illusory correlations:

> Availability provides a natural account for the illusory-correlation effect. The judgment of how frequently two events co-occur could be based on the strength of the associative bond between them. When the association is strong, one is likely to conclude that the events have been frequently paired. Consequently, strong associates will be judged to have occurred together frequently. According to this view, the illusory correlation between suspiciousness and peculiar drawing of the eyes, for example, is due to the fact that suspiciousness is more readily associated with the eyes than with any other part of the body [p. 1128].

Schemas may make schema-consistent instances more available than schema-inconsistent or schema-irrelevant stimuli by making schema-consistent examples easier to imagine, or by providing a strong association between two attributes, events, or things.

Crocker and Taylor (1978) have evidence that schemas make consistent instances more available and inconsistent instances less available in the judgment of covariation. Specifically, their subjects overestimated the frequency of schema-consistent instances and underestimated the frequency of schema-inconsistent instances. Subjects also thought the degree of covariation was stronger if they assessed a schema-consistent covariation than if they assessed a schema-inconsistent covariation, although the actual correlation in the stimuli was identical (see also Hamilton & Rose, 1978; Rothbart, Evans, & Fulero, 1979).

To summarize, people are likely to overestimate the magnitude of covariations that are schema-consistent, and underestimate the magnitude of covariations that are schema-inconsistent or schema-irrelevant. Schemas may lead people to overestimate the magnitude of schema-consistent covariations because schema-consistent evidence is more likely to be brought to bear on the covariation judgment, or because schema-consistent evidence is more available, so it is over-represented in the store of evidence when the judgment is made.

Comment on the Liabilities of Schematic Processing

Most of the biases described in this section can be explained by one simple, and at least on the evidence so far considered, justifiable assumption. This assumption is that a schema, as a normative structure against which incoming data are matched, contains only evidence of what an instance should look like, *not* evidence of what it *should not* look like. So-called biases in the search process can be explained in terms of a simple matching of one structure to another. As long as some fit between a stimulus configuration and a schema is obtained, the schema can be invoked to fill in default options, thereby leading to an illusory data base, a propensity for type 1 errors, and illusory correlations. Accordingly, no motivational construct need be resorted to in order to understand the liabilities of schematic processing. These biases, rather, can have a cognitive basis.

SUMMARY, CONCLUSIONS, AND FUTURE DIRECTIONS

This chapter has been devoted to a topic of increasing interest to social psychologists: social schemas. The goal was to review and extend what is known about social schemas and determine whether there exists within the literature the basis for a theory. In the first section, we defined a schema as a cognitive structure that represents some stimulus domain. It is organized through experience; it consists of a knowledge structure (i.e. a representation of the attributes of that stimulus domain); and it also includes plans for interpreting and gathering schema-related information. It may also provide a basis for activating actual behavior sequences or expectations of specific behavior sequences, i.e., scripts for how individuals behave in social situations (Schank & Abelson, 1977).

The second section reviewed the processing functions of schemas, specifically how they help the perceiver encode and represent incoming information. Schemas for persons, roles, and events are hierarchically ordered from the lower specific and anecdotal levels to more general abstract levels. Incoming data that matches schemas seems to be similarly hierarchically structured and, in addition, is structured in ways determined by the particular class of schemas to which it belongs; these structurings include balance, linear ordering, and temporal sequence; other structuring principles may also be uncovered. Schemas affect recall as well. Schemas also influence information-processing times but not in straightforward ways; schematic material is sometimes processed faster and sometimes slower than non-schema relevant material; some suggestions regarding mediating conditions were offered.

In the third section, we considered the interpretive and inferential functions of schemas. Schemas not only lead to differences in volume and selectivity of recall, they also add information to incoming stimulus configurations. These so-called default options then become indistinguishable from the actual attributes of the configuration. The rules governing such intrustions are a promising area for further research. Schemas fulfill a normative function, constituting a basis for evaluating incoming data. They provide bases for solving problems through the use of the representativeness and availability heuristics. Schemas enable the perceiver to project into the future, plan, develop appropriate action sequences, and shape the behavior of others.

The fourth section considered the liabilities of schemas. Schemas lead to faulty inferences when the wrong schema is brought to bear on a stimulus configuration. However, even when the appropriate schema is evoked, predictable errors occur. We argued that schemas provide an illusory data base, because they provide default options for missing data; they lead to inferences that are then, themselves, treated as data; and when they are salient, they are applied relatively indiscriminately to datasets for which the match to the schema is less than perfect. This point, along with additional data, led to the hypothesis that schematic processing produces a general propensity for type 1 errors: accepting data as consistent with a schema when it is either neutral or even inconsistent. Four sources for this bias were suggested. Finally, we argued that schemas are often responsible for various errors of perceived covariation, such as illusory correlation.

Taken together, these biases have profound implications for a number of different specific content areas. Faulty, but initially plausible medical diagnoses may go unrejected, possibly leading to fatal medical errors (Elstein, Shulman, &

Sprafka, 1978). Initial beliefs of guilt or innocence can, under some circumstances, prejudice jury members (Davis, Spitzer, Nagao, & Stasser, 1980). Policy-level decision-makers may incorporate only evidence that supports their position into their decisions and fail to utilize important information favoring another alternative as a result (Janis, 1972; Janis & Mann, 1977). Scientific theories may persist long after there is enough data available to discredit them (e.g., Kuhn, 1970). Visions of one's adversary as hostile or warmongering can lead to "defensive" retaliation. (See Jervis, 1976, and DiRivera, 1968, for a discussion of these issues in domestic and foreign policy.) The study of biases due to schematic processing in areas where such biases can have severe or fatal consequences may well be one of the most important areas in which research on schemas can move, particularly if the research focus can be directed toward methods that undo or lead to resisting such errors.

We can now return to the issue posed at the outset of this paper—namely, is there the basis for a schema theory? If we employ the minimum definition of a theory as a set of interrelated hypotheses, the answer must be a qualified *yes*. Not all the hypotheses are as straightforward as one might hope and many are highly speculative; the hypotheses do not relate to each other as well as they might. Nonetheless, a body of related hypotheses does exist. However, if one asks the question, do we have a good theory of schemas, the answer is unquestionably *no*.

To begin with, the conceptual clarity is minimal. To obtain a definition that subsumes all the so-called schema literature necessitates a vagueness in the definition not tolerable in a good theory. What are some directions in which work might progress to reduce this problem? A first step in dealing with this question requires dividing up the schema-like concepts into groups of friendly, orthogonal, and somewhat incompatible concepts. We consider such concepts as frames (Minsky, 1975), schemas as used by Neisser (1976), prototypes (e.g. Cantor & Mischel, 1977), and scripts (e.g. Bower, 1977; Schank & Abelson, 1977) to be friendly concepts not incompatible with any generalizations or speculations offered here. Principles of structure like balance, temporal ordering, grouping, and linear sequencing, we consider to be largely orthogonal, crosscutting the kinds of knowledge structures with which we have been concerned. The main class of concepts that we do not consider compatible are those that posit some underlying affective significance or value basis as a precondition to their operation on incoming data, the most notable and recent such competitor being attitudes. The main point of difference between an affectively based formulation and a schematic one is that schemas are cognitive structures that do not require affect or value relevancy as preconditions for activation. It is difficult to see how a formulation based on affective significance can handle findings such as selective recall of schema-relevant material that involves boring, redundant scripts like going to a movie or shopping in the supermarket. We would argue that many kinds of predictions, judgments, and explanations are based on schematic cognitive structures, not just affectively laden ones. An affectively based model's predictive capacity simply does not extend to unvalenced situations.[5]

Second, methods for measuring schemas independent of their processing functions should be established. Some beginning efforts in this area have been developed by Markus (1977) for self-schemata, Cantor & Mischel, (1977) for prototypes, and Bower et al. (1977) for scripts. In addition, assessing what schemas actually exist within particular content domains (e.g. political schemas; see Kinder, Fiske & Wagner [1978]) merits attention.

Third, we need a clear specification of what schemas are *not* and how they differ from seemingly related structural conceptions. The first is, in part, a measurement issue. Successful discrimination of people who hold schemas from aschematics and of issues for which people have schemas from those for which people do not have schemas can help define the limits of schematic processing and identify what people are doing when they are *not* reasoning schematically. For example, are they reasoning from partial or incomplete schemas and if so, what are the attributes of that kind of processing? Are they reasoning from a temporary theory or hypothesis that is erected for the occasion and if so, how does that kind of hypothesis-driven processing differ from processing according to more enduring structures like schemas? Are they reasoning more inductively and if so, what are they getting from the raw data that schematics are not getting, and how are they getting it?

A good theory also has the quality of being internally consistent and not generating contradictory propositions. At the moment, this is not true of the schemas literature. We know, for example, that schemas sometimes decrease data processing time and sometimes increase it, but we do not yet know why. The identification of the inconsistency, however, can lead to predictions regarding when one or the other effect will occur. The main issue created by lack of internal consistency is the need to specify the conditions under which a stimulus configuration will be modified to suit the schema versus when the schema will be modified to accommodate incoming data structures. Schemas do distort reality but they do not do so indefinitely. At some point, the schema is rejected and a new schema is sought out. Under some circumstances, the schema itself changes. What are the delimiting conditions that determine this restructuring?

The third criterion of a good theory is that it fit both old and new data. The fact that schema theory fits the old data should not surprise anyone, because schema theory consists solely of the consistencies that can be abstracted from the old data! That it fits new data may stem less from validity than from an unfortunate lack of rigor—a point that leads one to the fourth criterion.

The final criterion of a good theory is that it be testable and falsifiable. This is perhaps the most devastating criterion vis-à-vis the current state of the schema's

---

[5]Obviously, however, we are not precluding affective concerns as a possible basis for developing schemas, for some schemas being more salient than others, or for some schemas being more structured than others.

literature. The concept of schema and its processing functions currently provide the basis for nothing more than demonstration studies. Though predictions can be generated by schema theory, failure to show a hypothesized effect will likely be attributed to failing to specify the right schema or measurement error, rather than a failure of the theory itself. Until the theory is formalized in a falsifiable form, its heuristic value will be greatly limited. At least two possible directions can be identified that would improve this situation. One area of focus is the determinants of what schema will be evoked by a given stimulus configuration. Are these cognitive structures evoked by dominant cues in the configuration itself, are they determined by what schemas are dominant in the mind of the perceiver, or both? Perhaps a schema is evoked when a dominant cue in a stimulus configuration is a central attribute of a predominant schema. What makes cues salient? (See Taylor & Fiske, 1978.) What conditions lead to predominance of particular schemas? This is an area that is ripe for hypotheses and empirical investigation. For example, one hypothesis is that schemas or concepts that have been recently used in an unrelated context may be more easily evoked by a stimulus configuration than if the schema has not been recently used in processing information (Wyer & Srull, Chapter 5, this volume). A second hypothesis is that affect-laden schemas may predominate over nonaffect-laden schemas so that if two schemas are equally applicable to an ambiguous stimulus configuration, the more affectively toned schema will be evoked.

An additional focus for subsequent work should be how schemas develop and change with experience. Formal specification of the developmental component of the theory may be the potentially richest direction in which to move, because it can address not only how schematic functions develop, but how schemas change as well. Are schemas abstracted from repeated interactions with examples or from particularly good examples (examplars)? Are certain predictable kinds of features acquired before others? If so, what are their defining attributes?

Kurt Lewin once said there is nothing as useful as a good theory. In the case of the schema literature, one might say that there is nothing as useful as *not* having a good theory, because the weaknesses in the theory point out the directions that future research must take. Ultimately, the set of problems outlined in this last section will prove to be the most important and difficult for any schema theory to handle. Nonetheless, they must be handled if we are going to render the term "schema" anything more than a place-holding concept for the elusive structures of the mind.

ACKNOWLEDGMENTS

This chapter was prepared for the First Ontario Symposium on Personality and Social Psychology—Social Cognition: Cognitive Structure and Processes Underlying Person Memory and Social Judgment, August, 1978. Preparation was supported by NSF Research Grant No. BNS 77–09922. We are particularly grateful for the helpful comments of Susan Fiske, Jonathan Grudin, Dave Hamilton, Don Kinder, Hazel Markus, Fred Miller,

Darren Newtson, Lee Ross, David Sears, Eliot Smith, Mike Storms, John Winkler, and Bob Wyer.

REFERENCES

Abelson, R. P. Concepts for representing mundane reality in plans. In D. G. Bobrow & A. Collins (Eds.), *Representation and understanding: Studies in cognitive science*. New York: Academic Press, 1975.

Abelson, R. P. Script processing in attitude formation and decision-making. In J. S. Carroll, & J. W. Payne (Eds.). *Cognition and social behavior*. Hillsdale, N.J.: Lawrence Erlbaum Associates, 1976.

Ajzen, I. Intuitive theories of events and the effects of base-rate information on prediction. *Journal of Personality and Social Psychology*, 1977, *35*, 303–314.

Aronson, E., & Carlsmith, J. M. Performance expectancy as determinant of actual performance. *Journal of Abnormal and Social Psychology*, 1962, *65*, 178–183.

Aronson, E., & Linder, D. Gain and loss of esteem as determinants of interpersonal attractiveness. *Journal of Experimental Social Psychology*, 1965, *1*, 156–172.

Aronson, E., & Mettee, D. R. Dishonest behaviors as a function of differential levels of induced self-esteem. *Journal of Personality and Social Psychology*, 1968, *9*, 121–127.

Baddeley, A. D. The trouble with levels: A reexamination of Craik and Lockhart's framework for memory research. *Psychological Review*, 1978, *85*, 139–152.

Bartlett, F. C. *Remembering*. Cambridge: Cambridge University Press, 1932.

Baumgardner, M. H., Leippe, M. R., & Ostrom, T. M. *The role of criterial attributes in the organization of cognitive representations*. Paper read at Midwestern Psychological Association, Chicago, May 1976.

Becker, H. S. *Outsiders: Studies in the sociology of deviance*. New York: Free Press, 1963.

Bem, D. J., & Allen, A. On predicting some of the people some of the time: The search for cross-situational consistencies in behavior. *Psychological Review*, 1974, *81*, 506–520.

Bousfield, W. A. The occurrence of clustering in the recall of randomly arranged associates. *Journal of General Psychology*, 1953, *49*, 229–240.

Bower, G. H. *On injecting life into deadly prose: Studies in explanation-seeking*. Inviting address at meeting of Western Psychological Association, Seattle, April 1977.

Bower, G. H., Black, J. B., & Turner, J. T. Scripts in text comprehension and memory. *Cognitive Psychology*, 1979, *11*, 177–220.

Bransford, J. D., & Johnson, M. K. Considerations of some problems of comprehension. In W. G. Chase (Ed.), *Visual Information Processing*. New York: Academic Press, 1973.

Bruner, J. S. On perceptual readiness. *Psychological Review*, 1957, *64*, 123–52.

Bruner, J. S. & Potter, M. C. Interference in visual recognition. *Science*, 1964, *144*, 424–425.

Cantor, N., & Mischel, W. *From personality impression to social inference: The role of preexisting knowledge in structuring information-processing*. Unpublished manuscript, Stanford University, 1978.

Cantor, N., & Mischel, W. Prototypes in person perception. In L. Berkowitz (Ed.), *Advances in experimental social psychology*. (Vol. 12). New York: Academic Press, 1979.

Cantor, N., & Mischel, W. Traits as prototypes: Effects on recognition memory. *Journal of Personality and Social Psychology*, 1977, *35*, 38–48.

Carroll, J. S. The effect of imagining an event on expectations for the event: An interpretation in terms of the availability heuristic. *Journal of Experimental Social Psychology*, 1978, *14*, 88–96.

Carroll, J. S., & Payne, J. S. The psychology of the parole decision process: A joint application of attribution theory and information-processing psychology. In J. S. Carroll, & J. S. Payne (Eds.), *Cognition and social behavior*. Hillsdale, N.J.: Lawrence Erlbaum Associates, 1976.

Chapman, L. J. Illusory correlation in observational report. *Journal of Verbal Learning and Verbal Behavior,* 1967, *6,* 151–155.

Chapman, L. J., & Chapman, J. P. Genesis of popular but erroneous psychodiagnostic observations. *Journal of Abnormal Psychology,* 1967, *72,* 193–204.

Chapman, L. J., & Chapman, J. P. Illusory correlation as an obstacle to the use of valid psychodiagnostic signs. *Journal of Abnormal Psychology,* 1969, *74,* 271–280.

Cohen, C. E. *Cognitive basis of stereotyping.* Paper presented at the American Psychological Association Annual Meeting, San Francisco, September 1977.

Collins, A. M., & Quillian, M. R. Retrieval time from semantic memory. *Journal of Verbal Learning and Verbal Behavior,* 1969, *8,* 240–247.

Cottrell, N. B., Ingraham, L. H., & Monfort, F. W. The retention of balanced and imbalanced cognitive structures. *Journal of Personality,* 1971, *39,* 112–131.

Craik, F. M., & Tulving, E. Depth of processing and the retention of words in episodic memory. *Journal of Experimental Psychology,* 1975, *104,* 268–294.

Crocker, J., & Taylor, S. E. *Theory-driven processing and the use of complex evidence.* Paper presented at the American Psychological Association Annual Meeting, Toronto, August 1978.

Davis, J. H., Spitzer, C. E., Nagao, D., & Stasser, G. The nature of bias in social decisions by individuals and groups—an example from mock juries. In Brandstatter, Davis, & Schuler (Eds.), *Dynamics of Group Decisions.* Beverly Hills, Calif.: Sage, 1980.

Delia, J. C., & Crockett, W. H. Social schemas, cognitive complexity and the learning of social structures. *Journal of Personality,* 1973, *41,* 413–429.

Dennis, N. F. *Cards of Identity.* London: Weidenfeld Nicolson, 1955.

DeSoto, C. B. The predilection for single orderings. *Journal of Abnormal and Social Psychology,* 1961, *62,* 16–23.

DeSoto, C. B. Learning a social structure. *Journal of Abnormal and Social Psychology,* 1969, *60,* 417–421.

DeSoto, C. B., & Albrecht, F. Cognition and social ordering. In R. P. Abelson, F. Aronson, T. M. Newcomb, N. S. McGuire, M. J. Rosenberg, & Tim Tannenbaum (Eds.), *Theories of cognitive consistency: A sourcebook.* Skokie, Ill.: Rand McNally, 1968. (a)

DeSoto, C. B., & Albrecht, F. Conceptual good figures. In R. P. Abelson, F. Aronson, T. M. Newcomb, W. S. McGuire, M. J. Rosenberg, & T. M. Tannenbaum (Eds.), *Theories of cognitive consistency: A sourcebook.* Skokie, Ill.: Rand-McNally, 1968. (b)

DeSoto, C. B., Henley, N. M., & London, M. Balance and the grouping schema. *Journal of Personality and Social Psychology,* 1968, *8,* 1–7.

Deutsch, M., & Krauss, R. M. *Theories in social psychology.* New York: Basic Books, 1965.

DiRivera, J. H. *The psychological dimension of foreign policy.* Columbus: Merill, 1968.

Dooling, D. J., & Mullet, R. L. Locus of thematic effects in retention of prose. *Journal of Experimental Psychology,* 1973, *97,* 404–406.

Elstein, A. S., Shulman, L. S., & Sprafka, S. A. *Medical problem solving: An analysis of clinical reasoning.* Cambridge: Harvard University Press, 1978.

Fischoff, B. Attribution theory and judgment under uncertainty. In J. H. Harvey, W. J. Ickes, & R. F. Kidd (Eds.), *New directions in attribution research.* Hillsdale, N.J.: Lawrence Erlbaum Associates, 1976.

Fiske, S. T., & Kinder, D. R. *Schemas and political information processing.* Paper presented at the American Psychological Association Meeting, Toronto, August 1978.

Frederiksen, C. H. Representing logical and semantic structure of knowledge acquired from discourse. *Cognitive Psychology,* 1975, *7,* 371–458.

Garland, H., Hardy, A., & Stephenson, L. Information search as affected by attribution type and response category. *Personality and Social Psychology Bulletin,* 1975, *1,* 612–615.

Geva, N., Lingle, J. H., Ostrom, T. M., Leippe, M. R., & Baumgardner, M. H. *Information processing in social cognition: Thematic effects of person judgments on impression organization.* Unpublished manuscript, Ohio State University, 1978.

Goffman, E. *Stigma*. Englewood Cliffs, N.J.: Prentice-Hall, 1963.

Greenwald, A. G. Cognitive learning, cognitive response to persuasion, and attitude change. In A. Greenwald, T. Brock, & T. Ostrom (Eds.), *Psychological foundations of attitudes*. New York: Academic Press, 1968.

Hamilton, D. L., Katz, L. B., & Leirer, V. O. Organizational processes in impression formation. In R. Hastie, T. Ostrom, E. Ebbeson, R. Wyer, Jr., D. Hamilton, & D. Carlston (Eds.), *Person memory: The cognitive basis of social perception*. Hillsdale, N.J.: Lawrence Erlbaum Associates, 1980.

Hamilton, D. L., & Rose, T. R. *Illusory correlation and the maintenance of stereotypic beliefs*. Unpublished manuscript. University of California at Santa Barbara, 1978.

Hastie, R., & Anderson, C. *Recall of schema consistent and schema inconsistent material*. Research in progress.

Hastie, R., & Kumar, P. A. Person memory: Personality traits as organizing principles in memory for behaviors. *Journal of Personality and Social Psychology*, 1979, *37*, 25–38.

Hastorf, A. H., Schneider, D. J., & Polefka, J. *Person Perception*. Reading, Mass.: Addison-Wesley, 1970.

Henley, N. M., Horsfall, R., & DeSoto, C. B. Goodness of figure and social structure. *Psychological Review*, 1969, *76*, 194–204.

Higgins, E. T., & Rholes, W. S. Impression formation and role fulfillment: A "holistic reference" approach. *Journal of Experimental Social Psychology*, 1976, *12*, 422–435.

Innes, M. *What happened at Hazlewood*. New York: Penguin Books, 1946/1977.

Janis, I. L. *Victims of groupthink*. Boston: Houghton-Mifflin, 1972.

Janis, I. L., & Mann, L. *Decision making*. New York: The Free Press, 1977.

Jenkins, H. M., & Ward, W. C. Judgment of contingency between responses and outcomes. *Psychological Monographs*, 1965, *79* (1, Whole No. 594).

Jennings, D. L., Amabile, T., & Ross, L. The intuitive scientists's assessment of covariation: Data-based vs. theory-based judgments. In A. Tversky, D. Kahneman, & P. Slovic (Eds.), *Judgment under uncertainty: Heuristics and biases*. Book in preparation, 1980.

Jervis, R. *Perception and misperception in international politics*. Princeton, N.J.: Princeton University Press, 1976.

Jones, E. E., & Harris, V. A. The attribution of attitudes. *Journal of Experimental Social Psychology*, 1967, *3*, 1–24.

Kahneman, D., & Tversky, A. On the psychology of prediction. *Psychological Review*, 1973, *80*, 237–251.

Kearns, D. *Lyndon Johnson and the American dream*. New York: Harper & Row, Publishers, 1976.

Kelley, H. H. Causal schemata and the attribution process. In E. E. Jones, D. E. Kanouse, H. H. Kelley, R. E. Nisbett, S. Valins, & B. Weiner, (Eds.), *Attribution: Perceiving the causes of behavior*. Morristown, N.J.: General Learning Press, 1972.

Kinder, D. R., Fiske, S. T., & Wagner, R. G. *Social psychological perspectives on political leadership*. Unpublished manuscript, Yale University, 1978.

Kuethe, J. L. Social schemas. *Journal of Abnormal and Social Psychology*, 1962, *64*, 31–38.

Kuethe, J. L. Pervasive influence of social schemata. *Journal of Abnormal and Social Psychology*, 1964, *68*, 248–254.

Kuhn T. S. *The structure of scientific revolutions*. Chicago: University of Chicago Press, 1970.

Langer, E. J., & Abelson, R. P. A patient by any other name . . . : Clinician group difference in labeling bias. *Journal of Consulting and Clinical Psychology*, 1974, *42*, 4–9.

Lawler, E. *Motivation in work organizations*. Belmont, Calif.: Brooks-Cole, 1973.

Lingle, J. H., & Ostrom, T. M. *Principles of memory and cognition in attitude formation*. Unpublished manuscript, Ohio State University, 1977.

Little, K. B. Personal space. *Journal of Experimental Social Psychology*, 1964, *1*, 237–247.

Loftus, E. F., & Palmer, J. C. Reconstruction of automobile destruction: An example of the interaction between language and memory. *Journal of Verbal Learning and Verbal Behavior*, 1974, *13*, 585–589.

Mandler, J. M., & Johnson, N. S. Remembrance of things passed: Story structure and recall. *Cognitive Psychology*, 1977, *9*, 111–151.

Markus, H. Self-schemata and processing information about the self. *Journal of Personality and Social Psychology*, 1977, *35*, 63–78.

Markus, H. *Social schemas: Cognitive representations of social reality*. Unpublished manuscript, University of Michigan, 1974.

Markus, H., Sentis, K., & Hamill, R. *On thinking you are fat: Consequences for information processing*. Paper presented at the American Psychological Association Meeting, Toronto, August 1978.

Martin, J. *When prosperity fails: Distributional determinants of the perception of justice*. Unpublished doctoral dissertation, Harvard University, 1977.

Mettee, D. R., Taylor, S. E., & Freedman, H. Affect conversion and the gain-loss effect. *Sociometry*, 1973, *36*, 494–513.

Miller, G. A., Galanter, E., & Pribram, K. H. *Plans and the structure of behavior*. New York: Holt, Rinehart & Winston, 1960.

Minsky, M. A framework for representing knowledge. In P. H. Winston (Ed.), *The psychology of computer vision*. New York: McGraw-Hill, 1975.

Mitchell, T. R. Expectancy models of job satisfaction, occupational preference and effort: A theoretical methodological and empirical appraisal. *Psychological Bulletin*, 1974, *81*, 1053–1077.

Neisser, V. *Cognition and reality: Principles and implications of cognitive psychology*. San Francisco: Freeman, 1976.

Nisbett, R. E., & Ross, L. *Human inference: Strategies and shortcomings in social judgment*. Englewood Cliffs, N.J.: Prentice-Hall, 1979.

Owens, J., Bower, G. H., & Black, J. B. *The "soap opera" effect in story recall*. Unpublished manuscript. Stanford University, 1977.

Pettigrew, T. Social evaluation theory: Convergences and applications. *Nebraska Symposium on Motivation, 1967*. Lincoln: University of Nebraska Press, 1967.

Picek, J. S., Sherman, S. J., & Shiffrin, R. M. Cognitive organization and coding of social structures. *Journal of Personality and Social Psychology*, 1975, *31*, 758–768.

Poitou, J. P. Status congruence as a cognitive bias. *Journal of Personality and Social Psychology*, 1970, *16*, 592–597.

Potts, G. R. Information processing strategies used in the encoding of linear orderings. *Journal of Verbal Learning and Verbal Behavior*, 1972, *11*, 727–740.

Press, A. N., Crockett, W. H., & Rosenkrantz, P. S. Cognitive complexity and the learning of balanced and unbalanced social structures. *Journal of Personality*, 1969, *37*, 541–553.

Rabbie, J. M., & Horwitz, M. Arousal of ingroup–outgroup bias by a chance win or loss. *Journal of Personality and Social Psychology*, 1969, *13*, 269–277.

Radloff, R. Social comparison and ability evaluation. *Journal of Experimental Social Psychology*, 1966, (1), 6–26. (Supplement)

Rholes, W. S. *The influence of availability on causal attribution*. Paper presented at Eastern Psychological Association, Boston, April 1977.

Rogers, T. B., Kuiper, N. A., & Kirker, W. S. Self-reference and the encoding of personal information. *Journal of Personality and Social Psychology*, 1977, *35*, 677–688.

Rosch, E., Mervis, C. B., Gray, W. D., Johnson, D. M., & Boyes-Braem, P. Basic objects in natural categories. *Cognitive Psychology*, 1976, *8*, 382–439.

Rosenthal, R., & Jacobson, L. *Pygmalion in the classroom: Teacher expectation and pupils' intellectual development*. New York: Holt, Rinehart & Winston, 1968.

Ross, L. The intuitive psychologist and his shortcomings: Distortions in the attribution process. In L. Berkowitz (Ed.), *Advances in experimental social psychology* (Vol. 10). New York: Academic Press, 1977, 174–221.

Ross, L. Some afterthoughts on the intuitive psychologist. *Cognitive Theories in Social Psychology.* New York: Academic Press, 1978.

Ross, L. D., Amabile, T. M., & Steinmetz, J. L. Social roles, social control, and biases in social-perception processes. *Journal of Personality and Social Psychology,* 1977, *35,* 485–494.

Ross, L., Lepper, M., & Hubbard, M. Perseverance in self perception and social perception: Biased attributional processes in the debriefing paradigm. *Journal of Personality and Social Psychology,* 1975, *32,* 880–892.

Ross, L., Lepper, M. R., Strack, F., & Steinmetz, J. Social explanation and social expectation: Effects of real and hypothetical explanations on subjective likelihood. *Journal of Personality and Social Psychology,* 1977, *35,* 817–829.

Rothbart, M., Evans, M., and Fulero, S. Recall for confirming events: Memory processes and the maintenance of social stereotypes. *Journal of Experimental Social Psychology,* 1979, *4,* 343–355.

Rumelhart, D. E. Notes on a schema for stories. In D. G. Bobrow, & A. Collins, (Eds.), *Representation and understanding: Studies in cognitive science.* New York: Academic Press, 1975.

Sagan, C. *The dragons of Eden.* New York: Ballantine, 1977.

Schank, R. C. *Conceptual information processing.* Amsterdam: North-Holland, 1975 (a).

Schank, R. C. The structure of episodes in memory. In D. G. Bobrow, & A. Collins, (Eds.), *Representation and understanding: Studies in cognitive science.* New York: Academic Press, 1975 (b).

Schank, R., & Abelson, R. *Scripts, plans, goals and understanding: An inquiry into human knowledge structures.* Hillsdale, N.J.: Lawrence Erlbaum Associates, 1977.

Scheff, T. J. *Being mentally ill: A sociological theory.* Chicago: Aldine Publishing Company, 1966.

Schneider, W., & Shiffrin, R. M. Controlled and automatic human information processing: I. Detection, search, and attention. *Psychological Review,* 1977, *84,* 1–66.

Schur, E. M. *Labeling deviant behavior: Its sociological implications.* New York: Harper & Row, 1971.

Sears, D. O., & McConahay, J. B. *The politics of violence: The new urban blacks and the Watts riot.* Boston: Houghton-Mifflin, 1973.

Shaw, M. E., & Costanzo, P. R. *Theories of social psychology.* New York: McGraw-Hill, 1970.

Slovic, P., & Lichtenstein, S. Comparison of Bayesian and regression approaches to the study of human information processing in judgment. *Organizational Behavior and Human Performance,* 1971, *6,* 649–744.

Smedslund, J. The concept of correlation in adults. *Scandinavian Journal of Psychology,* 1963, *4,* 165–173.

Snyder, M. *When believing means doing: A cognitive social psychology of action.* Paper presented at the American Psychological Association Annual Meeting, San Francisco, September 1977.

Snyder, M., & Swann, W. B., Jr. When actions reflect attitudes: The politics of impression management. *Journal of Personality and Social Psychology,* 1976, *34,* 1034–1042.

Snyder, M., & Swann, W. B., Jr. Hypothesis testing processes in social interaction. *Journal of Personality and Social Psychology,* 1978, *36,* 1202–1212.

Snyder, M., Tanke, E. D., & Berscheid, E. Social perception and interpersonal behavior: On the self-fulfilling nature of social stereotypes. *Journal of Personality and Social Psychology,* 1977, *35,* 656–666.

Snyder, M., & Uranowitz, S. W. Reconstructing the past: Some cognitive consequences of person perception. *Journal of Personality and Social Psychology,* 1978, *36,* 941–950.

Sorrentino, R. M., & Short, J. C. The case of the mysterious moderates: Why motives sometimes fail to predict behavior. *Journal of Personality and Social Psychology,* 1977, *35,* 478–484.

Spiro, R. J. Remembering information from text: The "State of Schema" approach. In R. C. Anderson, R. J. Spiro, & W. E. Montague (Eds.), *Schooling and the acquisition of knowledge.* Hillsdale, N.J.: Lawrence Erlbaum Associates, 1977.

Sulin, R. A., & Dooling, D. J. Intrusion of thematic ideas in retention of prose. *Journal of Experimental Psychology*, 1974, *103*, 255–262.

Taylor, S. E. The availability bias in social psychology. In A. Tversky, D. Kahneman, & P. Slovic (Eds.), *Judgment under uncertainty: Heuristics and biases*. Book in preparation, 1980.

Taylor, S. E. Cognitive and contextual factors in the imputation of stereotypes. To appear in D. L. Hamilton (Ed.), *Cognitive bases of stereotyping*. Hillsdale, N.J.: Lawrence Erlbaum Associates, in press.

Taylor, S. E., & Crocker, J. *The processing of context information perception*. Manuscript submitted for publication, 1978.

Taylor, S. E., Crocker, J., & D'Agostino, J. Schematic bases of social problem solving. *Personality and Social Psychology Bulletin*, 1978, *4*, 447–451.

Taylor, S. E., & Fiske, S. T. Salience, attention, and attribution: Top of the head phenomena. In L. Berkowitz (Ed.), *Advances in experimental social psychology* (Vol. 11). New York: Academic Press, 1978.

Taylor, S. E., Fiske, S. T., Etcoff, N., & Ruderman, A. The categorical and contextual bases of person memory and stereotyping. *Journal of Personality and Social Psychology*, 1978, *36*, 778–793.

Taylor, S. E., Livingston, J., & Crocker, J. *The impact of schemas in prediction and reference*. Research in progress.

Tesser, A. Self-generated attitude change. In L. Berkowitz (Ed.), *Advances in experimental social psychology* (Vol. 11). New York: Academic Press, 1978.

Tesser, A., & Leone, C. Cognitive schemas and thought as determinants of attitude change. *Journal of Experimental Psychology*, 1977, *13*, 340–356.

Thompson, W. C., Reyes, R. M., & Bower, G. H. *Delayed effects of availability on judgment*. Paper presented at the annual meeting of the American Psychological Association, Toronto, August 1978.

Thorndyke, P. W. Cognitive structures in comprehension and memory of narrative discourse. *Cognitive Psychology*, 1977, *9*, 77–110.

Trope, Y. Inferences of personal characteristics on the basis of information retrieved from one's memory. *Journal of Personality and Social Psychology*, 1978, *36*, 93–106.

Tversky, A. Features of similarity. *Psychological Review*, 1977, *84*, 327–352.

Tversky, A., & Kahneman, D. Availability: A heuristic for judging frequency and probability. *Cognitive Psychology*, 1973, *5*, 207–232.

Tversky, A., & Kahneman, D. Judgment under uncertainty: Heuristics and biases. *Science*, 1974, *185*, 1124–1131.

Tversky, A., & Kahneman, D. Causal schemata in judgments under uncertainty. In M. Fishbein (Ed.), *Progress in social psychology*. Hillsdale, N.J.: Lawrence Erlbaum Associates, 1977.

Van Kreveld, D., & Zajonc, R. B. The learning of influence structures. *Journal of Personality*, 1966, *34*, 205–223.

Ward, W., & Jenkins, H. The display of information and the judgment of contingency. *Canadian Journal of Psychology*, 1965, *19*, 231–241.

Woll, S., & Yopp, H. The role of context and inference in the comprehension of social action. *Journal of Experimental Social Psychology*, 1978, *14*, 351–362.

Word, C. O., Zanna, M. P., & Cooper, J. The nonverbal mediation of self-fulfilling prophecies in interracial interaction. *Journal of Experimental Social Psychology*, 1974, *10*, 109–120.

Wyatt, D. F., & Campbell, D. T. On the liability of stereotype or hypothesis. *Journal of Abnormal and Social Psychology*, 1951, *46*, 496–500.

Zadny, J., & Gerard, H. B. Attributed intentions and informational selectivity. *Journal of Experimental Social Psychology*, 1974, *10*, 34–52.

Zajonc, R. B. Cognitive theories of social behavior. In G. Lindzey & E. Aronson (Eds.), *Handbook of social psychology* (Rev. ed.). Reading, Mass.: Addison-Wesley, 1968.

Zajonc, R. B., & Burnstein, E. The learning of balanced and unbalanced social structures. *Journal of Personality,* 1965, *33,* 153–163 (a).

Zajonc, R. B., & Burnstein, E. Structural balance, reciprocity, and positivity as sources of cognitive bias. *Journal of Personality,* 1965, *33,* 570–583 (b).

Zanna, M. P., & Pack, S. J. On the self-fulfilling nature of apparent sex differences in behavior. *Journal of Experimental Social Psychology,* 1975, *11,* 583–591.

4 Cognitive Representations of Persons

David L. Hamilton
University of California, Santa Barbara

For the last two decades, the study of person perception has been almost indistinguishable from the study of judgment processes. In particular, the focus of research during this period has been on the problem of how a perceiver integrates and combines several disparate pieces of information about a target person into a single judgment of that person.

This emphasis can be seen in several research areas concerned with person perception. It is clearly evident, for example, in research on clinical judgment. During the 1950s the primary concern of research on this topic was with the accuracy of clinical diagnoses. Beginning with Hoffman's (1960) influential paper on the "paramorphic representation" of the judgment process, research on clinical judgment shifted in the 1960s to an interest in how the clinician uses and combines the information available in the process of making a diagnostic judgment (cf. Goldberg, 1968; Hammond, Hursch, & Todd, 1964; Hoffman, Slovic, & Rorer, 1968; Slovic & Lichtenstein, 1971). A parallel trend can be seen in research on impression formation. Through the influence of Anderson (e.g., 1962, 1968) and others, the study of impression formation during this period became equivalent to the study of information integration in the judgment process. A third illustration of this trend is found in the literature on attribution processes. Stimulated by attribution models proposed by Jones and Davis (1965), Kelley (1967), Weiner, Frieze, Kukla, Reed, Rest, and Rosenbaum (1972), and others, this research has focused on how perceivers combine different kinds of information in making judgments of causality. The similarities among these different lines of research in the issues they have explored has been noted by several authors (e.g., Anderson, 1972, 1974a; Fischoff, 1976; Slovic & Lichtenstein, 1971). In each of these areas of person perception research, the

135

primary concern has been with the combinatory process through which several distinct items of information are integrated as the perceiver makes a single judgment regarding a target person.

It is obvious that the judgment process is an important component of person perception, and the voluminous literature that has accumulated during the last 20 years regarding the topics noted previously attests to both the complexity and the pervasiveness of that process. Certainly we have learned a great deal about how relatively simple quantitative models can rather effectively account for the data obtained in these studies (e.g., Anderson, 1974a, 1974b; Dawes & Corrigan, 1974; Fischoff, 1976; Goldberg, 1968), about the relative importance of various kinds of information and how they are differentially weighted in perceivers' judgments, and about the nature of perceiver biases in the judgment process (e.g., Chapman & Chapman, 1967, 1969; Kanouse & Hanson, 1972; McArthur, 1972; Nisbett, Borgida, Crandall, & Reed, 1976; Ross, 1977). It is not clear to me, however, that our research efforts should be so singularly focused on the judgment process. We may, it seems, have been overly optimistic about the extent to which we could understand person perception through an analysis of the integration process.

In this paper, I argue that a social-cognitive perspective on the person perception process can be quite useful in pointing out some aspects of this process that, for the most part, have been ignored and that need to be studied. In the next section, I briefly discuss how a social cognition approach can broaden the range of issues and processes investigated in this research area. I then describe some findings from my own research program, which grows out of this orientation.

SOME THOUGHTS ON A SOCIAL COGNITION APPROACH TO PERSON PERCEPTION

A social cognition approach to person perception would include consideration of all factors influencing the acquisition, representation, and retrieval of person information, as well as the relationship of these processes to judgments made by the perceiver. Many of the topics and issues that would be incorporated under this umbrella have been addressed by person perception researchers in the past. What is "new" in the current approach is the direct investigation of the cognitive structures and processes underlying person perception, often using experimental techniques borrowed from cognitive psychology. Approaching person perception from this perspective can, I believe, shed new light on some issues that have been of interest for a long time. That this has already begun to occur is well documented in the chapters comprising this volume.

In order to illustrate how a social cognition approach might broaden our understanding of person perception, I consider three topics where I believe such an approach would be beneficial. These topics are: first, how the nature of the perceiver's cognitive structure influences the acquisition and processing of information about the target person(s); second, how the perceiver develops, on the basis of the information available and the existing cognitive framework, a cognitive representation of the target person (or group), which is then stored in memory; and third, how information contained in that cognitive representation is retrieved from memory and used as a basis for making interpersonal judgments.

Consider first the influence of the perceiver's cognitive structure on the processing of information about others. The notion that characteristics of the perceiver might influence his or her interpersonal perceptions certainly is not new (Bruner & Taguiri, 1954) and has been recognized at least implicitly in each of the research literatures I referred to earlier. For example, the perceiver forming an impression of a stranger has well-developed expectancies about the nature of personality and what the presence of certain attributes implies about the person. Similarly, the clinician interpreting diagnostic test material in all likelihood construes those data within his preferred theoretical framework. Finally, the person making causal attributions does so within the context of his naive theories of causality. Thus the assumption that the perceiver's cognitive structure is an important component in person perception is widespread and has a long history.

In addition, there is a large research literature relevant to this question, for the study of implicit personality theories has been concerned specifically with such structures. As Schneider (1973) notes, however, the primary goal of most of this research has been to identify the dimensions underlying a subject's judgments of, say, trait co-occurrences. The major focus has been on the *assessment* of cognitive structures, attempting to determine the number and nature of the dimensions comprising implicit personality theories. In contrast, the influence of these dimensions on subsequent processing of information about others has received relatively little attention and has been assumed more than it has been investigated. Thus the study of implicit personality theories has been more concerned with the development of techniques for measuring one's cognitive structure than with investigating the effect of that structure on cognitive processing. One consequence of this orientation, I believe, is that the implicit personality theory literature has remained somewhat isolated from other research in person perception.

Recently, however, a considerable amount of research in social cognition has been addressed directly to the question of how cognitive structures influence the processing of information. I am, of course, referring to research on how social schemas govern the encoding, organization, and retention of information in a social context. Taylor and Crocker (Chapter 3, this volume) have provided an extensive review of this research, and it need not be reiterated here. For purposes of the present discussion, I would only point out that this research is focusing explicitly on what the implicit personality theory literature has always failed to adequately address, namely, the functional consequences of such structures for subsequent information processing. Hence, we now have the opportunity to bridge the gap between cognitive structure and information processing, between implicit personality theory and the impression formation process.

A second illustration concerns the question of how a perceiver forms a cognitive representation of a target person or group of persons. Again, the question is not new. Asch (1946), for example, was primarily concerned with this issue, and he attached great importance to it:

> This remarkable capacity we possess to understand something of the character of another person, to form a conception of him as a human being, as a center of life and striving, with particular characteristics forming a distinct individuality, is a precondition of social life. In what manner are these impressions established [p. 258]?

And again, "To know a person is to have a grasp of a particular structure (Asch, 1946, p. 283)."

Despite the abundant literature on impression formation, we still know relatively little about the nature of one's cognitive representations of others and how they develop. When the question is reformulated in terms of underlying cognitive processes, it becomes more amenable to empirical investigation. As the perceiver receives more and more information about another person, some of that information will be encoded and some of it will not. Some of what gets encoded will be retained and some of it will not. The incoming information will be processed in terms of the relevant schemas, which in turn will further influence the retention and organization of that information. The schematic structure will also be the basis for inferences the perceiver will make about the target person that go beyond the actual information available. What we have, then, is a complex interaction of stimulus information, cognitive structure, and cognitive processing that combine to generate a conception of the target person. It is this cognitive representation of the person that we refer to when we speak of an "impression" of another person.

There has been relatively little research investigating the nature of these cognitive representations in the context of social perception. Because much of the research I want to describe in this paper is concerned with this question, I will defer discussion and speculation about this topic until later sections.

A third area in which a social cognition approach to person perception raises new questions concerns the judgment process. As noted earlier, the vast majority of person perception studies in recent years have dealt in one way or another with the judgment process. However, the social cognition perspective adopted here indicates some additional issues that have not been investigated in this literature. Two examples are considered briefly here to illustrate this point.

The first issue concerns the information on which judgments of others are based. If one accepts the general process I have just described, that is, encoding and organization of stimulus information in terms of a schematic structure, resulting in a cognitive representation of the target person, then it seems plausible that at least under some conditions, subsequent judgments made about that person will be based on the perceiver's cognitive representation and not on the stimulus information per se. Again, this is not a terribly novel idea, but it has received little research attention. One reason for this neglect is that the experimental paradigms we have used have, in effect, been designed to minimize the role of the processes I have described and to maximize the influence of stimulus information. For example, the stimulus materials on which judgments are to be based—trait words in the impression formation literature, or MMPI profiles in the clinical judgment research—do not have the ambiguity of meaning or the potential for alternative interpretation that is characteristic of many real-life person perception contexts. In addition, the subject's judgments are typically made immediately after the stimulus descriptions have been presented. Both of these characteristics of the typical person perception experiment would increase the extent to which the subject's response is determined by the stimulus information at hand. In contrast, there are many person perception contexts in which the information available about a person is ambiguous or its meaning is unclear, and/or the perceiver is asked to make judgments of the person some period of time after the information has been received. Under these conditions one would expect that the impact of schema-based processing would be more noticeable, and that with the passage of time the distinction between what is known to be true and what is assumed to be true of the person would become increasingly fuzzy. In making interpersonal judgments under such circumstances, the perceiver would be relying heavily on his impression or cognitive representation of the person, and not simply on what he could remember of the factual information known about the person.

A second issue regarding the judgment process concerns what happens after the judgment has been made. After some judgment, attribution, diagnosis, etc., has been made by a perceiver, it seems likely that the judgment itself would become incorporated into the perceiver's conception of the target person. Thus, what originally was an inference or judgment by the perceiver can become a part of the cognitive representation on which subsequent judgments about the person will be based. Because our experimental procedures usually terminate as soon as the subject has made a judgment of the stimulus person, there has been very little opportunity to investigate sequential influences in the judgment process. Recent developments in social cognition provide the means for examining this process.

We still do not have a very good understanding of the relationship between cognitive representations and the judgment process, but the broader perspective on person perception afforded by the present approach provides the potential for greatly increasing our understanding of this and several other issues. Indeed, progress has already been made with regard to both of the issues just cited (e.g., Jaccard & Fishbein, 1975; Ostrom, Lingle, Pryor, & Geva, 1980; Wyer & Srull, Chapter 5, this volume). Of course, much remains to be done in unraveling the complexities of the processes referred to in this section. Nevertheless, I am encouraged that recent developments in social cognition, including the borrowing of techniques and methodologies from cognitive psychology and applying them to the analysis of social psychological phenomena, will permit direct investigation of many of the processes involved in person perception in ways that have not been possible before.

ORGANIZATION PROCESSES
IN THE DEVELOPMENT OF
COGNITIVE REPRESENTATIONS OF PERSONS

For the last few years my students and I have been studying processes influencing the development of cognitive representations of persons. Therefore, our work has focused on factors involved in the acquisition, organization, and representation of information received by a perceiver regarding target persons or groups. Some of this research, growing out of an interest in stereotyping, has been concerned with cognitive processing biases that can result in and maintain inaccurate representations of social groups. These studies are discussed at length elsewhere (Hamilton, 1976, 1979; Hamilton & Gifford, 1976; Hamilton & Rose, 1980) and are not reviewed here. In this paper, I want to present an overview of a series of experiments concerned with organizational processes in impression formation. A more complete description of this research program is reported in Hamilton, Katz, and Leirer (1980b).

Because the bulk of impression formation research has been concerned with quantitative models of information integration, the literature is almost devoid of theoretical discussions of the processes involved in the development of an overall impression of another person. The single major exception to this statement, of course, is Asch's (1946) classic paper. Although the general tenor of Asch's presentation is appealing, his discussions of underlying processes are somewhat vague and imprecise. Our research therefore began with our own intuitive assumptions about some of the cognitive processes involved in the acquisition and organization of information about another person. In the following paragraphs our initial thinking on this topic is presented as an introduction to our research program. I then summarize the findings we have obtained in a series of experiments, after which I offer some suggestions for a more systematic framework for understanding these processes.

We conceived of impression development as a process of integrating and organizing successively received information about a target person into a coherent cognitive representation of him or her. We assumed that the perceiver seeks coherence and organization in an impression and that, therefore, the perceiver assumes all items of information characterizing the person should "make sense" in relation to each other. This implies that the perceiver will attempt to relate each new piece of information to other information already acquired, as well as to the emerging cognitive representation of the person. The result of such a process would be a network of associations among the individual items of information as they are stored in memory. Moreover, such a network of interitem associations would presumably facilitate later recall of the information. Thus our initial assumptions were that impressions tend to be highly organized, that in achieving this organization the perceiver develops a network of associations among items of information known about the person, and that this characteristic of the resulting cognitive representation would facilitate recall of the descriptive information.

In contrast to the foregoing process, consider the typical memory study and the cognitive processes that may transpire in it. This also is a task in which the subject is actively acquiring information for a specific purpose, but in a memory experiment the task demands do not require that the subject develop a coherent structure in which all of the items can be organized. Thus, although interitem associations may be developed to some degree, depending on the mnemonic strategy used by the subject, a major feature differentiating these two contexts would seemingly be the extent to which organizational activity is inherent in the task demands placed on the subject. Consequently, we considered the procedures typically used in memory experiments to constitute a useful comparison condition. Based on the assumption that an organized network of interitem associations would facilitate retrieval of information from memory, our first prediction was that subjects instructed to form an impression of a person described by a series of items would be able to recall more of those items than would subjects, believing they were in a memory experiment, who were instructed to try to remember as many of the stimulus items as possible.

The findings that I will be reporting come from a series of experiments we have completed thus far (reported in Hamilton, Katz, & Leirer, 1980a; Hamilton, Leirer, & Katz, 1979; Hamilton & Lim, 1979). Because these studies have all used the same basic paradigm, I will describe our procedures at the outset. Although a number of manipulations have been included in the designs of these experiments, the hypothesis that subjects given impression formation instructions would evidence higher recall performance than subjects given memory instructions was tested in each of them.

Our procedures are fairly simple and straightforward. College student subjects, usually run in groups of five or so, come to the laboratory for an experiment ambiguously advertised as being concerned with "cognitive processes." Two groups of subjects are created by a manipulation of the instructions given to them. One group is told that the experiment is concerned with impression formation. It is explained that they will read a series of sentences describing a person and that they are to form an impression of that person on the basis of those descriptions. The other group is told that the experiment is concerned with memory for descriptions of action, that they will be shown a series of sentences describing behavioral acts, and that they should try to remember as many of them as they can. A series of sentence predicates, usually 15 or so in number, is presented to the subjects, one sentence at a time. Each of these sentence predicates describes one behavior or behavior pattern, such as the following: "rented an apartment near where he works"; "went to a movie with friends Saturday night"; "tries to keep informed on current events." After subjects have read the set of stimulus sentences, a brief filler task is given to eliminate short-term memory effects. This is followed by the major dependent variable of interest, free recall, which is assessed by asking subjects to write down as many of the sentences as they can remember.

Two additional aspects of the procedure should be noted. First, the stimulus items are presented in random order. Thus, the stimulus sequence does not have any obvious structure to it; it is not comparable to reading a coherent paragraph one sentence at a time. Second, although a subsequent recall task may be implied by the memory instructions, subjects in the Impression Formation condition had no indication that they would be asked to recall the stimulus items.

In all of these experiments we have found strong evidence that subjects in the Impression Formation condition recalled more of the stimulus items than subjects in the Memory condition. Figure 4.1 presents the results of seven separate tests of this hypothesis, obtained in five different experiments. In each of the comparisons shown in Fig. 4.1, samples of subjects given either impression formation or

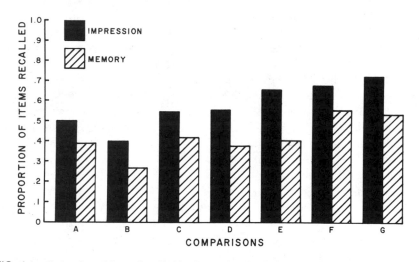

FIG. 4.1.   Proportion of Items Recalled by Impression Formation and Memory Groups in Seven Different Comparisons. Note: Comparisons A, B, and C are from Experiments 1, 2, and 3, respectively, of Hamilton, Katz, and Leirer (1980a). Comparison D is from the One Presentation condition of Hamilton, Leirer, and Katz (1979). Comparisons E, F, and G are based on the first trial recall performance of subjects in three conditions of Hamilton and Lim (1979) in which the stimulus items were behavior descriptions, trait words, and both behaviors and traits, respectively.

memory instructions were given one presentation of a series of items, after which the free recall measure was obtained. The proportion of items recalled by each group in shown in the figure. In each case this effect was quite strong and statistically significant. This difference has occurred consistently across several conditions and stimulus sets, and in one study in which the nature of the stimulus items was varied, it occurred regardless of whether the stimuli were behavior descriptions, trait attributes, or a combination of the two. Thus we feel confident that this finding is reliable.

These results, then, provide strong support for our first hypothesis and are consistent with our view that an inherent aspect of the impression formation process is the organization of the descriptive information into a coherent structure. However, this evidence does not provide any indication of how our subjects were organizing the information, and in fact, we can only infer differences in organization from the obtained differences in recall performance. Obviously, it would be desirable to have a means of more directly tapping into the organization process itself.

Intuitively it seems plausible that an impression would be organized into certain content themes based on the information known about the person, and that in achieving this organization the perceiver would use various person-relevant schemas. That is, we might assume that a perceiver would have one schema for storing information about a person's abilities and accomplishments, other schemas for processing information about social or interpersonal qualities, interests, physical appearance, and so forth. Information obtained about a person might then be organized and stored separately in terms of these categories. Organization of the information in this way would be useful and presumably would facilitate later retrieval of the information from memory, and hence may explain the superior recall performance of the Impression Formation, as compared to the Memory condition subjects in our experiments.

In order to evaluate this hypothesis, we have used a technique known in the memory literature as the analysis of clustering in free recall. In this technique, the experimenter constructs a sequence of stimulus items containing several instances of each of several a priori categories. For example, a typical memory study of this sort might have a stimulus list consisting of nouns referring to several different kinds of birds, musical instruments, countries, and pieces of furniture. These items are presented in a random order, and one then determines the extent to which the items are grouped or clustered into these categories in the subject's free recall protocol. To the extent that such clustering is present, the subject has organized and stored the stimulus items in terms of those categories.

In our experiments using this clustering paradigm, the stimulus items have been behavior descriptions representing different categories of personality content such as those mentioned earlier, for example, abilities, interpersonal characteristics, and interests. In the first of these studies (Hamilton, Leirer, & Katz, 1979) we presented, in scrambled order, four such items from each of four categories. Half of the subjects were given instructions to form an impression of a person described by the items, whereas the other half were told it was a memory experiment and they were to try to remember as many of the items as they could. For half of the subjects in each of these groups the stimulus set was shown once and for half of them it was shown twice before the free recall task was administered. This manipulation was included for the following reason. Clustering indices tend to be moderately correlated with the length of the recall list, and we knew from previous studies that following one presentation of the stimulus series subjects in the Impression condition recall more than those in the Memory group. It could be, then, that differences in clustering would be confounded with differences in recall performance. We anticipated that with a second presentation of the stimulus list the recall performance in the Memory condition would improve and approach that of subjects in the Impression condition. If so, then in that case any differences in clustering could not be due simply to differences in the length of the recall list. This is, in fact, exactly what we found, as shown in Fig. 4.2. On free recall, the impression and memory groups differed significantly if they saw the stimulus series once, but not if two presentations were given. However, on the clustering measure (Bousfield & Bousfield, 1966) subjects in the impression condition had significantly higher scores regardless of whether they had had one or two exposures to the stimulus items. These findings, then, demonstrate quite clearly that in forming an impression of another person one actively organizes the available information according to certain

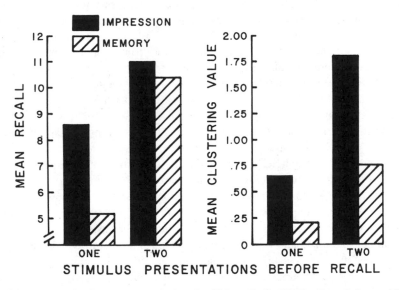

FIG. 4.2.   Mean Recall Performance and Clustering Values Obtained in Hamilton, Leirer, and Katz (1979) Experiment.

personality relevant schemas, and that such organization facilitates retention of that information.

There is, however, a theoretical ambiguity that remains regarding exactly what it is that differentiates subjects in our Impression and Memory conditions. Specifically the question is, do these groups differ in the *amount* or the *nature* of the organization that they are imposing on the stimulus information? That is, subjects in the Impression Formation condition may organize the information to a greater extent, or the two groups may be equivalent in the extent of organizational activity, but the Impression Formation subjects have better recall because they use schemas that provide a more effective organizational framework. Either possibility is both plausible and theoretically meaningful. The clustering paradigm cannot differentiate between them because the clustering measures determine only the extent to which the subject has organized the material in terms of the a priori categories established by the experimenter in the stimulus materials. Therefore, one cannot determine whether a low clustering score means that the subject did not organize the information or that the subject organized the items according to some other set of rules.

To examine this question, we (Hamilton & Lim, 1979) made use of another technique for investigating organization in memory, a method originally developed by Tulving (1962) and usually referred to in the literature as the analysis of subjective organization (Sternberg & Tulving, 1977). In this paradigm the same stimulus items are presented to the subject a number of times and free recall is assessed after each trial. On each trial the stimulus items are presented in a different order and similarities between recall protocols on adjacent trials are determined. The logic of the analysis is that, because the items occur in a different order with each presentation, if two items are recalled together on successive trials they must be stored together in memory. In contrast to the analysis of clustering, this paradigm permits one to determine the relative amount of organization that has occurred under various conditions, but one cannot determine the basis of that organization.

In their study, Hamilton and Lim (1979) combined the features of these two paradigms. For a series of eight trials subjects were presented with a sequence of 16 items that were ordered differently on each trial. Analysis of intertrial similarities in the sequence in which items were recalled would then provide a measure of subjective organization. In addition, we structured the set of stimulus items much like we did in the previous experiment, i.e., there were four items representative of each of four categories of personality content. Thus we could also determine the extent to which items were clustered into these a priori categories.

The results of the study were both clear and interesting. The free recall performance of Impression Formation subjects initially was superior to that of the Memory group, consistent with the findings from our other studies. As both groups improved over trials and approached asymptote performance, the difference between groups decreased and eventually disappeared. In contrast to this pattern, but confirming the results of the previous study, the analysis of clustering indicated that Impression Formation subjects consistently organized the stimulus material in terms of the four content categories to a greater extent than did subjects in the Memory condition. This difference was evident on the first trial and was consistently maintained through all trials. Finally, the analysis of subjective organization, based on intertrial similarities in the sequence of items in recall, showed that there was no difference between the Impression and Memory conditions.

These findings lead to the following interpretive conclusions. First, in attempting to perform the tasks indicated in the instructions given to them, subjects in both groups apparently attempted to organize the stimulus material in the course of forming an impression, on the one hand, or learning the stimulus list, on the other. In either case such organization can be a means of reducing the complexity of the task with which they were confronted. Second, it is clear that the two groups used different organizational schemas in performing their respective tasks. Although these analyses do not indicate what organizational rules were used by subjects in the Memory condition, we do know that Impression condition subjects organized and stored the stimulus information in terms of the four a priori content categories represented in the stimulus items, and that the Memory subjects did not. This suggests that the process of forming an impression activates certain personality relevant schemas that the perceiver will use in encoding and organizing the information available. Third, we can conclude that the schemas used by the Impression Formation subjects provided a more effective organizational framework than the memory rules developed by subjects in the Memory condition. This conclusion is based on the fact that, although the two groups were similar in subjective organization scores, the Impression Formation group evidenced better recall performance through the first several trials.

The results from these studies comparing Impression Formation and Memory conditions can be viewed as demonstrating that different task sets can influence how information is organized. As such, they are consistent with previous studies of "cognitive tuning," in which subjects instructed to either "receive" or "transmit" information about another person were shown to organize that information differently (Zajonc, 1960). Subsequent studies have shown that these tuning sets can influence one's perceptions of the target person (e.g., Cohen, 1961; Harvey, Hawkins, & Kagehiro, 1976), and there is some evidence that these sets have their primary effect during the encoding of information (Harkins, Harvey, Keithly, & Rich, 1977). The general question that arises, then, concerns how different kinds of processing sets that a perceiver might use under various circumstances might influence the way in which information is organized. Differences in how the perceiver organizes the information available presumably would not only influence the amount recalled but would also affect the nature of the cognitive representation one develops of a target person. The final study to be reported here was concerned with this question. Specifically, we investigated how person-relevant stimulus information is organized in memory under conditions when the self is and is not made salient as a basis for information processing.

Recently, Rogers and his colleagues (Rogers, Kuiper, & Kirker, 1977) have argued that the self is a "powerful agent in the organization of the person's world [p. 677]." In their studies, subjects were able to recall more of the stimulus items if, in processing the information, they had been induced to judge whether the items were descriptive of themselves than if they were led to evaluate certain other characteristics of the items, such as their structural properties or semantic meaning. Rogers et al. interpreted these results as indicating that self-referenced processing produces a stronger memory trace, and they suggest that the self-schema provides an important framework within which self-relevant information is organized. One inference that can be drawn from their discussion of self-referenced processing is that items that the subject regards as highly descriptive of himself would be stored separately from items considered as not self-descriptive.

There is another possible process that may underlie the findings reported by Rogers et al. (1977). The crucial factor producing superior recall may have less to do with the fact that the stimulus items were processed in relation to the self than that they were processed within an organized conceptual framework. As in the case of forming an impression of another person, all of the items were evaluated in relation to the same object, in this case the self, and hence were considered in terms of certain organizing schemas. This was not true of any of the other processing conditions included in the Rogers et al. experiments.

The question then becomes, how do subjects organize the information under various instructional set conditions? As previously noted, the implication of the Rogers et al. work is that when the self is made salient the information will be organized in terms of the items' descriptiveness of one's self. An alternative possibility is that, in processing self-descriptive information, the perceiver uses the same personality-relevant schemas that he would use in processing information about others. That is, the perceiver has a certain set of schemas related to the nature and content of personality—an implicit personality theory (Schneider, 1973) or personal construct system (Kelly, 1955), if you like—which the perceiver uses in processing information about persons, including himself. In this case, we would expect a set of descriptive items to be organized in memory in a similar fashion both when the items are presented as describing another person and when they are presented as possible descriptors of oneself.

To evaluate these two possible organizing schemas, we (Hamilton & Leirer, 1979) conducted a study in which four different instructional sets were included. Two of them were the same as we have used throughout this research program, the Memory set and the Impression Formation set. A third group of subjects was given Self-Referenced processing instructions. They were told that the study was concerned with "the way in which we evaluate information that may or may not be descriptive of ourselves," and were instructed to think about the extent to which each of the stimulus sentences was descriptive of themselves. Finally, a fourth group received instructions that combined features of the Impression Formation and the Self-Referenced conditions. These instructions were similar to the Impression Formation set, but in addition to forming an impression of the stimulus person they were to "compare that person to yourself in terms of how similar or dissimilar you think the person is to you." We call this the Impression and Self-Comparison condition. The stimulus set consisted of 24 behavior-descriptive sentence predicates, with six sentences from each of four personality content categories. All subjects received two presentations of the stimulus series before the free recall measure was administered. Following the recall task, subjects were given a page listing the 24 sentences and were asked to indicate the extent to which each item was descriptive of themselves.

Based on these measures, we conducted two different analyses of clustering in free recall. One analysis was the same as that used in the previous studies, determining the extent to which each subject's recall protocol was organized in terms of the four content categories represented in the stimulus sentences. For the second analysis we used the subject's ratings of the items to define three different groups of items: those he considered descriptive of himself, those he rated as not descriptive, and those that received intermediate ratings. The second clustering analysis determined the extent to which the subject's recall list was organized according to these three categories. If subjects in the Self-Referenced set condition, and perhaps also in the Impression and Self-Comparison condition, organized the stimulus items according to self-schemas based on self-descriptiveness or similarity to self, then the second analysis should yield high clustering values in these conditions. On the other hand, if subjects employed a common set of personality-relevant schemas in all of the person-related tasks, then the clustering values from the first analysis should be high in the Impression, the Self-Referenced, and the Impression and Self-Comparison conditions.

The results of the analyses, shown in Fig. 4.3, supported the second set of predictions. Specifically, the analysis of clustering in terms of the four content categories indicated that the mean clustering index for the Memory condition was significantly lower than those for the other three conditions, but that these three groups did not differ from each other. Thus, all three groups that were given person-related task instructions organized the stimulus information in terms of the major personality content themes represented in the items. In contrast, there were no differences among any of the groups on measures of clustering in terms of the self-descriptiveness categories, and the clustering values in this analysis were so consistently close to chance performance that it is clear that the subjects simply were not using these categories as an organizational framework. Thus,

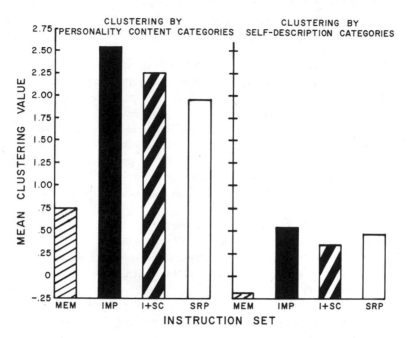

FIG. 4.3.   Comparison of Clustering by Personality Content Categories and Self-Descriptiveness Categories for Various Instruction Sets (based on Hamilton & Leirer, 1979). Note MEM = Memory instructions; IMP = Impression Formation instructions; I + SC = Impression and Self-Comparison instructions: SRP = Self-Referenced Processing instructions.

these findings support the hypothesis that perceivers have a set of schemas relevant to personality-related content, and that information pertinent to both oneself and to others is organized and stored in terms of these schemas.

TOWARD A CONCEPTUAL FRAMEWORK FOR UNDERSTANDING COGNITIVE REPRESENTATIONS OF PERSONS

The program of research described in the preceding section has produced a number of informative findings regarding the nature and organization of our cognitive representations of persons. These findings can be summarized as follows:

1. Subjects engaged in the task of forming an impression of a person described by a series of behavior descriptions were able to recall more of those items than subjects given the task of committing them to memory. This finding

we interpreted as being due to the process of imposing a meaningful organization on the stimulus information, a process we consider an inherent aspect of impression development.

2. Subjects' recall of the behavior descriptions was clustered according to prominent personality themes represented in those items to a greater extent in the Impression Formation than in the Memory condition, supporting the interpretation proposed for the previous finding.

3. Although we are not prepared at this point to reject the possibility that during impression formation subjects organize the stimulus items *more* than do subjects in a traditional memory task, the evidence presently available suggests that these two tasks differ in *how* the items are organized. As previously noted, impressions tend to be organized in terms of categories of personality content. And although it is less clear what types of organization are employed by subjects in a memory task, the recall findings indicate that they are less effective in facilitating later retrieval of the descriptive information.

4. Finally, subjects evaluating the self-descriptiveness of stimulus items employed the same organizational framework on a recall task as did subjects engaged in an impression formation task. This finding implies that persons have in their cognitive structures a number of schematic categories pertaining to personality content that they apply consistently in processing information about persons, both others and themselves.

These, then, are the empirical findings we have obtained in our research thus far. What do these findings imply about the process by which perceivers develop cognitive representations of persons? In this section, I present some tentative theoretical ideas about the interaction of cognitive structure and cognitive processing that are suggested by the results of these experiments. In attempting to develop a conceptual framework for thinking about impression development, I have drawn on the ideas of several authors who have discussed the nature of schemas and schema processing, and I have tried to apply these ideas to this topic. Similarities with the views of other authors will therefore be apparent. However, because I have borrowed from several different discussions of schema-based processing, the following ideas should not be construed as reflecting the application of any single theorist's viewpoint (other than my own).

Our approach to understanding the development of cognitive representations of persons utilizes the concept of schema as an element of cognitive structure. Rumelhart and Ortony (1977) have defined schemas as

data structures for representing the generic concepts stored in memory. They exist for generalized concepts underlying objects, situations, events, sequences of events, actions, and sequences of actions.... A schema contains, as part of its specification, the network of interrelations that is believed to generally hold among the constituents of the concept in question [p. 101].

Although the use of the term schema in social psychology tends to be vague, there exists a considerable amount of evidence that strongly suggests the need to recognize the existence of such cognitive structures containing the person's "world knowledge." In particular, schemas appear to play an important role in the encoding, comprehension, organization, and retrieval of social information (cf. Taylor & Crocker, Chapter 3, this volume).

Schema theories assume that each person has available in his or her cognitive structure an enormous number of schemas that can be used in interpreting experience and processing information. A subset of those schemas will represent concepts generally applicable to persons, and in the present discussion we are concerned only with these person schemas. Each of these schemas contains a number of "elements" that represent the person's accumulated knowledge, beliefs, and expectations pertaining to the content relevant to that schema. We assume that when a person is confronted with a task of construing a person and his or her behavior, this subset of schemas pertaining to person-objects will be activated and readily available for encoding, organizing, and representing incoming information. An incoming piece of information that "fits" or pertains to an element of a particular schema is said to *instantiate* that particular schema. The process by which this occurs is not well understood, but it is assumed that the perceiver will comprehend the meaning of that information in terms of the elements contained in that schema. The schema may then be the basis for drawing further inferences about the person. It is the information as interpreted within the context of the schema that will be represented in memory and available for later retrieval.

Two commonly cited properties of schemas should be mentioned at the outset. First, schemas can exist at varying levels of abstraction. Some schemas are fairly specific and therefore represent a rather narrow range of content; other schemas are more abstract and consequently have much broader application. We assume that this is true of person schemas as well. However, most person schemas of the type discussed in this section are assumed to be of a fairly abstract nature. Second, as implied by the preceding point, schemas can exist in hierarchical relation to each other. That is, the more specific, lower level schemas may be linked with more abstract, higher level schemas in subordinate/superordinate relationships. In addition, we assume that schemas that exist at the same level of abstraction can be linked with each other.

Given this cursory overview of the nature of schemas and how they function, how can this framework be applied to understanding the previously discussed findings and their implications for the development of cognitive representations of persons? In addressing this question, I want to discuss two topics. The first concerns the effect of the task instructions used in our research on the schematic processing of the stimulus information. The second topic concerns the process by which the person's schema structure interacts with the stimulus information in the development of a cognitive representation of the target person.

Consider first the effect of our task instructions. At the beginning of our experiments, the subjects receive instructions indicating either that the study is concerned with how we form first impressions—that their task will be to form an impression of a person described by a series of behavior descriptions—or that the experiment is concerned with memory—that their task will be to try to remember as many sentences as possible. This instructional manipulation can be understood as having an influence by activating different schematic structures for the task at hand. One consequence of the impression formation instructions is that the subset of the perceiver's schemas that are relevant to understanding person-objects will, to some extent, be called forth for coping with the anticipated information. Given these instructions, the perceivers know what ball park they'll be playing in, even before any information is received. Schemas having to do with international relations, car engines, and checkbook balancing can be set aside for the moment; right now schemas having to do with the personality and behavior of persons will be needed. The effect of these instructions, then, is that the domain of person-schemas is mildly activated and readied for encoding, interpreting, and organizing the incoming information. These schematic categories then prove to be quite useful in processing the stimulus items, particularly in the clustering studies in which the items in the stimulus set were intentionally constructed to include several instances reflecting each of several personality themes. Although we are less confident in speculating about the types of schemas called forth by the memory instructions, it seems likely that they would be concerned less with the nature of personality and more with strategies for maintaining verbal items in memory for later recall. In sum, one effect of the instructional manipulation used in these studies is that different sets of schemas are activated. In the case of the impression formation instructions the schemas activated are quite useful in organizing the stimulus items and representing that information in memory, which in turn has the effect of facilitating later recall of those items.

The task instructions can be viewed as having an effect similar to that observed in studies in which "point of view" (e.g., Bower, 1977), "perspective" (e.g., Anderson & Pichert, 1978; Pichert & Anderson, 1977), or "priming" (e.g., Higgins, Rholes, & Jones, 1977; Wyer & Srull, Chapter 5, this volume) manipulations have been shown to influence recall. One difference, however, is that, whereas these other manipulations presumably activate a single schema, task instructions such as those given to our impression formation subjects have the effect of calling forth a domain of schemas relevant to the particular task. Nevertheless, these manipulations all produce evidence of "top down" (Rumelhart & Ortony, 1977) or "conceptually driven" (Bobrow & Norman, 1975) processing.

The second, and more difficult, issue that needs to be addressed concerns the nature of the cognitive representation of a person that is the result of the impression formation process. I have suggested that each person has available a large number of schemas pertaining to personality concepts and other person-related content. The stimulus information acquired about the target person is processed in terms of this schematic structure, and the end product is a cognitive representation or impression of that person. How does this process take place, and what is the nature of the resulting cognitive representation?

The person-schemas I have discussed are, to use Rumelhart and Ortony's (1977) term, generic concepts. They are abstractions drawn from one's previous experiences and can apply to any instance of an object or event to which the schema is relevant. For example, a schema for Extraversion contains the person's knowledge and beliefs about the characteristics and behaviors typical of people who are extraverted, and can be applied to interpreting or anticipating the behavior of any particular person. As previously noted, these schemas are employed in processing information about a person during the impression-formation process. As the impression develops, however, a new cognitive structure is formed, one which we call a cognitive representation of the person. This structure has many of the properties of a schema in that, for example, it contains the perceiver's knowledge and beliefs about the object to which it applies, it can influence the interpretation of new information, it can be the basis for anticipating and governing future behavior, etc. However, it also differs from schemas as defined earlier in some important respects. For example, it applies to only one person (the target person) and hence as a person schema it would have the narrowest possible range of application. More important, it has a multicomponent structure that reflects the contribution of many of the more generic person schemas to its development. In what follows, I attempt to describe a process by which such a cognitive representation of a person might develop.

As noted earlier, a schema contains a number of elements representing various aspects of the person's knowledge and beliefs about a particular domain of content. Consider, as a hypothetical example, a schema we might call Athletic. This schema might include the following among its elements: "is in good physical condition"; "participates in competitive sports"; "exercises to keep in shape"; "is knowledgeable about sports events and personalities." Notice that none of these elements state specific facts—there are many competitive sports in which one might participate; there are many ways of exercising to keep in shape—but they all summarize categories of information or types of behavior consistent with the generic concept of being athletically inclined. When a subject acquires a specific piece of information about a target person, for example, that he "plays softball in a city recreation league," this item instantiates one of the elements of this schema ("participates in competitive sports"). When a schema is instantiated in this way, that schema becomes represented as a component of the cognitive representation of that person. The knowledge that the person "plays softball in a city recreation league" is then stored in that component of the cognitive representation. Later in the stimulus list, when the subject learns that the target person "jogs every morning before going to work," that information instantiates another element of the same schema ("exercises to keep in shape''). Because they instantiate the same schema, these two items would be stored together in memory, in the same component (''athletic'') of the cognitive representation. Other items dealing with different content would instantiate other schemas in the same way. Hence, additional components of the cognitive representation would be established, and items reflecting various categories of content would be organized and stored in terms of this structure. When later asked to recall information about the target person, the perceiver's retrieval process presumably would access one category of the cognitive representation and retrieve items contained in it, then access information stored in a second category, and so forth. Such a process would produce the significant amounts of clustering in recall observed in the impression formation conditions of the experiments reported earlier.

Thus, the process of impression development consists of the formation of a cognitive representation of the person, a new cognitive structure that contains the perceiver's knowledge and beliefs about the person. This representation is the end product of an interaction between the incoming stimulus information and the preexisting schematic structure of the perceiver. That is, items of stimulus information instantiate certain of the schemas, a process that determines which conceptual categories will be included in the resulting impression. Given this perspective, a number of points can be made about the relationship between one's overall schema structure and the structure of one's cognitive representation of a person. First, the more varied the stimulus information available about a stimulus person, the more numerous the schematic categories that will be instantiated, and hence the more differentiated and complex will be the cognitive representation of that person. Second, the more extensive the information within a particular category, the more richly articulated will be that component of the impression. Third, because the components of a cognitive representation of a person derive from the instantiation of preexisting schemas, it follows that each category represented in the impression of a person corresponds to a schema in the perceiver's cognitive structure. That is, a stimulus item cannot instantiate a schema that does not exist. Finally, the proportion of one's person-schemas represented in the impression will change with increasing familiarity with the target person. At least during the early stages of impression development, the cognitive representation of a person will contain far fewer categories than the total number of schemas the perceiver has available for construing person-related information. As the perceiver gets to know the target person better and more diverse kinds of information are acquired about that person, more and more schemas will, in time, become instantiated and those schemas will then be represented within the perceiver's impression of that person. The target person with whom the person is most familiar, of course, is the self, and therefore we might expect that the cognitive representation of one's self would contain components or categories corresponding to a large proportion of the schemas contained in the total cognitive structure of person-related schemas.

The process of impression development described here emphasizes the role of the instantiation of schemas by stimulus information as the means by which conceptual categories are incorporated in the cognitive representation. Although this process is viewed as the primary mechanism by which components of impressions are established, it is not the only process by which schematic categories or concepts can become represented in the structure of an impression. Within the domain of person-related schemas available for use by a perceiver, it is unlikely that any given schema would exist totally independently of the others. Rather it seems obvious that there are implicational relationships among schemas. We can conceive of such implicational linkages between schemas as existing in either of two forms. Two schemas may be directly linked to each other, or they may be related because they are both linked to the same superordinate schema. In either case, instantiation of one schema might imply that concepts contained in the other schema are likely to apply to the target person as well. If the implicational relationship of the first schema to the second is sufficiently strong, then the content of the second schema may to some extent become represented in the impression of the target person.

Thus, we are suggesting a distinction between two types of inferential processes by which the perceiver may go beyond the actual information available in "fleshing out" his conception of a target person. First, instantiation of a schema by a particular fact, for example, that the person plays softball in a city recreation league, may lead the perceiver to assume other things to be true of the person as well, based on the knowledge, beliefs, and expectations contained in that schema—that he enjoys athletic activities in general, that he reads the sports page of the newspaper, that he is in good physical condition, etc. Second, as noted in the preceding paragraph, instantiation of one schema may be the basis for inferences about the person regarding content contained in another schema with which it is implicationally related. The distinction drawn here is a sticky one that has not been adequately discussed in the literature on schema structures. In particular, because we do not presently have any adequate means of specifying the content of a particular schema, it is difficult to know whether any given inference is an instance of within-schema or between-schema inferencing.

To this point we have discussed cognitive representations of persons primarily in terms of the processing, storage, and retrieval of bits of factual information learned about a target person. Obviously our impressions of others are not restricted to such information but include more general conceptions of the person's personality and behavior patterns. Frequently the information received, as in descriptions from another person, occurs at the level of personality characteristics ("She's really smart") or behavior patterns ("He talks all the time"), rather than specific behaviors. Thus, the instantiating information need not be highly specific. In addition, the inferential processes noted earlier can result in a more general conception of a person. To return to our earlier example, knowledge that a person plays softball in a recreation league might be the basis for a more general conception ("He enjoys competitive sports") and perhaps more abstract characterizations ("He's a jock") as well. Thus, the overall cognitive representation is likely to include information and characterizations at varying levels of specificity or abstractness. What kinds of schematic inferences are likely to be made from various types of stimulus information remains to be determined.

In addition, we have said nothing about the role of evaluation in cognitive representations, yet evaluation is clearly of fundamental importance in understanding the nature of impressions. The problem of how evaluation is represented in these cognitive structures, and the relationship between evaluative and nonevaluative components of impressions, will need to be addressed in future research. Some recent evidence suggests that the problem may be more complex and the solution more elusive than might have seemed at first glance (cf. Anderson & Hubert, 1963; Dreben, Fiske, & Hastie, 1979; McArthur, Chapter 6, this volume).

The theoretical ideas presented in this section concerning the processing and representation of information about persons are viewed as a first step toward a conceptual framework for understanding how our conceptions of others develop. The presentation of these ideas has been fairly speculative and has gone considerably beyond the evidence at hand, and the resulting framework is obviously tentative and incomplete. The value of this approach to impression development will depend on the findings of research investigating the implications of these ideas and on subsequent refinement and elaboration of the conceptual framework. Moreover, we agree with Taylor and Crocker (Chapter 3, this volume) that, although the concept of schema-based processing has been useful in stimulating research, "schema theory" in its more general form is in need of further development and specification. The ultimate viability of the present approach will depend in part on these more general theoretical developments. Nevertheless, we are hopeful that the ideas presented here will have heuristic value in stimulating the kinds of thinking and investigation that will be necessary if this orientation is to prove to be useful.

ACKNOWLEDGMENTS

Preparation of this manuscript was supported in part by NIMH Grant 29418. The author is grateful to Terry Rose, Shelley Taylor, and Mark Zanna for their comments on an earlier version of the manuscript.

REFERENCES

Anderson, N. H. Application of an additive model to impression formation. *Science,* 1962, *138,* 817–818.
Anderson, N. H. A simple model for information integration. In R. P. Abelson, E. Aronson, W. J.

McGuire, T. M. Newcomb, M. J. Rosenberg, & P. H. Tannenbaum (Eds.), *Theories of cognitive consistency: A sourcebook*. Chicago: Rand McNally, 1968.

Anderson, H. H. Looking for configurality in clinical judgment. *Psychological Bulletin*, 1972, *78*, 93–102.

Anderson, N. H. Cognitive algebra: Integration theory applied to social attribution. In L. Berkowitz (Ed.), *Advances in experimental social psychology* (Vol. 7). New York: Academic Press, 1974. (a)

Anderson, N. H. Information integration theory: A brief survey. In D. H. Krantz, R. C. Atkinson, R. D. Luce, & P. Suppes (Eds.), *Contemporary developments in mathematical psychology*. San Francisco: Freeman, 1974. (b)

Anderson, N. H., & Hubert, S. Effects of concomitant verbal recall on order effects in personality impression formation. *Journal of Verbal Learning and Verbal Behavior*, 1963, *2*, 379–391.

Anderson, R. C., & Pichert, J. W. Recall of previously unrecallable information following a shift in perspective. *Journal of Verbal Learning and Verbal Behavior*, 1978, *17*, 1–12.

Asch, S. Forming impressions of personality. *Journal of Abnormal and Social Psychology*, 1946, *41*, 258–290.

Bobrow, D. G., & Norman, D. A. Some principles of memory schemata. In D. G. Bobrow & A. M. Collins (Eds.), *Representation and understanding: Studies in cognitive science*. New York: Academic Press, 1975.

Bousfield, A. K., & Bousfield, W. A. Measurement of clustering and of sequential constancies in repeated free recall. *Psychological Reports*, 1966, *19*, 935–942.

Bower, G. *"On injecting life into deadly prose": Studies in explanation-seeking*. Paper presented at Western Psychological Association Convention, Seattle, 1977.

Bruner, J. S., & Tagiuri, R. Person perception. In G. Lindsey (Ed.), *Handbook of social psychology* (Vol. 2). Reading, Mass.: Addison-Wesley, 1954.

Chapman, L. J., & Chapman, J. P. Genesis of popular but erroneous psychodiagnostic observations. *Journal of Abnormal Psychology*, 1967, *72*, 193–204.

Chapman, L. J., & Chapman, J. P. Illusory correlation as an obstacle to the use of valid psychodiagnostic signs. *Journal of Abnormal Psychology*, 1969, *74*, 271–280.

Cohen, A. R. Cognitive tuning as a factor affecting impression formation. *Journal of Personality*, 1961, *29*, 235–245.

Dawes, R. M., & Corrigan, B. Linear models in decision making. *Psychological Bulletin*, 1974, *81*, 95–106.

Dreben, E. K., Fiske, S. T., & Hastie, R. The independence of evaluative and item information: Impression and recall order effects in behavior-based impression formation. *Journal of Personality and Social Psychology*, 1979, *37*, 1758–1768.

Fischoff, B. Attribution theory and judgment under uncertainty. In J. H. Harvey, W. J. Ickes, & R. F. Kidd (Eds.), *New directions in attribution research* (Vol. 1). Hillsdale, N.J.: Lawrence Erlbaum Associates, 1976.

Goldberg, L. R. Simple models or simple processes? Some research on clinical judgments. *American Psychologist*, 1968, *23*, 483–496.

Hamilton, D. L. Cognitive biases in the perception of social groups. In J. S. Carroll & J. W. Payne (Eds.), *Cognition and social behavior*. Hillsdale, N. J.: Lawrence Erlbaum Associates, 1976.

Hamilton, D. L. A cognitive-attributional analysis of stereotyping. In L. Berkowitz (Ed.), *Advances in experimental social psychology* (Vol. 12). New York: Academic Press, 1979.

Hamilton, D. L., & Gifford, R. K. Illusory correlation in interpersonal perception: A cognitive basis of stereotypic judgments. *Journal of Experimental Social Psychology*, 1976, *12*, 392–407.

Hamilton, D. L., Katz, L. B., & Leirer, V. O. Cognitive representation of personality impressions: Organizational processes in first impression formation. *Journal of Personality and Social Psychology*, 1980. (a)

Hamilton, D. L., Katz, L. B., & Leirer, V. O. Organizational processes in impression formation. In

R. Hastie, T. M. Ostrom, E. B. Ebbesen, R. S. Wyer, Jr., D. L. Hamilton, & D. E. Carlston (Eds.), *Person memory: The cognitive basis of social perception.* Hillsdale, N. J.: Lawrence Erlbaum Associates, 1980. (b)

Hamilton, D. L., & Leirer, V. O. *Organization of information about self and others.* Unpublished manuscript, University of California at Santa Barbara, 1979.

Hamilton, D. L., Leirer, V. O., & Katz, L. B. *A clustering analysis of organizational processes in impression formation.* Unpublished manuscript, University of California at Santa Barbara, 1979.

Hamilton, D. L., & Lim, C. *Organizational processes in person impressions and memory: Differences in the amount or the nature of organization?* Unpublished manuscript, University of California at Santa Barbara, 1979.

Hamilton, D. L., & Rose, T. Illusory correlation and the maintenance of stereotypic beliefs. *Journal of Personality and Social Psychology,* 1980, *39,* 832–845.

Hammond, K. R., Hursch, C. J., & Todd, F. J. Analyzing the components of clinical inference. *Psychological Review,* 1964, *71,* 438–456.

Harkins, S. G., Harvey, J. H., Keithly, L., & Rich, M. Cognitive tuning, encoding, and the attribution of causality. *Memory and Cognition,* 1977, *5,* 561–565.

Harvey, J. H., Harkins, S. G., & Kagehiro, D. K. Cognitive tuning and the attribution of causality. *Journal of Personality and Social Psychology,* 1976, *34,* 708–715.

Higgins, E. T., Rholes, W. S., & Jones, C. R. Category accessibility and impression formation. *Journal of Experimental Social Psychology,* 1977, *13,* 141–154.

Hoffman, P. J. The paramorphic representation of clinical judgment. *Psychological Bulletin,* 1960, *57,* 116–131.

Hoffman, P. J., Slovic, P., & Rorer, L. G. An analysis-of-variance model for the assessment of configural cue utilization in clinical judgment. *Psychological Bulletin,* 1968, *69,* 338–349.

Jaccard, J. J., & Fishbein, M. Inferential beliefs and order effects in personality impression formation. *Journal of Personality and Social Psychology,* 1975, *31,* 1031–1041.

Jones, E. E., & Davis, K. E. A theory of correspondent inferences: From acts to dispositions. In L. Berkowitz (Ed.), *Advances in experimental social psychology* (Vol. 2). New York: Academic Press, 1965.

Kanouse, D. E., & Hanson, L. R. Negativity in evaluations. In E. E. Jones, D. E. Kanouse, H. H. Kelley, R. E. Nisbett, S. Valins, & B. Weiner (Eds.), *Attribution: Perceiving the causes of behavior.* Morristown, N. J.: General Learning Press, 1972.

Kelley, H. H. Attribution theory in social psychology. In D. Levine (Ed.), *Nebraska symposium on motivation.* Lincoln, Neb.: University of Nebraska Press, 1967.

Kelly, G. A. *The psychology of personal constructs.* New York: Norton, 1955.

McArthur, L. A. The how and what of why: Some determinants and consequences of causal attribution. *Journal of Personality and Social Psychology,* 1972, *22,* 171–193.

Nisbett, R. E., Borgida, E., Crandall, R., & Reed, H. Popular induction: Information is not necessarily informative. In J. S. Carroll & J. W. Payne (Eds.), *Cognition and social behavior.* Hillsdale, N. J.: Lawrence Erlbaum Associates, 1976.

Ostrom, T. M., Lingle, J. H., Pryor, J. B., & Geva, N. Cognitive organization of person impressions. In R. Hastie, T. M. Ostrom, E. B. Ebbesen, R. S. Wyer, Jr., D. L. Hamilton, & D. E. Carlston (Eds.), *Person memory: The cognitive basis of person perception.* Hillsdale, N. J.: Lawrence Erlbaum Associates, 1980.

Pichert, J. W., & Anderson, R. C. Taking different perspectives on a story. *Journal of Educational Psychology,* 1977, *69,* 309–315.

Rogers, T. B., Kuiper, N. A., & Kirker, W. S. Self-reference and the encoding of personal information. *Journal of Personality and Social Psychology,* 1977, *35,* 677–688.

Ross, L. The intuitive psychologist and his short-comings: Distortions in the attribution process. In L. Berkowitz (Ed.), *Advances in experimental social psychology* (Vol. 10). New York: Academic Press, 1977.

Rumelhart, D. E., & Ortony, A. The representation of knowledge in memory. In R. C. Anderson, R. J. Spiro, & W. E. Montague (Eds.), *Schooling and the acquisition of knowledge*. Hillsdale, N. J.: Lawrence Erlbaum Associates, 1977.

Schneider, D. J. Implicit personality theory: A review. *Psychological Bulletin, 1973, 79,* 294–309.

Slovic, P., & Lichtenstein, S. Comparison of Bayesian and regression approaches to the study of information processing in judgment. *Organizational Behavior and Human Performance, 1971, 6,* 649–744.

Sternberg, R. J., & Tulving, E. The measurement of subjective organization in free recall. *Psychological Bulletin, 1977, 84,* 539–556.

Tulving, E. Subjective organization in free recall of "unrelated" words. *Psychological Review, 1962, 60,* 344–354.

Weiner, B., Freize, I., Kukla, A., Reed, L., Rest, S., & Rosenbaum, R. M. Perceiving the causes of success and failure. In E. E. Jones, D. E. Kanouse, H. H. Kelley, R. E. Nisbett, S. Valins, & B. Weiner (Eds.), *Attribution: Perceiving the causes of behavior*. Morristown, N. J.: General Learning Press, 1972.

Zajonc, R. B. The process of cognitive tuning in communication. *Journal of Abnormal and Social Psychology, 1960, 61,* 159–167.

5

Category Accessibility: Some Theoretical and Empirical Issues Concerning the Processing of Social Stimulus Information

Robert S. Wyer, Jr.
Thomas K. Srull
University of Illinois at Urbana-Champaign

The impression one forms of a person is often thought to consist of a set of personality trait labels that, separately or in combination, provide the basis for affective reactions to the person, predictions about the person's behavior in different situations, inferences about other general attributes of the person, and one's own future behavior toward the person. The manner in which personality traits are used for these purposes has been investigated within a variety of conceptual frameworks and research paradigms (cf. Anderson, 1968; Asch, 1946; Byrne, 1971; Cantor & Mischel, 1977; Fishbein & Hunter, 1964; Rosenberg & Sedlak, 1972; Schneider, 1973). Less attention has been given to the factors that determine which traits are assigned to a person on the basis of information about the person's behavior, and thus comprise the impression being formed. Attribution theory (Bem, 1972; Jones & Davis, 1965; Jones & McGillis, 1976; Kelley, 1967) has of course been concerned with how situational context in which behavior occurs affects the extent to which it is regarded as more or less indicative of a particular trait. In many instances, however, a given behavior may be equally indicative of several different traits, not all of which may be considered at the time the behavior is observed. In such instances, a question arises concerning the factors that affect which of these traits are actually assigned to a person on the basis of the behavior. Additional questions concern the processes whereby these traits come to affect inferences about the actor, either in combination with, or independently of the behavioral information upon which they were based. The present paper is concerned with such matters.

Although the processes we assume to underlie impression formation are stated more formally later in this chapter, a brief outline of these processes may help to convey a feel for the issues of concern. When people observe or read about someone's behavior with (or perhaps even without) the intention of forming an impression of this person, they may first construe the implications of this behavior for one or more personality traits. They may then attempt to identify a prototypic individual or group, or someone they have known in the past that they believe possesses these traits. Once this identification is made, the actor may then be assumed to be similar to the person or group identified, and therefore may be attributed other characteristics that are associated with this person or group.

Thus, suppose a person in a restaurant is observed to send a steak back because it is too well done, making a snide remark to the waiter in the process. An observer might interpret the actor's behavior as being finicky about food, belligerent, and demeaning. Certain of these traits may be similar to those the observer uses to characterize a prototypic individual who is arrogant, domineering, and patronizing in his dealings with subordinates. However, other subsets may characterize a gourmet acquaintance who is contemptuous of restaurants that are careless about their preparation of food but who is sophisticated, congenial, and interesting to be with. In such an event, the impression formed of the actor may differ substantially, depending on the individual to whom he happens to be compared.

Although this general description of impression formation seems intuitively reasonable, it makes salient several ambiguities concerning the nature of the processes involved and the conditions in which they occur. An observed behavior may often be interpreted in many different ways. For example, the behavior of giving someone an answer to an examination question may be interpreted as either dishonest or as kind. Which interpretation happens to be made of the behavior may determine the actual or prototypic individual with whom the actor is compared, and consequently may affect the nature of other traits attributed to the actor. Moreover, the same trait or set of traits may be typical of more than one individual or group, each of which differs from the others with respect to other, unmentioned characteristics. To predict the nature of the impression one is likely to form on the basis of the observed behavior, it is therefore necessary to understand the factors that may affect which of several traits may be assigned on the basis of behavioral information, and which of several alternative representations of persons or groups associated with this trait is likely to be recalled and used as a basis for further judgments.

This paper reports a series of studies that are concerned with these questions. These studies identify certain factors that affect the interpretation and use of behavioral information in forming impressions of people, and help to circumscribe the conditions in which these factors have an influence. In addition, the research has implications for the processes underlying the encoding of social stimulus information and at what point they occur in the sequence of cognitive events previously outlined. To provide a context for conceptualizing the phenomena to be discussed, we first outline a theoretical framework that has implications for both these and other phenomena discussed elsewhere in this volume (cf. Ebbesen; Hamilton; Hastie; Higgins; Ostrom, Pryor, & Simpson; Ross; and Snyder)

A THEORETICAL DESCRIPTION OF SOCIAL INFERENCE PROCESSES

The formulation to be described is a summary of a more formal model of social information processing elaborated by Wyer and Srull (1980). It takes into account three interrelated assumptions that underlie both our own empirical work and that are reported elsewhere in this volume. Each assumption has both historical antecedents in cognitive psychology and empirical support in contemporary research.

Assumption 1. Social information is often interpreted and encoded into memory as a complex configuration of concepts, the features of which overlap but are not necessarily identical to those actually contained in the stimulus information. Thus, some aspects of the original information may not be contained in the encoded representation of it, whereas some features contained in the representation may not have been specified in the original information (cf. Bower, 1975). This assumption is hardly novel. Bartlett (1932) and Bruner (1957, 1958), for example, postulated the existence of cognitive *schemata,* or configural representations of prototypic objects and events, that provide the basis for interpreting information about particular objects and events that one encounters. A similar notion is found in Schank and Abelson's (1977) conceptualization of *scripts.* In both cases, a new social experience is assumed to be interpreted with reference to previously formed representations of persons or events that one has stored in memory. As a result, a representation of the new experience is formed that contains both aspects of the information actually presented and features of the script or schema used as a basis for interpreting and organizing it. Once such a representation is formed, its features may often be incorrectly recalled as having been specified in the original information. Thus, as Johnson, Bransford, and Solomon (1973) found, people who read that (e.g.) John pounded the nail into the wall may interpret this in terms of a prototypic schema of someone performing the act with a hammer, and therefore may subsequently recall that a hammer was actually mentioned in the original material.

Assumption 2. When people are called upon to judge a person, object, or event, they do not perform an exhaustive search of memory for all previously acquired information that is relevant to this judgment; rather, they sample only a subset of this information that is most easily accessible and, given that this subset is sufficiently consistent in its implications, may base their judgments on these implications alone. This assumption, which also has its roots in the early work of Bruner (1957), has more recently been the basis of extensive research by Tversky and Kahneman (1973, 1974). These researchers have found in several different studies that people's judgments of the frequency of occurrence of a type of object or event, and therefore perceptions of its representativeness, depend on how easily instances of this type can be recalled and not on an exhaustive search of the entire set of these instances stored in memory. The notion that judgments are based upon only a subset of the relevant information one has available is also found in Taylor and Fiske's (1979) analysis of "top of the head" phenomena. Moreover, it is implicit in self-perception theory (Bem, 1967), which assumes that people's self-judgments are based primarily upon the perceived implications of their most recent behavior, with previously acquired but less readily accessible information being virtually ignored (see also Salancik, 1974; Salancik & Conway, 1975).

Assumption 3.   Once information has been organized and encoded, this encoding, rather than the information itself, serves as the primary basis for subsequent judgments of the persons, objects, and events to which it is relevant. Although the original information as well as the encoding of it may initially have some effect on these judgments, the relative influence of the encoding will increase over time. A version of this assumption underlies the early work of Bartlett (1932), who postulated that once a person or object has been labeled with the name of a preexisting concept, subsequent inferences are likely to be based upon attributes associated with the concept to which the label refers rather than upon the actual attributes of the object labeled. Bartlett further assumed that once this label is assigned, the details of the original information are forgotten, with the result that the label and its implications have more influence. A similar notion is fundamental to research considered in detail later in this chapter. For example, Carlston (1980) and Higgins, Rholes, and Jones (1977) both found evidence that the trait labels used by subjects to encode a target person's behavior, rather than the actual behavior manifested by this person, tended to provide the basis for later judgments of the person. Moreover, in some instances this tendency increased with the time interval between the initial encoding of the behavior and the judgments subsequently reported. More complex representations may also persist to affect judgments independently of the information upon which they were originally based. For example, Ross and his colleagues (Ross, Lepper, & Hubbard, 1975; Ross, Lepper, Strack, & Steinmetz, 1977) have shown that subjects' explanations of both their own and another's behavior continue to affect judgments even after the information explained has been discredited. Similarly, Sherman, Ahlm, Berman, and Lynn (1978) have shown that the label attached to a social issue comes to function autonomously of the factors that led to the label

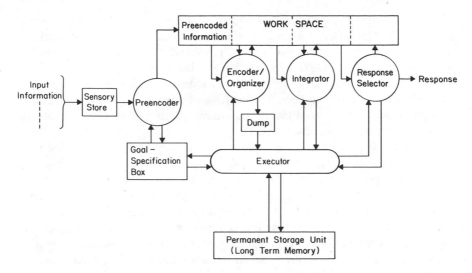

FIG. 5.1.   Flow diagram of proposed information-processing model. Processing units are enclosed in circles, and storage units in rectangles. (Only those paths of primary concern to this paper are presented.).

to initially be assigned, and therefore influences behavioral decisions to work on projects related to the issue.

The following formulation provides a framework for conceptualizing these phenomena and the bases for the assumptions to which they pertain. Because the formulation is described elsewhere (Wyer & Srull, 1980), and because many of its implications are not germane to the particular issues of concern in this chapter, we forego a detailed presentation of it here. Rather, we focus only on those aspects of the formulation that are particularly relevant to the assumptions noted in the foregoing section and that bear directly on the determinants and effects of the manner in which informatin is encoded.

The information-processing model we propose can be diagramed metaphorically as shown presented in Fig. 5.1. It consists of four interrelated storage units and five processing units. Many of these units correspond to components of the general information-processing system outlined by Bower (1975). We focus here on the units of primary relevance to the issues of concern in this chapter, with the others noted only briefly.

Storage Units

The storage units, which are represented by rectangles in Fig. 5.1, include a Sensory Store, a Goal Specification Box, a Work Space, and a Permanent Storage Unit. The Sensory Store is simply a receptacle for all sensory input that impinges on the organism, and its functions are not critical to our present puposes. The *Goal Specification Box* contains immediate processing objectives (e.g., to form an impression of a person, to predict whether a student would make a good research assistant, to decide whether a restaurant described by an acquaintance would be a good place to eat, etc.) and a representation of the procedures to be used for accomplishing them. The contents of this unit are used to direct the flow of information between the various storage units and processing units in pursuit of the processing objectives.

The *Work Space* is a rather complex temporary repository for both the raw input material to be processed (i.e., encoded, organized, integrated, etc.) and the output of this processing. This unit corresponds roughly to the working memory component described by Bower (1975) and the central processor of Newell and Simon (1972). Although the Work Space has limited storage capacity, material may be retained in it for some time if it is useful for the attainment of present or anticipated processing objectives. However, if the immediate processing objectives for which the material is relevant have been attained, or if the information is not expected to be used for some time, the contents of the Work Space will eventually be cleared. When this occurs, all material that has not previously been transmitted to Permanent Storage is lost. This latter assumption turns out to be extremely important, as we shall see.

The *Permanent Storage Unit,* which is analogous to long-term memory, is the most central to our present concerns. It therefore is discussed in somewhat more detail than the other model components. Our conceptualization is quite different than many other recent formulations in which long-term memory is viewed as a network of interrelated concepts, represented by nodes and interconnected by pathways denoting their association (cf. Anderson, 1976; Anderson & Bower, 1973; Collins & Loftus, 1975). With some modifications, such models can do a reasonable job of accounting for many phenomena of concern in social cognition research (Wyer & Carlston, 1979). However, in contrast to this more structured view, we conceptualize long-term memory as a set of content-addressable storage bins. Each bin is tagged in a way that specifically identifies the concept or set of concepts to which its contents refer. Thus, bins may pertain to particular individuals (Jimmy Carter, one's wife, etc.), or to prototypic persons or groups (Republicans, college professors, feminists, etc.), and to either specific events (last year's New Year's Eve party), or general ones (eating in a restaurant). The information contained in a bin may vary in both type and complexity. For example, a bin containing information about a person (Jimmy Carter, a college professor, etc.) may include general attributes of the person, prior judgments of him/her, visual images of the person, configural representations of the person's general characteristics or behavior in certain types of social situations, sequences of events in which the person participated, etc. Each configuration of attributes and events contained in a bin is referred to in this chapter as a *schema*. Each type of information described earlier, be it a single judgment or a schema, is considered to function as a single piece of information that is deposited in, or retrieved from, a bin as a single unit.

It is worth noting that a given piece of information may often be stored in more than one bin. For example, a representation of Mary slapping John at last year's New Year's Eve party might be stored in bins pertaining to "Mary," to "John," to "last year's New Year's Eve party," or to parties in general. Where material is stored depends on the information-processing objectives at the time it is received. For example, a judge who receives the information with the objective of forming an impression of John is likely to store it in the "John" bin, but may not store it in other possible bins. To this extent, the information will not be retrieved at a later point in time when information about Mary is sought. Although a detailed consideration of the implications of this aspect of the model is beyond the scope of this paper, its relevance to an understanding of information accessibility is obvious. (For an elaboration of these matters, see Wyer & Srull, 1980.)

In addition to bins pertaining to persons and events, we also postulate more general, semantic bins. These bins, which are of primary relevance to the research to be discussed in this chapter, contain concepts about attributes and behaviors, each of which has a name and is accompanied by features that serve as bases for interpreting new input information. For example, the trait concept "hostile" may have a set of features that include alternative names that identify the trait (e.g., "aggressive") and representations of behavior (e.g., propositional statements, imaginal examplars, etc.) that typify the trait. Such a configuration may be conceptualized as a *trait schema,* a term we use extensively later in this paper. It should be noted that the features of different trait schemata may overlap. That is, a single behavior may exemplify more than one trait, and thus may be contained in more than one trait schema. The implications of this are also noted.

A distinction should be made between trait schemata of the sort contained in a semantic bin and the schemata contained in a person bin. The material in semantic bins is not associated with particular individuals or groups; rather, these bins are analogous to mental dictionaries of trait and behavioral terms. Thus, a "hostile" schema in a semantic bin may consist of behaviors or intentions that typify hostility along with other trait terms that are synonymous with "hostile." However, none of these behaviors are specifically associated with any real or hypothetical individual. In contrast, a prototypic "hostile person" bin may also exist, the contents of which may consist of several schemata of either particular individuals one has known, or of hostile persons in general. These schemata may contain behavioral sequences at different levels of abstractness, configurations of traits that characterize such persons in different contexts, or both. Note that the traits in these hostile person schemata may not necessarily be synonymous with "hostile." Rather, they may often be denotatively unrelated attributes that are thought to characterize hostile individuals or types of hostile persons in various situations. In this regard, several different schemata may be contained in the same bin, the features of which may also be different.

Storage and Retrieval Processes.   Permanent Storage bins contain only the output of the processing units (the Encoder/Organizer, Integrator, and Response Selector) that has been transmitted to them after processing is completed. Thus, any material that has not at least been encoded will not be contained in Permanent Storage. Information is deposited in the bins in the order it is transmitted, so that the most recently used piece of information is always on top. This is important because bins containing information that is potentially relevant for the attainment of immediate processing objectives are searched from the top down. Thus, when two pieces of information are both potentially useful for attaining a particular processing objective, the more recently deposited piece is the first to be identified as relevant, and thus is the more likely to be used. Finally, if a piece of information is retrieved from any point in the bin for use in processing, it is returned to the top of the bin rather than to its original location, and thus becomes more accessible for later use. This assumption implies that the relative locations of concepts and schemata in long-term memory are subject to change as the result of processing information. As a result, the information that is retrieved at any given time is often likely to depend in part on what fortuitously happens at the time to be near the top of the bin from which material is being sought.

There is obviously a high degree of interrelatedness among concepts and the bins in which they are contained. The name of concepts contained in one bin may serve as tags that identify other bins. Thus, the bin pertaining to an acquaintance, Helga, may contain information that she is a native of Germany or is a student in psychology. However, ''German'' and ''psychology student'' may be tags of prototypic person bins that contain concepts and schemata associated with these types of persons. Alternatively, a ''German'' bin may contain the names of individual persons in this category, each of which identifies a bin containing information about these persons that has nothing to do with their nationality per se. Thus, our conceptualization of memory retains many features of other models that appear more structured. However, it can account for several phenomena that are hard to predict on the basis of prior formulations.

Processing Units

The five processing units comprising the system diagramed in Fig. 5.1 (the Preencoder, the Encoder/Organizer, the Integrator, the Response Selector, and the Executive Unit) can be described fairly briefly. The *Preencoder* consists of a system of filters that are capable of separating various types of input information. A primary function of this unit is to distinguish between information that is relevant to the objectives of information processing (which is sent to the Goal Specification Box) and information that is to be processed in the pursuit of these objectives (which is sent to the Work Space). However, more specialized filters that enable information of potential relevance to a processing objective to be identified may also be invoked.

The information sent to the Work Space by the Preencoder is operated on by one or more of three additional units, depending on the objectives to be attained. Of these processing units, the *Encoder/Organizer* is of greatest relevance to the questions of concern in this paper, (that is, how behavioral information is interpreted and its effects on judgments of the actor). Its function is to interpret or organize new information by comparing its features with those of previously formed concepts and schemata that exist in Permanent Storage. This is done in two stages. First, specific aspects of the information are encoded in terms of either trait or behavioral concepts drawn from semantic bins.[1] Thus, for example, features of information that one person helped another on an examination might be compared to features of either a schema associated with the trait "dishonest," one associated with "helpful," or one associated with "intelligent." The behavior may therefore be encoded by using any one of these labels, depending on which schema happens to be drawn from the semantic bin. In this regard, we assume that in most cases, the first concept drawn from a bin that is applicable for encoding the input material will be the one used, and that additional search is unlikely.[2]

After the individual pieces of stimulus information have been semantically encoded, the Encoder/Organizer may then interpret this information in terms of more complex configural concepts or schemata of the sort contained in person and event bins. Thus, a cluster of behavioral and trait features of a person may be encoded in terms of a schema associated with a general type of person ("college

---

[1]In later versions of this model, it may be necessary to take into account the possibility that certain configurations of information are encoded directly on the basis of material in person or event bins, without going through a preliminary stage of encoding individual features using concepts in the semantic bin. For example, close personal acquaintances may typically be recognized on the basis of a comparison of the configuration of their features with configurations contained in a "significant other" bin, without a prior encoding of the individual features comprising the configuration. However, this could be handled by postulating an additional semantic bin containing names of persons along with their "definitions" (e.g., configurations of physical features). Such a bin would function similarly to other semantic bins such as those containing the names and definitions of particular behaviors.

[2]When information presented cannot readily be encoded in terms of any existing concept, or when the processing objectives specified in the Goal Specification Box dictate that a particularly accurate encoding of the information be made, several potentially applicable schemata may be retrieved, and the stimulus information encoded in terms of whichever schema produces the best fit. However, this possibility is relatively unlikely under the conditions of concern in this paper, and it is therefore not discussed in detail.

professor,'' ''feminist,'' etc.) or a specific person one has known. Alternatively, information concerning time-based sequences of events, such as that a person is breaking up with his wife and the conditions surrounding it, may be encoded and organized in terms of a prototypic event schema (or ''script''; see Abelson, 1976).

Two points are important. First, the information to be encoded or organized may be externally generated, it may be previously acquired information that is retrieved from memory, or it may be a combination of both. For example, new information about an acquaintance, or an event one has heard about in the past, may be interpreted by retrieving previous information about the person or event, and invoking a prototypic schema that allows both the new and old information to be incorporated into a single representation. Thus, suppose I know from past experience that a particular person typically succeeds on a certain type of task and I have constructed a representation of this person as someone with high ability. If I then learn that the person has recently failed on similar tasks, I may interpret this latter information in terms of a prototypic schema of a person with high skill who initially performs well but becomes bored, loses motivation, and ends up doing badly. Alternatively, I may make a variety of situational attributions such as that the person was distracted or had too little sleep the night before to support my representation of the person as someone with high ability (cf. Jones, Rock, Shaver, Goethals, & Ward, 1968; Weiner & Kukla, 1970).

Second, the encoding of information in terms of prototypic schemata and concepts presumably involves a comparison of the features of the information presented with features of the schema. However, the schema may not include, nor even be relevant to, all the features of the information presented. On the other hand, the schema may include some features that are *not* included in the information being interpreted. Thus, although a schema may be deemed appropriate for encoding information about a person or event on the basis of common features, the ultimate representation of the person or event in terms of this schema may contain features that were not present in the original material, excluding some that were. Note that which features of the original information are retained in the encoding of it may depend on which of several alternative schemata happen to actually be used as a basis for encoding and organizing it.

Although the *Integrator* and *Response Selector* are of considerable importance in our general formulation of information processing, we forego a detailed discussion of them here. The Integrator is used when the encoded information has several alternative implications for a single judgment or decision, and the judge must combine these implications in some way to arrive at a single value. In some cases, algebraic combination rules may be invoked (for summaries of such rules, see Anderson, 1974; Wyer, 1974). The particular nature of these rules is likely to depend on the type of information presented and the type of judgment to be made (for a more detailed discussion of this possibility, see Wyer, 1974; Wyer & Carlston, 1979).

The Response Selector is activated when a judgment or decision must be communicated to another in a language the other can understand. In experimental situations, this translation often consists of mapping an internal representation of a judgment onto a response scale with predefined numerical or verbal labels. The process of making this translation and the factors that affect it have been the subject of substantial research in the area of social judgment (Ostrom & Upshaw, 1968; Parducci, 1965; Upshaw, 1969, 1978). Again, we do not fully develop the processes involved here. However, it is worth noting that these two bodies of social psychological research, one concerned with social judgment and the other with information integration, may ultimately both be incorporated into the general conceptualization we propose in a way that permits reasonably precise statements to be made concerning the functions of the two processing units.

Finally, the *Executive Unit* functions to identify and retrieve material from bins in Permanent Storage for use in processing. This material may consist either of previously acquired information that is to be further organized or integrated, or it may consist of concepts and prototypic schemata that are used to interpret and organize other information. Once a given stage of processing is completed, both the concepts and prototypic schemata used in processing the input information, and the results of this processing, are returned by the Executive Unit to appropriate bins in Permanent Storage. This is done in the order the processing takes place. Thus, if a schematic representation of a person is formed, followed by a single judgment of him/her on the basis of this representation, the schema is deposited first in a bin pertaining to the person and the judgment then stored on top of it.[3] As a result, the judgment rather than the schema is more likely to be retrieved when information about the person is sought in the future.

The particular Permanent Storage bins from which information is drawn, and to which it is returned, presumably depend on processing objectives, and are governed by information in the Goal Specification Box. Thus, for example, if the objective is to determine how good Mary would be as a graduate student, any new information about her (once it is encoded in terms of concepts in semantic bins) is compared with schemata drawn from a "graduate student" bin that pertain either to particular graduate students one has known in the past, or prototypic graduate students that are characterized as "good" or "bad." Once a schema that is applicable for encoding the information about Mary has been identified, the prototypic schema used for this purpose is returned to the top of the "graduate student" bin, whereas the representation of Mary is returned to the "Mary" bin from which it can later be retrieved for future use. Moreover, if a

---

[3]Here and elsewhere in this chapter, a semantic distinction is made between a "judgment," and an "encoding." It is recognized that a judgment, which typically involves the assignment of a stimulus configuration to some category, is a special form of encoding. The two terms are used primarily for convenience in communicating some of the ideas to be presented throughout this chapter.

formal judgment of Mary (e.g., "good student") has been made as a result of this process, the judgment will be stored in the "Mary" bin on top of the configural representation of her that originally led to this judgment.

General Implications of the Model

The social information-processing system we have described here is obviously quite sketchy. Indeed, even in the more formal presentation of the system (Wyer & Srull, 1980), several aspects need to be made more precise. In some cases, this precision can only be attained with the help of empirical data that bear upon some of the assumptions underlying it. However, even in its present form, the formulation has several general implications of relevance to the issues of concern in this volume, and to the research to be described later in this chapter. For example, note that the formulation incorporates all three of the general assumptions underlying research in social cognition cited at the beginning of this section. To summarize its more important implications:

1. If information about a person or event has been retrieved from Permanent Storage and reencoded or reorganized, the revised schema will then be deposited on top of any previous information in the bin pertaining to that person or event. Thus, the reencoded representation of the person or event, rather than the original encoding, is most likely to be retrieved in the future for use in making additional judgments. Moreover, once a judgment is made of a person or event on the basis of certain infromation, this judgment is deposited in Permanent Storage on top of the information on which it was based. Therefore, the judgment itself, rather than the information that led to it, is more likely to be recalled and used in the future.

2. If judgments of a person or event are made a short time after new information about the object is presented, and therefore before this information is cleared from the Work Space, the judgment may be based in part upon the original material as well as the subsequent encodings of it. Moreover, the material will be able to be recalled accurately, in its preencoded and preorganized form. However, after a period of time has elapsed and the Work Space has been cleared, only the encoded material deposited in Permanent Storage is available. As a result, the encoding of information is apt to have a greater effect on judgments over time, whereas implications of the original, preencoded information will have less effect. Similarly, the effect of encoding and organization of information on the recall of this information is also likely to increase over time.

3. Previously acquired concepts that have been recently used to encode or organize information for one purpose may often be retrieved from memory for use in processing additional information for a different purpose. However, unless subsequent information is acquired about the objects to which these concepts

pertain, the concepts will remain near the top of the bin in which they are contained. In such cases, they may still be readily retrieved and applied to new material, even though a substantial period of time has elapsed since they were previously activated.

In the remainder of this chapter, we first briefly cite a few representative studies to demonstrate the applicability of the formulation proposed to issues of concern in constructive and reconstructive memory, and the effects of prior judgments on subsequent ones. Then, we describe in more detail a recent series of studies we have personally conducted on the effects of category accessibility on the interpretation of person information. In combination, these studies bear on all three of the assumptions we have described as underlying social cognition theory and research, and they also help to evaluate certain aspects of the formulation proposed.

THE ROLE OF SCHEMATA IN MEMORY
FOR EPISODIC INFORMATION

As previously noted, the interpretation of information in terms of a schema may often assume the existence of features that were not stated explicitly in the information, but are required for the schema to apply. Once this encoding occurs, the added features become part of the representation of the person or event to which the information pertains. If this representation is deposited in Permanent Storage as a single unit, and if the information originally presented is subsequently cleared from the Work Space, the recall of this information will be based solely on the stored representation of it. Thus, it will include the added features as well as features of the original material, and these two sets of features may not be distinguishable.

Perhaps the best evidence concerning this possibility is a recent study by Spiro (1977), which also demonstrates the role of processing objectives in the representation and recall of information. In some conditions of this study, subjects read one of two ostensibly true studies about an engaged couple as part of an experiment described as being concerned with "reactions to situations involving interpersonal relations." In both stories, the man tells his financee that he does not want children. Then, in one story, the woman responds by saying that she shares the man's views. In the other, however, she becomes greatly upset and enters into a bitter argument with her husband-to-be. It seems reasonable to suppose that subjects with the objective of reacting to interpersonal relations may interpret this material with reference to prototypic event schemata they have formed in the past about engaged and married couples. In the first case, this schema may be of two persons who love one another, share similar values, get married, and live happily ever after. In the second case, however, it may be of two people who love one another but find they cannot agree on issues of importance, wind up in conflict, and ultimately separate.

After reading one of the two stories, participants performed an unrelated activity during which the experimenter ''incidentally'' remarked to some subjects that the couple described in the story eventually married and were still happily together, but remarked to others that the couple ultimately broke their engagement and had not seen each other since. Suppose subjects attempt to interpret the experimenter's remark in the context of the prior information they received. In some cases, the comment is consistent with expectations based on the prototypic schema described earlier, and no further interpretation or organization of the material would be expected. In the other cases, however, the experimenter's remark is inconsistent with the implications of the schema, and the remark therefore requires further assumptions in order to reconcile it with the original material. This may be done by invoking additional prototypic schemata concerning interpersonal conflict or reconciliation, the contents of which connect the original information with the experimenter's final statement, and thus provide an explanation of the outcome described. Alternatively, subjects may infer that certain aspects of the information presented were incorrect. Or, they may attempt to reinterpret the information in a manner that makes it consistent with one or the other of the original schemata. In any case, the revised representation of the two persons and their relationship would then be deposited as a unit in Permanent Storage.

After completing the interpolated task, subjects were dismissed and asked to return either 2 days, 3 weeks, or 6 weeks later. In this later session, they were asked to recall the story they had read earlier. In doing so, subjects were told explicitly to write down only material that was actually contained in the story, and not to include any personal reactions or inferences they might have made about the people and events involved.

What sort of predictions would be made on the basis of the formulation proposed here? Because subjects were dismissed without being asked to give their reactions to the interpersonal situation they read about, the processing objectives were presumably not attained by the end of the first session. The original information would therefore be temporarily retained in the Work Space, and thus able to be recalled and distinguished from the encoded representation of it. With the passage of time, however, the Work Space is likely to be cleared, and only the encoding of the information is retained in Permanent Storage. In this encoded representation, the original material and the features that were inferred during the process of encoding it cannot be distinguished, and thus more errors in recall should occur.

Consistent with the foregoing interpretation, recall errors increased over time, and these errors were typically of the sort expected to result from attempts to reconcile the experimenter's "incidental remark" with the original material. For example, when subjects were first told that neither party wanted children but were later led to believe the couple had broken their engagement, some recalled the original information as stating that the couple had actually disagreed about having children; others recalled it as stating that one party ultimately changed his/her mind about the desirability of having children. In contrast, when subjects were told that the couple disagreed but wound up happily married, they tended to add details that minimized the implications of the disagreement, recalling that "the problem was resolved when they found that (the woman) could not have children anyway," or that although one person thought the matter was important, the other did not (for these and other concrete examples, see Spiro, 1977, pp. 144–145). These responses are all quite plausible explanations for the outcome of the couple's interaction that one might expect to be invoked in an attempt to reconcile the unanticipated outcome with the initial information. What is striking is that these explanations were recalled as actually having existed in the information presented, despite explicit instructions not to include inferences or personal reactions.

It is important to note, however, that these effects should theoretically not occur unless the representation of the information formed in the course of attaining processing objectives and ultimately placed in Permanent Storage is one that requires the addition of these explanatory features. In the conditions previously described, the ostensible purpose of the experiment was to study reactions to interpersonal relations. The statement of this purpose undoubtedly led subjects to process the information with the objective of understanding the couple being described and the events involving them. However, if other objectives were involved, schemata containing the additional features might not be invoked, and recall errors of the sort described earlier should not occur. In fact, this appears to be the case. In other conditions of Spiro's study, subjects were told that the experiment was simply concerned with memory, thus giving them a set to remember the original material but not necessarily to encode it in terms of an explanatory schema. In these conditions, recall errors were fewer, and they were not systematically affected by the experimenter's "incidental" remark.

Although the study by Spiro did not deal directly with the use of behavioral information to infer traits of persons involved and the effects of these trait assignments on later judgments, the intrusions and distortions evident in the recall data obtained in this study clearly have implications for the traits of the parties involved (i.e., judgments of them as conciliatory, rigid, selfish, understanding, etc.). Moreover, these implications may differ, depending on the particular type of intrusions or distortions that occurred. To this extent, the study confirms the important role that cognitive representation of interpersonal behavior may have on social judgments of persons to whom the representation pertains.

EFFECTS OF PRIOR JUDGMENTS
ON SUBSEQUENT ONES

The proposed formulation implies that once a judgment of a person is made on the basis of behavioral information, the representation formed of the person in the course of making this judgment (rather than the information itself) is apt to be the primary basis for later inferences about the person. Moreover, the relative influence of this representation is likely to increase over the time interval between making this judgment and the subsequent inference. This is because the original information is more apt to have been cleared from the Work Space as time goes on, and thus is no longer available.

These effects are most apparent when the original information and the representation formed in order to make the initial judgment have different implications for the final inference. A recent study by Carlston (1977, 1980) nicely demonstrates this. Subjects first read six behavioral vignettes of a target person that, in combination, implied that the person was either: (1) both kind and dishonest; or (2) both unkind and honest. After receiving this information, they rated the target with respect to one of the two traits (either kindness or honesty). Then, either a few minutes or several days later, they again rated the target, this time along both of the dimensions pertaining to the traits to which the information was directly relevant, and also along other evaluative dimensions. If subjects base their final judgments solely on the implications of the original behavioral information, these judgments should not differ as a function of subjects' initial ratings. However, suppose that in making their initial judgments of the target, subjects construct representations of the target as someone who has the trait being judged (i.e., a kind person), based on a prototypic schema of someone who has this trait. Moreover, suppose they then recall this representation to use as a basis for their final ratings. In the absence of other information, people typically infer that persons characterized by a favorable attribute are apt to have other favorable attributes (i.e., that kind person are honest) and that persons with an unfavorable attribute are likely to have other unfavorable ones. To this extent, there should be a positive relation between the favorableness of subjects' initial ratings of the target person and the final ones. When subjects' initial judgments were relatively extreme, and thus had clear implications for their final inferences, this was in fact the case.[4]

In addition, Carlston found that the effect of initial judgments on subsequent ones increased over the time interval between the two sets of ratings. This finding is consistent with our hypothesis that after a period of time has elapsed, the Work Space is cleared and the original information is no longer directly available for making final judgments, leading the initial judgment to have more effect. This

---

[4]Although there are certain contingencies in the overall effects described here, as noted by Carlston (1980), the nature of these contingencies is also consistent with the formulation proposed.

interpretation is strengthened by supplementary data in the Carlston study indicating that subjects recalled their initial judgments with surprising accuracy, even after a week had elapsed since the time they were made. In contrast, the behavioral information was forgotten much more rapidly as time went on.

In yet another research paradigm, Ross, Lepper, and Hubbard (1975) gave subjects feedback that they were either typically successful or unsuccessful in distinguishing between true and false suicide notes. Then, in some conditions, subjects were debriefed, being given clear and explicit information that the feedback they had received was false and based solely on a predetermined random schedule. Despite this debriefing, subjects who were told they had been successful predicted they would do better on similar tasks in the future than those who were told they had done badly. This suggests that subjects constructed explanations for the outcomes they received (e.g., explanatory scripts or schemata) that led them to attribute themselves either high or low ability; these self-schemata then persisted to affect their predictions of future performance even after the original information was discredited. Analogous effects on subjects' judgments of others have been reported by Ross et al. (1977).

In sum, the present conceptualization suggests that once a person either explicitly or implicitly makes a trait judgment of a person on the basis of the person's behavior, the representation of the person underlying this judgment attains an autonomous status in relation to the original material. Moreover, the representation, and perhaps the judgment based on it, is deposited in the appropriate bin on top of previously acquired material, and thus is likely to be used for future inferences to which it is relevant. The fact that this occurs even after the original information has been discredited has intriguing implications for many areas of study by social psychologists, and the psychological processes underlying such effects are certain to be the focus of much future research.

THE EFFECTS OF CATEGORY ACCESSIBILITY ON THE INTERPRETATION OF NEW INFORMATION

The research just described was primarily concerned with the effect of an initial representation of information about a person or event on the subsequent recall and use of information about that *same* person or event. However, this restriction is unnecessary. Concepts or schemata that are acquired or retrieved from memory for a given purpose are presumably returned to Permanent Storage on top of the bin to which they are relevant. Thus, these concepts or schemata are much more likely to be retrieved in the future for use in making judgments to which they are applicable. Although the previous studies cited were interpreted in terms of the retrieval and use of representations stored in person and event bins, similar considerations arise in the case of material contained in semantic bins. Thus, for example, suppose the trait schema associated with ''honest'' has recently been used to interpret behavioral information about Andrew Young, after which it is redeposited on top of the semantic bin from which it was drawn. As a result, it is more likely to be retrieved for use in encoding subsequent information that another person (other than Young) has told his girlfriend that her new hair style is unattractive, than would the schema associated with "unkind," even though both schemata are applicable. Therefore, if the encoding rather than the original behavior is used as a basis for later judgments of the person, this person is more apt to be evaluated favorably than would otherwise have been the case. These considerations suggest that the judgments of people may often be affected by quite fortuitous events that happen to increase the accessibility of one or another concept that is subsequently used to encode new information.

An Initial Demonstration

A provocative demonstration of this possibility was reported by Higgins, Rholes, and Jones (1977). Subjects were first administered a "color-naming" task that required them to remember four trait names and six names of inanimate objects. In each of two (*Applicable Priming*) conditions, the trait terms could be used to describe the same set of behaviors. However, the terms in one condition were all favorable (*adventurous, self-confident, independent,* and *persistent*), whereas in the other they were all unfavorable (*reckless, conceited, aloof,* and *stubborn*). In two other (*Inapplicable Priming*) conditions, the four trait terms also had either favorable or unfavorable implications, but were inappropriate for describing the set of behaviors. After being exposed to one of these sets of trait terms as part of the "color-naming" task, subjects ostensibly took part in an unrelated study of "reading comprehension." Here, they were asked to read the following paragraph about a stimulus person, Donald, whose behavior could be readily encoded using the trait terms in either of the Applicable Priming sets. (The two applicable trait terms, which were of course not contained in the paragraph read by subjects, are given in parentheses following each behavioral description):

> Donald spent a great deal of his time in search of what he liked to call excitement. He had . . . risked injury, and even death, a number of times. . . . He was thinking perhaps he would do some skydiving or maybe cross the Atlantic in a sailboat (*adventurous/reckless*). By the way he acted, one could readily guess that Donald was well aware of his ability to do many things well (*self-confident/conceited*). Other than business engagements, Donald's contacts with people were rather limited. He felt he didn't really need to rely on anyone (*independent/aloof*). Once Donald made up his mind to do something, it was as good as done. . . . Only rarely did he change his mind, even when it might well have been better if he had (*persistent/stubborn*) [p. 145].

After reading the foregoing paragraph, half of the subjects in each priming condition characterized Donald's behavior in their own words, whereas the remaining judges did not. Then, all judges evaluated Donald. Finally, they attempted to recall the exact content of the paragraph they had read. Results were consistent with the hypotheses previously outlined. First, when the priming words were applicable for encoding the behavioral information, subjects who wrote descriptions of Donald typically used trait words or phrases that were either the same as or synonyms of the priming words, and the evaluative implications of these encodings were biased in the direction expected. When the priming words were inapplicable, however, the evaluative implications of the behavioral descriptions were if anything opposite in direction to those of the priming words. Finally, the overall evaluation of Donald increased with the favorableness of the implications of the priming words when these words were applicable for encoding Donald's behavior, but was minimally affected by the priming words when they were not applicable.

The findings reported by Higgins et al. (1977) suggest that the effect of information on one's attitudes and beliefs may be influenced substantially by prior, objectively irrelevant experiences that increase the accessibility of one or another set of concepts for use in interpreting this information. It is therefore of interest to explore in more detail the dynamics underlying the effects of category accessibility and the conditions in which these effects occur. A series of studies by the present authors are currently under way to explore several issues made salient by Higgins et al. (1977) in combination with the general conceptualization we outlined at the beginning of this chapter. They include the extent to which trait schemata can be made accessible by priming behavioral instances of these schemata as well as trait names, and the factors that affect the magnitude, duration, and generalizability of priming effects. In our discussion of this research, we also consider the utility of the proposed formulation of person memory in accounting for priming effects in relation to that of alternative formulations.

The Indirect Priming of Trait Schemata

Theoretical Considerations.   In the Higgins et al. (1977) study, specific trait terms that presumably could be used to describe the behavioral information presented about the target person were primed. However, the priming task theoretically does more than simply make particular words more accessible. In addition, it increases the accessibility of more general concepts, or schemata, to which these words refer. Thus, priming "honest" may not only increase the likelihood that this particular word is used to describe a behavior to which it is potentially applicable, but it may also increase the likelihood of using semantically related words (e.g., "trustworthy") that denote the same general schema. This is evidenced by Higgins et al.'s finding that when subjects were asked to describe the target person in their own words, they used trait terms that were identical to the priming words in less than half the cases. The majority of descriptors were synonyms or phrases with similar semantic implications to the priming words.

In addition to trait terms, such schemata contain prototypic behaviors that exemplify the trait. The similarity of these behaviors to those described in new information presumably determines the extent to which this information is encoded in terms of trait concept. However, if these behaviors are part of the schema, they should also have priming capabilities. That is, exposure to behavioral descriptions may activate a trait schema in which the behaviors are contained, and the increased accessibility of this schema may then lead other, more ambiguous behaviors to be interpreted in terms of that trait schema. This may be true even if the latter behaviors are presented in a completely unrelated context than in the first set.

Additional considerations arise in evaluating this possibility, however. First, many behaviors do not unambiguously reflect a given trait. That is, some aspects of a behavior, or representations of it, may be contained in several different schemata (cf. Carlston, 1980). For example, various aspects of the behavior "giving someone an answer on an examination" could exemplify "dishonest," "kind," or "intelligent," and thus could be contained in schemata associated with all of these traits. In other instances, features of a behavior may be remotely related to any trait schema, and thus may be unlikely to activate a schema unless they are accompanied by other schema-relevant information. Finally, behaviors may vary in the frequency with which they reflect a trait and thus in their typicality. For example, the behavior of kicking one's dog may almost always convey hostility, whereas the behavior of not paying one's rent until the landlord repaints his apartment may do so only in conjunction with other schema-relevant behaviors. Thus, the former behavior may be more likely to activate a "hostile" schema than the latter. More generally, a larger number of behaviors may need to be primed in order to activate a trait schema when these behaviors are ambiguous than when they are not.

These considerations suggest two things. First, the effect of priming trait-relevant behaviors on the interpretation of other trait-relevant information may increase with the number of different behaviors that are primed, and thus with the likelihood that the schema associated with the trait is activated.[5] Second, there may be substantial differences over traits (and schemata) in the amount of priming required to produce a given effect. Whereas some of these differences may be

---

[5]An increase in priming effects with the frequency of priming is also predicted by spreading activation formulations of memory (e.g., Collins & Loftus, 1975; Wyer & Carlston, 1979), which postulate that the more times a concept is activated, the greater the residual activation remaining at the location of this concept in memory, and therefore the more likely it is that the concept will be reactivated in the future. For further elaboration of this model and its implications, see the section under "A Comparison of the Storage Bin Model with Alternative Models of Memory."

idiosyncratic to the particular traits and behaviors involved, others may be more general. For example, unfavorable information may be generally less ambiguous than favorable information. This is suggested both by direct evidence (Wyer, 1973, 1974) and the results of impression formation experiments (Birnbaum, 1974; Wyer & Hinkle, 1976) that indicate that unfavorable information about persons has more influence on evaluations of them than does favorable information (see also Kanouse & Hanson, 1971). One reason for this is suggested by correspondent inference theory (Jones & Davis, 1965; Jones & McGillis, 1976). That is, favorable behavior is socially desirable, and thus engaging in this behavior may be attributed to an attempt to gain social approval. If this is generally the case, instances of an unfavorable trait may generally be more indicative of the trait, and thus more apt to activate the schema associated with it, than are instances of a favorable trait. To this extent, a greater number of behavioral instances may be required to activate schemata associated with favorable traits than to activate those associated with unfavorable traits.

Another fairly obvious determinant of priming effects is the time interval between the occurrence of priming and the acquisition of the information to be interpreted. The storage bin conceptualization of memory we have proposed implies that when several alternative concepts and schemata could potentially be used to interpret new information, the one that is nearest the top of the bin from which material is being drawn will be the one used. Priming may lead a relevant trait schema to be used for one purpose and then returned to the top of the semantic bin. However, with the passage of time, other trait schemata are also likely to be used, and thus to be deposited on top of the primed schema. Some of these more recently used schemata may also be applicable for encoding the new information. As a result, the accessibility and the use of a schema to encode stimulus material is likely to decrease over the time interval between its prior activation and the presentation of the new material.

Empirical Evidence.   The various possibilities described earlier were explored in two initial studies by Srull and Wyer (1979). Because the general procedure used in these studies was similar to that employed in subsequent experiments to be described, it may be worth presenting in some detail. Subjects in each study were initially recruited for a series of unrelated experiments, often extending over two experimental sessions. At the beginning of the first session, subjects were greeted by a male experimenter who introduced himself as a graduate student. The student indicated that although the participants were actually not assigned to him, the "real experimenter" had agreed to let him pretest a measure of how people perceive word relationships. Each item on the test, which was adapted from materials developed by Costin (1969), consisted of a set of four words, and the subject's task was to underline any three words that would make a complete sentence. Two alternative sentences could be constructed from each item. However, each sentence formed from some items (e.g., "leg break arm his'') necessarily described an instance of hostile behavior; each sentence formed from still other (*filler*) items (e.g., ''her found knew I'') was irrelevant to either of these traits.

Two separate studies were conducted, one in which hostility-related items were used as priming items, and the other in which kindess-related items were used. (The remaining filler items were common to both experiments.) To investigate the effect of differences in the amount of priming required to activate a schema, we varied both the total number of items in the test and the proportion of this number that were schema-related. Specifically, subjects completed a total of 30 or 60 items, either 20% (6 or 12) or 80% (24 or 48) of which were relevant to the concept to be activated. Schema-related and filler items were distributed unsystematically throughout the questionnaire.

After completing the sentence construction task, subjects were either turned over immediately to the ''real experimenter'' or were dismissed with instructions to return either one hour or one day later. In each case, the second experimenter (a female) indicated that the remainder of the experimental session consisted of three unrelated tasks, the first of which was described as an investigation of impression formation. In this task, subjects first read a paragraph describing the events in one afternoon of a target person's life. For one experiment, the paragraph described several behaviors that, based on normative data, were ambiguous with respect to hostility (e.g., refusing to let a salesman enter his apartment, refusing to pay the rent unless the landlord repainted his apartment, telling a garage mechanic he would have to go somewhere else if he couldn't fix his car the same day, demanding money back from a sales clerk, etc.). For the second experiment, vignettes describing behaviors that were ambiguous with respect to kindness were constructed in a similar fashion.[6] After reading the vignette, subjects first rated the target person along a series of trait dimensions, six of which (e.g., hostile, unfriendly, kind, considerate, etc.) were directly related to the target concepts and six of which (e.g., boring, selfish, interesting, intelligent, etc.) were evaluative but descriptively unrelated to either target concept. After making these ratings, subjects also estimated the hostility (or kindness) implied by additional individual behaviors that, based on normative ratings, were either ambiguous, or unambiguously high or low with respect to the amount of hostility (or kindness) they implied.

Ratings of the target person with respect to traits directly related to the primed concepts are shown for each experiment in Fig. 5.2 as a function of experimental variables. The general pattern of results is unequivocal and consistent with predictions. That is, the effect of priming on judgments increased with the number

---

[6]For each experiment, behaviors were defined as ambiguous if their mean normative rating with respect to hostility (or kindness) was relatively neutral, but these ratings had a high standard deviation (see Srull & Wyer, 1979, for a detailed discussion).

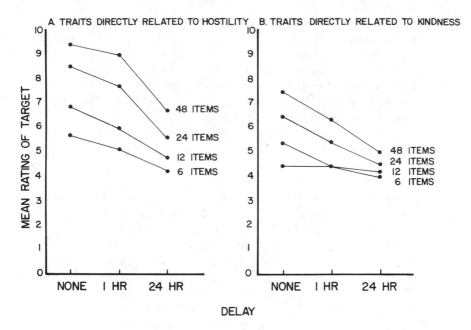

FIG. 5.2. Mean ratings of the target person with respect to: (A) traits directly related to hostility; and (B) traits directly related to kindness as a function of delay and number of schema-related priming items. (High values indicate greater estimates of the amount of the trait manifested by the target person.)

of schema-related items in the questionnaire, but decreased with the time interval between between the priming task and presentation of the target information. In addition, a comparison of the effect of priming hostility with the effect of priming kindness bears on our earlier speculations concerning the effects of ambiguity. For example, as few as 6 priming items were apparently sufficient to affect judgments of hostility, at least under no delay conditions. In contrast, the effect of priming kindness was negligible when the number of schema-related items was low (6 or 12). Furthermore, the effect of priming hostility was substantial even after a period of 24 hours, whereas the effect of priming kindness had dissipated almost entirely by this time. It is somewhat risky to generalize from these results, which pertain to only one trait at each level of favorableness. However, they are nonetheless consistent with our specualtion that more priming is often required to activate favorable trait schemata than unfavorable ones. Moreover, the more rapid attenuation of priming effects on kindness judgments suggests that instances of favorable traits are often relevant to several different schemata. Thus, other relevant concepts are likely to be activated in the 24 hour period between the priming task and stimulus presentation, decreasing the effect of the former priming.

Alternative Interpretations.   In evaluating the results of these initial studies, two alternative interpretations must be considered. Of these, the least interesting is that the results are an artifact of compliance with experimental demand characteristics. That is, if subjects had insight into the relvance of the initial (priming) task to the impression formation task, despite the elaborate precautions taken to make them appear unrelated, they may have inferred that the experimenter expected them to interpret the behavioral information in a manner consistent with the priming items and evaluated the target person accordingly. To investigate this possibility, subjects in the second experiment were asked after completion of the experimental session(s) to indicate which of the four tasks were most likely to be related to the same hypothesis. Following this question, they were also asked to indicate any other tasks that might have been related. Of 96 subjects run in the experiment, only five mentioned the priming task as related to any other task, and only one connected it to the impression formation task. Thus, subjects did not see the two tasks as intentionally related. Additional evidence against such a "demand" interpretation is provided in later experiments, to be reported shortly.

This does not mean, however, that subjects had no insight into the effect of the priming task on their later judgments. In an informal interview after the experiment, one participant spontaneously recalled noticing that she was interpreting the target's behavior as very kind while reading the stimulus vignette, and wondered if this was a result of forming the several kindness-related sentences contained in the previous task. However, she assumed that this effect was really fortuitous, and had no idea that it was part of the experiment. Thus, it appears that at least in some instances, subjects may have insight into the fact that their

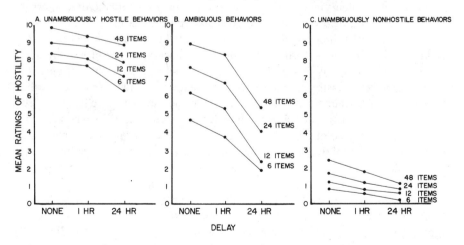

FIG. 5.3.   Mean hostility ratings of: (A) unambiguously hostile; (B) ambiguous; and (C) unambiguously nonhostile behaviors as a function of delay and number of hostility-related priming items.

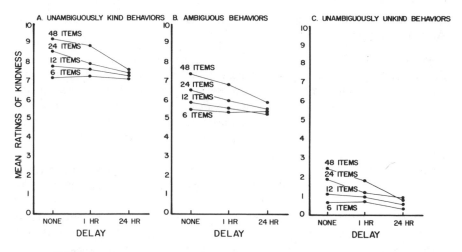

FIG. 5.4.   Mean kindness ratings of: (A) unambiguously kind; (B) ambiguous; and (C) unambiguously unkind behaviors as a function of delay and number of kindness-related priming items.

prior experience affects their interpretation of new information, although they do not connect this effect to the experimenter's hypothesis.

The second alternative interpretation is of more substantive importance and leads to still other considerations. Specifically, it is conceivable that the concepts made salient by the priming task have direct effects on evaluations of the target person that are *not* mediated by their effects on the interpretation of the information presented about the target. For example, subjects for whom the concept of hostility was activated may tend to rate a person as hostile regardless of the behavior manifested by this person. However, two sets of findings argue against this interpretation. First, if this were the case, it should also have been evident in the earlier study by Higgins et al. (1977). That is, the priming of favorable versus unfavorable trait terms should have affected evaluations of the target person regardless of the applicability for encoding the intervening behavioral information. However, as noted previously, priming affected judgments only when the terms being primed were potentially applicable.

Evidence that subjects did in fact interpret the behavioral information differently in the present experiments is provided by analyses of direct ratings of individual behaviors. The effects of experimental variables on these ratings, shown in Fig. 5.3 and Fig. 5.4, are similar to their effects on ratings of the target person. However, the ratings are more pronounced on judgments of ambiguous behaviors than on judgments of behaviors that have more clear implications for the rating being made. However, even these behaviors were apparently not totally unambiguous, and thus were also affected by priming to some extent.

Indirect Effects of Priming on Judgments
Along Other Trait Dimensions

The data reported by Higgins et al. (1977), suggest that priming does not have a direct influence on judgments of a person, but affects these judgments only through its mediating influence on the interpretation of information about the person. However, once a trait judgment is made on the basis of this interpretation, this judgment may have implications for other traits that are not directly related to either the material describing the person being judged, or the behavioral items in the priming task. This, of course, is suggested by Carlston's study described previously in the chapter. However, a judgment that the target possesses the trait being primed may reflect a perception of the target as representative of a prototypic person with that attribute (e.g., a "hostile person," a "kind person," etc.). Moreover, the schema associated with such a person may consist in part of other traits that, although not semantically related to the primed trait, are assumed to accompany the trait as a result of prior experience, and thus comprise one's implicit personality theory (Rosenberg & Sedlak, 1972). For example, although kind *behavior* is itself not typically related to intelligence, a kind *person* may be inferred to be intelligent as a result of "intelligence" being present in the prototypic schema of such a person. This reasoning implies that priming effects on judgments of a target with respect to a particular trait will generalize to judgments of other traits that are associated with it.

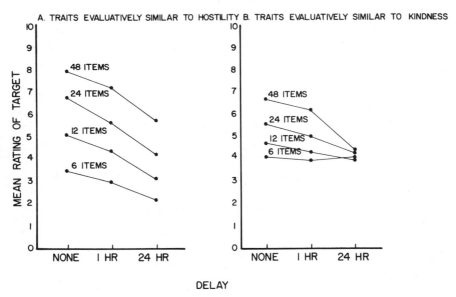

FIG. 5.5.   Mean ratings of the target person for: (A) traits evaluatively similar to hostility; and (B) traits evaluatively similar to kindness as a function of delay and number of schema-related priming items.

In fact, ratings of target persons with respect to traits that were evaluatively similar to the primed trait support this possibility. The effects of experimental variables on these ratings, shown in Fig. 5.5, were similar to, but significantly less in magnitude, than their effects on ratings of the primed trait (Fig. 5.2).

To summarize, then, the study by Higgins et al. (1977), shows that the priming of concepts does not have direct effects on judgments of persons along dimensions to which they are not applicable. However, the Srull and Wyer (1979) studies show that once information about a person is encoded in terms of a primed concept, the effects of this encoding on subsequent judgments may be quite widespread.

A Comparison of the Storage Bin Model with Alternative Models of Memory

Many, if not all, of the effects obtained in the studies described thus far could be interpreted on the basis of other conceptualizations of memory and encoding processes. One particularly attractive alternative is the spreading activation model of semantic memory proposed by Collins and Quillian (1969; see also Collins & Loftus, 1975), and extended by Wyer and Carlston (1979) into the area of person memory. According to such a formulation, concepts in memory are represented by nodes, and associations among these concepts by pathways connecting the nodes. Concepts are activated by excitation that is transmitted to them along these pathways from other activated concept nodes. The excitation at a given node must exceed a threshold value in order to be activated. Once a concept is deactivated (or is no longer being used), the excitation at its node dissipates gradually over time. However, during that period in which some residual excitation at the deactivated node remains, less excitation from other sources is required to reactivate it. The implications of this formulation are similar in many respects to those of the storage bin model we have proposed. That is, if one assumes that a trait concept node (e.g., ''hostile'') is connected to behavioral nodes by pathways, it follows that as more behavioral concepts are activated (that is, as the number of priming items increases), more excitation is transmitted to the concepts node, and thus the more likely it is that the node will be activated. Moreover, the shorter the time interval between the priming of this trait concept and the presentation of the stimulus information, the more residual excitation will remain at the concept node, and thus the more likely it is that excitation transmitted from related behavioral concepts will reactivate the concept.

However, several considerations suggest that such a formulation is less effective in accounting for the phenomena of concern here than the storage bin model. For one thing, rigorous applications of network-spreading activation models to lexical and semantic decision tasks (Collins & Quillian, 1969; Meyer & Schvanevelt, 1971; Schvanevelt & Meyer, 1973; Shoben, 1976) have yielded inconsistent evidence for priming effects with reaction time procedures. More important, the effects of priming on judgments obtained in these studies appear to disappear in a matter of seconds. In contrast, the effects of priming on judgments, obtained in the present studies, are often evident after a period of several hours. This suggests that the priming phenomena reported here may be due to factors other than those postulated on the basis of spreading activation models.

A second indication that the storage bin model is more useful in accounting for category accessibility effects on social stimulus judgments comes from the time interval between the encoding of the stimulus information and the judgment of the target person. According to the storage bin formulation, the original material as well as the encoding of it may affect judgments made a short time after the material is presented, because during this period the material may be temporarily retained in the Work Space. However, after a longer period of time, the Work Space may be cleared. Once this occurs, only the encoding of the information retrieved from Permanent Storage is available for use, and thus the encoding should have greater effect. Although such an increase in the effect of encoding over time would not be impossible to account for with a spreading excitation model, several untested ad hoc assumptions are necessary to do so (see Wyer & Carlston, 1979).

In fact, empirical evidence supports the hypothesis that temporal increases in encoding effects do occur in the conditions described earlier. In the study by Higgins et al. (1977), subjects returned 2 tweeks after making their initial judg-

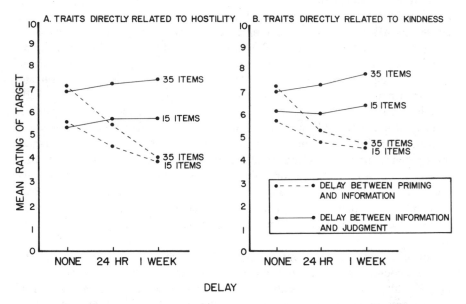

FIG. 5.6.   Mean ratings of the target person for: (A) traits directly related to hostility; and (B) traits directly related to kindness as a function of length of delay, type of delay, and number of schema-related priming items.

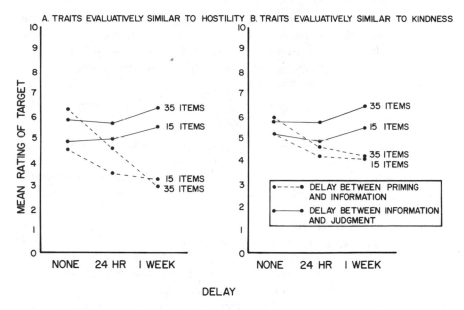

FIG. 5.7.   Mean ratings of the target person for: (A) traits evaluatively similar to hostility; and (B) traits evaluatively similar to kindness as a function of length of delay, type of delay, and number of schema-related priming items.

ments and repeated their evaluations of the target person. As expected, evaluations were more extreme in the direction of the priming concepts when they were made following the delay than when they were made immediately after the stimulus material was presented. To investigate these delay effects in the paradigm constructed by Srull and Wyer, we repeated the earlier studies using only two levels of priming (15 or 35 items). As before, some subjects completed hostility-related priming items and rated the target on traits either directly related or evaluatively similar to hostility. Others completed kindness-related priming items and rated the target on traits either directly related, or evaluatively similar, to kindness. As a replication of the earlier studies, one set of conditions varied— the time interval between priming and presentation of the stimulus material (no delay, 24 hour delay, or a 1-week delay). In addition, however, we added a second set of conditions in which the stimulus material was always presented immediately after the priming task, but the interval between stimulus presentation and the judgment of the target was varied. Mean ratings of the target person on traits directly related to hostility and kindness are plotted in Fig. 5.6 as a function of these variables. Mean ratings of the target on traits evaluatively similar to hostility and kindness are shown in Fig. 5.7. As in the earlier studies, the overall effect of priming decreased with the interval between the priming task and stimulus presentation, and the initial effect of differences in the amount of priming dissipated. In contrast, when subjects were allowed to encode the information immediately after the priming task, the overall effect of this encoding *increased* over time. Although the magnitude of this increase was not large, its reliability over priming concepts (hostility and kindness), and its consistency with the results reported by Higgins et al., suggest that it be considered seriously. As we have noted, a spreading activation formulation would have substantial difficulty in accounting for these data.

Temporal Locus of Encoding Effects

Thus far we have assumed that priming affects the encoding or interpretation of information at the time it is received, and that subsequent judgments are then based upon the encoded representation of the material. However, an alternative possibility is that both the primed concept and the original behavioral material are stored independently in memory until a judgment is requested. Then, the behavioral information is retrieved and reencoded, and the judgment is reported on the basis of this reencoding. If the latter interpretation is valid, the magnitude of priming effects should be a function of the accessibility of the primed concept at the time the information is retrieved and the judgment is made, rather than of its accessibility at the time the stimulus information is presented. There are two implications of this. First, priming effects should be a function of the interval between the priming task and the judgment (i.e., a function of the accessibility of the primed concept at the time this judgment is made) rather than of the time between the priming task and stimulus presentation. Second, priming should affect judgments when it occurs *after* the stimulus information is presented as well as before.

The first of these implications is called into question by the data reported in Fig. 5.6 and Fig. 5.7. As shown in these figures, the time interval between the priming task and the judgment was varied. However, in some conditions this variation was confounded with the length of the interval between the priming task and stimulus presentation, with the interval between stimulus presentation and judgment held constant. In other cases, it was confounded with the length of the interval between stimulus presentation and judgment, with the time between priming and stimulus presentation held constant. According to the alternative interpretation previously described, priming effects should decrease as delay increases under both conditions. However, although priming effects decreased over time in the first condition, they *increased* slightly in the second. Thus, the critical factor appears to be the interval between priming and stimulus presentation, and not between priming and the judgment.

The second implication was tested directly in a fourth study by the present authors. That is, the (hostility) priming task was varied at two levels (15 and 35 items) and administered *after* rather than before the stimulus information. In one set of conditions, the delay between the priming task and the final judgments was varied (no delay vs. 24-hour delay). In another set of conditions, the delay between the stimulus information and the priming task was varied. Because the behavioral information is apt to be recalled under long delay conditions, the

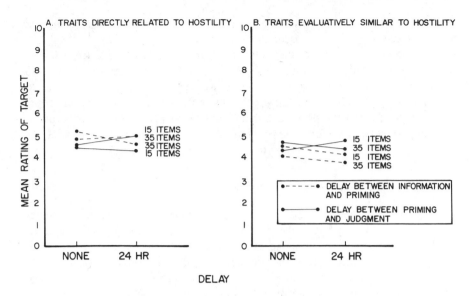

FIG. 5.8. Mean ratings of the target person for: (A) traits directly related to hostility; and (B) traits evaluatively similar to hostility as a function of length of delay, type of delay, and number of hostility-related priming items.

alternative interpretation implies that the effect of priming should be less in these conditions. However, as shown in Fig. 5.8, there was little difference in priming effects as a function of the length of delay, the type of delay, or the amount of priming. (Statistical analyses yielded no significant results involving any of these variables.) In other words, there was no evidence of any priming effects whatsoever when priming was administered after the stimulus information was presented.

These data, in combination with results of previous experiments, indicate that priming has an effect only if it precedes rather than follows the stimulus material. This provides strong evidence against the interpretation that reencoding of the stimulus material occurs at the time judgments are made, at least under the conditions of concern in this paper. Rather, the effect of increasing category accessibility appears primarily to affect the way in which information is encoded into memory at the time it is first received.[7] Moreover, once this encoding

---

[7]E. Tory Higgins (personal communication, January 3, 1979) has suggested that the failure for stimulus information to be reencoded after it is first received may occur only when the objectives for which the information is to be used (in this case, the goal of forming an impression of the person described) are stated at the outset. If the priming occurs after presenting the stimulus information, but before processing objectives are stated (in this case, before subjects are told to form an impression of the target, and thus before they encode the information in terms of traits), subjects may reencode the information in terms of whatever concepts are easily accessible at the time the objectives are imposed, and so priming effects may be more evident.

occurs, and the original information is cleared from the Work Space, its ultimate effect on judgments is increased.

Incidentally, the earlier study also provides additional evidence against a demand interpretation of priming effects obtained in previous studies. That is, if anything, the possibility that the experimenter is interested in the effect of the priming task on the interpretation of stimulus information should be more apparent here than when the priming task occurred first. Thus, the absence of any priming effects suggests that the previous pattern of results is not attributable to attempts by subjects to comply with experimenter expectancies.

The Generality of Concepts and Schemata Being Primed

The studies reported indicate that the accessibility of trait concepts and schemata can be systematically manipulated in a way that affects judgments of persons. However, we must ultimately understand more precisely the range of behaviors and situations to which these schemata apply. In this regard, our present conceptualization of a schema is admittedly rather underdeveloped. More attention must be given to the structure and organization of such schemata and the concepts contained in them. For one thing, certain behaviors may be more representative of a trait than others. It may ultimately be desirable to postulate a hierarchical schema in which concepts have various degrees of centrality, with more central concepts being better able to activate the schema than peripheral ones. This notion has been developed in more detail by Wyer and Carlston (1979) in the context of extending a spreading activation network model to the study of person memory.

The importance of clarifying the range of experiences to which schemata are typically applicable can be seen with reference to the first experiment conducted by Srull and Wyer, in which hostility-related concepts were primed. In the priming task used in this study, the sentences constructed pertained to hostility of a variety of types and toward a variety of objects. A question arises as to whether people have rather undifferentiated concepts of hostility, or whether they have several different, more circumscribed concepts. For example, aggressive acts toward persons or animals (e.g., kicking the cat) may reflect a different type of hostility than aggressive acts toward inanimate objects (e.g., kicking the car). To this extent, exposure to behaviors of the latter type may tend to affect the interpretation of information about people less than exposure to behaviors of the former type.

A more interesting consideration concerns the difference between one's own hostility and that of others. Suppose in a hypothetical experiment that some subjects are given priming items of the type "I him hit kicked," whereas others are given items of the type "me he hit kicked." The sentences constructed from the first type of item convey aggressive acts by oneself toward others, whereas those constructed from the second type convey hostile acts by another toward oneself. If priming of the sort considered in this paper activates general semantic schemata pertaining to hostility, that are independent of the objects toward whom it is directed, the two types of priming should have similar effects. However, it is conceivable that priming of the first type activates a self-schema that pertains only to one's own hostility, whereas priming of the second type activates concepts associated with others' hostility. To this extent, only the second type of priming would affect the interpretation of stimulus information about other persons (i.e., information of the sort presented in the studies reported here). On the other hand, the first type of priming, but not the latter, might affect the interpretation of one's own behavior, and therefore one's self-description. Research is currently underway to investigate these possibilities.

CONCLUSIONS

What have we learned about the determinants and effects of category accessibility as a result of the studies reported in this paper? Several conclusions seem justified:

1. Prior exposure to either the names of trait schemata or instances of these schemata may affect the interpretation of information to which the schemata are relevant, and therefore may influence judgments of persons to whom the information pertains. This may occur even when the information being interpreted is presented in a different context, and is ostensibly unrelated to the conditions in which the schemata were initially activated.

2. The accessibility of a trait schema, and therefore its use in interpreting behavioral information, is a positive function of the number of instances of the concept to which one has previously been exposed, but decreases as a function of the time interval between exposure to these instances and the presentation of the information to which the schema is relevant. On the other hand, once this information has been encoded in terms of the primed schema, the effects of this encoding appear to increase over the time interval between the encoding and the judgment of the person to whom it pertains.

3. The priming of trait concepts has very little, if any, effect on judgments of a target person unless these concepts are applicable for encoding specific information about this person. However, once this encoding has been made, and the person has been implicitly assigned the trait implied by the encoding, this judgment may serve as a basis for subsequent judgments of the person with respect to other traits that are descriptively unrelated to the behavioral information about the person, but are associated with the primed trait through prototypic schemata of people who possess this trait.

4. The effect of category accessibility on the interpretation of information occurs primarily at the time the information is initially encoded, rather than at the

time judgments are made. That is, there is no evidence that the information used in making a judgment is *re* encoded or reinterpreted on the basis of primed concepts that are salient at the time the judgment is made.

These various conclusions, as well as the other research in social cognition that we have noted briefly in this chapter, are consistent with the general formulation of information processing postulated by Wyer and Srull (1980), and outlined briefly at the beginning of this chapter. The formulation is still in its formative stages, and many loose ends need tying together. However, the consistency of its implications with the data currently available suggest that continued refinement of the model and exploration of its implications may be worthwhile.

Quite apart from the theoretical formulation underlying the research we have reported, the paradigm used in this research appears to be a fruitful one for investigating a variety of issues associated with the effect of catgory accessibility on judgments. In this regard, the prior use not only of trait schemata, but also more general schemata associated with social roles and stereotypes, may influence judgments through mechanisms similar to those described here. This possibility, along with others suggested by the formulation proposed in this chapter, are worthy of further investigation.

ACKNOWLEDGMENTS

This paper was supported by National Science Foundation Grant BNS 76-24001 to the first author, and USPHS Training Grants MH-14257 and MH-15140 to the second author. Appreciation is extended to Tory Higgins and Tom Ostrom for very helpful comments on an earlier version of this manuscript.

REFERENCES

Abelson, R. P. Script processing in attitude formation and decision-making. In J. S. Carroll & J. W. Payne (Eds.), *Cognition and social behavior*. Hillsdale, N.J.: Lawrence Erlbaum Associates, 1976.

Anderson, J. R. *Language, memory, and thought*. Hillsdale, N.J.: Lawrence Erlbaum Associates, 1976.

Anderson, J. R., & Bower, G. H. *Human associative memory*. Washington, D.C.: V. H. Winston, 1973.

Anderson, N. H. Application of a linear-serial model to a personality-impression task using serial presentation. *Journal of Personality and Social Psychology*, 1968, *10*, 354–362.

Anderson, N. H. Cognitive algebra: Integration theory applied to social attribution. In L. Berkowitz (Ed.), *Advances in experimental social psychology* (Vol. 7). New York: Academic Press, 1974.

Asch, S. E. Forming impressions of personality. *Journal of Abnormal and Social Psychology,* 1946, *41,* 258–290.

Bartlett, F. C. *Remembering: A study in experimental and social psychology.* Cambridge: Cambridge University Press, 1932.

Bem, D. J. Self-perception: An alternative interpretation of cognitive dissonance phenomena. *Psychological Review,* 1967, *74,* 183–200.

Bem, D. J. Self-perception theory. In L. Berkowitz (Ed.), *Advances in experimental social psychology* (Vol. 6). New York: Academic Press, 1972.

Birnbaum, M. H. The nonadditivity of personality impressions. *Journal of Experimental Psychology,* 1974, *102,* 543–561.

Bower, G. H. Cognitive psychology: An introduction. In W. K. Estes (Ed.), *Handbook of learning and recognitive processes* (Vol. 1). Hillsdale, N.J.: Lawrence Erlbaum Associates, 1975.

Bruner, J. S. *On perceptual readiness.* Psychological Review, 1957, *64,* 123–152.

Bruner, J. S. Social psychology and perception. In E. Maccoby, T. Newcomb, & E. Hartley (Eds.), *Readings in social psychology.* New York: Holt, Rinehart & Winston, 1958.

Byrne, D. *The attraction paradigm.* New York: Academic Press, 1971.

Cantor, N., & Mischel, W. Traits as prototypes: Effects on recognition memory. *Journal of Personality and Social Psychology,* 1977, *35,* 38–48.

Carlston, D. E. *The recall and use of observed behaviors and inferred traits in social inference processes.* Unpublished doctoral dissertation, University of Illinois, 1977.

Carlston, D. E. The recall and use of traits and events in social inference processes. *Journal of Experimental Social Psychology,* 1980, *16,* 303–329.

Collins, A. M., & Loftus, E. F. A spreading-activation theory of semantic processing. *Psychological Review,* 1975, *82,* 407–428.

Collins, A. M., & Quillian, M. R. Retrieval time from semantic memory. *Journal of Verbal Learning and Verbal Behavior,* 1969, *8,* 240–247.

Costin, F. The scrambled sentence test: A group measure of hostility. *Educational and Psychological Measurement,* 1969, *29,* 461–468.

Fishbein, M., & Hunter, R. Summation versus balance in attitude organization and change. *Journal of Abnormal and Social Psychology,* 1964, *69,* 505–510.

Higgins, E. T., Rholes, C. R., & Jones, C. R. Category accessibility and impression formation. *Journal of Experimental Social Psychology,* 1977, *13,* 141–154.

Johnson, M. K., Bransford, J. D., & Solomon, S. K. Memory for tacit implications of sentences. *Journal of Experimental Psychology,* 1973, *98,* 203–205.

Jones, E. E., & Davis, K. E. From acts to dispositions: The attribution process in person perception. In L. Berkowitz (Ed.), *Advances in experimental social psychology* (Vol. 2). New York: Academic Press, 1965.

Jones, E. E., & McGillis, D. Correspondent inferences and the attribution cube: A comparative reappraisal. In J. H. Harvey, W. J. Ickes, & R. F. Kidd (Eds.), *New directions in attribution research* (Vol. 1). Hillsdale, N.J.: Lawrence Erlbaum Associates, 1976.

Jones, E. E., Rock, L., Shaver, K. G., Goethals, G. R., & Ward, L. M. Pattern of performance and ability attribution: An unexpected primacy effect. *Journal of Personality and Social Psychology,* 1968, *10,* 317–340.

Kanouse, D. E., & Hanson, L. R. *Negativity in evaluations.* Morristown, N.J.: General Learning Press, 1971.

Kelley, H. H. Attribution theory in social psychology. In D. Levine (Ed.), *Nebraska Symposium on Motivation.* Lincoln: University of Nebraska Press, 1967.

Meyer, D. E., & Schvaneveldt, R. W. Facilitation in recognition between pairs of words: Evidence of a dependence between retrieval operations. *Journal of Experimental Psychology,* 1971, *90,* 227–234.

Newell, A., & Simon, H. A. *Human problem solving*. Englewood Cliffs, N.J.: Prentice-Hall, 1972.

Ostrom, T. M., & Upshaw, H. S. Psychological perspective and attitude change. In A. G. Greenwald, T. C. Brock, & T. M. Ostrom (Eds.), *Psychological foundations of attitudes*. New York: Academic Press, 1968.

Parducci, A. Category judgment: A range-frequency model. *Pyschological Review*, 1965, *72*, 407–418.

Rosenberg, S., & Sedlak, A. Structural representations of implicit personality theory. In L. Berkowitz (Ed.), *Advances in experimental social psychology* (Vol. 6). New York: Academic Press, 1972.

Ross, L., Lepper, M., & Hubbard, M. Perserverance in self perception and social perception: Biased attributional processes in the debriefing paradigm. *Journal of Personality and Social Psychology*, 1975, *32*, 880–892.

Ross, L., Lepper, M. R., Strack, R., & Steinmetz, J. Social explanation and social expectation: Effects of real and hypothetical explanations on subjective likelihood. *Journal of Personality and Social Psychology*, 1977, *35*, 817–829.

Salancik, G. R. Inference of one's attitude from behavior recalled under linguistically manipulated cognitive sets. *Journal of Experimental Social Psychology*, 1974, *10*, 415–427.

Salancik, G. R., & Conway, M. Attitude inferences from salient and relevant cognitive content about behavior. *Journal of Personality and Social Psychology*, 1975, *32*, 829–840.

Schank, R., & Abelson, R. *Scripts, plans, goals and understanding: An inquiry into human knowledge structures*. Hillsdale, N.J.: Lawrence Erlbaum Associates, 1977.

Schvaneveldt, R. W., & Meyer, D. E. Retrieval and comparison processes in semantic memory. In S. Kornblum (Ed.), *Attention and performance IV*. New York: Academic Press, 1973.

Schneider, D. J. Implicit personality theory: A review. *Psychological Bulletin*, 1973, *79*, 294–309.

Sherman, S. J., Ahlm, K., Berman, L., & Lynn, S. contrast effects and their relationship to subsequent behavior. *Journal of Experimental Social Psychology*, 1978, *14*, 340–350.

Shoben, E. J. The verification of semantic relations in a same-different paradigm: An asymmetry in semantic memory. *Journal of Verbal Learning and Verbal Behavior*, 1976, *15*, 365–379.

Spiro, R. J. Remembering information from text: The "State of Schema" approach. In R. C. Anderson, R. J. Spiro, & W. E. Montague (Eds.), *Schooling and the acquisition of knowledge*. Hillsdale, N.J.: Lawrence Erlbaum Associates, 1977.

Srull, T. K., & Wyer, R. S. The role of category accessibility in the interpretation of information about persons: Some determinants and implications. *Journal of Personality and Social Psychology*, 1979, *37*, 1660–1672.

Taylor, S. E., & Fiske, S. T. Salience, attention, and attribution: Top of the head phenomena. In L. Berkowitz (Ed.), *Advances in experimental social psychology* (Vol. 11). New York: Academic Press, 1979.

Tversky, A., & Kahneman, D. Availability: A heuristic for judging frequency and probability. *Cognitive Psychology*, 1973, *5*, 207–232.

Tversky, A., & Kahneman, D. Judgment under uncertainty: Heuristics and biases. *Science*, 1974, *85*, 1124–1131.

Upshaw, H. S. The personal reference scale: An approach to social judgment. In L. Berkowitz (Ed.), *Advances in experimental social psychology* (Vol. 4). New York: Academic Press, 1969.

Upshaw, H. S. Social influence on attitudes and on anchoring of congeneric attitude scales. *Journal of Experimental Social Psychology*, 1978, *14*, 327–339.

Weiner, B., & Kukla, A. An attributional analysis of achievement motivation. *Journal of Personality and Social Psychology*, 1970, *15*, 1–20.

Wyer, R. S. Category ratings as "subjective expected values": Implications for attitude formation and change. *Psychological Review*, 1973, *80*, 446–467.

Wyer, R. S. *Cognitive organization and change: An information processing approach*. Potomac, Md.: Lawrence Erlbaum Associates, 1974.

Wyer, R. S., & Carlston, D. E. *Social inference and attribution*. Hillsdale, N.J.: Lawrence Erlbaum Associates, 1979.

Wyer, R. S., & Hinkle, R. L. Informational factors underlying inferences about hypothetical persons. *Journal of Personality and Social Psychology*, 1976, *34*, 481–495.

Wyer, R. S., & Srull, T. K. The processing of social stimulus information: A conceptual integration. In R. Hastie, T. M. Ostrom, E. B. Ebbesen, R. S. Wyer, D. L. Hamilton & D. E. Carlston (Eds.), *Person memory: Cognitive basis for social perception*. Hillsdale, N.J.: Lawrence Erlbaum Associates, 1980.

PROCESSING FACTORS AND BIASES IN SOCIAL COGNITION

6

What Grabs You?
The Role of Attention in
Impression Formation and
Causal Attribution

Leslie Zebrowitz McArthur
Brandeis University

INTRODUCTION

Direct from Philadelphia—the presidential debates! Tonight's debate is being broadcast live from the Walnut Street Theatre, which has been chilled to a previously agreed upon temperature of 68°F! In the interests of fairness, both candidates have been made up and lit in exactly the same way. They're also sitting behind matching lecterns, and are wearing identical blue suits! Now then, which of you is Governor Carter? [Gary Trudeau, *Doonesbury,* 1976]

Can it really be that such trivial factors as lighting and clothing would influence perceptions regarding the outcome of a presidential debate? Surprisingly, the answer is *yes.* Due to the wealth of information available to us in social situations and our limited information-processing capacity,[1] salient, though trivial, stimuli often exert a strong influence upon our attentional focus. This phenomenon, selective attention, may be reflected in preferential registration, encoding, and/or recall of salient stimuli.[2] (See Taylor & Fiske, 1978, for a related discussion.)

---

[1] Although some have argued that people fail to process all of the available information due to a limited information-processing capacity (e.g., Treisman, 1969), and others have argued that there is no established limit to this capacity (eg. Neisser, 1967), all would agree that there is more information available to the organism than it processes.

[2] The terms "attention-drawing," "salient," and "figural" are used interchangeably throughout this chapter to denote those stimuli that are selectively attended.

The question is, what stimuli will be selectively attended? Heider (1944) has suggested that some answers may be given in object perception research: "In recent years, a great many studies have been made of the processes of organization in the perceptual field. It is the thesis of this paper that the principles involved in these studies can be applied profitably to the perception of other persons and their behavior . . . [p. 358]." The present chapter considers Heider's suggestion that there are parallels between object and person perception in the light of recent evidence. More specifically, research is reviewed that demonstrates that in the realm of person perception, as in object perception, perceivers selectively attend to intense, changing, complex, novel, and unit-forming stimuli. Research demonstrating parallels in the influence of the perceiver's expectancies and arousal level upon which stimuli are selectively attended is also reviewed. Moreover, it is argued that the impact that attention-drawing stimuli have upon perceptions of people parallel their impact upon perceptions of objects.[3]

To develop the foregoing arguments, the chapter begins with a brief survey of the determinants of selective attention in the realm of nonsocial stimuli together with anecdotal evidence regarding the impact of selective attention upon perceivers' judgments about objects. Two general determinants of selective attention are considered: (1) the characteristics of the available *stimuli;* and (2) the momentary *state of the perceiver*. Following this treatment of the object perception research, two areas of social perception are considered—impression formation and causal attribution. Within each of these areas, research is reviewed that examines judgments about people and behaviors that are selectively attended, either by virtue of their stimulus characteristics or by virtue of the perceiver's state.

Before moving on to examine this research evidence, two caveats are in order. One is that, throughout the literature review, the construct of selective attention is treated rather loosely in the sense that there is rarely an attempt to identify where in the processing of information selection occurs. In a final section on "mediation," the issue of whether selective attention to particular stimuli reflects selectivity in registration, encoding, and/or memory is addressed together with the question of how selectivity at any one of these levels can influence impressions and causal attributions. A second caveat is that, although many of the principles developed in this chapter have equal applicability to the relam of self-perception, these applications are not made explicit, and research that has focused on the role of attention in self-perception is not reviewed.

---

[3]Some clarification of the term "perception" is needed here. "Perceptions" of stimuli refer to *judgments* about them rather than perception in the sense of noticing. Thus, Neisser's (1976, p. 87) argument that "attention is nothing but perception," does not apply to the present usage of the term perception. The prevalence of the term "person-perception" to denote impressions and attributions in social psychological theories and research seemed to warrant any possible confusion entailed by this usage.

OBJECT PERCEPTION

Attention-Drawing Stimuli

Theory and research on selective attention in object perception has identified intensity, change, complexity, novelty, and unit-formation as stimulus attributes that draw attention.[4] These principles can be traced back to very early psychologists, such as Titchener (1908/1966), who argued: "sudden stimuli and sudden changes of stimulus exert an influence upon attention . . . the stimulus which moves has a remarkable power to draw the attention . . . and the fifth condition of clearness [attention] is the novelty, rarity, unaccustomedness, strangeness of stimuli . . . [pp. 26–29]." Consistent with Titchener's introspective insights, Gestalt psychologists have demonstrated that moving (i.e. changing) stimuli and contextually novel stimuli tend to be figural—that is to stand out from their surroundings. They have also shown that bright (i.e. intense) stimuli, highly articulated (i.e. complex) stimuli, warm-colored stimuli, nearer stimuli, and objects that form a unit are more likely to be seen as figural. The determinants of "unit" formation include similarity among stimulus elements, contiguity, and discriminability. Kahneman (1973) has aptly noted that the Gestalt concept of figural emphasis is akin to selective attention: "When part of a flat picture 'stands out' in perception it is seen as figure over its background. The subjective experience of attention is often described in the same terms: The attended object 'stands out.' [p. 76]." Research on selective attention has demonstrated this similarity: For example, Berlyne's (1970) research, using behavioral rather than the early phenomenological measures of attention, has revealed that people more readily notice novel (unexpected) stimuli, larger stimuli, brighter stimuli, colored stimuli, and more complex stimuli. Berlyne has sorted these attention-getting properties into two classes—*physical* properties, which are intrinsic to the stimulus such as brightness, color, and size; and *collative* properties, which depend upon comparison or collation of stimulus elements, such as complexity, unit formation, and novelty. One might expect that people or behaviors that have these attributes would draw more attention than those that do not, and research is reported, which demonstrates that this is so.

Perceiver Effects

Theory and research on selective attention in object perception has indentified the perceivers' expectations and arousal level as two important determinants of which stimuli will draw attention. Here, too, we can find some words of wisdom

---

[4]This is not meant to be an exhaustive list of attention-drawing stimulus attributes.

in the early writings of Titchener (1908/1966): "A sixth condition of clearness [attention] is the likeness of the incoming sensation to the idea, sensation, or image already present in the mind [p. 29]." Bruner (1957) has elaborated this proposition in his writings on perceptual readiness. According to Bruner, the "readiness," or set to see X results in X being more easily and quickly recognized, and a wider range of things being identified or misidentified as X. Research has shown this to be so. For example, the set to look for a particular visual stimulus improves the accuracy of recognition (eg. Eriksen & Collins, 1969; Neisser, 1967; Posner & Boies, 1971). The effects of manipulated set on attention have also been demonstrated in reversible-figure phenomena (Hochberg & Brooks, 1970; Leeper, 1935; Zinchenko, 1966). Direct instruction is one factor that can influence the perceiver's expectations, and this has often been the method employed in research. Other determinants noted by Bruner are the past frequency of occurrence of an event and its probability of occurrence in the momentary context.[5] In sum, when a stimulus array is ambiguous, the way it is seen is often determined by what the perceiver *expects* to see. This should be true in the perception of people as well as in the perception of nonsocial stimuli, and research consistent with this extrapolation is reviewed.

In addition to the perceiver's expectations, general *arousal* level is another variable that has been shown to influence the allocation of attention to nonsocial stimuli. Easterbrook (1959) proposed that an increase in drive[6] causes a restriction in the range of cues that the organism uses in guiding its action. When arousal is low, the range of cues attended to is high, and many nonsalient cues are processed; when "arousal" increases, the range of cues utilized narrows and nonsalient cues are more likely to be rejected. With further increases in arousal, continuing restriction of the range of cues attended causes even some salient cues to be ignored. Support for Easterbrook's hypothesis has been provided by research employing a variety of arousal manipulations (Bahrick, Fitts, & Rankin, 1952; Bruner, Matter, & Papanek, 1955; Bruning, Capage, Kozoh, Young, & Young, 1968; Bursill, 1958; Callaway & Stone, 1960; Callaway & Thompson. 1953; Cornsweet, 1969; Hockey, 1970; McNamara & Fisch, 1964). All of these

---

[5]Bruner also noted that the present significance of a stimulus to a perceiver can influence the "readiness" or set to see it. This effect is more appropriately viewed as the influence of *goals* upon attention—what the perceiver wants or needs to perceive rather than what is expected. There is evidence in object perception as well as in person perception that perceiver variables such as task set and desires do influence selective attention, but this research is not reviewed in the present chapter due to space limitations.

[6]"Drive" is defined by Easterbrook (1959) as "a dimension of emotional arousal or general covert excitement, the innate response to a state of biological deprivation or noxious stimulations, which underlies or occurs simultaneously with overt action and affects its strength and course. This emotional arousal is greater in neurotic than in normal subjects, greater than usual in subjects under stress or threat or in frustration, and in general greater in animals that have been 'motivated' by any of the usual deprivations, noxious stimulations, or other incentives than it is in unmotivated or resting animals of the same species [p. 184]."

studies reveal a focusing of attention under high arousal, which is manifested in less awareness of nonsalient stimuli and more responsivity to the salient stimuli. In the domain of social stimuli, one would expect aroused perceivers to attend to fewer people within a social setting, and those to whom they attend should be the most salient ones. Also, aroused perceivers should notice fewer of a given person's behaviors, and it is the most salient behaviors that should be noticed.

How Is the Attended Stimulus Perceived?

In extrapolating from research on selective attention to nonsocial stimuli to the realm of person perception, one must consider not only what stimuli will be attended, but also what impact increased attention to a particular person or a particular behavior will have upon social perceptions. The relevance of object perception research might seem more tenuous for this latter question than the former, because the contents of social perception would seem to be quite different from the contents of object perception. For example, as Heider (1958) has noted, people are perceived to have attributes that cannot be defined in physical terms, and the stimuli involved in person perception are usually more extended in time than those involved in object perception. Nevertheless, Gestalt psychologists' research in the realm of object perception does provide some interesting analogues to person perception. For example, Rubin (1915) argued that stimuli experienced as figural are more impressive than those experienced as ground; that everything about the figure is remembered better; and that feelings are attached to figures and not to grounds. Also, Koffka (1935) argued that: "fixation of one of two equivalent objects tended to make it the carrier of motion, whether it moved objectively or not [p. 283]." Extrapolating to the realm of person perception, one might expect that, like other figural stimuli, people or behaviors that "stand out" either as a result of some attention-drawing physical property or as a result of the perceiver's state will: (1) be more impressive and better recalled; (2) create stronger feelings in the perceiver; and (3) more often be perceived as causing the events in a social interaction. Considerable research in the areas of impression formation and causal attribution provides support for these analogues to object perception.

IMPRESSIONS

Attention-Drawing People

Magnitude of Impressions

The Gestalt principle that figural or salient stimuli are more impressive and better remembered suggests that attention-drawing people may create a "bigger" impression—that is, they may be seen as more prominent, and their attributes and behaviors may be more thoroughly and accurately perceived. The evidence in support of this hypothesis is mixed.

Prominence.   Several studies have exposed perceivers to staged interactions and assessed their impressions of each actor's prominence with measures such as ratings of the actor's talkativeness, the degree to which the perceiver had formed an impression of the actor, the degree to which the actor determined the information exchanged, and the degree to which the actor influenced or set the tone of the conversation.[7] Such measures have been employed in at least nine studies that varied the physical salience of actors engaged in a getting-acquainted conversation. Of these, only three have obtained significant effects. McArthur and Post (1977) found higher prominence ratings of a brightly lit than a dimly lit actor, and Taylor and Fiske (1975, Study 1) and Taylor, Crocker, Fiske, Sprinzen, and Winkler (1979, Study 1) found higher ratings for the salient actor, who was seated facing perceivers, than for the nonsalient actor, whose back was to them.[8] On the other hand, Storms (1973) found that perceivers who were shown videotapes that focused their attention on an actor's behavior for the second time did not rate the actor as more talkative than perceivers who were shown videotapes that refocused their attention onto a different actor. Similarly, Taylor and Fiske (1975, Study 2) found no effects of an actor's seating position; and McArthur and Post (1977, Studies 2–5) found no effects of an actor's motion, shirt-pattern complexity, contextually novel clothing, or contextually novel sex on various prominence ratings.

There are five studies in which actors' prominence has been assessed following their participation in more engaging interactions than the getting-acquainted conversations reviewed earlier, and all of these have obtained significant salience effects. Studies by Taylor and her associates (Taylor, Fiske, Close, Anderson, Ruderman, 1976; Taylor, Fiske, Etcoff, & Ruderman, 1978, Study 3) exposed perceivers to interesting, sometimes humorous ad-libbed discussions and found that the salient novel black in an all white group and the salient novel male or female in a group of the opposite sex were rated as more prominent on a number of measures than the same people were when they were less salient by virtue of appearing in racially or sexually integrated groups. Also, Taylor, Crocker, Fiske, Sprinzen, and Winkler (1979, Study 2) found that perceivers who were highly involved in a debate topic gave higher prominence ratings to the actor who faced them during the debate than to the less salient actor, and Taylor et al. (1979, Study 3) found that perceivers reported greater ease in rating and greater promi-

---

[7]The latter two measures of prominence have sometimes been combined with a measure of the degree to which the actor causes another's behavior to form a "Causal Role Index." Thus, some of the findings reported here may be redundant with those reported in the section on Causal Attributions.

[8]One could argue that greater attention to the forward-facing confederate reflects the greater *complexity* of a facial stimulus as compared with a head of hair or the greater *change* in a facial stimulus array, or its greater *brightness*. Although it is not certain exactly what stimulus attribute is the crucial determinant of greater attention to the forward facing actor, research utilizing this manipulation is reviewed inasmuch as it constitutes a large segment of the literature on the role of attention in impression formation and causal attribution.

nence for the actor who faced them during a personal self-disclosure conversation.

Recall. As in the case of prominence measures, greater recall about the verbalizations of an attention-drawing actor has been rare in studies presenting perceivers with getting-acquainted conversations. No effects were found in two experiments in which the seating arrangement drew attention more to one person than another (Taylor & Fiske, 1975, Study 1; Taylor, Crocker, Fiske, Sprinzen, & Winkler, 1979, Study 1). Likewise, McArthur and Post (1977) found no preferential recall of the comments made by the actor who drew attention by virtue of motion, a complexly patterned shirt, a contextually novel shirt color, or a contextually novel sex. However, there was greater recall about a brightly than a dimly illuminated actor in this series of studies, as well as greater recall about an actor seen on the TV monitor than one covered in the second study reported by Taylor and Fiske (1975).

Recall effects have been equally uncommon in studies manipulating the salience of an actor within a more affectively toned context. Although Taylor, Crocker, Fiske, Sprinzen, and Winkler (1979) found greater recall of the comments of the actor who faced perceivers during a two-person self-disclosure conversation (Study 3), they found no greater recall about the actor who faced perceivers during an involving debate (Study 2). Also, though Taylor, Fiske, Close, Anderson, and Ruderman (1976) found that more was recalled about a black actor's contributions to an ad-libbed discussion when he was salient by virtue of being the only black than when the group was racially integrated, there were no parallel effects in a second study that manipulated the actors' sex. Likewise, McArthur and Solomon (1978) found that perceivers of a heated argument showed no greater recall about an actor when she had the statistically novel physical attribute of either a leg brace or red hair than when she did not.

As Taylor and Fiske (1978) have noted, recall of verbal information may be less sensitive to manipulations of visual attention than recall of visual information would be. Consistent with this argument, McArthur and Ginsberg (1978) have demonstrated that a visual attention manipulation can increase visual recall, even though it has no impact upon verbal recall. Because visual information intrinsic to an actor, such as nonverbal behaviors, could in and of itself affect the degree of attention to the actor, visual recall was assessed in this study by measuring recall of visual stimuli proximal to an actor. A videotape was made of two men who were seated on chairs, facing one another while carrying on a getting-acquainted conversation. Above and slightly to the side of each speaker was a black and white photograph depicting a child-like drawing of an outdoor scene. The composition of each scene was very similar, but the particular objects in each differed. Attention to the actors was manipulated by varying the novelty of their hair color. One actor had novel, red hair, whereas the other had brown hair. It was expected that when the videotape was shown in color, subjects would fixate more on the red-haired than the brown-haired actor and thereby have more visual exposure to the picture behind the red-head. This differential exposure to the two pictures was not anticipated when the videotape was shown in black and white. Consistent with expectations, subjects' recognition of objects in the picture, which was behind the red-haired actor, was greater than recognition of objects in the picture behind the brown-haired actor when the videotape was shown in color, whereas there was a nonsignificant trend in the opposite direction when the videotape was shown in black and white. Although visual recall was thus sensitive to the visual-attention manipulation employed in this study, recall of the actors' verbalizations was not. An attention manipulation based upon seating arrangements has also revealed significantly greater visual recall about the salient forward-facing actor in the absence of any differential verbal recall (Fiske, 1978). It thus appears that perceivers' recall of visual information is a more sensitive indicator of their selective attention than is recall of verbal information when the salience manipulation is itself a visual one.

Additional evidence for greater recall of visual information regrading a highly attended stimulus person is provided by Rump and Delin (1973), who argued that people would attend more carefully to the behavior of a high- than a low-status person and, as a result, would more accurately recall the height of the high-status person. Students estimated the height of either a short or a tall person, who was described as a postgraduate lecturer (low-status) or as a professor (high-status). The height of the tall, high-status person was *overestimated* relative to that of the tall, low-status person. This effect has been reported before, and it has always been interpreted as reflecting a tendency to ''aggrandize'' high-status people. *But,* Rump and Delin also found that the height of the short, high-status person was *underestimated* relative to that of the short, low-status person. And, in both cases, subjects' judgments of the height of the high-status person were more accurate. Additional evidence that perceivers more accurately recall visual information about salient stimulus persons has recently been provided by Langer and Imber (1980) who examined visual recall about people who drew attention by virtue of a statistically novel attribute (e.g. being a millionaire, being a cancer victim).

Summary and Implications.   The evidence in support of the hypothesis that people with salient physical attributes create a ''bigger'' impression clearly is mixed. Fourteen studies have measured perceptions of an actor's prominence, employing a total of 41 analyzed measures. Of these, eight studies have supported the hypothesis on one or more measures for a total of 21 significant effects.

Although studies that have varied the physical salience of actors engaged in a relatively interesting and affectively toned social interaction account for only 56% of the prominence measures, whereas getting-acquainted conversations account for the remaining 44%, the more engaging social interactions account for 76% of the significant effects. Thus, it may be that prominence effects depend on the *quality of information* to which subjects are exposed: Actors may have to do something that can engage perceivers' affective responses and/or create a big impression before the effects of selective attention on prominence ratings will be observed.

Alternatively, it may be that the prominence effects depend on the *particular attention manipulation* that is employed. As McArthur and Post (1977) have noted, prominent people in the real world are generally seated facing us rather than with their backs to us, and it may be that it is the cultural associations to being at the "head of the table" rather than the greater salience of facial stimuli that mediates the impact of seating arrangements on prominence ratings (see for example, Bass, 1952). The prominence effects obtained in McArthur and Post's (1977) lighting study can be explained in a similar fashion, because prominent people in the real world are often literally "in the limelight." Consistent with the argument that prominence effects may reflect the cultural associations of a particular salience manipulation, those studies that varied attention to an actor by means of seating arrangements or lighting account for only 24% of the prominence measures, whereas they account for 43% of the significant effects. It thus appears that the tendency to perceive people with salient physical attributes as more prominent may be most apt to occur for particular kinds of social interactions and/or for particular manipulations of salience, and further research exploring the range of these prominence effects clearly is needed.

Only four out of eleven studies that have assessed recall of actors' verbalizations have found greater recall about the attention-drawing actor. These positive findings have been equally distributed among studies employing getting-acquainted conversations versus those employing more engaging social interactions as well as among manipulations of attention based on seating arrangement versus other variables. All in all, there is not much evidence consistent with the hypothesis that more will be recalled about the verbal behavior of an actor who draws visual attention than one who does not. However, there is some evidence that greater recall of visual information about such an actor may be a more reliable phenomenon. Research exploring a wider range of visual recall variables would be very useful, as would research exploring the impact of manipulations of *verbal* salience (eg. voice qualities) upon recall of *verbal* information.

Direction of Impressions

The Gestalt principle that "feelings are attached to figures and not to grounds" suggests that ratings of attention-drawing people on *evaluative* dimensions will be more extreme than those of less salient individuals. The available evidence provides considerable support for this hypothesis, although the confirmations are concentrated within studies that have exposed perceivers to relatively engaging social interactions as opposed to those that have presented getting-acquainted conversations in which the information exchanged is rather predictable, boring, and unemotional.

Getting-Acquainted Conversations: Supporting Evidence. Out of nine studies employing a getting-acquainted conversation, four have found no effects at all on behavioral evaluations (McArthur & Post, 1977, pattern complexity and novel shirt color experiments; Storms, 1973; Taylor & Fiske, 1975, Study 1) whereas five have found effects on at least one evaluative dimension. Some of the significant effects reveal more positive evaluations of the physically salient actor: Actors were rated as more friendly when they faced the perceiver than when they did not (Taylor, Crocker, Fiske, Sprinzen, & Winkler, 1979, Study 1), and when they moved than when they were stationary (McArthur & Post, 1977). Actors were also rated as more sincere and more easygoing when they were seated in a bright light than when they were in dim light (McArthur & Post, 1977). In three studies, evaluations of actors moved in a negative direction when they became more physically salient: The forward facing actor in the Taylor et al. (1979) study and the actor whose conversational partner was covered on the TV monitor in Taylor and Fiske's (1975) second experiment were both rated as more nervous than their nonsalient counterparts. Also, the salient, novel sex actor in McArthur and Post's (1977) research was rated as less friendly than the common sex actor.

Getting Acquainted Conversations: Summary and Implications. In assessing the effects in these studies, it is important to note that more positive and/or more negative evaluations of a physically salient person do not necessarily reflect more extreme evaluations. Ratings of the salient actor must deviate more from some neutral point than those of the nonsalient actor if one is to argue that the former are more extreme. In the studies, which have been reviewed thus far, evaluative impressions of the attention-drawing actor have differed from those of a less salient actor in seven instances, of which only one represents a decrease in extremity. Thus, it does seem fair to conclude that impressions of a physically salient actor will be more, rather than less, evaluatively extreme than those of a nonsalient actor. And, in some cases the evaluations will be more positive, whereas in others they will be more negative. However, this effect is far from universal within these getting-acquainted conversations. Nine studies have measured evaluative impressions, employing a total of 29 analyzed measures. Of these, five studies have supported the hypothesis on at least one measure for a total of only six significant extremity effects. The fact that supporting evidence has been obtained in only 21% of the possible instances adds an important caveat to the conclusion that attention increases the extremity of evaluations: This is true only for *some* of the behaviors of *some* stimulus persons.

As was true for prominence effects, the *quality of the actors' behavior* may be an important moderating variable: It may be that the stimulus person must do something that engages the perceiver's affective responses and/or that can be exaggerated in perceivers' impressions, and this may often not be the case in the rather banal, getting-acquainted conversations. What's more, in order to derive measuring instruments sensitive to extremity effects, the experimenter must have some notion of the dimensions on which impressions will be exaggerated with increased attention to the stimulus person; this is often unknown in the getting-acquainted conversations where the actors do not manifest any particular personality attributes. Research that has given perceivers richer information about the personalities of the salient and the nonsalient actors and which has given researchers a better basis for selecting dimensions of evaluation has yielded more consistent effects of selective attention on evaluative extremity.

Affectively Toned Conversations: Supporting Evidence. Five of the seven manipulations of perceivers' attention during their exposure to a relatively interesting, affectively toned, social interaction have yielded more extreme evaluations of the attention-drawing actor. On the negative side, subjects exposed to an interesting and involving debate did not rate the performance of the actor who faced them any more extremely than that of the actor whose back was to them (Taylor, Crocker, Fiske, Sprinzen, & Winkler, 1979, Study 2), and although perceivers formed more positive impressions of a forward-facing actor engaged in a personal self-disclosure conversation, these positivity effects did not reflect more extreme evaluations, (Taylor et al., 1979, Study 3).

On the positive side of the ledger, other research conducted by Taylor and her associates has revealed that perceivers exposed to an interesting and humorous ad-libbed discussion consistently have evaluated the behavior of salient persons more extremely than that of the nonsalient persons (Taylor, Fiske, Close, Anderson, & Ruderman, 1976; Taylor, Fiske, Etcoff, & Ruderman, 1978). For example, increasing the physical salience of a black stimulus person yielded an increase in positive affect: He was rated as making a more useful, original, and significant contribution to the discussion when the accompanying slide show depicted him as the novel black in a group of five whites than when it depicted him in a racially integrated group. In a second study that varied the sexual novelty of stimulus persons in the group, one of the actors tended to be perceived negatively whereas another tended to be perceived positively. The person who made a generally negative impression was rated as even less likable, less worthy of respect, colder, etc. in a group of opposite-sexed people than in a sexually integrated group. On the other hand, the person who made a generally favorable impression was rated even more positively when "standing out" in a group of opposite-sexed people than when the group was sexually mixed. Thus, selective attention to stimulus persons seems to increase the polarization of evaluations: Those who elicit positive feelings become more positively evaluated when they are physically salient, whereas those who elicit negative feelings become more negatively evaluated.

McArthur and Solomon (1978) found that the direction in which selective attention pushes evaluations varies not only with the general likability of a stimulus person but also with the specific attributes of that person, which are being evaluated. Characters with definite personalities were deliberately created in this study in which subjects were shown a videotaped discussion about the outcome of a bridge hand between two partners, one of whom emerged as an "aggressor" and the other as a "victim." During the discussion, the aggressor repeatedly criticized the victim's performance, and was sometimes downright insulting. The victim's behavior stood in marked contrast to the aggressor. She was basically friendly, passive, and displayed little competence at bridge. Attention to the victim was manipulated in this study by varying the novelty of her physical appearance in the population at large as opposed to within the immediate context, as had been done in earlier research. In the control condition, subjects watched a black and white videotape in which the aggressor and the victim were equivalent in the extent to which their physical appearance would draw attention. In the "brace salience" condition, the victim wore a leg brace which, being a relatively novel physical attribute, should draw perceivers' attention. Of course a leg brace carries certain connotations about the wearer, and one could argue that it is these connotations rather than selective attention per se that causes the perceiver's impressions to change when the victim wears a brace. For this reason, an additional manipulation of attention was employed, one that would not carry the same connotations as the leg brace, but that should also cause subjects to attend more to the victim than in the control condition. This was the "hair salience" condition, in which the black and white control videotape was shown in color, revealing the victim's red hair, which, like a leg brace, is a relatively novel physical attribute and should therefore attract attention.

The expectation that the victim's behavior would be evaluated more extremely when attention was drawn to her was confirmed both for the leg brace and for the hair color manipulations of attention. These increases in extremity were highly differentiated, becoming more positive on some dimensions and more negative on others. For an attribute on which control subjects rated the victim on the positive side of the midpoint—friendliness—experimental subjects who saw the brace or hair salience tapes rated her even more positively. For attributes on which control subjects rated the victim on the negative side of the midpoint— passivity and competence—experimental subjects rated her even more negatively.

Although it was difficult to predict exactly how differential attention to the victim would affect ratings of the aggressor's behavior, these ratings were also examined by McArthur and Solomon (1978). On the basis of an hydraulic model of attention, one could argue that drawing attention to the victim would decrease the extremity of ratings of the aggressor's behavior inasmuch as it would become less noticed. On the other hand, drawing attention to the friendly and passive behavior of the victim could produce a contrast effect whereby the aggressor seems more aggressive than she does in the control condition when the victim's passive behavior goes relatively unnoticed. Such an effect would be consistent with the literary ploy of introducing a character who serves as a "foil" to enhance, by contrast, the attributes of the hero. It would also be consistent with contrast effects in the realm of object perception where, for example, the perceived brightness or color of an object varies with its surround. The results provided support for the contrast hypothesis. The aggressor was rated as less friendly, less receptive, and somewhat more active when she interacted with an attention-drawing victim than in the control condition. Research conducted by Simpson and Ostrom (1976) supports the argument that this contrast effect reflects a *perceptual* effect, rather than an attempt to rate the two actors as differently as possible (a *response* effect).

Affectively Toned Conversations: Summary and Implications.   As was true for the effects of attention on impressions within the getting-acquainted conversation studies, the effects within the more affectively toned interactions typically represent extremity effects. Of 25 significant differences between impressions of a salient and nonsalient actor within these studies, only three reflected a decrease in extremity. Not only were increases in extremity the rule when manipulations of selective attention affected impressions, but moreover these effects were very frequent. Evaluative impressions were assessed on 39 measures following seven separate manipulations of selective attention. Five manipulations supported the extremity hypothesis on at least one measure for a total of 22 significant effects. Thus, supporting evidence has been obtained in 56% of the possible instances, in contrast to the 21% success rate for studies presenting perceivers with a getting-acquainted conversation. This pattern of results is actually quite compatable with the Gestalt principle that *feelings are attached to figures,* because one should expect more extreme impressions of figural actors only when their behavior produces some feelings in the perceiver.

Although the contrasting pattern of results for getting-acquainted conversations versus other social interactions suggests that the effects of selective attention upon the extremity of impressions may depend on the stimulus person's particular behaviors and the sensitivity of the impression measures to these behaviors, the effects do show a great deal of generality across attention-drawing attributes. Greater polarization in impressions of the salient person have been demonstrated for both classes of attention-drawing properties identified by Berlyne (1970). *Physical* attributes, such as the intensity of a stimulus person's illumination, have been shown to increase the extremity of evaluations, and so have *collative* attributes, such as the contextual or statistical novelty of the stimulus person's physical attributes. One would expect these effects to generalize to still other attention-drawing physical and collative attributes. For example, one would expect more polarized impressions of people who deviate from the norm on any number of physical attributes such as height, weight, age, attractiveness, etc.[9]

---

[9]Research conducted by McGuire and his associates (McGuire, McGuire, Child, & Fujloka, 1978; McGuire & Padawer-Singer, 1976) has demonstrated that a variety of novel physical attributes attract attention in children's spontaneous *self*-descriptions.

A Curvilinear Effect?   The tendency for increased attention to a stimulus person to increase the polarization of evaluative reactions is consistent with some research manipulating the frequency of perceivers' exposure to stimuli. For example, Perlman and Oskamp (1971) found that increased frequency of exposure to photos of negatively evaluated men—criminals—yielded decreases in attractiveness ratings, whereas increased frequency of exposure to photos of positively evaluated men—Who's Who designates—yielded increases in attractiveness ratings. Likewise, in the realm of object-perception, Brickman, Redfield, Harrison, and Crandall (1972) found that increased frequency of exposure to abstract paintings that were not well liked on initial viewing yielded decreases in attractiveness ratings, whereas increased frequency of exposure to photos of liked abstract paintings yielded increases in attractiveness ratings. Other research (Zajonc, Markus, & Wilson, 1974) has shown that these divergent exposure effects require that positive or negative affective associations accompany the repeated exposures. In the absence of such associations, increased exposure (i.e., *mere* exposure) seems to yield *increased* attractiveness, regardless of initial affect. Of course, in the usual contexts of person perception, one would expect initial positive and negative associations to accompany subsequent exposures— thus yielding the polarization effect.

In contrast to the impact on evaluative responses of repeated exposure to a visual stimulus, the semantic satiation literature has shown that when a verbal stimulus is repetitively presented over a short period of time, it loses its affective value or polarity (eg. Amster, 1964; Jakobovits, 1968). There are several possible explanations for the different effects of repeated exposure to visual versus verbal stimuli, one of which concerns their complexity. Words are less complex than the stimuli employed by Perlman and Oskamp and by Brickman et al. and these, in turn, are still less complex than those employed in the research manipulating the salience of a behaving stimulus person. More complex stimuli may require much more exposure for the satiation or habituation effect to occur (See Harrison, 1977, for a review of the effects of complexity). If so, one might expect a curvilinear relationship between attention and the polarization of evaluative reactions in person perception: As attention increases up to some optimal point, the polarity of evaluations will also increase, whereas after that point, increased attention will begin to produce decreases in the polarity of evaluations.

Although none of the person perception research has reported such a habituation effect, there is some indirect evidence that it may indeed occur. Anecdotal evidence comes from my research assistant who reported that, after watching the bridge game argument some forty odd times, she no longer perceived the aggressor as aggressive, and began to fear that she was showing the wrong videotape. More substantial, though still not conclusive, evidence comes from a strange pattern of correlations between the durations of visual fixation on stimulus persons and ratings of their behavior in research conducted by McArthur and Ginsberg (1978). In several instances, there was a positive correlation between duration of fixation on an actor and ratings of that actor's behavior in the control condition where the level of fixation was low to moderate, and a negative correlation between the duration of fixation on an actor and ratings of his or her behavior in the experimental condition, where that actor was salient and the duration of fixation was moderate to high. The hypothesis that there is a curvilinear relationship between attention to a person and the extremity of evaluation of that person's behavior certainly seems to warrant an explicit test. This would require systematically varying the duration of attention to a stimulus person across a wide range and observing the pattern of resultant evaluations.

Attention-Drawing Behaviors

The finding that physically salient actors are sometimes more positively evaluated, sometimes more negatively evaluated, and sometimes no differently evaluated than their nonsalient counterparts, suggests that an important question to raise in considering the impact of selective attention upon impressions is "what behaviors get exaggerated?" This may essentially be a question of what behaviors draw attention and, if so, the answer will be the same as for the question of what stimulus persons draw attention: Those behaviors which are intense, changing, complex, novel, or which form a unit should influence impressions more than their less attention-drawing counterparts.

Intensity, Novelty, and Change

An experiment conducted by Rothbart, Fulero, Jensen, Howard, and Birrell (1978) provides evidence that behaviors that are intense and/or novel have more influence upon social perceptions than those that are less attention-drawing. Subjects in this study were presented with several statements, each depicting a behavior engaged in by a different man. For half of the subjects, several of these behaviors were extreme criminal acts—e.g., murder, rape—whereas for the remaining subjects they were more moderate criminal acts—e.g., shoplifting, vandalism. Despite the fact that the same number of criminal acts were reported to both groups, estimates of the frequency of criminal acts were greater in the extreme than in the moderate condition, and more extreme than moderate criminal acts were recalled. Although it cannot be ascertained whether these results are due to the greater intensity or to the greater novelty of the more extreme crimes, it is clear that behaviors with one or both of these characteristics have a greater impact upon impressions of a group of people than do more moderate behaviors. By the same token, our impressions of a *given person* should be disproportionately influenced by that person's most novel or intense behaviors. Some evidence consistent with this extrapolation is provided by research on impression formation, which has revealed that highly evaluatively polarized events carry more weight in impression formation than those that are less evaluatively extreme, and that negatively evaluated events are more influential than positive ones (eg.

Hamilton & Zanna, 1972; Hodges, 1974; Manis, Gleason, & Dawes, 1966; Warr, 1974). Again, it is not clear whether these effects are due to the greater intensity and/or to the greater novelty of the more polarized and more negative behaviors (See Kanouse & Hanson, 1972, for a review of several explanations for the greater impact of negative cues on evaluations).

Research by Rosenberg, Nelson, and Vivekananthan (1968) has revealed that the contextual novelty of particular behaviors can determine the impact that they have upon impressions even when extremity (i.e., intensity) does not vary. These authors explored the defining characteristics of a central trait in Asch's (1946) early research in the context of data which plotted the adjectives employed by Asch in a three-dimensional space. They found that the central traits "warm" and "cold," which exerted more impact upon impressions than the "peripheral" intellectual traits with which they were presented, were no more extreme on the social dimension than the intellectual ones were on the intellectual dimension. On the basis of this evidence, they argued that the greater impact upon impressions of "warm" and "cold" should not be interpreted as reflecting their greater extremity. On the other hand, the finding that the traits "warm" and "cold" had more impact upon impressions when they were presented in the context of exclusively intellectual traits than when they were in the context of other social traits can be interpreted in terms of their relative novelty within each stimulus context. Thus, traits that are central—i.e., that exert the greatest impact upon impressions—may be those that draw more attention by virtue of their relative novelty. It should be noted that this greater impact of novel traits is limited to impressions of attributes which fall on the same dimension as they do, a finding that has implications for the range of impressions that novel behaviors will influence (Zanna & Hamilton, 1972).

Linking the foregoing research regarding the weighting of extreme and novel adjective trait terms in impression formation to the concept of selective attention rests upon the assumption that the weight attached to a particular trait term reflects the degree of attention paid to it. Some indirect support for this assumption can be found in the literature on order effects in impression formation, where instructions designed to equalize attention across an entire list of descriptive adjectives eliminated primacy effects—i.e., the greater weighting of early adjectives (e.g. Anderson & Hubert, 1963; Hendrick & Constantini, 1970). The link between weight and attention in impression formation has been demonstrated even more convincingly in recent research by Fiske (1980). Perceivers were shown a series of slides depicting people performing behaviors that varied in negativity and extremity. Perceivers' impressions of a stimulus person reflected greater weighting of behaviors that were extreme *or* negative, a finding that indicates that negative behaviors can carry more weight than positive ones independently of any difference in their intensity, because the two variables were manipulated orthogonally in this research. Moreover, Fiske found that a behavioral measure of attention, looking time, replicated the greater weight assigned to extreme and negative behaviors, which supports the assumption that the weight attached to a particular behavior in impression formation reflects selective attention to that behavior.

Some indirect evidence that changing behaviors exert more influence upon impressions than static ones is provided by research on gain–loss effects in interpersonal attraction: People whose behavior changes from critical to complementary or vice versa are evaluated more extremely than those whose behavior remains constant (eg. Aronson & Linder, 1965). There are, of course, many possible explanations for these particular effects other than greater attention to the changing behavior. More direct evidence that changing behaviors do indeed draw more attention is provided in a recent study by Wilder (1978) in which perceivers watched a videotape of someone collating questionnaires. The collating behavior either changed during the course of the videotape (from unpredictable to predictable or vice versa) or it remained constant throughout the tape (always unpredictable or always predictable). During the first half of the videotape, perceivers segmented the collating behavior into finer units when it was unpredictable than when it was predictable. During the second half of the videotape, they segmented it into finer units when it had changed than when it had not, irrespective of the actual nature of the behavior. Additional evidence that changing stimuli draw more attention than constant ones has recently been provided by Newtson, Rinder, Miller, and LaCross (1978), who found that perceivers' segmented a stimulus person's collating behavior into units that were marked by a highly visible change in the stimulus field.[10] While it seems reasonable to argue that the pattern of behavioral segmentation in these studies reflects greater attention to changing behavior, neither study investigated the impact of such selective attention upon impression formation, and further research on this subject would be a worthwhile addition to the suggestive findings of the Aronson and Linder (1965) study mentioned earlier.

Summary and Implications.   The available evidence is consistent with the hypothesis that intense, novel, or changing behaviors draw more attention than

---

[10]Further evidence that demonstrates the influence of unit-forming, changing, or complex behaviors upon selective attention is provided in a childhood game, the "Whoops Johnny" riddle. In this game, the demonstrator challenges some naive person to mimic his behavior, which consists of a moderately complex series of finger movements accompanied by verbalizations. The finger movements are not only somewhat complex, but they involve motion (changes), and they form a unit by virtue of similarity to one another and contiguity as well. As the completion of the finger movements, the "demonstrator" folds his or her arms, a simple, rather static act. The naive person usually manages after a few tries—if not the first—to successfully mimic the finger movements, but the final behavior of arm-folding can continue to elude him or her for many trials. Often it is only when the arm-folding behavior is performed by the demonstrator in a very exaggerated fashion that the naive person picks it up. Clearly, the more complex, changing, and unit-forming finger motions draw more attention.

more moderate, commonplace, or static ones. In addition, it has been found that negative behaviors draw more attention than positive ones, an effect that probably reflects the greater statistical novelty of negative events, because it is orthogonal to their intensity. Intense, novel, changing, or negative behaviors are looked at more, segmented into finer units, and better recalled. What's more, they exert a greater impact upon impressions of the person manifesting them than do that person's less salient behaviors. All of these findings have profound implications for impression formation, and their range of applicability warrants further investigation.

Unit Formation

Unit formation is another attention-drawing attribute that may provide certain behaviors with a greater impact upon impressions than others. For example, one might expect that an actor who performs six behaviors, three positive and three negative, will be rated more positively if the three positive behaviors form a *sequential unit* than if they do not. Likewise, one might expect the actor to be rated more positively if the three positive behaviors form a *unit of similar acts* than if they are three, equally positive, dissimilar ones. It should be noted that the most sensitive test of the capacity of unit-forming behaviors to influence impressions requires that their unit-formation not render any remaining behavior novel, because novel behaviors also draw attention.

In addtition to the possibility that particular behaviors may draw more attention by virtue of forming a unit among themselves, behaviors may also form a *unit with the actor*. And one would expect that those behaviors that more readily form a unit with the actor will draw more attention and exert a greater impact upon impressions. Evidence in support of this hypothesis has been provided in studies of illusory correlation, which refers to an erroneous inference about the relationship between two categories of events. More specifically, it has been demonstrated that pairs of events that draw more attention than others tend to be perceived as more strongly correlated than they really are (e.g., Chapman & Chapman, 1967; Chapman, 1967). In the realm of person perception, particular actor-behavior pairs that draw attention by virtue of forming a unit should be perceived as more strongly associated than other pairs, and the behaviors in the unit-forming pairs should thereby exert a stronger influence upon impressions.

Two bases of unit formation have been studied within the context of impression formation. One is *associative connections,* which is discussed at greater length in the section on perceiver expectations. The second is *shared infrequency.* More specifically, there is evidence that illusory correlation effects occur when people and behaviors form a unit by virtue of both being statistically infrequent. This basis for unit formation is analogous to the Gestalt principle that stimuli that are highly discriminable tend toward unit formation.

Hamilton and Gifford (1976) tested the shared infrequency hypothesis by showing perceivers a series of slides, each of which attributed a positive or negative behavior to a member of some abstract group, A or B. One class of behaviors (positive or negative) and one group of people (A or B) were less frequent than another. There was, however, an equal proportion of positive to negative behaviors for members of both groups, and thus no logical basis for forming different impressions of them. As expected, subjects perceived the infrequent group members and the infrequent behaviors as being more strongly associated than they really were: They overrecalled instances of infrequent behaviors by the minority group, and their evaluations of the minority group were more negative than those of the majority when the infrequent behaviors were negative ones and more positive than those of the majority when the infrequent behaviors were positive ones.

A conceptual replication of the Hamilton and Gifford Study (Jones, Scott, Solernou, Noble, Fiala, & Miller, 1977) examined the effects of shared infrequency upon recall and evaluations when the stimulus persons were described by personality traits rather than behaviors. Like Hamilton and Gifford, they found that subjects' recall of the number of statistically infrequent undesirable traits that had been attributed to the minority group was exaggerated, although subjects did not evaluate the minority group more negatively on a measure of likableness.

A second conceptual replication of the Hamilton and Gifford Study has been conducted by McArthur and Friedman (1980), who sought to ascertain the generalizability of the shared infrequency effect to more meaningful minority groups than the abstract groups A and B employed in the foregoing studies. To this end, subjects were presented with eight bogus case studies of "patients" from a mental health center with a picture of the patient attached to each history. Negative behaviors in the case histories were more infrequent than positive ones, and one demographic group in each set of eight patients was more infrequent than another. Race, sex, and age of the patients were the demographic variables that were manipulated. The expectation that impressions of the members of each demographic group would be more negative when they appeared infrequently was confirmed only for certain demographic groups. Consistent with Hamilton and Gifford's (1976) shared infrequency effect, all subjects' impressions of older patients and black patients as well as male subjects' impressions of women patients were more negative when these patients were in the minority than when they were in the majority. However, unlike earlier findings, subjects did not recall more negative behaviors by these groups when they were in the minority. Recall of the behaviors of young, white, or same-sex patients also failed to vary with their frequency of appearance. Moreover, impressions of younger, white, or same-sexed patients were more *positive*, rather than more negative, when they appeared infrequently. Because the positive behaviors were not infrequent, these latter illusory correlation effects cannot be attributed to a tendency for infrequent people to form a unit with infrequent behavior. However, a more general shared distinctiveness hypothesis can account for all of the impression data: when demographic groups were distinctive (i.e. salient) by virtue of infrequency, they were perceived to be more related than they really were to behaviors that were distinctive by virtue of associative connections to members of that group.[11] This interpretation of the results assumes that positive behaviors had stronger associative connections than negative ones to younger, white, and same-sexed patients, whereas the reverse was true for their demographic complements. Support for this assumption is provided by research documenting age, race, and sex stereotypes (Bennet & Ekman, 1973; Brigham, 1971; Broverman, Broverman, Clarkson, Rosenkrantz, & Vogel, 1970), as well as by the recall data. Although subjects' recall of the behavior of patients *within* each demographic group did not vary with that group's statistical frequency, there were differences in recall *between* demographic groups. Subjects tended to attribute fewer positive and more negative behaviors to older, black, and women patients than to their demographic complements.

Summary and Implications. The hypothesis that behaviors that form a unit with each other will exert a disproportionate influence upon impressions has not as yet been tested. However, the hypothesis that behaviors that form a unit with an actor will exert a disproportionate influence upon impressions has found support in research on illusory correlation effects. In particular, it has been found that behaviors that form a unit with an actor by virtue of their shared infrequency will exert an undue influence upon impressions of that actor *unless* there are counteracting associative bases for unit formation, as there were in McArthur and Friedman's (1980) research. It is important to note that the results of the McArthur and Friedman research suggest that the shared infrequency effect is merely one instance of a more general shared distinctiveness effect. Actors and behaviors that are similar merely by virtue of both being highly discriminable or salient may tend toward unit formation. If so, then actors who draw attention by virtue of any one of the attributes summarized in the preceding section on attention-drawing actors may be perceived as co-occurring more often than they really do with behaviors that draw attention by virtue of any one of the attributes discussed in this section. In short, the tendency for behaviors that are intense, changing, novel, negative, complex, or unit-forming to exert more influence upon impressions than their less attention-drawing counterparts should be particularly pronounced when the actor too draws attention by virtue of some salient attribute.

---

[11]It should be noted that these are not simple association effects. An illusory correlation effect derived from associative connections would have yielded only an overall difference in impressions of two demographic groups, not a difference that depended upon the infrequency of the group.

Perceiver Effects

The inherent or contextual salience of an actor's attributes or behavior—e.g., intensity or novelty—is not the only factor that influences perceivers' selective attention and hence their impressions. Another factor is the perceiver's set. For example, in McArthur and Friedman's study (1980), those behaviors that were expected, such as negative behaviors by an "outgroup" member or positive behaviors by an "ingroup" member, had the most impact on subjects' impressions of a salient person. In light of these findings, it would seem important to consider the influence of perceiver variables upon selective attention and impression formation. Two such variables are discussed, each of which has been shown to influence selective attention in object perception: expectancy and arousal.

Expectancy

Assimilation Effects. Considerable research has shown that perceivers' impressions of a stimulus person move in the direction of what they expect to observe. For example, Kelley (1950) found that students' impressions of a lecturer were much more favorable when they expected him to be "warm" than when they expected him to be "cold." More recently, Langer and Abelson (1974) found a similar effect upon clinicians' impressions of an interviewee. Traditional therapists, who were expecting to observe a "patient", evaluated the person as more disturbed than those who were expecting to observe a "job applicant." Similarly, Snyder, and Frankel (1976) found that subjects who watched a silent videotaped interview with the expectation that the topic of conversation was sex rated the interviewee as more upset and uncomfortable than those who expected the topic to be politics. The effect of expectations on subsequent perceptions has also been studied by Zadny and Gerard (1974), who found that labeling a stimulus person as a "music major" produced more recall of his music-related activities than did labeling him as either a "psychology," or a "chemistry" major, in which case there was more recall of his psychology- and chemistry-related activities, respectively. In a second study, these authors also found that labeling a social interaction as a "burglary" yielded more recall of the actors' potentially theft-related activities than did labeling it as "two people waiting for friends." Snyder and Uranowitz (1978) also found an effect of expectations upon recall. Subjects recalled more stereotypically lesbian behaviors when they were told that a woman was homosexual than when they were told she was heterosexual. However, this effect was obtained when perceivers' "expectancies" were manipulated *after* being exposed to information about the woman, whereas all of the other effects reported in this section obtained only when expectancies were manipulated *prior* to exposure to the stimulus persons.

Eisen and McArthur (1979) examined the impact of perceivers' expectations upon their evaluations of a salient versus a nonsalient stimulus person. Perceivers who expected to watch a videotaped trial and to determine a defendant's guilt rated the stimulus person as more responsible for a crime than those who were set to watch a social interaction and to form an impression of someone. What is more, the effects of expectations upon impressions of the stimulus person interacted with the person's salience. Given an impression set, the more time the defendant appeared on camera, the more positively he was evaluated whereas, given a trial set, the more visibly salient the defendant, the more negatively he was evaluated. It thus appears that the direction in which evaluations of people become polarized with increased attention to them can depend on the perceiver's cognitive set. The differential impact of salience upon impressions of the defendant in the two set conditions may be explained in terms of the information that perceivers were set to process. A trial set predisposed them to focus on criminal responsibility in the defendant's behavior on the night of the crime; the more they saw of him, the more negative information they seem to have discovered, which is consistent with the fact that the trial testimony was designed to produce a guilty verdict. An impression set, on the other hand, predisposed subjects to focus on personality dispositions in the defendant's courtroom behavior; the more they saw of him the more positive information they seem to have discovered, which is consistent with the fact that the defendant's background and demeanor painted him in a relatively positive light.

More direct evidence that perceivers' expectations influence selective attention has been provided in research by Massad, Hubbard, and Newtson (1979). Subjects in this study were exposed to a videotape depicting three geometric figures; a large triangle, a small triangle, and a circle, engaged in a series of movements (Heider & Simmel, 1944). Some subjects were set to view the large triangle as a bully picking on the small triangle and the circle, whereas others were set to view it as guardian of some treasure, which the small triangle and circle were trying to steal. Perceivers with these two sets differed not only in their impressions of the three geometric figures, but they also differed in their segmentation of the ''behaviors'' of the figures, thus providing evidence that expectations influence the registration of information. Further evidence for this argument was provided by the finding that subjects whose set was changed *after* viewing the videotape did not change their impressions of the geometric figures unless they had an opportunity to reexamine the videotape—that is to register the information differently.

Associative Bases.   In considering the role of expectations in person perception, an important issue to address is their genesis. In some of the earlier summarized research, the expectations were given to perceivers by the experimenter, and in real life our expectations often derive from explicit instructions from other people. In other studies, perceivers' expectations derived from *culturally transmitted associations* to labels or situations. For example, the *labels* ''patient'' and ''cold'' have different associations from the labels ''job applicant'' and ''warm,'' and these divergent associations may prime perceivers to expect and to notice different behaviors (i.e., the behaviors that form a unit with the actor may vary with the perceiver's set). Likewise, the *situations* of a "burglary," and a "trial" have different behaviors associated with them than "two people waiting," and a "social interaction," respectively. Other culturally transmitted associations may accrue to certain *groups of people,* such as blacks, women, and the aged.

Evidence that associative connections cause certain demographic groups to form a "unit" with certain behaviors was provided in the McArthur and Friedman (1980) study reported previously. Research by Taylor et al. (1978, Study 3) provides additional evidence that different behaviors are associated with males and females in our society. Perceivers in this study were exposed to an interesting ad-libbed discussion among six people whose sexual designation was varied. When a particular stimulus person was designated as a man, that person was perceived as more analytical, influential, and negative and as less sensitive, perceptive, and warm than when designated as a woman. One plausible interpretation of these findings is that cultural associations cause women to form a unit with sensitive, perceptive, and warm behaviors with the consequence that these behaviors drew the most attention when the stimulus person was designated as a woman, whereas cultural associations cause men to form a unit with analytical, confident, influential, and negative behaviors with the result that these behaviors drew the most attention when the stimulus person was designated as a man. More direct evidence that cultural associations cause particular behaviors to draw more attention for some groups of people than others is provided in a series of studies by Hamilton and Rose (1978), which demonstrated that traits culturally associated with particular occupational groups were *recalled* as describing those groups more often than other types of traits, and more often than other groups even though the actual frequency of descriptions did not differ.

In addition to culturally transmitted associations, there may be *other associative connections* that influence a perceiver's expectancies and thence impressions of certain groups of people. Chapman and Chapman's (1967) research provides ample evidence that certain symtomology is associated with certain physiognomic features. The reverse may also be true: Certain physical characteristics may lead perceivers to expect certain symptoms and/or certain behaviors. Secord (1958) has argued that these associations may not only be culturally transmitted, but that they may also reflect a more basic association to the physical attribute, derived from its *functional* or its *metaphorical* properties. For example, it has been found that people pictured wearing glasses are perceived to be more intelligent than people not wearing glasses (e.g., Birnbaum, Frechtman, & McArthur, 1978). This may reflect associations based upon the functional qualities of glasses: Glasses are used for reading, which is associated with intelligence. The folkloric stereotype that people who have red hair are hot-tempered may reflect associations based upon metaphorical generalization from red: The color red is fiery, which is associated with hot. *Affective* associations may also cause certain behaviors to draw more attention when they are manifested by people with particular physical characteristics. Considerable research has demonstrated that people's impressions of attractive people are much more positive than their impressions of unattractive people on a variety of evaluative dimensions that would seem to have no real connection with beauty. Perceptions of the intelligence, academic potential, likability, and aggressive tendencies of attractive individuals are all more favorable than perceptions of unattractive individuals. (See Berscheid & Walster, 1974, for a review of this literature.) This positive halo effect may well reflect associations based upon the affect produced by attractive people—e.g. looking at attractive people brings pleasure, which is associated with a whole range of positive attributes.

One can generate many well-known stereotypes using the foregoing associative principles. To the extent that such associations influence perceivers' expectancies, they have particularly interesting implications for perceptions of stimulus persons whose physical appearance not only has strong associative connections to particular behaviors but that also draws a lot of attention. Black has many associative connections, but a black-haired (Caucasian) person is not likely to attract much attention and will thereby be less vulnerable to stereotyping than the red-haired person whose relatively novel physical appearance not only draws attention, but moreover may draw attention to particular behaviors— namely hot-tempered ones. The result will be shared distinctiveness effects, such as those reported by Berscheid and Walster (1974), Hamilton and Gifford (1976), McArthur and Friedman (1980).

Behavioral Bases.   In addition to culturally, functionally, metaphorically, and affectively based associations, another factor that certainly influences what behaviors perceivers expect is the *stimulus person's past behavior*. Behaviors that are consistent with an actor's past behavior may exert a greater influence upon impressions than those that are inconsistent because the former receive more attention by virtue of being expected. Considerable research has demonstrated primacy effects in impression formation such that impressions are more influenced by early than by later information, unless perceivers are specifically instructed to attend equally to all the information. (See Jones & Goethels [1972] for a review of this literature.) One plausible explanation for these primacy effects is that the expectations produced by the early information cause perceivers to selectively attend to that later information, which is consistent with it. In keeping with this explanation are the findings of Cantor and Mischel (1977), who examined the impact of a perceiver's categorization of stimulus persons upon recall of the information presented about them. For example, when a stimulus person had been described by traits characterizing him as a prototypical extravert, perceivers were subsequently more confident that trait material conceptually related to extraversion had been presented than they were that conceptually unrelated material had been. The authors concluded that once a trait schema is primed, further material is identified with the stimulus person to the extent that it is associated with the preexisting schema.

The *perceiver's prior behaviors* as well as those of the stimulus person also contribute to expectancies. For example, Higgins, Rholes, and Jones (1977) found that perceivers' characterizations and evaluations of a stimulus person reflected the evaluative aspects of trait categories to which they had previously been exposed: Perceivers who read a description of someone after reading positive trait terms that were pertinent to describing him or her, evaluated the person more favorably than those who read the description after being exposed to pertinent negative trait terms. Likewise, Hamilton and Zanna (1974) found that the connotative meaning of an attribute is assimilated to the desirability of the context in which it is embedded. Thus, evaluations of a stimulus person are assimilated to the perceiver's cognitive set, whether that set is derived from the past behavior of the stimulus person or the perceiver.

Contrast Effects.   A paradox, which may have become obvious to the reader, needs to be addressed. The foregoing argument that expected behaviors draw the perceiver's attention conflicts with the earlier argument that novel and changing behaviors do so. After all, one form of novelty is deviation from expectation, and behavioral change is often more unexpected than constancy. The question is, when will the "novel" act draw the perceiver's attention and when will the "expected" act do so? The Gestalt "maximum–minimum" principle is pertinent here. According to Koffka (1935), there is a tendency in perceptual organization toward maximum or minimum simplicity: "Roughly speaking, a minimum simplicity will be the simplicity of uniformity, a maximum simplicity that of perfect articulation [p. 171]." Assimilation effects can be viewed as a minimum effect—behaviors are seen as uniform with expectations; contrast effects can be viewed as a maximum effect—behaviors are seen as strongly differentiated from expectations.

Werner (1924) has argued that assimilation effects appear when the difference between elements is small, contrast when it is great. Similar effects occur within the realm of person perception. When behaviors are either ambiguous or not too discrepant from expectations, perceivers show an assimilation effect: They notice what they expect to find and pay less attention to behaviors that do not fit their expectations. But, when an actor's behavior includes some that clearly fall outside of this range of assimilation (Sherif & Hovland, 1961), then perceivers' attention is drawn more to the extreme, "novel" behaviors than to the commonplace and/or expected ones. An example of behaviors that clearly fall outside of the range of expected ones is provided in the well-known submariner-astronaut study (Jones, Davis, & Gergen, 1961), in which unexpected out-of-role behavior exerted a stronger influence upon impressions than expected in-role behavior. This "contrast" effect can be attributed to the greater perceptual salience of the unexpected behaviors. However, one would expect it to be replaced with an effect of "assimilation to expectancies" if the behaviors manifested either did not deviate so much from expectancies or were rather ambiguous.

Summary and Implications.   The available evidence indicates that a perceiver's expectancies exert an important influence upon impression formation. When behavioral stimuli are relatively ambiguous, perceivers selectively attend to those behaviors that they expect to find, and these exert a disproportionate influence upon their impressions. On the other hand, when behavioral stimuli are unambiguous, those that deviate markedly from expectations draw more attention and have a stronger influence upon impressions than the expected ones. A variety of factors can influence impression formation by way of affecting a perceiver's expectations. These include explicit instructions, culturally transmitted associations, associations based upon metaphorical, functional, and affective properties of a stimulus person's physical appearance, a stimulus person's past behavior, and the perceiver's own recent behavior. These influences upon impression formation merit further investigation, especially because there is substantial evidence for a self-fulfilling prophecy effect in which those impressions borne out of expectations tend to be fulfilled (e.g. Snyder, Tanke, & Berscheid, 1977).

Arousal

As noted in the introduction, Easterbrook (1959) has proposed that an increase in drive causes a restriction in the range of cues to which the organism attends, and supporting research has revealed that it is the most salient cues that are attended. Generalizing to the realm of person perception, McArthur and Solomon (1978) predicted that aroused perceivers would tend to rate stimulus persons more extremely than nonaroused perceivers, because the attention of the former group should be narrowed to focus upon the stimulus person's most salient characteristics and should exclude subtle nuances of behavior. The arousing effects of loud noise did not confirm this hypothesis, a finding that was attributed to the tendency for the noise to interfere with subjects' ability to hear the social interaction to which they were exposed. However, the arousing effects of self-consciousness, induced by videotaping subjects while they watched the same interaction, did confirm the hypothesis. An aggressor who was seen as basically unfriendly, competent, and active was rated as even more unfriendly, more competent, and more active by aroused perceivers. Similarly, a victim who was seen as basically friendly, incompetent, and passive was rated as even more friendly, less competent, and more active by aroused perceivers.

A study by Whitehead, Holmes, and Zanna (1978) has revealed that the direction in which perceivers' arousal pushes their impressions can depend upon another perceiver variable, namely expectancies. The tendency for perceivers to rate a stimulus person as warmer when they expected him to be warm than when they did not was stronger when they were aroused by threat of electric shock than when they were not aroused. Thus, in this study, arousal narrowed perceivers' attention to the cues that their expectancies made salient, whereas in McArthur and Solomon's (1978) study, arousal narrowed perceiver's attention to behavioral cues that were inherently salient.

Employing a somewhat different measure of narrowed attention, Vallacher (1978), like McArthur and Solomon (1978), found effects of a self-consciousness manipulation: Subjects who thought they were being videotaped while watching a series of five stimulus persons tended to make "either-or" judgments of these people's standing on a number of dimensions, whereas those who did not think they were being videotaped tended to manifest finer discriminations in their ratings.

Summary and Implications. According to Easterbrook, a wide variety of arousal states should narrow observers' attention to the most dominant cues. However, there is clearly need for additional research that investigates the range of this effect. One might expect, for example, a curvilinear effect such that at the most extreme levels of arousal impressions will become *less* polarized. Easterbrook's theory would actually anticipate this, because he argued that when arousal increases beyond the level that causes nonsalient cues to be ignored, some salient cues come to be ignored as well. Thus, extreme levels of arousal may so constrict attention that it no longer even focuses upon the most salient behaviors, thus reducing the extremity of impressions.

CAUSAL ATTRIBUTIONS

Attention-Drawing People

There is a great deal of evidence for a person-perception analogue to Koffka's (1935) argument that "fixation of one of two equivalent objects tends to make it the carrier of motion, whether it moves objectively or not [p. 283]." The stimuli that are attended by perceivers of a social interaction also tend to be seen as causal.

Direct support for this effect was first reported by Storms (1973), who tested Jones and Nisbett's (1972) proposition that actor–observer differences in causal attributions are at least partly due to differences in attentional focus. According to Jones and Nisbett, observers attribute an actor's behavior to the actor's own disposition, because their attention is focused on the actor, who is salient or "figural" against the ground of the situation. Actors, on the other hand, attribute their own behavior to situational causes, because they attend to their environment, which for them is salient or figural. Consistent with this argument, Storms found that when observers' attention was focused onto the actor's environment by showing them a videotape of the environment as the actor sees it, the observers attributed the actor's behavior more to situational causes than when their attention was not refocused onto the actor's situation. Although a complementary trend for dispositional attributions was obtained, reflecting somewhat greater dispositional attribution when attention was focused on the actor than when it was focused on the situation, these effects were not significant.

Other research has varied the degree to which perceivers attend to an actor versus the actor's environment by manipulating the stimulus characteristics of each rather than by manipulating their physical availability, as Storms did. Consistent with object perception research demonstrating that changing stimuli attract attention, Arkin and Duval (1975) found that perceivers attributed more causality for an actor's art work choices to a situation containing dynamic, changing stimulus elements—a videotaped depiction of art works—than to one that was stable—photos of art works. As in Storms' study, no significant effects on dispositional attribution were observed.

McArthur and Post (1977) conducted a series of five experiments in which the attention-drawing stimuli in an actor's environment consisted of other people. The results revealed that when an actor's environment—i.e. another actor—drew perceivers' attention, they made more situational attributions for the actor's behavior during a getting-acquainted conversation than when it did not. More specifically, when an actor conversed with someone who was brightly lit, moving, wearing a striped shirt, or who formed a Gestalt "unit" with others present, then the actor's behavior was attributed more to situational causes than when he conversed with someone who was dimly lit, stationary, wearing a grey shirt, or who did not form a "unit" with others present. Two different bases of unit formation yielded this latter effect. In one study, it was shirt color: There was more situational attribution for the behavior of an actor whose shirt was a different color from those worn by a "unit" of three others than for the behavior of an actor who appeared with people whose shirts varied in color. In a second study, the basis of unit formation was the actor's sex. There was more situational attribution for the behavior of an actor who was the opposite sex from a "unit" of three others than for the behavior of an actor who appeared with people of both sexes. Although dispositional attribution trends complementary to the situation attribution effects were obtained in all of the McArthur and Post studies, none approached significance.

The finding that causal attributions for a stimulus person's behavior vary with the tendency for their companions to form a unit has also been reported in research by Taylor, Fiske, Close, Anderson, and Ruderman (1976), which exposed perceivers to an ad-libbed brainstorming session. Causal attributions for the behavior of a black actor, whose environment consisted of a "unit" of five whites, were compared with attributions for the behavior of the same actor when his environment was racially mixed. Consistent with the findings of McArthur and Post (1977), there was a slight tendency for perceivers to make more situational attributions for the behavior of the black actor when his companions formed a unit than when they did not.

The research reviewed thus far has revealed that when people interact with someone who draws attention by virtue of clothing, movement, or association with a physically cohesive group, then their behavior tends to be attributed more to situational causes than when they interact with someone who draws less attention. Presumably, these "situational" causes are causes in the attention-drawing partner, and some research by McArthur and Solomon (1978) has explicitly tested this by asking subjects to what extent each of three factors had caused the actor's behavior: the actor's own *personality,* the *situation,* and the behavior and personality of the *partner* with whom the actor was interacting. This research differed from previous studies in two additional important respects. One is the nature of social interaction in which the effects of attention were examined. As Taylor and Fiske (1978) have noted, most of the effects of attention on causal attributions have been demonstrated in the context of commonplace, redundant, and boring "getting-acquainted" conversations. McArthur and Solomon tested the generalizability of these effects to a more interesting, unusual, and informationally complex social situation. The typical "getting-acquainted" conversation was replaced with a heated discussion about the outcome of a bridge hand between two partners, one of whom emerged as an "aggressor," and the other as a "victim." The level of emotions in this discussion was high and the information exchanged about what had transpired in the bridge game was complicated. Another important difference between this research and previous studies was the manipulation of attention that was employed. As noted previously, attention to the victim in this study was manipulated by means of a statistically novel attribute: a leg brace or red hair.

The expectation that the aggressor's behavior would be attributed more to causes in the victim when attention was drawn to the victim was confirmed both for the leg brace and for the hair color manipulation of attention. Interestingly, the "partner attribution" measure seems to have usurped any effects of attention on the less specific situational attribution measure for, unlike past research in which there was no partner attribution measure, the situational attribution measure revealed no effect. Consistent with past research, the attentional manipulations had no impact on dispositional attributions. It thus appears that perceivers' causal attributions for the behavior of individuals engaged in a social interaction will vary with the degree of attention to those individuals even when the interaction is a rather heated argument. The aggressor's antisocial behavior was blamed more on the victim when the victim was salient than when she was not. It is important to note that this tendency to "blame" a salient victim of aggression cannot readily be explained in terms of negative stereotypes of "crippled people" and "redheads." Not only does it require quite a stretch of the imagination to generate overlapping stereotypes of these two groups of people, but in addition it should be recalled that the victim was rated as more friendly and more passive when she wore a leg brace or had red hair than when she didn't. Therefore the stereotypes "unfriendly," or "overassertive" cannot be mediating the attribution effects. More important, ratings of the victim's behavior were not significantly correlated with the tendency to attribute the aggressor's behavior to her.

That blaming of a salient victim was demonstrated for a novel physical attribute as inconsequential as red hair suggests that its impact may be very widespread: One would also expect more blaming of victims who deviate from the norm on any number of physical attributes such as height, weight, age, ethnicity, etc. On the brighter side, when such "deviant" individuals are the recipients of kind behavior, they should be perceived as more deserving than more physically ordinary people.

Two paradigms varying the extent to which stimulus persons capture perceivers' attention have failed to find more situational attribution for the nonsalient actor's behavior. Taylor and Fiske (1975) and Taylor, Crocker, Fiske, Sprinzen, and Winkler (1979) manipulated attentional focus by varying perceivers' seating positions and found no difference between situational attributions for the behavior of an actor who faced the perceiver and those for an actor whose back was to the perceiver. This lack of effect may be attributed to the fact that situational attribution is probably an insensitive indicator of attentional effects in the point of view paradigm, where the "situations" of both the salient and nonsalient actors are very similar: both consist of the other actor plus a circle of six observers. A better measure of the extent to which each actor's behavior is attributed to external causes may be a "partner attribution" measure such as that employed by McArthur and Solomon (1978). And, in point of fact, Taylor and her associates have found effects on such a measure, although their question has been phrased "to what extent did this actor cause his/her partner's behavior?" rather than as "to what extent was this actor's behavior caused by his/her partner?" The former question comprised part of a causal index on which Taylor and her associates have repeatedly found salience effects: The attended actor is perceived as causing the partner's behavior more than the nonattended actor is.

Another paradigm that failed to obtain the standard effects of attention on situational attribution is that employed by Eisen and McArthur (1979), who manipulated perceivers' attention to a stimulus person by varying the length of time the person appeared on camera in a videotaped mock trial. There were no effects of this salience manipulation on situational or dispositional attribution for the defendant's behavior, although it did influence impressions of the actors. One possible explanation for the failure of this manipulation is that, as in the Taylor and Fiske paradigm, situational attribution may have been an insensitive indicator of attentional effects: Whether the defendant was on camera 5 minutes or 10 minutes, the situation of "being on trial" undoubtedly was perceived as a potent cause of his behavior.

Summary and Implications

Koffka's (1935) argument that "fixation of one of two equivalent objects tended to make it the carrier of motion, whether it moved objectively or not," seems to have an analogue in the realm of person perception. The bulk of the evidence indicates that when environmental stimuli draw attention, they are perceived as causing the actor's behavior. Thus, situational attribution is higher when an actor interacts with salient than with nonsalient persons or objects. This effect has been demonstrated for stimuli which draw attention by virtue of their *physical* properties—e.g., bright lights—as well as for stimuli which draw attention by virtue of their *collative* properties—e.g., "unit" formation and statistical novelty. Not only do these effects replicate across a variety of salience manipulations, but moreover they replicate across a variety of social situations, including observations of getting-acquainted conversations, artwork choices, brainstorming, and verbal aggression.

The tendency to make more situational attributions for the behavior of an actor who is interacting with attention-drawing stimuli is not reliably complemented by tendency to make more dispositional attributions for the behavior of an attention-drawing actor. In all of the studies that manipulated the presence of attention-drawing stimuli, none revealed significant effects on dispositional attributions, although several did show trends in the expected direction. One clear conclusion from this is that situational and dispositional causes are not psychological reciprocals of one another. Indeed, their average intercorrelation in the studies reporting this data have not been significant. Another implication of these findings is that attending to someone does not strengthen the perception that his or her behavior is dispositionally caused in the same way that attending to someone's environment strengthens the perception that his or her behavior is situationally caused. Upon reflection, this fact is not really so surprising. Attending to someone's environment can reveal proximal, situational causes for that persons' behavior. But, attending to a person doesn't really reveal dispositional causes for that person's behavior. These are in some sense "distal" causes, not to be gleaned merely from looking more at the person's overt behavior. Another possible contributor to the failure of attentional manipulations to influence attributions to dispositional causes is the "fundamental attribution error." It has been noted that perceivers tend to underestimate the impact of situational factors and to overestimate the role of dispositional factors in controlling behavior (Ross, 1977). Thus, it may be that drawing attention to an actor's environment can offset the tendency to underestimate situational causes, whereas drawing attention to an actor cannot further augment the estimation of dispositional causes, which are already inflated.

Attention-Drawing Behaviors

The research reviewed in the preceding section has revealed that the tendency to attribute causality to people varies with the degree to which their *physical appearance* draws attention. One would also expect causal attributions to vary with the degree to which a person's *behaviors* draw attention. More specifically, one would expect behaviors that are intense, changing, complex, novel or which form a unit to yield more causal attributions to a stimulus person than their less attention-drawing counterparts. This hypothesis has received surprisingly little attention in the research literature.

There has been considerable research on the effects upon causal attributions of the *intensity* of an action's consequences, but unfortunately, the findings are very contradictory: Sometimes there is more causal attribution to the perpetrator when the consequences are severe—or intense—than when they are mild, and sometimes there is more attribution to the victim. (See Wortman, 1976, for a summary of this literature.) It may be that the direction of the effect depends on the degree to which the consequences draw attention to the perpetrator versus the degree to which they draw attention to the victim. If they form a unit with the perpetrator, then one would expect that with increasing intensity, perpetrator attribution would increase. If, on the other hand, they form a unit with the victim, one would expect that with increasing intensity, victim attribution would increase. For this formulation to provide any predictive power requires that one be able to determine the conditions under which the consequences of an action will form a unit with the perpetrator versus the victim. Variables such as contiguity and similarity may be useful in this attempt. For example, the more temporally or spatially separated the act is from its consequences, the more likely the consequences are to form a unit with the recipient than the perpetrator. Similarity of the act to the perpetrator versus the recipient may also have an influence on unit formation: For example, the stronger the associative connections the act has to the perpetrator, the more apt its consequences are to form a unit with the perpetrator.

In addition to the possible impact of the intensity of an action's consequences upon causal attributions, other research indicates that attention to and causal attributions for an actor's behavior may vary with the amount of *change* in the behavior. For example, Wilder's (1978) study, noted earlier, revealed not only that subjects divided an actor's behavior into more units when it changed than when it was constant, but it also revealed that the number of units was positively correlated with dispositional attributions of causality. Other research has also reported greater unitization of changing, unpredictable behavior, but the effects on causal attributions has not been consistent (see Newtson, 1976, for a review of this literature). Sometimes changing behaviors receive more dispositional attribution, and sometimes they receive more situational attribution. The effect seems to depend on other features of the behavior, and more research is clearly needed to clarify the relationship between the degree of change that an actor's behavior manifests and causal attributions.

Summary and Implications.   Although there has been considerable research documenting the impact of attention-drawing people upon causal attributions, there is surprisingly little evidence bearing on the impact of attention-drawing behaviors. Given the impact of these variables upon impression formation, further research clearly seems warranted. One would expect, for example, that more causality will be attributed to actors who perform intense, novel, complex, changing, and unit-forming behaviors than to those whose behaviors are more subdued, ordinary, simple, static, and/or fragmented. And, given the shared distinctiveness illusory correlation effects documented in the research on impression formation, one would expect these effects to be especially pronounced when the actor's appearance, as well as his behavior, draws attention.

Perceiver Effects

Like the impact of attention-drawing behaviors upon causal attributions, that of the perceiver's expectations has received little attention in the research literature. To the extent that perceivers attend more to expected events, such events may be more apt to be seen as causal than unexpected ones. A study by Enquist, Newtson, and LaCross (1978) provides some evidence for this hypothesis. Subjects in this study were exposed to a videotape that depicted an accident occurring while two people explored a room. Some subjects had no particular expectancy, others were set to expect one person, Rick, to be responsible for the accident, and still others were set to expect Bob to be the culprit. While watching the videotape, subjects had two buttons, one labeled Bob, and the other labeled Rick, and they were instructed to press the appropriate button whenever an actor performed a meaningful action. The results revealed that the behavior of the actor whom subjects expected to be responsible was segmented more finely and better recalled than that of the other actor, thus providing evidence of greater attention to expected events. In addition, subjects rated the actor to whom they attended more as more responsible for the accident. Evidence that these attributional effects reflect differential registration of information consistent with expectancies is provided by the finding that when the expectancy manipulations were provided *after* the videotape, they had no effect upon attributions of responsibility.

Although there is evidence that the observer's arousal level influences the polarization of their impressions, there is no evidence that arousal influences causal attributions. McArthur and Solomon (1978) had expected that the tendency to attribute an aggressor's behavior more to a salient than a nonsalient victim would be stronger for aroused than nonaroused perceivers, but this hypothesis was not confirmed either for the self-consciousness or the noise arousal manipulation.

Summary and Implications

The role of the perceiver's expectancies in causal attribution has been surprisingly disregarded. Although there is some evidence that people attend more to expected events and thereby perceive them as more causal, the only manipulation that has been employed to vary perceiver's expectations is an instructional one. As the section on impression formation has revealed, there are many other bases for perceivers' expectations, and these may have important implications for causal attributions in the real world. For example, Heider (1944) suggested that events may be attributed to the actor with whom they have the strongest associative connections: "A crime can be blamed on a person because of physical similarity; he looks as if he could have committed this crime [p. 7]." Cultural, functional, metaphorical, and affective associations to a person's physical appearance may each contribute to this type of effect, and they merit serious investigation. Further research testing the hypothesis that perceivers' arousal will augment causal attributions to attention-drawing stimuli also seems worthwhile, even though the existing evidence does not support this hypothesis.

MEDIATION

The evidence reviewed in this chapter reveals that principles of selective attention together with Gestalt "laws" concerning the properties of figural stimuli have the power to account for a wide variety of data on impression formation and causal attribution. The question remains as to the mediation of these effects. This question is actually twofold: first is the question of *where* in information processing does selective attention occur; and second is the question of *how* selective attention produces the effects upon impressions and causal attributions that have been reviewed.

Where?

There are three points at which the perceiver may selectively attend to salient persons and behaviors. One is at *registration* of information: The perceiver may pick up more information about salient stimuli and/or the perceiver's perceptual organization of the available stimuli may vary with their salience. A second point at which selectivity may occur is at the *encoding* of information: The perceiver may store and/or interpret information about salient stimuli differently—e.g., it may be more available, and/or it may be weighted more heavily. A third point at which selectivity may operate is in the *recall* of information: The perceiver may be able to remember more information about salient stimuli. In considering these three possible loci of attentional selectivity, it is important to note that they are not mutually exclusive. There could be selectivity at registration, more at encoding, and still more at recall. Also, whatever selectivity occurs at one point will be reflected further down the line. For example, whatever information a perceiver fails to pick up will certainly receive no weight and will not be recalled. Although much of the available research evidence has not really been oriented toward answering the question of where in the processing of information selectivity occurs, some data pertinent to this question has been gathered.

Evidence for selectivity during *registration* of information has been provided by research that has recorded perceivers' visual fixation during exposure to salient and nonsalient stimuli. For example, McArthur and Ginsberg (1978) recorded the duration of subjects' visual fixation on the left half of a TV monitor both when the actor on the left possessed an attention-drawing attribute and when he or she did not. Subjects fixated longer on an actress when she wore a striped shirt than when she wore a less complex, gray one; they also fixated longer on a red-haired, red-beared actor when his novel hair color was visible than when the same videotape was shown in black and white; and, they fixated longer on an actress when her leg brace was visible than when it was obscured by a standing ashtray. Other evidence that observers look more at statistically novel stimulus persons has been provided by Langer, Taylor, Fiske, and Chanowitz (1976) who found that, when subjects' staring was unobserved, they stared longer at photographs of handicapped or pregnant stimulus persons than at photos of normal persons. Taylor and Langer (1977) also reported that subjects stared more at a pregnant than nonpregnant women. Additional evidence for preferential registration of salient people is provided by Enquist, Newtson, and LaCross (1978), who found that perceivers exposed to a social interaction segmented more finely the behavior of an actor who was expected to cause an accident than that of another actor. This may reflect greater pick-up of information about the salient actor, because it seems reasonable to argue that behavioral sequences, which are broken into finer units, are drawing more continuous attention than those that are viewed more grossly. It also indicates that the perceptual organization of information at registration varies with the actor's salience.

In addition to the foregoing evidence for preferential registration of salient persons, Fiske (1980) has provided evidence for preferential registration of salient behaviors in her finding that perceivers spend more time looking at slides depicting extreme or negative behaviors than those which depict more moderate or positive ones. Other evidence for preferential registration of salient behaviors is provided by Wilder's (1978) finding that changing behaviors are unitized more finely. This may reflect greater pick-up of information about salient behaviors. And, like other unitization work by Newtson and his colleagues, it also indicates that the perceptual organization of behaviors at registration varies with their salience (eg. Massad, Hubbard, & Newtson, 1979; Newtson, Rinder, Miller, & LaCross, 1978).

Evidence for selective attention to particular behaviors during the *encoding* of information has been provided by studies demonstrating that extreme, novel, negative, or early behaviors in a sequence are weighted more heavily in perceiver's impressions than their less salient counterparts. Although this differential weighting may represent selectivity over and above that manifested during registration, it may also simply be a consequence of the selective registration of these behaviors. Some evidence consistent with the latter argument is provided by research that eliminated preferential weighting of early trait information by tasks designed to equalize registration of all of the traits in the list (eg. Anderson & Hubert, 1963; Hendrick & Constantini, 1970).

Evidence for selective attention to particular behaviors during the *recall* of information is scarce. The research evidence that allows one to distinguish between selection during recall and selection during registration and/or encoding comes from studies that have varied attention by manipulating the perceiver's expectancies. In several studies (eg. Enquist, Newtson, & LaCross, 1978; Massad, Hubbard, & Newtson, 1979; Snyder & Frankel, 1976; Zadny & Gerard, 1974), perceivers have been given an expectancy either before or after exposure to a social interaction. The results have revealed that when perceivers are given an expectancy before exposure, their impressions, attributions, and/or recall are assimilated to that expectancy, although this does not occur for those given an expectancy after exposure. This implies that the selective attention produced by these manipulations of perceivers' expectations operated during the registration and/or encoding of information, not during recall.

In contrast to the foregoing findings, Snyder and Uranowitz (1978) recently found that perceivers' recall was influenced by the information that a woman was a lesbian when this ''expectancy'' for certain behaviors was given *after* reading her life history. It may be that selective attention during recall is most apt to occur when the expectancy engages a well-developed schema that controls the memory search. This would be more true when the expectancy concerns heterosexual versus homosexual behavior, as it did in Snyder and Uranowitz' study, than it would be when it concerns theft-related versus waiting behavior, as it did in Zadny and Gerard's research, or nonverbal behavior in an interview about politics versus sex, as it did in Snyder and Frankel's research.

Summary and Implications.   The available evidence indicates that attentional selection typically operates during registration and/or encoding of information, and only occasionally during recall. This is not to say that attention-drawing stimuli are not recalled better than those that do not draw attention. Indeed, recall effects have been demonstrated in several studies. Rather, this is to say that many, if not most, effects of selective attention upon recall represent selection occurring earlier in the processing of information—i.e. during registration or encoding—rather than selection occurring during the recall process itself. To determine whether or not there is selective attention at encoding that is not merely a reflection of selection at registration requires further research assessing the impact of salient stimuli upon social judgments in the absence of selective registration. Such research is difficult to design, because it is impossible to precisely control stimulus registration except in a very artificial context—eg. tachistoscopic stimuli.

How?

The second mediation question concerns how it is that people who draw more attention tend to create bigger and more extreme impressions and to be perceived as more causal than less attention-drawing people. And, how is it that behaviors that draw more attention tend to exert more influence upon impressions and causal attributions than those that are less salient? The answer to this question is not totally independent of the answer to the question of where selectivity occurs. Four possible answers to the ''how?'' question are considered: (1) information about salient stimuli is more likely to be remembered; (2) the perceptual organization of information at the time it is registered is influenced by stimulus salience; (3) information is encoded such that information about salient stimuli is more available; and (4) information is encoded such that information about salient stimuli is more linked to the perceiver's affective reactions.

If selectivity during information processing were such that practically no information was remembered about the nonsalient people or behaviors, it is self-evident that these people would not create a big or extreme impression or be seen as causal and that these behaviors would not exert much influence upon impressions or causal attributions. Of course, reality is not this clear-cut. Recall measures reveal that information about nonsalient stimulis *is* remembered. Indeed, attentional manipulations often influence impressions and attributions without even producing any preferential recall of the salient person's behaviors.

One possible flaw in the research assessing recall is that measures of *verbal* recall have typically been employed. Given that the attentional manipulations have typically been visual ones, one would expect measures of visual recall to be a more sensitive index of perceivers' selective attention to salient stimuli. Consistent with this argument, McArthur and Ginsberg (1978) and Fiske (1980) have found preferential recall of visual information about a salient actor in the absence of preferential recall of verbal information. However, in these studies, as in those employing measures of verbal recall, the correlations between recall and impression or attribution measures were not significant. It is therefore difficult to argue that the social judgment effects are mediated by differential recall of information.

Of course, it may be that the information that subjects have been asked to recall is not sufficiently relevant to their impressions and/or attributions to even be expected to correlate with them. More research that taps recall of behaviors, which one would logically expect to be influencing these social perceptions, clearly is needed. Although the final answer awaits further research, the existing evidence suggests that the impact of selective attention upon social perceptions does not derive merely from the *amount* of information perceivers can recall about salient versus nonsalient people and their behaviors.

Although there is not much support for the argument that the impact of selective attention upon social perceptions reflects the amount of information recalled, these effects may reflect the *perceptual organization* of this information at the time it is registered. This perceptual mediation is most compelling in the case of the causal attribution effects. In the context of a dynamic social interaction, each person's behavior is typically both cause and effect: Each person reacts to the other, and that reaction causes a reaction in the other. The power of certain stimuli to draw attention may cause the perceiver to organize the interaction chain in terms of the salient person's influence on the nonsalient person, rather than vice versa.[12] For example, in Fig. 6.1, the behavioral exchanges tend to be perceptually organized into units reflecting the causal influence of the salient actor on the nonsalient actor (0= = = =o), rather than into units reflecting the causal influence of the nonsalient actor on the salient actor (o– – – –0), regardless of who actually begins the interaction. As a consequence, the salient actor may be seen as exerting more causal influence than the nonsalient actor even though their actual influence is equal. Although there is really no direct evidence for this mediation of the effects of selective attention on causal attribution, Newtson's unitization work does reveal that attention-drawing stimuli affect perceptual organization, and additional research that assesses the pattern of organization of events in a dyadic interaction as a function of the salience of the actors would seem worthwhile.

FIG. 6.1. Segmentation of a dyadic interaction into causal influence units as a function of the salience of each member of the dyad.

0= = = =o– – – –0= = = =o– – – –0= = = =o– – – –0= = = =o– – – –0

o– – – –0= = = =o– – – –0= = = =o– – – –0= = = =o– – – –0= = = =o

0= = = =o is the causal influence of the salient actor on the nonsalient actor.
o– – – –0 is the causal influence of the nonsalient actor on the salient actor.

Although the impact of attention-drawing stimuli upon perceptual organization may prove to account for at least some of their effects upon social judg-

---

[12]The author would like to thank William DeJong for suggesting this perceptual mediation of the tendency to perceive salient stimuli as causal.

ments, another possible mediation is their impact upon the *encoding* of information. The failure to find consistent differences in the quantity of information recalled about salient and nonsalient stimuli has led Taylor and Fiske (1978) to suggest that it is "availability" or the ease with which information is brought to mind (Tversky & Kahneman, 1973), rather than whether or not it can be recalled, that mediates the effects of salient stimuli on social perceptions. More specifically, Taylor and Fiske have suggested that, given manipulations of visual attention, visual images of the salient stimuli are more available in memory than visual images of the nonsalient stimuli. As noted earlier, some support for this hypothesis has been provided in demonstrations of preferential recall of visual material about salient persons in the absence of preferential recall of verbal material, but it was also noted that visual recall did not correlate any more highly with social perceptions than verbal recall. In addition to the need for more research that taps recall of visual behaviors that one would logically expect to influence social perceptions, Taylor and Fiske's hypothesis requires research-employing measures specifically designed to probe the "availability" of information in memory—i.e., how accessibly it is encoded—rather than whether or not it can be retrieved. Reaction time measures would be appropriate for this purpose.

Another possible encoding answer to the question of how selective attention influences social judgments is related to what Berlyne (1970) has called "learning" in his discussion of selective attention. More specifically, Berlyne argued that responses to a stimulus array may become more strongly associated with salient than nonsalient stimuli. Such an effect provides a plausible mediation for the impact of salient stimuli upon evaluative impressions. If the perceiver's affective responses to an actor or a behavior are more strongly associated with these social stimuli when they are salient than when they are not, this could produce a tendency to rate salient actors more extremely and to weight salient behaviors more heavily in impression formation. Although this classical conditioning mediation has no directly supporting evidence, research on animal learning has demonstrated stronger conditioning to salient than nonsalient components of a complex stimulus array (eg. Rescorla & Wagner, 1972). Moreover, the affective conditioning mediation is compatible with several patterns of results in the existing data. For example, it is consistent with the finding that attentional manipulations have more impact upon impressions when perceivers are exposed to affectively toned interactions than when they are exposed to banal getting-acquainted conversations. It is also compatible with the finding that perceivers' recall about attention-drawing people and behaviors is relatively independent of their evaluative responses (see, for example, Dreben, Fiske, & Hastie, 1979), because divergent affective associations could influence perceiver's ratings of stimulus persons independently of their explicit recall of those persons' behaviors. Such an effect would be consistent with Zajonc's (1979) distinction between affective and cognitive judgments.

The hypothesis that the impact of selective attention upon impressions is affectively mediated would seem to merit an explicit test. A paradigm that would be useful in this regard is one in which perceivers' affective reactions were monitored during their exposure to salient and nonsalient actors performing emotionally evocative behaviors. One would predict that perceivers would manifest more reactivity to the salient actor, even though the actual behaviors did not differ, and that subsequent exposure to the actors in a neutral context would yield a stronger classically conditioned emotional response to the salient than the nonsalient actor.

Summary and Implications.   Four possible answers to the ''How?'' question have been suggested: (1) information about salient stimuli may be more apt to be recalled and thus has more impact upon all social judgments; (2) information may be perceptually organized in a manner that highlights the causal role of salient stimuli; (3) information about salient stimuli may be encoded such that it is more cognitively available to the perceiver and thus has more impact upon all social judgments; (4) information about salient stimuli may be encoded such that it is more linked to the perceiver's affective responses, and thus has more impact upon evaluative, impression judgments. The available research doesn't really provide a sound basis for choosing among these four possible mediations, although there is some evidence against the first one. Also, the low intercorrelations among impression, attribution, and recall measures renders the cognitive availability explanation less plausible than others because it assumes a common mediator for all of these social judgments. Thus, research probing the viability of a perceptual organization explanation for the impact of salient stimuli upon causal attributions and the viability of an affective encoding explanation for the impact of salient stimuli upon impression extremity may prove to be the most fruitful.

CONCLUSIONS

Several commonalities between the perception of social and nonsocial stimuli have been documented in this chapter. Just as perceivers selectively attend to intense, changing, complex, novel, and unit-forming stimuli in the realm of object perception, so do they selectively attend to such stimuli in the realm of person perception. And just as perceivers' expectations and arousal determine what nonsocial stimuli will be selectively attended, so do they determine what social stimuli will be. Moreover, the impact that Gestalt psychologists have shown these stimuli to have upon our perceptions of objects have intriguing analogues in our perceptions of people.

Though striking, these commonalities are not very well represented in much of the theory and research on person perception. Not only did Gary Trudeau and all of his readers find the cautionary measures invoked in the presidential debates rather laughable, but probably many of the psychologically sophisticated readers of this chapter did as well. Indeed, even Heider, who acknowledged a similarity between object perception and person perception, stressed that there are important differences in the nature of the proximal stimuli that are employed in the perceptions of objects and persons. In particular, Heider (1958) maintained that: "While we believe that we get to know something about a person from the shape of his face, or even the color of his hair, these physiognomic properties are far outweighed by his actions as clues to his personality [p. 23]."

It is of course true that persons are perceived to have attributes that cannot be defined in physical terms. However, the research reviewed in this chapter reveals that a brighter light on Jimmy Carter, or an unusually colored suit, or a more boldly striped tie, could, by virtue of their capacity to draw attention, exert a surprisingly strong influence upon perceivers' impressions of him and their causal attributions for his behavior during the debate. Likewise, behaviors that are selectively attended to either by virtue of their physical properties (such as a novel regional accent) or the perceiver's state could exert a stronger influence upon impressions and causal attributions than their less salient counterparts. Research exploring the mediation of these effects may provide valuable data for information-processing theories. Equally valuable would be research that explores both the range of events in social perception which can be predicted from principles of selective attention and figural emphasis, as well as the consequences of these processes for social interaction. It all depends, of course, on "what grabs you."

ACKNOWLEDGMENTS

I would like to thank Teresa Amabile, Reuben Baron, William DeJong, Susan Fiske, David Hamilton, and Shelley Taylor for their very helpful comments on an earlier draft of this chapter. Preparation was supported by an NIMH Research Grant MH26621.

REFERENCES

Amster, H. Semantic satiation and generation: Learning? Adaptation? *Psychological Bulletin*, 1964, *62*, 273–286.

Anderson, N. H., & Hubert, S. Effects of concomitant verbal recall on order effects in personality impression formation. *Journal of Verbal Learning and Verbal Behavior*, 1963, *2*, 379–391.

Arkin, R. M., & Duval, S. Focus of attention and causal attributions of actors and observers. *Journal of Experimental Social Psychology*, 1975, *11*, 427–438.

Aronson, E., & Linder, D. Gain and loss of esteem as determinants of interpersonal attractiveness. *Journal of Experimental Social Psychology*, 1965, *1*, 156–171.

Asch, S. E. Forming impressions of personality. *Journal of Abnormal and Social Psychology*, 1946, *41*, 258–290.

Bahrick, H. P., Fitts, P. M., & Rankin, R. E. Effect of incentives upon reactions to peripheral stimuli. *Journal of Experimental Psychology*, 1952, *44*, 400–406.

Bass, B. N., & Klubick, S. Effects of seating arrangements on leaderless group discussions. *Journal of Abnormal and Social Psychology*, 1952, *47*, 724–727.

Bennett, R. & Eckman, J. Attitudes toward aging: a critical examination of recent literature and implications for future research. In C. Eisendorfer and M. P. Lawton (Eds.) *The Psychology of Adult Development and Aging*, Washington D.C.: American Psychological Association, 1973.

Berlyne, D. E. Attention as a problem in behavior theory. In D. I. Mostofsky (Ed.), *Attention: Contemporary theory and analysis*, New York: Appleton Century Crofts, 1970.

Berscheid, E., & Walster, E. Physical attractiveness. In L. Berkowitz (Ed.), *Advances in experimental social psychology* (Vol. 7). New York: Academic Press, 1974.

Birnbaum, G., Frechtman, J., & McArthur, L. Z. *Stereotypic traits associated with glasses or blond hair*. Manuscript in preparation, 1978.

Brickman, P., Redfield, J., Harrison, A. A., & Crandall, R. Drive and predisposition as factors in the attitudinal effects of mere exposure. *Journal of Experimental Social Psychology*, 1972, *8*, 31–44.

Brigham, J. C. Ethnic stereotypes. *Psychological Bulletin*, 1971, *76*, 15–38.

Broverman, I. K., Broverman, F. E., Clarkson, P. S., Rosenkrantz, P. S., & Vogel, S. R. Sex-role stereotypes and clinical judgments of mental health. *Journal of Consulting and Clinical Psychology*, 1970, *34*, 1–7.

Bruner, J. S. On perceptual readiness. *Psychological Review*, 1957, *64*, 123–152.

Bruner, J. S., Matter, J., & Papanek, M. L. Breadth of learning as a function of drive level and mechanization. *Psychological Review*, 1955, *62*, 1–10.

Bruning, J. L., Capage, J. W., Kozoh, G. F., Young, P. F., & Young, W. E. Socially induced drive and range of cue utilization. *Journal of Personality and Social Psychology*, 1968, *9*, 242–244.

Bursill, A. E. The restriction of peripheral vision during exposure to hot and humid conditions. *Quarterly Journal of Experimental Psychology*, 1958, *10*, 113–129.

Callaway, E., & Stone, G. Re-evaluating the focus of attention. In L. Uhr & J. G. Miller (Eds.), *Drugs and behavior*. New York: John Wiley, 1960.

Callaway, E., & Thompson, S. V. Sympathetic activity and perception: An approach to the relationships between autonomic activity and personality. *Psychosomatic Medicine*, 1953, *15*, 443–455.

Cantor, N., & Mischel, W. Traits as prototypes: Effects on recognition memory. *Journal of Personality and Social Psychology*, 1977, *35*, 38–48.

Chapman, L. J. Illusory correlation in observational report. *Journal of Verbal Learning and Verbal Behavior*, 1967, *6*, 151–155.

Chapman, L. J., & Chapman, J. P. Genesis of popular but erroneous psycho-diagnostic observations. *Journal of Abnormal Psychology*, 1967, *72*, 193–204.

Cornsweet, D. J. Use of cues in the visual periphery under conditions of arousal. *Journal of Experimental Psychology*, 1969, *80*, 14–18.

Dreben, F. K., Fiske, S. T., & Hastie, R. The independence of evaluative and item information. Impression and recall order effects in behavior-based impression formation. *Journal of Personality and Social Psychology*, 1979, *37*, 1758–1768.

Easterbrook, J. A. The effect of emotion on cue utilization and the organization of behavior. *Psychological Review*, 1959, *66*, 183–201.

Eisen, S. V., & McArthur, L. Z. Evaluating and sentencing a defendant as a function of his salience and the preceiver's set. *Personality and Social Psychology Bulletin*, 1979, *5*, 48–52.

Enquist, G., Newtson, D., & LaCross, K. *Prior expectations and the perceptual segmentation of ongoing behavior*. Unpublished manuscript, University of Virginia, 1978.

Eriksen, C. W., & Collins, J. F. Visual perception rate under two conditions of search. *Journal of Experimental Psychology,* 1969, *80,* 489–492.

Fiske, S. T. Attention and weight in person perception: The impact of negative and extreme behavior. *Journal of Personality and Social Psychology,* 1980, *38,* 889–908.

Fiske, S. T. Personal communication based upon unpublished data, 1978.

Hamilton, D. L., & Gifford, R. K. Illusory correlation in interpersonal perception: A cognitive basis of stereotypic judgments. *Journal of Experimental Social Psychology,* 1976, *12,* 392–407.

Hamilton, D. L., & Rose, T. L *Illusory correlation and the maintenance of stereotypic beliefs.* Unpublished manuscript, University of California, Santa Barbara, 1978.

Hamilton, D. L., & Zanna, M. P. Differential weighting of favorable and unfavorable attributes in impressions of personality. *Journal of Experimental Research in Personality,* 1972, *6,* 204–212.

Hamilton, D. L., & Zanna, M. P. Context effects in impression formation: Changes in connotative Meaning. *Journal of Personality and Social Psychology,* 1974, *29,* 649–654.

Harrison, A. A. Mere Exposure. In L. Berkowitz (Eds.), *Advances in experimental social psychology,* (Vol. 10). New York: Academic Press, 1977.

Heider, F. *Perceiving the other person.* In R. Tagiuri & L. Petrullo (Eds.), *Person Perception and Interpersonal Behavior.* Stanford: Stanford University Press, 1958.

Heider, F. Social perception and phenomenal causality. *Psychological Review,* 1944, *51,* 358–374.

Heider, F., & Simmel, M. An experimental study of apparent behavior. *American Journal of Psychology,* 1944, *57,* 243–259.

Hendrick, C., & Constantini, A. F. Effects of varying trait inconsistency and response requirements on the primacy effect in impression formation. *Journal of Personality and Social Psychology,* 1970, *15,* 158–164.

Higgins, E. T., Rholes, W. S., & Jones, C. R. Category accessibility and impression formation. *Journal of Experimental Social Psychology,* 1977, *13,* 141–154.

Hochberg, J., & Brooks, F. Perspective reversal and intercue distance. In D. I. Mostofsky, *Attention: Contemporary theory and analysis.* New York: Appleton–Century–Crofts, 1970.

Hockey, G. R. J. Effect of loud noise on attentional selectivity. *Quarterly Journal of Experimental Psychology,* 1970, *22,* 28–36.

Hodges, B. Effect of valence on relative weighting in impression formation. *Journal of Personality and Social Psychology,* 1974, *30,* 378–381.

Jakobovitz, L. A. Effects of mere exposure: A comment. *Journal of Personality and Social Psychology,* 1968, *9,* 30–32.

Jones, E. E., Davis, K. E., & Gergen, K. J. Role playing variations and their informational value for person perception. *Journal of Abnormal and Social Psychology,* 1961, *63,* 302–310.

Jones, E. E., & Goethels, G. R. Order effects in impression formation: Attribution context and the nature of the entity. In E. E. Jones, D. E. Kanouse, H. H. Kelley, R. E. Nisbett, S. Valins, & B. Weiner (Eds.), *Attribution: Perceiving the causes of behavior.* Morristown: N.J.: General Learning Press, 1972.

Jones, E. E., & Nisbett, R. E. The actor and the observer: Divergent perceptions of the causes of behavior. In E. E. Jones, D. E. Kanouse, H. H. Kelley, R. E. Nisbett, S. Valins, & B. Weiner (Eds.), *Attribution: Perceiving the causes of behavior.* Morristown, N.J.: General Learning Press, 1972.

Jones, R. A., Scott, J., Solernou, J., Noble, A., Fiala, J., & Miller, K. Availibility and formation of stereotypes. *Perceptual and Motor Skills,* 1977, *44,* 631–638.

Kahneman, D. *Attention and effort.* Englewood Cliffs, N.J.: Prentice-Hall, 1973.

Kanouse, D. E., & Hanson, L. R. Negativity in evaluations. In E. E. Jones, D. E. Kanouse, H. H. Kelley, R. E. Nisbett, S. Valins, & B. Weiner (Eds.), *Attribution: Perceiving the causes of behavior.* General Learning Press: Morristown, N. J.: 1972.

Kelley, H. H. The warm cold variable in first impressions of persons. *Journal of Personality,* 1950, *18,* 431–439.

Koffka, K. Perceived Motion. In *Principles of gestalt psychology*. New York: Harcourt Brace & Co., 1935.

Langer, E. J., & Abelson, R. P. A patient by any other name . . . clinician group difference in labeling bias. *Journal of Consulting and Clinical psychology*, 1974, *42*, 4–9.

Langer, E. J., & Imber, L. Role of mindlessness in the perception of deviance. *Journal of Personality and Social Psychology*, 1980, *39*, 360–367.

Langer, E. J., Taylor, S. E., Fiske, S. T., & Chanowitz, B. Stigma, staring, and discomfort: A novel stimulus hypothesis. *Journal of Experimental Social Psychology*, 1976, *12*, 451–463.

Leeper, R. A study of a neglected portion of the field of learning: The development of sensory organization. *Journal of Genetic Psychology*, 1935, *46*, 42–75.

Manis, M., Gleason, T. C., & Dawes, R. M. The evaluation of complex social stimuli. *Journal of Personality and Social Psychology*, 1966, *3*, 404–419.

Massad, C. M., Hubbard, M., & Newtson, D. Selective perception of events. *Journal of Experimental Social Psychology*, 1979, *15*, 513–532.

McArthur, L. Z., & Friedman, S. Illusory correlation in impression formation: Variations in the shared distinctiveness effect as a function of the distinctive person's age, race, and sex. *Journal of Personality and Social Psychology*, 1980, *39*, 615–624.

McArthur, L. Z., & Ginsberg, E. *Visual attention to people with a salient physical attribute.* Manuscript in preparation, Brandeis University, 1978.

McArthur, L. Z., & Post, D. L. Figural emphasis and person perception. *Journal of Experimental Social Psychology*, 1977, *13*, 520–535.

McArthur, L. Z., & Solomon, L. K. Perceptions of an aggressive encounter as a function of the victim's salience and the perceiver's arousal. *Journal of Personality and Social Psychology*, 1978, *36*, 1278–1290.

McGuire, W. J., McGuire, C. V., Child, P., & Fujloka, T. Salience of ethnicity in the spontaneous self-concept as a function of one's ethnic distinctiveness in the social environment. *Journal of Personality and Social Psychology*, 1978, *36*, 511–521.

McGuire, W. J., & Padawer-Singer, A. Trait salience in the spontaneous self-concept. *Journal of Personality and Social Psychology*, 1976, *33*, 743–754.

McNamara, H., & Fisch, R. Effect of high and low motivation on two aspects of attention. *Perceptual and Motor Skills*, 1964, *19*, 571–578.

Neisser, U. *Cognitive psychology*. New York: Appleton-Century-Crofts, 1967.

Neisser, U. *Cognition and reality*. San Francisco: W. H. Freeman & Co. 1976.

Newtson, D. Foundations of attribution: The perception of ongoing behavior. In J. H. Harvey, W. J. Ickes, & R. F. Kidd (Eds.), *New directions in attribution research* (Vol. 1). New York: John Wiley & Sons, 1976.

Newtson, D., Rindner, R., Miller, R., & LaCross, K. Effects of availability of feature changes on behavior segmentation. *Journal of Experimental Social Psychology*, 1978, *14*, 379–388.

Perlman, D., & Oskamp, S. The effects of picture content and exposure frequency on evaluations of Negroes and whites. *Journal of Experimental Social Psychology*, 1971, *7*, 503–514.

Posner, M. I., & Boies, S. J. Components of attention. *Psychological Review*, 1971, *78*, 391–408.

Rescorla, R. A., & Wagner, A. R. A theory of Pavlovian conditioning: Variations in the effectiveness of reinforcement and non-reinforcement. In A. H. Black & W. F. Prokasy (Eds.), *Classical conditioning II: Current theory and research*. New York: Appelton, 1972.

Rosenberg, S., Nelson, C., & Vivekananthan, P. S. A multidimensional approach to the structure of personality impressions. *Journal of Personality and Social Psychology*, 1968, *9*, 283–294.

Ross, L. The intuitive psychologist and his shortcomings: Distortions in the attribution process. In L. Berkowitz (Ed.), *Advances in experimental social psychology* (Vol. 10). New York: Academic Press, 1977.

Rothbart, M., Fulero, S., Jensen, C., Howard, J., & Birrell, P. From individual to group impressions: Availability heuristics in stereotype formation. *Journal of Experimental Social Psychology*, 1978, *14*, 237–255.

Rubin, E. [Figure and ground.] In D. C. Beardslee & M. Wertheimer (Eds. and trans.), *Readings in perception*. Princeton: D. Van Nostrand Co., Inc. 1958. (Reprinted and abridged from *Visuell Wahrgenomonene Figuren*. Copenhagen: Gyldendalske, 1915.)

Rump, E. E., & Delin, P. S. Differential accuracy in the status-height phenomenon and an experimenter effect. *Journal of Personality and Social Psychology*, 1973, *28*, 343–347.

Secord, P. Facial features and inference processes in interpersonal perception. In R. Tagiuri & L. Petrullo (Eds.), *Person perception and interpersonal behavior*. Stanford: Stanford University Press, 1958.

Sherif, M., & Hovland, C. *Social judgment*. New Haven: Yale University Press, 1961.

Simpson, D. D., & Ostrom, T. M. Contrast effects in impression formation. *Journal of Personality and Social Psychology*, 1976, *34*, 625–629.

Snyder, M. L., & Frankel, A. Observer bias: A stringent test of behavior engulfing the field. *Journal of Personality and Social Psychology*, 1976, *34*, 857–864.

Snyder, M., Tanke, E. D., & Berscheid, E. Social perception and interpersonal behavior: On the self-fulfilling nature of social stereotypes. *Journal of Personality and Social Psychology*, 1977, *35*, 656–666.

Snyder, M., & Uranowitz, S. W. Reconstructing the past: Some cognitive consequences of person perception. *Journal of Personality and Social Psychology*, 1978, *36*, 941–950.

Storms, M. Videotape and the attribution process: Reversing actors and observers' points of view. *Journal of Personality and Social Psychology*, 1973. *27*, 165–175.

Taylor, S. E., Crocker, J., Fiske, S. T., Sprinzen, M., & Winkler, J. D. The generalizability of salience effects. *Journal of Personality and Social Psychology*, 1979, *37*, 357–368.

Taylor, S. E., & Fiske, S. T. Point of view and perceptions of causality. *Journal of Personality and Social Psychology*, 1975, *32*, 439–445.

Taylor, S. E., & Fiske, S. T. Salience, attention, and attribution: Top of the head phenomena. In L. Berkowitz (Ed.), *Advances in experimental social psychology* (Vol. 11). New York: Academic Press, 1978.

Taylor, S. E., Fiske, S. T., Close, M. M., Anderson, C., & Ruderman, A. J. *Solo status as a psychological variable: The power of being distinctive*. Unpublished manuscript, Harvard University, 1976.

Taylor, S. E., Fiske, S. T., Etcoff, N. L., & Ruderman, A. J. The categorical and contextual basis of person memory and stereotyping. *Journal of Personality and Social Psychology*, 1978, *36*, 778–793.

Taylor, S. E., & Langer, E. J. Pregnancy: A social stigma? *Sex Roles*, 1977, *3*, 27–35.

Titchener, E. B. Attention as sensory clearness. In *Lectures on the Elementary Psychology of Feeling and Attention*, New York: Macmillan, 1908. (Reprinted in P. Bakan *Attention: An Enduring Problem in Psychology*. Princeton: D. Van Nostrand Co., 1966.)

Treisman, A. M. Strategies and models of selective attention. *Psychological Review*, 1969, *76*, 282–299.

Tversky, A., & Kahneman, D. Availability: A heuristic for judging frequency and probability. *Cognitive Psychology*, 1973, *5*, 207–232.

Vallacher, R. R. Objective self awareness and the perception of others. *Personality and Social Psychology Bulletin*, Winter 1978, *4*, 63–67.

Warr, D. Inference magnitude, range, and evaluative direction as factors affecting relative importance of cues in impression formation. *Journal of Personality and Social Psychology*, 1974, *30*, 191–197.

Werner, H. Ueber Strukturgesetze und deren auswirkung in den sog, geometrischoptischen Tauschungen. *Z. Psychol.*, 1924, *94*, 248–264.(As cited in F. Heider, Social perception and phenomenal causality. *Psychological Review*, 1944, *51*, 358–374.)

Whitehead, L. A., Holmes, J. G., & Zanna, M. P. *The effects of arousal and expectations on interpersonal perception*. Paper presented at the annual meeting of the Canadian Psychological Association, Ottawa, June 1978.

Wilder, D. A. Effect of predictability on units of perception and attribution. *Personality and Social Psychology Bulletin,* 1978, *4,* 281–284.

Wortman, C. Causal attributions and personal control. In J. H. Harvey, W. J. Ickes, & R. F. Kidd (Eds.), *New directions in attribution research* (Vol. 1). New York: John Wiley & Sons, Inc., 1976.

Zadny, J., & Gerard, H. B. Attributed intentions and informational selectivity *Journal of Experimental Social Psychology,* 1974, *10,* 34–52.

Zajonc, R. B. *Feeling and thinking: preferences need no inferences.* Distinguished Scientific Contribution Award address presented at the meeting of the American Psychological Association, New York, September 1979.

Zajonc, R. B., Markus, H., & Wilson, W. R. Exposure effects and associative learning. *Journal of Experimental Social Psychology,* 1974, *10,* 248–263.

Zanna, M. P., & Hamilton, D. L. Attribute dimensions and patterns of trait inferences. *Psychonomic Science,* 1972, *27,* 353–354.

Zinchenko, V. Perception as action. Proceedings of the International Congress of Psychology, Moscow, 1966, Symposium, 30, 64–72. Cited in D. I. Mostofsky. *Attention: Contemporary Theory and Analysis.* New York: Appleton–Century–Crofts, 1970, 113.

7
Cognitive Processes in Inferences About a Person's Personality

Ebbe B. Ebbesen
University of California, San Diego

This chapter is concerned with the way in which individuals generate personality impressions of people whose behavior they have observed. Because the task of generating personality ratings is common to both personality and social psychological research, evidence from both of these fields is used in the development of the ideas presented here.

RESEARCH ON PERSONALITY

Although the agreement is far from complete, many personality theorists conceive of traits (and other personality attributes) as psychological properties of people that function as causes of behavior (Allport, 1966; Cattell, 1950). In addition, trait constructs are believed to be scientifically useful because knowledge of the location of a given individual (or group) on particular trait dimensions allows the psychologist to infer the presence of a wide variety of additional attributes of that individual (or group). For example, a person who ranks high on the extraversion dimension should frequently attend parties, might have a job involving frequent contact with other people, should be considered outgoing and friendly by his/her peers, might tend to be more egotistical and so on. Although the situation may moderate the degree to which behaviors caused by a trait emerge, the position of an individual on the underlying dimension should remain relatively constant from situation to situation as well as over time.

Measures of Personality

Several different measurement procedures have been employed to determine the location of individuals on personality dimensions. Three of the most common are: (1) the self-report in which individuals judge their own attributes and/or report their own behaviors; (2) the other-person-report, in which peers, parents, teachers, employers and such indicate the presence and extent of the individual's attributes and/or behaviors; and (3) direct observation of behavior, in which the frequency of behaviors indicative of the traits of interest are tallied by trained observers in relevant settings.

The fact that self- and other-person-reports are frequently used as personality measurement devices is of considerable importance given that personality theories emphasize the behavior of individuals and not the processes by which raters construct their responses to questionnaires. Because traits and other personality constructs are usually offered as explanations for individual differences in behavior, most personality theorists who utilize rating measures must implicitly assume that the raters' responses are based on properties of relevant behavioral indicators.[1] Although specific models for the cognitive processes that might underlie such a relationship between behavior and a person's ratings have not been part of personality theory, several assumptions, similar to the following, seem to be required: (1) raters have stored in memory some cognitive representation of each individual being judged by virtue of having observed and interacted with these individuals; (2) one or more properties of these representations varies with the frequency of behavioral indicators of relevant personality characteristics; and (3) when asked to fill out personality tests, raters retrieve these representations and base their reports (in at least a monotonic and more likely a linear manner) on the properties of these representations that vary with the frequency of behavioral indicators. If these or similar assumptions are not made about the cognitive process guiding the construction of personality test responses, there would be little reason to expect ratings to reflect behavioral measures of personality. The model must assume that people who frequently perform actions indicative of, say, honesty, will be the same people whom raters remember as possessing attributes that tend to produce responses on personality tests interpreted by researchers as reflecting extreme honesty.

It is of interest to note that trait theorists need not specify the nature of the representation that raters have of the people being rated. It is only necessary to assume that properties of these representations correlate with the actual frequencies of the behaviors thought (by the researchers) to be indicative of the personality constructs of interest.

---

[1]It is possible to argue that raters are sensitive to properties of behavior other than absolute frequency, e.g., duration, intensity, relative frequency (compared to other behaviors and/or other people); however, although not a formal part of many personality theories, traits are often used to explain and are often measured by the frequency of behavioral events.

Some Empirical Results

Evidence for the scientific utility of trait and other similar personality constructs have come primarily from two somewhat different methodologies, both of which are based on the correlation between different measures of one or more traits. Using various combinations of the three previously mentioned types of personality measures, one methodology focuses on the trait theory assumption that individual differences in the degree of particular traits are relatively constant over time and situations. People high on a given trait dimension should remain high on that dimension over time, over different measures of that dimension, and over settings. The second methodology focuses on another major assumption of trait theory, namely, that knowledge of people's positions on one trait dimension can supply information to the personality theorist about where the people will fall on other personality dimensions. A particular *pattern* of associations among *different* personality constructs should remain constant over time, measures, settings, and samples of people.

Consistency Within Constructs.   Because rating and questionnaire measures of personality are assumed to tap the same personality constructs that cause individual differences in behavior, the use of different measures of the same trait should not substantially change the empirical relationships among constructs that are found.

Recently, however, several extensive reviews of the former methodology (e.g., Bem & Allen, 1974; Mischel, 1968; Vernon, 1964) have concluded that although there is some temporal consistency in individual differences on various trait dimensions, the consistency that is found is not very large and, furthermore, whatever consistency there is gets smaller, in general, when: (1) different types of measures of the same trait construct are used; (2) the situation in which different measures are taken changes; and (3) behavioral measures are used instead of self- and other-person-reports (e.g., Block, 1977; Sears, 1963). Two conclusions reached from this type of evidence are that situations control the behavior of individuals rather than (or more than) traits (e.g., Bowers, 1973; Mischel, 1968) and *measurement* factors (rather than personality characteristics) common to seemingly different measures of the same construct often account for a large part of the covariation among measures (Mischel, 1968).[2]

---

[2]As an aside, it is important to note that situational control and trait control of behavior are not necessarily incompatible, as each is usually studied. For example, a change in the context could cause most people to behave in a more (or less) extraverted manner without disrupting the ordering of individual differences. People high in extraversion can remain high across situations even though the average (over people) amount of extraversion displayed varies. It is only when the change in context (time and/or measure) has *different* effects on different individuals that the usefulness of the trait construct will be undermined. The fact that correlations over settings and measures are generally so low (rarely higher than .30) implies that such interactions are common.

Consistency of Associations Among Different Constructs.   Although the size of the correlation between different measures of particular traits seems small, in general (Mischel, 1968), and may vary in size depending on the particular pair of measures that are used or the settings in which they are obtained (e.g., Fiske, 1973; Mischel, 1973; Mischel, Ebbesen, & Zeiss, 1976), the pattern of associations among different traits seems to be far more stable across measures (e.g., Huba & Hamilton, 1976; Mischel, 1968), particularly when self- and other-person-reports serve as the primary measurement tools.[3] For example, Huba and Hamilton (1976) reported that the associational pattern among 12 of Murry's needs remained quite stable across different measurement devices (e.g., the Personality Research Form, the Adjective Check List, self-ratings, Edwards Personal Preference Schedule, and peer ratings) and across different samples of subjects (even though the absolute size of the correlations varied quite a bit from measure to measure). Norman (1963) also reported finding highly consistent patterns of intertrait associations across several samples of raters and ratees using traits and measures quite different from those analyzed by Huba and Hamilton (1976).

On the other hand, when direct behavioral measures (e.g., frequency counts) have been used in addition to self- and other-person-reports, the results are quite different. For example, Shweder (1975) reported that the patterns of correlations among different personality constructs obtained from peer and self-ratings were completely different from the patterns of correlations among the identical constructs but measured by behavioral frequency estimates. D'Andrade (1974) has reported similar findings with different personality constructs.

Alternative Interpretations

When the results from both types of studies are examined together, a consistent pattern seems to emerge. The stability of traits across measures, time, and settings and the consistency of the associations among different traits are higher when raters provide the raw data than when direct frequency counts of behavior are used (e.g., Block, 1977; Mischel, 1968; Vernon, 1964). Two quite different explanations for this general pattern of results have been proposed.

One view argues that the use of a standard set of cross-situationally stable personality characteristics that are assumed to form theoretically useful nomological networks should be abandoned (e.g., Bem & Allen, 1974; Mischel, 1968; Shweder, 1978). In this view, the tendency to find significant correlations be-

---

[3]The fact that correlations between different measures of the same trait construct are relatively inconsistent and generally small has little bearing on the consistency of the pattern of associations among different trait constructs. Patterns can remain even though the absolute sizes of correlations vary considerably.

tween two "different" rating measures of the same personality construct is thought to be due to the measures having more artifactual features in common than is apparent.[4] In addition, the stable patterns of associations among personality constructs typically obtained when rating measures are used are assumed to represent *conceptual* systems that link various personality terms to one another and that are shared by the raters. Thus, these patterns of data are not assumed to reflect the internal structure of people's personality (e.g., D'Andrade, 1965; Fiske, 1978; Mischel, 1968, 1973; Mulaik, 1964; Vernon, 1964). This is why behavioral measures that do not allow the conceptual biases of raters to affect the results do not produce comparable results to rating measures.[5]

A second view argues that ratings can and do reflect the structure of personality and that the studies that have employed direct behavioral measures of personality have been deficient in one way or another (e.g., Bem & Allen, 1974; Block, 1977; Block, Weiss, & Thorne, 1979), thereby producing results that have not matched those obtained from rating measures.

Personality as the Conceptual Bias of the Rater.   Several well-known and replicable findings not strictly within the domain of personality research are consistent with the first explanation. First, the pattern of ratings that individuals generate about people whom they know very well (e.g., themselves, good friends) typically resembles the pattern of ratings of complete strangers and hypothetical stereotypes (Mulaik, 1964; Passini & Norman, 1966). Second, direct measures (e.g., semantic similarity ratings) of the conceptual relationships among words used to define personality constructs often matches the pattern of correlations among those constructs (D'Andrade, 1965; Ebbesen & Allen, 1977; Shweder, 1975; Shweder & D'Andrade, 1979). This result is found even when the correlations are based upon data from highly standardized personality tests, e.g., the M.M.P.I. (Shweder, 1975) and the Edwards Personal Preference Schedule (Ebbesen & Allen, 1977). Finally, measures of implicit personality theory (Schneider, 1973) also yield patterns of associations among personality constructs that are very similar to patterns of correlations among direct measures of the same constructs (e.g., Ebbesen & Allen, 1977). In short, across several different methods of measuring conceptual associations among personality terms, people's beliefs about which personality characteristics are associated and

---

[4]For example, "different" tests may have some items that are virtually identical (Ebbesen, 1971). In addition, raters may base many of their responses on characteristics of the ratees that have little to do with the ratees' behaviors, e.g., sex and physical attractiveness.

[5]Bem and Allen (1974) argue that the lack of consistency in behavioral measures reflects the fact that different constructs may be useful for different people. If the appropriate subset of individuals can be found for each construct, then consistency in individual differences in behavior will be found. One can still ask, however, why rating measures tend to yield higher correlations and greater consistency.

which are not tend to predict which characteristics actually are associated (as measured by tests based on self- and other-person-reports).[6]

Another form of evidence consistent with the first explanation comes from studies that show that people's memory for the co-occurence of events (e.g., words, sentences, pictures, and such) seem to be influenced by the similarity in the meaning of the events as well as by the actual co-occurrence frequency of the events (e.g., Berman & Kenny, 1976; Chapman, 1967; Chapman & Chapman, 1967, 1969; Cohen, 1977; Hamilton & Gifford, 1976; Shweder, 1978). In addition, people seem to remember having witnessed events (which they really did not) because the events fit their expectations about what should have occurred (e.g., Bartlett, 1932; Bransford & McCarrell, 1974; Cantor & Mischel, 1977; Cohen, 1977; Hamilton, 1977; Loftus & Palmer, 1974; Markus, 1977; Rogers, Rogers, & Kuiper, 1979; Snyder & Uranowitz, 1978). Thus, if they remember one characteristic of an individual, they may be likely to infer other characteristics because the latter are expected to occur with the former.

In other words, several converging sources of evidence suggest that people are biased observers of other people's behaviors (e.g., Ross, 1977). These biases might well explain why rating measures and behavioral measures tend to yield different results. Raters *construct* consistencies where few actually exist (Mischel, 1968, 1973). If this view is correct, the processes by which raters construct their inferences should play a central role in theories of personality.

Personality as Stable Dispositions.   Because the second explanation for the greater consistency in rating than direct behavioral measures of personality rests primarily on a criticism of previous research, strong direct empirical support for it is difficult to find. Nevertheless, it is important to examine the nature of the types of assumptions that are typically invoked to support this explanation. First, it has been suggested that the relationships between traits and behavioral indicators may depend on other factors, e.g., moderator variables (Kogan & Wallach, 1964; Wallach, 1962), the situational context in which behaviors occur (Endler & Hunt, 1969; Mischel, 1973), and the sample of people to whom the trait is being applied (Bem & Allen, 1974). A particular behavioral indicator may have multiple causes, only one of which is the relevant personality dimension, and most important, these causes may interact (Magnusson & Endler; 1977). Unless these other factors are adequately assessed and controlled for by appropriate measurement procedures, correlations between different measures of the same construct and between different constructs will tend to be severely attenuated and

---

[6]It is of some importance to note that semantic and implicit personality associational networks do *not* resemble behavioral networks. In other words, conceptual and rating matrices are similar to each other but neither is similar to matrices based on behavioral frequency counts.

distorted.[7] This may be less of a problem, however, when rater-based measures are used because raters may either adjust their responses to take account of other causal influences or base their responses on intuitive averages of large samples of behavior. For example, as is well known to attribution researchers, raters often discount behaviors that are under situational control but that otherwise would be indicative of particular trait characteristics (e.g., Kelley, 1967).

Second, the behavioral indicators that have been used in most previous empirical studies of personality may have been far too narrowly defined (Block, Weiss, & Thorne, 1979). Specific personality attributes may control broad classes of behavior and the frequency of any particular type of behavior within a broad class may be only weakly related to the location of an individual on the personality dimension (Gormly & Champagne, 1974; McGowan & Gormly, 1976). Thus, the number of times a person returns lost wallets may be only weakly related to that person's honesty because the behavior of returning wallets is controlled by other factors as well as by honesty. However, the average number of times that this person returns lost wallets, avoids cheating on exams, accurately completes his/her income tax report, truthfully answers his/her child's questions about the origin of babies, does not invent excuses for arriving late to meetings, and so on may well be strongly related to this person's honesty.[8]

Third, if personality traits are related to broad behavioral categories, those properties of the raters' cognitive representations of individuals on which they base their questionnaire and test responses may be correlated with the number of occurrences of these *broad* behavioral categories rather than with the frequency of particular instances within them. Furthermore, if more than one behavioral indicator is needed to define a personality construct, the rule governing how different indicators within a category are to be combined may not be simple addition. Different indicators within a category may be weighted differently

---

[7]As this chapter was being copyedited, a very important series of studies providing some of the missing empirical evidence for this position were published by Epstein (1979). He showed that the reliability of single behavioral items measured one time were very low. Because most personality studies employing direct behavioral measures typically measure behaviors only one or two times, Epstein argued that the low correlations for behavioral indices might reflect the poor reliability of the measures. By measuring behaviors five to ten times, split-half reliabilities were increased from about .20 to around .85. More important, behavioral measures averaged over many measurement sessions tended to correlate reasonably well (about .45) with more traditional self-report measures of personality.

[8]This assumption is, of course, quite common in formal test theory. Multiple items are required before a reliable indicator of a measured attribute can be obtained. A similar argument has been proposed with regard to the relationship between attitudes (which have many traitlike features) and behavior (e.g., Ajzen & Fishbein, 1977; Fishbein & Ajzen, 1975). Indeed, as Weigel and Newman (1976) reported and Bagozzi and Burnkrant (1979) note, much higher correlations have been found between multiple behavior categories and attitude ratings (= .65) than between single behavior categories and attitude ratings (= .18).

(Bagozzi & Burnkrant, 1979). For example, rare behavioral events that contribute little to the overall frequency of the broad category might receive relatively greater weight by raters (Collins, Whalen, & Henker, 1980).   If such rare events are less influenced by other (none trait) causes of behavior, then ratings would tend to provide more valid indicators of the trait than a simple unweighted frequency count of relevant actions.

PROCESSES BY WHICH RATERS
CONSTRUCT RESPONSES

Although there are several empirical consequences of both of the former explanations, those of primary interest in this chapter concern the way in which raters construct their personality judgments. One view argues that the consistencies in rater-based measures comes about because the process by which raters construct their responses is influenced by a number of cognitive biases. If these biases could be eliminated, the consistencies in rating-based measures of personality would disappear (Shweder, 1978). The other view argues that the consistency in rating-based measures reflects the true structure of personality because raters are more sensitive than most researchers have been to the various causal factors that control behavior. If behaviors were measured in the same manner as observers used them, the consistencies found with raters would be duplicated (and even improved) in the behavioral domain (Block et al., 1979; Epstein, 1979).

Some Places Cognitive Biases Might Influence Ratings

If one accepts the cognitive bias explanation, it is of interest to ask exactly how such biases might cause raters to produce the pattern of results that they do. Several reasonable classes of cognitive process models can be generated. One class of models argues that raters are selective in the information that they attend to and encode while observing behavior (e.g., Berscheid, Graziano, Monson & Dermer, 1976; Cohen, 1977; Cohen & Ebbesen, 1979; Ebbesen, 1980; Mischel, Ebbesen, & Zeiss, 1972, 1976; Newtson & Engquist, 1976; Tsujimoto, 1978). In particular, behavioral events that are consistent with previously held beliefs, expectations, stereotypes, and/or implicit theories are more likely to be encoded (and therefore remembered at a later time) than are events that are inconsistent with previously acquired information. Thus, if observers believe a person is friendly, they may be more likely to attend to actions that not only imply friendliness but equally importantly they may attend to actions that are related to those attributes that are conceptually linked to friendliness, e.g., generosity, kindness, warmth, etc. In other words, implicit personality theory and other beliefs about people might influence which behavioral events receive greatest attention. Then, when observers are asked to evaluate particular individuals, they will tend to remember the individuals as having emitted patterns of behavior consistent with their prior expectations, categorizations, and beliefs.

Another class of models argues that prior beliefs, expectations, and such have their primary effects during the retention interval: the time between exposure to the behavior and the test (e.g., Hamilton, Katz, & Leirer, 1980; Rogers, Rogers, & Kuiper, 1979). In this view, behavioral information that is consistent with previously acquired beliefs and theories is more likely to be *retained* than information that is inconsistent with such beliefs. The exact process that produces such selective retention varies across models from selective rehearsal strategies to the assumption that consistent information is associatively linked with more information already stored in memory and therefore is less likely to be forgotten than inconsistent information.

A third class of models that has received little attention until recently assumes that prior knowledge of the conceptual relationship among attributes has its effects at the point when observers are constructing their answers to various test questions (Ebbesen, 1980). For example, observers might select answers so as to generate a consistent picture of the ratee. Alternatively, the strategy that raters use to search through memory might be biased. Because most attention has been given to the first two classes of models (e.g., Cantor & Mischel, 1977; Carlston, 1980; Cohen & Ebbesen, 1979; Markus, 1977; Snyder & Uranowitz, 1978), I concentrate, in this chapter, on the last.

Retrieval and Decision Processes

One model of retrieval assumes that during interactions with people raters build up and store "generalized impressions" of these individuals that are relatively abstract and free of behavioral details. The exact form of the representations need not be specified in detail. They might be thought of as lists of features (Ebbesen & Allen, 1979; Smith, Shoben, & Rips, 1974), points in multidimensional space (Rosenberg & Sedlack, 1972), prototypes (Cantor & Mischel, 1979) or something else. Regardless, the essential aspect of the representations is that they are global reflections of the individuals that can be retrieved and cognitively operated on as a single unit. One might think of the content of these representations as being impressionistic and/or evaluative (Zajonc, 1980).

An alternative view argues that people have available in memory representations of individuals that contain information about behavioral details. For example, continuous or "stop-action" visual images of interactions, along with verbal content, might be available. A somewhat different notion assumes that bins for different types of action might be filled as an interaction unfolds (Wyer & Srull, 1980). Regardless of the form of these representations, in this view, their contents are not global and cannot be treated as single units. Instead, they contain many behavioral details, each of which is cognitively treated as a separate fact about the person. Of course, several additional views can be created by combining these two extremes.

If a cognitive process model of personality evaluations is to be complete, it is important that it include assumptions that specify how the items that typically appear on personality tests are themselves represented in memory (e.g., Ebbesen & Allen, 1979) as well as how the individuals being rated are represented. For example, trait terms might be thought of as lists of features (say behaviors), nodes in a network, points in multidimensional space, lists of persons remembered as possessing the relevant attributes, individuals prototypical of the category, a point on an evaluative dimension, or possibly prototypical behaviors or scripts (Shank & Abelson, 1977). Different views intuitively suggest somewhat different models of the rating process.

Ratings from "Generalized Impressions."   If traits are thought to be represented in semantic memory in a global fashion, e.g., a point in multidimensional space or a node in a network, and if raters are also assumed to retain "generalized impressions" of individuals, one reasonable model of the rating process assumes that raters retrieve the generalized impression of the ratee and compare it to the representations of each personality characteristic being evaluated.[9] The greater the similarity of the two representations (one for the ratee and one for the characteristic) the more trait the ratee would seem to have. If the same generalized impression is used for all of the questions about a particular ratee and if the rule used to compute the similarity of the two representations does not involve the differential weighting (across questions) of different components of the representations, then the pattern of associations (computed over ratees) among different traits will tend to match the pattern of the rater's beliefs about the similarities among the traits themselves (Ebbesen, 1980). This is because traits whose representations are initially similar to each other will tend to be seen as equally similar or dissimilar to the generalized impression. If two traits are initially opposite in meaning, however, and one is seen as similar to the generalized impression, then the other will tend to be seen as different from the generalized impression. If different raters tend to share beliefs about the similarity among different traits, then the pattern of correlations produced by averaging ratings over several different raters will tend to match the pattern of the average *conceptual* similarities among the traits. On the other hand, if a different similar-

---

[9]Raters must be able to construct (or retrieve) cognitive representations of the attributes being evaluated. Thus, raters must "know" what the meanings of terms such as, extravert, honest, and dominant, are. The exact form that this prior semantic knowledge takes is of little importance to the present models, however.

ity rule is used or if different questions elicit different representations of the person being rated, then the "generalized impression" model would not predict that the pattern of associations among ratings would match the structure of implicit personality.

In short, this "generalized impression" model (along with specific assumptions about the similarity rule used to generate responses) can account for the finding that the structure of personality derived from ratings often matches the semantic structure of the terms used in the personality tests. An interesting aspect of this model is that it does not assume the existence of special cognitive biases or processes that act selectively on new or remembered information about people. Implicit personality information, for example, is not biasing the way in which a rater remembers or attends to another person's behavior. In fact, it doesn't *bias* anything. It is simply that responses to questions whose representations in semantic memory are similar to each other will tend to covary over the ratees if the responses are based on a global similarity decision process and the same representation of any given ratee is used by a rater for each question.[10]

Ratings from Memory for Behavioral Details.   If the content of the representations of people that raters construct are assumed to contain behavioral details, then different models of the process by which raters construct responses seem reasonable.[11] In one version, raters would search through the "list" of retrieved behaviors and base their response on some aspect of parts of that "list." For example, if one assumes that traits are represented in semantic memory as prototypical behaviors, a high rating might be given for a particular trait if a sufficiently good match between the trait's prototype and one of the behaviors in the ratee's "list" is found. Unlike the global similarity model outlined earlier, this model predicts that the pattern of associations among ratings will match the structure of implicit personality only if the behaviors in the remembered "lists" co-occur in appropriate ways.

Rather than matching one prototype to instances in a "list," a somewhat different model assumes that raters might "count-up" the number of behaviors in

---

[10]This model does not require that the representations of different ratees be similar to each other. In fact, it expects the representations to be quite different. If two traits are similar to one representation, they might be quite dissimilar to another. The point is that the similarity of such traits to the different representations will tend to covary, whereas traits which are neither strongly similar nor dissimilar to each other will not tend to covary.

[11]The assumption that the unique facts that are retained consist of behavioral details instead of other facts is not a necessary one in the context of this model. The facts could include aspects of the ratee's physical appearance, job, house, and so on. Nevertheless, it is intuitively reasonable to assume that behavioral details form at least a part of the evidence used to construct personality ratings.

the list that imply that the trait is present. The more behaviors in the list the more extreme the rating. In one version of this model, the same remembered behavior may affect the ratings given to different traits. If behaviors are more likely to be counted as indicative of a particular trait if they have already been counted for semantically similar traits, then this model predicts a pattern of associations among trait ratings that would tend to match the semantic structure of those traits. Behavioral indicators of different but similar traits would *cognitively* co-occur because the same *remembered* behavior would serve as an indicator of the different traits.

Characteristics of Retrieval Models

Several features of the foregoing models are important. First, none of these models propose that the processes *bias* the way in which raters attend to, retain, or retrieve information about ratees. They do not invoke availability heuristics (Kahneman & Tversky, 1973), selective attention, illusory correlation (Chapman, 1967), or some other process that causes observers to inaccurately report the information to which they have been exposed. Second, the feature of the models that accounts for the previously discussed results in personality research has little to do with whether raters can or can not accurately remember the *behavior* of ratees (cf. Shweder, 1978). Thus, research that demonstrates that people's memory for facts about themselves and others can be biased by prior expectations and beliefs, may be irrelevant to understanding the causes of the consistent structure in rater-based measures of personality. The causal process may not depend on cognitive biases that affect memory for the behavior of individuals. It is possible that the structural consistency is a consequence of the retrieval and decision processes that raters use when constructing responses. In such models, the apparent effect that previously stored semantic relationships have on the structure of personality ratings depends on whether the same remembered evidence is used to construct ratings of semantically similar traits and whether the rules used to evaluate the evidence are global (i.e., do not differentially weight different parts of the evidence). As can be seen, trait ratings might be based on a global representation of a ratee that may or may not be related to the ratee's behavior or on a more detailed representation of the ratee's behavior that accurately reflects behaviors observed by the rater. In both cases, whether the resulting pattern of trait ratings (over ratees) will or will not reflect the preexisting semantic structure of the traits (or the actual co-occurrence structure of the behaviors) depends on the exact nature of the decision and inference processes that raters use when constructing their responses. In short, a major portion of the evidence used by critics of trait and other personality theories to suggest that the perceived structure in personality comes about because observers *construct* behavioral consistency where none exists says very little both about the kind of evidence raters use to generate their personality inferences and about the way in which they use that evidence.

RESEARCH ON THE CONSTRUCTION
OF PERSONALITY

Some of the studies that Claudia Cohen, Robert Allen, and I have recently completed at the University of California, San Diego speak more directly to these issues.[12] The remainder of this chapter explores some of the implications of this work for the present discussion.

Behavior Scanning and Similarity

It may be possible to discriminate between models that assume that the evidence that raters use to construct their responses is something resembling a generalized impression and models that assume that the evidence consists of a set of behavioral facts by measuring how long it takes raters to construct their responses. If raters do cognitively review a representation of a ratee's behavior that consists of several different elements, then the time that the raters take to construct an inference based on such evidence should be longer the more behavioral information that they review. The purpose of such a review might be to match aspects of the trait representation with an element of the set of remembered behavioral events (as might happen if traits are represented in memory as behavioral prototypes) or it might be to compare, in some way, a combination of various elements in the set of behaviors with a representation of the trait (as might happen if traits are represented in memory as feature lists).

On the other hand, if raters construct their trait evaluations by computing the similarity of a ''generalized impression'' of the ratee to the representations of the traits (e.g., by computing the distance between two points in multidimensional space or the length of the path between two nodes in a network or by comparing the affective values of the two representations), the amount of behavioral evidence that produced the ''impression'' should have little effect on the *time* the subjects take to emit their response—although the amount and type of evidence might well affect the *type* of response that is emitted.[13] If the amount of informa-

---

[12]Claudia Cohen is now at Douglass College, Rutgers University, and Robert Allen is at Bell Laboratories, Murry Hill, New Jersey.

[13]This does not mean, however, that other factors will play no role in the reaction times. As Ebbesen and Allen (1979) discuss, the time taken to make similarity decisions can be affected by several factors.

tion in the representation of a ratee does not increase with the amount of behavioral information that the rater has been exposed to (as might be expected if the content of the representations consisted of affective reactions or nodes in a network), then the length of time the rater takes to construct his or her answer on the basis of that representation would not be expected to increase as a function of the length of the behavioral segment.

Extensive research involving memory for digits, letters, words, and paragraphs has shown that true and false reaction-times to questions that ask whether a particular element was present in a studied list generally increase as the length of the list increases (e.g., Sternberg, 1974). One might expect a similar result for sequences of remembered behavior if the amount of behavioral evidence that observers retain in memory increases as the length of the observed behavioral segment increases. That is, the longer the observed sequence, the longer observers of the sequence should take to decide whether a given action was or was not in that sequence. Allen and Ebbesen (in press) found exactly this result.

Observers watched different lengths of videotaped segments of actors' behaviors. After exposure to a given segment, observers indicated whether specific actions had occurred in that segment (half actually did) by pressing buttons connected to a computer. A significant linear relationship was found between the temporal length of the segment about which observers were answering questions and the time it took observers to decide whether the action had occurred.

Even though these results suggest that the amount of remembered behavioral information increases as the length of the segment increases and that observers review the remembered content when asked whether a particular individual engaged in a particular action, observers may construct answers to more global personality questions in a completely different manner. Specifically, observers might retain two (or more) representations of actors or be able to retrieve different parts of one representation (e.g., an episodic encoding and a semantic, affective, or impressionistic encoding; Ebbesen, 1980). If so, the raters might base answers to trait questions on different remembered evidence than answers to questions about behavioral details.

To obtain evidence on this issue, Allen and Ebbesen (in press) asked the observers of their videotapes to answer a series of trait and motivational questions, as well as the behavioral detail questions. In particular, following each behavioral segment, the observers were asked to indicate whether statements about a particular actor (the tapes depicted two people interacting) in the segment were true or false (again by pressing buttons). For example, one statement read "Was he forgetful?" and another read "Was she critical?". Observers were instructed to answer these questions solely on the basis of the previously seen segment. Reaction-times to these questions were recorded as before. As with questions about specific actions, observers took longer to decide whether a ratee was or was not a particular personality type the longer the segment of behavior on which the responses were based.

These results suggest that the observers were constructing answers to the personality questions by reviewing a representation of the ratee's behavior and that the number of cognitive elements in that representation increased with the length of the behavioral segment. Although the slopes of the two reaction-time functions (one for the behavioral detail questions and one for the trait questions) suggested that the trait questions were being answered on the basis of the exact same evidence as the behavioral questions—the slopes were not significantly different—additional evidence collected by Allen and Ebbesen (in press) strongly suggested that not all trait questions were treated alike by the ratees. Specifically, trait terms that were rated (by an independent group of subjects) as being easy to infer from only one sample of a person's behavior yielded a *different* pattern of results than trait terms that could be inferred only from many different samples of a person's behavior. Reaction times increased as the length of the behavioral segment increased for the latter trait terms but not for the former ones. The length of the behavioral segment had no effect on the amount of time that it took raters to construct answers to "concrete" personality characteristics: ones that could be easily inferred from a single behavior.

To explain these results, Allen and Ebbesen (in press) suggested that a two-stage decision process (Atkinson & Juola, 1974; Smith, Shoben, & Rips, 1974) might guide the construction of trait responses. In the first stage, the representation of the trait is compared to a generalized impression of the actor. If the similarity of the two representations are above or below a true or a false cutpoint, the rater responds yes or no (respectively). If, however, the similarity estimate falls between these two cutpoints (making it unclear whether a yes or no response is correct), a second stage is entered in which additional evidence is examined before a response is made. Allen and Ebbesen assumed that this additional evidence is a more detailed representation of the behavioral segment—one in which the number of unique elements depends on the length of the behavioral segment. Thus, only traits that are moderately similar to the generalized impression should produce reaction times that increase with the length of the behavioral segment. To complete the argument, they also suggested that (in their experimental task, at least) "concrete" traits would tend to be either very similar or very dissimilar to a generalized impression whereas more "abstract" traits would tend to be *moderately* similar to the generalized impression because the latter have multiple implications and only some of their implications might be represented in the generalized impression.

Allen and Ebbesen (in press) reported two additional findings in support of their model. First, as would be expected if a two-stage model were involved and "concrete" traits were more frequently answered after only first-stage processing, the average reaction-time for "concrete" traits was shorter than for "abstract" traits. Second, if the first-stage process involves a computation of the similarity of the trait to a generalized impression (and a global similarity rule is used in this stage), then the pattern of associations among trait evaluations that exit from the first stage (the "concrete" traits) should be similar to the pattern of semantic relationships already existing among the terms. Allen and Ebbesen found that these two patterns were similar to each other. If, in addition, the ratings for the more abstract traits that were produced from the second, "behavior-scanning," stage are based on a process that weights or matches different elements of the remembered behavior to different trait items, then the pattern of trait responses from this stage should be quite unlike the pattern of semantic relationships already existing among the terms. This result was also found.

The idea that observers may store two rather different representations of an actor's behavior in memory can be made more intuitive if one thinks of the global representation as an affective reaction or an evaluative memory and the detailed representation as a list of specific actions. In this view, the structure of trait ratings of known individuals may match that of implicit personality theory because a large component of the meaning of trait terms is evaluative (Hastorf, Osgood, & Ono, 1966) and because trait ratings are usually made by computing the affective similarity of each trait term to the global representation of the person being judged. Such a unidimensional similarity-judgment rule would be equivalent to a global similarity rule and therefore the structure of the ratings produced by such a process would tend to match preexisting semantic or implicit personality structures.

The reaction time differences between the "concrete" and the "abstract" trait words can also be explained by the foregoing view if we assume that the concrete trait words are more affect laden (that is, have more extreme affective values) than the abstract trait words. If such were the case, the abstract trait words might tend to be only moderately similar to the affective or global representation of the actor and therefore they would be more likely to require second-stage processing before a response could be constructed. This would cause response times to the abstract trait terms to be longer and to be more influenced by the length of the behavior segment than responses times to the concrete trait terms.

In summary, although other models can explain the results, a model that assumes that raters have two representations of each ratee (rather than one) available in memory and that one representation is more global, evaluative, and semantic and the other is more detailed and episodic can explain the results. Furthermore, whether a response to a given trait item will reflect the global or the detailed representation may depend on how similar the representation of the trait is to the global representation.

Dual-Representations of People

It should not be concluded from these results, however, that different *trait terms* are represented in memory in different ways. Although they may well be, the two-stage model explains the results without requiring this assumption. On the other hand, the two-stage model does assume that raters hold (at least) two quite different representations of ratees in memory. If two representations (or if different aspects of one) are available to raters, it is important to ask whether raters can be induced to construct their evaluations more on the basis of one or the other representation.

Another aspect of a model that assumes that two representations are available concerns the extent to which the two representations can be retained in memory by the raters. The subjects in the Allen and Ebbesen study were tested for their impressions almost immediately after having been exposed to the ratee's behavior. If, as seems intuitively likely, behavioral details are less well retained than a more global representation (we are often able to remember how we feel about someone without remembering the exact behaviors that led to the feeling), it is possible that in most personality test situations only a few, if any, behavioral details are actually available to the raters when they construct their responses. It is important, therefore, to examine the effect that the time between exposure and testing has on the nature of the process raters use to construct their responses.

Some features of a recent study by Cohen and Ebbesen (1979) and a follow-up by Ebbesen, Cohen, and Allen (1979) are relevant to both of the foregoing issues, namely, controlling which representation is used by raters and the role of the delay between exposure and testing. With regard to the former issue, both studies suggest that it might be possible to induce raters to construct personality inferences from different sources of remembered evidence about a ratee by giving the raters different observational goals. They found that observers who were instructed to form a detailed *impression* of an actor whose behavior they had observed produced a pattern of correlations among different personality ratings that was similar to: (1) the pattern of semantic similarities among the personality terms; (2) the pattern of rated co-occurences of the terms; and (3) the pattern of correlations among ratings of the same personality terms produced by a group of subjects who had not observed the behavior of the ratees, but who knew the sex of the actors and a brief one sentence description of the content of the behavioral segment.[14] Thus, raters who were trying to form an impression of a ratee, constructed personality ratings whose structure matched the structure of

---

[14]A major difference between the data structure used to generate the pattern of correlations among different traits in this study and that typically used in personality research should be noted. In personality research, one rater (or the average of a group of raters) constructs ratings of many different ratees. Correlations are then computed over ratees within the rater. In the research cited here, many raters construct ratings of one or two different ratees. Correlations are then computed over raters within the ratee. Whereas this difference may prove to be important in future research, the present approach makes little notice of it. In *both* cases, it is assumed that different representations of the *ratee* produce variation in the ratings. In the personality case, these different representations are all in the same person's head, whereas in the present case, each is in a different person's head. The fact that similar results can be obtained with both procedures lends weak support to the present approach.

preexisting conceptual relationships among the terms. In contrast, the pattern of ratings produced by a group of observers who were told to memorize the actor's behavior (instead of form an impression of the actor) was significantly less similar to each of the three previously described normative or conceptual patterns. In short, it was possible, by instructing observers to memorize an actor's behavior, to alter the previously consistent finding that the structure of rater-based measures of personality is virtually identical to the conceptual structure of the personality terms used. Observers who watched an actor while trying to memorize his behavior generated a pattern of ratings that was only marginally similar to the pattern of conceptual associations among the terms.

Several different interpretations of these important results are possible. Additional findings from these studies reduce the plausibility of some of them, however. One class of interpretations (Cohen & Ebbesen, 1979; Ebbesen, 1980) argues that the set to memorize a person's behavior decreases the likelihood that subjects are influenced by those attentional, encoding, and/or memory biases that are normally employed by people—and more likely to be present in the impression set condition. For example, the observers in the memory set condition may have remembered the actor's behavior more accurately than observers in the impression set condition. Thus, both types of observers may have constructed their ratings on the basis of the same type of evidence (memory for behavioral details); however, the contents of the evidence that the impression set subjects remembered may have been more biased by illusory correlation, schema-driven memory biases, and/or similar processes. The fact that subjects in the behavior memory set condition correctly recognized more behavioral details in a post-exposure recognition test than subjects in the impression set condition supports this interpretation.

Further support for this view is found in the effects of variations in the length of the interval between exposure to the behavior and testing on memory for behavioral details and on the match of the pattern of correlations among ratings to preexisting conceptual structures. Not surprisingly, memory for behavioral details decreased (equally in both set conditions) as the time since exposure to the behavior increased. In addition, the pattern (in both set conditions) of correlations among the personality ratings also became more similar to the structure of preexisting conceptual associations. In fact, after about 1 week, the pattern of correlations was as similar to the pattern of semantic and other conceptual associations as typically occurs in personality research (cf. Shweder & D'Andrade, 1979). As memory for the behavior of the actors became less accurate with time, the structure of the personality ratings became more conceptual. In short, a 1-week delay was sufficient to produce results virtually identical to those typically obtained in more traditional personality research.

Although these findings seem to support the single-representation-plus-cognitive-bias interpretation, one aspect of the Ebbesen et al. (1979) results does not. After a delay, a significant difference between the two set conditions still existed in the accuracy with which the observers could remember behavioral details; however, there was *no* comparable difference in the extent to which the pattern of personality correlations matched the structure of conceptual associations. The patterns were equally similar to conceptual structures.

If the match between semantic, co-occurrence, and/or stereotypic norms and correlations among personality ratings of known individuals primarily depends on cognitive biases that distort memory for the *behavior* of the individuals, then one might have expected the difference between the two set conditions in memory for behavioral details (after a week's delay) to produce detectable differences in the match between personality correlations and appropriate normative baselines. As already described, this did not occur.

Although it is possible to explain this and the other findings by adding floor effect or other processes to the cognitive-bias explanation, the model that postulates the presence of two representations of the ratee rather than one can explain the results as well. If two (or more) different representations of a ratee are available to a rater, it is conceivable that an observer's memory for behavioral details may reflect the contents of one representation while the same observer's ratings of personality may reflect the contents of another representation. If so, there would be no expectation that the two types of measures should yield equivalent results. Even though the set manipulations may have directly caused subjects to attend to and/or remember different features of the actor's behavior there is no need to assume that the personality ratings were based on this behavioral information. The effect of the set instructions on the personality ratings may have originated from a different process.

In particular, the personality rating results can be explained with the previously discussed two-stage model by assuming that the instructions to memorize the actor's behavior increased the likelihood (relative to the impression instructions) that trait inferences were constructed from a "behavior-scanning" inference process. One way this might have been accomplished is if the cutpoints in the first stage were widened by the memory-set instructions. The weakened effect of the set instructions on the personality rating structures after a week's delay, can be explained by the same process. It seems likely that the set instructions would have much less of an impact on the location of the cutpoints after a delay. Finally, because the long delay reduced the amount of behavioral information available to the subjects (as evidenced by their poorer memory for behavioral details), the delay may have caused subjects to considerably *narrow* the distance between the cutpoints in *both* set conditions, thereby causing them to answer most of the trait questions on the basis of the generalized impression.[15]

---

[15]Of course, there are other models that can explain these results as satisfactorily as the present one. Some assume that the delay causes the organization of the personality impression information to become more like the structure of preexisting beliefs about personality. Others assume a more complicated link between behavior and trait inferences. Nevertheless, the present model is an interesting one because it emphasizes the possibility of different types of remembered evidence and because it explains the well-replicated structure of personality inferences without involving cognitive and memorial biases.

Retrieval Processes and Questions
About a Rater's Behavior

The previous discussions have centered on the process by which trait ratings are constructed; however, some personality tests ask raters to indicate whether (and sometimes how often) ratees emit various (typically broadly defined) behaviors. It is conceivable that answers to such questions are constructed in a different manner than answers to more global trait evaluations. On the other hand, several studies have shown that the structure of such behavior ratings are equally similar to the semantic structure of the terms used in the questions as is the structure of personality trait ratings (see Shweder & D'Andrade, 1979, for a review). Thus, it is important to ask how answers to broad questions about behavior might be constructed.

As with trait ratings there are several possibilities. The typical explanation of such results invokes cognitive biases and memory distortions that cause the organization of behavioral facts to become more like semantic organization, implicit personality theory, scripts, or some other preexisting structure that is assumed to be in memory (e.g., Cohen, 1977; Cohen & Ebbesen, 1979; Hamilton, et al., 1980; Snyder & Uranowitz, 1978). On the other hand, even though such attentional and/or memory biases might affect what is remembered, a careful review of the research that demonstrates the effects of such biases shows that their impact on what is remembered is small compared to the impact of the content of the behavior that is observed (e.g., Cohen, 1977). That is, the content of the observed behavior is a far more powerful determinant of how subjects respond on memory tests than are the prior expectations and/or memory structures subjects bring to the test. The number of expectation-consistent errors is typically much smaller than the number of expectation-inconsistent correct responses. Although it is conceivable that small biases might produce enough distortion in what is remembered to cause the structure of behavior ratings to match conceptual structures, other models that do not rely on such biases can explain the effects as well. In particular, as in the case of trait ratings, a retrieval model that assumes that a common set of evidence is used for each behavior rating in such a manner that different parts of the evidence are given equal weight will tend to produce a structure that matches the semantic structure of the behavioral terms themselves.

One way to enhance the plausibility of such a model is to consider in more detail how subjects might construct behavior ratings. Ebbesen (1980) suggested that at least four different classes of information about a ratee might be used as evidence on which to base a response. As an example, suppose the item asks a rater to indicate whether the ratee is the type who gives generous monetary tips. The rater might answer on the basis of: (1) one or more specific memories of the ratee giving a tip; (2) other specific recalled behaviors that imply the size of the tip the ratee was given (e.g., a recollection that the ratee gave a large sum of money to a beggar or that a waiter greeted the ratee with a big smile and welcomed her by name); (3) general or more global characteristics of the ratee (e.g., the rater might retrieve a general impression which implies that the ratee is generous); and (4) beliefs about baserates (e.g., the rater may believe most people tip 15% and having no direct recollection of the ratee's actions assume the ratee conforms to the norm). If observers tend to construct behavior ratings by relying on a generalized impression or by using behaviors that might serve as indicators of several different but related traits, the pattern of behavior ratings will tend to match the pattern of semantic associations among the behavioral terms.

In short, there are some types of ratee-specific information that will, if used by raters, tend to cause behavior ratings to seem to be biased by preexisting semantic structures. Raters may be constructing their ratings on the basis of perfectly well-remembered facts about the ratee but still produce a pattern of ratings that matches the pattern of semantic associations among the terms. Additional research is needed to determine whether such retrieval processes actually do contribute to the structure of behavior ratings and if so, to what extent.

IMPLICATIONS

Several aspects of the preceding sections of this chapter have implications both for personality research and for understanding how raters generate personality ratings.

Personality Research

The two contrasting interpretations of personality research outlined earlier both assume that any specific behavior of individuals is very likely a function of multiple causes. Both agree that situational factors, measurement factors, cognitive factors, motivational factors, and such act directly and interactively to determine behavior. The personality model assumes that, in addition to these causes, stable personality characteristics also contribute to the variance in behavior. The two interpretations also differ in their views of raters. The personality model assumes that ratings can and often do bypass these other causes of behavior and therefore reflect the stable and consistent features of personality. In contrast, the alternative view argues that the consistent part of ratings do not reflect features of personality but are instead a direct result of the operation of various cognitive biases of the raters (e.g., Shweder, 1978). Considerable additional study of these views is needed before one or both can be rejected. Each is capable of explaining most of the results that have been obtained in the personality area.

On the other hand, several claims often made by proponents of one or the other view can be rejected on the basis of current evidence. In particular, the demonstration that cognitive biases influence ratings and memory for behavioral details may be of little use in trying to understand the nature of the information on which raters base their personality ratings. As noted earlier, it is possible to explain the fact that the structure of personality ratings reflect conceptual structures without invoking the operation of a cognitive bias that prevents the ratings from reflecting features of the ratee's personality. The fact that people are poor detectors of correlations among events (Shweder, 1978) is unimportant because raters rarely have to indicate the correlation among events when rating people. In addition, demonstrations of cognitive biases often indicate that the amount of bias is small and that the content of the information presented to observers has a large impact on the content of memory. In short, it may be a mistake to conclude from the existing evidence in personality research what the nature of the information on which personality ratings are based is and how that information is used in the rating-construction process.

Alternatively, research that has examined the rating process does suggest tentative conclusions for these issues. Apparently, raters do not usually construct personality ratings by retrieving "lists" of behaviors nor storage registers filled with specific remembered actions. Ratings of particular characteristics do not tend to correlate with the frequency of *specific* behavioral indicators and more important, for some kinds of characteristics, the time raters take to construct a response does not increase with the amount of behavior that they have stored in memory. Even though an independent memory test showed that raters remembered many of the behavioral details they had observed, some personality trait items (the more "concrete" ones) were apparently answered without a search through that behavioral information(Allen & Ebbesen, in press). Furthermore, the decay in memory for behavioral details seems to be fairly rapid (Ebbesen et al., 1979), suggesting that even if raters tried to base their ratings directly on remembered actions they would not be able to do so when a brief delay (of say a week) was imposed between exposure to the behavior and the rating session (Ebbesen et al., 1979).

None of these conclusions condemn the use of ratings in personality research, however. It is quite possible to construct a model of the rating process that assumes that raters rely on a "generalized impression" or some similar unitary and abstract representation but that also produces information of interest to personality theorists. For example, the *content* of such a representation might well vary with the frequency of broadly defined behavioral categories (even though specific previously observed exemplars of that category are no longer available in memory). This would be similar to assuming that the meaning of or affective reaction to the behaviors are retained in memory even though the details are lost. As a specific example of such a model, suppose ratees were represented as points in multidimensional space and each new set of behavioral events moved the points to new locations. Then, even though ratings might be based on the distance between the location of a rated characteristic and the location of a ratee in this space, the resulting rating would still contain information about the ratee's behavior (although the exact nature of the behavioral information would be hard to extract). If there is no need to claim that all traits express themselves in behavior in a direct (one-to-one) manner, then the ratings constructed from a model similar to the foregoing could provide a useful view of personality. In particular, individual differences in ratings on a given dimension would tend to reflect individual differences in broad categories of behavior, even though the factor structure of ratings might be completely unrepresentative of the *structure* of specific behavioral events. In other words, it is possible to explain the relatively high temporal stability of individual differences in personality ratings (e.g., Block et al., 1979) and the fact that the structure of those ratings match preexisting semantic or implicit personality structures (e.g., Ebbesen & Allen, 1977; Shweder & D'Andrade, 1979) with a model that assumes that trait ratings are based on global memory representations of the rated individuals. Furthermore, there is no need to assume that the content of such global representations bare no relationship to individual differences in the behaviors of the rated individuals.

On the other hand, this is but one of many models consistent with current evidence. There is no *necessary* link between behavioral attributes and the content of a rater's representation (or representations) of a ratee. The content of a representation might reflect attributes of the ratee other than his/her behavior. However, a brief glance at the social psychological literature will show that attitude and trait attributions are very sensitive to the content of the ratee's behavior. Although rarely of primary interest and often included only as a control, most attribution studies find large effects of the content of the actor's behavior on ratings of the actor (moderated by other factors of interest to attribution theorists; e.g., Jones & Harris, 1967). In addition, in the personality area McGowan and Gormly (1976) found that peer ratings of a trait did correlate highly (.70) with a broadly defined behavioral category consisting of ten specific behaviors. Furthermore, it is quite possible that the validity as well as the reliability of ratings of personality attributes can be increased by averaging the ratings of a large number of raters (Horowitz, Inouye, & Siegelman; 1979). In short, there is fairly strong evidence that the extremity of personality ratings can reflect, in part, the content of the behavior that raters observe.

As can be seen from the previous discussion the kinds of conclusions that are reasonable to draw about a ratee's behavior from rater responses can depend on how the raters constructed their responses. For example, whether it is reasonable to conclude that the factor structure obtained from personality rating measures reflects the structure of behavior or, alternatively, the semantic structure of words depends on knowing the *exact* manner in which the raters generated their responses. At the very least, personality researchers might include in factor studies an analysis of the semantic structure of the terms that were employed in the tests. Although evidence of high similarity between the factor and semantic structures (see Ebbesen & Allen, 1977, for one technique to assess the similarity of the structures) would be ambiguous, evidence of low similarity would eliminate certain models from consideration and strengthen some of the conclusions the personality researcher might make.

Alternatively, personality research might do well to shift emphasis from ratings of personality (until more is known about the rating process) to discovering which specific behaviors tend to go into which broad behavioral categories. If one accepts the personality model described here, then discovering how to put together specific behaviors becomes very important. Yet (except for Epstein, 1979) to my knowledge very little personality research has tried to apply the test-refinement models (e.g., Jöreskog, 1974) often used with paper-and-pencil tests to direct measures of behavior (see Green, 1978 for a similar point). Why not begin by borrowing behavior-item pools from, say, the MMPI or other standard tests but use direct behavioral assessment rather than *ratings* of the behaviors? Clearly, this would be a very difficult task but one that would avoid the problems inherent in rating measures and one that might provide important evidence capable of deciding whether the structure of personality is in behavior or the rater's head.[16]

The Rating Process

Much of the recent surge of interest among social psychologists in cognitive processes has been focused on encoding and retention processes (e.g., Hastie, Ostrom, Ebbesen, Wyer, Hamilton, & Carlston, 1980). Errors and biases in memory and ratings have been explained largely in terms of these two points in the information-processing system. In this chapter, I have tried to show that retrieval and decision processes should be given equal attention. Many of the phenomena typically invoked to support encoding and memory biases can be explained by appropriate retrieval and decision models. It is premature to assume most rater biases originate in the encoding and retention stages.

One example of this point is implicit personality theory. It has sometimes been assumed that implicit personality theory represents the (or at least one) way

---

[16]This recommendation need only be followed if one's interest is in developing a useful model of the structure of personality. If one's goal is to find a rating measure capable of predicting a specific criterion behavior in a specific setting, then some of Mischel's (1968), or Bem and Allen's (1974) suggestions seem quite reasonable. For example, one might simply ask individuals how they intend to behave in the particular setting at a particular time. In other words, it is quite possible for very specific rating measures to predict narrowly defined behavioral indicators even though trait ratings do not predict narrowly defined behavioral indicators. As noted in the text, the process by which raters construct behavior ratings may not be the same as the process by which they construct trait ratings.

in which information about people is stored in memory. Thus, ratings of the likelihood that two traits or personality features will co-occur in individuals are assumed to tap into this memory structure. These assumed structures are then used to explain other phenomena, such as memory biases that seem to conform to personality stereotypes (e.g., Cantor & Mischel, 1977; Cohen & Ebbesen, 1979). Biasing manipulations (e.g., set instructions and prior information about an actor) are assumed to "activate" these preexisting structures and thereby affect the kind of personality information that observers retain. In other words, implicit personality (or any other previously stored structure related to person information) is assumed to guide the types of information about specific others that the observer retains in memory by organizing the incoming information in particular ways and/or by selectively storing certain parts of the incoming information and/or by "filling in gaps" in the incoming information with unobserved but expected information.

Another view of implicit personality theory is that it is an artifact of the meaning of trait words and the way in which subjects construct responses to questions about personality (Ebbesen & Allen, 1979). In this view, implicit personality theory does not describe the nature of the personality information that people remember about other people. Instead, it represents the fact that all words, including trait words, share *semantic* features to different degrees. Then, when asked to relate these words to various entities (other trait words, specific known individuals, stereotypes, etc.), the semantic relationships among the *words* will tend to emerge in the structure of the responses provided that the responses are constructed in particular ways (already discussed). In other words, the common assumption that biases in ratings and/or memory arise because specific memory structures (other than the semantic relations among words) are activated and thereby cause distortions and fabrications in what is remembered about a specific person is not a necessary one. The structure of personality information that people remember about others (and themselves) may bear little resemblance to the structure of implicit personality theory (or any other proposed structures). Lists of behaviors, prototypes, points in multidimensional space, scripts, and random structures can all be made compatible with existing data. In addition, the nature of the personality information that people store about specific well-known individuals may be completely different than the implicit personality structures that are typically found in personality rating studies. As Cohen and Ebbesen (1979) and Ebbesen et al. (1979) demonstrated, people can, in the appropriate circumstances, construct ratings whose structure is quite unlike implicit personality theory. Such ratings might well reflect the nature of the personality information that is available to raters but that they seldom use. Alternatively, it is equally plausible that the ratings reflect differences in the nature of the information that the raters have retained in memory.

The foregoing indeterminacy in locating the cause of the structure in personality ratings may be an inherent limitation of cognitive models. It may not be possible to determine, empirically, the form of cognitive structures and the processes that operate on them (Anderson, 1978, 1979). Many memory-structure-plus-process models may always be capable of providing equally accurate predictions of results. Part of the problem is that there are many more unobservable constructs in these models than the methods are capable of discriminating.

On the other hand, there are several conclusions that the research cited here supports with somewhat less ambiguity. One of the most important of these is that personality inferences and memory for specific behaviors appear to be based on different processes, retrieved evidence, or both. That is, personality ratings do not seem to be based on the same evidence (or derived from a common pool of evidence in the same way) as responses to questions about the specific behaviors of the ratee. Although the two-stage model in which the first-stage evidence consists of an abstract representation of a ratee and the second consists of a more detailed (episodic) representation of the ratee (Allen & Ebbesen, 1979) can be used to explain both the behavioral and trait rating results (see Ebbesen, 1980), no direct evidence that behavioral items are treated exactly like trait items has been reported. Trait ratings may be more likely than memory for behavioral details to be based on an abstract representation of the ratee. In addition, different types of normative information may be used to guide the "guesses" that raters construct when answering the two types of response items.

Another conclusion is that the nature of the process models that are proposed to account for personality ratings depend to some extent on the way in which the trait items, themselves, are assumed to be represented in memory. As was discussed previously, certain process models seem to work better with the assumption that trait items are stored as feature lists, points in multidimensional space, or samples of known individuals who possess the trait (Ebbesen & Allen, 1979); others seem to follow from the assumption that traits are represented as a prototypical behavior, script, or a list of behaviors.

The previous point highlights the fact that specifics of retrieval processes can be intimately related to assumptions about the nature of the information that is stored in memory. The latter is related, in turn, to assumptions about the way in which behavioral information is encoded while it is being observed (Ebbesen, 1980). In short, it may only be possible to assess the empicial utility of specific models of different parts of the personality rating system in the context of *given* assumptions about other parts of the system. Unless the other parts of the system are specified in considerable detail, alternative models for the part being studied will always be capable of explaining the results merely by altering assumptions about other parts of the system. The use of concepts such as schema, implicit personality theory, causal theories, prototypical traits, and so on in the absence of specific assumptions about retrieval and decision processes should therefore be avoided.

ACKNOWLEDGMENTS

Preparation of this paper was facilitated by National Institute of Mental Health Grant MH 26069. I would like to thank George Mandler and Steven Bruun for their comments on an earlier draft of this manuscript.

REFERENCES

Allen, R. B., & Ebbesen, E. B. Cognitive processes in person perception: Retrieval of personality trait and behavioral information. *Journal of Experimental Social Psychology*, in press.

Allport, G. W. Traits revisited. *American Psychologist*, 1966, *21*, 1–10.

Anderson, J. R. Arguments concerning representations for mental imagery. *Psychological Review*, 1978, *85*, 249–277.

Anderson, J. R. Further arguments concerning representations for mental imagery: A response to Hayes-Roth and Pylyshyn. *Psychological Review*, 1979, *86*, 395–406.

Ajzen, I., & Fishbein, M. Attitude-behavior relations: A theoretical analysis and review of empirical research. *Psychological Bulletin*, 1977, *84*, 888–918.

Atkinson, R. C., & Juola, J. F. Search and decision processes in recognition memory. In D. H. Krantz, R. C. Atkinson, D. C. Luce, and P. Suppes (Eds.), *Contempory developments in mathmatical psychology* (Vol. 1). San Francisco: Freeman, 1974.

Bagozzi, R. P., & Burnkrant, R. E. Attitude organization and the attitude-behavior relationship. *Journal of Personality and Social Psychology*, 1979, *37*, 913–929.

Bartlett, F. C. *Remembering*. Cambridge: Cambridge University Press, 1932.

Bem, D. J., & Allen, A. On predicting some of the people some of the time: The search for cross-situational consistencies in behavior. *Psychological Review*, 1974, *81*, 506–520.

Berman, J. S., & Kenny, D. A. Correlational bias in observer ratings. *Journal of Personality and Social Psychology*, 1976, *34*, 263–273.

Berscheid, E., Graziano, W., Monson, T., & Dermer, M. Outcome dependency: Attention, attribution, and attraction. *Journal of Personality and Social Psychology*, 1976, *34*, 978–989.

Block, J. An illusory interpretation of the first factor of the MMPI: A reply to Shweder. *Journal of Consulting and Clinical Psychology*, 1977, *45*, 930–935.

Block, J., Weiss, D. S., & Thorne, A. How relevant is a semantic similarity interpretation of personality ratings? *Journal of Personality and Social Psychology*, 1979, *37*, 1055–1074.

Bowers, K. S. Situationism in psychology: An analysis and a critique. *Psychological Review*, 1973, *80*, 307–336.

Bransford, J. D., & McCarrell, N. S. A sketch of a cognitive approach to comprehension: Some thoughts about understanding what it means to comprehend. In W. D. Weimer & D. S. Palermo (Eds.), *Cognition and the symbolic processes*. Hillsdale, N.J.: Lawrence Erlbaum Associates, 1974.

Cantor, N., & Mischel, W. Traits as prototypes: Effects on recognition memory. *Journal of Personality and Social Psychology*, 1977, *35*, 38–48.

Cantor, N., & Mischel, W. Prototypes in person perception. In L. Berkowitz (Ed.), *Advances in experimental social psychology*. New York: Academic Press, 1979.

Carlston, D. Events, inferences, and impression formation. In R. Hastie, T. M. Ostrom, E. B.

Ebbesen, R. S. Wyer, Jr., D. L. Hamilton, & D. E. Carlston (Eds.), *Person memory: The cognitive bases of social perception.* Hillsdale, N.J.: Lawrence Erlbaum Associates, 1980.

Cattell, R. B. *Personality: A systematic theoretical and factual study.* New York: McGraw-Hill, 1950.

Chapman, L. J. Illusory correlation in observational report. *Journal of Verbal Learning and Verbal Behavior,* 1967, *6,* 151–155.

Chapman, L. J., & Chapman, J. P. Genesis of popular but erroneous psychodiagnostic observations. *Journal of Abnormal Psychology,* 1967, *72,* 193–204.

Chapman, L. J., & Chapman, J. P. Illusory correlation as an obstacle to the use of valid psychodiagnostic signs. *Journal of Abnormal Psychology,* 1969, *74,* 271–280.

Cohen, C. E. Cognitive basis of stereotyping: An information processing approach to social perception. (Doctoral dissertation, University of California, San Diego, 1976). *Dissertation Abstracts International,* 1977, *38,* 412B–413B. (University Microfilms No. 77-13, 681).

Cohen, C. E., & Ebbesen, E. B. Observational goals and schema activation: A theoretical framework for behavior perception. *Journal of Experimental Social Psychology,* 1979, *15,* 305–329.

Collins, B. E., Whalen, C. K., & Henker, B. Ecological and pharmacological influences on behaviors in the classroom: The hyperkinetic behavioral syndrome. In J. Antrobus (Ed.), *The eco-system of the "sick kid."* New York: Jossey-Bass, 1980.

D'Andrade, R. G. Trait psychology and componential analysis. *American Anthropology,* 1965, *67,* 215–228.

D'Andrade, R. G. Memory and the assessment of behavior. In H. M. Blalock, Jr., (Ed.), *Measurement in the social sciences.* Chicago: Aldine, 1974.

Ebbesen, E. B. *The effects of levels of success-failure on selective memory for and self-adoption of positive and negative information about oneself.* Unpublished doctoral dissertation, Stanford University, 1971.

Ebbesen, E. B. Cognitive processes in understanding ongoing behavior. In R. Hastie, T. M. Ostrom, E. B. Ebbesen, R. S. Wyer, Jr., D. L. Hamilton, & D. E. Carlston (Eds.), *Person memory: The cognitive basis of social perception.* Hillsdale, N.J.: Lawrence Erlbaum Associates, 1980.

Ebbesen, E. B., & Allen, R. B. Cognitive processes in implicit personality trait inferences. *Journal of Personality and Social Psychology,* 1979, *37,* 471–488.

Ebbesen, E. B., & Allen, R. B. *Further evidence concerning Fiske's question: "Can personality traits ever be empirically validated?"* (Technical Memorandum 77-1229-4). Murry Hill, N.J.: Bell Laboratories, 1977.

Ebbesen, E. B., Cohen, C. E., & Allen, R. B. *Cognitive processes in person perception: Behavior scanning and semantic memory.* Unpublished manuscript, University of California, San Diego, 1979.

Endler, N. S., & Hunt, J. McV. Generalizability of contributions from sources of variance in the S-R inventories of anxiousness. *Journal of Personality,* 1969, *37,* 1–24.

Epstein, S. The stability of behavior: I. On predicting most of the people much of the time. *Journal of Personality and Social Psychology,* 1979, *37,* 1097–1126.

Fishbein, M., & Ajzen, I. *Belief, attitude intention, and behavior: An introduction to theory and research.* Reading, Mass.: Addison-Wesley, 1975.

Fiske, D. W. Can personality constructs be validated empirically? *Psychological Bulletin,* 1973, *80,* 89–92.

Fiske, D. W. *Strategies for personality research.* San Francisco: Jossey-Bass, 1978.

Green, B. F. In defense of measurement. *American Psychologist,* 1978, *33,* 664–670.

Gormley, J., & Champagne, B. *Validity in personality trait ratings: A multicriteria approach.* Paper presented at the meeting of the Eastern Psychology Association, Philadelphia, April 1974.

Hamilton, D. L., & Gifford, R. K. Illusory correlation in interperson perception: A cognitive basis of stereotypic judgments. *Journal of Experimental Social Psychology,* 1976, *12,* 392–407.

Hamilton, D. L. *Illusory correlation as a basis for social stereotypes.* Paper presented at meetings of the American Psychology Association, San Francisco, August 1977.

Hamilton, D. L., Katz, L., & Leirer, V. Organizational processes in impression formation. In R. Hastie, T. M. Ostrom, E. B. Ebbesen, R. S. Wyer, Jr., D. L. Hamilton, & D. E. Carlston (Eds.), *Person memory: The cognitive basis of social perception.* Hillsdale, N.J.: Lawrence Erlbaum Associates, 1980.

Hastie, R., Ostrom, T. M., Ebbesen, E. B., Wyer, R. S., Jr., Hamilton, D. L., & Carlston, D. E. (Eds.). *Person memory: The cognitive basis of social perception.* Hillsdale, N.J.: Lawrence Erlbaum Associates, 1980.

Hastorf, A. H., Osgood, C. E., & Ono, H. The semantics of facial expressions and the prediction of the meanings of stereoscopically fused facial expressions. *Scandinavian Journal of Psychology,* 1966, *7,* 179-188.

Horowitz, L. M., Inouye, D., & Siegelman, E. Y. On averaging judges' ratings to increase their correlation with an external criterion. *Journal of Consulting and Clinical Psychology,* 1979, *47,* 453-457.

Huba, G. J., & Hamilton, D. L. On the generality of trait relationships: Some analyses based on Fiske's paper. *Psychological Bulletin,* 1976, *83,* 868-876.

Jones, E. E., & Harris, V. A. The attribution of attitudes. *Journal of Experimental Social Psychology,* 1967, *3,* 1-24.

Jöreskog, K. G. Analyzing psychological data by structural analysis of covariance matrices. In D. H. Krantz, R. C. Atkinson, R. D. Luce, & E. P. Suppes (Eds.), *Contemporary developments in mathematical psychology* (Vol. 2). San Francisco: W. H. Freeman, 1974.

Kahneman, D., & Tversky, A. On the psychology of prediction. *Psychological Review,* 1973, *80,* 237-251.

Kelley, H. H. Attribution theory in social psychology. In D. Levincs (Ed.), *Nebraska Symposium on Motivation.* Lincoln: University of Nebraska Press, 1967.

Kogan, N., & Wallach, M. A. *Risk-taking: A study in cognition and personality.* New York: Holt, Rinehart & Winston, 1964.

Loftus, E., & Palmer, J. Reconstruction of automobile destruction. *Journal of Verbal Learning and Verbal Behavior,* 1974, *13,* 585-589.

Magnusson, D., & Endler, S. Interactional psychology: Present status and future prospects. In D. Magnusson & N. S. Endler (Eds.), *Personality at the crossroads: Current issues in interactional psychology.* Hillsdale, N.J.: Lawrence Erlbaum Associates, 1977.

Markus, H. Self-schemata and processing information about the self. *Journal of Personality and Social Psychology,* 1977, *35,* 63-78.

McGowan, J., & Gormley, J. Validation of personality traits: A multicriteria approach. *Journal of Personality and Social Psychology,* 1976, *34,* 791-795.

Mischel, W. *Personality and assessment,* New York: Wiley, 1968.

Mischel, W. Toward a cognitive social learning reconceptualization of personality. *Psychological Review,* 1973, *80,* 252-283.

Mischel, W., Ebbesen, E. B., & Zeiss, A. M. Selective attention to the self: Situational and dispositional determinants. *Journal of Personality and Social Psychology,* 1972, *27,* 129-142.

Mischel, W., Ebbesen, E. B., & Zeiss, A. M. Determinants of selective memory about the self. *Journal of Consulting and Clinical Psychology,* 1976, *44,* 92-103.

Muliak, S. A. Are personality factors raters' conceptual factors? *Journal of Consulting Psychology,* 1964, *28,* 506-511.

Newtson, D. A., & Engquist, G. The perceptual organization of ongoing behavior. *Journal of Experimental Social Psychology,* 1976, *12,* 436-450.

Norman, W. T. Toward an adequate taxonomy of personality attributes: Replicated factor structures in peer nomination personality ratings. *Journal of Abnormal and Social Psychology,* 1963, *66,* 574-583.

Passini, F. T., & Norman, W. T. A universal conception of personality structure? *Journal of Personality and Social Psychology,* 1966, *4,* 44–49.

Rogers, T. B., Rogers, P. J., & Kuiper, N. A. Evidence for the self as a cognitive prototype: The "false alarms effect." *Personality and Social Psychology Bulletin,* 1979, *5,* 53–56.

Rosenberg, S., & Sedlack, S. Structural representations of implicit personality. In L. Berkowitz (Ed.), *Advances in experimental social psychology* (Vol. 6). New York: Academic Press, 1972.

Ross, L. The intuitive psychologist and his shortcomings: Distortions in the attribution process. In L. Berkowitz (Ed.), *Advances in experimental social psychology* (Vol. 10). New York: Academic Press, 1977.

Schneider, D. J. Implicit personality theory: A review. *Psychological Bulletin,* 1973, *79,* 294–309.

Sears, R. R. Dependency motivation. In M. R. Jones (Ed.), *Nebraska Symposium on Motivation.* Lincoln: University of Nebraska Press, 1963.

Shank, R., & Abelson, R. *Scripts, plans, goals, and understanding.* Hillsdale, N.J.: Lawrence Erlbaum Associates, 1977.

Shweder, R. A. How relevant is an individual difference theory of personality? *Journal of Personality,* 1975, *43,* 455–484.

Shweder, R. A. *Fact and artifact in personality assessment: The influence of conceptual schemata on individual difference judgments.* Paper presented at American Psychology Association Meetings, Toronto, August 1978.

Shweder, R. A., & D'Andrade, R. G. Accurate reflection or systematic distortion? A reply to Block, Weiss and Thorne. *Journal of Personality and Social Psychology,* 1979, *37,* 1075–1084.

Smith, E. E., Shoben, E. J., & Rips, L. J. Structure and process in semantic memory: A feature model for semantic decisions. *Psychological Review,* 1974, *81,* 214–241.

Snyder, M., & Uranowitz, S. Reconstructing the past: Some cognitive consequences of person perception. *Journal of Personality and Social Psychology,* 1978, *36,* 941–950.

Sternberg, S. Memory scanning: New findings and current controversies. *Quarterly Journal of Experimental Psychology,* 1974, *27,* 1–32.

Tsujimoto, R. N. Memory bias toward normative and novel trait prototypes. *Journal of Personality and Social Psychology,* 1978, *36,* 1391–1401.

Vernon, P. E. *Personality assessment: A critical survey.* New York: Wiley, 1964.

Wallach, M. A. Commentary: Active-analytical versus passive-global cognitive functioning. In S. Messick & J. Ross (Eds.), *Measurement in personality and cognition.* New York: Wiley, 1962, 199–215.

Weigel, R. H., & Newman, L. S. Increasing attitude-behavior correspondence by broadening the scope of the behavioral measure, *Journal of Personality and Social Psychology,* 1976, *33,* 793–802.

Wyer, R. S., Jr., & Srull, T. K. The processing of social stimulus information: A conceptual integration. In R. Hastie, T. M. Ostrom, E. B. Ebbesen, R. S. Wyer, Jr., D. L. Hamilton, & D. E. Carlston (Eds.), *Person memory: The cognitive bases of social perception.* Hillsdale, N.J.: Lawrence Erlbaum Associates, 1980.

Zajonc, R. B. Feeling and thinking: Preferences need no inferences. *American Psychologist,* 1980, *35,* 151–175.

8 Seek, And Ye Shall Find: Testing Hypotheses About Other People

Mark Snyder
University of Minnesota

> *It is the theory which*
> *decides what we can find.*
>
> —Albert Einstein

In the course of social relationships, individuals often attempt to make judgments about the personal attributes of other people. At times, this quest for knowledge may involve the active testing of hypotheses about other people. When individuals form early impressions of their new acquaintances, they may wish to test hypotheses based upon expectations about their acquaintances' personal dispositions: Is this new acquaintance as friendly as a mutual friend has led me to believe? Is that new acquaintance as boring as every other graduate of the same college? Similarly, when individuals find themselves questioning the accuracy of existing beliefs about friends, they may wish to test hypotheses based on alternate interpretations of their natures: Is this friend whom I have always liked really as mean-tempered as everyone now tells me? Is that friend's unexpected change in behavior a sign of a corresponding change in character? In fact, whenever individuals find themselves wondering whether particular attributes are characteristic of other people or whether other individuals are particular types of people (Is this person sufficiently conscientious to do the job? Is that person a genuine intellectual?), they essentially have formed hypotheses about the personal attributes of other people. Having formed hypotheses about other people, individuals then may proceed to test these hypotheses. In particular, individuals systematically may use their subsequent social interactions as opportunities to actively collect behavioral evidence with which to test their hypotheses. This essay is

277

concerned with the processes by which individuals actively test hypotheses about other people.

Having formed a hypothesis about another person, how might an individual test it actively using social interaction? Consider the case of an individual who wishes to test the hypothesis that another person is friendly and sociable. Jim has been told by Brian that Chris is a sociable and outgoing person. Now, Jim knows that Brian is hardly the world's shrewdest judge of character. In fact, Jim knows that Brian's assessments of other people's personalities are as often wrong as right. Accordingly, Jim decides to regard Brian's pronouncement about Chris as a hypothesis to be tested. How, then, is Jim to test the hypothesis that Chris has a sociable and outgoing nature? Perhaps he will use their first conversational encounter as an opportunity to actively test his hypothesis. He might plan his hypothesis-testing strategy by saying to himself: "If Chris is as sociable and outgoing as Brian has claimed, then Chris probably goes to lots of parties. I'll steer the conversation in the direction of parties. If Chris goes to parties, then I will know that Brian was right when he said that Chris is a sociable and outgoing type of person." In accord with this strategy, at some appropriate time in the conversation, Jim might say "Tell me about a party you went to" and Chris might oblige with an account of a party. Jim then might conclude that he has confirmed the hypothesis that Chris is sociable and outgoing.

However, had this same Chris been reputed to be shy and retiring, Jim might have found himself testing this hypothesis by asking about the times that Chris wanted to be alone. He then might have found that, in keeping with a shy and retiring disposition, Chris indeed did spend time alone. In each case, as a direct consequence of Jim's hypothesis-testing efforts, Chris' actions have provided actual *behavioral confirmation* for Jim's initial hypothesis. After all, most (if not all) people have been to some parties and have spent some time alone in their lifetimes. Moreover, most (if not all) people will be particularly likely to talk about parties when asked to do so in conversation. Similarly, they will be particularly likely to talk about quieter times when conversations move in that direction.

This hypothetical scenario illustrates the key aspects of just one strategy of testing hypotheses in social interaction. As a hypothesis-tester, Jim asked Chris a series of questions designed to determine whether or not Chris' actual behavior and life experiences matched those of a characteristically sociable and outgoing person. In choosing and asking his questions, Jim formulated and enacted a *confirmatory* hypothesis-testing strategy. The defining characteristic of a confirmatory strategy for testing hypotheses in social interaction is the preferential soliciting of behavioral evidence whose presence would tend to confirm the hypothesis under scrutiny. That is, to test the hypothesis that another person was friendly and sociable by means of a confirmatory strategy, an individual would devote (as did Jim) most of his conversation to probing for instances of the presence of sociable and outgoing behaviors. For example, the individual might ask (as did Jim) about those times when the other person went to parties, those times when the other person sought out new friends, etc. To the extent that such a confirmatory hypothesis-testing strategy yielded relatively many hypothesis-confirming instances of friendly and sociable actions, the hypothesis-tester would accept the hypothesis under consideration.

Why write a scenario to illustrate a confirmatory hypothesis-testing strategy? Why not write a scenario illustrating a *disconfirmatory* hypothesis-testing strategy in which an individual would preferentially solicit behavioral evidence whose presence tends to disconfirm the hypothesis? After all, most (if not all) hypotheses about personal attributes (e.g., this person is sociable and outgoing) have readily available alternative competing hypotheses (e.g., this person is shy and retiring). Thus, to test the hypothesis that another person was friendly and sociable by means of a disconfirmatory strategy, individuals would devote most of their conversation to probing for instances of the presence of shy and retiring behaviors. For example, an individual might ask about times when the person had wanted to spend time alone, had avoided meeting new people, etc. To the extent that such a disconfirmatory hypothesis-testing strategy yielded relatively few such hypothesis-disconfirming instances of shy and retiring actions, the individual would accept the hypothesis under consideration.

Or, why not write a scenario illustrating an "equal-opportunity" strategy of soliciting hypothesis-confirming and hypothesis-disconfirming evidence with equal diligence? Thus, to test the hypothesis that another person was friendly and sociable by means of an "equal-opportunity" strategy, individuals would devote equal amounts of their conversation to probing for instances of friendly-sociable and shy-retiring behaviors before deciding whether or not to accept the hypothesis. After all, in the absence of relevant empirical evidence, the confirmatory, the disconfirmatory, and the "equal-opportunity" strategies are all possible and plausible approaches to testing hypotheses about other people.

As it happens, the choice to write a scenario illustrating the enactment and the consequences of a confirmatory hypothesis-testing strategy is an outcome of a series of experimental investigations. The activities of the principal characters in this illustrative scenario are representative of the typical activities of participants in these investigations. In these studies, individuals were provided with hypotheses to test about the personalities of other people (targets). These individuals then prepared to test these hypotheses (that their targets were extraverts, or that their targets were introverts) by choosing a series of questions to ask their targets during a later interview (for details of the basic procedural paradigm, see Snyder & Swann, 1978b).

In these investigations, individuals planned to test their hypotheses by preferentially soliciting behavioral evidence whose presence would tend to confirm their hypotheses. To test the hypothesis that their targets were extraverts, individuals were particularly likely to choose questions that one typically asks of people already known to be extraverts (e.g., "What would you do if you wanted to liven things up at a party?''). To test the hypothesis that their targets were introverts, individuals were particularly likely to choose precisely those questions that one typically asks of people already known to be introverts (e.g., ''What factors make it hard for you to really open up to people?''). That is, participants planned to test their hypotheses by preferentially soliciting behavioral evidence whose presence would tend to confirm the hypothesis under scrutiny.

Moreover, these confirmatory hypothesis-testing procedures channeled social interaction between hypothesis-testers and targets in ways that caused the targets to provide actual behavioral confirmation for the hypothesis-testers' hypotheses. Targets who were being ''tested'' for extraversion actually came to behave in relatively sociable and outgoing fashion. Targets who were being ''tested'' for introversion actually came to behave in relatively shy and reserved fashion.

Evidently, an individual's active attempts to test a hypothesis about another individual may initiate a chain of events that channel subsequent social interaction in ways that cause the target of that hypothesis to provide behavioral confirmation for the hypothesis-tester's hypothesis. How pervasive is the commitment to confirmatory hypothesis-testing strategies? What are the psychological processes that underlie and generate both the preferential soliciting of hypothesis-confirming behavioral evidence and the interpersonal consequences of hypothesis-testing activities? What are the theoretical implications of these investigations of hypothesis-testing processes in social interaction for understanding the nature of social knowledge? It is the intent of this essay to provide answers to these questions. Consider, first, the empirical efforts to chart the unfolding dynamics of hypothesis-testing processes in social interaction; and, then, the theoretical and meta-theoretical implications of investigations of hypothesis-testing processes.

FORMULATING STRATEGIES FOR TESTING HYPOTHESES ABOUT OTHER PEOPLE: A PARADIGMATIC INVESTIGATION

A series of empirical investigations have examined the strategies that individuals formulate to test hypotheses about other people with whom they anticipate social interaction. In an initial paradigmatic demonstration, Snyder and Swann (1978b, Experiment 1) provided participants with hypotheses about other individuals (targets). Participants then prepared to test their hypotheses by planning a series of questions to ask the target in (what they believed to be) a forthcoming interview. Specifically, the experimenter informed participants that they would be taking part in an investigation of how people come to know and understand each other. The experimenter explained that one way to learn about other people is to ask them questions about their likes and dislikes, their favorite activities, their life experiences, and their feelings about themselves. Each participant would attempt to find out what another person (supposedly waiting in another room) was like by asking questions designed to determine whether that person was the type whose personality was outlined on a card provided by the experimenter. These personality profiles provided the participants with hypotheses about the other individual.

The personality profile was one of two that had been prepared in advance. Some participants learned that it would be their task to assess the extent to which the target's behavior and life experiences matched those of a prototypic extravert. According to the personality profile (Snyder & Swann, 1978b):

> Extraverts are typically outgoing, sociable, energetic, confident, talkative, and enthusiastic. Generally confident and relaxed in social situations, this type of person rarely has trouble making conversation with others. This type of person makes friends quickly and easily and is usually able to make a favorable impression on others. This type of person is usually seen by others as characteristically warm and friendly [p. 1203]

Other participants learned that their assignment would be to determine the extent to which the target's behavior and life experiences matched those of a prototypic introvert. According to the personality profile (Snyder & Swann, 1978b):

> Introverts are typically shy, timid, reserved, quiet, distant, and retiring. Usually this type of person would prefer to be alone reading a book or have a long serious discussion with a close friend rather than to go to a loud party or other large social gathering. Often this type of person seems awkward and ill at ease in social situations, and consequently is not adept in making good first impressions. This type of person is usually seen by others as characteristically cool and aloof [p. 1204].

The experimenter then explained that the profile (the hypothesis) dealt in abstract generalities and global characteristics. However, getting to know someone involves finding out concrete information and specific facts about what that person actually thinks, feels, and does. Accordingly, the participant would choose 12 questions that would help find out whether the target's specific beliefs, attitudes, and actions in life situations matched the general characteristics described in the profile.

The experimenter then provided participants with a list of "Topic Areas Often Covered by Interviewers," from which to choose their 12 questions. The questions on the topic sheet inquired about a wide range of beliefs, feelings, and actions within the domains of personal experience and interpersonal relationships. Undergraduate rater-judges previously had classified these questions into three categories:

1. Extraverted Questions.   These questions were ones that the rater-judges thought typically would be asked of people *already known* to be extraverts: for example, "What kind of situations do you seek out if you want to meet new people?"; "In what situations are you most talkative? What is it about these situations that makes you like to talk?".

2. Introverted Questions.   According to the rater-judges, these questions characteristically would be asked of individuals *already known* to be introverts: for example, "What factors make it hard for you to really open up to people?"; "What things do you dislike about loud parties?".

3. Neutral questions.   Questions for which there was no consensus that it was an extraverted question or an introverted question and those classified by the rater-judges as irrelevant to introversion and extraversion were classified as neutral questions: for example, "What are your career goals?"; "What do you think the good and bad points of acting friendly and open are?".

Participants then selected the 12 questions that they estimated would provide them with the information to best test the hypothesis about the target. The experimenter then informed each participant that the interview would not actually take place, and thoroughly debriefed each participant.

What strategies did participants formulate to test their hypotheses about targets with whom they anticipated social interaction? In accord with a confirmatory strategy, participants preferentially chose to solicit behavioral evidence whose presence would tend to confirm their hypotheses. Thus, participants planned to ask *extravert-questions* much more frequently when planning to test the hypothesis that their targets were *extraverted individuals* than when preparing to test the hypothesis that their targets were introverted individuals. Similarly, participants chose to ask *introvert-questions* more frequently when planning to test the hypothesis that their targets were *introverted individuals* than when preparing to test the hypothesis that their targets were extraverted individuals. And, despite the fact that participants could have allocated many of their choices to neutral questions, they tended not to exercise this option. Moreover, participants chose neutral question with equally rare frequency whether they were testing the extravert or the introvert hypothesis.

This paradigmatic investigation provided clear evidence that individuals systematically formulate confirmatory strategies for testing hypotheses about other people. To test the hypothesis that their targets were extraverts, participants were particularly likely to choose to ask precisely those questions that one typically asks of people already known to be extraverts. Similarly, to test the hypothesis that their targets were introverts, participants were particularly likely to choose to ask precisely those questions that one typically asks of people already known to be introverts.

IN SEARCH OF THE LIMITS OF
CONFIRMATORY HYPOTHESIS TESTING

How pervasive is the commitment to confirmatory hypothesis-testing strategies? In the initial investigation (Snyder & Swann, 1978b, Experiment 1), participants chose to ask questions that solicited hypothesis-confirming evidence about twice as often as they chose to ask questions that solicited hypothesis-disconfirming evidence. A series of subsequent investigations have attempted to define the boundary conditions within which hypothesis-testers will choose to preferentially solicit hypothesis-confirming behavioral evidence. Each investigation has attempted to identify circumstances in which hypothesis-testers will *avoid* confirmatory strategies. Yet, despite repeated and diverse attempts to accomplish this goal, these investigations not only failed to yield even one circumstance in which hypothesis-testers avoid confirmatory strategies, but also failed to identify even one procedure that successfully diminishes the magnitude of the preferential soliciting of hypothesis-confirming evidence.

Origins of the Hypothesis

Hypotheses differ in their origins. Some hypotheses emerge from more credible sources than do others. Consider again the case of Jim and his hypothesis that Chris is a friendly and sociable individual. Surely, Jim would have had more faith that this hypothesis accurately captured Chris' nature if the hypothesis had emerged from a credible source (perhaps a demonstrably reliable and valid personality assessment device) rather than from the intuitions of his friend Brian (who, it will be recalled, had a rather undistinguished track record of accurately perceiving other people). Will the origins of a hypothesis influence the strategies that individuals formulate to test that hypothesis?

In an experiment designed to answer this question (Snyder & Swann, 1978b, Experiment 1), participants were provided with hypotheses about other people within the basic question-choosing procedural prardigm. Some participants prepared to test the hypothesis that their targets were extraverts, whereas others, the hypothesis that their targets were introverts. However, the experimenter also provided participants with information about the (supposed) origins of the personality profile (which, it will be recalled, constituted the hypothesis to be tested). Some participants learned that the hypothesis was based upon ''a summary of the results of a personality test the other person took last week.'' The intent here was to give the hypothesis some credibility by having it ''emerge'' from the target's own actions. Moreover, pretesting had indicated that the undergraduate population from which participants in this investigation were recruited continue to have considerable faith in the validity of personality assessment procedures. Accordingly, these participants ought to have had some reason to believe that their hypotheses accurately captured their targets' natures.

By contrast, other participants learned that the hypothesis was simply a description of a hypothetical type of person. The intent here was to make clear that the hypothesis had no connection whatsoever to any actions of the target. These participants were given no reasons to believe that the hypothesis was either true or false. Their task simply was to discover whether or not their targets were like a hypothetical type of person. The hypothesis, rather than emerging from some actions of the target that might suggest that it would prove true, appeared to emerge, so to speak, "from thin air."

The origins of the hypothesis being tested had *no* noticeable effect on the questioning strategy that individuals adopted to test their hypotheses. Hypothesis-testers were just as likely to formulate confirmatory strategies of preferentially soliciting the presence of hypothesis-confirming evidence when there were no reasons to anticipate the outcome as when they had some reason to expect that their hypotheses were true. In either case, they planned to preferentially ask extravert-questions to test the hypothesis that their targets were extraverts, and introvert-questions to test the hypothesis that their targets were introverts.

Certainty of the Hypothesis

It seems to matter not at all whether or not individuals have any reason to suspect that their hypotheses would prove to be accurate. Hypotheses that emerge from thin air are accorded the same treatment as hypotheses that emerge from credible personality assessment devices. But, would individuals avoid confirmatory hypothesis-testing strategies if they had compelling reasons to believe that their hypotheses will prove to be inaccurate? In an investigation of this possibility (Snyder & Swann, 1978b, Experiment 3) participants chose the set of questions that they would use to test the hypothesis that their targets were extraverts. Their task was identical to that of the basic procedural paradigm, except that some participants learned information that was designed to graphically convey the certainty that their hypotheses would prove to be inaccurate or would prove to be accurate.

To make it seem quite *unlikely* that their targets were extraverts, some participants learned that she was a member of a sorority of which only 7 of 30 members were extraverts. Accordingly, they were to find out if she was one of the very few extraverts in the sorority. By contrast, to make it seem quite *likely* that their targets actually were extraverts, some participants learned that she was a member of a sorority of which fully 23 of 30 members were extraverts. Accordingly, they were to find out if she was one of the very many extraverts in the sorority.

There is no doubt that participants in this investigation understood the implications of the information about the composition of the sorority. Participants who believed that there were very many extraverts in the sorority estimated that it was much more likely that their specific targets were extraverts than did participants who believed that there were very few extraverts in the sorority. Yet, this knowledge of the likelihood that their hypotheses would prove accurate or inaccurate had no demonstrable effect on the formulation of strategies for testing these hypotheses. Participants were as likely to formulate confirmatory strategies of preferentially searching for the presence of hypothesis-confirming evidence when they knew that it was quite unlikely that their targets were extraverts (that is, when they knew that there were very few extraverts in the target's sorority) as when they knew that it was quite likely that their targets were extraverts (that is, when they knew that there were very many extraverts in the target's sorority) as when they had no information about the presumptive accuracy or inaccuracy of their hypotheses (that is, when [in the basic procedural paradigm] they learned nothing about the target). In each case, hypothesis-testers planned to ask equally many more extraverted questions and equally fewer introverted questions than their counterparts who attempted (in the basic procedural paradigm) to test the hypothesis that their targets were introverts.

Incentives for Accuracy

Would individuals continue to formulate confirmatory strategies for testing hypotheses about the personalities of other people if they were offered substantial incentives for testing their hypotheses as "accurately" as possible? To evaluate this possibility, some participants in an investigation of hypothesis testing (Snyder & Swann, 1978b, Experiment 4) learned that the researchers would award "$25 to the person who develops the set of questions that tell the most about . . . the interviewee. [p. 1209]." Thus, they should "try to be as accurate as possible in finding out what they interviewee is like [p. 1209]." Some participants were offered this incentive to test the hypothesis that their targets were extraverts, and others, to test the hypothesis that their targets were introverts.

Participants in this investigation did not abandon their confirmatory strategies for testing their hypotheses about their targets when offered a $25 incentive for accuracy. In fact, they were no less likely to preferentially solicit the presence of hypothesis-confirming behavioral evidence from their targets than were individuals who had not been offered such large incentives for accuracy. With or without substantial incentives for accuracy, individuals planned to ask more extravert-questions to assess their targets' extraversion than to assess their introversion; at the same time, they planned to ask more introvert-questions to determine their targets' introversion than to determine their extraversion. Apparently, the offer of substantial monetary incentives was not sufficient to even diminish, let alone override, the propensity to preferentially solicit the presence of hypothesis-confirming evidence.

Testing Competing Hypotheses

Surely, there must be some way to induce individuals to eschew their confirmatory strategies for testing their hypotheses about other people. Typically, in these investigations, participants have had access to one of the two personality profiles (either that of the prototypic extravert or that of the prototypic introvert) and have designed interview strategies to determine whether or not their targets were the type of person described in the personality profile. Perhaps, it might be argued, participants planned to preferentially solicit evidence whose presence would tend to confirm their hypotheses because they had no alternative hypotheses to consider. What if, instead of providing participants with a hypothesis, one were to provide them with *both* personality profiles and ask them to find out whether their specific targets were more similar to the prototypic extravert or more similar to the prototypic introvert? How would participants proceed to evaluate equally probable competing hypotheses about their targets?

In an investigation designed to answer this question (Snyder & Swann, 1977a) participants chose the questions that they would ask of their targets in (what they believed to be) a forthcoming interview. Some participants received both the extraverted personality profile and the introverted personality profile, with the instructions that both profiles "describe two hypothetical persons familiar to us all—the extravert and the introvert. Your task will be to find out if the other person is more like an extravert or more like an introvert."

What interview strategies did these participants formulate when they had competing hypotheses about their targets' personalities? Did they formulate "equal-opportunity" strategies and sample questions representatively from both the extraverted and introverted domains? Or, did they preferentially sample questions from one domain or other, perhaps because they had assumed (for purposes of planning an interview strategy) that their targets were either extraverts or introverts? As it happened, even when faced with competing hypotheses to test, individuals continued to preferentially solicit behavioral evidence from one domain. Participants who were assigned the task of testing competing hypotheses formulated interview strategies equivalent to those of participants who attempted to test the sole hypothesis that their targets were *extraverts*. In either case, participants chose to ask more extravert-questions than did participants who attempted to test the sole hypothesis that their targets were introverts. Moreover, in either case, participants planned to ask fewer introvert-questions than did participants who attempted to test the sole hypothesis that their targets were introverts.

It appears that participants coped with competing hypotheses by acting as if they were testing only one hypothesis—the extravert hypothesis. But why the extravert hypothesis? Why not the introvert hypothesis? One explanation of this outcome may be eliminated with ease. It is unlikely that participants assumed that extraverts appear in the world with greater frequency than introverts, and therefore chose to sample questions from the extravert-domain. After all, in an earlier investigation, participants had been totally insensitive to concrete information about the frequency of extraverts in the sorority to which the target belonged.

There is, however, a more viable explanation of the outcome of this investigation. Perhaps, when comparing the two hypotheses, participants may have found it somewhat easier to imagine specific behaviors that are characteristic of extraverts than to imagine specific behaviors that are characteristic of introverts. After all, in the personality profiles that constituted the hypotheses, extraverts were defined by that which they do (i.e., "Extraverts are typically outgoing, sociable, energetic, confident, talkative, and enthusiastic") and introverts were defined by what they don't do (i.e., "Introverts are typically shy, timid, reserved, quiet, distant, and retiring"). Perhaps, because it is easier to think of extraverted behaviors than introverted behaviors, hypothesis-testers may have chosen to preferentially solicit evidence from the domain of extraversion when faced with both the extravert and the introvert hypothesis.

Knowledge of Disconfirming Attributes

Even in the face of competing hypotheses, individuals plan to preferentially solicit evidence whose presence would tend to confirm only one of the competing hypotheses. Nevertheless, there may exist a related procedure for inducing individuals to avoid confirmatory hypothesis-testing strategies. So far, in these investigations, the hypotheses have been framed in terms of those attributes that characteristically are thought to be *present* in, respectively, prototypic extraverts (e.g., "extraverts are typically outgoing, sociable, energetic, confident, talkative, and enthusiastic") and prototypic introverts (e.g., "introverts are typically shy, timid, reserved, quiet, distant, and retiring"). Thus, at the same time as the hypotheses have explicitly defined those attributes whose presence would confirm the hypothesis, they have been mute about those attributes whose presence would disconfirm the hypothesis under consideration. An individual who desired, for whatever reason, to solicit disconfirming evidence would be forced to self-generate on his or her own that set of attributes that would provide disconfirming evidence. Such an individual, when faced with the extravert hypothesis and a list of all those attributes whose presence reflects extraversion, would have to quickly bring to mind all those attributes whose presence would indicate that a person is not an extravert (e.g., the presence of shy, reserved, quiet, cool, and aloof behaviors).

Perhaps, it might be argued, participants in these investigations planned to preferentially solicit confirming evidence because (as a result of the hypotheses having been framed in terms of confirming attributes) those attributes that would constitute confirming evidence simply were more cognitively available to them than were those attributes that would constitute disconfirming evidence. What if, instead of providing individuals with hypotheses framed exclusively in terms of confirming attributes, one were to provide them with hypotheses that were framed both in terms of confirming attributes and in terms of disconfirming attributes? What if, for example, the extravert hypothesis not only made clear what an extravert *is* but also made equally clear what an extravert is *not?*

To probe the strategies that individuals would use to test such hypotheses, Snyder and Campbell (1980) had participants choose sets of questions to test either the hypothesis that their targets were extraverts or the hypothesis that their targets were introverts. For some participants, the personality profile that constituted the hypothesis to be tested provided information both about those attributes whose presence would confirm the hypothesis and those attributes whose presence would disconfirm the hypothesis. Thus, the personality profile of the hypothetical extravert affirmed the presence of all those attributes that characterize a prototypic extravert (e.g., "are typically outgoing, sociable, energetic, confident, talkative, and enthusiastic") at the same time as it denied the presence of all those attributes that characterize a prototypic introvert (e.g., "are rarely shy, timid, reserved, quiet, distant, and retiring"). Similarly, the personality profile of the hypothetical introvert affirmed the presence of all those attributes that characterize a prototypic introvert (e.g., "is usually seen by others as characteristically cool and aloof") at the same time as it denied the presence of all those attributes that characterize a prototypic extravert (e.g., "is rarely seen by others as characteristically warm and friendly").

What interview strategies did these participants formulate to test hypotheses that were framed in terms of both confirming and disconfirming attributes? Surely, any participants who wished to formulate disconfirmatory or "equal-opportunity" strategies had all the ammunition that they needed to choose a set of questions that would embody such strategies. But, such was not the case. Confirmatory hypothesis-testing strategies were as prevalent in the sample of individuals who participated in this investigation as they had ever been.

Even when the hypotheses made clear those attributes whose presence would confirm and those attributes whose presence would disconfirm the hypothesis under scrutiny, participants planned to preferentially solicit evidence that would tend to confirm their hypotheses. Participants chose more extravert-questions to test the hypothesis that their targets were extraverts than to test the hypothesis that their targets were introverts. At the same time, participants planned to ask more introvert-questions to test the hypothesis that their targets were introverts than to test the hypothesis that their targets were extraverts. Moreover, these manifestations of the formulation of confirmatory hypothesis-testing strategies were as evident for these participants whose hypotheses defined both confirming and disconfirming attributes as they were for other participants whose hypotheses defined only the confirming attributes.

The procedure of providing participants with hypotheses framed in terms of both confirming and disconfirming attributes was not sufficient to even diminish, let alone override, the propensity to preferentially solicit behavioral evidence whose presence would confirm these hypotheses. But what would happen if participants were provided with hypotheses framed exclusively in terms of attributes that would disconfirm the hypotheses? To answer this question, Snyder and White (1978) provided participants with either the extravert hypothesis or the introvert hypothesis framed exclusively in terms of attributes typically thought to be *absent* in, respectively, with prototypic extraverts (e.g., rarely shy, timid, reserved, quiet, distant, retiring, etc.) or with prototypic introverts (e.g., rarely outgoing, sociable, energetic, confident, talkative, enthusiastic, etc.). Again, participants systematically formulated confirmatory strategies: they chose extravert-questions more frequently to test the extravert hypothesis than to test the introvert hypothesis, and introvert-questions more frequently to test the introvert hypothesis than to test the extravert hypothesis. This preferential soliciting of hypothesis-confirming evidence occurred despite the fact that the hypotheses contained not one single reference to confirming attributes. Evidently, the propensity to preferentially solicit hypothesis-confirming behavioral evidence is *not* a consequence of framing hypotheses exclusively in terms of hypothesis-confirming attributes.

The Lengths to Which One Must Go

Over and over again, individuals who participated in these investigations formulated confirmatory hypothesis-testing strategies. It seemed to matter not at all to these individuals where their hypotheses originated, how likely it was that their hypotheses would prove accurate or inaccurate, whether substantial incentives for accurate hypothesis-testing were offered, or whether the hypotheses explicitly defined disconfirming attributes. As far as these individuals were concerned, a hypothesis was a hypothesis was a hypothesis. They accorded all hypotheses equal status when preparing a strategy to solicit information with which to test these hypotheses. In each case, participants planned to preferentially solicit (by means of the questions that they chose to ask their targets) behavioral evidence whose presence would tend to confirm their hypotheses. Even when faced with competing hypotheses of equal credibility, participants continued to preferentially solicit behavioral evidence from one domain. Moreover, even when one goes beyond the testing of hypotheses about other people to the testing of hypotheses about one's self, individuals preferentially accumulate confirming evidence to test hypotheses about their own personal attributes (cf. Snyder & Skrypnek, 1979).

Is there any procedure that will induce individuals to avoid the preferential soliciting of evidence from one behavioral domain? Yes. But, oh, the lengths to which one must go to accomplish this feat. The only procedure that successfully induces individuals to avoid the preferential soliciting of behavioral evidence from one domain is one that provides them with *no* hypotheses to test. When participants chose that series of questions that they would ask to find out about their targets in the absence of any hypotheses about their targets' personalities (that is, in the absence of a profile), they came closer than any other group of participants in this series of investigations to formulating an "equal-opportunity" interview strategy of sampling questions representatively from both the extravert- and the introvert-domain (Snyder & Swann, 1977b). In comparison with participants who chose their questions in order to test hypotheses about their targets' extraverted or introverted natures, these participants asked fewer of those questions that would have provided confirming evidence for either hypothesis and more of those questions that would have provided disconfirming evidence for either hypothesis.

Thus, it was only when participants were given no hypotheses to test that they even approached the formulation of interview strategies that avoided a preferential sampling of behavioral evidence from one or other domain. Of course, the fact that individuals may avoid confirmatory strategies when they are not attempting to test any hypotheses hardly constitutes the identification of a circumstance in which individuals avoid confirmatory strategies when *they are attempting* to test hypotheses about other people. If any procedure exists for inducing individuals to eschew confirmatory hypothesis-testing strategies in favor of either disconfirmatory or "equal-opportunity" hypothesis-testing strategies, that procedure has yet to appear.

THE CONSEQUENCES OF CONFIRMATORY STRATEGIES FOR TESTING HYPOTHESES ABOUT OTHER PEOPLE

Time and again, investigations of strategies for testing hypotheses about other people have yielded the same outcome. To test their hypotheses, individuals who participated in these experiments wanted to ask their targets precisely those questions that they would have asked of someone for whom the hypothesis was already known to be true. Consider, now, the consequences of enacting these confirmatory hypothesis-testing strategies in social interaction.

So far, hypothesis-testers in these investigations never had the opportunity to interrogate their targets. What would happen if one were to allow hypothesis-testers the opportunity to interview their targets and "collect the data" that their confirmatory strategies would provide them? Would these confirmatory evidence-gathering procedures generate behaviors that would erroneously confirm their hypotheses? Would targets who are being "tested" for extraversion actually come to behave in relatively sociable and outgoing fashion? Would targets who are being "tested" for introversion actually come to behave in relatively shy and reserved fashion? After all, the more often one inquires about the target's extraversion, the more often the target will have opportunities to provide instances of extraverted behavior. Similarly, the more often one inquires about the target's introversion, the more often the target will have opportunities to provide instances of introverted behaviors. Confirmatory hypothesis-testing strategies may constrain targets to behave in ways that provide actual behavioral evidence for the hypothesis under consideration.

In order to more systematically probe these processes, Snyder and Swann (1978b, Experiment 2) conducted an experimental investigation of hypothesis-testing processes in social interaction. Hypothesis-testers first formulated their hypothesis-testing strategies and then carried out these strategies by actually interviewing their targets.

Hypothesis-Testing in Social Interaction

In this investigation, participants were scheduled in pairs of previously unacquainted individuals. To insure that they would have no contact before their interaction, they had been instructed to arrive at separate experimental rooms that were located on different corridors. Each participant was assigned randomly to one of two roles: hypothesis-tester or target. Half of the hypothesis-testers were instructed to assess the extent to which their targets' behavior and experiences matched those of the prototypic extravert. The other half of the hypothesis-testers were instructed to assess the extent to which their targets' behavior and experience matched those of a prototypic introvert. At the same time as the hypothesis-testers were choosing questions to ask their targets during the forthcoming interviews, the experimenter informed participants assigned to the role of target that they would be interviewed by another student. Targets were instructed simply to answer all the questions in as informative, open, and candid a manner as possible.

All dyads then participated in interviews in which the hypothesis-testers asked the 12 questions that they had chosen and the targets answered these 12 questions. These interviews were conducted by means of microphones and headphones connected through a stereophonic tape recorder. All interviews were tape-recorded, with each participant's voice on a separate channel of tape. To assess the extent to which the answers of the targets provided actual behavioral confirmation for the attributes of the hypothesis-testers' hypotheses, a panel of naive judges listened to tape recordings of the interviews. These listener-judges heard *only* the track of the tape containing the targets' voices, and rated each target on a variety of attributes associated with extraversion and introversion: for example, talkative–quiet; unsociable–sociable; friendly–unfriendly; poised–awkward; introverted–extraverted; enthusiastic–apathetic; shy–outgoing; energetic–relaxed; cold–warm; and unconfident–confident.

It is now possible to chart processes of hypothesis testing in social interaction. Consider, first, the effects of the hypothesis-testers' hypotheses on the hypothesis-testing strategies formulated by the hypothesis testers and, then, on the targets' behavioral self-presentation during the interviews, as measured by the listener-judges' evaluations of the tape recordings. By now, it should come as no surprise to learn that hypothesis-testers formulated confirmatory strategies to test hypotheses about their targets' natures. In accord with this strategy, hypothesis-testers chose to ask extravert-questions more frequently when planning a strategy to test the hypothesis that their targets were extraverted individuals than when formulating a strategy to test the hypothesis that their targets were introverted individuals. Moreover, hypothesis-testers chose to ask introvert-questions more frequently when planning a strategy to test the hypothesis that their targets were introverts than when preparing to test the hypothesis that their targets were extraverts.

These hypothesis-testers attempted to evaluate the accuracy of their hypotheses about their targets by preferentially soliciting evidence whose presence would tend to confirm their hypotheses. And, indeed, during the interview the targets provided precisely the behavioral evidence that would appear to confirm the hypotheses being tested by the hypothesis-testers. For, the listener-judges' ratings of the targets' contributions to the interviews provided clear evidence that targets hypothesized to be extraverts actually presented themselves in more extraverted fashion than did targets hypothesized to be introverts. Evidently, the targets' answers to the hypothesis-testers' questions did provide actual behavioral confirmation for the hypotheses being tested by the hypothesis-testers. Moreover, it should be recalled that these behavioral differences were detectable by naive listener-judges who had access *only* to tape-recordings of the targets' contributions to the interviews.

As a consequence of the confirmatory strategies used by the hypothesis-testers to gather evidence with which to test their hypotheses, targets presented themselves in ways that provided actual behavioral confirmation. But, did the hypothesis-testers regard their hypotheses as having been confirmed by the target's actions? Apparently so. For, when all was said and done, the experimenter (during the post-experimental debriefing session) asked hypothesis-testers what they had learned about their targets' characteristic nature. Those who had tested the hypothesis that their targets were extraverts, on the average, regarded their targets as more extraverted by nature than did their counterparts who had tested the hypothesis that their targets were introverts.

The sequential outcomes of this experimental investigation provide empirical documentation for each and every stage of the unfolding drama of the hypothesis-testing process in social interaction: the hypothesis-tester's formulation of confirmatory strategies, the hypothesis-tester's use of confirmatory data-gathering procedures in social interaction with the target of the hypothesis, and the target's behavioral confirmation of the hypothesis being tested. In light of this demonstration of the self-confirming nature of hypotheses about other people, it becomes easier to understand why so many popular beliefs about other people (in particular, clearly erroneous social and cultural stereotypes) are so stubbornly resistant to change. Even if one were to develop sufficient doubt about the accuracy of these beliefs to proceed to actively test them, one nevertheless might be likely to gather all the evidence one needs to confirm and retain these beliefs. And, in the end, one may be left with the secure (but totally unwarranted) feeling that these beliefs must be correct because they have survived (what may seem to the individual) perfectly appropriate and even rigorous procedures for assessing their accuracy.

The "Professional" Hypothesis-Tester

The adoption of confirmatory hypothesis-testing strategies, and the interpersonal consequences that accompnay them, may not be limited to everyday attempts to understand the personalities of people with whom one interacts. In their professional activities, many individuals routinely interview others to test hypotheses about their natures. Employers interview job candidates to test hypotheses about their suitability for particular jobs (e.g., Does this applicant have the attributes that define the ideal executive?). Clinical psychologists and psychiatrists interview their clients to test hypotheses about the links between their past experiences and their current complaints (e.g., Does this person have the background that typically yields psychosomatic disorders?).

Consider the case of interactions between clinicians and their clients. There has been considerable concern with the extent to which clients' behaviors come to match the conceptual frameworks and theoretical orientations of their therapists (cf. Frank, 1974; Scheff, 1966). Somehow, therapists elicit from their clients material confirming their views. Accordingly, client values come to match those of their therapists (cf. Bandura, Lipsher, & Miller, 1960; Rosenthal, 1955; Welkowitz, Cohen, & Ortmeyer, 1967). Even the dreams that clients report come to contain increasing amounts of "approved" material (cf. Whitman, Kramer, & Baldridge, 1963). Accordingly, the kinds of improvement reported by clients tend to confirm the therapists' theoretical orientation. Patients in psychoanalysis express increasing amounts of formerly "unconscious" material as therapy progresses (Frank, 1974). By contrast, those individuals who improve in client-centered therapy report reduced discrepancies between their real self and their ideal self, which is precisely the change predicted by the theory underlying this form of treatment (Rogers & Dymond, 1954).

A similar view of the relationship between physician and client also has been suggested by Balint (1957). According to Balint, every doctor has a "theory" of how a patient ought to behave when sick. Furthermore, Balint (1957) claims that these beliefs exert powerful influences on all aspects of the doctor's activities with patients: "It was almost as if every doctor had revealed knowledge of what was right and what was wrong for patients to expect and to endure and further, as if he had a sacred duty to convert to his faith all the ignorant and unbelieving among his patients [p. 216]." It is this process that Balint has christened the "apostolic" mission of medicine.

Research on hypothesis-testing in social interaction may suggest the processes by which such outcomes may be generated. Having diagnosed the client's "problem," the therapist may selectively and preferentially solicit confirming evidence. This activity may be guided by a hypothesis about what kinds of "backgrounds" lead up to what kinds of current "problems." For example, the psychiatrist who believes (erroneously) that adult gay males had bad childhood relationships with their mothers may meticulously probe for recalled (or fabricated) signs of tension between their gay clients and their mothers, but neglect to so carefully interrogate their heterosexual clients about their maternal relationships. No doubt, any individual could recall some friction with his or her mother, however minor or isolated the incidents.

The point is that all individuals have childhood histories with events and experiences that could "account for" aspects of their adult lifestyles in need of "explanation." Yet, a search for the past that explains the present is only done when some contemporary event needs a historical explanation. Accordingly, "searchers" don't realize the extent to which their hypotheses would be confirmed even when there was no current problem to be explained. As evidence for this proposition, consider the study of Renaud and Estess (1961) who conducted life history interviews with 100 men chosen precisely because their adult lives gave no indications whatsoever of "problems." These men were in excellent health, were occupationally and educationally superior in their accomplishments, had no histories of mental or psychological conflict, complained of no problems of personal, social, marital, or occupational adjustment.

But with what kinds of events and experiences were the childhood histories of these "normal" individuals filled? Quite simply, the childhood histories of these men were laden with the kinds of "traumatic events" and "pathogenic factors" that are found ordinarily in the histories of psychiatric patients who are disabled by their symptoms. In fact, Renaud and Estess (1961) found that the life histories of these 100 "normals" were rife with:

> overt parental discord as seen in divorce or separation; covert parental discord as manifested in lengthy periods of withdrawal; seclusiveness or lack of mutuality; excessively rigid or overindulgent patterns of discipline, or both; resolution of oedipal anxieties through overidentification with one parent to the exclusion of the other; unresolved sibling rivalries; repressive and unrealistic approaches to sexual information and sexual practices; frequent maternal physical complaints of a type recognized today as related to tension and conflict [p. 795].

In short, as Renaud and Estess (1961) observed: "these data abound with material such as we are accustomed to encounter in the histories of psychiatric patients [p. 795]." In fact, Renaud and Estess quite candidly admitted that, had these men come to them complaining of "colitis, ulcers, phobias, work inhibitions, incapacitating shyness, etc. [p. 795]," they would have found no trouble finding evidence of the "background factors" that are supposed to predispose one to these problems. Of course, these men did not suffer from any of these problems, so (other than for purposes of a research investigation into the pathogenicity of the childhoods of apparent "normals") no one would ever have bothered to probe into their backgrounds. As long as one only probes into the backgrounds of "troubled" adults, it will be all too easy to blame any and all contemporary problems on whatever "pathogenic" background is demanded by one's hypothesis that links current symptoms and historical causes.

HYPOTHESIS TESTING:
A THEORETICAL ANALYSIS

The time has come to consider, from a theoretical perspective, the processes that might underlie and generate the hypothesis-testing strategies documented in our empirical investigations. Why do individuals preferentially solicit evidence whose presence would tend to confirm their hypotheses about other people? The following theoretical analysis is an attempt to account for why individuals are so pervasively and stubbornly committed to confirmatory hypothesis-testing strategies. The central theses of this analysis are quite simply that: (1) the processes of human thought foster, promote, and almost ensure the ready and willing adoption of confirmatory strategies by hypothesis-testers, and (2) the structural organization of human social behavior almost guarantees that targets can and will display a vast repertoire of hypothesis-confirming actions.

Consider the perspective of an individual who is contemplating a hypothesis about another person in anticipation of testing the accuracy of that hypothesis. This individual's choice of a hypothesis-testing strategy, no doubt, reflects beliefs about what types of evidence are particularly relevant and informative for purposes of accepting or rejecting the hypothesis under scrutiny. There is every reason to believe that this individual will believe that it is the presence of confirming evidence that is particularly informative and relevant for purposes of hypothesis testing. That is, he or she most likely operates with an implicit "philosophy of science" that dictates that hypotheses about other people survive according to their ability to accumulate confirming evidence.

Considerable evidence from the research literature on logical reasoning supports this assertion. In research on concept formation and concept utilization, people prefer and use positive instances of concepts over negative ones (cf. Hovland & Weiss, 1953). Moreover, confirming instances generally have more impact on inductive conclusions than do disconfirming instances (cf. Gollob, Rossman, & Abelson, 1973); and, covariation between positive instances leads to estimates of greater relationships than does covariation between negative or mixed instances (cf. Jenkins & Ward, 1965; Smedslund, 1963). Furthermore, in judgments of similarity, individuals preferentially look for common features rather than distinctive features (e.g., Tversky, 1977). Similarly, investigations of logical reasoning (e.g., Wason & Johnson-Laird, 1972) show that, in attempting to decide whether general propositions (e.g., all Norwegian men are handsome) are true, individuals almost always look for instances that could verify the proposition (e.g., Norwegian men who are handsome) and almost never look for falsifying instances (e.g., nonhandsome men who are Norwegian). Even researchers in the behavioral sciences tend to design empirical investigations that seek to confirm, rather than to disconfirm, their hypotheses (Greenwald, 1975; Mahoney, 1976). Finally, people in general experience considerable difficulty in understanding and making valid and permissible inferences from negative propositions (cf. Clark & Clark, 1977).

Generalizing from these diverse investigations on reasoning and comprehension, it seems that individuals regard confirming evidence as more relevant than disconfirming evidence in testing hypotheses about other people. In fact, direct tests of this proposition are provided by the research of Snyder and Cantor (1979). In two separate investigations, individuals read an account of events in 1 week in the life of a woman named Jane. This narrative provided them with an extensive store of historical information about Jane's actions in different situations and with different people over a period of time. Thus, participants in those experiments had the opportunity to learn about Jane's activities when she was alone and with others, when she interacted with strangers and with friends, when she was at work and when she was in social situations, etc. The story intentionally contained instances of Jane behaving in clearly extraverted and introverted fashion. Jane's extraverted and introverted actions occurred in different situations and at different times during the week chronicled in the story. Thus, for example, Jane eagerly engaged in animated conversation with another patient in the doctor's office, but refrained from socializing with some acquaintances during a coffee-break at the office. In fact, there were equal numbers of extraverted and introverted actions in the story.

Two days later, participants were provided with hypotheses about Jane: They received either the hypothesis that she was well suited to apply for a job that required the personal attributes of a prototypic extravert, or the hypothesis that she was well suited to apply for a job that required the personal attributes of a prototypic introvert. Participants then were required to report from memory all those facts that they had previously learned from the story that they regarded as *relevant* to deciding whether Jane was well suited to apply for the job under consideration. Participants preferentially reported as relevant those facts that would tend to *confirm* their hypotheses. Participants asked to report factual information relevant to testing the hypothesis that Jane was an extravert were particularly likely to report instances of Jane behaving in accord with their construct of the prototypic extravert. By contrast, participants asked to report factual information relevant to testing the hypothesis that Jane was an introvert were particularly likely to report instances of Jane behaving in accord with their construct of the prototypic introvert. This outcome occurred despite the fact that all participants had access to equivalent amounts of hypothesis-confirming and hypothesis-disconfirming evidence that they had learned before they were provided with any hypotheses about Jane.

Evidently, as the investigations of Snyder and Cantor (1979) suggest, people do believe that the presence of confirming evidence is particularly relevant and informative for purposes of testing hypotheses about others. (See Snyder and Campbell (1979) for other investigations of the hypothesis-tester's beliefs about the relevance and informativeness of different types of evidence.) Moreover, individuals seem to define the task of testing a hypothesis as one of building the case in support of that hypothesis by preferentially accumulating evidence whose presence would confirm the hypothesis under scrutiny (cf. Snyder & Cantor, 1979). Accordingly, in anticipating the behavior of the target, the hypothesis-tester may be much more likely to think of instances in which the target behaves in accord with the hypothesis than to think of instances in which the target violates the hypothesis. In so doing, the individual may draw upon richly detailed and well-articulated conceptions of prototypic personality types (e.g., the prototypic extravert, the prototypic introvert, etc.) for knowledge of specific behavioral manifestations of global personality attributes (cf. Cantor & Mischel, 1977). Thus, an individual who anticipates interaction with a target hypothesized to be an extravert may bring to mind all those actions by which a hypothetical extravert might manifest an extraverted disposition.

If representations of the target behaviorally confirming the individual's hypothesis are more cognitively "available" than representations of the target violating the hypothesis, then there is every reason to believe that the individual will overestimate the likelihood that the target will, in fact, behave in ways that confirm the hypothesis. Considerable evidence suggests that individuals use "availability" as a heuristic for estimating frequency: Events that are easy to bring to mind are thought to occur with greater frequency than events that are difficult to bring to mind (cf. Tversky & Kahneman, 1973). If so, by virtue of contemplating the forthcoming interaction with the target in the light of the hypothesis, the individual not only will regard confirming evidence as particularly relevant for testing the hypothesis but also will believe that these hypothesis-confirming actions will occur in great numbers and that these hypothesis-confirming behaviors will be representative of the target's true personal nature (cf. Ross, Lepper, Strack, & Steinmetz, 1977).

To the extent that the individual believes that hypothesis-confirming behaviors are *both* relevant to the hypothesis-testing task *and* typical of the target's activities, he or she may consider it not unreasonable to confine the conversation to those topics about which the target can provide the most informative and meaningful facts. Accordingly, an individual may use social interaction as an opportunity to preferentially solicit evidence that confirms the hypothesis under consideration.

Such a preferential evidence-gathering procedure may generate a sample of evidence in which hypothesis-confirming evidence will be over-represented and hypothesis-disconfirming evidence will be under-represented: There is every reason to believe that most people, as targets, will be "generous" in providing specific instances of hypothesis-confirming actions. There is sufficient situation-to-situation variability in human social behavior that most people about whom hypotheses are tested will have behaved, in some situations and at some times, consistently with the hypothesis under consideration (c.f. Mischel, 1968). However, these same people probably will have behaved, in other situations and at other times, in ways that would tend to disconfirm that same hypothesis. Accordingly, to the extent that the individual preferentially solicits hypothesis-confirming instances of the target's behavior, such a data-gathering procedure will be particularly successful in generating a sample of data in which confirming evidence is over-represented and in which disconfirming evidence is under-represented. Of course, it will be this sample of data upon which the individual will base the decision to accept or reject the hypothesis in question. Accordingly, the individual may accept this hypothesis more readily than the actual events in the target's life truly warrant.

HYPOTHESIS TESTING AND THE
SOCIAL NATURE OF SOCIAL KNOWLEDGE

Confirmatory hypothesis-testing strategies and their consequences are not confined to the domain of hypotheses about the personal attributes of other people. Indeed, the same preferential search for confirming evidence that characterizes attempts to test hypotheses about the world of people seems to characterize attempts to test hypotheses about the world of objects. In their attempts to establish the truth or falsity of general "if . . . then" propositions, people overwhelmingly search for specific instances that would verify the truth of the proposition and neglect to search for instances that would falsify the proposition under consideration. For example, had you participated in an experiment described by Wason and Johnson-Laird (1972):

> four cards would have been placed in front of you, showing the following symbols:
>
> E   K   4   7
>
> You know that each of these cards has a letter on one of its sides and a number on its other side, and you are then presented with the following rule which refers only to the four cards:
>
> *If a card has a vowel on one side, then it has an even number on the other side.*
>
> Your task is to name those cards, and only those cards, which need to be turned over in order to determine whether the rule is true or false [p. 173].

Almost without exception, in such circumstances, problem-solvers say either *"E and 4"* or *"only E."* Both answers are wrong. The correct answer is *"E and 7."* Any odd number on the other side of E *falsifies* or disconfirms the rule in precisely the same fashion as does any vowel on the other side of the *7*. Time and again in their investigations of problem solving, Wason and Johnson-Laird (1972) have observed seemingly intelligent individuals (including professional logicians) attempt to determine whether rules are true or false by searching only for evidence that could verify or confirm the truth of the rule at the same time as they neglected to search for more logically compelling evidence that could falsify or disconfirm the truth of the rule. Thus, participants seem not to understand that no matter how many confirming instances one has discovered, it still takes only one disconfirming instance to falsify the rule. Thus even with an even number on the other side of *E* and a vowel on the flip side of *4*, the "if vowel... then even" rule would still be falsified by a vowel on the other side of *7*.

In their logical reasoning, individuals in experiments devised by Wason and Johnson-Laird (1972) appear to fall victim to the cognitive processes described centuries ago by Sir Francis Bacon:

> The human understanding, when any proposition has been laid down, ... forces everything else to add fresh support and confirmation ... it is the peculiar and perpetual error of the human understanding to be more moved and excited by affirmatives than negatives, whereas it ought duly and regularly to be impartial; *nay in establishing any true axiom the negative instance is the most powerful* [1620/1853, emphasis added]

There is, on first consideration, a striking similarity between the activities of individuals assigned to test hypotheses about letters, numbers, and other attributes of physical reality and the activities of individuals assigned to test hypotheses about extraversion, introversion, and other attributes of social reality. In either case, individuals formulate and enact confirmatory strategies for testing their hypotheses. In either case, the adoption of confirmatory strategies increases the likelihood that hypotheses will be confirmed erroneously by the evidence generated by those strategies. Yet, the similarities may be only superficial ones. Although the strategies adopted may appear to be similar, the consequences of these strategies are strikingly different in the two domains. And, it is these differing consequences that make social reality and the world of people fundamentally and inherently different from physical reality and the world of objects.

To appreciate the differing consequences of confirmatory strategies for testing hypotheses about objects and about people, one must look not to what people *do* (that is, to the confirmatory strategies that they formulate and enact) but rather to what people do *not do* (that is, to the disconfirmatory strategies that they do not formulate and enact). There is no doubt that a disconfirmatory strategy (that is, one that preferentially searches for disconfirming evidence) is the logically appropriate one for problems of the type devised by Wason and Johnson-Laird

(1972). If individuals searched for instances that would falsify or disconfirm hypothetical rules, they would be less likely to accept erroneous propositions about events in the physical world.

But, what would happen if individuals assigned experimentally to test hypotheses about the personalities of other people were to adopt disconfirmatory strategies for testing their hypotheses? In such a strategy, individuals preferentially solicit evidence that disconfirms or invalidates their hypotheses. Thus, with a disconfirmatory strategy, an individual given the task of determining whether or not another person was an extravert would choose questions typically asked of individuals already known to be introverts. Similarly, another individual would attempt to determine whether or not the target was an introvert by choosing questions typically asked of individuals already known to be extraverts.

Were such disconfirmatory strategies enacted in social interaction, the outcome, of course, would be *behavioral disconfirmation*. Interviewers testing the hypothesis that their targets were extraverts would create targets who presented themselves in relatively introverted fashion. Interviewers testing the hypothesis that their targets were introverts would create targets who presented themselves in relatively extraverted fashion. As a consequence of hypothesis-testers having adopted disconfirmatory strategies, targets would come to behave in ways that erroneously *disconfirm* the hypotheses under scrutiny.

Apparently, for purposes of testing hypotheses in social interaction, disconfirmatory strategies are no less reactive (i.e., constraining of the outcomes of hypothesis-testing) than are confirmatory strategies. The only difference is that, whereas confirmatory strategies will yield hypothesis-confirming outcomes too frequently, disconfirmatory strategies will generate hypothesis-disconfirming outcomes too frequently. Why is a search for disconfirming evidence a nonreactive (or unconstraining) strategy in the case of testing the truth of logical propositions but a highly reactive (or constraining) strategy in the case of testing the accuracy of hypotheses about people? The answer, quite simply, is that *people are not objects*. Objects, and accordingly the truth value of propositions about them, exist independently of our transactions with them. There will or will not be even numbers on the other side of cards with vowels on their faces no matter which cards I choose to examine to determine whether the rule is correct.

However, the nature of social reality is somewhat different from that of physical reality. The behavior of other people is very much a product of our own actions toward them. How others present themselves to us is, in large measure, a product of how we first treat them. If I preferentially probe for instances of your friendly and sociable actions, I will see and hear a rather different ''you'' than if I preferentially probe for instances of your shy and retiring actions. In general, to the extent that an individual preferentially solicits instances from one domain of behavior and experience in an attempt to test a hypothesis about another person, such instances will be over-represented in that person's self-presentation.

But what of the potential for a nonreactive strategy of hypothesis testing in social interaction? It should be clear by now that both the confirmatory strategy and the disconfirmatory strategy are highly reactive procedures for testing hypotheses about other people. It should be readily apparent too that an "equal-opportunity" strategy of sampling representatively from the domain of confirming and disconfirming evidence is no less reactive a strategy. If participants in a typical experiment on hypothesis testing were to ask equal numbers of extravert- and introvert-questions, they would only succeed in providing their targets with equal opportunities to appear extraverted and introverted. "Half and half" interview strategies would succeed only in creating "half and half" people.

In fact, any hypothesis-testing strategy that involves actual social interaction will be, by the very nature of the involvement of the hypothesis-tester with the target, a reactive strategy. Whatever actions the hypothesis-tester takes toward the target, they will serve to constrain and channel the target's behavior. Perhaps, the only procedure for faithfully testing a hypothesis is to observe a target who is unaware of being observed. Ideally, the hypothesis-tester would observe the target in interaction with a wide variety of other individuals who might have diverse hypotheses and beliefs about the target and attempt to "average" the target's self-presentation in these diverse contexts. Such a sleuth-like approach seems unlikely to be adopted on a wide scale.

These considerations of the reactive nature of the procedures by which individuals test hypotheses about other people, as well as the differences between testing hypotheses about objects and testing hypotheses about people, help to make clearer just what it is that is inherently and fundamentally social about *social* knowledge. Investigations of hypothesis-testing processes in social interaction serve to sensitize us to the links between the domain of thought and the domain of action. To the extent that individuals chronically formulate and enact confirmatory strategies for assessing the accuracy of their hypotheses and beliefs about other people, they create for themselves a world in which hypotheses become self-confirming and beliefs become self-perpetuating. (For other demonstrations of the self-perpetuating nature of beliefs, see Snyder, 1981; Snyder & Swann, 1978a; Snyder, Tanke, & Berscheid, 1977; Snyder & Uranowitz, 1978.)

The outcomes of investigations of the terpersonal consequences of beliefs suggest that beliefs can and do create social reality: The very events of the social world (specifically, the behaviors of others with whom we interact in social relationships) may be reflections and products of our images of the social world (specifically, our beliefs, hypotheses, and theories about other people). Social knowledge is *social* knowledge precisely because of its intimate involvement in the construction of social reality in ongoing relationships. This, of course, means that social thought cannot be studied meaningfully in static circumstances of minimal personal involvement. This approach prevents us from witnessing the intimate interplay between social knowledge and social behavior in ongoing interpersonal relationships. Instead, cognitively oriented social psychologists ought to attend to the influence of thought on the unfolding dynamics of continuing sequences of social interaction. Only then can a cognitive social psychology be a truly *social* psychology. For, it is as if the events of social interaction and interpersonal relationships are the stage on which the unfolding drama of the structure and process of human social thought are played out and revealed to interested spectators.

ACKNOWLEDGMENTS

This research and the preparation of this manuscript were supported in part by National Science Foundation Grants SOC 75-13872, "Cognition and Behavior: When Belief Creates Reality," and BNS 77-11346, "From Belief to Reality: Cognitive, Behavioral, and Interpersonal Consequences of Social Perception," to Mark Snyder. For their comments on the manuscript, many thanks to Terri Amabile, Mike Ross, Lee Ross, and Mark Zanna.

REFERENCES

Bacon, F. [*Novum organum.*] In J. Devey (Ed. and trans.), *The physical and metaphysical works of Lord Bacon.* London: Henry G. Bohn, 1853. (Originally published, 1620.)

Balint, M. *The doctor, his patient, and the illness.* New York: International Universities Press, 1957.

Bandura, A., Lipsher, D. H., & Miller, P. E. Psychotherapists' approach-avoidance reactions to patients' expressions of hostility. *Journal of Consulting Psychology*, 1960, *24*, 1–8.

Cantor, N., & Mischel, W. Traits as prototypes: Effects on recognition memory. *Journal of Personality and Social Psychology*, 1977, *35*, 38–48.

Clark, H. H., & Clark, E. V. *Psychology and language: An introduction to psycholinguistics.* New York: Harcourt Brace Jovanovich, Inc., 1977.

Frank, J. D. *Persuasion and healing.* New York: Schocken Books, 1974.

Gollob, H. F., Rossman, B. B., & Abelson, R. P. Social inference as a function of the number of instances and consistency of information presented. *Journal of Personality and Social Psychology*, 1973, *27*, 19–33.

Greenwald, A. G. Consequences of prejudice against the null hypothesis. *Psychological Bulletin*, 1975, *82*, 1–20.

Hovland, C. I., & Weiss, W. Transmission of information concerning concepts through positive and negative instances. *Journal of Experimental Psychology*, 1953, *45*, 175–182.

Jenkins, H. M., & Ward, W. C. Judgment of contingency between responses and outcomes. *Psychological Monographs*, 1965, *79*, (1, Whole No. 594).

Mahoney, M. J. *Scientist as subject: The psychological imperative.* Cambridge, Mass.: Ballinger, 1976.

Mischel, W. *Personality and assessment.* New York: Wiley, 1968.

Renaud, H., & Estess, F. Life history interviews with one hundred normal American males: "Pathogenicity" of childhood. *American Journal of Orthopsychiatry*, 1961, *31*, 796–802.

Rogers, C. R., & Dymond, R. (Eds.), *Psychotherapy and personality change.* Chicago: University of Chicago Press, 1954.

Rosenthal, D. Changes in some moral values following psychotherapy. *Journal of Consulting Psychology*, 1955, *19*, 431–436.

Ross, L., Lepper, M. R., Strack, F., & Steinmetz, J. Social explanation and social expectation: Effects of real and hypothetical explanations on subjective likelihood. *Journal of Personality and Social Psychology,* 1977, *35,* 817–829.

Scheff, T. J. *Being mentally ill: A sociological theory.* Chicago: Aldine, 1966.

Smedslund, J. The concept of correlation in adults. *Scandinavian Journal of Psychology,* 1963, *4,* 165–173.

Snyder, M. On the self-perpetuating nature of social stereotypes. In D. L. Hamilton (Ed.), *Cognitive processes in stereotyping and intergroup behavior.* Hillsdale, N.J.: Lawrence Erlbaum Associates, 1981.

Snyder, M., & Campbell, B. H. *Testing hypotheses about other people: The hypothesis-tester's philosophy of science.* Unpublished manuscript, University of Minnesota, 1979.

Snyder, M., & Campbell, B. H. Testing hypotheses about other people: The role of the hypothesis. *Personality and Social Psychology Bulletin,* 1980, *6,* 421–426.

Snyder, M., & Cantor, N. Testing hypotheses about other people: The use of historical knowledge. *Journal of Experimental Social Psychology,* 1979, *15,* 330–342.

Snyder, M., & Skrypnek, B. J. *Testing hypotheses about the self:* Assessments of job suitability. Unpublished manuscript, University of Minnesota, 1979.

Snyder, M., & Swann, W. B., Jr. Unpublished data, University of Minnesota, 1977. (a)

Snyder, M., & Swann, W. B., Jr. Unpublished data, University of Minnesota, 1977. (b)

Snyder, M., & Swann, W. B., Jr. Behavioral confirmation in social interaction: From social perception to social reality. *Journal of Experimental Social Psychology,* 1978, *14,* 148–162. (a)

Snyder, M., & Swann, W. B., Jr. Hypothesis-testing processes in social interaction. *Journal of Personality and Social Psychology,* 1978b, *36,* 1202–1212. (b)

Snyder, M., Tanke, E. D., & Berscheid, E. Social perception and interpersonal behavior: On the self-fulfilling nature of social stereotypes. *Journal of Personality and Social Psychology,* 1977, *35,* 656–666.

Snyder, M., & Uranowitz, S. W. Reconstructing the past: Some cognitive consequences of person perception. *Journal of Personality and Social Psychology,* 1978, *36,* 941–950.

Snyder, M., & White, P. Unpublished data, University of Minnesota, 1978.

Tversky, A. Features of similarity. *Psychological Review,* 1977, *84,* 327–352.

Tversky, A., & Kahneman, D. Availability: A heuristic for judging frequency and probability. *Cognitive Psychology.* 1973, *5,* 207–232.

Wason, P. C., & Johnson-Laird, P. N. *Psychology of reasoning: Structure and content.* London: D. T. Batsford, 1972.

Welkowitz, J., Cohen, J., & Ortmeyer, D. Value system similarity: Investigation of patient–therapist dyads. *Journal of Consulting Psychology,* 1967, *31,* 48–55.

Whitman, R. M., Kramer, M., & Baldridge, B. Which dream does the patient tell? *Archives of General Psychiatry,* 1963, *8,* 277–282.

9 # Self-centered Biases in Attributions of Responsibility: Antecedents and Consequences

Michael Ross
University of Waterloo

> *The altogether unique kind of interest each human mind feels in those parts of creation which it can call me or mine may be a moral riddle, but it is a fundamental psychological fact. No mind can take the same interest in his neighbor's me as in his own. The neighbor's me falls together with all the rest of things in one foreign mass, against which his own me stands out in startling relief.*
>
> —William James (1890/1950, p. 289).

Social and business relationships often demand joint decision making and coordinated group action. In this chapter, I am concerned with systematic biases in attributions of responsibility that may be associated with such activities. Specifically, I suggest that allocations of responsibility for a group product tend to be self-centered: Individuals take more credit than other participants attribute to them.

Misunderstandings stemming from joint efforts in science provide anecdotal evidence of this bias. Consider: You have collaborated on a research project with a student or faculty member; the question arises as to who should be "first author" on the publication (i.e., Who contributed more to the final product?). Often, it seems to be the case that both of you feel entirely justified in claiming that honor. Moreover, because you are convinced that your memory of each participant's contributions must be shared by your colleague (there being only one reality), it is naturally assumed that the other person is deliberately attempting to take advantage of you.

In the history of science, there are many instances of such disputes. For example, in 1923 two Canadians, Banting and Macleod, were awarded the Nobel prize for their discovery of insulin. Upon receiving the prize, Banting contended that Macleod, who was head of the laboratory, had been more of a hinderance than a help. On the other hand, Macleod managed to omit Banting's name in speeches describing the research leading up to the discovery of insulin (Harris, 1946). In recent years there have been similar disputes, including a rancorous debate over Roslynd Franklin's contribution to the unraveling of D.N.A. (Sayre, 1975).

Although examples of disagreements among scientists are well documented, the prevalence of the phenomenon remains unclear. It is my suspicion that scientists are not aberrant (at least in this regard); self-centered perceptions of responsibility are likely following any joint venture. What is, perhaps, unique about science is the need to rank-order authorship, with its ensuing professional implications. This requirement is generally lacking in the more casual, joint endeavors that occur in everyday life. Consequently, participants may remain unaware of their discrepant views, and the ubiquity of egocentric biases in attributions of responsibility is not apparent.

Nor is the basis of the phenomenon evident. The participants in scientific disputes frequently attribute a divergence in opinion to their opponent's malevolence. This may well be a valid interpretation. Some individuals are likely to cheat and lie when the stakes are high, for example, when Nobel prizes are at issue. Certainly, the image of the scientist, dispassionate and objective, unyielding in his commitment to discovering the truth, has taken a beating in recent years (Mahoney, 1976).

Conceivably the source of the conflict often resides elsewhere, however. Perceptions may be at variance even in the absence of deliberate deceit. As a result, self-centered judgments of responsibility may occur in relatively mundane settings where the participants seem well intentioned and the extrinsic benefits are less apparent.

In the present chapter, I assess the pervasiveness of a self-centered bias in attributions of responsibility and discuss its antecedents and consequences. The ultimate goal is to understand a particular dynamic of social interaction that may promote conflict and misunderstanding among group members.

PERVASIVENESS OF SELF-CENTERED BIASES
IN JUDGMENTS OF RESPONSIBILITY

Fiore Sicoly and I conducted research with two quite different subject populations to assess the ubiquity of biases in attributions of responsibility: (1) ongoing social relationships; and (2) ad hoc groups (Ross & Sicoly, 1979). We obtained strong evidence of self-centered biases in judgments of responsibility in both settings.

In one experiment, spouses were asked to estimate their responsibility for 20 activities relevant to married couples (e.g., cleaning house, caring for children, planning leisure activities, making important decisions that affect both individuals, causing conflicts). As expected, individuals tended to accept more responsibility for these activities than their spouses attributed to them. Similarly, in a laboratory experiment on decision making, subjects reported that they had exerted much greater control over the course and content of the discussion than their coparticipants ascribed to them (Ross & Sicoly, 1979, Experiment 4). As anticipated, then, judgments of responsibility for everyday activities may be self-centered; further, the bias is found in close, as well as in transitory, relationships.

How does the group's level of performance affect members' attributions of responsibility? Ross and Sicoly (1979) found that judgments of responsibility were self-centered when no explicit performance feedback was provided. Moreover, spouses evinced self-centered biases even on negatively evaluated items (eg., causing conflicts that occur between both individuals). On the other hand, there is considerable evidence that people accept less responsibility for a failure than for a success (eg., Miller & Ross, 1975; Schlenker & Miller, 1977). As a result, judgments of responsibility are likely to be less self-centered when the group outcome is clearly inferior.

DETERMINANTS OF THE SELF-CENTERED BIAS IN JUDGMENTS OF RESPONSIBILITY

What processes mediate self-centered judgments of responsibility? In attempting to answer this question, it is difficult not to implicate memory. To allocate responsibility for a joint endeavor, well-intentioned participants presumably attempt to recall the contributions each made to the final product. (Actually the assessment may be ongoing; nonetheless, assuming an end-point tallying simplifies discussion and does not distort the concepts and processes.) Some aspects of the interaction may be recalled more readily, or be more available, than others, however. Specifically, individuals may recall a greater proportion of their own contributions than of the contributions of other participants. There are at least two general processes that may be operating to increase the availability of one's own contributions: (1) selective encoding and retrieval of information; and (2) informational disparities.

Selective Encoding and Retrieval

For a number of reasons, the availability of the person's own inputs may be facilitated by differential encoding and storage of self-generated responses. First, individuals' own thoughts (about what they are going to say next, daydreams, etc.) or actions may distract their attention from the contributions of others.

Second, individuals may rehearse or repeat their own ideas or actions; for example, they might think out their position before verbalizing and defending it. Consequently, their own inputs may receive more "study time," and degree of retention is strongly related to study time (Carver, 1972). Third, encoding and retrieval may be biased by expectancies. Perhaps individuals enter endeavors with Walter Mitty fantasies: They may expect to contribute more than their coparticipants (e.g., lead their team to victory); at the very minimum, their self-expectations may exceed the expectations others hold for them. Such exalted expectations can have many sources, including previous experiences that justify these hopes, or wishful thinking. One possible consequence, though, is that the divergent expectations of self and others may produce enhanced encoding of, and memory for, self-generated inputs. Nisbett and L. Ross (1980), Taylor and Crocker (Chapter 3, this volume), and Snyder (Chapter 8, this volume) have recently documented how theories or expectations can guide encoding and retrieval of information so as to produce confirmation of these theories.

Finally, motivational factors may mediate biases in storage and retrieval. One's sense of self-esteem may be enhanced by focusing on, or weighting more heavily, one's own inputs (cf. Miller & Ross, 1975). Similarly, a concern for personal efficacy (deCharms, 1968; White, 1959) could lead individuals to dwell on their own contributions to a joint product and, hence, bias encoding and recall.

Informational Disparities

There may also be differences in the information available to participants in a joint endeavor. Individuals have greater access to their own thoughts and strategies than do observers. Further, participants in a common enterprise may differ in their knowledge of the frequency and significance of each other's independent contributions. Enhanced recall of self-generated inputs could well be the result of such informational disparities.

AVAILABILITY AND JUDGMENTS
OF RESPONSIBILITY

The preceding discussion outlines a number of factors that may be operating to render one's own outputs more available and more likely to be recalled than the inputs of others. A self-centered bias in availability, in turn, could produce biased attributions of responsibility for a joint product. As Tversky and Kahneman (1973) have demonstrated, people use availability, that is "the ease with which relevant instances come to mind [p. 209]," as a basis for estimating frequency. Thus, if self-generated inputs are, indeed, more available, they should be judged to be more frequent; and, as a result, individuals should claim more responsibility for a mutual product than other participants would attribute to them.

To assess availability, Sicoly and I obtained subjects' recall of their own and of the other participants' inputs to joint endeavors (Ross & Sicoly, 1979). Thus, the married couples in the experiment described earlier were asked to report instances of the contributions made by each spouse to the various activities. As anticipated, subjects dwelled on their own behaviors, an indication that their own inputs to these activities were more available. Similarly, members of laboratory dyads reported more of their own statements than of their partner's when they were required to provide verbatim recall of past discussions.

Does the availability bias occur only when the group product is evaluated positively? The answer is a qualified *no*. Verbatim memory for group problem-solving discussions was self-centered even when the subjects were led to believe that their dyads' solutions were of poor quality. Negative feedback did reduce the extent of the bias, however (Ross & Sicoly, 1979, Experiment 2).

Finally, there is also some evidence in support of the hypothesized causal relation between the bias in recall and the bias in judgments of responsibility. The two biases were significantly correlated in the study with married couples: The greater the tendency to recall self-relevant behavior, the greater the overestimation in perceived responsibility, $r(35) = .50$, $p < .01$.

The causal relation was assessed more directly in an experiment on selective retrieval of information from memory. Graduate students were prompted to think either about their own contributions to their B.A. theses or about the contributions of their supervisors. The students were induced to engage in such differing retrieval by variations in the form in which questions were posed. In the self-focus condition subjects were asked to indicate their own contribution to each of a number of activities related to their B.A. theses (Example question: I suggested _____ percent of the methodology used in the study.) In the supervisor-focus condition, subjects were asked to report the extent of their supervisor's contributions to each of these activities (Example question: My supervisor suggested _____ percent of the methodology used in the study.). As anticipated, subjects subsequently allocated more (approximately twice as much) overall responsibility for the thesis to themselves in the self-focus than in the supervisor-focus condition. Thus attributions of responsibility were related to the availability in recall of each participant's contributions (Ross & Sicoly, 1979, Experiment 5).

THE INTERACTION HYPOTHESIS

The research that I have summarized to this point reveals that (1) egocentric biases in attributions of responsibility occur following group interactions; (2) availability tends to be self-centered; (3) there is a direct relation between availability and attributions of responsibility. Although all of this is most promising, there is an alternative way to conceptualize the responsibility data. I have labeled this alternate interpretation the interaction hypothesis.

It is a truism that what people do affects what other people do. Our successes or failures often depend on the actions of others. Consequently, it may be invalid to assume that the inputs of spouses, researchers, or participants in group efforts should add to 100%.

One way to think about the interaction problem in a group context is to consider a joint endeavor between A and B. The final product may reflect A's unique contribution, B's unique contribution, and an emergent contribution, AB, that would not have occurred in the absence of either A or B. Because the interactive element requires the inputs of both participants, it may be appropriate that each accepts full credit for AB. Thus, if A is asked to indicate his or her degree of responsibility for the final product, A may take credit for A and AB; similarly B may take credit for B and AB. As a result the total amount of responsibility to be distributed exceeds 100%. Indeed, there are instances in which each participant should possibly accept 100% of the credit for a joint outcome: For example, how do you divide responsibility for the decision to get married when, if either partner says no, there is no marriage?

The interaction hypothesis raises two quite separate issues in the group context:

1. Perhaps what we have been labeling self-centered biases in responsibility attributions is an artifact of the measurement techniques employed. We have assumed that if A and B each assign themselves, for instance, 60% of the credit for a given product, their attributions of responsibility are egocentric. Each is accepting 60% of the responsibility and allocating the other person only 40%. This assumption may be invalid: A and B might appreciate the interactive nature of their endeavor; they may think it quite appropriate that the other person take 60% of the credit as well (or at least considerably more than 40%).

2. Alternatively, the interactive nature of joint endeavors could contribute to the responsibility biases evinced in the present research, yet the attributions may remain egocentric in the sense that the participants fail to recognize that interactions are jointly determined. Each person may take credit for the emergent components and explicitly fail to credit (or underestimate) the other participant's contributions. In its extreme form, this implies A accepts credit for A and AB; whereas, A assigns B credit for B only. The basis of such misperceptions could reside in the memorial processes described earlier: the individual's own inputs to the emergent contribution may be more readily available in recall than the inputs of other participants.

The first alternative, the artifact hypothesis, requires that people understand and recognize the interactive elements of joint endeavors. There is reason to believe, however, that people tend to perceive relative contributions in additive rather than interactive terms. For example, the continuing nature–nurture controversy in psychology demonstrates that even sophisticated observers may fail to recognize interactions. As Hebb (1953) pointed out 25 years ago:

> So far as I can now see, even to ask the question, in the form in which it is usually asked, is a symptom of confusion; a confusion, it may be added, to which I have contributed as handsomely as I was able. . . . Is it fifty percent environment, fifty percent heredity, or ninety to ten, or what are the proportions? This is exactly like asking how much of the area of a field is due to its length, how much to its width. The only reasonable answer is that the two proportions are one hundred percent environment and one hundred percent heredity. They are not additive; any bit of behavior whatever is fully dependent on both [p. 43–44].

Similarly, Bowers (1973) has proposed that the trait versus situationist conflict that has been waged in the personality literature for decades may be best resolved by an interactionist account. The important point from the current perspective, though, is that the history of these debates reveals a general reluctance (or inability) on the part of many of the participants to think in interactive terms. This reluctance may reflect what Kelley (1973) has described as a tendency to prefer simple schema. Social observers tend to make person or situation attributions rather than person × situation attributions.

More directly relevant to the realm of social interaction, Alec Lumsden and I (Ross & Lumsden, 1979) recently asked members of intramural basketball teams at the University of Waterloo to describe the turning point in their last game. Their open-ended responses were then coded to determine if the subjects attributed the turning point to the actions of their own team, their opponent's team, or both teams. Again one-sided causation was the rule: 89% of the subjects ascribed the turning point to the actions of either their teammates or of their opponents; only 8% of the subjects clearly implicated both teams in their descriptions of the turning point (the remaining 3% being no response or unclassifiable).

The pretest from the Ross and Sicoly (1979) study on married couples also provided evidence, anecdotal in nature, pertinent to the interaction issue. Do spouses believe that each may validly accept primary responsibility for the various joint activities? Apparently not. At the conclusion of each of the pretest sessions, we encouraged spouses to compare their answers to the responsibility questions. All too often, the result was a heated debate in which each spouse expressed dissatisfaction with the other's "inflated" responses. (This experience led us to revise the questionnaire and to avoid such comparisons in the experiment proper.)

Finally, in the actual experiment, husbands and wives were asked to predict the responsibility judgments of their spouses (these data are reported in Sicoly & Ross, 1978). Both spouses assumed a much greater congruency of perceptions than actually occurred (eg., if a husband accepted 60% of the responsibility for an activity, he tended to assume that his wife assigned herself approximately 40% of the responsibility).

In summary, group members seem not to fully appreciate the interactive nature of their endeavor. Their judgments of responsibility are more likely to be additive than multiplicative. Hence, if the interactive element enhances egocentrism, it is probably through the medium of differential availability. This enhancement and its interpretation remain to be empirically validated.

DETERMINANTS OF THE AVAILABILITY BIAS

Alec Lumsden and I have recently explored the self-fulfilling prophesy interpretation of biased availability (Ross & Lumsden, 1979). According to this explanation, high expectations of one's performance may lead to selective encoding and retrieval that will serve to confirm one's expectations. We sought to examine this proposition in a field setting with the following properties: The event would be important, the participants would know each other reasonably well, and it would be possible for us to assess the participants' expectations, actual performance, and recall of performance.

These considerations led us to a sport setting. The subjects were males at the University of Waterloo (undergraduates, graduates, and faculty members) who were participants in an intramural basketball league. The 38 participating teams had played five weekly games prior to our study and some held practices between games. Because this study is not reported elsewhere, I describe it in some detail.

The subjects were contacted by phone a few days prior to their final, regularly scheduled game. They were told that we were assessing the accuracy of players' performance expectations for themselves and for their teammates. Each participant was asked to estimate the number of points he would score in the next game and the number of points each of his teammates would score (own and teammate judgments were presented in counterbalanced order). Subjects were asked to provide three estimates for each target person: an optimistic estimate ("If he/you were really on, how many points do you think he/you might score?"), a realistic estimate ("Realistically, how many points do you think he/you will score?"), and a pessimistic estimate ("If he/you were having a bad night, how many points do you think he/you would score?"). The three judgments were obtained in a counterbalanced order. To assess the accuracy of subjects' estimates, we sent observers who recorded individual scoring totals to each game.(The league organizers had recently chosen to downplay individual performances; typically, official scorers kept track of team totals only.) Three or four days after the game, we telephoned a random subset of the subjects again (subjects were not led to expect this callback). They were asked various questions about the game, including the number of points they and their teammates had scored.

The self-fulfilling prophecy interpretation implies: (1) that players should be more optimistic about their own future performances than their teammates would be; and (2) that players' expectations should predict recall of their own performance, independently of their actual performance. In support of the first proposition, players' optimistic predictions for their own performances were indeed higher than those provided for them by their teammates ($p < .001$). An appropriate analysis of the second proposition relates *realistic* expectations to recall, with actual performance partialed out. The resulting partial correlation between players' realistic expectations for and their recall of their own performance was nonsignificant, $r = .21$ (pessimistic and optimistic expectations were also poor predictors of recall, $p = $ n.s.); on the other hand, a similar partial correlation between players' expectations for and their recall of their teammates' performances was quite strong ($r = .68$, $p < .01$).

Thus, the results provide evidence for a self-fulfilling prophecy interpretations, but with the wrong group of people! There are two likely, though admittedly post hoc, explanations for this reversal. First, the players may not know how many points their teammates scored; as a result, players may base their recall for their teammates largely on pregame expectations. In addition, their memory for their own scoring totals may have been too vivid to allow for the possibility of error and assimilation.

We can evaluate this explanation by examining the relation between actual performance and recall, partialing out expectations. The correlation should be low, if recall is unrelated to actual performance. The relation was strong, however, both for players' recall of their teammates' performances ($r = .73$, $p < .01$) and for players' recall of their own performances ($r = .82$, $p < .01$). Thus, players seem relatively well attuned to their own and to their teammates' scoring totals; differences on this dimension do not appear to be large enough to account for the finding that expectations predict recall only of one's teammates' performances.

Alternatively, the players may have held more coherent expectations for their teammates' performances than for their own performances. In support of this position, note that players' expectations for their own performances were relatively diffuse: They were capable of being more pessimistic ($p < .001$) as well as more optimistic about their own performances than were their teammates. As a result, perhaps only expectations for others form a relatively stable schema toward which recall may be assimilated.

If this interpretation is valid and generalizable beyond a sporting context, it has an intriguing implication for actor–observer differences in perceptions. Recall of another's behavior may be related to prior expectations, whereas recall of one's own behavior may be independent of prior expectations (when actual performance is controlled for). This suggests: (1) that observers may be more inclined than actors to perceive their expectations as having been confirmed; and,

(2) that, as a result, observers may see more cross-situational stability in an actor's behavior than the actor himself. In this way, the expectancy-recall link could contribute to the actor–observer discrepancy in attribution documented by Jones and Nisbett (1971).

In sum, the data from this study provide suggestive evidence for a relation between expectations and recall. Moreover, the strength of the relation may differ for actors and observers. The study provides no evidence, however, that self-centered biases in recall are the result of a self-fulfilling prophecy mechanism.

GROUP-CENTERED BIASES
IN AVAILABILITY AND RESPONSIBILITY

In the quote presented at the beginning of this chapter, William James suggests that individuals are most attentive to matters relating to self. This proposition is consistent with the results of the availability assessments in the Ross and Sicoly experiments described in the foregoing. The dichotomy that James presents between me and not me ("the neighbor's me falls together with all the rest of things in one foreign mass") seems overdrawn, though. One can differentiate among the "not-me's" and such distinctions may have important implications for availability and attributions of responsibility.

One obvious distinction is that between ingroups and outgroups. There is substantial reason to believe that biases in availability could occur at this group level because most of the sources of bias at the individual level may have their parallel at the group level. For example, the strategies and actions of one's own group members are likely to be more salient (due to informational disparities and differential attention) than are those of members of outgroups. Moreover, if the actions of one's own group are more available, the ingroup should be judged to be more responsible for the outcomes of intergroup competitions than its opponents.

Competitive athletics provides an interesting context in which to examine group effects. We have conducted two field experiments with basketball players as subjects. In the first study, we asked the players on 12 intercollegiate teams to describe an important turning point in their last game (Ross & Sicoly, 1979). The questionnaire was distributed 2 or 3 days after the game. An examination of the data revealed that within a team the players were recalling quite different events. Nonetheless, 80% of the players recalled turning points that they believed were caused by the actions of their own team. Representative answers are provided in Table 9.1.

In the second study, the subjects were participants in an intramural basketball league at the University of Waterloo (Ross & Lumsden, 1979). This study was designed, in part, to correct an interpretational ambiguity in the original experi-

TABLE 9.1
Recall of the Turning Pont in a Basketball Game

Representative responses to the question:
"Briefly describe one important turning point in the last game and indicate in which period it occurred."

A. Answers from players on winning teams:
—When we switched defenses (second half).
—We applied full-court zone press in the first half when the first few minutes were crucial in our favor—set the tempo for the game.
—A turning point occurred in the second half when we had a time out and discussed using a triangle and two defense—it was a new defense for us and so we were testing its effectiveness.
—Turning point in the last game was our continuous full court zone press, which caused the other team to turn the ball over many times and allowed us to take advantage of these situations and score baskets.

B. Answers from players on losing teams:
—The beginning of the game when we fell behind.
—Lost our control and then became frustrated to the point where we couldn't execute.
—At the very beginning we started out poorly and fell behind. The sloppy, non-thinking mistakes, we multiplied as the game went on. The whole game was a disaster.
—In the second half we had discipline both on our fast break and on our press. We got three quick baskets in a row. However, this was not exactly a turning point in the game, as it did not last.

---

ment. It is difficult to know whether to characterize the turning point question in the initial study as an availability probe or a responsibility probe because it seems to involve both recall *and* an attribution of responsibility for the outcome of the game. In the second study, players were simply asked, "Recall in one sentence a single event or play that sticks out in your mind from the last game," a more direct assessment of availability. In addition, subjects were asked to describe the turning point of the game. These measures were obtained 3 or 4 days after the game.

The results supported the earlier findings. Eighty-two percent of the subjects recalled a single event in which the actions of their own team were figural (interestingly, about one-half of these events explicity involved the subject personally); only 5% of the subjects recalled an event that centered on the opposing team; the remaining 13% of the subjects recalled an event in which both teams were described as playing a significant role (See Table 9.2 for representative answers).

The turning point question yielded weaker but parallel results to those obtained in the first study. Sixty-eight percent of the subjects recalled turning points that they described as caused by the actions of their own team; only 21% recalled turning points that they attributed to the actions of the opposing team. Finally, none of the measures reported here, for either study, were affected by the outcome of the game.

TABLE 9.2
Recall of a Salient Event in a Basketball Game

Representative responses to the question:
"In one sentence describe a single event or play that sticks out in your mind."

—One of our guards was going for a basket and got tripped into the wall.

—Near the end of the second half I took the ball down the court and made a long pass . . . a nice play on my part.

—When I missed the lay-up.

—Our shooting went cold in the second half.

—The palming of the ball by one of the opposing players. He was never called.

—Our captain hit a shot from about over 20 feet out.

—I passed directly to a guy on the other team.

—Near the end of the game I came for a lay-up and coming down completely knocked the shit out of this guy.

—The consistency of a teammate's shooting.

The sports pages of a newspaper provide further examples of group-centered biases in judgments of responsibility. For instance, the following quotes appeared in the *Toronto Globe and Mail* (Feb. 10, 1979) report of a game between a hockey team from the Soviet Union and a team from the National Hockey League: "The NHL team played well because we allowed them to do so" (Valentine Stych, deputy chairman of the U.S.S.R. sports committee). "A key to the game was the way we cut off centre ice and dominated the neutral zone" (Scotty Bowman, NHL coach).

In summary, group biases in attributions of responsibility and in availability appear to mirror the biases found at the individual level. There is a need to explore these group biases further. Do they occur in nonsporting contexts? Are they affected by the strength of the relationships among group members? Is there a connection between biases at the individual and group levels? That is, are individual biases in availability and responsibility reduced and ingroup biases enhanced as the strength of the unit relation between group members increases? Would nonparticipant ingroup members (e.g., spectators at an athletic event) evince similar biases?

EXCEPTIONS

The research described in this chapter documents the pervasiveness of egocentric biases in attributions of responsibility. In fact, they seem too pervasive; all of us have witnessed exceptions. Newspaper headlines blare: "Begin Blames Sadat for

the Breakdown of Peace Negotiations.'' Many of us have been unhappy participants in, or observers to, marital disputes in which warring spouses blame each
other for their problems. Further, the conflicts between teenagers and their parents, with the ensuing denials of responsibility, are legend. The exceptions need
not be negative. Think of the movie star who, on receiving an Oscar, minimizes
his or her own contributions to the award-winning picture, or the fullback in
football who attributes his successes to his offensive lineman.

One could discount these examples, argue that the denials reflect public
stances rather than genuine feelings. Thus, the patching-up process that follows
the familial disputes previously described, often includes acknowledgments by
both parties that they may have been too hasty to blame the other. Nonetheless, it
seems evident that there are situations in which responsibility attributions are
genuinely nonegocentric.

And this is not surprising from the present perspective. It may be argued that
responsibility attributions are sometimes egocentric and sometimes not, because
availability is sometimes egocentric and sometimes not. Although we have little
evidence as yet concerning when availability is nonegocentric, it is possible to
speculate. Three factors seem likely to affect the degree to which availability is
self-centered: intentionality, participant involvement, and valence of outcome.

INTENTIONALITY

When our actions have an impact on others that we do not anticipate, we may
accept less responsibility for the result than others would assign to us. Kelley and
Stahelski (1970) demonstrated this phenomenon experimentally. When an initially cooperative individual interacted with a competitive individual in a Pris-
oner's Dilemma game, the cooperative individual was, for defensive reasons,
quickly forced to compete. Yet, the competitor failed to note that his own
behavior had provoked the other's competitive responses. The cooperator, on the
other hand, was aware of the competitor's impact on the course of their interaction. In short, the individual affected was more aware of the unintended impact
of the actor's (competitor's) behavior than was the actor. Kelley and Stahelski
(1970) concluded that ''the results may illustrate what may be a common phenomenon in personality and social psychology, that a personality predisposition
acts through its influences upon the person's social behavior to determine the
information he gains from his social environment and, thereby, the beliefs he
comes to hold about his world [p. 66].''

PARTICIPANT INVOLVEMENT

In much of the research described in this chapter, subjects have engaged in
complex social interactions: They alternated between the roles of speaker (or
actor) and listener (or observer), and their attention may have been directed at

planning and executing their own responses. In contrast, perhaps less involved observers would have been able to concentrate on other persons in their environment, with the consequence that recall would be other-directed rather than self-directed. Also, observers may be less self-absorbed when their own responses require little attention as, for example, when they enact well-practiced behaviors (Langer, 1978, suggested that a wide range of social behaviors require minimal thought).

VALENCE OF OUTCOME

"In every (election) campaign there's a hundred fuck-ups. If you win no one ever remembers them [Halberstram 1979, p. 228]." This bit of wisdom is offered by a presidential candidate in Michael Halberstram's fictional account of a U.S. election. In psychology, the study of the relation between valence of outcome and recall has a rather checkered history, falling largely within the domain of research on repression (Erdelyi & Goldberg, in press; Holmes, 1972, 1974). It is possible to speculate, however, that in its less extreme forms the impact of outcome may be accounted for by selective retrieval: As suggested by the Halberstram quotation, individuals ask themselves different questions following success (Where did we go right?) than following failure (Where did we go wrong?). Failure focuses attention on errors and on "could-have-beens."

The present concern is the relation between outcome valence and the degree to which recall is self-centered. There is considerable evidence that people accept more responsibility for success than for failure (Miller & Ross, 1975). This self-serving propensity could be facilitated by selective retrieval: Individuals may choose (perhaps quite unconsciously) to access more self-generated inputs after group successes than after group failures.

Consistent with this reasoning, Ross & Sicoly (1979) found that recall was less self-centered when subjects were led to believe that their group had performed poorly than when they were informed that that their group had performed well. Nevertheless, recall remained significantly self-centered, even after failure; following group failure subjects recalled a higher proportion of their own statements than of their partner's statements.

Of course, the foregoing focus is on the quantity of recall; yet valence may affect what, as well as how much, is remembered. Self-esteem may be maintained by recall that highlights one's own successes and one's partners' errors. We have not examined verbatum recall in sufficient detail to know if this occurs. Future research should be concerned more with the content and less with the amount of recall.

In summary, beliefs about responsibility are guided by the information that is readily available to the actor. As the research described in this chapter indicates, the information available is often egocentric. Yet, it need not be so. Self-centered attributions of responsibility will be less probable to the extent that: (1) the individual's attention is diverted from him- or herself during the course of the interaction; (2) the individual overlooks the impact of his or her own actions on others; or (3) the individual is prompted to focus on the contributions of the other participants during retrieval and assignments of responsibility.

CONSEQUENCES OF SELF-CENTERED BIASES IN RESPONSIBILITY

In considering the implications of self-centered attributions of responsibility, one should not overlook its advantages. Most important, a self-centered bias is likely to facilitate efforts at control. If I see myself as responsible, I may engage in efforts to improve my own, or my group's, outcomes rather than wait for someone else to come to my aid. In addition, the bias may enhance group satisfaction rather than engender disharmony. In many group settings, participants do not explicitly allocate responsibility for their endeavors. As a result, they can happily continue to feel more appreciated by their cohorts than they truly are.

There are drawbacks, however. Unrealistic assessments of personal responsibility can be upsetting in situations of failure. This is exemplified in the following remarks by Carl Yastremski of the Boston Red Sox:

> The game used to eat me up. If I had a bad day it would just destroy me inside. If I went 0-for-4, I'd get so messed up, it would still affect me mentally the next day. If I went 4-for-4 I was so 'up,' it carried me over too. Everything was 'me.' What did *I* do, was all that mattered.
>
> I don't know how far into my career it was—maybe 10 years—when I finally learned the secret. The thing that drives you nuts in this game is not giving credit to the other guy. Now when I go 0-for-4 I remind myself that the pitcher had performed well, I give him the credit instead of tearing myself apart [Quoted in *The Toronto Globe and Mail,* March 24, 1979, S5].

Second, we may engage in unwarranted devaluation of others to the extent that we fail to appreciate fully their contributions. In support of this contention, Kipnis, Castell, Gergen, and Mauch (1976) found that perceived control of marital decision making was related to lowered evaluations of the worth of one's spouse.

Finally, the self-centered bias in responsibility attributions can be injurious to group cohesion. In our study of married couples, Sicoly and I obtained evidence that in many marriages at least one of the spouses received less recognition for his or her efforts than he or she believed was deserved. Although the spouses may never become aware of these divergent views, there is a potential for discontent if the discrepancy in perceptions does become known. Ratings of marital satisfaction suggested that this potential was realized in some marriages, at least (Sicoly & Ross, 1978). The greater the incongruence in perceptions of responsibility, the less happy the wife was with her marriage ($r = -.41$, p $< .01$). This relation was not obtained for husbands. Because both spouses assigned primary responsibility for the household activities under consideration to the wife, it is the wife who may be particularly upset if her unequal share of the load is not fully recognized by her spouse.

In conclusion, even individuals in close relationships are unlikely to realize that their differences in judgment could arise from honest evaluations of information that is differentially available. In fact, all of the negative effects of self-centeredness stem from this lack of awareness. A simple appreciation of the pervasiveness of the bias, and of one's own susceptibility, may yield quite different attributions for its occurrence. Bitterness and accusation could be replaced by enlightened debates over the evidence supporting the competing truth-claims.

ACKNOWLEDGEMENTS

The research and the preparation of this manuscript were supported in part by Social Science Research Council Grant S76-1138. I would like to thank Alec Lumsden, James Olson, and Mark Zanna for their comments on earlier versions of this chapter.

REFERENCES

Bowers, K. S. Situationism in psychology: An analysis and a critique. *Psychological Review,* 1973, *80,* 307–336.

Carver, R. P. A critical review of mathagenic behaviors and the effect of questions upon the retention of prose material. *Journal of Reading Behavior,* 1972, 4, 93—119 .

deCharms, R. C. Personal causation: *The internal affective determinants of behavior.* New York: Academic Press, 1968.

Erdelyi, M. H., & Goldberg, B. Let's not sweep repression under the rug: Towards a cognitive psychology of repression. In J. F. Kihlstrom & F. J. Evans (Eds.), *Functional disorders of memory.* Hillsdale, N.J.: Lawrence Erlbaum Associates, 1980.

Halberstram, M. *The wanting of Levine.* New York: Berkeley Publishing Corporation, 1979.

Harris, S. *Banting's miracle: The story of the discovery of insulin.* Toronto: J. M. Dent & Son, 1946.

Hebb, D. O. Heredity and environment in animal behavior. *British Journal of Animal Behavior,* 1953, *1,* 43–47.

Holmes, D. S. Repression or interference: A further investigation. *Journal of Personality and Social Psychology.* 1972, *22,* 163–170.

Holmes, D. S. Investigations of repression: Differential recall of material experimentally or naturally associated with ego threat. *Psychological Bulletin,* 1974, *81,* 623–653.

James, W. *The principles of psychology* (Vol. 1). New York: Dover Publications Inc., 1890/1950.

Jones, E. E., & Nisbett, R. E. *The actor and the observer: Divergent perceptions of the causes of behavior.* Morristown, N.J.: General Learning Press, 1971 .

Kelley, H. H. The processes of causal attribution. *American Psychologist,* 1973, *28,* 107–128

Kelley, H. H., & Stahelski, A. J. Social interaction basis of cooperators' and competitors' beliefs about others. *Journal of Personality and Social Psychology,* 1970, *16,* 66–91.

Kipnis, D., Castell, P. T., Gergen, M., & Mauch, D. Metaphoric effects of power. *Journal of Applied Psychology,* 1976, *61,* 127–135.

Langer, E. J. Rethinking the role of thought in social interaction. In J. H. Harvey, W. J. Ickes, & R. F. Kidd (Eds.), *New directions in attribution research* (Vol. 2). Hillsdale, N.J.: Lawrence Erlbaum Associates, 1978.

Mahoney, M. J. *Scientist as subject.* Cambridge, Mass: Ballinger, 1976.

Miller, D. T., & Ross, M. Self-serving biases in the attribution of causality: Fact or fiction? *Psychological Bulletin,* 1975, *28,* 213–225.

Nisbett, R. E., & Ross, L. *Human inference: Strategies and shortcomings of social judgment.* Englewood, N.J.: Prentice-Hall, 1980.

Ross, M., & Lumsden, A. Unpublished data, University of Waterloo, 1979.

Ross, M., & Sicoly, F. Egocentric biases in availability and attribution. *Journal of Personality and Social Psychology,* 1979, *37,* 322–336.

Sayre, A. *Roslynd Franklin and D.N.A.* New York: Norton, 1975.

Schlenker, B., & Miller, R. S. Egocentrism in groups: Self-serving biases or logical information processing? *Journal of Personality and Social Psychology,* 1977, *35,* 755–764.

Sicoly, F., & Ross, M. *Interpersonal perceptions of division of labor and marital satisfaction.* Unpublished manuscript, University of Waterloo, 1978.

Tversky, A., & Kahneman, D. Availability: A heuristic for judging frequency and probability. *Cognitive Psychology,* 1973, *5,* 207–232.

White, R. W. Motivation reconsidered: The concept of competence. *Psychological Review,* 1959, *66,* 297–33.

10 Impression Formation, Impression Management, and Nonverbal Behaviors

Robert M. Krauss
Columbia University

One of the earliest phenomena addressed by a self-consciously cognitive social psychology—and one that continues to be an important research focus for contemporary cognitive social psychologists—is the the process by which we form impressions of others. To the best of my knowledge the problem was first formulated explicitly by Solomon Asch (1952), and, in my judgment, that formulation has not been improved upon appreciably in the intervening quarter century. Asch wrote:

> Out of the diverse aspects of an individual we form a view of him as a particular kind of person, with relatively enduring properties. It is with persons who have identity and individuality that we establish significant relations. . . .
>
> Ordinarily our view of a person is highly unified. Experience confronts us with a host of actions in others, following each other in relatively unordered succession. In contrast to this unceasing movement and change in our observations we emerge with a product of considerable order and stability. Although he possesses many tendencies, capacities and interests, we form a view of *one* person, a view that embraces his entire being or as much of it as is accessible to us. . . . How do we organize the various data of observation into a single, relatively unified impression? [p. 206-207]

In addition to posing the central question in the study of impression formation, Asch provided us with an experimental technique that, with minor variations, is still in use today. The technique, which I am sure is familiar to most readers, is simplicity itself. A subject is presented with a list of trait adjectives said to characterize a hypothetical person—for example, he or she is said to be "intelligent," "skillful," "industrious," "warm," "determined," "practical," and "cautious." The subject is then asked to rate the same person on a number of additional traits—is he or she generous, wise, happy, sociable, serious, imaginative, honest, etc.? By varying the characteristics attributed to the person and the relationships among them, we can infer the process by which these disparate elements are organized into a "product of considerable order and stability."

Almost a decade after Asch's initial statement of the problem, a sociologist, Erving Goffman, presented a view of the process from a rather different perspective, that of the individual who presents himself before others. As Goffman (1961) pointed out, the individual in interaction with others

> may wish them to think highly of him, or to think he thinks highly of them, or to perceive how in fact he feels toward them. . . . Regardless of the particular objective which the individual has in mind and of his motive for having this objective, it will be in his interests to control the conduct of others . . . this control is achieved largely by influencing the definition of the situation which the others come to formulate, and he can influence this definition by expressing himself in such a way as to give them the kind of impression that will lead them to act voluntarily in accordance with his own plan. *Thus, when an individual appears in the presence of others, there will usually be reason for him to mobilize his activity so that it will convey an impression to others which it is in his interests to convey* [pp. 3–4, italics added].

Thus as Heider (1958) among others pointed out, the parallel between social perception and the perception of the physical world holds only up to a point. A rock, untouched by human hands, should look like what it is, and if we mistake it for something else it is either because we have been insufficiently observant or because a natural coincidence has disguised it. But apart from the most metaphoric of usages, it would be silly to suspect that a rock resembled a frog in order to make us believe that it was a frog. For a physical stimulus, we can assume that its appearance is what it is apart from any consideration of us. It probably is true, as the poet Longfellow tells us, that "Things are not as they seem." But it is only when the object of our perception is another person (or something produced by another person) that a thing appears to be something in order to make us believe it *is* that. The mortician, who promises to arrange a simple, dignified, and economical funeral for the dear departed, may indeed be the sincere, sympathetic, and dedicated fellow his visage and manner proclaim. Alternatively, he may be a pious-sounding hypocrite who exploits others' grief for his own profit. It is only in the social psychological laboratory that one can safely say "This person is sincere, sympathetic, and dedicated. Therefore he must be honest." In the real world, people who behave that way often end up as major shareholders in the Brooklyn Bridge.

There is another important difference between impression formation in the laboratory and in the real world. Notwithstanding the current craze for T-shirt self-expressivism, people don't ordinarily walk around labeled with trait adjectives—and when they do, the descriptions tend to be less than credible. Typically we believe people to be intelligent, industrious, warm, and so forth not because they are labeled semantically as such, but on the basis of inferences we draw from our observations of their behavior. And such inferences must necessarily be highly complex because the traits themselves are multifaceted and ill-defined. Perhaps intelligence can be measured objectively, although I don't think IQ is what we mean when we call someone we know "intelligent." But how does one know if a person is warm or sincere or industrious?

It seems self-evident that there must be a relationship between impression formation, on the one hand, and impression management, on the other. Without the existence of observable behaviors that are understood by most people to reflect internal predispositions—regardless of whether or not they actually do—our impressions of others would be totally idiosyncratic. The man I judged "warm" another might judge "cold," and vice-versa. And although there is far from perfect agreement on the impressions different people form of the same others, certainly there is enough agreement enough of the time to suggest there is a reasonable consensus on the behaviors that constitute evidence for the presence of particular personal traits and states. More important, if this were not the case, impression management would be unworkable. In order for a mortician to appear "solicitious," there must be some set of behaviors that can be reliably expected to yield an impression of solicitiousness.

The research I discuss here begins with a series of studies of interactions in which one party attempted to deceive the other. We were interested in two questions: First, were there nonverbal behaviors that were reliably associated with deceptive utterances? And second, were there nonverbal behaviors that tended to be perceived as indicators of deception, regardless of whether or not they were actually so associated? The first of these questions is actually a classic problem in applied psychophysiology, popularly known as "lie detection." Traditionally, the approach has been to attempt to discriminate false from truthful responses by examining changes in psychophysiological indices of arousal. There is, of course, a voluminous research literature in this area. The second question—whether there exist behaviors that people believe to be indicators of deception—has received rather scant attention, although to a social psychologist it is the more interesting.

By deceptive behavior, I refer to behavior that is intended to foster in another a belief or understanding that the deceiver himself believes to be untrue. And this interpersonal element is really an intrinsic part of the definition. Deception, or attempted deception, cannot be defined simply as stating that which is untrue or even stating that which one knows to be untrue. We often say things that are at least technically untrue (when we tell jokes or use hyperbole, for example) knowing that what we say will not be taken literally by our listeners. Viewed from this interpersonal perspective, deception may be seen as a particular kind of self-presentation—that is, an attempt to convey the impression that one is a truthful person. The task of the deceiver is to manage the impression he or she conveys; the task of the other party, the "impression former," is to perceive the true state of affairs as accurately as ability and circumstances permit.

How do people in everyday life judge whether the people with whom they interact are telling the truth?

To a large extent, we judge that someone is attempting to deceive us on the basis of two factors: (1) What we perceive to be the a priori plausibility of an utterance; and (2) What we perceive as the speaker's motive for saying it—that is to say, the value to the speaker of what Ayer (1955) terms the utterance's perlocutionary force. So when a used car salesman tells us a vehicle that looks like a well-used New York City taxi was owned by a retired schoolteacher who used it only to go to church on Sundays, we are likely—given the implausibility of the statement, on the one hand, and our perception of the salesman's motive for saying it, on the other—to judge that he is lying. The operation of such a "discounting principle" is shown nicely in an experiment by Robert Kraut (1978). Kraut had listeners judge the honesty, sincerity, etc. of a confederate who, in the course of a simulated job intereview stated either that she occasionally smoke marijuana or that she abstained from its use entirely. Immediately prior to this, the interviewer had stated a pro- or anti-marijuana attitude. Observers were more likely to judge the job candidate to be lying when her statements were self-serving—either denying that she used marijuana after the interviewer voiced disapproval or admitting that she used it occasionally after the interviewer said she approved of such use. Highest marks for honesty were given to the candidate who confessed to being an occasional user after the interviewer had expressed her disapproval. The principle subjects employ in making such judgments seems reasonably straightforward: To the extent that a statement can be seen as extrinsically motivated (i.e., to the degree that its acceptance can be expected to bring about some desired state of affairs), it is likely to be seen as untruthful. This principle, of course, fits nicely within the general framework of attribution theory (Jones & Nisbett, 1971).

But quite apart from *what* people say or the circumstances in which they say it, it is popularly believed that one can tell whether a statement is true or false by *how* it is said. And Kraut's study also demonstrated quite elegantly the operation of a nonverbal factor in the perception of deception. By carefully editing his audiotapes, Kraut was able to create versions in which there was either a long hesitation before the interviewee stated whether or not she smoked marijuana, or no hesitation. The effect of the hesitation on listeners' perception of deception was interesting. When the job candidate's statement was self-serving—that is, when she admitted to using marijuana after the interviewer had voiced a positive attitude toward its use or claimed not to use it when the interviewer had expressed her disapproval—the hesitation increased the likelihood that judges would perceive her to be lying. But when it preceded a statement that ran counter to the job candidate's self-interest, the hesitation tended to strengthen the impression of truthfulness and candor.

And of course the relevance of nonverbal behaviors to the perception of deception and truthfulness is not limited to hesitations in speech. By popular belief, at least, the deceiver unconsciously reveals himself in a variety of ways—by his failure to meet our gaze, by covering his mouth with his hands, and so forth. Nor are these beliefs confined to the lay public. So astute an observer of human behavior as Sigmund Freud (1905) claimed: "He that has eyes to see and ears to hear may convince himself that no mortal can keep a secret. If his lips are silent, he chatters with his fingertips; betrayal oozes out of him at every pore [p. 78]."

But if it is the case that there are behaviors associated with deception, or behaviors people believe to be so associated, and if these behaviors can to some extent be simulated or controlled, the potential deceiver may employ them in a strategic fashion to enhance the effectiveness of his deception. Thus, it is the existence of behaviors that are perceived as indicators of deception, along with the possibility that these behaviors can be at least to some extent controlled, that makes it reasonable to regard deception under the more general framework of self presentation.

With these considerations in mind, Valerie Geller, Christopher Olson, and I (Krauss, Geller, & Olson, 1976) decided to do a study addressed to a rather simple question: To what extent do visible cues aid in detecting deception? Most of us appear to feel we stand a better chance of detecting a lie in a face-to-face conversation than in one conducted over a telephone. Perhaps this is because we believe that the behavioral cues associated with deception come primarily from the body rather than the voice, or because we feel the more information we have the better. But whatever the reason, the belief is widely held. Our experimental situation was structured as an interview. Both interviewer and interviewee were naive subjects—male and female undergraduates at Columbia University. The interview schedule contained five questions on each of four topic areas: Politics, Religion, Personal Future, and Values. The questions all concerned the interviewee's personal beliefs or plans for the future. Interviewers were instructed to ask the questions using the wording and the order given in the interview schedule and not to improvise additional questions. Two of the four topics were designated as deception topics for each pair, and interviewees were instructed to falsify their answers on these topics. Truth and deception topics were counterbalanced across subjects. The interviewer was told that the interviewee would be lying on two of four topics, but of course not which ones. After each answer, the interviewer rated its truthfulness on a seven-point scale. All interviewer–interviewee pairs were of the same sex.

In about half of the pairs, the interviews took place face-to-face across a table. Head and shoulder frontal views of both subjects were videotape recorded. The two signals were fed into a special effects generator, which composited them into a single side-by-side split-screen image for use in a subsequent experiment. In the remainder of the pairs, subjects sat in separate rooms and communicated over a high-quality audio channel. Cameras in the separate rooms recorded each subject, and the composited images were virtually indistinguishable from those recorded with both subjects in the same room. We refer to these conditions as face-to-face and intercom, respectively. Cross-cutting the communication modality variable is a second manipulated variable we have called arousal, but which could probably be as well described by a number of other terms. Whatever one chooses to call it, what we wanted to do was to engage the subject's motivation to deceive well by making the deception more consequential than simply complying with the experimenter's request. So we did what social psychologists traditionally do—that is, we deceived our subjects by telling them that the ability to deceive successfully was an indicator of general intellectual ability and creative aptitude, implying that it was related to success in a number of careers. We also informed our "aroused" subjects that their videotapes would be "evaluated" by a research team at Columbia's Psychiatric Institute. All of this was, of course, sheer nonsense and subjects were so informed in a step-by-step debriefing at the conclusion of the experiment.

The dependent variable measure is what we call the Detection Index. It consists of the sum of the truthfulness ratings for those questions on which the interviewee was answering truthfully minus the sum of the ratings for those answers on which the interviewee was lying. We use this measure because it seems to tap the ability to discriminate truthful from untruthful utterances and to control for particular subjects' biases in using the seven-point scale—whether one tends to be particularly suspicious or trusting.

Let us turn to the results. First, with respect to the communication modality variable (whether subjects communicated face-to-face or over an intercom) and to our great surprise, we found significantly more accurate detection of deception in the intercom condition than in the face-to-face condition. Contrary to our expectation, being in the actual presence of the interviewer did not make it more difficult for the interviewee to convey the impression of being truthful when actually he or she was not. Indeed, our result indicates that just the opposite was true.

Parenthetically, a recent study done in our laboratory indicates that this effect is not confined to strategic manipulation of the impression of honesty. Valerie Geller, in a recent doctoral dissertation (Geller, 1977), has shown that it is easier to convey the impression of dominance or submissiveness in a face-to-face setting than it is over an audio link. Geller used an interview situation much like ours, but instead of instructing her interviewees to lie, she induced them to give the impression of being strongly dominant or submissive personalities. At the end of the interview, which concerned the same sort of mundane matters as did our first study, interviewers were asked to rate their partners on a number of measures of dominance–submissiveness. Interviewees were better able to impression manage—i.e., to appear either more dominant or more submissive—in the face-to-face condition. Looking at the relation between how dominant or submissive a subject was judged to be by his interviewer and that subject's score on the Schutz FIRO-B dominance scale (which we will take as an index of the subject's "true" dominance–submissiveness), Geller found significant correlations for control subjects who were not induced to give any particular impression and for subjects in the intercom condition. For interviewees in the face-to-face condition, the correlation is not significantly different from zero.

Taken together, the results of these two studies indicate that if one is motivated to make a self-presentation that is inconsistent with his or her internal predisposition (as truthful or dominant when one is not), it can be more readily accomplished face-to-face than, say, over a telephone. Or, to put it another way, it is easier to "see through" another's guise from the information in the vocal channel alone. However, we are not yet in a position to say why this is so, and there is more than one possibility. For example, it may be that the face-to-face situation creates an "information overload." That is, the interviewer is presented with more information than can be processed simultaneously and, in trying to deal with it all, deals with none of it efficiently. A second possibility is that visible behaviors are readily controlled, at least in low affect situations such as ours, and consequently are intrinsically misleading. Still another possibility focuses on the easy-to-forget fact that, whereas in the face-to-face condition the interviewer can visually monitor the interviewee, it is also the case that situation is symmetrical—the interviewee can also see the interviewer. Perhaps the feedback the interviewee gains this way helps in perpetrating an effective deception. These are but three possible explanations of these findings; there are others.

To return to our deception study, we were somewhat surprised to find no significant effect for our arousal manipulation; nor did it enter significantly into interactions with other variables. This might be taken as evidence of the ineffectuality of our manipulation. However, in the next experiment we discuss, raters viewing videotapes of subjects in the present experiment did respond differently to interviewees sampled from the aroused and nonaroused conditions. We pursue this matter further in a moment.

With these findings in hand, Geller, Olson, and I proceeded to a second study in which we presented a sample of the videotape recordings obtained previously to groups of naive subjects and asked them to rate the truthfulness of the responses on the same scale the interviewers in the first experiment had used. In all, we used 64 question-answer segments, which constituted a balanced sample of male respondents in the various conditions of the first study. Each stimulus person appeared twice: once telling the truth and once lying. Our raters were male and female clerical and managerial employees of the New Jersey Bell Telephone Company, and they were run in groups of six to eleven. The stimulus materials were presented to raters in one of three conditions: audio only—raters heard the stimulus person's response but did not see the video portion; video only—raters saw the video portion, but did not hear the response; and audio-video—raters both heard the response and saw the person making it. In the two conditions in which there was a video display, the side of the split screen containing the image of the interviewer was covered so raters saw only the interviewee.

The analysis of variance for this experiment is, as you can imagine, large and complex, including a number of control factors from both the first and second studies that I have not mentioned. The ANOVA produced enough significant main and interaction effects to be both gratifying and distressing—especially if one is trying to communicate the outcome of the experiment in a summary presentation such as this. I therefore present only those effects that are most relevant to the present discussion; to do otherwise would result in a presentation of inordinate length and opacity. But the effects I omit do not change or qualify these results in any substantial way.

Of greatest interest here, is the way two factors—Communication Modality and Rating Condition—interact. This interaction is shown in Fig. 10.1. Note two things: First, it is clear that cues to deception are available in an interviewee's visible behavior; but it also seems the case that such cues are readily controllable. The greatest accuracy is displayed by raters who saw but could not hear the responses of interviewees in the intercom condition—interviewees who were not, you will recall, being visually monitored by their interviewers. The visible behaviors of interviewees in the face-to-face condition—who could be seen by their interviewers—are not particularly informative. Second, it seems clear that raters do not always make good use of the information available to them. Note that for

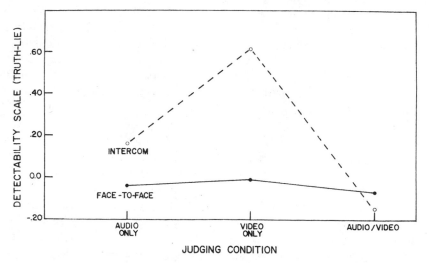

FIG. 10.1.   Detectability for Face-to-Face and Intercom subjects as a function of judgment condition.

intercom interviewees, rater accuracy is substantially greater in the video-only condition than in the audio-video condition. Yet the same *visual* information was available to raters in the two conditions, the only difference being that raters in the audio-visual condition had vocal information as well. It seems apparent that audio-visual raters weighted vocal information more heavily than visual information. This conjecture is supported by an examination of the correlations of ratings in the three rating conditions. The product-moment correlation between ratings in the audio-only and audio-video conditions is .71; between video-only and audio-video, the value is .40. Both values are significantly greater than zero, but the audio-only ratings accounts for about three times as much of the variance in truthfulness ratings in the audio-video condition.[1]

Finally, a main effect was found for interviewee's arousal condition: Across all rating conditions, the Detection Index was higher for aroused interviewees than for those who had not been given the arousal manipulation. The effect was greater for subjects in the intercom condition than for those in the face-to-face condition; the interaction between those two conditions is significant.

Geller, Olson, and I also subjected our stimulus videotape to another sort of analysis. Naive judges rated each of the 64 segments on nine attributes: fluency, nervousness, emphaticness, seriousness, attractiveness, facial mobility, nervous hand gestures, gaze direction, and facial shielding. Each judgment was made by at least four judges and done on the basis of minimal information; that is, fluency was judged from the audio track without visual information, whereas judgments of facial mobility were made without a sound track, and so forth. Instructions to the judges were also minimal. They were encouraged to adopt any criteria for fluency, nervousness, etc. they felt appropriate. Inter-rater reliability was adequate but varied considerably among the nine attributes.

These data enable us to respond to the two questions raised earlier: Which attributes are significantly correlated with truthfulness ratings and which attributes actually discriminate among truthful and untruthful responses? Let us begin by addressing ourselves to the first question. It will be recalled that the truthfulness ratings were made under three different rating conditions; the correlations we report here are from the audio-visual rating condition. Where informative correlations were found in one of the other rating conditions, they are noted. The nine rated attributes are listed in Fig. 10.2; the asterisks indicate statistically significant correlations. Where the correlation is negative, this is indicated by a minus sign in parentheses.

As that figure indicates, segments judged high on fluency, seriousness, and emphaticness, low on nervousness, and having relatively short latencies tend to be judged truthful in the audio-video rating condition. For video-only raters, judged

---

[1]We have considerable more confidence in the reliability of this interaction effect than its somewhat marginal probability value ($p < .08$) would ordinarily engender because it is the second time we have observed it. In a prior study, using only half of these stimulus segments and a very different sample of raters, virtually the same configuration of results was found.

**FLUENCY
GAZE LENGTH
FACIAL MOBILITY
NERVOUS HAND GESTURES
FACIAL SHIELDING
**SERIOUSNESS
 *NERVOUSNESS (−)
ATTRACTIVENESS
**EMPHATICNESS
 *RESPONSE LATENCY (−)
RESPONSE LENGTH
 $*p < .05$ (two-tailed).
 $**p < .01$ (two-tailed).

FIG. 10.2. Judged attributes and measured properties correlated with truthfulness ratings in the audio-video rating condition.

nervousness is not related to truthfulness ratings but nervous hand gestures and response length are, negatively in the case of the former and positively in the case of the latter. Correlations for the audio-only and the audio-video rating condition differ little. It's interesting to note that some of the attributes popularly believed to be signs of deceptive behavior and that people are likely to say they look for when attempting to detect deception (for example, gaze direction and facial shielding) are not reliably correlated with subjects' ratings.

When we turn to the question of which attributes actually distinguish between lying and truth-telling, a quite different picture emerges. The relationships are weak and specific to treatment conditions. In Fig. 10.3, we list those attributes that differ significantly between truthful and deceptive segments. Fluency is judged to be greater when truth-telling than when lying, but only for subjects who have undergone the arousal manipulation. The popular favorites, gaze direction and facial shielding, in fact do not discriminate at all. Judged nervousness does, but only in interaction with the Communication Modality variable. Inter-

 *FLUENCY (T > L IN HI AROUSAL ONLY)
GAZE LENGTH
FACIAL MOBILITY
NERVOUS HAND GESTURES
FACIAL SHIELDING
SERIOUSNESS
 *NERVOUSNESS (INTERCOM: L > T; F/F: T > L)

 *ATTRACTIVENESS (T > L IN HI AROUSAL ONLY)
EMPHATICNESS
RESPONSE LATENCY
RESPONSE LENGTH
 $*p < .05$

FIG. 10.3. Judged attributes and measured properties that differentiate significantly between lying and truth-telling.

viewees in the intercom condition are judged to be more nervous when they are lying than when telling the truth, as one would expect. However, in the face-to-face condition, the difference is in the opposite direction: Interviewees are judged significantly *less* nervous when lying. Again our subjects demonstrate their ability to suppress visible cues to deception when the situation warrants.

Attractiveness is typically considered a biasing factor and was included because we expected it to be related to our judges' ratings—predicting that attractive interviewees would be judged more truthful. In fact they were not and it's ironic that they weren't because judged attractiveness *does* discriminate between truth-telling and lying—at least for interviewees who have undergone the arousal induction. The same subjects are judged to be more attractive when telling the truth than when lying; no differences were found for nonaroused subjects.

We also decided to examine the extent to which the act of deception was reflected in our subjects' voices—more specifically, how lying affected fundamental voice frequency. Fundamental voice frequency (or vocal pitch) is an interesting variable from the point of view of impression formation and impression management. To begin with, a number of studies have shown that pitch does, in fact, vary to some extent with an individual's internal state. For example, Williams and Stevens (1969) compared radio transmissions to aircraft pilots, who were encountering serious in-flight difficulty, to transmissions by the same pilots before difficulty was encountered. In all cases, pitch was higher in the former. Hecker, Stevens, von Bismarck, and Williams (1968) had subjects monitor a series of meters and report their readings. Stress was manipulated by increasing time pressure. Fundamental frequency tended to covary with stress. And Ekman, Friessen, and Scherer (1976) performed a pitch analysis on the voices of subjects in the Ekman and Frienssen (1974) experiment and found elevated pitch levels during deception.

A second aspect of changes in fundamental voice frequency that makes it an interesting variable from the point of view of impression formation and impression management is that it is perceived by naive listeners as an indication of stress, nervousness, or anxiety. For example, we have been analyzing the telephone transmissions of the Consolidated Edison power controller during the hour that preceded the fateful blackout of New York City on the evening of July 13, 1977 (Streeter, Krauss, Apple, & Macdonald, 1978). One of the things we did was to take all of the power controller's 303 utterances during that hour and edit them onto an audio tape in random order, deleting the speech of the other party to the conversation. We then had naive listeners rate these randomly ordered utterances for the degree to which the speaker appeared to be under stress. (Because virtually all of what was said was in a highly specialized technical jargon, our raters could not evaluate the actual urgency of the situation from its content, so their ratings are not confounded by this variable.) The correlation between the two variables is +.48. No other predictor—among more than a dozen acoustical and semantic variables we examined—correlated so highly.

TABLE 10.1
Mean Truth-Minus-Lie Pitch Differences (in Hz) by Experimental
Condition (from Streeter et al., 1977)[a]

Interview	Interviewee		
	Aroused	Nonaroused	M
Face-to-face	−4.8 (5)	−.1 (4)	−2.5
Intercom	−7.1 (7)	−1.0 (6)	−4.1
M	−6.0	−.6	−3.3

[a]N = 8 per cell. Values in parentheses indicate number of interviewees in that cell who had higher pitch values while lying than while truthtelling.

A third aspect of pitch that is of interest to us is that it can, to some extent at least, be controlled voluntarily. An actor attempting to similate fear or surprise will elevate his or her pitch (Fairbanks, 1940), and I strongly suspect (although we have not actually done the experiment) that naive subjects, less well trained in vocal expression, will do the same. The fact that pitch can be controlled voluntarily means, of course, that it can be employed in impression management.

Going back to our deception experiment, we calculated the average pitch for each of the utterances on our 64-segment tape (Streeter, Krauss, Geller, Olson, & Apple, 1977). Differences in pitch between truthful and deceptive utterances in the four conditions of that experiment are shown in Table 10.1. Overall, we found significantly higher pitch on deceptive utterances than on truthful ones. On the average, pitch was 3.3 Hz higher when subjects lied than when they told the truth. But as Table 10.1 indicates, the effect was not uniform across the conditions of the experiment. Interestingly, subjects in the arousal condition—that is, who were strongly motivated to deceive successfully—showed the greatest increase in pitch: 6.0 Hz, on the average. The increase found for nonaroused subjects was an order of magnitude smaller. Did judges use these pitch changes in deciding whether or not a subject was lying? As nearly as we can tell, they did not. The correlation between ratings of truthfulness and pitch was − .01. However, when we presented subjects with speech that had been filtered, so that its content was unintelligible (preserving such vocal features as loudness, intonation, tempo, length, and, of course, pitch), we found a modest but significant correlation of − .26 between an utterance's average fundamental frequency and its rated truthfulness: the higher the pitch, the less truthful it was judged.

How can we understand the process by which perceivers infer an internal state from an overt behavioral attribute like pitch? How do we know when someone is being truthful, or nervous, or whatever? Bill Apple, Lynn Streeter, and I designed an experiment to shed some light on this process. To do so we exploited another virtue of pitch as a nonverbal variable in impression formation and management—the fact that thanks to modern speech synthesis technology pitch can be manipulated in precisely the manner an experimenter wishes without disturbing other vocal characteristics. You will appreciate that in natural speech such vocal properties as pitch, amplitude, and speech rate tend to covary, and it's virtually impossible for a speaker voluntarily to vary pitch while holding rate and amplitude constant. A procedure developed at Bell Laboratories called Linear Predictive Coding permits one to represent natural speech in digital form in terms of a small set of parameters. By manipulating the values of the appropriate parameters, one can increase or decrease pitch or amplitude independently. The altered digitized representation can then be synthesized to produce speech that sounds quite natural.

We (Apple, Streeter, & Krauss, 1979) applied this procedure to the speech of 27 male college students answering two interview questions. The first question was "What would you do if you suddenly won or inherited a large sum of money?" The second was "What do you think of college admissions quotas designed to favor minority groups?" What we were attempting to do was to find two questions that differed along a dimension of personal involvement and in this regard we were reasonably successful. Table 10.2 shows some speech statistics for responses to the two questions. It will be seen that answers to the Money question were briefer, had a shorter latency, and were more rapidly articulated and lower pitched than those to the Quota question. An independent sample of subjects from the same population judged the latter to be both more cognitively complex and more emotionally involving than the former.

For one-third of our subjects, we *increased* the fundamental frequency of their responses by a factor of 20%; for another third we *decreased* it by 20%; for the remaining one-third, pitch was left *unchanged*. These altered responses were then synthesized and assembled in random order on an audiotape. These stimulus tapes have been used in a number of experiments. I should also add that pitch was not the only vocal property we manipulated, but at this time I forego discussion of the others. We played these pitch-altered tapes to a large number of subjects,

TABLE 10.2
Premanipulation Characteristics of Responses to Quota and Money
Questions (from Apple et al., 1979)
(N = 27 responses per question)

| | *Quota* | | *Money* | | |
	Mean	*S.D.*	*Mean*	*S.D.*	*t-diff.*
Response Length (Syll)	111.1	40.7	84.6	42.7	3.89**
Response Time (Sec)	36.8	13.8	25.6	13.2	4.68**
Speech Rate (Syll/Sec)	3.0	0.50	3.4	0.74	2.12*
Fund. Freq. (Hz)	112.2	14.9	107.4	14.6	5.60***

  * < .05, two-tailed.
  ** < .01, two-tailed
  *** < .001, two-tailed

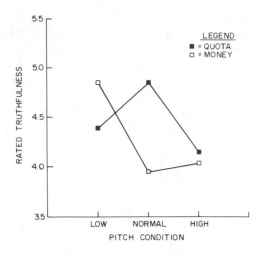

FIG. 10.4.   Truthfullness ratings for "Quota" and "Money" questions as a function of pitch condition.

asking different groups of subjects to make different sorts of judgements. Some subjects were asked to judge how truthful the response was; others were asked to indicate how nervous the respondent appeared to be; still others were asked how fluent, how emphatic, and how serious they found the response.[2]

As we expected, elevated pitch tends to have a quite deleterious affect on attributions made to speakers. For example, as pitch goes up, the judged truthfulness of the answer goes down. But the situation becomes a bit more complicated when we look at judgements made of responses to the Money and Quota questions separately. This is shown in Fig. 10.4. It appears that pitch level affects responses to the Quota and Money questions somewhat differently. On both, elevated pitch results in quite low truthfulness ratings, but normal levels of pitch are affected somewhat differently. This initially struck us as strange, because elevated pitch leads to the perception that the speaker is under stress and we expected our judges to perceive stress as an indication of lying. We did not ask subjects to estimate the stress speakers were under, but we did have one group rate how nervous the speakers seemed. We found a quite robust main effect for pitch (the higher the pitch, the more nervous the speaker was perceived to be), with no pitch by question interaction. Apparently our subjects perceive speakers to be increasingly nervous with increasing pitch, regardless of the particular question they are answering. Why, then, do they not perceive truthfulness as monotonic negative function of pitch?

The explanation, we believe, requires an attributional framework. Our raters understand that the Quota and Money questions are two quite different sorts of questions. The latter produced a low level of personal involvement; there is little affect associated with the answer. This is certainly not the case for the Quota

---

[2]For further details of method and results, see Apple et al. (1979).

question. Even before the Bakke decision, the question of special quotas for minority students was a matter of intense concern and discussion among Columbia undergraduates, most of whom are politically to the left, on the one hand, and white, middle-class, and planning to on to graduate or professional school, on the other hand. The Quota question catches our speakers neatly between their social values and their self interests. This speculation is borne out by the striking differences in speech statistics for answers to the two questions referred to earlier.

Harold Kelley's ''discounting principle'' posits that to the extent a situation contains a number of factors, any one of which might plausibly have resulted in an observed outcome, the less likely is any single factor to be perceived as the cause of that outcome. With fewer potential causes present, the cause-to-effect attribution will be more compelling. We speculated that our listeners would be more likely to discount higher pitch levels for responses to the Quota question than to the Money question. With the Quota question, relatively higher pitch can be attributed in part to the effect of answering a ''loaded'' question. For the less involving Money question, such an attribution is less plausible.

To pursue this speculation we examined ratings made by judges of Seriousness, Emphaticness, and Fluency, the same attributes we had found in our previous study to be highly correlated with judgements of truthfulness. For all, we found significant Pitch by Question interactions that are strikingly similar in form to the ones found for truthfulness judgements.

It should go without saying that our attribution explanation of the effects of pitch variation on perceived internal state is at this point little more than a plausible speculation. Our studies used only two questions and it seems likely that they varied on a number of dimensions. The obvious next step is to demonstrate in a systematic way that listeners take properties of questions into account in interpreting the significance of acoustic variations in the answer. It also seems

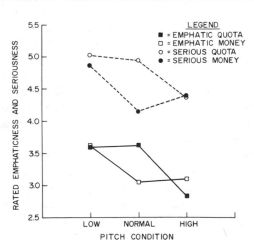

FIG. 10.5. Seriousness and Emphaticness ratings for ''Quota'' and ''Money'' questions as a function of pitch condition.

reasonable to expect that listeners will take into account a variety of other sorts of contextual features. Such research is currently underway.

It should also be clear that voice fundamental frequency is only one of the vocal properties that may affect a listener's perception of a speaker's internal state or more enduring predisposition. We would expect such qualities as loudness and speech rate to produce similar effects, and from data I have not discussed here, we know that speech rate can profoundly affect both perceptions of a message's veracity and its speaker's characteristics. In addition, there are more exotic vocal characteristics dear to the heart of the phonetician, such as ''breathiness,'' ''raspiness,'' and ''precision of articulation,'' that we have not begun to consider.

The point of all this is that, in the real world, person perception does not occur in a vacuum. Our perceptions of others typically are based on data of one sort or another. Ordinarily, when we say that someone is intelligent, or warm, or aggressive, we can point to behaviors that support our attributions. Certainly, we need to know how people integrate such attributes to produce a ''single, relatively unified impression.'' But to understand how we form impressions of people in the real world, and how in the real world people affect the impressions others form of them, we need to know more about where those perceived attributes come from.

To close, I'd like to touch on two different but related topics. The first consists of some questions raised for future research on impression management and impression formation by the work I've discussed. The second consists of some more general thoughts about the study of social cognition.

Clearly we have done little more than scratch the surface in our attempt to understand the processes by which people project and form impressions, and we must be cautious not to generalize too broadly from the results we have obtained. Our findings suggest that at least under some circumstances people are able to discriminate between the false and truthful utterances of others and that, to some extent, it is the presence of uncontrolled nonverbal behaviors of the sort Ekman & Friesen (1974) term ''leakage'' and ''deception cues'' that enable them to do this. But in reviewing the research done in our own laboratory (much of which has not been discussed) and elsewhere, we are forced to agree with Kraut's (unpublished) assessment that in all likelihood there are no nonverbal cues consistently and cross-situationally associated with deceptive utterances. Contrary to what is proclaimed in the popular press, there are no ''tell-tale signs'' of lying; the gullible layman (or psychologist, for that matter) who interprets a speaker's hand-shielding of his mouth or a failure to maintain eye contact as a sign of deceit, will reject many true statements as untruthful and fail to detect many lies in the bargain. Fortunately, people tend to be a good deal wiser than this. For it seems clear from our own work and that of others (Kraut, 1978) that subjects' interpretation of nonverbal cues is very much context-dependent—and sensibly so.

But if the study of nonverbal behavior can tell us little about lie detection per se, it does seem to be considerably more informative about what might be termed ''lie perception''—i.e., the behaviors that seem to produce in others the perception that one is being untruthful, regardless of whether or not that actually is the case. From our own work and that of others, we have a pretty fair idea of at least some of the behaviors that are related to judgements of truthfulness. And from this, I suppose, we could advise a speaker on what he or she should do to avoid being judged a liar. For example, one should speak fluently and emphatically, and keep response latencies short (except perhaps preceding damaging admissions); one should keep vocal pitch down and avoid the appearance of being nervous.

As was pointed out earlier, the fact that such behaviors are to some extent controllable makes them useful in the process of impression management. But it is not yet clear to what extent subjects actually consciously or unconsciously avail themselves of these means. Earlier, we speculated that subjects under stress who wanted to appear calm would try to keep their voices from rising, but we have no direct evidence that this is so; Bill Apple and I have an experiment planned to test this hypothesis.

I find it interesting that my own work has brought me back to address an old and familiar question in the study of social cognition—namely, how the perceiver integrates the variety of verbal and nonverbal cues he or she receives to arrive at a unitary attribution of another's internal state. One would expect that such attributions become especially problematic when the signals carried in different nonverbal channels are contradictory. For example, how do we apprehend the internal state of one who appears (visually) to be calm and relaxed, but whose voice sounds nervous? It would seem that a schematic information-processing approach could offer a good deal of insight into how such attributions might be formed.

Bill Apple (1979), in a just-completed doctoral dissertation, pursued this question in a series of experiments. (I describe his research briefly in order to make a point; it is reported in detail elsewhere.) Apple first collected videotapes of a large number of subjects answering an affectively neutral interview question. From this pool, he was able to select groups of speakers who appeared visibly quite nervous, moderately nervous, or quite calm, when judged from video alone. By taking each speaker's voice off the audio track and LPCing it (see foregoing) he was able to produce three versions of the same response, in which pitch was either shifted up or down by 20%, or left unaltered. He then carefully dubbed the voices back onto the audio track, taking care to maintain lip synchrony. By this process he was able to obtain a set of stimulus tapes of speakers whose visible nervousness and vocal nervousness varied orthogonally. Apple employed several measures that could reasonably be expected to reveal evidence of schematic information processing (e.g., response latency, recognition memory, etc.). Somewhat to our surprise, however, all of his results could be accounted for by a simple additive model; there was no tendency for the two sources to interact, as one would expect if the information were being processed schematically. Of course, additive effects are not necessarily inconsistent with schematic processing. But if only additive effects are found, they can be accounted by a very simple model and there is no need to invoke one that is more complex.

I raise this point because it seems to me that the current vogue for invoking exotic processing notions like schemata may come to vitiate the usefulness of what is, to be sure, a valuable concept. If it is applied indiscriminately to all situations in which people process information about others, the concept may become a vague metaphor and lose whatever integrative power it has.

The final point I want to make concerns the study of person perception. The tradition of research on trait inference or implicit personality theory begun by Asch (1952), referred to at the beginning of this paper, may have misled us—not because the research it generated is uninteresting (certainly that is not the case), but rather because it has led us to believe we were studying perception when we were not. In order to accept the notion that the integration of trait information is fundamentally a perceptual act, it seems to me one must assume that traits and other internal dispositions are not themselves complex inferences, integrating a variety of sorts of information, possessing a dynamic of their own. By presenting our subjects with the *product* of the perceptual process—i.e., the inference—and asking him or her to operate on it, we may be eliminating the very thing that is most interesting about the perception of people.

Perhaps there is a moral in this and, because this is the first Ontario Symposium on Social Cognition, I am emboldened to draw it. It seems to me that as social psychology has become increasingly cognitive in its orientation, it has become increasingly less concerned with what historically has been one of its central foci—namely, the study of social interaction. More and more (granted, with notable exceptions) our experiments seem to be populated by wraiths, embodied only by a lists of trait adjectives, descriptions forming the cells of the attribution cube, and the like. Infrequently do our subjects actually see other people and less frequently still do they interact with them. Certainly people make messy stimuli, less tractable than the idealized representations of them we often employ. But as Snyder (Chapter 8, this volume) among many others has pointed out, in our interaction with others we can and frequently do affect them as stimuli. Indeed it is precisely people's capacity to respond to, and be affected by, us that makes social perception different from the perception of the physical world (Heider, 1958).

There are those who predict that social psychology will, in a relatively short time, become a branch of cognitive psychology. I am not one of those who would regard this as a fate worse than death. But I do hope that we will try to apply the insights of cognitive psychology—the concepts, theories, and methods—to the study of the behavior that is central to our lives as social beings.

ACKNOWLEDGMENTS

All of the research discussed in this paper was done collaboratively. I gratefully acknowledge the contributions of Bill Apple, Valerie Geller, Chris Olson, and Lynn Streeter. I am also grateful for the comments of Peter Bricker, Nancy Morency, and Myron Wish. This research received support from Bell Laboratories.

REFERENCES

Asch, S., *Social psychology*. Englewood Cliffs, N.J.: Prentice-Hall, 1952.

Apple, W. *Perceiving emotion in others: Integration of verbal, nonverbal and contextual cues*. Unpublished doctoral dissertation, Columbia University, 1979.

Apple, W., Streeter, L. A., Krauss, R. M. The effects of pitch and speech rate on personal attributions. *Journal of Personality and Social Psychology*, 1979, *37*, 715–727.

Ayer, A. J. What is communication? In *Studies in communication*. Communication and Research Centre, University College, London: Secker & Warburg, 1955.

Ekman, P., & Friesen, W. V. Detecting deception from body or face. *Journal of Personality and Social Psychology*, 1974, *29*(3), 288–298.

Ekman, P., Friesen, W. V., & Scherer, K. Body movements and voice pitch in deceptive interaction. *Semiotica*, 1976, *16*, 23–27.

Fairbanks, G. Recent experimental investigations of vocal pitch in speech. *Journal of the Acoustical Society of America*, 1940, *11*, 457–466.

Freud, S. (1905). Fragment of an analysis of a case of hysteria. *Collected papers* (Vol. 3). New York: Basic Books, 1959.

Geller, V. The role of visual access in impression management and impression formation. Unpublished doctoral dissertation, Columbia University, 1977.

Goffman, E. *The presentation of self in everyday life*. Garden City, N.Y.: Anchor (Doubleday), 1961.

Hecker, M. H. L., Stevens, K. N., von Bismarck, G. & Williams, C. E. Manifestations of task-induced stress in the acoustic speech signal. *Journal of the Acoustical Society of America*, 1968, *44*(4), 993–1001.

Heider, F. *The psychology of interpersonal relations*, New York: Wiley, 1958.

Jones, E. E., & Nisbett, R. E. *The actor and the observer: Divergent perceptions of the causes of behavior*. Morristown: General Learning Press, 1971.

Krauss, R. M., Geller, V., & Olson, C. T. *Modalities and cues in the detection of deception*. Paper presented at the meeting of the American Psychological Association, Washington, D.C., September 1976.

Kraut, R. E. Verbal and nonverbal cues in the perception of lying. *Journal of Personality and Social Psychology*, 1978, *36*, 380–391.

Streeter, L. A., Krauss, R. M., Apple, W., & Macdonald, N. *Acoustical and perceptual indicators of stress*. Paper given at meetings of the Acoustical Society of America, Honolulu, Hawaii, October 1978.

Streeter, L. A., Krauss, R. M., Geller, V., Olson, C., & Apple, W. Pitch changes during attempted deception. *Journal of Personality and Social Psychology*, 1977, *35*, 345–350.

Williams, C. E., & Stevens, K. N. On determining the emotional state of pilots during flight: An exploratory study. *Aerospace Medicine*, 1969, *40*(12), 1369–1372.

11 The "Communication Game": Implications for Social Cognition and Persuasion

E. Tory Higgins
University of Western Ontario

Language is a unique and critical feature of interpersonal relations. It is, thus, surprising that the area of psychology most directly concerned with interpersonal relations, social psychology, has paid so little attention to the nature and consequences of language. The purpose of this paper is to consider the role of language in two major aspects of interpersonal relations—interpersonal judgments and persuasion. Both the interpersonal effects of language and the information-processing factors underlying these effects are considered. A number of specific issues are examined. Some of these issues concern the impact of a message on the listener. Does the influence of a message vary depending on whether its style is appropriate for the communication situation or topic? How do listeners' judgments of the communicator's intent affect their response to the message? Do the presuppositions of a message affect its persuasiveness? What happens when listeners' expectations about the communicator are disconfirmed?

The consideration given to the role of language in interpersonal relations has been mainly restricted to implications for the listener. There is, of course, a vast literature on the effects of counterattitudinal advocacy on the communicator (e.g., Festinger, 1957; Janis & King, 1954), but language has much broader implications for the communicator. Some of these are examined in this paper. In referential communication, for example, what happens when a communicator tailors the message to suit the listener's characteristics? What happens when communicators, in order to follow the rules of communication, attempt to produce clear and concise messages?

Finally, the paper considers issues of relevance to both communicators and listeners. One of these issues concerns the effects of message labeling (e.g., literal vs. figurative labeling). Another issue concerns the implications of different communicative goals (e.g., "task" goals, "social relationship" goals) for memory and persuasion. In order to examine these and other issues, one must first consider the nature of the communication process itself.

The "Information Transmission" Approach

The study of verbal communication processes in social psychology has been greatly influenced by the "information transmission" approach used to investigate communication accuracy (cf. Mehrabian & Reed, 1968; Rosenberg & Cohen, 1966) and the effects of communication on persuasion (cf. Eagly & Himmelfarb, 1978; Hovland, Janis, & Kelley, 1953; McGuire, 1966, 1969, 1972).[1] This approach reflects the mathematical model of communication conveyed in the following diagram (cf. DeVito, 1970; Shannon & Weaver, 1949):[2]

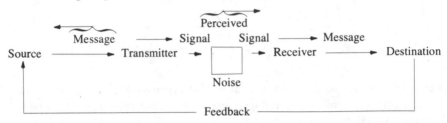

Most research concerned with communication accuracy or referential communication has been based on the "information transmission" approach (Higgins, Fondacaro, & McCann, 1981). In most studies of referential communication, the communicator must provide sufficient information about the target stimulus or referent to enable the recipient, on the basis of the message, to identify or construct the referent (cf. Flavell, Botkin, Fry, Wright, & Jarvis, 1968; Glucksberg, Krauss, & Higgins, 1975; Olson, 1970). The amount of information contained in a message is defined in terms of uncertainty reduction; that is, in terms of how effectively the message zeroes in on the referent by ruling out nonreferents (cf. Cherry, 1957; Shannon & Weaver, 1949). Accurate referential communication requires that communicators tailor their message to take into consideration both the recipient's personal characteristics (e.g., friend vs. stranger; child vs. adult) and the nature of the communication task (e.g., identify-

---

[1]There have also been many studies on impression formation from verbal input (cf. Asch, 1946; Anderson, 1974; Higgins & Rholes, 1976; Wyer, 1974). However, this research has been concerned with judgments based on lexical integration rather than the communication process per se.

[2]I prefer the description, "information transmission," to the usual description, "information processing," because it more clearly reflects this approach's concern with the communicator's success in transmitting the message content, and because the "communication game" approach is also concerned with information processing but without the emphasis on the communicator's effective transmission of the message content.

ing a person at a crowded party vs. in one's office; describing a route to be driven vs. to be drawn). The recipients must also take into consideration both "individual-related" and "task-related" information in interpreting the message. Moreover, they must provide the communicator with feedback concerning their interpretation of the message and, when necessary, request additional information about the referent (cf. Glucksberg et al., 1975; Higgins, 1977a, 1978b).

A number of factors or processes have been postulated to underly referential communication or communication accuracy: vocabulary size, verbal comparison (i.e., comparing the extent to which the message refers to the referent vs. to the nonreferents), perceptual comparison (i.e., determining which features of the referent distinguish it from the nonreferents), and "role-taking" (i.e., taking into consideration the attributes of one's communicative partner; cf. Flavell et al., 1968; Glucksberg et al., 1975; Higgins, 1978b; Higgins & Akst, 1975; Rosenberg & Cohen, 1966).

In the area of persuasion, the "information transmission" process has most often been discussed in terms of Lasswell's (1948) characterization: Who (source) says what (message) in what channel (channel or modality) to whom (receiver) with what effect (destination or impact)? The factors most often suggested as underlying the effects of such "information transmission" on persuasion are attention, comprehension, retention, and willingness to yield (cf. Eagly & Himmelfarb, 1978; Hovland et al., 1953; McGuire, 1969). The emphasis of this approach is on the communicator's or source's effectiveness in transmitting a message containing persuasive arguments that are understood and accepted by the recipient, with persuasion depending upon the comprehensibility, validity, and convincingness of the arguments contained in the message, as well as on the recipient's motivation to hold the "correct" position on the issue.[3]

The "Communication Game"

Although the information transmission approach has typically served as the underpinnings of social psychological research concerned with communication, other aspects of the communication process not captured by this approach have received attention in the fields of speech-communication, philosophy, linguistics, and sociology. These other aspects include cultural conventions for appropriate language use with different message topics and in different social situations, as well as social exchange goals of communication other than information transmission (e.g., "social relationship" goals and "face" goals). An approach that

---

[3]In this summary of the "information transmission" approach, I have purposely abstracted some general features of this approach. I do not mean to imply that this approach has been followed in exactly this manner, or that the limitations and restrictions of the approach have not been recognized or responded to.

incorporates these additional aspects of communication as well as those aspects included in the "information transmission" approach conceptualizes communication as a "game." For example, Wittgenstein (1953) spoke of the "language-game" in order to emphasize the face that the use of words occurs within a general framework of actions. Goffman (1959), and Garfinkle (1967), as well as other symbolic interactionists (cf. Burke, 1962; Lyman & Scott, 1970) have also argued that interpersonal communication involves "gamesmanship" and following the "rules of the game."

In describing communication as a "game," these and other authors wish to emphasize that communication is purposeful social interaction occurring within a socially defined context, involving interdependent social roles and conventional rules, stratagems, and tactics for making decisions and obtaining various goals. A review of various papers proposing different aspects of a "game-" like approach to communication suggests that the following four general assumptions are typically made:

1. Communication involves shared patterns of expectations, rules, or conventions concerning the participants' social roles and the appropriate language to be used, with appropriate language use requiring that both the linguistic and extralinguistic context be taken into account (cf. Austin, 1962; Cushman & Whiting, 1972; Gumperz & Hymes, 1972; Morris, 1938; Peirce, 1940; Rommetveit, 1974; Ruesch & Bateson, 1968; Searle, 1970; Watzlawick, Beavin, & Jackson, 1967).

2. Communication requires coorientation and monitoring between the participants, with each participant taking into account the other's characteristics (Cushman & Whiting, 1972; Delia, 1976; Mead, 1934; Piaget, 1926; Rommetveit, 1974) and, especially, their communicative intentions (cf. Grice, 1971; Merleau-Ponty, 1962; Searle, 1970; Silverstein, 1976).

3. Communication functions not only to transmit information, but also to create and define a relationship among the participants, with the content and relationship being interdependent (cf. Blumer, 1962; Bolinger, 1975; Garfinkel, 1967; Gumperz & Hymes, 1972; Hawes, 1973; Watzlawick et al., 1967).

4. Communication is a simultaneous, interdependent process of social interaction in which the participants intersubjectively and collaboratively determine the purpose and social reality or "meaning" of the interchange (cf. Blumer, 1962; Burke, 1962; Garfinkel, 1967; Goffman, 1959; Hawes, 1973; Merleau-Ponty, 1962; Rommetveit, 1974; Watzlawick et al., 1967).

The factors that mediate the "communication game" include the processes considered in the "information transmission" literature: labeling or categorization, verbal comparison, perceptual comparison, attention, comprehension, retention, and "role-taking." However, the "role-taking" involved in the "communication game" consists of more than just taking into consideration the attributes of one's communicative partner; it also includes judging oneself from the perspective of one's communicative partner. This self-judgment aspect of role-taking is one reason why the communication process has effects on the communicator as well as on the message recipient. In addition to these factors, the "communication game" includes fulfilling communicative roles, defining the communicative situation, judging message appropriateness (e.g., judging whether the message is appropriate for the context, the topic, the modality, etc.), judging motives and intentions, and responding to confirmation or disconfirmation of cultural expectations.

The factors and processes involved in information transmission are an important part of the "communication game." Transmitting information about objects and events and advocating particular positions on issues are among the major purposes of communication. Among the rules of communication are those dictating that messages should be accurate, comprehensible, and valid, and that communicators and recipients should take into consideration the attributes of their communicative partner. In addition, categorization, attention, comprehension, and retention of the message are clearly important processes underlying communication. As previously discussed, many of these factors and processes have been extensively examined (cf. Eagly & Himmelfarb, 1974, 1978; Glucksberg et al., 1975; McGuire, 1969), although their implications have mainly been considered with regard to communication accuracy and persuasion rather than social judgment and person memory. The implications of the other aspects of the "communication game," however, have scarcely been considered with respect to either persuasion or social judgment and person memory. For this reason, the present chapter concentrates on the implications of those aspects of the "communication game" that have received relatively little attention in the "information transmission" literature, as well as those "information transmission" processes, such as categorization, whose implications for social judgment and person memory have seldom been examined.

It must be emphasized that the "communication game" approach at this stage is, at best, a loose, flexible, and preliminary framework for raising new issues and research questions. It is not, therefore, a model in the sense of involving a system of clear, logically related definitions, assumptions, and postulates. The four general assumptions of the "communication game" approach outlined earlier can be combined into two general features—the general rules of the "communication game" (combining the first and second assumptions), and the "communication game" as purposeful social interaction (combining the third and fourth assumptions). The discussion of the implications of the "communication game" for persuasion, social judgment, and person memory is organized in terms of these two general features.

GENERAL RULES OF THE
"COMMUNICATION GAME"

A review of the literature suggests the following general rules of the "communication game" (cf. Austin, 1962; Cushman & Whiting, 1972; Grice, 1971; Gumperz & Hymes, 1972; Rommetveit, 1974; van Dijk, 1977):

For communicators:

1. Communicators should take the audience's or recipient's characteristics into account.
2. Communicators should convey the truth as they see it.
3. Communicators should try to be understood (i.e., be coherent and comprehensible).
4. Communicators should give neither too much nor too little information.
5. Communicators should be relevant (i.e., stick to the point).
6. Communicators should produce a message that is appropriate to the context and circumstances.
7. Communicators should produce a message that is appropriate to their communicative intent or purpose.

For message recipients:

1. Recipients should take the communicator's or source's characteristics into account.
2. Recipients should determine the communicator's communicative intent or purpose.
3. Recipients should take the context and circumstances into account.
4. Recipients should pay attention to the message and be prepared for receiving it.
5. Recipients should try to understand the message.
6. Recipients, when possible, should provide feedback to the communicator concerning their interpretation or understanding of the message.

The foregoing list of rules of the "communication game" is not meant to imply either that these are the only rules of verbal communication or that people are consciously aware of these rules. The list of rules is also not meant to suggest that successful and/or acceptable communication requires that all of these rules be followed in every communicative interchange. In fact, in many cases it is not possible to follow all of the rules, and some rules must and will take precedence over others depending on the circumstances and the purpose of the communicative interaction (cf. Higgins et al., 1981). Thus, unlike formal games, such as baseball, chess, bridge, etc., there is no explicit, well-defined set of rules that must all be followed to play the game properly. Let us now examine some of these rules more closely and consider how they might affect persuasion, person memory, and social judgment.

Communicators Should Take the Recipient's Characteristics Into Account (Communicator Rule 1)

It is well recognized that to be an effective communicator one should tailor one's message to suit the characteristics of the recipient (cf. Mead, 1934; Piaget, 1926), and there is substantial evidence that communicators do, in fact, modify their message to suit the recipient (cf. Flavell et al., 1968; Glucksberg et al., 1975; Higgins, 1977a). One sort of message modification that is particularly relevant to the present paper is the modification of one's message to suit the recipient's attitude. For example, communicators will modify their message about an issue toward the recipient's position on the issue (Manis, Cornell, & Moore, 1974; Newtson & Czerlinsky, 1974). Similarly, communicators will modify their characterization of a person so as to generally agree in evaluative tone with the recipient's attitude toward the person (Higgins & Rholes, 1978). For example, if the target person's behavior could be characterized as either confident or conceited, a communicator is likely to label the person as "confident" when the recipient clearly likes the person, but as "conceited" when the recipient clearly dislikes the person.

What are the implications of such message modification? One might think that following the rules for effective communication would simply enhance the communicative interaction. However, it appears that message modification can have unintended negative consequences for the communicator's own objectivity. We have examined the effects of message modification on memory and social judgments in two studies. In one study (Higgins & Rholes, 1978), subjects summarized information about a stimulus person for a recipient who purportedly either liked or disliked the stimulus person. The stimulus information contained descriptions of a fictional undergraduate called "Donald," who was supposedly a member of a particular group of students whose personalities and interpersonal relations had been studied over a long period. The recipient was supposedly also a member of this group, and it was the communicators' task to summarize the information about the stimulus person so that the recipient could guess which group member was being described.

The descriptions in the "Donald" essay contained both evaluatively ambiguous descriptions, where for each description either a positive or negative label was appropriate, and evaluatively unambiguous descriptions, where for some descriptions only a positive label was appropriate and for other descriptions only a negative label was appropriate. For example, one of the evaluatively ambiguous descriptions was for "independent/aloof"—"Other than socially prescribed engagements, Donald's contacts with others are rather limited. He feels he does not need to rely on anyone''—and another evaluatively ambiguous description was for "persistent/stubborn"—"Once Donald makes up his mind to do something it is as good as done, no matter how long it might take or how difficult the going might be. Only rarely does he change his mind even when it might well be better if he did." One of the evaluatively positive unambiguous descriptions was for "athletic"—"Donald was fairly athletically inclined during high school. He played baseball, basketball, and tennis, and lettered in baseball and basketball during his last two years"—and one of the evaluatively negative unambiguous descriptions was for "short-tempered"—"Donald occasionally gets angry for little reasons. He is especially angered when his suggestions, ones he feels strongly about, are not acted upon by his friends."

The communicators modified their summaries of the stimulus information to be evaluatively consistent with their recipient's attitude toward the stimulus person. As shown in Table 11.1, communicators labeled both the ambiguous and unambiguous descriptions to be evaluatively consistent with their recipient's attitude, including more positive labels and less negative labels in their messages when their recipient purportedly liked the stimulus person. For the ambiguous descriptions, this involved communicators selecting whichever label among the alternative labels for a particular description was evaluatively consistent with the recipient's attitude. For the unambiguous descriptions, this involved communicators labeling those descriptions that were evaluatively consistent with the recipient's attitude and *not* labeling those descriptions that were evaluatively inconsistent with the recipient's attitude.

Due to the effects of categorization on memory (cf. Bartlett, 1932; Higgins, Rholes, & Jones, 1977; Higgins & King, 1981; Neisser, 1967), we expected that such message modification to suit the recipient's attitude would affect the communicators' own memory and judgments of the stimulus person. Indeed, as shown in Table 11.2, there was a highly significant tendency for communicators' reproductions to be evaluatively distorted in the direction of their recipient's attitude if they actually wrote their message (Message condition). This effect was not observed, however, if subjects simply intended to write a message (No Message condition). Thus, the recipients' attitude toward the stimulus person only affected communicators' own memory of the stimulus person if the com-

TABLE 11.1
Message Labeling (Higgins & Rholes, 1978)

Message Recipient's Opinion	Ambiguous		Unambiguous	
	Positive label	Negative label	Positive label	Negative label
Like	1.3	0.6	1.8	0.4
Dislike	0.8	1.5	1.3	1.8

TABLE 11.2
Reproduction Distortions (Higgins & Rholes, 1978)

Message Recipient's Opinion	Message		No Message	
	Positive Distortions	Negative Distortions	Positive Distortions	Negative Distortions
Like	2.4	0	0.8	0.6
Dislike	0.3	1.9	0.8	0.5

municators modified their categorizations of the stimulus person to suit their recipient's attitude. Similarly, there was a significant tendency for communicators' own attitudes toward the stimulus person to be evaluatively consistent with their recipient's attitude if they actually produced a message, but not if they simply intended to communicate.

Additional results strongly supported the interpretation that categorization mediated the message modification effects on communicators' memory and judgments. Significant positive relations were found between the evaluative tone of communicators' reproductions of the stimulus information and the evaluative tone of their message. In addition, communicators' attitudes toward the stimulus person were positively related to the evaluative tone of their message. Finally, consistent with expectations concerning the effects of categorization over time (Bartlett, 1932; Higgins et al., 1977; Higgins & King, in press), the effects of message modification on communicators' memory and liking of the stimulus person increased over a 2-week period. That is, the communicators' memory and liking of the stimulus person were more evaluatively consistent with their message when the period between message production and responses on the reproduction and attitude measures was 2 weeks rather than only 20 minutes. In addition, the correlation between the evaluative distortion in communicators' messages and the evaluative distortion in their reproductions increased significantly over time [from $r = +.18$(ns) to $r = +.74$, $p < .001$].

In the Higgins and Rholes (1978) study, as well as in previous studies of "audience effects" (e.g., Manis et al., 1974; Zimmerman & Bauer, 1956), the effects of only an initial audience were examined. It is an implicit assumption in Zimmerman and Bauer's (1956) conceptualization of "audience effects" that the first or initial audience is critical; that is, the effects of message formulation to suit the audience involve a primacy effect. This assumption has never been empirically tested, however, and there is considerable evidence from research on both memory and social judgment that recency effects can also occur, especially when there is a long delay between the first and second input (cf. Jones & Goethals, 1972; Miller & Cambell, 1959). It is also possible that there would be an averaging effect (cf. Anderson, 1974). Nevertheless, a number of information-processing considerations would predict that primacy effects would predominate (cf. Bartlett, 1932; Fredericksen, 1975; McGuire, 1969). In fact, it may be that communicators will not modify their message to the same extent for the second recipient as for the first recipient. This issue is presently being examined by having communicators, at various time intervals, describe the stimulus person to successive recipients with opposite opinions of the stimulus person.

Communicators will also modify their message to suit the information needs of their recipient. For example, even children will vary their message depending on whether their recipient is a young child or an adult (Sachs & Devin, 1976; Shatz & Gelman, 1973), whether their recipient is blindfolded or not (Maratsos, 1973), and whether their recipient has information in common with them or not (Higgins, 1977a). In a recent study, we examined whether communicators would vary their message description of a stimulus person depending on whether the recipient had been exposed to the same or different information about the person, and, if so, what effect such message modification would have on the communicators' own memory and impressions of the person (Higgins, McCann, & Fondacaro, 1980).

Undergraduates agreed to participate in a study on "interpersonal communication." Upon their arrival, the subjects were assigned either the role of "speaker" or the role of "listener" for the subsequent communication task. The speaker and listener were put into separate rooms connected by intercom. Both speakers and listeners were told they would receive an essay describing another undergraduate. Speakers were told that their task was to summarize their impression of the stimulus person for the listener. The listeners were told their task was to determine their communicator's impression of the stimulus person from the message. Each speaker–listener pair was either told that their partner had been given the same information about the stimulus person (Same condition) or different information about the stimulus person (Different condition). All subjects, in fact, received the same information. The information given to subjects was the "Donald" essay described earlier. Prior to the communication, all subjects read the "Donald" essay and, after a few minutes, were asked to reproduce the essay exactly, word for word (Premessage measure). The speakers then communicated their impression of "Donald" to the listener over the intercom, with no feedback from the listener being permitted. Following the communication, all subjects were again asked to reproduce the essay about "Donald" exactly, word for word (Postmessage measure).

Each message and reproduction was scored in terms of whether each of the 12 descriptions in the "Donald" essay was deleted (deletions), distorted to be more evaluatively positive or negative (positive and negative distortions), or reproduced without evaluative distortion (unchanged). (For examples of the scoring, see Higgins & Rholes, 1978.) As expected, communicators did vary their message depending on whether their recipient had the same or different information about the stimulus person. Communicators were significantly less likely to change the stimulus information when communicating their impression of the stimulus person if they believed their recipient had received different information about the stimulus person (mean number of "unchanged" descriptions = 6.5) than if they believed their recipient had received the same information (mean number of "unchanged" descriptions = 5.2). It appears that, at least under these circumstances, communicators are more careful to "stick to the facts" and present a relatively complete picture of the stimulus person if they believe their recipient has different information about the stimulus person. After all, it is especially important for communicators to give a complete, accurate account of the information they have when their message can provide additional information for the listener. In addition, the risk of disagreement is greater when the listener has different information, and "sticking to the facts" is probably the most defensible position to take. (Of course, if a communicator was trying to deceive the recipient, the communicator would be less likely to provide an accurate account of the information for a recipient with different information because the recipient would be less likely to catch any inaccuracies.)

Does such message modification affect the communicator's own memory of the stimulus person? As shown in Table 11.3, communicators in the Different condition were less likely to change the stimulus information in their Postmessage reproductions than communicators in the Same condition, even though they were, if anything, more likely to change the stimulus information in their Premessage reproductions (i.e., a significant Same/Different × Premessage/Postmessage interaction for "unchanged" recall). Thus, the more communicators "stick to the facts" when stating their impression about a stimulus person, the more accurate is their memory of the stimulus person over time. As further evidence that this difference in recall between speakers in the Same condition versus speakers in the Different condition is due to message modification, and not simply being informed that one's communicative partner has the same or different information about the stimulus person, an analysis of the listeners' reproductions of the stimulus information revealed no significant main

TABLE 11.3
Number of "Unchanged"
Descriptions[a]
(Higgins, McCann,
& Fondacaro, 1980)

	Premessage Reproduction	Postmessage Reproduction
Same	7.7	6.9
Different	7.4	7.6

[a]Maximum possible "unchanged" descriptions is 12.

effects or interactions involving the Same/Different variable. Thus, believing one's communicative partner has either the same or different information about the stimulus person affects recall only when subjects modify their verbal encoding of the stimulus information in response to this belief. The presence for speakers, but not for listeners, of a Same/Different effect on recall as a function of message production (Premessage vs. Postmessage) was reflected in a significant Speaker/Listener × Same/Different × Premessage/Postmessage interaction.

In sum, when communicators modify their message to suit the characteristics of their message recipient, this message modification does not have implications only for communicative accuracy and appropriateness. It also has implications for the communicators' own memory and judgments. The results of our studies indicate that communicators' memory and judgments of a stimulus person become increasingly consistent with the description of the stimulus person contained in their (modified) message. Thus, the verbal communication process can affect the communicator's memory and judgments as well as the recipient's memory and judgments, and this is true for referential communication as well as counterattitudinal persuasive communication.

When communicators take into consideration the characteristics, attitudes, and potential reactions of the recipient, they are traditionally considered to be "role-taking" (Flavell et al., 1968; Mead, 1934). However, "role-taking" can involve more than this (cf. Flavell et al., 1968; Higgins, 1981; Mead, 1934; Piaget, 1926; Shantz, 1975). In particular, "role-taking" has been used to refer to a process whereby one attempts to judge and experience events from the viewpoint of another person. In this sense, "role-taking" involves not simply judging other persons' characteristics, attitudes, etc., but involves seeing the world through their eyes.

An important variety of this latter type of role-taking occurs when people take the viewpoint of others in judging their own behavior (Mead, 1934). If communicators take the viewpoint of the recipient in judging their message, then some of the variables that affect recipients' responses to a message (e.g., the communicator's expertise and attractiveness) could affect communicator's responses to their own message, thus affecting the self-persuasion process. For example, there may be greater self-persuasion when communicators believe the recipient considers them to be attractive or knowledgeable on the topic than when communicators believe the recipient considers them to be unattractive or ignorant on the topic. Gross, Riemer, and Collins (1973), for instance, found that there was greater self-persuasion from producing a counterattitudinal essay when the communicators believed the audience considered them sincere than when they believed the audience considered them insincere. Thus, if communicators take the role of the recipient and judge themselves and their message from their recipient's standpoint (cf. Turner, 1956), self-persuasion will vary as a function of the communicators' beliefs concerning the recipient's response to them. This is in contrast to the effects on self-persuasion from Bem's (1965; 1972) "self-perception" process where communicators' self-judgments would depend on their behavior and the situational constraints on their behavior, and where the judgment is made from the communicators' own standpoint (just as if they were observing and judging another person). In fact, because communicators' own beliefs can be different from their judgment of the recipient's belief (cf. Wyer, Henninger, & Hinkle, 1977), self-persuasion could vary depending on whether communicators' self-judgments were a result of "role-taking," or "self-perception."

Recipients Should Take the Communicator's Characteristics, Motives, and Intentions Into Account (Recipient Rules 1 & 2)

Because the recipient is aware that the communicator is likely to follow the rule of modifying the message to suit the recipient, such message modification also has implications for the recipient's interpretation of the message. If recipients know that the communicator is aware of their attitude toward a person or issue, they should reevaluate, or even discount, a similar attitude reflected in the communicator's message. Consistent with this prediction, Newston and Czerlinsky (1974) found that when subjects were given a communicator's message on an issue that had been directed to an audience with an extreme opinion on the issue, and were asked to judge the communicator's true opinion, they "corrected" their judgment away from the opinion of the audience. This process of reevaluation also suggests that communicators would be more effective when their persuasive messages are "overheard" by the recipient, or when they advocate a position they know disagrees with the recipient's attitude. Under these conditions, the position taken in the communicators' messages could not simply result from following the message modification rule and, thus, would be more likely to reflect the communicators' true opinion. There is, in fact, considerable evidence supporting this prediction (cf. Eagly, Wood, & Chaiken, 1978; Mills & Jellison, 1967; Walster & Festinger, 1962). Furthermore, because communicators would not need to modify their message for an issue that was irrelevant to the recipient, a recipient would be more likely in such cases to judge the message as reflecting the communicator's true opinion and, thus, be more persuaded, as Brock and Becker (1965) have found.

Similarly, it is also necessary for the recipient to consider alternative reasons why the message was produced when attempting to determine the communicator's intent. Communication or speech acts presuppose intent or purpose, and determining the communicator's intention is a critical part of understanding the message (Grice, 1975; Merleau-Pointy, 1962; Searle, 1970; Silverstein, 1976). Austin (1962) points out that because speech is an action, it is liable to be done under duress, by accident, by mistake, etc., just like any other action.

Influenced by causal attribution theories (e.g., Heider, 1958; Jones & Davis, 1965; Kelley, 1967), there has been a growing recognition that the persuasiveness of a message is affected by recipients' causal explanations concerning why the communicator expressed a particular opinion on an issue (cf. Eagly, Wood, & Chaiken, 1978). For example, Eagly and Himmelfarb (1978) suggest that recipients are affected by whether they judge the communicator's expressed opinion to reflect the communicator's true feelings versus situational constraints. As just discussed, one such situational constraint is the recipient's opinion.

An important issue in the area of communication and persuasion is whether the effectiveness of a persuasive message is reduced when the recipient judges the communicator to have a persuasive intent. Evidence on this issue has been mixed (cf. McGuire, 1966), perhaps because there has been a tendency simply to contrast general persuasive intent with nonpersuasive intent. However, the recipient could judge the communicator to have many different kinds of persuasive intent (cf. Austin, 1962; Searle, 1970), and the specific judged intent could be a critical factor in determining the recipient's response. For example, recipients of a persuasive message on some political issue may respond differently if they believe the communicator's purpose is to defeat them (a competitive orientation) versus to gain their support (a cooperative orientation). One factor influencing recipients' attributions of intent may be their judgments of the communicator's characteristics. For example, if the communicator is judged to belong to a different political group, the recipient is more likely to attribute a competitive persuasive intent.

Not only can the recipients' judgments of the communicator's characteristics and intentions affect their response to the message (e.g., their willingness to yield; their confidence in the validity of the message arguments), but they can also affect their actual interpretation of the message. Such judgments are an integral, pervasive aspect of the communication process, and the recipient will actively determine the communicator's characteristics and intentions *in order to* interpret the message. Judgments of the communicator's characteristics can affect the recipient's interpretation of the message because they place the interaction within a particular frame of reference (Lyman & Scott, 1970). For example, following a conference on the crisis in the middle East, one would interpret the statement, "The talks went very well," differently if said by an Israeli spokesman than if said by an Egyptian spokesman because of the assumed difference in bias. The importance of communicator characteristics for the interpretation of a message is emphasized in Asch's (1952) discussion of how the attribution of authorship may alter the "cognitive content" of a statement.

In sum, recipients must also take communicators' characteristics into account. Because one characteristic of communicators is their motive to suit the recipient through message modification, recipients may alter their judgment of the communicator's true opinion when they believe this motive is operating. This variation in recipients' judgment of the communicator is one example of a general tendency for recipients to vary their judgment of the communicator's dispositions or intent depending on the extent of situational constraints on message production. Recipients' judgments of the communicator's intent can affect not only their response to a message, but also their interpretation of the message.

Communicators Should Convey the Truth as They See It (Communicator Rule 2)

The communication and persuasion literature suggests that a major concern of message recipients in judging the communicator is whether the communicator is telling the truth. However, communicators are not responsible for strictly telling the truth, but, rather, for telling the truth "as they see it." This important point is reflected in Eagly et al.'s (1978) recent distinction between two kinds of communicator bias inferred by message recipients—a "knowledge bias" versus a "reporting bias." "Knowledge bias" refers to a recipient's judgment that the communicator's knowledge about the message topic is incomplete, inaccurate, or, generally, nonveridical. "Reporting bias" refers to a recipient's judgment that the communicator is unwilling to provide an accurate account of the message topic; that is, the communicator is knowingly conveying a distorted or biased version of his or her knowledge about the message topic.

"Knowledge bias," without "reporting bias," satisfies the rule that people should tell the truth *as they see it,* whereas "reporting bias" breaks this rule. One would, therefore, expect recipients to make more negative judgments of the communicator when they judge the communicator to have a "reporting bias" than when they judge the communicator to have a "knowledge bias." Indeed, Eagly et al. (1978) found that recipients judged the communicator (a mayoral candidate) as more insincere and manipulative when his behavior suggested a "reporting bias" (e.g., advocating a proenvironment position to a strongly proenvironment audience during an election year) than when his behavior suggested a "knowledge bias" (e.g., having a long history of supporting proenvironment causes).

Eagly et al. (1978) also found that recipients were less persuaded when they judged the communicator to have either a "knowledge bias" or a "reporting bias" than when they made neither judgment of bias. This decrease in persuasive impact of the biased messages would appear to derive from different factors for "knowledge bias" and "reporting bias." As discussed previously, if a communicator is judged as having modified his message to suit the audience (i.e., a "reporting bias"), the position advocated in the message is not considered to reflect the communicator's true position. Consistent with this interpretation, subjects judged the communicator as having the least freedom to express his true opinion when he tailored his message to suit the audience's opinion. On the other hand, if a communicator is known to have always supported a particular position, the information contained in the message is judged to be one-sided, incomplete, and generally, nonveridical.

The rule that communicators should convey the truth as they see it emphasizes two factors—sincerity and truth. Sincerity is clearly essential, but is it sufficient to tell the truth? In many cases it is not sufficient for a communicator to simply tell the truth. As a result of conversational postulates, implicatures, and presuppositions, a statement can be misleading even if it is true (cf. Gordon & Lakoff, 1975; Grice, 1975). Gordon and Lakoff (1975) provide the following example. Suppose you are witness to a murder and, when someone asks you what happened, you reply, "Someone tried to kill Harry." This reply is a true statement because if someone murdered Harry, he certainly tried to kill him. However, it is misleading because it conveys the impression that the attempt was unsuccessful. Thus, to avoid misleading the recipient, it is necessary that communicators follow Rule 4—do not give too little information.

Is it enough, then, that a communicator "tell the truth, the whole truth, and nothing but the truth?" Telling the whole truth is neither always necessary nor advisable. In referential communication, for example, it is poor communication to describe all of the referent's properties, because many of these properties do not discriminate the referent from the nonreferent, and, thus, are not relevant (Rule 5). In fact, it is even poor communication to describe all the discriminating properties of the referent if a subset of these properties is sufficient to allow the recipient to identify the referent correctly (cf. Glucksberg et al., 1975). For example, if one wants an apple from a bowl of fruit containing only one apple, it is poor communication to say, "Give me the round, red apple with the brown stem [Higgins, 1976b]." As Grice (1975) points out, telling the whole truth when part of the truth would fulfill the communicative purpose can be misleading because it suggests to the recipient that there was some particular reason for providing the additional information. Therefore, to avoid misleading the recipient, it is important for communicators to follow the other half of Rule 4—do not give too much information.

It would thus appear that a communicator must follow Rule 2 ("convey the truth as you see it") *and* Rule 4 ("give neither too much nor too little information") in order not to mislead the recipient. This suggests that the truth is still critical, but neither too much nor too little should be conveyed. However, in order to follow Rule 3 ("try to be understood"), and Rule 7 ("communicate in a manner appropriate to the communicative intent or purpose"), a communicator may, in fact, have to distort the truth. For example, if communicators wish to formulate a clear, unified message (Rule 3), they may have to polarize the information and/or ignore contradictory facts. There is considerable evidence from studies of "cognitive tuning" that speakers, as compared to listeners, will form a distorted, one-sided impression of a stimulus person prior to communication, with this distorted impression being communicated in their message (e.g., Brock & Fromkin, 1968; Cohen, 1961; Harvey, Harkins, & Kagehiro, 1976; Higgins, McCann, & Fondacaro, 1980; Leventhal, 1962; Zajonc, 1960). A communicator may also distort stimulus information in order to facilitate the recipient's identification of the referent (Rule 7). For example, by evaluatively distorting their description of the stimulus person to match the recipient's attitude, communicators in the Higgins and Rholes (1978) study increased the likelihood that their recipient would correctly identify the stimulus person; that is, a decrease in descriptive accuracy can increase referential accuracy.

It would be interesting to examine whether recipients' judgments of communicators' "reporting bias" vary depending upon the purpose of the message. In the Higgins and Rholes (1978) study, the purpose of the message was to facilitate the recipient's identification of the stimulus person. In Eagly et al.'s (1978) study, however, the supposed purpose of the candidate's message was to convey his true views on a controversial issue. Recipients are less likely to make negative, dispositional judgments in the former case because a reporting bias is appropriate to the agreed purpose of the message (i.e., it is dictated by Rule 7).

In sum, communicators may be judged negatively by the recipient if they either do not tell the truth "as they see it" or do tell the truth but convey a false impression by providing too little or too much information. Recipients' response to an inaccurate message will vary, however, depending upon their judgment of the communicator's motive for the inaccuracy.

Communicators Should Be Clear and Concise
(Communicator Rules 3 & 4);
Recipients Should Be Prepared for Receiving the Message
(Recipient Rule 5)

As we have seen previously, the communicator rules emphasizing that communicators should be clear and concise have implications for the recipients' judgments of the communicator's intent, as well as implications for the accuracy of the communicator's message. These rules, however, also have implications for the communicator's own memory and judgments of the stimulus information. These implications will be examined in two sections. The first section compares the effects on communicators from following these rules with the effects on the recipient from following a different rule (i.e., recipients should be prepared for receiving the message), a comparison that is central to the "cognitive tuning" literature. The second section examines a major means of accomplishing the clarity and conciseness demanded by the communicator rules; namely, labeling the stimulus information.

Cognitive Tuning

The "cognitive tuning" literature suggests that because communicators are supposed to produce clear, concise messages, they polarize and distort stimulus information to a greater extent than recipients who are supposed to be open to change and prepared for a wide range of possible information contained in the message. The "cognitive tuning" studies, however, have usually involved more than these different role expectations for the communicator and recipient (cf. Higgins et al., in press); in particular, they have used a procedure whereby the recipients, but not the communicators, expect to receive additional information about the stimulus person. Because subjects are more likely to integrate information about a stimulus person into a unified impression if they feel they have all the relevant information than if they know they will later receive additional information, this difference in expectations about receiving additional information could account for the results of the "cognitive tuning" studies. As another part of the Higgins et al. (1980) study, we independently examined the effects of differences in expectations about receiving additional information and differences in the normative expectations associated with the communicator and recipient roles.

As described in the foregoing section, subjects were assigned either the role of "communicator" or the role of "recipient." Both communicators and recipients were told they would receive an essay describing another undergraduate. Communicators were told that their task was to summarize their impression of the stimulus person for the recipient, whereas recipients were told their task was to determine their communicator's impression of the stimulus person from the message. Both communicators and recipients were either told that they would later receive additional information about the stimulus person from the experimenter ("Expectation" condition), or they were told nothing at all ("No expectation" condition). All subjects, in fact, only received the initial "Donald" essay previously described. After reading the essay, and prior to communication, all subjects were asked to write down their impression of "Donald." It is the results of this Premessage measure of subjects' impressions that is most comparable to the measure taken by previous "cognitive tuning" studies.

All subjects' impressions were scored in terms of whether they contained trait terms spontaneously labeling the stimulus descriptions, and whether the trait labels were evaluatively positive or negative. When possible the labels were scored on the basis of Anderson's (1968) likeableness ratings of trait labels, where labels above or below the median were scored as positive and negative, respectively. Otherwise, a judge (blind to experimental condition) rated the label as positive or negative. Inter-rater agreement was over 90%. Across all experimental conditions, a strong "positivity" bias was found, with subjects' impressions containing significantly more positive labels ($M = 2.5$) than negative labels ($M = 1.5$). Thus, in general, subjects' labeling of the stimulus person

TABLE 11.4
Impression Labeling (Higgins, McCann, & Fondacaro, 1980).

Communication role	Expectation			No Expectation		
	Positive Label	Negative Label	Pos.-Neg. Difference	Positive Label	Negative Label	Pos.-Neg. Difference
Communicator	2.6	1.5	1.1***	2.7	1.5	1.2*
Recipient	2.2	1.9	0.3ᵃ	2.3	1.1	1.2**

* $t = 2.53$, $p < .05$ two-tailed.
** $t = 2.85$, $p < .02$ two-tailed.
*** $t = 2.98$, $p < .01$ two-tailed.
ᵃ $t < 1$, $p > .30$ two-tailed.

conveyed a positive impression of the stimulus person that was more coherent and definite than the evaluatively inconsistent stimulus information. However, as shown in Table 11.4, this positivity bias was not present in every condition. Consistent with the "cognitive tuning" literature, there was a positivity bias in the Communicator/No Expectation condition, but there was no positivity bias in the Recipient/Expectation condition. Moreover, in contrast to recipients, communicators positively distorted their impression of the stimulus person even when they expected to receive additional information about the stimulus person (the Communicator/Expectation condition). Communicators, of course, should formulate a clear, unified message for the recipient even when they expect to receive additional information. Consistent with this interpretation, communicators' subsequent messages were, indeed, positively "polarized," containing significantly more positive labels ($M = 2.3$) than negative labels ($M = 1.7$).

Table 11.4 also indicates that there *was* a positivity bias in the Recipient/No Expectation condition. Thus, recipients who did not expect to receive additional information about the stimulus person positively distorted their impression of the stimulus person to the same extent as did communicators. Therefore, in contrast to the communicators whose positivity bias appears to have been determined by the rules of their communicative role (i.e., be clear, concise, and coherent), the recipients' positivity bias appears to have been determined by whether they expected to receive additional information about the stimulus person.

Labeling

One way in which communicators can make their message more concise is to label the stimulus information. Communicators may be reluctant, however, to transmit definitive judgments concerning a stimulus (i.e., label the stimulus information) when they expect later to receive additional information about the stimulus. It is, perhaps, for this reason that communicators' messages in the Higgins et al. (1980) study contained significantly fewer labels in the "Expectation" condition ($M = 3.1$) than in the "No Expectation" condition ($M = 5.0$). When communicators do increase the conciseness of their messages through labeling, does this affect the communicator's own memory and judgments of the stimulus information? The difference in the amount of message labeling between the "Expectation" and "No Expectation" conditions in the Higgins et al. (1980) study does appear to have affected the communicators' own memory for the stimulus information. When subjects were later asked to reproduce the stimulus information, the reproductions of communicators in the "No Expectation" condition were significantly more distorted than the reproductions of communicators in the "Expectation" condition. That is, the greater the labeling, the greater the distortion of the stimulus information. Thus, this study, as well as the Higgins and Rholes (1978) study, suggests that labeling does affect the communicator's own memory and judgments. What are the processes underlying the effects of labeling and do the effects vary for different types of labeling? The purpose of this section is to examine these issues.

The effects of labeling on memory has long been a major issue in cognitive psychology. In one of the first studies on labeling by Carmichael, Hogan, and Walter (1932), subjects were shown a set of ambiguous drawings, and prior to each drawing, the experimenter gave the subjets one of two alternative labels for the drawing (e.g., "dumbbells" vs. "eyeglasses"). When subjects were later asked to reproduce each drawing, the reproductions were distorted to resemble more closely a typical member of the category designated by the experimenter's label. In another labeling study by Thomas, DeCapito Caronite, LaMonica, and Hoving (1968), subjects either were told they would be shown a "green" color or were told they would be shown a "blue" color on a forthcoming slide, and that in a subsequent test of generalization they would have to respond whenever they recognized this particular stimulus color. All subjects were then shown the same ambiguous green-blue color. In the subsequent generalization test, subjects made more false recognitions for colors resembling the category designated by the experimenter's label. In a more recent study by Loftus and Palmer (1974), subjects were shown a film depicting a traffic accident. Following each film, subjects answered a series of questions about the accident. The critical question concerned the speed of the cars involved in the collision. For different subjects, the label used to refer to the collision varied: "About how fast were the cars going when they (contacted; hit; bumped; collided; smashed) each other?". Subjects' estimates of the speed varied depending upon the label provided by the experimenter. For instance, the speed estimates were higher for the "smashed" label than for the "hit" label.

The results of these and similar studies (e.g., Kelley, 1950) can be, and have been, interpreted in terms of the mediational effect of labeling on memory. However, because the labels were supplied to subjects by the experimenter, the labeling took place within the context of interpersonal communication and, thus, more than the mediational effect of labeling could be involved (cf. Higgins et al., 1977). In fact, these studies can be reinterpreted in terms of communication and social influence. There is, after all, considerable evidence that people's judgments, including judgments of physical stimuli, can be significantly influenced by the judgments of experts or power figures (cf. Collins & Raven, 1969), and an experimenter is likely to be perceived by subjects as both an expert and a power figure.[4] Furthermore, as with social influence generally, the nature of the conformity may vary across subjects, at least in part as a function of whether they consider the experimenter to be an expert, a power figure, or an attractive, high status figure. For example, subjects who consider the experimenter to be an expert may be more likely to "internalize" the label (cf. Kelman, 1958; McGuire, 1969) and take it as providing evidence about reality (Deutsch & Gerard's [1955] "informational social influence"). In addition, when experimenters, or communicators in general, select a particular label for a stimulus, it is interpreted as a signal of how they wish the recipient to process the stimulus information (Brown, 1958; Jörg & Hörman, 1978). Let us now consider how the effects of labeling may vary for different types of labeling.

Single Labels and Labels With Modifiers. Communicators may encode stimulus information in terms of either single labels or more general phrases involving a label plus a modifier. For example, a communicator may choose to describe a stimulus person as "fascinating" rather than "extremely interesting." It may be that people over time remember the specific label (or head term) better than the modifier. For example, people who judge a stimulus person to be "very interesting" may over time remember the person was interesting without remembering *how* interesting. If this is the case, then people who label a stimulus person as "very interesting" and people who label the same stimulus person as "fairly interesting" will both tend later to remember the person as being generally interesting; that is, there will be a convergence of their memory and judgments over time. On the other hand, the use of more extreme labels with modifiers could lead to a divergence of memory and judgments over time. For example, people who judge a stimulus person as "somewhat fascinating" may later remember the person as being fascinating, whereas people who judge a stimulus person as "somewhat boring" may later remember the person as being boring. Thus, describing a stimulus as "fascinating" rather than "extremely interesting" in order to produce a more clear, concise message could have a substantial effect over time on the communicator's memory and judgments of the stimulus person.

---

[4]It is possible to directly manipulate subjects' categorization of stimulus objects outside the context of interpersonal communication through the use of an unobtrusive verbal exposure or priming technique (Higgins et al., 1977).

Referential and Persuasive Labeling.   The emphasis in the labeling literature has been on the referential function of labels; that is, labeling is discussed as if its only function were to designate the class membership of an object or event. But labeling also has a persuasive function. When the experimenter in Thomas et al.'s (1968) study, for example, labels the ambiguous color, he is not only providing information about the stimulus' class membership. He is also giving his *opinion* as to what class of colors the stimulus *should* be classified with. It is, perhaps, for this reason that labels are so influential. It is one thing to decide whether a communicator's labels are accurate or inaccurate. It is quite another thing to accept or reject the communicator's opinion.

The persuasive function of labeling is especially evident with personality trait labels. When a communicator labels another person as "aggressive" or "kind," he is expressing his opinion concerning the underlying intentions or dispositions of the person. The communicator, after all, does not have direct access to information indicating the person's intentions or dispositions, but must infer them from the behavior and context (cf. Heider, 1958; Jones & Davis, 1965). Perhaps, the most striking example of this persuasive function of labels is verbal stereotypes. As Brown (1958) points out, to state that the Chinese are "superstitious" both expresses the opinion that they have particular religious beliefs and rituals and expresses the opinion that these beliefs and rituals are irrational and result from ignorance. Similarly, to state that Europeans are "dirty" both expresses an opinion about the frequency of their baths or showers, and expresses the opinion that they do not care about cleanliness and/or have inferior methods of personal hygiene. The recipient of such statements is not faced simply with accepting or rejecting the communicator's opinion about the target group's behavior, but must also accept or reject the communicator's opinion concerning the implications and inferences that should be drawn concerning the target group.

Symbolic and Nonsymbolic Properties of Labels.   Labels, like all words, can have nonsymbolic properties as well as symbolic properties (Higgins & Huttenlocher, 1975; Huttenlocher & Higgins, 1978). Activation of a label's meaning involves a symbolic process. A label, however, can also activate a nonsymbolic associative process acquired through previous co-occurrence of the label with other stimuli and events. Although it is misleading to talk as if labels have a distinct "emotive" meaning (cf. Higgins & Rholes, 1976), labels can cause an emotional reaction in the recipient that is, to some extent at least, independent from its literal meaning. Labels can become associated with positive or negative affect through prior linguistic co-occurrence with evaluatively positive or negative words (Yavuz & Bousfield, 1959), or through prior extralinguistic co-occurrence with positive or negative events (e.g., Lowenfeld, 1961; Reece, 1954). For example, a person could acquire a negative affective reaction to a particular ethnic label either because the person has frequently heard it used in combination with evaluatively negative words (e.g., "lazy," "stupid," "crooked," "drunken"), or has heard it used in the context of an unpleasant event involving a member of the ethnic group (e.g., avoiding a drunk in the park; warding off a panhandler; being cheated; hearing about a riot on the news). In addition, certain paralinguistic features of communication (e.g., intonation, pitch, facial expressions) can signal a negative attitude on the part of the communicator and, through their co-occurrence with a particular label, cause the label to become associated with negative affect. In fact, whenever there are alternative labels available, a communicator's choice of label is often a signal to the recipient, intentional or unintentional, regarding the communicator's attitude toward the referent of the label.

Literal and Figurative Labeling. Our understanding of the effects of labeling on memory and social judgments may also be enhanced by distinguishing between "literal" and "figurative" labeling. "Literal" labeling of a stimulus occurs when the label functions to categorize the stimulus as a member of the class of stimuli designated by the label. "Figurative" labeling of a stimulus occurs when the label functions to suggest a resemblance between the stimulus and members of the class designated by the label. In Thomas et al.'s (1968) study, a light on the borderline between blue and green was labeled either "blue," or "green". Such labeling is "literal" because the stimulus could be considered to be an actual member of the class designated by the label. In Carmichael et al.'s (1932) study, ambiguous line drawings were labeled as "eyeglasses," "table," "broom," etc. In a classic labeling study by Ranken (1963), abstract drawings were assigned the labels "fish," "dog," "rooster," etc. Such labeling is "figurative" because these drawings were *not* actual members of the object class designated by the label, but, rather, resembled the shape of class members.[5]

Literal and figurative labeling do not differ in their general effects on memory. Both literal labeling (cf. Higgins & Rholes, 1978) and figurative labeling (cf. Bahrick & Boucher, 1968; Ranken, 1963) tend to improve recall for the stimulus as a general entity (i.e., as a member of the class designated by the label) but reduce accuracy for the specific properties of the stimulus (i.e., distortion toward the prototypic features of the class designated by the label). Literal and figurative labeling, however, do differ in their pragmatic function and, perhaps, also in their specific effects on memory processes.

Although a class of objects must have a configuration of defining properties in common and/or some family resemblance (Rosch & Mervis, 1975), there is usually variability among class members. Furthermore, although the entire set of

---

[5]It should be noted that even if Ranken's drawings had been realistic, rather than abstract, representations of animals, the labeling would still have been figurative because the drawings would still have been drawings and not animals.

objects are members of the class, some members have properties that are more "characteristic" of the class and are, thus, more "typical" or "ideal" examplars of the class (Rosch, 1973; 1975b; Smith, Shoben, & Rips, 1974). By "literally" labeling a stimulus, the communicator is proposing that the stimulus' properties meet the criteria sufficiently to be considered an actual member of the class designated by the label. The stimulus' properties, however, need not be the same as the "typical" members of the class and need not be "characteristic" of the class.

Alternatively, by "figuratively" labeling a stimulus, the communicator is proposing that the stimulus is not an actual member of the class designated by the label but that its properties resemble the "characteristic" properties of members of the class designated by the label and that the stimulus resembles "typical" class members. If the label is accepted, the stimulus will be remembered as resembling "typical" members of the class designated by the label. Thus, if a label is used figuratively to encode a stimulus, it may cause more distortion toward the "typical" members of the class designated by the label than if the label is used literally (assuming that people remember not only the label but the pragmatic function of the label).

The effects on memory from "figurative" versus "literal" labeling were examined in a study by Higgins and Lee (1976). Purportedly as part of a study on "long-term memory for visual forms," 20 undergraduates were shown a series of 10 stimuli consisting of different geometric shapes of varying color. Embedded within the series were two target stimuli, which appeared in the third and eighth positions in the series. The target stimuli were moderate distortions of the capital letter "L" and the number "4." These stimuli were selected as targets because they could be labeled either literally (e.g., the stimulis is the number four) or figuratively (e.g., the stimulus resembles the number four). In the "literal set" condition the experimenter used literal labels for the nontarget stimuli, whereas in the "figurative set" condition the experimenter used figurative labels for the same nontarget stimuli. For example, an octagon drawing was "literally" labeled "octagon" and "figuratively" labeled "stopsign"; a round patch of yellow was "literally" labeled "yellow" and "figuratively" labeled "grapefruit." The target stimuli were assigned the same labels (i.e., "L"; "four"), with the expectation that subjects would interpret the pragmatic function of these labels as either literal or figurative depending on whether they were in the "literal set" condition or "figurative set" condition, respectively.

After subjects were shown the series of labeled stimuli, they were given both a reproduction task and a recognition task, with the order of these tasks alternating between subjects. (No order effects were found.) In the reproduction task, subjects were asked to reproduce each target stimulus as accurately as possible. In the recognition task, subjects were asked, for each target stimulus, to select the stimulus they saw from among an array of stimuli containing the target stimulus and nine additional stimuli varying in similarity to the standard exemplar of the stimulus class designated by the label. As hypothesized, both subjects' reproductions and stimulus selections in the recognition task were significantly (all p's $< .05$) more distorted away from the target stimuli toward the standard examplars in the "figurative set" condition than in the "literal set" condition. These results were replicated in a second study involving the same basic design and procedure.

Thus, at least for the stimuli used in our study, figurative labeling caused even more distortion than literal labeling toward the typical or standard member of the class designated by the label. Would figurative labeling also cause more distortion when used to label people? For example, many occupational roles, such as "businessman," consist of behaviors and attributes that define role membership (e.g., engaged in commerce or industry), as well as behaviors and attributes that are considered typical or characteristic of role occupants (e.g., methodical, practical, materialistic). The implications of a person being labeling as a "businessman" may be very different if the recipient interprets the label literally (i.e., the target person's profession *is* business) than if the recipient interprets the label figuratively (i.e., the target person's profession is *not* business, but his behavior and attributes resemble that of a businessman). Under certain conditions, the recipient may be as likely, or even more likely, to infer that the target person possesses those attributes assumed to be characteristic of businessmen when the label is interpreted figuratively than when the label is interpreted literally (cf. Higgins & King, 1981).

"Leading" Labeling and "Misleading" Labeling.   In Loftus and Palmer's (1974) study, different subjects were given different labels for the traffic collision, and were asked how fast the cars were going. Each label refers to contact between two objects, but the labels differ in the force behind the contact (e.g., "smashed" involves more force than "bumped"), and the amount of force has implications for the speed of the cars. The different questions in the Loftus and Palmer study, as well as in similar studies, have been referred to as "leading" questions. The labeling in such questions, however, might be better called "misleading" because it misleads the recipient concerning the stimulus information. After all, the cars in the Loftus and Palmer study collided with a particular force, and, thus, the labels vary in how accurately they describe the actual force of the collision. Some labels are relatively inaccurate but are presented to recipients as if they were accurate, and, therefore, these labels are misleading.

A question involving a "leading" label would contain a label that leads the recipient to categorize the stimulus information in terms of the label, but the label would not be presented to recipients as necessarily being an accurate description of the stimulus information. A recent study by Higgins and Rholes (see Higgins & King, in press) demonstrates the effects of such "leading" labels. Sixty undergraduates read the essay used in the Higgins and Rholes (1978) study. After reading the stimulus information, subjects were asked to rate Donald on a number of scales from "not at all x" to "extremely x." For all subjects, the endpoints for the scales relevant to the positive unambiguous information were positive (e.g., "athletic") and the endpoints for the scales relevant to the negative unambiguous information were negative (e.g., "short-tempered"). However, the endpoints for the scales relevant to the ambiguous information were negative for half the subjects (e.g., "conceited," "aloof") and positive for half the subjects ("confident," "independent"). As expected, subjects' immediate reproductions of the four ambiguous descriptions were significantly more positive when they rated the stimulus person on scales with positive endpoints (number of positive distortions − number of negative distortions, $M = +.9$) than when they rated the stimulus person on scales with negative endpoints (positive − negative distortions, $M = 0$)—a difference of .9. The reproductions were generally more negative one week later, but the difference in reproductions was even greater: positive endpoints, $M = +.4$; negative endpoints, $M = -1.3$—a difference of 1.7. This increased effect over time is consistent with a categorization interpretation (cf. Higgins et al., 1977; Higgins & King, 1981; Higgins & Rholes, 1978), but not a "demand effect" interpretation. In addition, there was no difference in reproduction of the unambiguous stimulus information for which all subjects received the same scales. This indicates that the results for the ambiguous stimulus information were due to differences in categorization and not to a general "halo effect." Thus, "leading" labels, as well as "misleading" labels, can affect recipients' memory.

In sum, achieving conciseness through labeling can have various effects on the memory and social judgments of both recipients and communicators depending on the type of labeling (single labels/labels with modifiers; symbolic/nonsymbolic; referential/persuasive; literal/figurative; leading/misleading).

Communicators and Recipients Should Take the Context and Circumstances into Account (Communicator Rule 6; Recipient Rule 3)

There has been a surprising lack of research concerning the effect of context on persuasion. This may be due, in part, to the fact that context was not explicitly considered in the "information transmission" approach to communication. Some aspects of context are implicitly included as part of the channel and receiver variables. For instance, the research concerned with the relative effectiveness of face-to-face persuasion versus mass media persuasion (cf. McGuire, 1969) is an example of a situational factor. There has also been research on how evaluatively positive or negative contexts affect persuasion. For example, there is evidence that persuasive messages are more effective if the recipient is in a pleasant situation (e.g., enjoying lunch) versus a neutral or unpleasant situation (e.g., Janis, Kaye, & Kirschner, 1965). There is also evidence that self-persuasion following the production of a counterattitudinal message will vary depending on whether the surrounding context is pleasant or unpleasant (cf. Cooper, Fazio, & Rhodewalt, 1978; Zanna & Cooper, 1976).

These effects of context on persuasion are relatively independent of the communication process. However, context can also affect message persuasiveness through its integral role in determining message appropriateness. Language use is interwoven with the accompanying activities and context, and both the appropriateness and meaning of a speech event is dependent on the surrounding nonlinguistic activities (cf. Bolinger, 1975; Ervin-Tripp, 1969; Hintikka, 1973; Hymes, 1974; van Dijk, 1977; Wittgenstein, 1953). Diversity of speech is the hallmark of sociolinguistics. Different speech styles (including codes, varieties, and registers) and keys (i.e., the tone, manner, or spirit of a speech act) are appropriate for different settings (i.e., the physical circumstances, including the time and place, of a speech act) and different scenes (i.e., the cultural definition of an occasion). Different speech styles are also appropriate for different genres (i.e., speech categories, such as poem, prayer, lecture), and social relationships (varying in intimacy, familiarity, etc. [Hymes, 1974; Trudgill, 1974]). For example, speech style should vary depending on the formality of the situation and social relationship (cf. Bolinger, 1975). There is also evidence that for different genres (lecture vs. speech vs. sermon) and different situations (classroom vs. social organization), different characteristics of the source (trustworthiness vs. expertness) are considered to be most important (Applbaum & Anatol, 1972).

The social context of an interaction between communicator and recipient often includes an additional party to the exchange—the "audience" who attends to the interchange but does not directly participate in it. In most studies of communication, the experimenter functions in the role of audience. In referential communication, the experimenter observes and records the interchange between subjects placed in the roles of communicator and recipient. In persuasive communication, the experimenter is a spectator to an interchange between the source of a persuasive message (who is often physically absent) and the subjects in the role of recipient.

Although the experimenter's role as audience has often been overlooked in interpreting persuasive effects of communication occurring in laboratory settings, some approaches have considered the experimenter to be a critical factor affecting subjects' responses. For example, Rosenberg (1965) proposed that subjects' responses in certain dissonance conditions are motivated by a desire to avoid negative judgments by the experimenter (i.e., "evaluation apprehension"). Wyer (1974) has suggested that informing subjects that the message they are about to receive is intended to persuade them may often suggest to them that the experimenter supports the position advocated in the message. If subjects feel that the experimenter wishes them to agree with this position, they are more likely to comply with the message, at least temporarily. On the other hand, if they feel that agreement would make them appear gullible or wishy-washy to the experimenter, they are less likely to comply.

Distinguishing among the roles of communicator, recipient, and audience may also have implications for attribution theory. Jones and Nisbett (1971) make a distinction between active and passive observers, where the active observer is actively interacting with the actor (i.e., a mutual contingency interaction), whereas the passive observer is "not in a position to respond to the actor and the actor is unaware of his specific presence [p. 87]." The recipient in communicative interaction is clearly an active observer. However, the audience in a communicative interaction may or may not be a passive observer, as defined by Jones and Nisbett. In fact, the experimenter in the role of audience is not a passive observer in this sense. Nevertheless, the experimenter's role as audience is different from the recipient's role, and could involve a different attribution process.

Context and circumstances are important to consider when examining the effects of message style on persuasion. There has been very little research on the effects of message style on persuasion (cf. Eagly & Himmelfarb, 1978; McGuire, 1969; Sandell, 1977) or on how message style interacts with other variables, such as topic, purpose, situation, social roles, etc. (cf. McGuire, 1969). The results of some previous studies, however, could be due, at least in part, to an interaction between style and other variables. For example, Sandell (1977) investigated the effect of "persuasive" style on attitude change by constructing messages in "persuasive" and "nonpersuasive" styles, and found that the "persuasive" style was, if anything, *less* effective, and even produced "boomerang" effects in a number of cases (cf. Higgins, 1978a). The "persuasive" style, however, was actually an advertising or commercial style (e.g., frequent use of adjectives, ellipses, and extreme modifiers) that subjects may have found inappropriate given the formality and seriousness of many of the topics and supporting arguments (e.g., the need for water purification). It may be that when message style is inappropriate to the situation or the message content, recipients make negative judgments of the source and/or pay little attention to the message.

Style could also be a contributing factor to the results of other recent studies. Chaiken and Eagly (1976) gave subjects either an "easy" or "difficult" message (i.e., varying in comprehensibility) presented via the written or oral mode (audiotape and videotape). With "difficult" messages, there was more persuasion with the written than the oral presentation, whereas with "easy" messages there was more persuasion with the oral than the written presentation. The style of the "difficult" messages, however, appears to have been more appropriate to the relatively formal written mode, whereas the style of the "easy" messages appears to have been more appropriate to the relatively informal oral mode (Borchers, 1936; Gruner, Kibler, & Gibson, 1967; Higgins, 1978b). Thus, rather than comprehensibility per se being critical, it could be that recipients are less persuaded by (and less attentive to) messages with styles inappropriate to the mode of presentation than messages with styles appropriate to the mode of presentation (cf. Chaiken & Eagly, p. 611). Miller, Maruyama, Beaber, and Valone (1976) investigated the relation between speaking rate and attitude change and found that "rapid" speech (approximately 190 words per minute) was more effective than "slow" speech (approximately 105 words per minute). Miller et al. (1976) suggest that "rapid" speech functions as a credibility cue. They also state, however, that radio announcers have an average speech rate of approximately 160 words per minute and the tapes subjects listened to were purportedly made by a radio station. Furthermore, recipients prefer a speech rate of approximately 175 words per minute for both oral reading and impromptu speaking and least prefer a speech rate of approximately 100 words per minute (Lass & Prater, 1973). Thus, subjects in the Miller et al. (1976) study may simply have reacted more favorably to a message produced at a rate appropriate for the genre. Finally, Bradac, Konsky, and Davies (1976) found that for advocating adoption of a new textbook, a message with high lexical and syntactic diversity was judged as more appropriate than a message with low lexical and syntactic diversity, and although the messages contained the same arguments, the more appropriate message was judged as containing more effective arguments.

The relation between speech style and context may also be important for self-persuasion. Use of an inappropriate style could decrease the influence of the message on the communicator by decreasing the communicator's commitment to the message, or generally reducing the communicator's embracement of the communicator role. Communicators could even purposely use a particular style to separate their "self" from their "role" as communicator. Such "role distance" (Goffman, 1961) could reduce dissonance when communicators produce a counterattitudinal message, especially if the recipient or audience indicates that the communicators were successful in disassociating their "self" from the message. Similarly, there is less self-persuasion when communicators of a counterattitudinal message believe their role enactment was unskillful than when they believe it was skillful (cf. Berger, 1972; Heslin & Amo, 1972). Finally, if different contexts and circumstances demand different labeling, communicators' memory and judgments regarding a topic of discussion may vary depending on the situation in which the topic was discussed.

Communicators and recipients must also take the context into account in referential communication. As discussed previously, a communicator's referential description of a target stimulus should vary depending on the characteristics of the alternative stimuli from which it needs to be distinguished (i.e., the nonreferent array). A communicator, for example, who wishes to be given the small McIntosh apple in a bowl of fruit should refer to the apple differently if it is the only apple in the bowl than if it is one of a variety of apples in the bowl. Similarly, a communicator should refer to a target person differently depending on the characteristics of the other people from whom the person needs to be distinguished (cf. Manis & Armstrong, 1971; Olson, 1970; Rosenberg & Cohen, 1966). For example, a communicator may refer differently to a stimulus person among a group of people depending on the characteristics of the other group members. If the stimulus person is moderately attractive, the communicator may refer to him/her as "attractive" if the other group members are less attractive, but as "unattractive" if the other group members are more attractive. If the stimulus person is both attractive and smart, the communicator may refer to him/her as "attractive" if the other group members are smart but not attractive, but as "smart" if the other group members are attractive but not smart.

Such variation in message labeling as a function of context could affect the communicator's own later judgments and memory for the stimulus person (cf. Higgins & Rholes, 1978). Variation in context, however, could also directly affect people's judgments of a stimulus person through a perceptual comparison or distinctiveness effect (cf. Livesley & Bromley, 1973; Manis & Armstrong, 1971; McGuire & Padawer-Singer, 1976; Sherif & Hovland, 1961). In order to specifically determine the effects on memory and judgments of message modification as a function of context, one might compare subjects who have a referential communicative purpose in distinguishing the stimulus person from others in the group with subjects who have a noncommunicative purpose (e.g., to make an interpersonal attraction judgment).

There are some interesting implications of communicators' modifying their message to suit the nonreferent context. If communicators label a stimulus person in one context and later recollect the label in a very different context, while forgetting the original context, then their memory of the stimulus person might be distorted to suit the new referential meaning of the label in the present context. This could account, at least in part, for the common phenomenon of people being surprised when they meet an old acquaintance after many years. For example, a professor who remembers his former undergraduate advisor as being brilliant may be surprised and disappointed after meeting him at a conference for the first time since graduation. As an undergraduate, he talked to friends about his "brilliant" advisor who was clearly more knowledgeable than anyone else he knew at the time. As a professor, he now has several colleagues who are considerably more impressive than his advisor. However, he has continued to remember the advisor as being "brilliant," and recollects the advisor's attributes so as to be consistent with the meaning of this label in the current context of professors. Because the advisor is only average with respect to the present set of alternatives, there is a large discrepancy between the remembered attributes and the actual attributes. Such distortion can also occur with regard to self-perception. For example, a woman who was called "bad" by her parents for naughty behavior as a child might believe she possesses personality traits designated by this term when used in her present adult context.

Although we have only begun to directly investigate these implications of changes in referential context, there is some support in the literature for different aspects of this proposal. Ostrom (1970) has shown that people will attempt to behave in a manner consistent with their previous self-labels even after the referential meaning of the labels has been modified. The results of Sherman, Ahlm, Berman, and Lynn (1978) suggest that people forget that their present attitude judgment was influenced by the prior attitude context in which the judgment was made, and use the attitude judgment as a guide for their present behavior.

In sum, recipients' reactions to a persuasive message and judgments of the communicator are affected not only by the message per se, but also by whether the style of the message is appropriate to the communicative context and circumstances; recipients judge the communicator more negatively and are less influenced when the message style is inappropriate. The use of an inappropriate message style could also decrease self-persuasion. Taking context into account in referential communication could also have important consequences for interpersonal judgments and attitudes, especially when the context of the initial stimulus description differs from the context of later recollections and judgments based on the description.

Communicators Should Produce Messages
Appropriate to Their Specific Purpose
(Communicator Rule 7)

Communication does not simply involve saying something. It also involves doing something. That is, there is a distinction between the information in a message and the act that making the message constitutes (Austin, 1962; Frentz & Farrell, 1976; Morris, 1964; Pearce, 1973). Austin (1962) distinguishes between locutionary acts (i.e., saying something) and illocutionary acts (i.e., the use or force of an utterance). He also distinguishes among a variety of performatives (i.e., utterances that perform an action) in terms of their illocutionary force, such as "exercitives" (e.g., advocating or urging a certain course of action) and "expositives" (e.g., expounding views, informing). Searle (1976) makes a similar distinction between "directives" and "representatives."

Various aspects of an utterance, including paralinguistic features such as tone of voice, cadence, and stress, can change its illocutionary force. Inappropriate use of such features could lead to a negative reaction from the recipient. For example, a communicator intending only to expound his/her view on an issue (an "expositive" or "representative") may use a tone of voice and stress that the recipient interprets as advocating a particular course of action (an "exercitive" or "directive"), which could induce reactance in the recipient. An important characteristic of performatives is that they are neither true nor false (Austin,

1962, p. 6) and, thus, the recipient's reaction to a performative is not a function of the message's "validity." Certain performatives, however, require that the communicator have particular feelings, thoughts, and intentions in order for the communicator to be judged as sincere (Austin, 1962; Searle, 1976). Because performatives are actions, they elicit reactions and lead the recipient to focus on the origin of the act. Thus, judgments of the source by the recipient becomes an integral part of the communication process (Recipient Rule 1). In addition, performatives must be uttered in appropriate circumstances (Communicator Rule 6). For example, certain performatives (e.g., a command) are inappropriate to the status or position of the communicator (e.g., a private) relative to the recipient (e.g., a general [Searle, 1976]).

Even when a statement or assertion is true, it may be judged as insincere and may be reacted to negatively if it involves a "presupposition" that is not satisfied (Austin, 1962). Many statements involve both a focal proposition and a presupposed proposition. Thus, the statement, "This is the best paper I have read this year," presupposes that the speaker has read other papers this year. If this is not the case, the statement may be true, but would be judged as misleading and insincere. Similarly, a comparison of two persons' traits or characteristics often involves not only an assertion concerning the relative positions of the persons along the dimension of comparison (i.e., relational information) but also presuppositions or implications concerning the overall positions of the persons along the dimension (i.e., positional information [cf. Clark, 1969; Flores D'Arcais, 1970; Higgins, 1977b; Huttenlocher & Higgins, 1971]). For example, the statement, "John is more brilliant than Bob," not only asserts that John is more intelligent than Bob, but also suggests that both John and Bob are very intelligent. If John is more intelligent than Bob but both are rather stupid, then the statement would be considered unacceptable and misleading (Higgins, 1977b).

Although there is evidence that the presuppositions contained in statements can affect perceptual judgments (e.g., Hornby, 1974), memory (e.g., Offir, 1973), and even deductive reasoning (e.g., Higgins, 1976a), there has been little concern with the effect of presuppositions on persuasion and social judgments. Hornby (1974) suggests that presuppositions may influence a listener's tendency to accept or question the truth of a statement, and could be used by speakers to lead their listeners to accept questionable conclusions, especially if the presuppositions do not invite questioning. For example, a recipient who believes that Bob is more intelligent than John may reject the comparative assertion that John is more intelligent than Bob when given the statement, "John is brighter than Bob," but may unknowingly accept the presupposition that John is bright. On the other hand, if a listener recognized that the presupposition was false, the listener might judge the speaker as manipulative, thus causing a "boomerang" effect. Thus, communication factors that affect whether a recipient questions the presuppositions contained in a message could determine the effect of a false presupposition on persuasion. For example, because under normal circumstances a written message is more accurately and fully comprehended than an oral message (Chaiken & Eagly, 1976; Higgins, 1978b), one would expect false presuppositions to be more effective for oral than written messages.

Other pragmatic rules of conversation can affect recipients' reactions to a message. For example, in a study by Pryor and Kriss (1977), the speaker's focus of concern, person or object, was varied through the use of active or passive sentences (e.g., "Sue likes the restaurant"; "The restaurant is liked by Sue"), and the recipient's attributions to the potential causal agents (person or object) were influenced by the relative importance of the person or object implied in the speaker's choice of focus (e.g., there was greater person attribution by recipients when the person was the focus).

In sum, if performatives (i.e., utterances that perform an action) are not accompanied by the appropriate paralinguistic features and by the appropriate feelings, thoughts, etc. on the part of the communicator, the communicator will be judged as insincere. The communicator will also be judged as insincere or manipulative if the presuppositions contained in the message are false, even if the assertion is true. Factors that affect a recipient's attention to and questioning of the presuppositions contained in a message could greatly influence the impact of the message.

THE "COMMUNICATION GAME" AS PURPOSEFUL SOCIAL INTERACTION

Communication initiates and defines a social relationship (cf. Ruesch & Bateson, 1968; Watzlawick et al., 1967). Moreover, a prerequisite of verbal communication, as for any social interaction, is the recognition that the other participants have goals they wish to achieve through the interaction. One of these goals may be to initiate or maintain a social bond (i.e., "social relationship" goals) and another goal may be to achieve a common definition of social reality (i.e., "social reality" goals). In fact, a major purpose of social interaction or social affiliation in general is to achieve consensus concerning social reality (the "pressure toward uniformity"), especially when physical reality is ambiguous and difficult to interpret (cf. Festinger, 1950; Schachter, 1959). For example, communicative behavior (comments and questions) increases when there is disconfirmation of expectations (Stamm & Pearce, 1971) or deviancy from consensus (Schachter, 1951). Other goals include "face" goals where the communicative interaction is used for impression management, self-presentation, and self-esteem maintenance (cf. Goffman, 1967; Lyman & Scott, 1970), "task" goals where the communicative interaction is used to achieve particular practical goals such as group problem-solving (cf. Collins & Raven, 1969), and "entertainment" goals where people communicate for the intrinsic pleasure of it (cf. Tubbs & Moss, 1977).

The "entertainment" goal of communication has frequently been overlooked in communication models. It may be that an important factor in the effects of communication on memory and social judgments is the participants' affective reaction to the communicative interaction (rather than simply the content of the information transmitted). For example, given that a communicator's message contained the same basic information and categorizations about a target person, the communicator may later remember and judge the target person more favorably if the general conversation about the target person was pleasant than if it was unpleasant.

This entertainment aspect of communication is one way in which communication is a "game." However, communication is also a "game" in the sense that it involves individuals making decisions and evolving strategies for obtaining goals within a social interactive setting. It involves choice behavior and interdependence between the players where each player can affect, but not totally determine, their own and other players' outcomes (cf. McClintock, 1972). The interdependence can be a zero-sum game (e.g., a debate) or a nonzero-sum game (e.g., a collaborative discussion). The implications of the "interdependence of outcomes" and "choice behavior" aspects of communication is discussed in another paper (Higgins et al., 1981). In this paper, the implications of the social relationship aspects of communication are considered. As a social relationship, the following factors become important to consider: (1) a major function of communication is to initiate and define the social relationship and share a common definition of social reality; (2) communication is part of the general culture, with its own specific rules, expectations, and conventions for behavior.

Sharing a Social Bond and a Definition of Social Reality

Participants in a communicative interaction establish a social relationship and some commonality by the very fact of engaging in communication (Rommetveit, 1974). Communication means "to make common or shared," and this involves sharing a social bond and a definition of the relationship, as well as exchanging information (Ruesch & Bateson, 1968). A desire to maintain the social bond and share a common definition of social reality should motivate participants to agree on their judgments and opinions. Thus, entering into a communicative interaction should cause convergence of opinions and judgments among the participants, as long as the participants are motivated to maintain the social relationship. The mode of attitude change might vary, however, depending on the recipient's interaction goal (Kelman, 1958): internalization (resulting from the motivation to have a correct, and objectively verifiable, position on an issue); identification (resulting from the motivation to establish a role relationship with the other participant); and compliance (resulting from the motivation to receive immediate awards and avoid immediate sanctions by publicly acquiescing to the advocated position, without private commitment to it). In addition, if the positions and judgments of the participants are considered illegitimate or beyond each other's latitude of acceptance (Sherif & Hovland, 1961), the participants may withdraw from the social relationship and, thus, end any motivation for consensus.

If participants in a communicative interaction are motivated to agree in order to maintain the social bond and create a common social reality, then convincing arguments that logically support the position advocated in the message may be unnecessary. In fact, participants may often provide reasonable arguments supporting their position in order to elicit positive judgments from the other participants that would promote the social relationship and avoid rejection (i.e., "intelligent," "serious," "responsive"), rather than providing arguments in order to convince the others of the validity of their position. That is, message content may affect persuasion as much through its impact on the recipient's feelings about the communicator as through the information it transmits about the issue. It is interesting in this regard that there is little evidence that the effectiveness of a persuasive message in changing recipients' attitudes is related to their recall of the arguments contained in the message (cf. Eagly & Chaiken, 1975; Greenwald, 1968; McGruire, 1969).[6] In addition, a study by Norman (1976) suggests that when the goal is identification with an attractive source, rather than internalization of an expert's opinion, the number of arguments contained in the message is not important. McGuire (1969) suggests that recipients may use the source of a message as a cue to accept or reject the message's conclusion, and may only find it necessary to learn and absorb the message's arguments when unable to clearly evaluate the source. Of course, if recipients are unable to clearly evaluate the source, they may hesitate to commit themselves to the social relationship, and, thus, would no longer be motivated to agree with the source for the sake of the relationship. In such cases, the persuasiveness of the arguments may be the only factor remaining that could influence the recipient.

One would not expect the message arguments to be particularly important if participants are not motivated to discover the "truth" as much as they are motivated to get along with each other and arrive at a consensus concerning social reality. One also would not expect the message arguments to be particularly important if participants focus on the intent or purpose of the message rather than the content per se, as discussed earlier. This focus on the purpose of the message and the social relationship among the participants rather than on the

---

[6]Himmelfarb and Eagly (1974) point out some methodological and conceptual reasons why a weak relation between recall and persuasion would not be surprising even if the arguments contained in the message were an important factor affecting persuasion. Nevertheless, the absence of a relation raises the possibility that learning, or even agreeing with, the message arguments may not be critical for persuasion. Greenwald (1968) suggests that this lack of relation is due to recipients rehearsing cognitive content beyond that of the persuasive message itself when trying to relate the new information contained in the message to their existing attitudes, knowledge, beliefs, etc.

message arguments could apply to self-persuasion as well as to persuasion of others. For example, there are a number of studies that have found little relation between the content of counterattitudinal messages (i.e., its degree of support for or commitment to the position advocated; the convincingness or strength of its arguments) and the amount of communicators' attitude change (e.g., Elms & Janis, 1965; Higgins, Rhodewalt, & Zanna, 1979; Zanna & Cooper, 1974). This suggests that the intent or purpose of the counterattitudinal message and its consequences for the recipient, rather than the content per se, is the critical factor.

In order to arrive at a common definition of social reality and remove obstacles to the social relationship, participants are motivated to determine the position of the other participants and modify their own position to be in greater agreement. This process should occur not only during actual communicative interaction, but also in the expectation of such interaction. Indeed, there is considerable evidence that people will change their beliefs toward the position to be advocated in a message they expect to receive, or toward the position held by a person with whom they expect to communicate (cf. Cialdini, Levy, Herman, & Evenbeck, 1973; Cooper & Jones, 1970; McGuire & Millman, 1965). One would expect that the more emotional or controversial the issue, the more motivated potential interactants would be to achieve prior consensus through belief change. One would also expect that potential interactants would not be motivated to establish a social bond or collaborate on a common definition of social reality with a disreputable source, and, thus, would not be motivated to change their beliefs. Consistent with these expectations, McGuire and Millman (1965) found more anticipatory belief change for emotional than nonemotional issues, and found little anticipatory belief change when the source was a criminal. Finally, because the belief change is motivated by the desire to establish a social bond, if people do not think they will actually engage in communication there should be little motivation for them to change their beliefs, and if their expectation of future communication with another person is cancelled there should be little motivation for them to maintain any belief change that occurred when they anticipated communication. The results of studies by Cooper and Jones (1970) and Cialdini et al. (1973) are consistent with these predictions.

This factor of communication anticipation might also account in part for a difference in results between Zimmerman and Bauer's (1956) original study and our recent study (Higgins & Rholes, 1978) of "audience" effects. In Zimmerman and Bauer's study, communicators who intended to summarize information on an issue for recipients with a particular opinion on the issue distorted the information in recall toward their recipients' opinion, whereas, in our study, communicators who intended to summarize information for the recipient (but did not actually produce the message) did not distort the information in recall toward their recipient's opinion. When the communicators recalled the stimulus information in Zimmerman and Bauer's study, however, they still expected to communicate (i.e., interact) with the recipients, whereas when the communicators recalled the stimulus information in our study they no longer expected to communicate with the recipient.[7]

Although communication involves sharing a social bond and a definition of the relationship, it does not necessarily involve sharing a common attitude toward the message itself (Higgins et al., 1981). Constructing and producing a message may be similar to constructing and producing any object or event. As a self-made product, a message is likely to have a special significance to its creator. To the communicator a message is "my product" whereas to the recipient the message is "his or her product." Thus, one would expect the communicator to be more committed to and ego-involved with the message than the recipient, and therefore, more likely to both accept the information contained in the message and remember it. This communicator–recipient difference is one possible factor underlying some very interesting findings in a recent study by Ross and Sicoly (1979). They found that when members of a problem-solving team were later asked how much they had contributed to the success of the project, the sum of the members estimated percentage share of the product was consistently greater than 100%; that is, the members overestimated their contribution to the product. Because each member's contribution to the project typically would occur when enacting the role of speaker, it is possible, as Ross and Sicoly suggest, that the overestimations were due to a message being better remembered (and more highly evaluated) by the speaker than the listener.

Ross and Sicoly's findings, however, could also be due to another potential communicator–recipient difference; specifically, communicators and recipients can have different communicative goals, or have the same basic goals but assign different importance to them. For example, one participant may give greater weight to the "task" goal, whereas the other participant may give greater weight to the "social relationship" goal, just as a small group can have both a task-oriented leader and a relationship-oriented leader (Bales, 1950). If so, then both participants may be accurately estimating their share in attaining what they personally judge to be the goal of the communicative interaction. This could occur even if both participants focus on the same type of goal, such as a "task" goal, because the participants could have different notions of the nature of the task goal, including what aspects of the task are most important or should be emphasized.

In sum, because participants in a communicative interaction are motivated to arrive at a consensus on social reality and to maintain their social bond, they may focus on the implications of the message for the communicator's characteristics

---

[7]Another explanation for the difference in results, mentioned in Higgins and Rholes (1978), is that communicators in the "intent only" condition of our study did not have time to formulate a message prior to recall, whereas there was a long delay in Zimmerman and Bauer's study prior to recall, during which communicators could have formulated their message.

and intent rather than on the actual information transmitted in the message. In addition, in order to reach consensus and remove obstacles to the relationship, participants are motivated to modify their own position to be in greater agreement with their communicative partner, even when only anticipating the communicative interaction. Communicators and recipients, however, may not share the same commitment to the message itself nor share the same communication goals, thus causing differences in their acceptance and memory of the message.

Cultural Conventions and Expectations

Communication is part of a cultural system of social action, and its functions and effects cannot be fully understood apart from its relation to the general culture or subculture (Bernstein, 1970; Cazden, 1970; Higgins, 1976b; Scribner & Cole, in press; Silverstein, 1976). For example, in many cultures communicators are expected to sacrifice most, if not all, of the rules of the communication game discussed earlier for the sake of politeness or decorum. There are cultural rules of social interaction for the participants as a function of their age, sex, social status, power, etc. that must also be reflected in their communicative behavior. This factor was discussed previously with respect to message appropriateness being determined by the social and physical context and circumstances. In addition, expectations and cultural conventions that are not specific to the communication process may, nevertheless, determine how communication affects persuasion and social judgment. Expectations can be "normative" (i.e., an obligatory behavior or characteristic whose absence leads to sanctions) or simply "probabilistic" (i.e., a typical or modal behavior or characteristic). For example, adults in our culture have a normative expectation that young children should not make noise during a church service, although children typically do, and adults have a probabilistic expectation that young children's favorite snack is candy, although they would be pleased if a child preferred fresh fruit. Expectations are generated from stored information involving both general cultural knowledge and personal experience. According to many recent models of comprehension, this stored information is used to go beyond the information directly provided in a message to infer additional information, draw implications, and formulate predictions about what information will follow (cf. Bransford, Barclay, & Franks, 1972; Bransford & McCarrel, 1974; Markham, 1981; Paris & Lindauer, 1976). For example, given the statement, "While banging in a nail, Tom hit his _____," one would infer that the instrument was a hammer and that Tom missed the nail, predict that the next word is "thumb", and draw the implication that Tom was subsequently in pain and angry. If the recipient's expectations and inferences are confirmed, a "click of comprehension" occurs (Brown, 1958). If not, the recipient may experience confusion and/or irritation, and new expectations and inferences will be generated.

Expectations can underlie impression formation from verbal descriptions (cf. Higgins & Rholes, 1976). For example, expectations underlie the impression formed from a message describing a person's characteristics and social role. Even though "casual" is generally a positively evaluated characteristic and "surgeon" is a positively evaluated role, people do not expect a surgeon to be casual (either normatively or probabilistically), and form a negative impression of a "casual surgeon" (Higgins & Rholes, 1976). Disconfirmation of an expectation (whether normative or probabilistic) is a salient event that the observer feels a need to explain. Thus, if a communicator who is a member of a particular social category or role behaves in a manner that disconfirms the recipient's expectations for members of that category or role, the recipient may make negative judgments of the communicator and respond negatively to the message. For example, Norman (1976) found that including arguments in a message advocating reduced sleep increased the amount of attitude change (relative to a "no arguments" condition) when the purported source of the message was an expert on the functions of sleep. In contrast, when the purported source was an attractive, but nonexpert, undergraduate, there was a high level of attitude change regardless of whether arguments were included. It could be that recipients expect an expert on a topic to present supporting arguments, but do not expect an attractive, nonexpert to do so. Thus, an absence of supporting arguments may have led to a negative judgment of the communicator, and a decrease in the effectiveness of the message, only for the expert communicator where the recipients' expectations were disconfirmed.

Higgins, Monaghan, and Rholes (1976) recently conducted a study that directly examined the effect of confirmation and disconfirmation of expectations on recipients' judgments of the communicator. Princeton undergraduates in their second or third year were given a written statement on the issue of federally subsidized national health insurance. The purported source of the essay was either a professor or a first-year undergraduate at the university. The essays advocated either a pro or con position on the issue. For each position advocated, two different essays were constructed containing the same basic arguments but varying in style. One essay was written in a simple, informal style similar to a popular, weekly newsmagazine, whereas the essay was written in a complex, formal style resembling a stuffy academic paper:

> Today Americans are paying almost twice as much for hospital service as they paid a decade ago. Some people in this country have no health insurance at all because they can't afford it, and others have illnesses that prevent them from being insured at all [Simple Pro].
>
> At the present time, Americans are being charged approximately two-fold for services rendered in a hospital as compared to what they were charged a decade previously, and, ironically enough, a considerable number of people have no medical insurance at all due to myriad other fiscal demands or a health condition that relegates them to an uninsurable category [Complex Pro].

An independent sample of 20 undergraduates rated the different essays and judged the "complex" essay to be significantly more complex and difficult to comprehend than the "simple" essay (all $ps < .05$). Another independent sample of 20 undergraduates were asked to rate the likelihood that a professor or a first-year undergraduate would write a simple or a complex message. Subjects clearly, and significantly, expected a professor to write a complex message rather than a simple message ($p < .005$), and expected a first-year undergraduate to write a simple message rather than a complex message ($p < .005$).

Eighty experimental subjects were told that in order to examine whether a recent decline in student–faculty interaction was due to a difference in perspective concerning contemporary social issues, we were having various undergraduates and faculty members write their opinions on a number of issues that would later be evaluated by both students and faculty. Subjects were told they would first read an essay on national health insurance, ostensibly written by a professor or first-year undergraduate, and would later write their own essays on another issue. After reading the essay, and prior to writing their own essays, subjects filled out a questionnaire "so that we can determine exactly how undergraduates and faculty respond to the arguments of other undergraduates and faculty." Subjects responded on 11-point scales from 0 (not at all "x") to 10 (extremely "x") for both "manipulativeness" and "expertise."

Subjects judged the "professor" as being significantly more manipulative ($p < .05$) when the essay was written in a simple style (disconfirming expectations) than when the essay was written in a complex style (confirming expectations)—$M = 7.0$ and $M = 6.1$, respectively. In contrast, subjects judged the "undergraduate" as being signifcantly more manipulative ($p < .01$) when the essay was written in a complex style (disconfirming expectations) than when the essay was written in a simple style (confirming expectations)—$M = 6.6$ and $M = 4.7$, respectively. Thus, there was a significant Source × Style interaction $F(1,71) = 5.69$, $p < .05$, with subjects judging a source as more manipulative when the essay was written in a style disconfirming expectations (i.e., a simple style for the "professor" and a complex style for the "undergraduate"). Subjects also judged the "professor" as having significantly less expertise ($p < .05$) when the essay was written in a simple style (disconfirming expectations) than when the essay was written in a complex style (confirming expectations)—$M = 3.7$ and $M = 4.6$ respectively. There was no significant effect of style on attributions of expertise for the "first year undergraduate," perhaps because the complex style made the "first year undergraduate" seem more intelligent at the same time that the style's disconfirmation of expectations caused a negative reaction. These results indicate that confirmation and disconfirmation of expectations about the type of message a particular kind of communicator would or should produce can influence the recipient's judgments of the communicator's characteristics and intent.

GENERAL SUMMARY AND CONCLUSIONS

The purpose of this paper has been to examine some of the effects of verbal communication on recipients' *and* communicators' attitudes, social judgments, and memory. These issues were considered from the perspective of the "communication game." This approach subsumes the more traditional "information transmission" aspects of communication, but also emphasizes that communication is purposeful social interaction, which is part of the general culture, occurs within a socially defined context, and involves conventional rules for obtaining various interdependent goals. Although the approach presented here is neither a formal nor complete model of communication, it does provide a framework for generating new insights into the way communication affects interpersonal relations.

A number of implications of the "communication game" for recipients' attitudes, judgments, and memory were considered. According to the "communication game" approach, one major factor in recipients' responses to the communicator and the message is their judgment of the communicator's goals and communicative intent. For example, a persuasive message may be more effective if recipients believe the underlying orientation of the communicator is cooperative (e.g., to gain an ally) than if they believe it is competitive (e.g., to beat an opponent). In addition, if recipients believe the communicator is modifying the message to suit their opinion, they will shift their judgment of the communicator's true opinion away from their own opinion. Moreover, recipients' judgments of the communicator's intent can also affect their actual interpretation of the message.

A number of factors can affect recipients' judgments of the communicator's purpose or intent, which, in turn, can affect their response to the message. Recipients may judge a communicator to be manipulative or insincere if the communicator either conveys a false impression by providing too little or too much information, inserts a false presupposition into the message, or uses a message style that is inappropriate for the communicative context and circumstances. Communicators will also be considered manipulative if they disconfirm their recipient's expectations concerning the type of message they should produce given their category membership (e.g., the type of essay a professor should write).

Another major factor in recipients' response to the communicator and the message is their motivation to establish or maintain a social bond with the communicator and/or share a consensus on social reality. These "social relationship" and "social reality" goals can lead recipients to modify their own attitudes and judgments to be in greater agreement with the communicator, even when they are only anticipating the communicative interaction. Moreover, recipients' concern with both these goals and the communicator's intent may often lead them to focus on the message as a basis for judging the communicator's characteristics rather than as a source of propositional information on some issue.

The effects of a message on recipients' judgments and memory can vary as a function of the type of labeling involved in the message. Recipients' (and communicators') memory for a person may vary depending on whether the person was described using a single label (e.g., "beautiful") or a label with a modifier (e.g., "extremely attractive"). The effect of labeling a stimulus person on recipients' memory may also vary depending on whether the label is interpreted as "literal" (i.e., the person is an actual member of the class designated by the label) or "figurative" (i.e., the person resembles members of the class designated by the label but is not an actual member of the class). Labels can have effects on recipients as a function of both their symbolic properties (e.g., their meaning and reference) and their nonsymbolic properties (e.g., their affective associations). Finally, recipients' judgments and memory can be affected by both "leading" labels (i.e., labels that lead the recipient to categorize a stimulus person in terms of the label) and "misleading" labels (i.e., labels that are inaccurate descriptions of a stimulus person but are presented to recipients as if they were accurate).

The "communication game" also has implications for the communicator. It is well known that advocating a counterattitudinal position on some issue can lead communicators to shift their own attitude toward the position advocated. However, self-persuasion from communication is not restricted to the case of counterattitudinal advocacy. In various types of communication, including referential communication, communicators will modify their message to accomplish various communication goals, including both "task" goals and "social relationship" goals, and this message modification will affect the communicator. For example, when communicators modify their description of a stimulus person in order to make the message more coherent and concise for the recipient or to suit the recipient's characteristics (e.g., to suit the recipient's attitude toward the stimulus person), the communicators' own attitudes, judgments, *and* memory of the stimulus person become increasingly consistent with their message descriptions. Communicators' memory of a stimulus person is also affected when they modify the amount of their labeling (e.g., reducing the amount of their labeling because they expect to receive additional information about the stimulus person).

Taking into consideration the recipient's characteristics when formulating one's message is one kind of "role-taking" that has implications for communicators' self-persuasion. Another type of "role-taking" is taking the viewpoint of others in judging one's own behavior. If communicators take their recipient's standpoint in judging themselves and their message, self-judgments and self-persuasion could vary as a function of their beliefs about the recipient's response to them (e.g., whether or not the recipient considers them to be an expert on the topic).

Social psychologists have generally taken an "information transmission" approach to communication, and the implications of this approach for persuasion have been examined rather extensively. The "communication game" approach to communication suggests a number of additional implications of the communication process for the attitudes, judgments, and memory of both recipients and communicators. At present, very few of these implications have been directly investigated. Turning our attention to some of these issues may provide a fuller understanding and deeper appreciation of the remarkable extent to which language influences interpersonal relations.

ACKNOWLEDGMENTS

The research by the author reported in this chapter was supported by Grant R01 MH 31427 from the National Institute of Mental Health. I am grateful to Alice Eagly, Susan Fiske, Reid Hastie, Lorraine Rocissano, Mark Zanna, and, especially, Bob Wyer for helpful comments and suggestions.

REFERENCES

Anderson, N. H. Cognitive algebra: Integration theory applied to social attribution. In L. Berkowitz (Ed.), *Advances in experimental social psychology*. New York: Academic Press, 1974.

Anderson, N. H. Likableness rating of 555 personality-trait words. *Journal of Personality and Social Psychology*, 1968, *9*, 272–279.

Applbaum, R. F., & Anatol, K. W. E. The factor structure of source credibility as a function of the speaking situation. *Speech Monographs*, 1972, *39*, 216–222.

Asch, S. E. Forming impressions of personality. *Journal of Abnormal and Social Psychology*, 1946, *41*, 258–290.

Asch, S. E. *Social psychology*. Englewood Cliffs, N.J.: Prentice-Hall, 1952.

Austin, J. L. *How to do things with words*. Oxford: Oxford University Press, 1962.

Bahrick, H. P., & Boucher, B. Retention of visual and verbal codes of the same stimuli. *Journal of Experimental Social Psychology*, 1968, *78*, 417–422.

Bales, R. F. *Interaction process analysis: A method for the study of small groups*. Cambridge, Mass.: Addison-Wesley, 1950.

Bartlett, F. C. *Remembering*. Cambridge: Cambridge University Press, 1932.

Bem, D. J. An experimental analysis of self-persuasion. *Journal of Experimental Social Psychology*, 1965, *1*, 199–218.

Bem, D. J. Self-perception theory. In L. Berkowitz (Ed.), *Advances in experimental social psychology*, New York: Academic Press, 1972.

Berger, C. R. Toward a role enactment theory of persuasion. *Speech Monographs*, 1972, *39*, 260–276.

Bernstein, B. A sociolinguistic approach to socialization: With some reference to educability. In F. Williams (Ed.), *Language and poverty: Perspectives on a theme*. Chicago: Markham Publishing Co., 1970.

Blumer, H. Society as symbolic interaction. In A. M. Rose (Ed.), *Human behavior and social processes*. London: Routledge & Kegan Paul, 1962.

Bolinger, D. *Aspects of language* (2nd ed.). New York: Harcourt Brace Jovanovich, 1975.

Borchers, G. An approach to the problem of oral style. *Quarterly Journal of Speech*, 1936, *22*, 114–117.

Bradac, J. J., Konsky, C. W., & Davies, R. A. Two studies of the effects of linguistic diversity upon judgments of communicator attributes and message effectiveness. *Communication Monographs*, 1976, *43*, 70–79.

Bransford, J. D., Barclay, J. R., & Franks, J. J. Sentence memory: A constructive versus interpretive approach. *Cognitive Psychology*, 1972, *3*, 193–209.

Bransford, J. D., & McCarrell, N. S. A sketch of a cognitive approach to comprehension: Some thoughts about understanding what it means to comprehend. In W. B. Weiner & D. S. Palermo (Eds.), *Cognition and the symbolic process*. Hillsdale, N.J.: Lawrence Erlbaum Associates, 1974.

Brock, T. C., & Becker, L. A. Ineffectiveness of "overheard" counterpropaganda. *Journal of Personality and Social Psychology*, 1965, *2*, 654–660.

Brock, T. C., & Fromkin, H. L. Cognitive tuning set and behavioral receptivity to discrepant information. *Journal of Personality*, 1968, *36*, 108–125.

Brown, R. *Words and things*. Glencoe, Ill.: The Free Press, 1958.

Brown, R. W. How shall a thing be called? *Psychological Review*, 1958, *65*, 14–21.

Burke, K. *A grammar of motives and a rhetoric of motives*. Cleveland: World, 1962.

Carmichael, L., Hogan, H. P., & Walter, A. A. An experimental study of the effect of language on the reproduction of visually perceived form. *Journal of Experimental Psychology*, 1932, *15*, 72–86.

Cazden, C. B. The situation: A neglected source of social class differences in language use. *Journal of Social Issues*, 1970, *26*, 35–60.

Chaiken, S., & Eagly, A. H. Communication modality as a determinant of message persuasiveness and message comprehensibility. *Journal of Personality and Social Psychology*, 1976, *34*, 605–614.

Cherry, C. *On human communication*. Cambridge, Mass.: M.I.T. Press, 1957.

Cialdini, R. B., Levy, A., Herman, C. P., & Evenbeck, S. Attitudinal politics: The strategy of moderation. *Journal of Personality and Social Psychology*, 1973, *25*, 100–108.

Clark, H. H. Linguistic processes in deductive reasoning. *Psychological Review*, 1969, *76*, 387–404.

Cohen, A. R. Cognitive tuning as a factor affecting impression formation. *Journal of Personality*, 1961, *29*, 235–245.

Collins, B. E., & Raven, B. H. Group structure: Attraction, coalitions, communication, and power. In G. Lindzey & E. Aronson (Eds.), *Handbook of social psychology* (2nd ed., Vol. 4.). Reading, Mass.: Addison-Wesley, 1969.

Cooper, J., Fazio, R. H., & Rhodewalt, F. Dissonance and humour: Evidence for the undifferentiated nature of dissonance arousal. *Journal of Personality and Social Psychology*, 1978, *36*, 280–285.

Cooper, J., & Jones, R. A. Self-esteem and consistency as determinants of anticipatory opinion change. *Journal of Personality and Social Psychology*, 1970, *14*, 312–320.

Cushman, D., & Whiting, G. C. An approach to communication theory: Toward consensus on rules. *Journal of Communication*, 1972, *22*, 217–238.

Delia, J. G. A constructivist analysis of the concept of credibility. *Quarterly Journal of Speech*, 1976, *62*, 361–375.

Deutsch, M., & Gerard, H. A study of normative and informational influence upon individual judgment. *Journal of Abnormal and Social Psychology*, 1955, *51*, 629–636.

DeVito, J. A. *The psychology of speech and language*. New York: Random House, 1970.

Eagly, A. H., & Chaiken, S. An attribution analysis of the effect of communicator characteristics on opinion change: The case of communicator attractiveness. *Journal of Personality and Social Psychology*, 1975, *32*, 135–144.

Eagly, A. H., & Himmelfarb, S. H. Current trends in attitude theory and research. In S. Himmelfarb, & A. Eagly (Eds.), *Readings in attitude change*. New York: John Wiley & Sons, 1974.

Eagly, A. H., & Himmelfarb, S. Attitudes and opinions. *Annual Review of Psychology*, 1978, *29*.

Eagly, A. H., Wood, W., & Chaiken, S. Causal inferences about communicators and their effect on opinion change. *Journal of Personality and Social Psychology*, 1978, *36*, 424–435.

Elms, A. C., & Janis, I. L. Counter-norm attitudes induced by consonant versus dissonant conditions of role-playing. *Journal of Experimental Research in Personality*, 1965, *1*, 50–60.

Ervin-Tripp, S. M. Sociolinguistics. In L. Berkowitz (Ed.), *Advances in experimental social psychology*. New York: Academic Press, 1969.

Festinger, L. Informal social communication. *Psychological Review*, 1950, *57*, 271–282.

Festinger, L. *A theory of cognitive dissonance*. Stanford: Stanford University Press, 1957.

Flavell, J. H., Botkin, P. T., Fry, C. L., Wright, J. W., & Jarvis, P. E. *The development of role-taking and communication skills in children*. New York: John Wiley & Sons, 1968.

Flores D'Arcais, G. B. Linguistic structure and focus of comparison in processing of comparative sentences. In G. B. Flores D'Arcais & W. J. M. Levelt (Eds.), *Advances in psycholinguistics*. Amsterdam: North-Holland Publishing Co., 1970.

Frederiksen, C. H. Effects of context-induced processing operations on semantic information acquired from discourse. *Cognitive Psychology*, 1975, *7*, 139–166.

Frentz, T. S., & Farrell, T. B. Language-action: A paradigm for communication. *Quarterly Journal of Speech*, 1976, *62*, 333–349.

Garfinkel, H. *Studies in ethnomethodology*. Englewood Cliffs, N.J.: Prentice-Hall, 1967.

Glucksberg, S., Krauss, R. M., & Higgins, E. T. The development of referential communication skills. In F. Horowitz, E. Hetherington, S. Scarr-Salapatek, & G. Siegel (Eds.), *Review of child development research* (Vol. 4). Chicago: University of Chicago Press, 1975.

Goffman, E. *The presentation of self in everyday life*. Garden City, N.Y.: Doubleday and Co., Inc., 1959.

Goffman, E. *Encounters: Two studies in the sociology of interaction*. New York: Bobbs-Merrill, 1961.

Goffman, E. *Interaction ritual: Essays on face-to-face behavior*. Garden City, N.Y.: Doubleday, 1967.

Gordon, D., & Lakoff, G. Conversational postulates. In P. Cole & J. L. Morgan (Eds.), *Syntax and semantics* (Vol. 3): *Speech acts*. New York: Academic Press, 1975.

Greenwald, A. G. Cognitive learning, cognitive response to persuasion, and attitude change. In A. G. Greenwald, T. C. Brock, & T. M. Ostrom (Eds.), *Psychological foundations of attitudes*. New York: Academic Press, 1968.

Grice, H. P. Logic and conversation. The William James Lectures, Harvard University, 1967–68. In P. Cole & J. L. Morgan (Eds.), *Syntax and semantics* (Vol. 3): *Speech acts*. New York: Academic Press, 1975.

Grice, H. P. Meaning. In D. D. Steinberg & L. A. Jakobovits (Eds.), *Semantics: An interdisciplinary reader in philosophy, linguistics, and psychology*. London: Cambridge University Press, 1971.

Gross, A. E., Riemer, B. X., & Collins, B. E. Audience reaction as a determinant of the speaker's self-persuasion. *Journal of Experimental Social Psychology*, 1973, *9*, 246–256.

Gruner, C. R., Kibler, R. J., & Gibson, J. W. A quantitative analysis of selected characteristics of oral and written vocabularies. *Journal of Communication*, 1967, *17*(2), 152–158.

Gumperz, J. J., & Hymes, D. (Eds.), *Directions in sociolinguistics: The ethnography of communication*. New York: Holt, Rinehart, & Winston, 1972.

Harvey, J. H., Harkins, S. G., & Kagehiro, D. K. Cognitive tuning and the attribution of causality. *Journal of Personality and Social Psychology*, 1976, *34*, 708–715.

Hawes, L. C. Elements of a model for communication processes. *Quarterly Journal of Speech*, 1973, *59*, 11–21.

Heider, F. *The psychology of interpersonal relations*. New York: Wiley, 1958.

Heslin, R., & Amo, M. F. Detailed test of the reinforcement-dissonance controversy in the counterattitudinal advocacy situation. *Journal of Personality and Social Psychology*, 1972, *23*, 234–242.

Higgins, E. T. Effects of presupposition on deductive reasoning. *Journal of Verbal Learning and Verbal Behavior*, 1976, *32*, 125–132. (a).

Higgins, E. T. Social class differences in verbal communicative accuracy: A question of "Which question?". *Psychological Bulletin*, 1976, *83*, 695–714. (b).

Higgins, E. T. Communication development as related to channel, incentive, and social class. *Genetic Psychology Monographs*, 1977, *96*, 75–141. (a).

Higgins, E. T. The varying presuppositional nature of comparatives. *Journal of Psycholinguistic Research*, 1977, *6*, 203–222. (b).

Higgins, E. T. Role-taking and social judgment: Alternative developmental perspectives and processes. In J. H. Flavell & L. Ross (Eds.), *New directions in the study of social-cognitive development*. New York: Cambridge University Press, 1981.

Higgins, E. T. Does persuasive style have a "boomerang" effect? *Contemporary Psychology*, 1978, *23*, 655–657. (a)

Higgins, E. T. Written communication as functional literacy: A developmental comparison of oral and written communication. In R. Beach & P. D. Pearson (Eds.), *Perspectives on literacy*. Minneapolis: College of Education, University of Minnesota, 1978. (b)

Higgins, E. T., & Akst, L. *Comparison processes in the communication of kindergartners*. Paper presented at meetings of the Society for Research in Child Development, Denver, April 1975.

Higgins, E. T., Fondacaro, R., & McCann, D. Rules and roles: The "communication game" and speaker-listener processes. In W. P. Dickson (Ed.), *Children's oral communication skills*. New York: Academic Press, in press.

Higgins, E. T., & Huttenlocher, J. *Symbolic and other associative processes*. Unpublished manuscript, University of Chicago and Princeton University, 1975.

Higgins, E. T., & King, G. Accessibility of social constructs: Information processing consequences of individual and contextual variability. In N. Cantor & J. Kihlstrom (Eds.), *Cognition, social interaction, and personality*. Hillsdale, N.J.: Lawrence Erlbaum Associates, 1981.

Higgins, E. T., & Lee, B. *Figurative versus literal labeling: Pragmatic effects on memory*. Unpublished manuscript, Princeton University, 1976.

Higgins, E. T., McCann, D., & Fondacaro, R. *The "communication game": When role-taking and role enactment affect information processing*. Unpublished manuscript, University of Western Ontario, 1980.

Higgins, E. T., Monaghan, R. A., & Rholes, W. S. *Judgments of communicators as a function of communicator status and message style*. Unpublished manuscript, Princeton University, 1976.

Higgins, E. T., Rhodewalt, F., & Zanna, M. P. Dissonance motivation: Its nature, persistence, and reinstatement. *Journal of Experimental Social Psychology*, 1979, *15*, 16–34.

Higgins, E. T., & Rholes, W. S. Impression formation and role fulfillment: A "holistic reference" approach. *Journal of Experimental Social Psychology*, 1976, *12*, 422–435.

Higgins, E. T., & Rholes, W. S. "Saying is believing": Effects of message modification on memory and liking for the person described. *Journal of Experimental Social Psychology*, 1978, *14*, 363–378.

Higgins, E. T., Rholes, W. S., & Jones, C. R. Category accessibility and impression formation. *Journal of Experimental Social Psychology*, 1977, *13*, 141–154.

Himmelfarb, S., & Eagly, A. H. *Readings in attitude change*. New York: John Wiley & Sons, 1974.

Hintikka, J. *Logic, language-games and information*. London: Oxford University Press, 1973.

Hornby, P. A. Surface structure and presupposition. *Journal of Verbal Learning and Verbal Behavior*, 1974, *13*, 530–538.

Hovland, C. I., Janis, I. L., & Kelley, H. H. *Communication and persuasion: Psychological studies of opinion change.* New Haven, Conn.: Yale University Press, 1953.

Huttenlocher, J., & Higgins, E. T. Adjectives, comparatives, and syllogisms. *Psychological Review,* 1971, *78,* 487–504.

Huttenlocher, J., & Higgins, E. T. Issues in the study of symbolic development. In W. A. Collins (Ed.), *Minnesota Symposia on child psychology.* (Vol. 11). Hillsdale, N.J.: Lawrence Erlbaum Associates, 1978.

Huttenlocher, J., & Weiner, S. L. Comprehension of instructions in varying contexts. *Cognitive Psychology,* in press.

Hymes, D. *Foundations in sociolinguistics: An ethnographic approach.* Philadelphia: University of Pennsylvania Press, 1974.

Janis, I. L., Kaye, D., & Kirschner, P. Facilitating effects of "eating while reading" on responsiveness to persuasive communications. *Journal of Personality and Social Psychology,* 1965, *1,* 181–186.

Janis, I. L., & King, B. T. The influence of role-playing on opinion change. *Journal of Abnormal and Social Psychology,* 1954, *49,* 211–218.

Jones, E. E., & Davis, K. E. From acts to dispositions: The attribution process in person perception. In L. Berkowitz (Ed.), *Advances in experimental social psychology.* New York: Academic Press, 1965.

Jones, E. E., & Goethals, G. R. Order effects in impression formation: Attribution context and the nature of the entity. In E. E. Jones, D. E. Kanouse, H. H. Kelley, R. E. Nisbett, S. Valins, & B. Weiner (Eds.), *Attribution: Perceiving the causes of behavior.* Morristown, N.J.: General Learning Press, 1972.

Jones, E. E., & Nisbett, R. E. The actor and the observer: Divergent perceptions of the causes of behavior. In E. E. Jones, D. E. Kanouse, H. H. Kelley, R. E. Nisbett, S. Valins, B. Weiner (Eds.), *Attribution: Perceiving the causes of behavior.* Morristown, N.J.: General Learning Press, 1971.

Jörg, S., & Hörmann, H. The influence of general and specific verbal labels on the recognition of labeled and unlabeled parts of pictures. *Journal of Verbal Learning and Verbal Behavior,* 1978, *17,* 445–454.

Kelley, H. H. The warm–cold variable in first impressions of persons. *Journal of Personality,* 1950, *18,* 431–439.

Kelley, H. H. Attribution theory in social psychology. In D. Levine (Ed.), *Nebraska symposium on motivation,* 1967, *15,* 192–238.

Kelman, H. C. Compliance, identification, and internalization: Three processes of attitude change. *Journal of Conflict Resolution,* 1958, *2,* 51–60.

Lakoff, G. Presupposition and relative well-formedness. In D. D. Steinberg & L. Jakobovits (Eds.), *Semantics: An interdisciplinary reader in philosophy, linguistics, and psychology.* London: Cambridge University Press, 1971.

Lass, N. J., & Prater, C. E. A comparative study of listening rate preferences for oral reading and impromptu speaking tasks. *The Journal of Communication,* 1973, *23,* 95–102.

Lasswell, H. D. The structure and function of communication in society. In L. Bryson (Ed.), *Communication of ideas.* New York: Harper, 1948.

Leventhal, H. The effects of set and discrepancy on impression change. *Journal of Personality,* 1962, *30,* 1–15.

Lively, W., & Bromley, D. *Person perception in childhood and adolescence.* New York: John Wiley & Sons, 1973.

Loftus, E. F., & Palmer J. C. Reconstruction of automobile destruction: An example of the interaction between language and memory. *Journal of Verbal Learning and Verbal Behavior,* 1974, *13,* 585–589.

Lowenfeld, J. Negative affect as a causal factor in the occurrence of repression, subception, and perceptual defense. *Journal of Personality*, 1961, *29*, 54–63.

Lyman, S. M., & Scott, M. B. *A sociology of the absurd*. New York: Appleton-Century-Crofts, 1970.

Manis, M., & Armstrong, G. W. Contrast effects in verbal output. *Journal of Experimental Social Psychology*, 1971, *7*, 381–388.

Manis, M., Cornell, S. D., & Moore, J. C. Transmission of attitude-relevant information through a communication chain. *Journal of Personality and Social Psychology*, 1974, *30*, 81–94.

Maratsos, M. P. Nonegocentric communication abilities in preschool children. *Child Development*, 1973, *44*, 697–700.

Markman, E. M. Comprehension monitoring. In W. P. Dickson (Ed.), *Children's oral communication skills*. New York: Academic Press, 1981.

McClintock, C. G. Game behavior and social motivation in interpersonal settings. In C. G. McClintock (Ed.), *Experimental social psychology*. New York: Holt, Rinehart & Winston, 1972.

McGuire, W. J. Attitudes and opinions. *Annual Review of Psychology*, 1966, *17*, 475–514.

McGuire, W. J. The nature of attitudes and attitude change. In G. Lindzey & E. Aronson (Eds.), *The handbook of social psychology*. Reading, Mass.: Addison-Wesley, 1969.

McGuire, W. J. Attitude change: The information-processing paradigm. In C. G. McClintock (Ed.), *Experimental Social Psychology*. New York: Holt, Rinehart & Winston, 1972.

McGuire, W. J., & Millman, S. Anticipatory belief lowering following forewarning of a persuasive attack. *Journal of Personality and Social Psychology*, 1965, *2*, 471–479.

McGuire, W. J., & Padawer-Singer, A. Trait salience in the spontaneous self-concept. *Journal of Personality and Social Psychology*, 1976, *33*, 743–754.

Mead, G. H. *Mind, self, and society*. Chicago: University of Chicago Press, 1934.

Mehrabian, A., & Reed, H. Some determinants of communication accuracy. *Psychological Bulletin*, 1968, *70*, 365–381.

Merleau-Ponty, M. *Phenomenology of perception*. London: Routledge & Kegan Paul, 1962.

Miller, N., & Campbell, D. T. Recency and primacy in persuasion as a function of the timing of speeches and measurements. *Journal of Abnormal and Social Psychology*, 1959, *59*, 1–9.

Miller, N., Maruyama, G., Beaber, R. J., & Valone, K. Speed of speech and persuasion. *Journal of Personality and Social Psychology*, 1976, *34*, 615–624.

Mills, J., & Jellison, J. M. Effect on opinion change of how desirable the communication is to the audience the communicator addressed. *Journal of Personality and Social Psychology*, 1967, *6*, 98–101.

Morris, C. Foundations of the Theory of Signs. *International Encyclopedia of Unified Science* (Vol. 1, No. 2). Chicago: University of Chicago Press, 1938.

Morris, C. *Signification and significance*. Cambridge, Mass.: The MIT Press, 1964.

Neisser, U. *Cognitive psychology*. New York: Appleton-Century-Crofts, 1967.

Newtson, D., & Czerlinsky, T. Adjustment of attitude communications for contrasts by extreme audiences. *Journal of Personality and Social Psychology*, 1974, *30*, 829–837.

Norman, R. When what is said is important: A comparison of expert and attractive sources. *Journal of Experimental Social Psychology*, 1976, *12*, 294–300.

Offir, C. E. Recognition memory for presuppositions of relative clause sentences. *Journal of Verbal Learning and Verbal Behavior*, 1973, *12*, 636–643.

Olson, D. R. Language and thought: Aspects of a cognitive theory of semantics. *Psychological Review*, 1970, *77*, 257–273.

Ostrom, T. M. Perspective as a determinant of attitude change. *Journal of Experimental Social Psychology*, 1970, *6*, 280–292.

Paris, S. G., & Lindauer, B. K. The role of inference in children's comprehension and memory for sentences. *Cognitive Psychology*, 1976, *8*, 217–227.

Pearce, W. B. Consensual rules in interpersonal communication: A reply to Cushman and Whiting. *Journal of Communication*, 1973, *23*, 160–168.

Peirce, C. S. Logic as semiotic: The theory of signs. In J. Buchler (Ed.), *The philosophy of Peirce: Selected writings*. London: Routledge & Kegan Paul, 1940.

Piaget, J. *The language and thought of the child*. New York: Harcourt Brace, 1926.

Pryor, J. B., & Kriss, M. The cognitive dynamics of salience in the attribution process. *Journal of Personality and Social Psychology*, 1977, *35*, 49–55.

Ranken, H. B. Language and thinking: Positive and negative effects of naming. *Science*, 1963, *141*, 48–50.

Reece, M. M. The effect of shock on recognition thresholds. *Journal of Abnormal and Social Psychology*, 1954, *49*, 165–172.

Riley, D. A. Memory for form. In Leo Postman (Ed.), *Psychology in the making*. New York: Alfred A. Knopf, 1962.

Rommetveit, R. *On message structure: A framework for the study of language and communication*. New York: John Wiley & Sons, 1974.

Rosch, E. Cognitive reference points. *Cognitive Psychology*, 1975, *7*, 532–547. (a)

Rosch, E. Cognitive representations of semantic categories. *Journal of Experimental Psychology: General*, 1975, *104*, 192–233. (b).

Rosch, E. On the internal structure of perceptual and semantic categories. In T. E. Moore (Ed.), *Cognitive development and the acquisition of language*. New York: Academic Press, 1973, 111–144.

Rosch, E., & Mervis, C. B. Family resemblances: Studies in the internal structure of categories. *Cognitive Psychology*, 1975, *7*, 573–605.

Rosenberg, M. J. When dissonance fails: On eliminating evaluation apprehension from attitude measurement. *Journal of Personality and Social Psychology*, 1965, *1*, 28–42.

Rosenberg, S., & Cohen, B. D. Referential processes of speakers and listeners. *Psychological Review*, 1966, *73*, 208–231.

Ross, M., & Sicoly, F. Egocentric biases in availability and attribution. *Journal of Personality and Social Psychology*, 1979, *37*, 322–336.

Ruesch, J., & Bateson, G. *Communication: The social matrix of psychiatry*. New York: W. W. Norton & Company, 1968.

Sachs, J., & Devin, J. Young children's use of age-appropriate speech styles in social interaction and role-playing. *Journal of Child Language*, 1976, *3*, 81–98.

Sandell, R. *Linguistic style and persuasion*. New York: Academic Press, 1977.

Schachter, S. Deviation, rejection, and communication. *Journal of Abnormal and Social Psychology*, 1951, *46*, 190–207.

Schachter, S. *The psychology of affiliation*. Stanford: Stanford University Press, 1959.

Scribner, S., & Cole, M. Literacy without schooling: Testing for intellectual effects. *Harvard Educational Review*, in press.

Searle, J. R. *Speech acts: An essay in the philosophy of language*. Cambridge: Cambridge University Press, 1970.

Searle, J. R. A classification of illocutionary acts. *Language in Society*, 1976, *5*, 1–23.

Shannon, C. E., & Weaver, W. *The mathematical theory of communication*. Urbana, Illinois: University of Illinois Press, 1949.

Shantz, C. U. The development of social cognition. In E. M. Hetherington (Ed.), *Review of child development research*. Chicago: University of Chicago Press, 1975.

Shatz, M., & Gelman, R. The development of communication skills: Modifications in the speech of young children as a function of listener. *Monographs of the Society for Research in Child Development*, 1973, *38*, Serial No. 152.

Sherif, M., & Hovland, C. I. *Social judgment: Assimilation and contrast effects in communication and attitude change*. New Haven: Yale University Press, 1961.

Sherman, S. J., Ahlm, K., Berman, L., & Lynn, S. Contrast effects and their relationship to subsequent behavior. *Journal of Experimental Social Psychology*, 1978, *14*, 340–350.

Silverstein, M. Shifters, linguistic categories, and cultural description. In H. A. Selby & K. H. Basso (Eds.), *Meaning in anthropology.* Albuquerque: University of New Mexico, 1976.

Smith, E. E., Shoben, E. J., & Rips, L. J. Comparison processes in semantic memory. *Psychological Review,* 1974, *81,* 214–241.

Stamm, K. R., & Pearce, W. B. Communicative behavior and co-orientational states. *Journal of Communication,* 1971, *21,* 208–220.

Thomas, D. R., DeCapito Caronite, A., LaMonica, G. L., & Hoving, K. L. Mediated generalization via stimulus labeling: A replication and extension. *Journal of Experimental Psychology,* 1968, *78,* 531–533.

Trudgill, P. *Sociolinguistics: An introduction.* Harmondsworth, Middlesex, England: Penguin Books, 1974.

Tubbs, S. L., & Moss, S. *Human communication* (2nd ed.). New York: Random House, 1977.

Turner, R. H. Role-taking, role standpoint, and reference-group behavior. *American Journal of Sociology,* 1956, *61,* 316–328.

van Dijk, T. A. Context and cognition: Knowledge frames and speech act comprehension. *Journal of Pragmatics,* 1977, *1,* 211–232.

Walster, E., & Festinger, L. The effectiveness of "overheard" persuasive communications. *Journal of Abnormal and Social Psychology,* 1962, *65,* 395–402.

Watzlawick, P., Beavin, J. H., & Jackson, D. D. *Pragmatics of human communication.* New York: W. W. Norton, 1967.

Wittgenstein, L. *Philosophical investigations.* New York: MacMillan, 1953.

Wyer, R. S., Jr. *Cognitive organization and change: An information processing approach.* Hillsdale, N.J.: Lawrence Erlbaum Associates, 1974.

Wyer, R. S., Jr. Henninger, M., & Hinkle, R. An informational analysis of actors' and observers' belief attributions in a role-playing situation. *Journal of Experimental Social Psychology,* 1977, *13,* 199–217.

Yavuz, H. S., & Bousfield, W. A. Recall of connotative meaning. *Psychological Reports,* 1959, *5,* 319–320.

Zajonc, R. B. The process of cognitive tuning and communication. *Journal of Abnormal and Social Psychology,* 1960, *61,* 159–167.

Zanna, M. P., & Cooper, J. Dissonance and the pill: An attribution approach to studying the arousal properties of dissonance. *Journal of Personality and Social Psychology,* 1974, *29,* 703–709.

Zanna, M. P., & Cooper, J. Dissonance and the attribution process. In J. H. Harvey, W. J. Ickes, & R. F. Kidd (Eds.), *New directions in attribution research.* Hillsdale, N.J.: Lawrence Erlbaum Associates, 1976.

Zimmerman, C., & Bauer, R. A. The effect of an audience on what is remembered. *Public Opinion Quarterly,* 1956, *20,* 238–248.

COMMENTARY

12

Social Cognition:
A Need to Get Personal

E. Tory Higgins
Nicholas A. Kuiper
James M. Olson
The University of Western Ontario

The spectrum of topics considered at the First Ontario Symposium was extremely broad, ranging from an assessment of the effects of fundamental voice frequency on impression formation (Krauss, this volume) to an examination of self-centered biases (Ross, this volume) and cognitive representations for organizing and storing information about others (e.g., Ostrom, Pryor, & Simpson, this volume). Although the range of topics was diverse, a number of common underlying themes were evident. One of the more prominent themes to emerge was the extensive borrowing of theoretical concepts and experimental paradigms from cognitive psychology. This borrowing has served to facilitate the investigation of cognitive structures and processes that underlie social judgements and memory for persons.

Illustrative of this trend is the borrowing of the concept of schema or prototype from cognitive investigators (Bartlett, 1932; Posner & Keele, 1968). In the present volume, Hastie as well as Taylor and Crocker, offer extensive and general overviews detailing how this concept has been incorporated and utilized in social cognition research and theorizing. At a more specific level, Ebbesen (this volume), Hamilton (this volume), and Ostrom et al. (this volume) have suggested that one's cognitive organizations or schemata for people may play an important role in the processing and recall of information about a new individual. Current work investigating the effects of social categorization and labeling on person memory (Higgins, this volume; Wyer & Srull, this volume) also attests to the impact of the "Bartlett" tradition on social cognition. Hopefully, this type of borrowing may resolve the potential problems of stagnation and disillusionment that some investigators have argued plague the social-personality domain (Sechrest, 1976).

Whereas social cognition researchers have borrowed extensively from the cognitive sphere, the application of these concepts and paradigms to social-personality issues has generally proceeded with a keen awareness of some of the potential limitations and shortcomings that may result. For example, Snyder (this volume) has commented on the need for social cognition researchers to tie thoughts or cognitions explicitly to future behaviors and actions. Several other participants at the symposium stressed the limitations of cognitive borrowing (Hastie, this volume; Higgins, this volume; Krauss, this volume; Taylor & Crocker, this volume; Zajonc, 1980). One such limitation concerns the relative neglect of an affective component in cognitive-based models. This shortcoming may be of minimal importance in the cognitive domain, where the nonsocial information typically encountered in the lab is relatively bland and affectless (Sarbin, Taft, & Bailey, 1960). The "personal" nature of the materials dealt with in the social and personality domains, however, make this factor more important in social cognition.

Accordingly, several chapters in the present volume have briefly raised the issue of affect in social cognition. Representative is Higgins's discussion of the relation between labeling and affect. Similarly, Ostrom et al. have briefly commented on how affect or emotion may influence the organization of social information about others. Finally, McArthur has proposed that emotionally significant social stimuli are more readily noticed than neutral ones.

At a more general level, these comments concerning the role of affect seem to point to the rather "impersonal" nature of a social cognition approach that relies heavily on concepts and paradigms borrowed from another domain. This approach can be considered "impersonal" in the sense that such factors as affect, degree of self-reference, and personal experiences (whether momentary or historical) are typically *not* addressed in model building. Yet, these may be the precise factors that are deeply involved in *social* information processing. For example, the interaction between stored knowledge structures or schemata and subsequent stimulus information may vary depending on how the structures or schemata were initially acquired—that is, depending on the personal learning history or experiences of the judge. In addition, social stimuli may be processed differently depending on the affective state of the judge during encoding, storage, and retrieval. Finally, social stimuli may be processed differently by the same person, or the same stimulus may be processed differently by different persons, depending on the personal relevance of the stimulus to the observer.

It is possible that the failure to incorporate these "personal" factors into social cognition could severely hamper the development of a comprehensive and realistic account of the processing of social information. Fortunately, however, the recognition of this potential is evident in the increasing number of recent attempts to focus specifically on some of these "personal" factors. For example, a major theme at the 1979 Princeton Conference on Personality and Cognition

(Cantor & Kihlstrom, 1981) concerned the role of individual differences and self-reference in social cognition. Similarly, one of the symposia topics at the 1979 APA convention pertained to the relation between social cognition and affect (Fiske, 1979). Considered together, these examples highlight an emerging trend in social cognition—one that emphasizes "personal" aspects.

In accordance with this emerging trend, the purpose of the present chapter is to explore in greater detail three categories of personal factors. These are personal experience, affect, and personal relevance. The first major section of the chapter deals with such personal experience variables as degree of familiarity and mode of acquisition of social knowledge. This section considers the impact of degree of personal experience (familiarity) on personal information processing. It also examines the role of acquisition (mode of personal experience) in social cognition. Much of the current research in social cognition has investigated the effects of cognitive structures or schemata on social judgments and memory, but the issue of how these social categories were originally formed has been relatively neglected. The present chapter represents a preliminary attempt to overcome this limitation by delineating a number of factors that may play an important role in the acquisition of social categories and expectations. The impact of these factors on subsequent processing of personal and social information is considered as well.

Another major area of concern is the role of affect in social cognition. In an attempt to integrate some of the literature on emotions and affect with current work in social cognition, several potentially important underlying dimensions of affect are proposed. These are outlined and their possible effects on the different stages in the information-processing sequence are considered. The final section of the chapter considers the role of personal relevance. This section comments on the close relation between affect and personal relevance and also discusses the role of self-reference in processing personal information about both the self and others.

Prior to addressing these issues, a number of important caveats should be raised. Because the purpose of this chapter is to provide a commentary on some of the emerging trends in social cognition, it is not our intent to offer a detailed and exhaustive review of the literature in these and related areas. Rather, our survey should be considered selective in nature, and one that hopefully provides a preliminary framework for developing future avenues of research. Although all of these areas fall within the general rubric of "personal" factors in social cognition, they are admittedly diverse in actual content. In turn, this suggests that the chapter might be viewed as a compendium of potential research avenues. As such, many of the ideas are presented in a speculative fashion in order to stimuluate the reader to further thought on these issues. Thus, any translation of these ideas into experimental hypotheses would require additional conceptualization and development.

THE ROLE OF PERSONAL EXPERIENCE
IN SOCIAL COGNITION

In the person perception and impression formation literatures, subjects are typically asked to make ratings or judgments about hypothetical or fictitious target persons (Wiggins, 1973). Although this paradigm has provided us with a wealth of information, it has some limitations (Fiske & Cox, 1979; Ostrom et al., this volume). For example, one such limitation is that trait lists of fictitious others cannot fully represent real-life initial encounters with strangers (Krauss, this volume; Secord & Backman, 1974). More important, however, this technique may tend to underestimate the role of personal experience in contributing to real-world social judgments and inferences. In this respect, both the degree and mode of personal experience may be critical. For example, in the real world, our interactions are not restricted solely to meeting strangers. Rather, the degree of personal experience (or familiarity) varies. Some interactions may invovlve strangers or unknown others, whereas others involve casual acquaintances or best friends. These differences in degree of personal experience may have an important bearing on the way social and personal information is processed. Accordingly, the first section of this chapter highlights some work that focuses on this factor and shows how it might relate to social cognition.

A second major aspect of personal experience concerns the manner or mode in which social information is acquired. In the laboratory, information about the social stimulus is usually provided directly to the subject (or judge). This feature raises a number of issues concerning the process of acquiring social information. Whereas a standardized presentation format might be employed in the lab setting, there are a variety of ways in which social information can be acquired in real life. Furthermore, these differences in the mode of acquisition may affect the subsequent use of stored information for making social judgments and inferences. Thus, this aspect of personal experience is discussed in some detail. This discussion focuses on several possible modes of personal experience, along with their potential influence on subsequent information processing.

Degree of Personal Experience

There is some evidence in the social and personality literature suggesting that degree of personal experience (familiarity) can affect the processing and organization of information about others. For example, in the realm of implicit personality theory, simpler multivariate structures have been demonstrated for unknown others than for personal acquaintances (Hastorf, Schneider, & Polefka, 1970; Koltuv, 1962). Further, the validity of trait inferences increases as the target becomes more familiar (Jackson, Neill, & Bevan, 1973; Norman & Goldberg, 1966). Finally, the tendency to ascribe traits to others depends on how well the person is known (Fiske & Cox, 1979; Nisbett, Caputo, Legant, & Marecek,

1973). Considered together, these studies argue strongly for the importance of degree of personal experience as a social variable.

In two current research programs (Kuiper & Rogers, 1979; Ostrom et al., this volume), target familiarity has been varied to assess the effects of degree of experience on the organization and processing of information about others. Ostrom et al. (this volume) propose that increased familiarity results in the utilization of a different organizational framework for storing and retaining information about the target person. Their proposal that "person nodes" tend to be employed mainly with known others receives empirical support from a series of recall analyses showing greater clustering by persons for familiar others. In a similar fashion, Kuiper and Rogers (1979) found enhanced recall for personality judgments about a familiar target compared to recall levels for an unknown target. These findings are consistent with a model of other-processing that postulates the development of a specific cognitive structure to organize, represent, and process personal information about familiar others. This structure facilitates the efficient processing of information, but only in the case where the prior degree of personal experience has been considerable (Kuiper & Derry, 1981).

Overall, the findings of both Kuiper and Rogers (1979) and Ostrom et al. (this volume) reinforce the notion that familiarity or degree of personal experience may be a critical variable in social cognition. Their independent demonstrations of systematic recall differences across levels of this variable attest to its potentially important role in personal information processing.

Modes of Personal Experience

Much of the research in social cognition has been concerned with the influence of stored social categories, beliefs, expectations, etc., on the processing of new social information. Relatively little attention has been paid either to how these stored constructs are acquired (i.e., alternative modes of acquisition) or to how mode of acquisition influences the interaction between the constructs and subsequent stimulus information. Mode of acquisition can influence both the effects of the stored beliefs on the encoding and interpretation of subsequent stimulus information (i.e., assimilation effects) and the effects of subsequent stimulus information on the modification of these beliefs (i.e., accommodation effects). This section considers each of these types of influence.[1]

It might be noted that we are not suggesting that mode of acquisition is a separate variable from stored information. After all, differences in acquisition

---

[1]Recent social cognition models have, perhaps, overemphasized the assimilation aspect of adaptation to social reality, with the accommodation aspect of adaptation receiving insufficient consideration. Certainly, accommodation plays a critical role in the course of social development (Piaget, 1962). It is possible that the balance shifts from accommodation to assimilation for any particular schema when the information contained in the schema is sufficient for goal attainment. Such issues need to be addressed in future research.

experiences cannot influence the subsequent processing of new information unless such differences are reflected in long-term storage. Social research on the
effects of cognitive structures on information processing, however, has only
rarely considered the acquisition process as another aspect of the stored information that might influence subsequent information processing (e.g., Greenwald,
1968; Regan & Fazio, 1977). Yet, it is well-known that trace storage is different
from trace utilization—as evident, for example, in differences between cued
recall and free recall (Tulving & Pearlstone, 1966)—and mode of acquisition is
one factor underlying this difference.

Overall, then, our purpose in this section of the chapter is to exemplify the
potential significance of the mode of acquisition variable for social cognition.
This is done by considering the implications of several acquisition dimensions for
the interaction between stored constructs and stimulus input. These dimensions
are: (1) induction versus propositional transmission; (2) simultaneous versus
successive instances; (3) partial versus continuous congruent instances; and (4)
concentrated versus dispersed instances. Following our discussion of these dimensions, we consider the relations among mode of acquisition, construct accessibility, and performance.

Induction Versus Propositional Transmission

Beliefs about particular people or social groups can be induced through
knowledge of instances or directly acquired as a proposition. For example, over a
number of days, a person could hear from a friend about another person's
behavior, and, each time, the described behavior of the target seems unfriendly.
Alternatively, the person could simply be told by the friend that the target is
unfriendly. In each case, the person might form the belief that the target is
unfriendly.

These cases differ, however, in a variety of ways. In the former "induction"
case, the belief is a conclusion derived from the person's own reasoning and
judgmental processes, whereas in the latter "propositional transmission" case,
the belief is a transmitted conclusion derived from another person's reasoning
and judgmental processes. The former "induced" belief, therefore, may be held
with greater confidence and may involve greater personal commitment. It might
also be better remembered. With an "induced" belief, concrete instances are
available to the subject as cues to retrieve or even to regenerate the belief. The
availability of concrete instances should increase the "vividness" of the belief,
and vivid information is more likely to be remembered than pallid information
(cf. Nisbett & Ross, 1980). There is also evidence that recognition and free recall
memory for events is greater when the cognitive events (e.g., associative responses) are self-generated than when they are provided by the experimenter (cf.
Paivio, 1971; Slamecka & Graf, 1978). In addition, recognition and recall of
self-generated events receive higher confidence ratings (Slamecka & Graf,
1978). This latter finding may account, in part, for the fact that active participa-

tion in presenting counterattitudinal arguments results in greater self-persuasion than simply being exposed to counterattitudinal arguments (e.g., Janis & King, 1954; King & Janis, 1956).

From a different perspective, "propositional transmission" could, under some circumstances (e.g., when transmitted by a liked or respected source), have informational and/or normative conformity effects on the receiver (cf. Deutsch & Gerard, 1955), thereby increasing the receiver's confidence in and commitment to the belief. It is also possible that, though people form their own beliefs on the basis of very few instances, they assume that others' beliefs are based on a relatively large number of instances. As a result, their confidence in the data base supporting a propositional belief could be increased. Such confidence in the data base, in turn, might increase their resistance to disconfirming instances, because the greater the perceived pool of confirming instances, the less representative a disconfirming instance will appear.

Thus, confidence in one's belief about a person or group and subsequent resistance to disconfirming instances may be affected by different factors for beliefs derived from "induction" versus "propositional transmission." Whether and when these factors apply, and which factors have the greatest influence, are important questions for future research.

Simultaneous Versus Successive Instances

The previous discussion of acquisition was restricted to the case of successive exposure to instances. Instances can also occur simultaneously, however, as when everyone laughs together at someone's joke. This simultaneous versus successive difference may have differential effects on social information processing. For example, Feldman, Higgins, Karlovac, and Ruble (1976) found that high consensus was more likely to lead to entity attributions (e.g., the car is attractive) when the consensus information was presented successively (one person at a time agreeing with the target's response) than when the consensus information was presented simultaneously (everyone agreeing with the target's response at the same time). A particular instance is likely to be more distinctive for successive instances than for simultaneous instances. In addition, each of the successive instances may be stored separately in episodic memory (cf. Tulving, 1972), whereas the simultaneous instances may be stored together as a single episode. For these reasons, successive instances may be more accessible and better remembered over time.

There might also be a difference between successive instances involving a relatively short period between instances (massed instances) and those involving a relatively long period between instances (spaced or distributed instances).[2] This difference would be captured in the phrases "I have noticed recently that . . . "

---

[2]For a discussion of various interpretations of the analogous "spacing effect" on memory with multiple presentations of the same item, see Hintzman (1974).

versus "Over the years I have noticed that... ". Successive instances spaced over a long period may be especially resistant to change because a subsequent series of disconfirming instances could be construed as merely a brief period of disconfirming instances versus the long period of confirming instances. In addition, although massed instances may have greater immediate salience and accessibility, spaced instances may be more memorable over time because they are more distinct. This would depend, however, on several confirming instances being built up and remembered prior to the appearance of a disconfirming instance. Otherwise, other factors could determine the impact of massed versus spaced instances. For example, disconfirming instances can have a greater impact following spaced than massed acquisition if the spaced acquisition promotes a recency effect in memory (cf. Dreben, Fiske, & Hastie, 1979; Jones & Goethals, 1972; Miller & Campbell, 1959).

Partial Versus Continuous Congruent Instances

To this point, we have considered only the case where knowledge is acquired through exposure to confirming instances. Yet, a belief can form from a set of previous instances that includes both congruent and incongruent cases (although the congruent instances would have to be more salient and/or frequent). Analogous to the difference between partial and continuous reinforcement, a belief formed on the basis of partial congruent instances might be more resistant to disconfirmation and rejection than a belief formed on the basis of continuous congruent instances. To take an example from the behavioral domain, Kerns (1975) has shown that children who have observed a model receive partial (or variable ratio) reinforcement for emitting a particular response will persist in emitting that response in the absence of any reinforcement for a much longer period (both in terms of time and number of responses) than will children who have observed a model receive continuous reinforcement for emitting the response.

One way of conceptualizing the difference between these two acquisition conditions is that the children in the continuous reinforcement condition believe that "x *always* leads to y", whereas children in the partial reinforcement condition believe that "x *often* leads to y." If so, then one negative instance (i.e., x but not y) would not count as a disconfirming instance in the partial reinforcement condition; rather, only a sequence of negative instances would disconfirm the belief.

The schedule of congruent and incongruent instances underlying the acquisition of a schema might also affect the relative memorability of the subsequent congruent and incongruent instances. For example, instances that are clearly incongruent with a stored schema might be more salient and memorable following continuous than partial schema acquisition. When the instances are less clearly incongruent, however, they may be more susceptible to congruent distortion following continuous schema acquisition.

Concentrated Versus Dispersed Instances

In acquiring an impression of a person or a group, the set of instances one encounters can be concentrated or dispersed across the discrete units of information considered in forming the impression. For example, keeping the total number of trait instances constant, an impression of a person may be formed from concentrated instances (i.e., a large number of instances per trait for a small number of traits) or from dispersed instances (i.e., a small number of instances per trait for a large number of traits). If people encode and store the input instances simply in terms of their desirability, then it should not matter whether the impression was formed through concentrated or dispersed instances. If each instance is stored in terms of the trait it exemplifies, on the other hand, then impressions acquired through concentrated versus dispersed instances could differ in some important ways. For example, suppose that judges are exposed to a sequence of trait instances about a target person that contains, overall, a greater number of undesirable traits. All judges are exposed to the same number of trait instances and the same percentage of undesirable instances, but some are exposed to concentrated instances whereas others are exposed to dispersed instances. The initial impression of the target person formed by all judges is likely to be negative. Because specific instances are likely to be forgotten more quickly than the target person's traits, however, the impression of the target person is likely to be more resistant to change for judges exposed to dispersed instances than for judges exposed to concentrated instances. In addition, the impression acquired through dispersed instances is likely to be more accessible, as more traits are available to act as retrieval cues.

Behavioral instances can also be concentrated or dispersed across situations. For example, keeping the total number of instances of a particular trait constant, a dispositional judgment of a person may develop from a large number of instances of a trait observed in each of a few situations (situationally concentrated instances) or a small number of instances of a trait observed in each of many situations (situationally dispersed instances). One would expect that a dispositional judgment would be held more confidently when it is acquired from situationally dispersed instances than situationally concentrated instances, because the behavior would appear to have greater cross-situational stability (cf. Kelley, 1967).

One's impression of a group might also be formed either from concentrated instances (i.e., a large number of instances per group member for a small number of group members) or from dispersed instances (i.e., a small number of instances per group member for a large number of group members). If each instance is stored in terms of the trait it exemplifies and the individual group member associated with it, then this factor could be important. For example, Rothbart, Fulero, Jensen, Howard, and Birrell (1978) presented all subjects with the same number of trait instances and group member-trait instance pairings. In the "single exposure" condition, every trait instance was associated with a different group member (i.e., dispersed instances), whereas in the "multiple exposure" condition, every instance of a particular trait was associated with a particular group member (i.e., concentrated instances). When the overall memory load was low, subjects stored each instance with the associated group member. Rothbart et al. (1978) found that "single exposure" (or dispersed instances) led to higher attractiveness ratings for the group than "multiple exposure" (or concentrated instances) when more desirable than undesirable trait instances were presented. These results suggest that the proportion of desirable or undesirable group members influences judgments of the attractiveness of the group over and above the proportion of desirable or undesirable trait instances associated with the group as a whole.

One might also expect that a group impression acquired through dispersed instances will be more stable over time than an impression acquired through concentrated instances, because information about individual group members should be forgotten more slowly than information about particular trait instances. In addition, the impression of the group as a whole might be more accessible in the dispersed instances condition, as there are a greater number of group members to act as retrieval cues for the general group impression. On the other hand, beliefs about individual group members may be more accessible and resistant to change in the concentrated instances condition, because there are more instances stored per individual to maintain the belief and to act as retrieval cues.[3]

In general summary, there are a variety of acquisition dimensions that have implications for the interaction between stored knowledge and subsequent stimulus information. Although these dimensions are largely independent, some acquisition modes are more likely to co-occur in nonlaboratory environments than are others, whereas other modes cannot co-occur (e.g., propositional transmission and modes involving induction from instances). Impression formation has been the social judgment area most clearly concerned with the issue of acquisition. As mentioned previously, research in this area has traditionally focused on only one type of acquisition—viz. beliefs or impressions formed from a short list of trait terms provided by the experimenter (cf. Anderson, 1971; Asch, 1946; Fishbein & Hunter, 1964; Hamilton & Zanna, 1974, Wyer, 1974). Such acquisition typically involves induction from partially congruent, dispersed, and massed successive trait instances that are based upon another per-

---

[3]The variable of concentrated versus dispersed instances also has implications for the subsequent impact of novel congruent and incongruent instances. For example, Gurwitz and Dodge (1977) provided subjects with the same number of stereotype-related instances confirming (or disconfirming) their previously acquired sorority stereotype. In the concentrated condition, the instances were all associated with a single sorority member, whereas in the dispersed condition, each instance was associated with a different sorority member. Confirming instances had more influence on the stereotype when they were concentrated.

son's experience with the target person. Although this mode of acquisition occurs in the real world, other modes also frequently underlie impression formation. In fact, this mode is more likely to be a source of stored information about others than stored information about the self, which could account, in part, for the processing differences between self-relevant and other-relevant stimulus information that have been found (cf. Kuiper & Rogers, 1979). There is a clear need for future research on impression formation to consider other modes of acquisition and to compare the effects on impression formation of different modes.

Relation Between
Acquisition, Accessibility, and Judgments

It is evident from the aforementioned description of acquisition modes that the "state" of social knowledge can derive from a variety of sources. For example, the accessibility of a schema can be affected by various aspects of acquisition. What are some implications of the fact that there are alternative sources for a particular cognitive state? As a preliminary consideration of this question, we examine traditional sources of increased construct accessibility.

There are a variety of factors that can increase a construct's accessibility, such as functional importance, frequency of activation, recency of activation, etc. (cf. Higgins & King, 1981). The fact that a construct's accessibility can derive from alternative sources can lead to systematic errors and biases in social judgment. Tversky and Kahneman (1973), for example, point out that when a category is made accessible by a factor other than frequency, perceivers may, nonetheless, judge the category to be frequent because of its accessibility. Chapman and Chapman (1969) and Hamilton and Gifford (1976) have found that the salience or distinctiveness of two categories can increase the accessibility of the association between them, leading to false judgments regarding the frequency of their co-occurrence (i.e., to an "illusory correlation"). Furthermore, accessible information will be given more weight in social judgment, even if its accessibility was due to recency rather than its functional importance (cf. Austin, Ruble, & Trabasso, 1977). Finally, a category made accessible by prior verbal exposure is more likely to be used to encode stimulus information, even though the defining characteristics of the category were not more evident in the stimulus information (cf. Higgins, Rholes, & Jones, 1977). In recognition of such findings, it is hoped that future research in social cognition will consider the implications of the fact that alternative sources exist for various cognitive states. The foregoing discussion has attempted to illustrate the relevance of this issue for construct accessibility. It may have equal relevance to other states of cognitive structures and schemata (e.g, confidence, salience).

Relation Between
Acquisition and Performance Contexts

There is considerable evidence suggesting that the accessibility of stored information can depend on the relation between the circumstances of acquisition and the circumstances of utilization. The work of Tulving and his colleagues on "encoding specificity" (cf. Tulving & Thompson, 1973; Watkins & Tulving, 1975) relates to this issue. These authors propose that the accessibility of a category or event depends on the relation between the mode of acquisition and the mode of performance. A performance context similar to the acquisition context provides additional retrieval cues to increase the accessibility of stored events (Tulving & Thompson, 1973), especially if the event and the encoding context later used as a retrieval cue form an integral encoded unit (Moscovitch & Craik, 1976).

Thus, the particular circumstances under which an event is acquired (within a particular context; while in a particular state) can affect how easily the event is later retrieved. For example, free recall of a target series of events is less impaired by interference from another series of events if the target series occurs in a clearly different context or point in time than the interfering series (Strand, 1970). There is also evidence for better performance on memory tasks when the subjects' state during testing is the same as their state during acquisition (Bower, Monteiro, & Gilligan, 1978), even when that state is one of intoxication (Goodwin, Powell, Bremer, Hoine, & Stern, 1969). Further, information that is important for enacting a particular social role, and that is acquired while enacting the role, may subsequently be better remembered while re-enacting that role than while enacting a different role. For example, Anderson and Pichert (1978) assigned subjects to the role of either burglar or homebuyer before reading a story that contained some information important to the burglar role and other information important to the homebuyer role. Recall of the parts of the story relevant to the role assigned at recall was better when this role was the same as the role assigned at acquisition.

Overall, these findings have several implications for further work in social cognition. First, they suggest that caution should be employed in drawing inferences from memory data in which the performance context (e.g., instructions for a recall or recognition test) differs substantially from the acquisition context. Under these conditions, a researcher may infer from poor memory performance that the information of interest is not stored in memory. It may be the case, however, that the information is actually in memory, but that this has been masked by the poor match between acquisition and performance contexts (Watkins & Tulving, 1975). Second, they suggest that it may be informative to manipulate systematically the relation between acquisition and performance contexts. By comparing the memory results for various combinations of acquisition and performance, one might be able to discover the information-processing consequences of alternative modes of acquiring information.

THE ROLE OF AFFECT IN SOCIAL COGNITION

A second "personal" aspect of social cognition that deserves increased attention in future research is the role of affect. One of the features of the social environment that contributes to its richness and complexity is that much social information carries with it a large affective or emotional component (Hastorf et al., 1970; McArthur, this volume; Sarbin et al., 1960). In contrast, the bulk of materials or stimuli typically encountered in a cognitive experiment are relatively bland or affectless (cf. Taylor & Crocker, this volume). If affect forms such a crucial component in the social cognition setting, it would seem useful to examine systematically some of the parameters and effects of affect on social information processing.

Psychologists have long been concerned with the role of affect in memory. Early attempts to address the affect-memory relation can be found in the works of Bartlett (1932), Freud (1914), Ratliff (1938), and Thorndike (1927), among others. Moreover, the concern with the importance of affect in memory has been a natural outgrowth of many different substantive interests. Theorists have been led to address the affect-memory relation by interests in clinical problems (e.g., Freud, 1959; Rapaport, 1959), "normal" cognitive processing (e.g., Bartlett, 1932; McGeoch & Irion, 1952), perception (e.g., Erdelyi, 1974; Postman, Bruner, & McGinnies, 1948), emotions (e.g., Arnold, 1960; Izard, 1977; Mandler, 1975), social motivation (e.g., Atkinson, 1953; Kanungo, 1968; Tomkins & Izard, 1965), and attitudes (e.g., Levine & Murphy, 1943; Malpass, 1969). Thus, the notion that affect influences information processing and memory historically has had a pervasive impact on psychological theory and research.

When viewed in the context of this historical tradition, recent theory and research in the area of social cognition gives affect little role in models of human information processing. Many theorists have focused upon nonmotivational factors in explaining social cognition and many models have not given explicit attention to affect. As Manis (1977) points out, this trend represents, at least in part, a healthy corrective from the earlier tendency to invoke affect-laden constructs at every turn. A number of critics (e.g., Erdelyi & Goldberg, 1979; Fiske, 1979; Manis, 1977; Zajonc, 1980) have argued that affect and other motivational variables must be taken into account if human social cognition is to be accurately characterized, however. Moreover, the notion that affect plays a role in information processing has intuitive appeal and plausibility. For example, Isen, Shalker, Clark, and Karp (1978) have shown that giving subjects a small gift improves their evaluations of the performance and service records of products they own.

The authors hypothesize that positive feelings make positive cognitions more accessible in memory.

Have recent models and research in social cognition, then, given sufficient consideration to the role of affect? To be sure, affect has received some attention, but perhaps not commensurate to its intuitive importance. This does not mean that the attention that has been given to affect in recent models is inappropriate: It may be that an intuitive analysis overemphasizes the role of such motivational variables (cf. Dawes, 1976; Miller & Ross, 1975). Indeed, nonmotivational factors seem sufficient to account for many aspects of social cognition. This point is well illustrated by several chapters in the present volume. Taylor and Crocker, for example, argue cogently that the liabilities of schematic processing can be explained by the single assumption that schemata contain evidence only of what an instance should look like, and not evidence of what it should not look like—no motivational construct is needed to explain the biases. Similarly, Ross argues that motivational processes do not appear to be necessary determinants of the egocentric bias in attributions of responsibility—nonmotivational processes (such as selective retrieval) seem to be the explanations best supported by the data.

Thus, one important reason for what may seem like neglect of affect and other motivational factors in social cognition is that they are not needed to account for many features of information processing. Another reason, however, may be that there are some difficulties associated with incorporating affect into information-processing models, even when it seems to be necessary. For example, the precise meaning of "affect" is unclear; the location of affect's possible influence in the multistage information-processing system is unclear; and it is difficult to specify the nature of the impact that affect might have on information processing. These issues are considered in the following sections.

The Meaning of Affect

Many terms that implicate affect, directly or indirectly, can be found in the psychological literature: Attitudes, autonomic arousal, drives, emotions, "energized" cognitions, feelings, goals, needs, purposes, and values. For our analysis, we use the term *affect* to refer to the phenomenological experience of physiological arousal. Only rarely has this variable been explicitly incorporated into cognitive or social information-processing models (e.g., Bower, 1978; Tomkins & Izard, 1965; Wyer & Carlston, 1979). Note that we are excluding from our definition of *affect* the notion of goal orientation. This "purposeful" sense of motivation is incorporated in some models of social cognition (cf. Wyer & Srull, this volume), has recently been receiving increased attention (e.g., Hamilton, this volume; Higgins, this volume; Jeffery & Mischel, 1979 ; Ostrom et al., this volume), and, of course, has long been a major concern of the psychology of learning. Our discussion, however, is restricted to phenomenological experiences of physiological arousal. Specifically, we attempt to identify some of the dimensions underlying affective experiences that may have implications for the processing of social information.

Two comments about our analysis are necessary. First, it is largely speculative, as little research has been done examining affect's role in social cognition. Thus, our aim is to identify some of the dimensions that might be included in future research and model building. The dimensions we consider are intensity, valence, duration, and causal specificity. Second, our analysis is not intended to be exhaustive. Rather than providing a comprehensive classification scheme, we hope to indicate how some of the dimensions influence social information processing.

Intensity.   Intensity is one of the dimensions underlying affect (Russell, 1978). Affective experiences can range from weak to strong. For example, certain emotional states (e.g., rage) can be characterized as more intense than others (e.g., dissatisfaction).

Valence.   Affect can also vary in valence, ranging from negative (unpleasant) through neutral to positive (pleasant). This dimension probably constitutes the most common basis for classifying affective experiences (Averill, 1975). Thus, joy is considered a positive state whereas sadness is considered negative; compliments are presumed to produce positive feelings whereas insults are presumed to produce negative feelings; achieving a goal is considered to be pleasant whereas goal-frustration is considered to be unpleasant, etc. Much research has examined the implications of affective valence for human information processing. Indeed, early work on the affect-memory relation was largely concerned with the valence dimension (cf. Dutta & Kanungo, 1975).

Duration.   Affect can also range from a temporary experience to a relatively enduring state. For example, some emotions are often temporary (e.g., anger, happiness, etc., may be deeply felt but then subside) whereas states of depression or anxiety may persist over longer periods of time.

Causal Specificity.   The dimension of causal specificity refers to the extent to which the cause of the affective experience can be specified by the individual. Thus, it relates to the cognitive interpretation of the affective state. Affect can vary from object-specific to nonspecific. For many affective experiences, the source of the state can be identified unambiguously (at least in the individual's mind) and the affect will be labeled accordingly. Examples of such source-specific affect include the feelings that result from evaluative (good–bad) judgments, emotional experiences that imply a target (e.g., anger, satisfaction), and the affective component of attitudes. On the other hand, some affective experiences are "nonspecific"—the source of the state is not apparent to the individual. For example, various clinical syndromes (e.g., anxiety attacks, depressions, etc.) are sometimes characterized by an inability to specify the cause of the felt arousal (cf. Costello, 1976; Kenny, 1963). "Specificity," of course, is defined subjectively in terms of the individual. Thus, the affect of persons in misattribution studies (cf. Valins & Nisbett, 1972; Zanna & Cooper, 1976) will be causally specific if they attribute their state to a particular cause, even though there may be multiple possible causes and even if they are incorrect.

Location and Nature of Affect's Influence on Information Processing

Phenomenological experiences of physiological arousal (i.e., affective experiences) can vary along each of the above four dimensions. This analysis may clarify the meaning of "affect", but it does not address the questions of where and how affect might influence the processing of social information. The present section considers these issues in a preliminary fashion within the framework of the identified dimensions.

Several authors in this volume comment upon possible locations of affect's influence on social cognition. For example, McArthur suggests that the affective significance of stimuli can guide attention, with more significant objects receiving greater study. Higgins proposes that the affective response to a conversation might influence whether positive or negative aspects of the memory content are later retrieved.

Clearly, affect might enter the system at various points. It is interesting to note, therefore, that few investigators have examined the role of affect beyond the input stage. As Dutta and Kanungo (1975) have commented: "In almost all studies in this area, manipulations of affective variables have been employed at the time of stimulus registration and hardly any attempt has been made to study the effect of manipulation of affect either on the storage or on the retrieval mechanism [p. 2]."

The notion that human information processing involves a number of conceptually distinct stages is widely accepted. Most models of memory encompass three basic phases. Dutta and Kanungo (1975), for example, distinguish between an acquisition phase, a retention phase, and a recall phase. Erdelyi (1974) labels these phases the input, consolidation, and output stages. For the purposes of our analysis, we adopt this latter terminology.

Intuitively, affect could influence any of these information-processing stages (cf. Erdelyi, 1974; Eysenck, 1976). For example, affectively important stimuli could receive more attention and increased efforts at comprehension and understanding than unimportant objects. Similarly, emotionally charged events might produce more rehearsal and rumination than neutral events. Finally, affect could bias retrieval processes, such as by making affectively significant schemata more accessible. The problem thus becomes one of specifying the characteristics of affective experiences that may be particularly important at a given stage. The dimensions previously identified may be useful in this regard.

One point needs to be addressed at the outset. It is clear that the different stages of information processing are not independent. Thus, an event that influences the input stage of memory will influence the consolidation and output stages as well. For example, failure to attend to some object will mean that memory traces will not be available for future retrieval. To take another example, output is facilitated if the circumstances of output match the circumstances of input (i.e., encoding specificity or state-dependent learning). In the following analysis, such "indirect" and interdependent effects are not discussed. Rather, the influence of the dimensions on the different stages are considered *as if* the dimensions were manipulated during that stage. It can be assumed that an effect on an early stage (input or consolidation) will have indirect effects on subsequent stages. Again, the following analysis is not meant to be exhaustive. Rather, our purpose is to identify one or more dimensions that may be important at each stage, in order to exemplify how affect might influence information processing.

Input Stage.   At the input stage of information processing, the intensity of a perceiver's affective state might influence attention. For example, research suggests that physiological arousal narrows the focus of attention, thereby increasing attention to "relevant" stimuli and decreasing attention to "irrelevant" stimuli (cf. Easterbrook, 1959). Applying these findings to social cognition, a plausible hypothesis is that the more a perceiver is aroused, the more stimuli relevant to an active schema will be noticed relative to schema-irrelevant stimuli. In this regard, McArthur and Solomon (1978) found some evidence for arousal increasing the extremity of a perceiver's impressions of target persons, although aroused subjects did not manifest a stronger tendency to attribute causality to a physically salient stimulus person than nonaroused subjects, as might be expected from Easterbrook's hypothesis.

The valence of the perceiver's affective state might also influence how stimuli are perceived (cf. Messick, 1965; Schiffenbauer, 1974). For example, Schiffenbauer (1974) reports that subjects' manipulated emotional states (positive vs. negative valence) strongly influenced their judgments of others' emotional states, with subjects attributing emotions to others that had the same valence as the emotion they were experiencing.

Finally, the causal specificity dimension might have implications for the input stage of information processing. In particular, it seems likely that the more unambiguously the cause of an affective state can be specified by an individual, the more attention will be directed toward cause-relevant stimuli. For example, anger at a particular individual might increase attention directed toward that person. If the emotional upset cannot be labeled clearly, however, then attention is less likely to be restricted to particular environmental stimuli. In some cases, the absence of a specific cause for one's affective state can lead to an information search to find the cause (cf. Barefoot & Straub, 1971; Schachter & Singer, 1962), which, in turn, can influence the encoding of stimulus information.

Consolidation Stage.   At the consolidation stage of information processing, the intensity of an individual's affective state might be important. For example, arousal might increase cognitive activity. Cacioppo (1979) found that accelerated heart-rate improved performance on reading comprehension and sentence generation tasks and increased counterargumentation to counterattitudinal messages (thereby reducing persuasion).

The duration of the affect could also influence the consolidation stage, to the extent that an enduring affective state produces greater rehearsal, rumination, and/or organization in memory. For example, the longer a state of depression or anxiety persists for an individual, the more likely it may be that the self-concept will be organized around "depressed" or "anxious" schemata (cf. Kuiper & Derry, 1981).

Causal specificity might also influence the consolidation stage of information processing. In particular, the more unambiguous the cause of an affective state, the more the cause may serve as an "organizing theme" or "node" in memory (cf. Anderson & Bower, 1973; Collins & Loftus, 1975; Lingle & Ostrom, 1981; Ostrom et al., this volume). In fact, if the cause of an emotional state is unambiguous, then the cause rather than the experience itself might serve as the central organizing node in memory.

Output Stage.   At the output stage of information processing, intense affect might restrict the range of retrieval cues that can be used to access stored information and/or increase the likelihood that well-learned or dominant schemata and responses will be activated and emitted. For example, Eysenck (1976) has argued that high levels of arousal have the effect of biasing the subject's search process toward readily accessible sources of stored information.

Affective valence also seems likely to influence the output stage. Support for this hypothesis comes from the work on psychodynamic defenses, especially repression (Freud, 1959). The concept of repression involves the notion that psychologically painful events or memories will not be accessible for retrieval. Although this concept has not received much attention in recent cognitive research, Erdelyi and Goldberg (1979) argue that available evidence strongly supports the hypothesis that "motivated forgetting" is a relatively common phenomenon. Additional support for a valence-output relation comes from the study by Isen et al. (1978) described earlier. It will be recalled that these authors proposed that giving subjects a small gift aroused positive feelings that in turn made positive cognitions more accessible in memory. Further, Gerard, Green, Hoyt, and Conolley (1973) found that subjects shown attractive, unattractive, and neutral faces overestimated the exposure frequencies of both the positively and negatively valenced faces and underestimated the frequency of the neutral faces. This suggests that the strongly valenced stimuli were more accessible for recall, thereby increasing their judged frequency (Tversky & Kahneman, 1973). Thus, the valence of either an individual's affective mood or the affect associated with an object/event/schema seems likely to influence the output stage of human information processing.

THE ROLE OF PERSONAL RELEVANCE
IN SOCIAL COGNITION

The third and final "personal" aspect of social cognition considered in this chapter concerns personal relevance. The degree of personal relevance of social stimuli may have an important bearing on the manner in which social information is interpreted, organized, and stored in memory. Illustrative is research on pragmatics in language. This work has demonstrated that the retention of surface structure material (in natural conversations) is at least equivalent to deep structure retention, but *only* for phrases and utterances that have a high degree of personal relevance for the listener (Keenan, MacWhinney, & Mayhew, 1977).

Personal relevance may also impact on various other parameters of social knowledge. For example, heightened self-involvement might increase the clarity of social category knowledge (cf. Sherif & Hovland, 1961), as well as the salience and confidence with which it is held (Fiske, 1981). This, in turn, could increase the accessibility of the information and its resistance to change (whether from disconfirming instances, counterattacks, or decay over time). Indeed, there is some recent evidence that attitudes acquired through direct, personal involvement are better defined and more confidently held than attitudes acquired without such involvement. Moreover, attitudes acquired through personal involvement are more predictive of subsequent behavior (cf. Fazio & Zanna, 1978; Regan & Fazio, 1977).

A further important aspect of personal relevance concerns its close relationship to the affective loading of social stimuli for the perceiver (Erdelyi, 1974; Zajonc, 1980). A recurring theme in the "self literature" is that increases in the perceived relevance of an event to the self lead to heightened affect or emotionality (Cooley, 1902; Epstein, 1973; James, 1890; Rogers, 1951; Snygg & Coombs, 1959). This theme is also evident in Dutta and Kanungo's (1975) research on the relation between affect and memory performance, where they find that highly self-relevant stimuli produce the greatest affect and the highest levels of recall.

The hypothesized relation between degree of self-reference, affect, and subsequent memory performance has received some indirect empirical support from several studies outside the cognitive domain. Consistent with the Dutta and Kanungo (1975) proposal that increased self-relevance produces heightened affect (and subsequent enhancement of memory performance), it has been demonstrated that: (1) self-relevant traits are more resistant to incongruent information and yield an increased number of specific behavioral examples on a free recall task (Markus, 1977); (2) self-referent decisions or instructions result in enhanced recall (Kuiper & Rogers, 1979; Rogers, Kuiper, & Kirker, 1977) and recognition performance (Rogers, 1977), compared to other rating tasks or instructions; and (3) people tend to overestimate their own contribution to a joint venture and have more accurate recall of self-statements (Ross, this volume).

One mechanism that might account for some of these effects is selective attention to material with higher affective overtones (i.e., of greater self-relevance). In this respect, McArthur (this volume) proposes that ''people and/or behaviors that have emotional significance for the perceiver should likewise receive differential attention from those that don't.'' At present, it is not precisely clear where in the information-processing sequence these effects of selective attention enter. Thus, one issue for future research on personal relevance and affect concerns the specification of where and how this factor is involved. Possibilities range from selective perception during encoding and/or organization to greater accessibility of self-relevant information during retrieval or output (McArthur, this volume; Ross, this volume).

Another important issue that should receive further attention relates to the effects of personal relevance on the processing of social information about other people. Although the studies cited earlier document effects for processing information about oneself, it is also possible that personal relevance might influence the processing of information about others. Such a hypothesis receives some support from person-perception research indicating that highly self-referential traits emerge earlier and more frequently in free descriptions of known others (Dornbusch, Hastorf, Richardson, Muzzy, & Vreeland, 1965; Hastorf, Richardson, & Dornbusch, 1958; Lemon & Warren, 1974; Shrauger & Patterson 1974). In addition, there is evidence that individuals often use their own view of self as a reference point in interpreting or predicting others' responses (Heider, 1958; Higgins, 1981; Ross, 1977; Snygg & Coombs, 1959). Comparisons of others to the self also form the keystone of Festinger's (1954) ''social comparison'' theory and Jones and Gerard's (1967) ''comparative appraisal'' self-development theory.

Recent work in social cognition has also provided some support for the role of personal relevance or self-reference in processing social information about other people. For example, it has been suggested that an individual's self-schema or prototype functions to organize personal information about others in memory (Hamilton, this volume; Kuiper & Rogers, 1979; Markus, 1977; Ostrom et al., this volume; Rogers, Kuiper, & Rogers, 1979). Although clustering methods have not provided much support for this proposal (Hamilton, this volume; Kuiper & Rogers, 1979), the generally positive person perception and attribution findings suggest that it might be valid. One strategy for future research is the "neomentalistic" research approach (Paivio, 1975), in which various stages in the information-processing sequence are tapped by different dependent measures. One possibility is that the effects of personal relevance are most pronounced in earlier encoding stages, rather than during retrieval. For example, highly self-relevant trait dimensions or categories may be more accessible in memory (Higgins & King, 1981; Kuiper & Derry, 1981; Ross, this volume), thereby facilitating social judgments about others in terms of these dimensions or categories.

CONCLUDING REMARKS

This chapter has examined some of the "personal" aspects of social cognition that are only beginning to receive explicit attention in models of human information processing. Personal experience, affect, and personal relevance all have implications for the way that social information is encoded, stored, and retrieved. Although these factors have been addressed in some studies, the emphasis in most recent models has been on relatively "impersonal" factors.

One aim of the chapter was to clarify the conceptual status of the personal factors. Thus, for example, some alternative modes of acquiring schemata were described and various dimensions that underlie affective experiences were discussed. These analyses illustrated the complexity of the personal factors. Their inclusion in models of social cognition will not be straightforward. Yet, it would seem that such complexity is needed to characterize more accurately human information processing. It was noted earlier that one of the unique features of social cognition is the richness and complexity of its subject matter. Theorists should expect, therefore, that elaborate models will be needed to represent such processing.

The second aim of the chapter was to consider some of the implications of the personal factors for social cognition. Thus, a number of hypotheses about the effects of personal experience, affect, and personal relevance on information processing were presented. Future research can assess the validity of these hypotheses. The important point is that if cognitive social psychology is to fulfill its "social" component, then a more "personal" approach will be needed. Such factors deserve more than benign neglect.

ACKNOWLEDGMENTS

The authors are grateful to Claudia Cohen, Susan Fiske, Tom Ostrom, and Bob Wyer for helpful comments and suggestions. Order of authorship is alphabetical.

REFERENCES

Anderson, J. R., & Bower, G. H. *Human associative memory.* Washington, D.C.: Winston & Sons, 1973.

Anderson, N. H. Two more tests against change of meaning in adjective combinations. *Journal of Verbal Learning and Verbal Behavior,* 1971, *10,* 75–85.

Anderson, R. C., & Pichert, J. W. Recall of previously unrecallable information following a shift in perspective. *Journal of Verbal Learning and Verbal Behavior,* 1978, *17,* 1–12.

Arnold, M. B. *Emotion and personality.* New York: Columbia University Press, 1960.

Asch, S. E. Forming impressions of personality. *Journal of Abnormal and Social Psychology,* 1946, *41,* 258–290.

Atkinson, J. W. The achievement motive and recall of interrupted and completed tasks. *Journal of Experimental Psychology,* 1953, *46,* 381–390.

Austin, V. D., Ruble, D. N., & Trabasso, T. Recall and order effects as factors in children's moral judgments. *Child Development,* 1977, *48,* 470–474.

Averill, J. R. A semantic atlas of emotional concepts. *JSAS Catalog of Selected Documents in Psychology,* 1975, *5,* 330. (Ms. No. 421).

Barefoot, J. C., & Straub, R. B. Opportunity for information search and the effect of false heart-rate feedback. *Journal of Personality and Social Psychology,* 1971, *17,* 154–157.

Bartlett, F. C. *Remembering.* Cambridge, England: Cambridge University Press, 1932.

Bower, G. H. Contacts of cognitive psychology with social learning theory. *Cognitive Therapy and Research,* 1978, *2,* 123–146.

Bower, G. H., Monteiro, K. P., & Gilligan, S. G. Emotional mood as a context for learning and recall. *Journal of Verbal Learning and Verbal Behavior,* 1978, *17,* 573–585.

Cacioppo, J. T. Effects of exogenous changes in heart-rate on facilitation of thought and resistance to persuasion. *Journal of Personality and Social Psychology,* 1979, *37,* 489–498.

Cantor, N., & Kihlstrom, J. F. (Eds.). *Personality, cognition, and social interaction.* Hillsdale, N.J.: Lawrence Erlbaum Associates, 1981.

Chapman, L. J., & Chapman, J. P. Illusory correlation as an obstacle to the use of valid psychodiagnostic signs. *Journal of Abnormal Psychology,* 1969, *74,* 271–280.

Collins, A. M., & Loftus, E. A spreading activation theory of semantic processing. *Psychological Review,* 1975, *82,* 407–428.

Cooley, C. H. *Human nature and the social order.* New York: Scribner, 1902.

Costello, C. *Anxiety and depression: The adaptive emotions.* Montreal: McGill-Queens University Press, 1976.

Dawes, R. M. Shallow psychology. In J. S. Carroll & J. W. Payne (Eds.), *Cognition and social behavior.* Hillsdale, N.J.: Lawrence Erlbaum Associates, 1976.

Deutsch, M., & Gerard, H. B. A study of normative and informational influence upon individual judgment. *Journal of Abnormal and Social Psychology,* 1955, *51,* 629–636.

Dornbusch, S. M., Hastorf, A. H., Richardson, S. A., Muzzy, R. E., & Vreeland, R. S. The perceiver and the perceived: Their relative influence on categories of interpersonal perception. *Journal of Personality and Social Psychology,* 1965, *1,* 434–440.

Dreben, E. K., Fiske, S. T., & Hastie, R. The independence of evaluative and item formation: Impression and recall order effects in behavior based impression formation. *Journal of Personality and Social Psychology,* 1979, *37,* 1758–1768.

Dutta, S., & Kanungo, R. N. *Affect and memory: A reformulation.* Oxford: Pergamon Press, 1975.

Easterbrook, J. A. The effect of emotion on cue utilization and the organization of behavior. *Psychological Review,* 1959, *66,* 183–201.

Epstein, S. The self concept revisited: Or a theory of a theory. *American Psychologist,* 1973, *28,* 404–416.

Erdelyi, M. H. A new look at the new look: Perceptual defense and vigilance. *Psychological Review,* 1974, *81,* 1–25.

Erdelyi, M. H., & Goldberg, B. Let's not sweep repression under the rug: Towards a cognitive theory of repression. In J. F. Kihlstrom & F. J. Evans (Eds.), *Functional disorders of memory*. Hillsdale, N.J.: Lawrence Erlbaum Associates, 1979.

Eysenck, M. W. Arousal, learning, and memory. *Psychological Bulletin*, 1976, *83*, 389–404.

Fazio, R. H., & Zanna, M. P. Attitudinal qualities relating to the strength of the attitude-behavior relationship. *Journal of Experimental Social Psychology*, 1978, *14*, 398–408.

Feldman, N. S., Higgins, E. T., Karlovac, M., & Ruble, D. N. Use of consensus information in causal attributions as a function of temporal presentation and availability of direct information. *Journal of Personality and Social Psychology*, 1976, *34*, 694–698.

Festinger, L. A theory of social comparison processes. *Human Relations*, 1954, *7*, 117–140.

Fishbein, M., & Hunter, R. Summation vs. balance in attitude organization and change. *Journal of Abnormal and Social Psychology*, 1964, *69*, 505–510.

Fiske, S. T. Effects of political involvement on political perception. In N. Cantor & J. F. Kihlstrom (Eds.), *Personality, cognition, and social interaction*. Hillsdale, N.J.: Lawrence Erlbaum Associates, 1981.

Fiske, S. T. (Chair). *Social cognition and affect*. Symposium presented at the 87th annual convention, American Psychological Association, New York, 1979.

Fiske, S. T., & Cox, M. G. The effect of target familiarity and descriptive purpose on the process of describing others. *Journal of Personality*, 1979, *47*, 136–161.

Freud, S. *On the psychopathology of everyday life*. New York: Macmillan, 1914.

Freud, S. Repression. In *Collected papers* (Vol. 4). New York: Basic Books, 1959.

Gerard, H. B., Green, D., Hoyt, M., & Conolley, E. S. Influence of affect on exposure-frequency estimates. *Journal of Personality and Social Psychology*, 1973, *28*, 151–154.

Goodwin, D. W., Powell, B., Bremer, D., Hoine, H., & Stern, J. Alcohol and recall: State-dependent effects in man. *Science*, 1969, *163*, 1358–1360.

Greenwald, A. G. Cognitive learning, cognitive response to persuasion, and attitude change. In A. G. Greenwald, T. C. Brock, & T. M. Ostrom (Eds.), *Psychological foundations of attitudes*. New York: Academic Press, 1968.

Gurwitz, S. B., & Dodge, K. A. Effects of confirmations and disconfirmations on stereotype-based attributions. *Journal of Personality and Social Psychology*, 1977, *35*, 495–500.

Hamilton, D. L., & Gifford, R. K. Illusory correlation in interpersonal perception: A cognitive basis of stereotypic judgments. *Journal of Experimental Social Psychology*, 1976, *12*, 392–407.

Hamilton, D. L., & Zanna, M. P. Context effects on impression formation: Changes in connotative meaning. *Journal of Personality and Social Psychology*, 1974, *29*, 649–654.

Hastorf, A. H., Richardson, S. A., & Dornbusch, S. M. The problem of relevance in the study of person perception. In R. Tagiuri & L. Petrullo (Eds.), *Person perception and interpersonal behavior*. Stanford: Stanford University Press, 1958.

Hastorf, A. H., Schneider, D. J., & Polefka, J. *Person perception*. Reading, Mass.: Addison-Wesley, 1970.

Heider, F. *The psychology of interpersonal relations*. New York: Wiley, 1958.

Higgins, E. T. Role-taking and social judgment: Alternative developmental perspectives and processes. In J. H. Flavell & L. Ross (Eds.), *New directions in the study of social-cognitive development*. New York: Cambridge University Press, 1981.

Higgins, E. T., & King, G. Accessibility of social constructs: Information processing consequences of individual and contextual variability. In N. Cantor & J. F. Kihlstrom (Eds.), *Personality, cognition, and social interaction*. Hillsdale, N.J.: Lawrence Erlbaum Associates, 1981.

Higgins, E. T., Rholes, W. S., & Jones, C. R. Category accessibility and impression formation. *Journal of Experimental Social Psychology*, 1977, *13*, 141–154.

Hintzman, D. L. Theoretical implications of the spacing effect. In R. L. Solso (Ed.), *Theories in cognitive psychology: The Loyola Symposium*. Potomac, Md.: Lawrence Erlbaum Associates, 1974.

Isen, A. M., Shalker, T. E., Clark, M., & Karp, L. Affect, accessibility of material in memory, and behavior: A cognitive loop? *Journal of Personality and Social Psychology*, 1978, *36*, 1–12.

Izard, C. E. *Human emotions*. New York: Plenum Press, 1977.

Jackson, D. N., Neill, J. A., & Bevan, A. R. An evaluation of forced-choice and true–false item formats in personality assessment. *Journal of Research in Personality*, 1973, *7*, 21–30.

James, W. *The principles of psychology*. New York: Holt, 1890.

Janis, I. L., & King, B. T. The influence of role-playing on opinion change. *Journal of Abnormal and Social Psychology*, 1954, *49*, 211–218.

Jeffery, K. M., & Mischel, W. Effects of purpose on the organization and recall of information in person perception. *Journal of Personality*, 1979, *47*, 397–419.

Jones, E. E., & Gerard, H. B. *Foundations of social psychology*. New York: Wiley, 1967.

Jones, E. E., & Goethals, G. R. Order effects in impression formation: Attribution context and the nature of the entity. In E. E. Jones, D. E. Kanouse, H. H. Kelley, R. E. Nisbett, S. Valins, & B. Weiner (Eds.), *Attribution: Perceiving the causes of behavior*. Morristown, N.J.: General Learning Press, 1972.

Kanungo, R. N. Retention of affective material: Role of extraversion and intensity of affect. *Journal of Personality and Social Psychology*, 1968, *8*, 63–68.

Keenan, J., MacWhinney, B., & Mayhew, D. Pragmatics in memory: A study of natural conversation. *Journal of Verbal Learning and Verbal Behavior*, 1977, *16*, 549–560.

Kelley, H. H. Attribution theory and social psychology. In D. Levine (Ed.), *Nebraska Symposium on Motivation* (Vol. 15). Lincoln: University of Nebraska Press, 1967.

Kenny, A. *Action, emotion, and will*. London: Routledge and Kegan Paul, 1963.

Kerns, C. D. Effects of schedule and amount of observed reinforcement on response persistence. *Journal of Personality and Social Psychology*, 1975, *31*, 983–991.

King, B. T., & Janis, I. L. Comparison of the effectiveness of improvised versus non-improvised role playing in producing opinion changes. *Human Relations*, 1956, *9*, 177–186.

Koltuv, B. Some characteristics of intrajudge trait intercorrelations. *Psychological Monographs*, 1962, *76*, (33, Whole No. 552).

Kuiper, N. A., & Derry, P. A. The self as a cognitive prototype: An application to person perception and depression. In N. Cantor & J. F. Kihlstrom (Eds.), *Personality, cognition, and social interaction*. Hillsdale, N.J.: Lawrence Erlbaum Associates, 1981.

Kuiper, N. A., & Rogers, T. B. Encoding of personal information: Self-other differences. *Journal of Personality and Social Psychology*, 1979, *37*, 499–514.

Lemon, N., & Warren, N. Salience, centrality, and self-relevance of traits in construing others. *British Journal of Social and Clinical Psychology*, 1974, *13*, 119–124.

Levine, J. M., & Murphy, G. The learning and forgetting of controversial material. *Journal of Abnormal and Social Psychology*, 1943, *38*, 507–517.

Lingle, J. H., & Ostrom, T. M. Principles of memory and cognition in attitude formation. In R. E. Petty, T. M. Ostrom, & T. C. Brock (Eds.), *Cognitive responses in persuasion*. Hillsdale, N.J.: Lawrence Erlbaum Associates, 1981.

Malpass, R. S. Effect of attitude on learning and memory: The influence of instruction-induced sets. *Journal of Experimental Social Psychology*, 1969, *5*, 441–453.

Mandler, G. *Mind and emotion*. New York: Wiley, 1975.

Manis, M. Cognitive social psychology. *Personality and Social Psychology Bulletin*, 1977, *3*, 550–566.

Markus, H. Self-schemata and processing information about the self. *Journal of Personality and Social Psychology*, 1977, *35*, 63–78.

McArthur, L. Z., & Solomon, L. K. Perceptions of an aggressive encounter as a function of the victim's salience and the perceiver's arousal. *Journal of Personality and Social Psychology*, 1978, *36*, 1278–1290.

McGeoch, J. A., & Irion, A. L. *The psychology of human learning*. New York: Longmans, 1952.

Messick, S. The impact of negative affect on cognition and personality. In S. S. Tomkins & C. E. Izard (Eds.), *Affect, cognition, and personality: Empirical studies.* New York: Springer Publishing Co., 1965.

Miller, D. T., & Ross, M. Self-serving biases in the attribution of causality: Fact or fiction? *Psychological Bulletin,* 1975, *82,* 213–225.

Miller, N., & Campbell, D. T. Recency and primacy in persuasion as a function of the timing of speeches and measurements. *Journal of Abnormal and Social Psychology,* 1959, *59,* 1–9.

Moscovitch, M., & Craik, F. I. M. Depth of processing, retrieval cues, and uniqueness of encoding as factors in recall. *Journal of Verbal Learning and Verbal Behavior,* 1976, *15,* 447–458.

Nisbett, R. E., Caputo, C., Legant, P., & Marecek, J. Behavior as seen by the actor and as seen by the observer. *Journal of Personality and Social Psychology,* 1973, *27,* 154–164.

Nisbett, R. E., & Ross, L. *Human inference: Strategies and shortcomings of social judgment.* Englewood Cliffs, N.J.: Prentice-Hall, 1980.

Norman, W. T., & Goldberg, L. R. Raters, ratees, and randomness in personality structure. *Journal of Personality and Social Psychology,* 1966, *4,* 681–691.

Paivio, A. *Imagery and verbal processes.* New York: Holt, Rinehart & Winston, 1971.

Paivio, A. Neomentalism. *Canadian Journal of Psychology,* 1975, *29,* 263–291.

Piaget, J. *Play, dreams and imitation in childhood.* New York: W. W. Norton & Co., 1962.

Posner, M. I., & Keele, S. W. On the genesis of abstract ideas. *Journal of Experimental Psychology,* 1968, *77,* 353–363.

Postman, L., Bruner, J. S., & McGinnies, E. Personal values as selective factors in perception. *Journal of Abnormal and Social Psychology,* 1948, *43,* 142–154.

Rapaport, D. *Emotions and memory.* New York: International University Press, 1959.

Ratliff, M. M. The varying function of affectively toned olfactory, visual and auditory cues in recall. *American Journal of Psychology,* 1938, *51,* 695–701.

Regan, D. T., & Fazio, R. H. On the consistency between attitudes and behavior: Look to the method of attitude formation. *Journal of Experimental Social Psychology,* 1977, *13,* 28–45.

Rogers, C. R. *Client-centered therapy.* New York: Houghton Mifflin, 1951.

Rogers, T. B. Self-reference in memory: Recognition of personality items. *Journal of Research in Personality,* 1977, *11,* 295–305.

Rogers, T. B., Kuiper, N. A., & Kirker, W. S. Self-reference and the encoding of personal information. *Journal of Personality and Social Psychology,* 1977, *35,* 677–688.

Rogers, T. B., Kuiper, N. A., & Rogers, P. J. Symbolic distance and congruity effects for paired-comparisons judgments of degree of self-reference. *Journal of Research in Personality,* 1979, *13,* 433–449.

Ross, L. The intuitive psychologist and his shortcomings: Distortions in the attribution process. In L. Berkowitz (Ed.), *Advances in experimental social psychology* (Vol. 10). New York: Academic Press, 1977.

Rothbart, M., Fulero, S., Jensen, C., Howard, J., & Birrell, P. From individual to group impressions: Availability heuristics in stereotype formation. *Journal of Experimental Social Psychology,* 1978, *14,* 237–255.

Russell, J. A. Evidence of convergent validity on the dimensions of affect. *Journal of Personality and Social Psychology,* 1978, *36,* 1152–1168.

Sarbin, T. R., Taft, R., & Bailey, D. E. *Clinical inference and cognitive theory.* New York: Holt, Rinehart & Winston, 1960.

Schachter, S., & Singer, J. E. Cognitive, social and physiological determinants of emotional state. *Psychological Review,* 1962, *69,* 379–399.

Schiffenbauer, A. Effect of observer's emotional state on judgments of the emotional state of others. *Journal of Personality and Social Psychology,* 1974, *30,* 31–35.

Sechrest, L. Personality. *Annual Review of Psychology,* 1976, *27,* 1–27.

Secord, P. F., & Backman, C. W. *Social psychology.* New York: McGraw-Hill, 1974.

Sherif, M., & Hovland, C. I. *Social judgment: Assimilation and contrast effects in communication and attitude change.* New Haven, Conn.: Yale University Press, 1961.

Shrauger, J. S., & Patterson, M. B. Self-evaluation and the selection of dimensions for evaluating others. *Journal of Personality,* 1974, *42,* 569–585.

Slamecka, N. J., & Graf, P. The generation effect: Delineation of a phenomenon. *Journal of Experimental Psychology: Human Learning and Memory,* 1978, *4,* 592–604.

Snygg, D., & Coombs, A. W. *Individual behavior: A perceptual approach to behavior* (Rev. ed.). New York: Harper, 1959.

Strand, B. Z. Change of context and retroactive inhibition. *Journal of Verbal Learning and Verbal Behavior,* 1970, *9,* 202–206.

Thorndike, E. L. The law of effect. *American Journal of Psychology,* 1927, *39,* 212–222.

Tomkins, S. S., & Izard, C. E. (Eds.). *Affect, cognition, and personality: Empirical studies.* New York: Springer Publishing Co., 1965.

Tulving, E. Episodic and semantic memory. In E. Tulving & W. Donaldson (Eds.), *Organization of memory.* London: Academic Press, 1972.

Tulving, E., & Pearlstone, Z. Availability versus accessibility of information in memory for words. *Journal of Verbal Learning and Verbal Behavior,* 1966, *5,* 381–391.

Tulving, E., & Thompson, D. M. Encoding specificity and retrieval processes in episodic memory. *Psychological Review,* 1973, *80,* 352–373.

Tversky, A., & Kahneman, D. Availability: A heuristic for judging frequency and probability. *Cognitive Psychology,* 1973, *5,* 207–232.

Valins, S., & Nisbett, R. E. Attribution processes in the development and treatment of emotional disorder. In E. E. Jones, D. E. Kanouse, H. H. Kelley, R. E. Nisbett, S. Valins, & B. Weiner (Eds.), *Attribution: Perceiving the causes of behavior.* Morristown, N.J.: General Learning Press, 1972.

Watkins, M. J., & Tulving, E. Episodic memory: When recognition fails. *Journal of Experimental Psychology: General,* 1975, *104,* 5–29.

Wiggins, J. S. *Personality and prediction.* Reading, Mass.: Addison-Wesley, 1973.

Wyer, R. S., Jr. Changes in meaning and halo effects in personality impression formation. *Journal of Personality and Social Psychology,* 1974, *29,* 829–835.

Wyer, R. S., Jr., & Carlston, D. E. *Social inference and attribution.* Hillsdale, N.J.: Lawrence Erlbaum Associates, 1979.

Zajonc, R. B. Feeling and thinking: Preferences need no inferences. *American Psychologist,* 1980, *35,* 151–175.

Zanna, M. P., & Cooper, J. Dissonance and the attribution process. In J. H. Harvey, W. J. Ickes, & R. F. Kidd (Eds.), *New directions in attribution research* (Vol. 1). Hillsdale, N.J.: Lawrence Erlbaum Associates, 1976.

Author Index

A

Abelson, R. P., 43, 50, 51, 72, 77, *80, 87,* 91,
  92, 97, 112, 115, 119, *128, 132,* 163, 170,
  194, 196, 221, *244,* 256, *276,* 295, *302*
Adams, N., 24, *37,* 51, *87*
Ahlm, K., 164, *196,* 373, *391*
Ajzen, I., 44, *80,* 108, 122, *128,* 253, *273, 274*
Akst, L., 345, *388*
Albrecht, F., 95, *129*
Allen, A., 111, *128,* 249, 250, 251, 252, 270,
  273
Allen, R. B., 251, 255, 256, 259, 260, 261,
  263, 264, 268, 269, 270, 271, 272, *273, 274*
Allport, D. A., 57, *80*
Allport, G. W., 60, 61, *80,* 247, *273*
Alper, T. G., 71, *80*
Amabile, T. M., 120, 121, *130, 132*
Amo, M. F., 371, *388*
Amster, H., 214, *241*
Anatol, K. W. E., 369, *385*
Anderson, J. R., 4, 6, 24, 30, 31, *34,* 42, 43,
  48, 53, *80,* 166, *194,* 272, *273,* 412, *416*
Anderson, N. H., 4, 5, *34,* 64, *80,* 135, 136,
  156, *156,* 161, 170, *194,* 216, 236, *241,*
  344, 351, 360, *385,* 404, *416*
Anderson, R. C., 73, *80,* 99, *130,* 152, *157,
  158,* 206, 207, 211, 228, *245,* 406, *416*
Andesman, P., 57, *83*
Anhansel, J., 71, *84*

Applbaum, R. F., 369, *385*
Apple, W., 333, 334, 335, 336, 339, *341*
Aristotle, 42, *80*
Arkin, R. M., 228, *241*
Armstrong, G. W., 372, *390*
Arnold, M. B., 407, *416*
Aronson, E., 92, 93, 109, 113, *128,* 217, *241*
Asch, S. E., 4, 5, 6, *35, 47, 80,* 138, 140, *157,*
  161, *195,* 216, *242,* 323, 340, *341,* 344,
  356, *385,* 404, *416*
Atkinson, J. W., 407, *416*
Atkinson, R. C., 261, *273*
Austin, J. L., 346, 348, 355, 356, 373, 374,
  385
Austin, V. D., 405, *416*
Averill, J. R., 409, *416*
Ayer, A. J., 326, *341*

B

Backman, C. W., 398, *419*
Bacon, F., 299, *302*
Baddeley, A. D., 102, *128*
Bagozzi, R. P., 253, 254, *273*
Bahrick, H. P., 204, *242,* 365, *385*
Bailey, D. E., 396, 407, *419*
Baldridge, B., 293, *303*
Bales, R. F., 379, *385*
Balint, M., 293, *302*
Balser, E., 10, *35*

Bandura, A., 293, *302*
Barclay, J. R., 49, 59, *80, 81,* 380, *386*
Barefoot, J. C., 412, *416*
Bartlett, F. C., 41, 42, 49, 54, *80,* 89, *128,*
   163, 164, *195,* 252, *273,* 350, 351, 352,
   385, 395, 407, *416*
Bass, B. N., 209, *242*
Bateson, G., 346, 375, 376, *391*
Battig, W. F., 14, *36*
Bauer, R. A., 351, 378, *392*
Baumeardner, M. H., 64, 65, *84,* 117, *128, 129*
Beaber, R. J., 371, *390*
Beach, L. R., 40, *80*
Bear, G., 60, *80*
Beavin, J. H., 346, 375, *392*
Becker, H. S., 114, *128*
Becker, L. A., 355, *386*
Bell, S. M., 56, *84*
Bem, D. J., 72, *81,* 111, *128,* 161, 164, *195,*
   249, 250, 251, 252, 270, *273,* 355, *385*
Bennett, R., 220, *242*
Berger, C. R., 371, *385*
Berkowitz, H., 12, *35*
Berlyne, D. E., 203, 213, 239, *242*
Berman, J. S., 252, *273*
Berman, L., 164, *196,* 373, *391*
Bernstein, B., 380, *385*
Berschied, E., 113, *132,* 224, 226, *242, 245,*
   254, *273,* 301, *303*
Bevan, A. R., 398, *418*
Bever, T. G., 42, *81*
Biederman, I., 54, 56, *81*
Billig, M., 61, *81, 87*
Birnbaum, G., 233, *242*
Birnbaum, M. H., 181, *195*
Birrell, P., 26, *37,* 62, 63, *86,* 215, *244,* 403,
   404, *419*
Black, J. B., 50, 53, 75, 77, *81,* 91, 92, 96, 97,
   98, 99, 100, 105, 106, 126, *128, 131*
Block, J., 249, 250, 251, 253, 254, 269, *273*
Blumer, H., 346, *385*
Bobrow, D. G., 42, 77, *81, 85,* 152, *157*
Boies, S. J., 204, *244*
Bolinger, D., 346, 369, *386*
Borchers, G., 370, *386*
Borgida, E., 136, *158*
Botkin, P. T., 344, 345, 349, 354, *387*
Boucher, B., 265, *385*
Bourne, L. E., Jr., 52, *81*
Bousfield, A. K., 8, 9, *35,* 144, *157*
Bousfield, W. A., 7, 8, 9, 12, 13, *35,* 95, 98,
   128, 144, *157,* 364, *392*

Bower, G. H., 6, 30, 31, *34,* 42, 44, 48, 50, 52,
   53, 73, 75, 77, *80, 81, 86, 87,* 91, 92, 93, 96,
   97, 98, 99, 100, 105, 106, 115, 119, 125,
   126, *128, 131, 133,* 152, *157,* 163, 165, 166,
   194, 195, 406, 408, 412, *416*
Bowers, K. S., 249, *273,* 311, *320*
Boyes-Braem, P., 93, *131*
Bradac, J. J., 371, *386*
Bransford, J. D., 42, 48, 49, 55, *81, 82, 84,* 98,
   128, 163, *195,* 252, *273,* 380, *386*
Bremer, D., 406, *417*
Brickman, P., 214, *242*
Brigham, J. C., 220, *242*
Brock, T. C., 11, *35,* 355, 359, *386*
Bromley, D., 372, *389*
Brooks, F., 204, *243*
Broverman, F. E., 220, *242*
Broverman, I. K., 220, *242*
Brown, R., 363, 380, *386*
Brown, R. W., 364, *386*
Brown, S. C., 9, 18, *37*
Bruce, D., 10, 12, *35*
Bruner, J. S., 61, *81,* 92, 115, *128,* 137, *157,*
   163, 164, *195,* 204, *242,* 407, *419*
Bruning, J. L., 204, *242*
Bull, M. P., III, 31, *38*
Burke, K., 346, *386*
Burnkrant, R. E., 253, 254, *273*
Burnstein, E., 59, 60, *87, 88,* 96, *134*
Bursill, A. E., 204, *242*
Byde, R. W., 64, *81*
Byrne, D., 5, *35,* 161, *195*

C

Cacioppo, J. T., 412, *416*
Calfee, R. C., 52, *81*
Calkins, M. W., 47, *81*
Callaway, E., 204, *242*
Campbell, B. H., 288, 297, *303*
Campbell, D. T., 60, *81,* 93, 116, *133,* 351,
   390, 402, *419*
Cantor, N., 46, 65, *81,* 91, 92, 93, 96, 98, 104,
   108, 110, 125, 126, *128,* 161, *195,* 224,
   242, 252, 255, *273,* 296, 297, *302, 303,* 397,
   416
Capage, J. W., 204, *242*
Caputo, C., 398, *419*
Carlsmith, J. M., 92, 93, 109, *128*
Carlston, D. E., 4, 6, *36, 38,* 164, 166, 170,
   180, 187, 188, 192, *195, 197,* 255, 270, *273,*
   275, 408, *420*

Carmichael, L., 54, *81*, 362, 365, *386*
Carroll, J. S., 15, *36*, 103, 112, *128*
Carver, R. P., 308, *320*
Castell, P. T., 319, *321*
Cattell, R. B., 247, *274*
Cazden, C. B., 380, *386*
Cermak, L. S., 77, *81*
Chaiken, S., 355, 356, 357, 359, 370, 375, 377, *386, 387*
Chalmers, D. K., 64, *81*
Champagne, B., 253, *274*
Chanowitz, B., 235, *244*
Chapman, J. P., 34, *35*, 108, 121, *129*, 136, *157*, 218, 223, *242*, 252, *274*, 405, *416*
Chapman, L. J., 34, *35*, 108, 121, *129*, 136, *157*, 218, 223, *242*, 252, 258, *274*, 405, *416*
Charness, N., 57, *82*
Chase, W. G., 56, *82*
Cherry, C., 344, *386*
Child, P., 74, *85*, 213, *244*
Cialdini, R. B., 378, *386*
Clark, E. V., 296, *302*
Clark, H. H., 296, *302*, 374, *386*
Clark, K. B., 71, *82*
Clark, M., 407, 412, *418*
Clarkson, P. S., 220, *242*
Clary, E. G., 12, *35*
Clayton, T., 54, *86*
Close, M. M., 206, 207, 211, 228, *245*
Cofer, C. N., 10, 11, 12, 13, *35, 36, 37*
Cohen, A. R., 11, *35*, 146, *157*, 359, *386*
Cohen, B. D., 344, 345, 372, *391*
Cohen, B. H., 12, 13, *35*
Cohen, C. E., 11, *35*, 68, *82*, 99, 105, 115, *129*, 252, 254, 255, 263, 264, 266, 268, 271, *274*
Cohen, J., 293, *303*
Cohen, L. J., 44, *82*
Cohen, R. L., 54, *82*
Cole, M., 9, *36*, 380, *391*
Colle, H. A., 8, *35*
Collins, A. M., 6, 31, *35*, 92, *129*, 166, 180, 187, *195*, 412, *416*
Collins, B. E., 254, *274*, 354, 363, 375, *386, 387*
Collins, J. F., 204, *242*
Coltheart, V., 52, *82*
Conolley, E. S., 412, *417*
Constantini, A. F., 216, 236, *243*
Conway, M., 164, *196*
Cook, S. W., 71, *88*
Cooley, C. H., 413, *416*

Coombs, A. W., 413, 414, *420*
Cooper, J., 113, *133*, 369, 378, *386, 392*, 410, *420*
Copper, R. M., 54, *82*
Cornell, S. D., 349, 351, *390*
Cornsweet, D. J., 204, *242*
Corrigan, B., *136, 157*
Costanzo, P. R., 90, *132*
Costello, C., 410, *416*
Costin, F., 181, *195*
Cottrell, N. B., 96, *129*
Coulson, D., 14, *37*
Cowan, C. L., 12, *38*
Cowan, T. M., 12, *35*
Cox, M. G., 398, *417*
Craik, F. I. M., 68, 77, *81, 82*, 102, *129*, 406, *419*
Crandall, R., *136, 158*, 214, *242*
Crocker, J., 93, 99, 101, 108, 115, 120, 121, 122, 123, *129, 133*, 206, 207, 210, 211, 230, *245*
Crockett, W. H., 59, *86*, 96, *129, 131*
Crutchfield, R., 5, *36*
Cushman, D., 346, 348, *386*
Czerlinsky, T., 349, 355, *390*

D

D'Agostino, J., 101, 108, 115, *133*
Dallett, K. M., 10, *35*
D'Andrade, R. G., 250, 251, 264, 266, 269, *274, 276*
Dangel, T. R., 14, *35*
Daniel, T. C., 54, *82*
Davies, R. A., 371, *386*
Davis, J. H., 125, *129*
Davis, K. E., 135, *158*, 161, 181, *195*, 225, *243*, 356, 364, *389*
Dawes, R. M., 49, *82*, 136, *157*, 216, *244*, 408, *416*
Dean, P. J., 13, *36*
DeCapito Caronite, A., 362, 364, 365, *392*
deCharms, R. C., 5, *35*, 308, *320*
Delia, J. G., 96, *129*, 346, *386*
Delin, P., 208, *245*
Demarest, I. H., 55, *83*
Dennis, N. F., 113, *129*
Dermer, M., 254, *273*
Derry, P. A., 399, 412, 415, *418*
DeSoto, C. B., 58, *82, 83*, 92, 95, 96, *129, 130*
Deutsch, M., 90, *129*, 363, *386*, 401, *416*
Devin, J., 352, *391*

DeVito, J. A., 344, *386*
DiRivera, J. H., 125, *129*
Divesta, F. J., 14, *35, 37*
Dixon, N. F., 61, *82*
Dodge, K. A., 404, *417*
Dolinsky, R., 13, *36*
Dominowski, R. L., 52, *82*
Dooling, D. J., 68, *87,* 98, 99, 105, *129, 133*
Dornbusch, S. M., 414, *416, 417*
Downing, L. L., 12, *35*
Dreben, E. K., 64, *82,* 156, *157,* 239, *242,* 402, *416*
Dutta, S., 409, 410, 413, *416*
Duval, S., 228, *241*
Dymond, R., 293, *302*

E

Eagly, A. H., 344, 345, 347, 355, 356, 357, 359, 370, 375, 377, *386, 387, 388*
Earhard, M., 13, *36*
Easterbrook, J. A., 204, 226, *242,* 411, *416*
Ebbesen, E. B., 4, 11, *35, 36,* 74, *85,* 250, 251, 254, 255, 256, 259, 260, 261, 263, 264, 266, 268, 269, 270, 271, 272, *273, 274, 275*
Ebbinghaus, H., 42, 47, *82*
Ebenholtz, S. M., 47, *80*
Eckman, J., 220, *242*
Edwards, A. L., 71, *82*
Edwards, W., 44, *82*
Eisen, S. V., 221, 230, *242*
Ekman, P., 333, 338, *341*
Elms, A. C., 378, *387*
Elstein, A. S., 125, *129*
Endler, N. S., 252, *274, 275*
Enquist, G., 233, 235, 236, *242,* 254, *275*
Epstein, S., 253, 270, *274,* 413, *416*
Erdelyi, M. H., 61, *82,* 318, *320,* 407, 410, 412, 413, *416, 417*
Eriksen, C. W., 204, *242*
Ervin-Tripp, S. M., 369, *387*
Estes, W. K., 42, 53, *82*
Estess, F., 294, *302*
Etcoff, N. L., 13, 32, *38,* 61, *87,* 95, *133,* 206, 211, 223, *245*
Evans, M., 62, 63, *86,* 99, 100, 123, *132*
Evenbeck, S., 378, *386*
Eysenck, M. W., 410, 412, *417*

F

Fairbanks, G., 333, *341*
Farrell, T. B., 373, *387*

Fazio, R. H., 369, *386,* 400, 413, *417, 419*
Feldman, N. S., 401, *417*
Festinger, L., 343, 355, 375, *387, 392,* 414, *417*
Fischoff, B., 107, *129,* 135, 136, *157*
Fisch, R., 204, *244*
Fishbein, M., 44, *80,* 139, *158,* 161, *195,* 253, *273, 274,* 404, *417*
Fiske, D. W., 250, 251, *274*
Fiske, S. T., 13, 32, *38,* 61, 64, 73, *82, 87,* 95, 106, 110, 111, 126, 127, *129, 130, 133,* 156, *157,* 164, *196,* 201, 206, 207, 208, 210, 211, 216, 223, 228, 229, 230, 235, 239, *242, 243, 244, 245,* 397, 398, 402, 407, 413, *416, 417*
Flavell, J. H., 41, *82,* 344, 345, 349, 354, *387*
Flores D'Arcais, G. B., 374, *387*
Fodor, J. A., 42, *81*
Fondacaro, R., 344, 348, 352, 353, 359, 360, 361, 362, 376, 379, *388*
Frandel, A., 221, 236, *245*
Frankel, F., 9, *36*
Frank, J. D., 293, *302*
Franks, J. J., 42, 48, 49, 55, 59, *81, 82,* 380, *386*
Frase, L. T., 14, *36, 50, 82*
Frechtman, J., 223, *242*
Frederiksen, C. H., 50, *82,* 96, 99, *129,* 352, *387*
Freedman, H., 109, *131*
Freize, I., 135, *159*
Frentz, T. S., 373, *387*
Freud, S., 327, *341,* 407, 412, *417*
Frey, P. W., 57, *83*
Friedman, A., 54, *83*
Friedman, S., 219, 220, 221, 223, 224, *244*
Friesen, W. V., 333, 338, *341*
Fromkin, H. L., 11, *35,* 359, *386*
Fry, C. L., 344, 345, 349, 354, *387*
Fujioka, T., 74, *85,* 213, *244*
Fulero, S., 26, *37,* 62, 63, *86,* 99, 100, 123, *132,* 215, *244,* 403, 404, *419*

G

Galanter, E., 91, 92, 114, *131*
Gardner, R. C., 61, *87*
Garfinkel, H., 346, *387*
Garland, H., 103, *129*
Garner, W. R., 43, 47, *83*
Garrett, M. A., 42, *81*
Gauld, A., 49, *83*
Geller, V., 327, 328, 334, *341*
Gelman, R., 352, *391*

Gerard, H. B., 66, *88,* 99, 100, 115, 119, *133,* 221, 236, *246,* 363, *386,* 401, 412, 414, *416, 417, 418*
Gergen, K. J., 225, *243*
Gergen, M., 319, *321*
Gerjouy, T. R., 9, *36*
Geva, N., 6, *37,* 64, 65, *84, 85,* 117, *129,* 139, *158*
Gibson, J. W., 370, *387*
Gifford, R. K., 62, *83,* 140, *157,* 219, 224, *243,* 252, *274,* 405, *417*
Gilligan, S. G., 73, *81,* 406, *416*
Ginsberg, E., 207, 214, 235, 237, *244*
Gleason, T. C., 216, *244*
Glucksberg, S., 344, 345, 347, 349, 358, *387*
Goethals, G. R., 170, *195,* 224, *243,* 351, *389,* 402, *418*
Goffman, E., 114, *130,* 324, *341,* 346, 371, 375, *387*
Goldberg, B., 318, *320,* 407, 412, *417*
Goldberg, L. R., 135, 136, *157,* 398, *419*
Goldin, S. E., 57, *83*
Gollob, H. F., 295, *302*
Gomulicki, B. R., 49, *83*
Gonzalez, R., 12, *36*
Goodwin, D. W., 406, *417*
Gordon, D., 358, *387*
Gormley, J., 253, 269, *274, 275*
Graf, P., 400, *420*
Gray, W. D., 93, *131*
Graziano, W., 254, *273*
Green, B. F., 270, *274*
Green, D., 412, *417*
Greenwald, A. G., 72, *83,* 118, *130,* 296, *302,* 377, *387,* 400, *417*
Gregg, L. W., 52, *83*
Grice, H. P., 346, 348, 355, 358, *387*
Gross, A. E., 354, *387*
Gruner, C. R., 370, *387*
Gumperz, J. J., 346, 348, *387*
Gurwitz, S. B., 404, *417*

H

Halberstram, M., 318, *320*
Halper, F., 54, *86*
Hamill, R., 101, *131*
Hamilton, D. L., 4, 11, *36,* 62, 68, *83,* 91, 95, 98, 99, 123, *130,* 140, 141, 142, 143, 144, 145, 147, 149, *157, 158,* 216, 219, 223, 224, 225, *243, 246,* 250, 252, 255, 266, 270, *274, 275,* 404, 405, *417*
Hammond, K. R., 135, *158*

Hanawalt, N. G., 55, *83*
Hanson, L. R., 136, *158,* 181, *195,* 216, *243*
Hardy, A., 103, *129*
Harkins, S. G., 11, *36,* 146, *158,* 359, *387*
Harrison, A. A., 214, *242, 243*
Harris, S., 306, *320*
Harris, V. A., 120, *130,* 269, 275
Hartman, G. W., 71, *88*
Harvey, J. H., 11, *36,* 146, *158,* 359, *387*
Hastie, R., 4, 6, *34, 36,* 46, 64, 67, 69, 75, 78, *82, 83,* 99, 100, *130,* 156, *157,* 239, *242,* 270, *275,* 402, *416*
Hastorf, A. H., 121, *130,* 262, *275,* 398, 407, 414, *416, 417*
Hawes, L. C., 346, *387*
Hayes, J. R., 15, *36*
Hayes-Roth, B., 78, *87*
Hebb, D. O., 311, *320*
Hecker, M. H. L., 333, *341*
Heider, F., 5, *36,* 43, 59, *83,* 202, 205, 222, 234, 241, *243,* 324, 340, *341,* 356, 364, *388,* 414, *417*
Helson, H., 42, *83*
Hendrick, C., 216, 236, *243*
Henker, B., 254, *274*
Henley, N. M., 58, *83,* 95, 96, *129, 130*
Henninger, M., 355, *392*
Herman, C. P., 378, *386*
Herstein, J. A., 15, *36*
Heslin, R., 371, *388*
Higgins, E. T., 110, *130,* 152, *158,* 164, 178, 179, 185, 186, 187, 188, *195,* 225, *243,* 344, 345, 347, 348, 349, 350, 351, 352, 353, 354, 358, 359, 360, 361, 362, 363, 364, 365, 366, 367, 368, 370, 372, 374, 375, 376, 378, 379, 380, 381, *387, 388, 389,* 401, 405, 414, 415, *417*
Himmelfarb, S. H., 344, 345, 347, 356, 370, 377, *387, 388*
Hinkle, R. L., 181, *197,* 355, *392*
Hintikka, J., 369, *388*
Hintzman, D. L., 401, *417*
Hochberg, J., 204, *243*
Hockey, G. R. J., 204, *243*
Hodges, B., 216, *243*
Hodun, A., 60, *80*
Hoffman, P. J., 135, *158*
Hogan, H. P., 54, *81,* 362, 365, *386*
Hoine, H., 406, *417*
Holmes, D. S., 318, *320*
Holmes, J. G., 226, *245*
Hopcroft, J. E., 42, *83*
Hörmann, H., 55, *84,* 363, *389*

Hornby, P. A., 374, *388*
Horowitz, L. M., 269, *275*
Horsfall, R., 58, *83,* 96, *130*
Horwitz, M., 95, *131*
Hoving, K. L., 362, 364, 365, *392*
Hovland, C. I., 225, *245,* 295, *302,* 344, 345, 372, 377, *389, 391,* 413, *420*
Howard, J., 26, *37,* 62, 63, *86,* 215, *244,* 403, 404, *419*
Hoyt, M., 412, *417*
Huba, G. J., 250, *275*
Hubbard, M., 72, *86,* 116, 118, 119, *132,* 164, 177, *196,* 222, 236, *244*
Hubert, S., 64, *80,* 156, *157,* 216, 236, *241*
Hunter, R., 161, *195,* 404, *417*
Hunt, J. McV., 252, *274*
Hursch, C. J., 135, *158*
Huttenlocher, J., 58, *83,* 364, 374, *388, 389*
Hyde, T. S., 11, *36*
Hymes, D., 346, 348, 369, *387, 389*

I

Ingraham, L. H., 96, *129*
Innes, M., 89, *130*
Inouye, D., 269, *275*
Irion, A. L., 407, *418*
Isen, A. M., 407, 412, *418*
Izard, C. E., 407, 408, *418, 420*

J

Jaccard, J. J., 139, *158*
Jackson, D. D., 346, 375, *392*
Jackson, D. N., 398, *418*
Jacobson, L., 113, *131*
Jakobovitz, L. A., 214, *243*
James, W., 305, *320,* 413, *418*
Janis, I. L., 125, *130,* 343, 344, 345, 368, 378, *387, 389,* 401, *418*
Jarvis, P. E., 344, 345, 349, 354, *387*
Jeffery, K. M., 408, *418*
Jellison, J. M., 355, *390*
Jenkins, H. M., 122, *130, 133,* 296, *302*
Jenkins, J. J., 11, *36,* 42, 43, 48, 53, 57, *83, 84*
Jennings, D. L., 121, *130*
Jensen, C., 26, *37,* 62, 63, *86,* 215, *244,* 403, 404, *419*
Jervis, R., 92, 114, 125, *130*
Johnson, D. M., 93, *131*
Johnson-Laird, P. N., 296, 298, 299, *303*

Johnson, M. K., 42, 49, *81, 84,* 98, *128,* 163, *195*
Johnson, N. J., 51, *84*
Jones, C. R., 152, *158,* 164, 178, 179, 185, 186, 187, 188, *195,* 225, *243,* 350, 351, 363, 368, *388,* 405, *417*
Jones, E. E., 71, *84,* 120, *130,* 135, *158,* 161, 170, 181, *195,* 224, 225, 227, *243,* 269, *275,* 314, *320,* 326, *341,* 351, 356, 364, 370, *389,* 402, 414, *418*
Jones, R. A., 62, *84,* 219, *243,* 378, *386*
Jöreskog, K. G., 270, *275*
Jörg, S., 55, *84,* 363, *389*
Juola, J. F., 261, *273*

K

Kagehiro, D. K., 11, *36,* 146, *158,* 359, *387*
Kahneman, D., 42, 44, 77, *84, 88,* 107, 108, 115, 122, *130, 133,* 164, *196,* 203, 239, *243, 245,* 258, *275,* 297, *303,* 308, *321,* 405, 413, *420*
Kanouse, D. E., 136, *158,* 181, *195,* 216, *243*
Kanungo, R. N., 407, 409, 410, 413, *416, 418*
Karlovac, M., 401, *417*
Karp, L., 407, 412, *418*
Katona, G., 47, *84*
Katz, L. B., 11, *36,* 68, *83,* 91, 95, 98, *130,* 140, 141, 142, 143, 144, *157,* 255, 266, *275*
Kaye, D., 368, *389*
Kearns, D., 118, *130*
Keele, S. W., 55, *85,* 395, *419*
Keenan, J., 413, *418*
Keithly, L., 146, *158*
Kelley, H. H., 5, *36,* 43, *84,* 92, *130,* 135, *158,* 161, *195,* 221, *243,* 253, *275,* 311, 317, *321,* 344, 345, 356, 362, *389,* 402, *418*
Kelly, G. A., 34, *36,* 147, *158*
Kelman, H. C., 363, 376, *389*
Kenny, A., 410, *418*
Kenny, D. A., 252, *273*
Kerns, C. D., 402, *418*
Kibler, R. J., 370, *387*
Kihlstrom, J. F., 397, *416*
Kinder, D. R., 111, 126, *129, 130*
King, B. T., 343, *389,* 401, *418*
King, G., 350, 351, 367, 368, *388,* 405, 415, *417*
Kintsch, W., 6, *36,* 42, 51, *84*
Kipnis, D., 319, *321*
Kirker, W. S., 4, 31, 34, *37,* 74, *86,* 101, 105, *131,* 147, *158,* 414, *419*

Kirschner, P., 368, *389*
Klubick, S., 209, *242*
Koffka, K., 42, 47, 54, *84*, 205, 225, 227, 231, *243*
Kogan, N., 252, *275*
Kohler, R., 71, *84*
Koltuv, B., 398, *418*
Konsky, C. W., 371, *386*
Korchin, S. J., 71, *80*
Kozoh, G. F., 204, *242*
Kraft, R. N., 57, *84*
Kramer, M., 293, *303*
Krauss, R. M., 90, *129*, 327, 333, 334, 335, 336, *341*, 344, 345, 347, 349, 358, *387*
Kraut, R. E., 326, 338, *341*
Krech, D., 5, *36*
Kriss, M., 375, *391*
Kuethe, J. L., 95, *130*
Kuhn, T. S., 119, 125, *130*
Kuiper, N. A., 4, 31, 34, *37*, 74, *86*, 101, 105, *131*, 147, *158*, 252, 255, *276*, 399, 405, 412, 414, 415, *418, 419*
Kukla, A., 135, *159*, 170, *196*
Kumar, P. A., 46, 67, 69, 75, *83*, 99, 100, *130*

L

LaCross, K., 27, *37*, 217, 233, 235, 236, *242, 244*
Laird, J. D., 72, *88*
Lakoff, G., 358, *387, 389*
LaMonica, G. L., 362, 364, 365, *392*
Langer, E. J., 115, 119, *130*, 221, 235, *244, 245*, 318, *321*
Lass, N. J., 371, *389*
Lasswell, H. D., 345, *389*
Lauer, P. A., 14, *36*
Lawler, E., 109, *130*
Leamer, E. E., 44, *84*
Lee, B., 366, *388*
Leeper, R., 204, *244*
Legant, P., 398, *419*
Leippe, M. R., 64, 65, *84*, 117, *128, 129*
Leirer, V. O., 11, *36*, 68, *83*, 91, 95, 98, *130*, 140, 141, 142, 144, 147, 149, *157, 158*, 255, 266, *275*
Lemon, N., 414, *418*
Leone, C., 12, *38*, 110, *133*
Lepper, M. R., 72, *86*, 111, 116, 118, 119, *132, 164*, 177, *196*, 297, *303*
Leventhal, H., 359, *389*
Levine, J. M., 71, *84*, 407, *418*

Levy, A., 378, *386*
Lichtenstein, S., 107, 115, *132, 135, 159*
Lim, C., 141, 142, 144, *158*
Lindauer, B. K., 380, *390*
Linder, D., 109, *128*, 217, *241*
Lindman, H., 44, *82*
Lingle, J. H., 4, 6, *36, 37*, 64, 75, *84, 85*, 117, 118, *129, 130*, 139, *158*, 412, *418*
Lippman, W., 3, *36*
Lipsher, D. H., 293, *302*
Little, K. B., 95, *130*
Lively, W., 372, *389*
Livingston, J., 93, 99, 115, *133*
Lockhart, R. S., 68, *82*
Loftus, E. F., 6, 31, *35*, 55, *84*, 105, *130*, 166, 170, 180, 187, *195*, 252, *275*, 362, 367, *389*, 412, *416*
Loftus, G. R., 54, 56, *84*
London, M., 95, 96, *129*
Lowenfeld, J., 364, *390*
Lumsden, A., 311, 312, 314, *321*
Lyman, S. M., 346, 356, 375, *390*
Lynn, S., 164, *196*

M

Macdonald, N., 333, *341*
MacWhinney, B., 413, *418*
Magnusson, D., 252, *275*
Mahoney, M. J., 296, *302, 306, 321*
Malpass, R. S., 407, *418*
Mandler, G., 13, *36*, 407, *418*
Mandler, J. M., 51, 54, 55, 56, *84, 130*
Manis, M., 216, *244*, 349, 351, 372, *390*, 407, *418*
Mann, L., 125, *130*
Maratsos, M. P., 352, *390*
Marecek, J., 398, *419*
Markman, E. M., 380, *390*
Markus, H., 4, 31, 34, *36*, 74, *85*, 91, 93, 101, 109, 111, 126, *131*, 214, *246*, 252, 255, *275*, 414, *418*
Marshall, G. R., 11, 12, *36, 37*
Massad, C. M., 222, 236, *244*
Martin, J., 109, *131*
Maruyama, G., 371, *390*
Matter, J., 204, *242*
Mauch, D., 319, *321*
Mayer, R. E., 58, *85*
Mayhew, D., 413, *418*
Mazur, J. E., 69, 75, 78, *83*

McArthur, L. Z., 73, *85*, 136, *158* , 206, 207, 209, 210, 211, 212, 214, 219, 220, 221, 223, 224, 226, 227, 228, 229, 230, 234, 235, 237, *242, 244*, 411, *418*
McCann, D., 344, 348, 352, 353, 359, 360, 361, 362, 376, 379, *388*
McCarrell, N. S., 49, *81*, 252, *273*, 380, *386*
McClintock, C. G., 376, *390*
McConahay, J. B., 109, *132*
McConnell, H. K., 72, *81*
McGeoch, J. A., 47, *85*, 407, *418*
McGillis, D., 161, 181, *195*
McGinnies, E., 407, *419*
McGowan, J., 253, 269, *275*
McGuire, C. V., 213, *244*
McGuire, W. J., 74, *85*, 213, *244*, 344, 345, 347, 352, 356, 363, 368, 370, 372, 377, 378, *390*
McNamara, H., 204, *244*
Mead, G. H., 346, 349, 354, *390*
Mehrabian, A., 344, *390*
Merleau-Ponty, M., 346, 355, *390*
Mervis, C. B., 40, *86, 93, 131*, 365, *391*
Messik, S., 411, *419*
Mettee, D. R., 109, 113, *128, 131*
Metzler, J., 56, *85*
Meyer, D. E., 187, *195, 196*
Miller, D. T., 307, 308, 318, *321*, 408, *419*
Miller, G. A., 91, 92, 114, *131*
Miller, K., 62, *84*, 219, *243*
Miller, N., 351, 371, *390*, 402, *419*
Miller, P. E., 293, *302*
Miller, R., 27, *37*, 217, 236, *244*
Miller, R. S., 52, *86*, 307, *321*
Mill, J., 42, *85*
Millman, S., 378, *390*
Mills, J., 355, *390*
Minsky, M., 50, 54, 55, *85*, 91, 92, 104, 125, *131*
Mischel, W., 46, 65, 74, *81, 85*, 91, 92, 93, 96, 98, 104, 108, 110, 125, 126, *128*, 161, *195*, 224, *242*, 249, 250, 251, 254, 255, 270, 271, *273, 275*, 297, 298, *302*, 408, *418*
Mitchell, T. R., 109, *131*
Monaghan, R. A., 381, *388*
Monfort, F. W., 96, *129*
Monson, T., 254, *273*
Monteiro, K. P., 73, *81*, 406, *416*
Moore, J. C., 349, 351, *390*
Morris, C., 346, 373, *390*
Moscovitch, M., 406, *419*
Moss, S., 375, *392*

Mueller, J. H., 11, 14, *37*
Muliak, S. A., 251, *275*
Mullet, R. L., 98, *129*
Murphy, G., 71, *84*, 407, *418*
Muzzy, R. E., 414, *416*
Myers, J. L., 14, *37*

N

Nagao, D., 125, *129*
Neill, J. A., 398, *418*
Neisser, U., 41, 44, *85*, 90, 125, *131*, 201, 202, 204, *244*, 350, *390*
Nelson, C., 216, *244*
Nelson, T. O., 56, *85*
Newell, A., 42, 43, 44, *85*, 166, *196*
Newman, L. S., 253, *276*
Newtson, D., 27, *37, 57, 85*, 217, 222, 233, 235, 236, *242, 244*, 254, *275*, 349, 355, *390*
Nisbett, R. E., 90, *131*, 136, *158*, 227, *243*, 309, 314, *321*, 326, *341*, 370, *389*, 398, 400, 410, *419, 420*
Nitsch, K. E., 49, *81*
Noble, A., 62, *84*, 219, *243*
Norman, D. A., 42, 77, *81, 85*, 152, *157*
Norman, R., 377, 381, *390*
Norman, W. T., 250, 251, *275, 276*, 398, *419*

O

O'Banion, K., 52, *81*
Offir, C. E., 374, *390*
Oldfield, R. C., 41, 49, *85*
Olson, C. T., 327, 334, *341*
Olson, D. R., 344, 372, *390*
Ono, H., 262, *275*
Ortmeyer, D., 293, *303*
Ortony, A., 43, *86*, 150, 152, 153, *159*
Osgood, C. E., 262, *275*
Oskamp, S., 214, *244*
Ostrom, T. M., 4, 6, 17, 24, *36, 37*, 64, 65, 75, *84, 85*, 117, 118, *128, 129, 130*, 139, *158*, 171, *196*, 213, *244*, 270, *275*, 373, *390*, 412, *418*
Owens, J., 97, 98, *131*

P, Q

Pack, S. J., 113, *134*
Padawer-Singer, A., 74, *85*, 213, *244*, 372, *390*
Paivio, A., 400, 415, *419*

Palmer, J. C., 55, 84, 105, *130,* 252, *275,* 362, 367, *389*
Papanek, M. L., 204, *242*
Parducci, A., 171, *196*
Paris, S. G., 380, *390*
Park, D. C., 48, *85*
Parker, R. E., 54, 56, *84*
Passini, F. T., 251, *276*
Patterson, M. B., 414, *420*
Paul, I. H., 41, *85*
Payne, J. S., 103, *128*
Pearce, W. B., 373, 375, *390, 392*
Pearlstone, Z., 47, *88,* 400, *420*
Peirce, C. S., 346, *391*
Perlman, D., 214, *244*
Perlmutter, J., 14, *37*
Pettigrew, T., 109, *131*
Pezdek, K., 14, *37,* 55, *85*
Piaget, J., 43, 44, *85,* 346, 349, 354, *391,* 399, *419*
Piala, J., 62, *84,* 219, *243*
Picek, J. S., 4, *37,* 59, *85,* 92, 96, 99, 105, *131*
Pichert, J. W., 152, *157, 158,* 406, *416*
Pittenger, J. B., 57, *83*
Pitts, P. M., 204, *242*
Poitou, J. P., 96, *131*
Polefka, J., 121, *130,* 398, 407, *417*
Posner, M. I., 40, 55, *85,* 204, *244,* 395, *419*
Post, D. D., 73, *85*
Postman, L., 47, 54, 61, *80, 81, 86,* 407, *419*
Post, D. L., 206, 207, 209, 210, 228, 229, *244*
Potter, M. C., 115, *128*
Potts, G. R., 58, *86,* 96, 99, 105, *131*
Powell, B., 406, *417*
Powers, W. T., 44, *86*
Prater, C. E., 371, *389*
Press, A. N., 59, *86,* 96, *131*
Pribram, K. H., 91, 92, 114, *131*
Prichert, J. W., 73, *80*
Pryor, J. B., 6, 17, 24, *37,* 64, *85,* 139, *158,* 375, *391*
Puff, C. R., 10, 12, *35, 37*
Quillian, M. R., 92, *129,* 187, *195*
Quine, W. V. O., 76, *86*

R

Rabbie, J. M., 95, *131*
Radloff, R., 109, *131*
Rankin, H. B., 365, *391*
Rankin, R. E., 204, *242*
Rapaport, D., 407, *419*

Ratliff, M. M., 407, *419*
Raven, B. H., 363, 375, *386*
Reece, M. M., 364, *391*
Reed, D. A., 56, *85*
Reed, H., 136, *158,* 343, *390*
Reed, L., 135, *159*
Reed, S. K., 40, 55, *86*
Refield, J., 214, *242*
Regan, D. T., 400, 413, *419*
Reicher, G. M., 10, 12, *35*
Reid, M., 59, *80*
Reitman, J. S., 48, *86*
Renaud, H., 294, *302*
Rescorala, R. A., 239, *244*
Restle, F., 50, 52, *86*
Rest, S., 135, *159*
Reyes, R. M., 106, *133*
Rhodewalt, F., 369, 378, *386, 388*
Rholes, C. R., 164, 178, 179, 185, 186, 187, 188, *195*
Rholes, W. S., 106, 109, *130, 131,* 152, *158,* 225, *243,* 344, 349, 350, 351, 352, 359, 362, 363, 364, 365, 367, 368, 372, 378, 379, 381, *388,* 405, *417*
Richardson, S. A., 414, *416, 417*
Rich, M., 146, *158*
Riemer, B. X., 354, *387*
Riley, D. A., 54, *86, 391*
Rindner, R., 27, *37,* 217, 236, *244*
Rips, L. J., 255, 261, *276,* 366, *392*
Riskey, D. R., 64, *86*
Ritchey, G. H., 56, *84*
Robertson, D. R., 58, *87*
Robinson, J. A., 12, *37*
Rock, I., 54, *86*
Rock, L., 170, *195*
Roencker, D. L., 9, 18, *37*
Rogers, C. R., 293, *302,* 413, *419*
Rogers, P. J., 252, 255, *276,* 414, *419*
Rogers, T. B., 4, 31, 34, *37,* 74, *86,* 101, 105, *131,* 147, *158,* 252, 255, *276,* 399, 405, 414, *418, 419*
Rommetveit, R., 346, 348, 376, *391*
Rorer, L. G., 135, *158*
Rosch, E., 40, 52, *86,* 93, *131,* 365, 366, *391*
Rose, T., 99, 123, *130,* 140, *158,* 223, *243*
Rosenbaum, R. M., 135, *159*
Rosenberg, M. J., 369, *391*
Rosenberg, S., 4, 5, 34, *37,* 69, *86,* 161, 186, *196,* 216, *244,* 255, *276,* 344, 345, 372, *391*
Rosenkrantz, P. S., 59, *86,* 96, *131,* 220, 242
Rosenthal, D., 293, *302*

Rosenthal, R., 113, *131*
Ross, L., 72, *86*, 90, 111, 115, 116, 118, 119, 120, 121, *130*, *131*, *132*, 136, *158*, 177, *196*, 231, *244*, 252, *276*, 297, *303*, 309, *321*, 400, 414, *419*
Ross, M., 306, 307, 308, 309, 311, 312, 314, 318, 320, *321*, 379, *391*, 408, *419*
Rossman, B. B., 295, *302*
Rothbart, M., 26, *37*, 62, 63, *86*, 99, 100, 123, *132*, 215, *244*, 403, 404, *419*
Royer, J. M., 14, *37*
Rubin, E., 205, *244*
Rubin, Z., *86*
Ruble, D. N., 401, 405, *416*, *417*
Ruderman, A. J., 13, 32, *38*, 61, *87*, 95, *133*, 206, 207, 211, 223, 228, *245*
Ruesch, J., 346, 375, 376, *391*
Rumelhart, D. E., 43, 44, 51, *86*, 96, 97, 99, *132*, 150, 152, 153, *159*
Rump, E. E., 208, *245*
Russell, J. A., 409, *419*
Rywick, T., 64, *87*

S

Sachs, J., 352, *391*
Sadler, O., 12, *37*
Sagan, C., 114, *132*
Sakuoura, J. S., 72, *83*
Salancik, G. R., 164, *196*
Sandell, R., 370, *391*
Sarbin, T. R., 396, 407, *419*
Savage, L. J., 44, *82*
Sayre, A., 306, *321*
Schachter, S., 375, *391*, 412, *419*
Schank, R., 43, 50, 51, 77, *87*, 91, 92, 96, 97, 99, 112, 124, 125, *132*, 163, *196*, 256, *276*
Schaye, P., 64, *87*
Scheff, T. J., 114, *132*, 293, *303*
Schiffenbauer, A., 411, *419*
Schlenker, B., 307, *321*
Schneider, D. J., 121, *130*, 137, 147, *159*, 161, *196*, 251, *276*, 398, 407, *417*
Schneider, W., 102, *132*
Schorr, D., 24, *37*, 51, *87*
Schultz, C. B., 14, *35*, *37*
Schur, E. M., 114, *132*
Schvaneveldt, R. W., 187, *195*, *196*
Scott, J., 219, *243*
Scott, M. B., 346, 356, 375, *390*
Scott, W. A., 5, *37*
Scribner, S., 380, *391*

Searle, J. R., 346, 355, 356, 373, 374, *391*
Sears, D. O., 109, *132*
Sears, R. R., 249, *276*
Sechrest, L., 395, *419*
Secord, P., 223, *245*, 398, *419*
Sedlak, A., 4, 5, *37*, 69, *86*, 161, 186, *196*
Sedlack, S., 255, *276*
Seelman, V., 71, *87*
Sentis, K. P., 60, *87*, 101, *131*
Shalker, T. E., 407, 412, *418*
Shank, R., 256, *276*
Shannon, C. E., 344, *391*
Shantz, C. U., 354, *391*
Shatz, M., 352, *391*
Shaver, K. G., 170, *195*
Shaw, M. E., 90, *132*
Sheikh, A. A., 61, *87*
Shepard, R. N., 56, *87*
Sherer, K., 333, *341*
Sherif, M., 225, *245*, 372, 377, *391*, 413, *420*
Sherman, S. J., 4, *37*, 59, *85*, *88*, 92, 96, 99, 105, *131*, 164, *196*, 373, *391*
Shiffrin, R. M., 4, *37*, 59, *85*, 92, 96, 99, 102, 105, *131*, *132*,
Shimmerlik, S. M., 14, *37*
Shoben, E. J., 187, *196*, 255, 261, *276*, 366, *392*
Short, J. C., 111, *132*
Shrauger, J. S., 414, *420*
Shuell, T. J., 8, 13, *37*
Shulman, L. S., 125, *129*
Shweder, R. A., 250, 251, 252, 254, 258, 264, 266, 267, 268, 269, *276*
Sicoly, F., 306, 307, 309, 311, 314, 318, 320, *321*, 379, *391*
Siegelman, E. Y., 269, *275*
Silverstein, M., 346, 355, 380, *392*
Simmel, M., 222, *243*
Simon, H. A., 42, 43, 44, 52, 56, *82*, *83*, *85*, 166, *196*
Simpson, C., 52, *86*
Simpson, D. D., 9, 25, 26, 27, 30, 32, *37*, 213, *244*
Singer, J. E., 412, *419*
Skrypnek, B. J., 289, *303*
Slamecka, N. J., 400, *420*
Slovic, P., 107, 115, *132*, 135, *158*, *159*
Smedslund, J., 122, *132*, 296, *303*
Smith, E. E., 24, *37*, 51, *87*, 255, 261, *276*, 366, *392*
Smith, K. H., 52, 53, 75, *87*
Snyder, M., 70, *87*, 100, 105 112, 113, 114,

115, 122, *132,* 221, 226, 236, *245,* 252, 255, 266, *276,* 279, 280, 281, 283, 284, 285, 286, 288, 290, 291, 296, 297, 301, *303*
Snyder, M. L., 221, 236, *245*
Snygg, D., 413, 414, *420*
Solernou, J., 62, *84,* 219, *243*
Solomon, L. K., 207, 211, 212, 226, 227, 229, 230, 234, *244,* 411, *418*
Solomon, S. K., 42, *84,* 163, *195*
Sorrentino, R. M., 111, *132*
Spiro, R. J., 104, *132,* 173, 175, *196*
Spitzer, C. E., 125, *129*
Spitz, H. H., 9, *36*
Sprafka, S. A., 125, *129*
Sprinzen, M., 206, 207, 210, 211, 230, *245*
Srull, T. K., 163, 165, 167, 172, 181, 182, 187, 194, *196, 197,* 255, *276*
Stahelski, A. J., 317, *321*
Stamm, K. R., 375, *392*
Stasser, G., 125, *129*
Stein, N. L., 55, *84*
Steinfeld, G. J., 55, *87*
Steinmetz, J. L., 111, 116, 120, *132,* 164, 177, *196,* 297, *303*
Stephenson, G. M., 49, *83*
Stephenson, L., 103, *129*
Stern, J., 406, *417*
Sternberg, R. J., 8, *37,* 145, *159*
Sternberg, S., 260, *276*
Stevens, K. N., 333, *341*
Stoll, J., 62, *84*
Stone, G., 204, *242*
Storms, M., 206, 210, 227, *245*
Strack, F., 111, 116, *132,* 297, *303*
Strack, R., 164, 177, *196*
Strand, B. Z., 406, *420*
Straub, R. B., 412, *416*
Streeter, L. A., 333, 334, 335, 336, *341*
Sulin, R. A., 68, *87,* 99, 105, *133*
Swann, W. B., Jr., 113, 114, 122, *132,* 279, 280, 281, 283, 284, 285, 286, 290, 291, 301, *303*

T

Taft, R., 71, *87,* 396, 407, *419*
Tagiuri, R., 137, *157*
Tajfel, H., 61, *81, 87*
Tanke, E. D., 113, *132,* 226, *245,* 301, *303*
Taylor, S. E., 13, 32, *38,* 61, 73, *87,* 93, 95, 99, 101, 106, 108, 109, 110, 115, 120, 121, 122, 123, 127, *129, 131, 133,* 164, *196,* 201,

206, 207, 210, 211, 223, 228, 229, 230, 235, 239, *244, 245*
Tesser, A., 12, *35, 38,* 40, *87,* 91, 110, *133*
Thomas, D. R., 362, 364, 365, *392*
Thompson, C. P., 9, 18, *37*
Thompson, D. M., 406, *420*
Thompson, J. W., 41, *87*
Thompson, S. V., 204, *242*
Thompson, W. C., 106, *133*
Thorndike, E. L., 407, *420*
Thorndyke, P. W., 51, 78, *87,* 96, 99, *133*
Thorne, A., 251, 253, 254, 269, *273*
Titchener, E. B., 203, 204, *245*
Todd, F. J., 135, *158*
Tolman, E. C., 44, *87*
Tomkins, S. S., 407, 408, *420*
Trabasso, T., 52, *87,* 405, *416*
Treisman, A. N., 201, *245*
Trope, Y., 108, *133*
Trudgill, P., 369, *392*
Tsujimoto, R. N., 58, 65, *87,* 254, *276*
Tubbs, S. L., 375, *392*
Tulving, E., 8, 12, 13, *37, 38,* 47, *88,* 102, *129,* 145, *159,* 400, 401, 406, *420*
Turner, R. H., 354, *392*
Turner, T. J., 50, 53, 75, 77, *81,* 91, 92, 96, 97, 99, 100, 105, 106, 126, *128*
Tversky, A., 40, 42, 44, 77, *84, 88,* 107, 108, 111, 115, 122, *130, 133,* 164, *196,* 239, *245,* 258, *275,* 296, 297, *303,* 308, *321,* 405, 413, *420*

U, V, W

Ullman, J. D., 42, *83*
Upshaw, H. S., 171, *196*
Uranowitz, S. W., 70, *87,* 100, 105, 115, *132,* 221, 236, *245, 252,* 255, 266, *276,* 301, *303*
Valins, S., 410, *420*
Vallacher, R. R., 227, *245*
Valone, K., 371, *390*
vanDijk, T. A., 51, *84,* 348, 369, *392*
VanKreveld, D., 96, *133*
Vernon, P. E., 249, 250, 251, *276*
Vivekananthan, P. S., 216, *24'*
Vogel, S. R., 220, *242*
von Bismarck, 333, *341*
von Restorff, H., 47, *88*
Vreeland, R. S., 414, *416*
Wagner, A. R., 239, *244*
Wagner, R. G., 126, *130*
Wald, J., 57, *83*

Wallace, W. P., 47, 53, *88*
Wallach, M. A., 252, *275, 276*
Walster, E., 224, *242,* 355, *392*
Walter, A. A., 54, *81,* 362, 365, *386*
Waltz, D., 55, *88*
Waly, P., 71, *88*
Ward, L. M., 170, *195*
Ward, W. C., 122, *130, 133,* 296, *302*
Warr, D., 216, *245*
Warren, N., 414, *418*
Wason, P. C., 296, 298, 299, *303*
Watkins, M. J., 406, *420*
Watson, W. S., 71, *88*
Watzlawick, P., 346, 375, *392*
Weaver, W., 344, *391*
Weigel, R. H., 253, *276*
Weiner, B., 135, *159,* 170, *196*
Weiss, D. S., 251, 253, 254, 269, *273*
Weiss, W., 295, *302*
Welkowitz, J., 293, *303*
Werner, H., 225, *245*
Whalen, C. K., 254, *274*
Whitehead, L. A., 226, *245*
White, P., 289, *303*
White, R. W., 308, *321*
Whiting, G. C., 346, 348, *386*
Whitman, J. R., 47, *83*
Whitman, R. M., 293, *303*
Whitmarsh, G. A., 12, 13, *35*
Whitten, W., 48, *85*
Wiggins, J. S., 398, *420*
Wilde, J., 58, *87*
Wilder, D. A., 33, *38,* 217, 232, 236, *245*
Williams, C. E., 333, *341*
Wilson, W. R., 214, *246*
Winkler, J. D., 206, 207, 210, 211, 230, *245*
Winston, P. H., 42, *88*

Wittgenstein, L., 40, *88,* 346, 369, *392*
Wixon, D. R., 72, *88*
Woll, S., 99, *133*
Wood, W., 355, 356, 357, 359, *387*
Woodworth, R. S., 54, 57, *88*
Word, C. O., 113, *133*
Wortman, C., 232, *246*
Wright, J. W., 344, 345, 349, 354, *387*
Wulf, F., 54, *88*
Wyatt, D. F., 93, 116, *133*
Wyer, R. S., 4, 6, *36, 38,* 163, 165, 166, 167,
    172, 180, 181, 182, 187, 188, 192, 194, *196,*
    197, 255, 270, *276,* 344, 355, 369, *392,* 404,
    408, *420*
Wylie, R. C., 74, *88*

Y, Z

Yarmey, A. D., 31, *38*
Yavus, H. S., 364, *392*
Yopp, H., 99, *133*
Young, P. F., 204, *242*
Young, W. E., 204, *242*
Zadny, J., 66, *88,* 99, 100, 115, 119, *133,* 221,
    236, *246*
Zajonc, R. B., 11, *38,* 59, *86, 88,* 92, 96, *133,*
    134, 146, *159,* 214, 239, *246,* 255, *276,*
    359, *392,* 396, 407, 413, *420*
Zangwill, O. L., 41, 49, *85, 88*
Zanna, M. P., 113, *133, 134,* 216, 225, 226,
    243, 245, 246, 369, 378, 388, *392,* 404, 410,
    413, *417, 420*
Zeiss, A. M., 74, *85,* 250, 254, *275*
Zillig, M., 71, *88*
Zimmerman, C., 351, 378, *392*
Zinchenko, V., 204, *246*

Subject Index

A

Action schemas, 97
Adjusted Ratio of Clustering (ARC), 9-10, 15, 17, 18, 23, 26
Affect, role of, 34
  in social cognition, 407-413
ARC (*see* Adjusted Ratio of Clustering)
Attention, selective, role of
  in causal attribution, 201-202, 227-241
  in impression formation, 201-202, 205-227, 234-241
  in object perception, 202, 203-205
  in person perception, 201-202, 205-227, 234-241
Attitude schemas, 71-72
Attributions, causal, role of attention in, 201-202, 227-241
"Audience effects," studies of, 351-352, 378

B

Bias
  communicator, 357
  group-centered, 314-317
  knowledge, 357
  reporting, 357, 359
  self-centered, responsibility and, 305-320
  type I error, 118-121, 123
Blocking of information, temporal, 10-11

C

Category accessibility, 161-194
  effects on interpretation of new information, 177-193
Category concept acquisition, 52
Category salience (memory strategy), 13
Central tendency (prototype) schemata, 40, 43
Centrality, trait, 4
Clinical judgment, research on, 135
Clustering in free recall, 6, 7-10, 15, 23-24
  analysis of, 143-144, 148
  measures of, 8-10
Clustering research, contribution to person perception, 10-15
Cognition, social (*see* Social cognition)
Cognitive processes in personality inferences, 247-272
Cognitive representations of persons, 135-156
  conceptual framework for understanding, 149-156
  evaluation of, 156
  organization processes in development of, 3-34, 140-149
"Cognitive tuning," studies of, 146, 360-361
Communication, " information transmission approach to, 344-345, 385
"Communication game," 343-385
  as purposeful social interaction, 375-382
  rules of the, 348-375

Communicator bias, 357
Competing categories (memory strategy), 13–14
Complex linguistic schemata, 48–52
Conditional probability index, 76–77
Context node, 30
Covariation, errors in assessment of, 121–123
Crossed information, 32

D

Descriptor organization, 24, 25–27, 30, 33
  stereotyping and, 32
Descriptors, 16, 17, 21–22, 24
  speed of recognition, 24

E

Emotional factors, influence of, 34
Encoding effects, temporal locus of, 190–192
Event-schema relationships, 43–44
"Event" schemas, 91, 96
Event sequences, memory for, 57–58
Experience, personal, role in social cognition, 398–407

F

Fact node, 30
Familiarity, as determinant of organization of person information, 16–24, 398–399
Feature nodes, 6
First impressions, 4, 16, 152
Form, memory for, 54–55
Free recall, clustering in (*see* Clustering in free recall)

G

Game, communication (*see* "Communication game")
Grammatical schema, 52–53
Group-centered bias, 314–317

H

Hypotheses about other people
  centainty of the, 284–285
  competing, 286–287
  origins of, 283–284
  testing, 277–302
Hypothesis, interaction, 309–312

Illusory data base, 117–118, 123
Impression formation (*see also* Social information)
  management of, 323–340
  processes in, 140, 161–162
  research on, 135, 138, 140–145
  selective attention in, 201–202, 205–227, 234–241
Impression schemata, behavioral events and, 66–71
Impressions
  first, 4, 16, 152
  person (*see* Person impressions)
  trait-biased, 64–66
Individual differences, 33–34
Individual person schemata, 20, 21, 22, 23, 24, 64–71, 151–154
Information
  crossed, 32
  nested, 32
  social (*see* Social infomration)
  temporal blocking of, 10–11
Information processing, affect's influence on, 410–413
"Information transmission" approach (communication), 344–345, 385
Interaction hypothesis, 309–312
Interpersonal relations, communication and, 343–385

J, K

Judgment processes, study of, 135–136, 138–139
Judgments, prior, effects on subsequent ones, 176–177
Knowledge bias, 357

L

Labeling, 361–368
  figurative, 365–367
  'leading,' 367–368
  literal, 365–367
  'misleading,' 367–368
  persuasive, 364
  referential, 364
  types of, 363–368
Labels
  nonsymbolic properties of, 364–365

symbolic properties of, 364–365
  with modifiers, 383
Language, interpresonal relations and, 343
Learning trials, number of, 12
Linear ordering principles, 58–59
Linguistic schemata, complex, 48–52
Location node, 30, 31

M

Management, impression, 323–340
Memory
  associative, 30–31
  comparison of models of, 187–190
  for event sequences, 57–58
  for form, 54–55
  human, schematic principles in, 39–80
  for scenes, 55–57
  strategies, 13–15
Message modification, 349–354

N

Name discriminability, 19, 21, 23, 24
Nested information, 32

O

Object node, 30, 31
Object perception, selective attention in, 202,
    203–205
Other-person-reports, 248, 250

P

Perception (*see* Object perception; Person per-
    ception)
Performatives, 373–375
Person features, 4, 6, 30, 31
"Person gestalt," 5, 6, 15
Person impressions, 4, 91
  research practices, 5
  theories of, 5
  unity of, 4
Person information, familiarity as determinant of
    organization of, 16–24
Person node, 6, 30
Person organization
  alternatives to, 24–30
  behavioral consequences of, 33

Person perception, 3–34, 135
  areas of research, 135–136
  contribution of clustering research to, 10–15
  selective attention in, (*see* Attention,
      selective)
  Social cognition approach to, 136–140
Person schemas, 20, 21, 22, 23, 24, 64–71, 91,
    151–154
Personal experience, role in social cognition,
    398–407
Personal relevance, role in social cognition,
    413–415
Personality
  cognitive processes in inferences about,
      247–272
  measures of, 248
  research on, 247–272
Perspective schemata, 72–73
Persuasion
  "communications game" and, 343–385
  "information transmission" process and, 345
Point-of-view schemata, 71–75
Predicate node, 30, 31
Presentation, order of, 4
Presuppositions, 374–375
Priming
  applicable, 178
  effects of, 178–187, 193
  inapplicable, 178
  indirect, of trait schemata, 179–186
Probabilities, 43–44
Procedural schemata, 40, 41, 43
Processing
  controlled, 102
  hypothesis-driven, 89
  schematic, 89–127
    liabilities of, 114–123
  self-referenced, 147–148
  social information
    model of, 163–173
    schematic basis of, 89–127
Prototype schemata, 40

R

"Ratio of Repetition" measure, 8
Reality, social, 375
  definition of, 376–380
Recall, free, clustering in (*see* Clustering in free
    recall)
Reporting bias, 357, 359

Research
    clustering, contribution to person perception,
        10–15
    impression formation, 135, 138, 140–145
    judgment process, 135–136, 138–139
    person perception, 135–136
    personality, 247–272
    verbal learning and memory, 47–54
    word list learning, 47
Responsibility, self-centered biases in, 305–320
Role schemas, 91
"Role-taking," 354

S

Salient categories (memory strategy), 13
Scenes, memory for, 55–57
Schema(s)
    action, 97
    attitude, 71–72
    central tendency, 40, 43
    cognitive, effects on memory, 39–80
    complex linguistic, 48–52
    concept of, 89–93
    definitions of, 40, 49, 91, 123–124, 150
    event, 91, 96
    functions of, 93–114
        encoding and representation, 94–103
        inferential and interpretive, 103–114
        structuring, 97
    grammatical, 52–53
    impression, and behavioral events, 66–71
    instantiation of, 151, 159
    normative aspect of, 109–110
    origins of the construct of, 41–43
    person, 20, 21, 22, 23, 24, 64–71, 91, 151–
        154
    perspective, 72–73
    point-of-view, 71–75
    procedural, 40, 41, 43
    properties of, 151
    relationships between events and, 43–44
    role, 91
    role in memory for episodic information,
        173–175
    self-concept, 74–75, 91, 101
    social, 91–127
    social balance, 59–60
    social group, 58–64
    template, 40–41, 43
    trait, indirect priming of, 179–186
    types of, 39–41

    visual, 54–58
    wrong, errors due to using, 115–117
Schema-relatedness index, 76
Schematic processing, 89–127
SCR (see Stimulus Category Repetition)
Selective attention (see Attention, selective)
Self, as form of social information organization,
    31–32, (see also Personal relevance)
Self-centered biases, responsibility and, 305–
    320
Self-concept schemata, 74–75, 91, 101
Self-judgments, 355
Self-persuasion, 354–355
Self-referenced processing, 147–148
Self-reports, 248, 250
Serial order (memory strategy), 13
Similarity-attraction paradigm, 5
Social balance schemata, 59–60
Social cognition
    "communications game" and, 343–385
    personal factors and, 395–415
    role of affect in, 407–413
    role of personal experience in, 398–407
    role of personal relevance in, 413–415
Social cognition approach (person perception),
    136–140
Social group schemata, 58–64
Social inference processes, theoretical descrip-
    tion of, 163–173
Social information
    organization of, 3–34
    processing
        model of, 163–173
        schematic basis of, 89–127
Social reality, 375
    definition of, 376–380
Social schemas, 91–127
Stereotyping, 32, 140, 365
    group, 60–64
Stimulus Category Repetition (SCR), 8–9, 18
Subject node, 30
Subjective organization, analysis of, 145–146

T

Task orientation, 11–12
Template schemata, 40–41, 43
Temporal blocking of information, 10–11
Temporal organization, 24–25, 27–30
Testing, hypotheses about other people, 277–
    302
Theory, in social science, 90, 126–127

Time node, 30, 31
Trait centrality, 4
Trait judgment task, 5
Trait schemata, indirect priming of, 179-186
Traits (*see also* Personality)
    as causes of behavior, 247-249
Type I error biases, 118-121, 123

V, W

Verb node, 30, 31
Verbal learning and memory research, 47-54
Visual schemata, 54-58
Word list learning research, early, 47